Here, silent, speak the great of other years,
the story of their steep ascent
from the unknown to the known,
erring perchance in their best endeavor,
succeeding often, where to their fellows
they seemed most to fail.

Here, the distilled wisdom of the years,
the slow deposit of knowledge
gained and writ by weak, yet valorous men,
who shirked not the difficult emprize.

Here is offered you the record of their days and deeds,
their struggle to attain that light
which God sheds on the mind of man,
and which we know as Truth.

Unshared must be their genius; it was their own;
but you, be you brave and diligent,
may freely take and know
the rich companionship of others' ordered thought.

Lines written by George Stewart
Carved over the fireplace in the Historical Library
at the Yale University School of Medicine
MCMXLI

BRITISH SOCIETY OF GASTROENTEROLOGY PRESIDENTS 1937–2004

	DATE	PRESIDENT		DATE	PRESIDENT		DATE	PRESIDENT
1.	1937	A Hurst	22.	1962	H Taylor	43.	1983	JE Lennard Jones
2.	1938	JA Ryle	23.	1963	WA Bourne	44.	1984	RB McConnell
3.	1940–42	A Hurst	24.	1964	CE Newman	45.	1985	EL Blair
4.	1943	H Tidy	25.	1965	WM Capper	46.	1986	GP Crean
5.	1945	T Izod Bennett	26.	1966	F Avery Jones	47.	1987	J Alexander-Williams
6.	1946	A Abrahams	27.	1967	I Fitzgerald	48.	1988	JJ Misiewicz
7.	1947	E Spriggs	28.	1968	N Tanner	49.	1989	JH Baron
8.	1948	TL Hardy	29.	1969	HT Howat	50.	1990	R Williams
9.	1949	G Evans	30.	1970	NF Coghill	51.	1991	R Shields
10.	1950	J McNee	31.	1971	AA Harper	52.	1992	JR Bennett
11.	1951	W MacAdam	32.	1972	WI Card	53.	1993	M Hobsley
12.	1952	AH Douthwaite	33.	1973	S Sherlock	54.	1994	MS Losowsky
13.	1953	LSP Davidson	34.	1974	WT Cooke	55.	1995	IAD Bouchier
14.	1954	SW Patterson	35.	1975	SC Truelove	56.	1996	PM Smith
15.	1955	LJ Witts	36.	1976	JC Goligher	57.	1997	RH Dowling
16.	1956	T Hunt	37.	1977	G Watkinson	58.	1998	MJS Langman
17.	1957	CF Illingworth	38.	1978	W Sircus	59.	2000	L Turnberg
18.	1958	C Dodds	39.	1979	CC Booth	60.	2001	ATR Axon
19.	1959	HW Rodgers	40.	1980	BC Morson	61.	2002	DP Jewell
20.	1960	H Edwards	41.	1981	AE Read	62.	2003	RN Allan
21.	1961	E Bulmer	42.	1982	CG Clark	63.	2004	NA Wright

This book is dedicated to all those British physicians and scientists who devoted their lives to the study of gastroenterology and in particular to Sir Arthur Hurst, whose vision was instrumental in the establishment of the discipline in Britain.

HISTORIA VERO TESTIS TEMPORUM

LUX VERITATIS,

VITA MEMORIAE,

MAGISTRA VITAE*

* History is the witness of times,
The light of truth,
The life of memory,
The mistress of life.

Cicero, *De Oratore* (55 BCE)

Irvin M Modlin, MD, MA (Litt) (*Hon Causa*), PhD, FRCS (Ed), FRCS (Eng), FCS (SA), FACS
Professor of Gastroenterological Surgery
Dir, Gastric Surgical Pathobiology Research Group
Yale University School of Medicine
Department of Surgery
PO Box 208062
New Haven, Connecticut 06520-8062
United States

Mark Kidd, PhD
Gastric Surgical Pathobiology Research Group
Yale University School of Medicine
PO Box 208062
New Haven, Connecticut 06520-8062
United States

Editorial Director: Irvin M Modlin
Conceptual development: Irvin M Modlin
Art direction: Sudler & Hennessey, London
Editing and coordination: Irvin M Modlin & Mark Kidd
Copy editing: Sudler & Hennessey, London
Illustration design and configuration: Irvin M Modlin & Mark Kidd
Illustration research and composition: Irvin M Modlin & Mark Kidd
Cover design: Irvin M Modlin & Mark Kidd
Layout and origination: Sudler & Hennessey, London
Separation and lithography: Quadrant Design and Print Solutions, Hertford
Production: Sudler & Hennessey, London
Printed by Quadrant Design and Print Solutions, Hertford.

Published by ALTANA Pharma Limited.

ALTANA Pharma
Investing in patients

 ALTANA

ISBN 0-9546783-0-3

Diverse and Sundry Reflections on British Medicine with Especial Attention to Gastroenterology

Irvin Mark Modlin

Mark Kidd

ACKNOWLEDGEMENTS

JOHN LITTLEFIELD

I am mindful of the fact that the seeds of this book and my fascination with British medicine were planted almost more than two decades ago when Dick Welbourn and Steve Bloom were misguided enough to offer to train at the Hammersmith and thus provide me with one of the most felicitous experiences of my life. Their early support and friendship provided a basis for what has been a wonderful odyssey through the seas of life and knowledge. Chris Booth was inspirational at many different levels and to this day remains both an icon and a force of nature. Hugh Baron taught me the meaning of erudition and inspired in me a desire to not only understand acid secretion but also perpetuate the memory of Prout, while John Spenser struggled with great kindness and patience to convert my fumbling into a passable surgical skill. Subsequently, Nick Wright, perceiving in me some pathological features, provided great insight into the arcana of growth factors and introduced me to the celestial world of the Athenaeum and the rustic elegance of Snowshill, where long evenings culminated in numerous great scientific advances. All of which were sadly lost on the empty plains of Bordeaux. To these and many more friends and colleagues throughout Britain too numerous to mention I owe more than can be expressed in mere words.

I am particularly indebted to John Littlefield, without whose interest and amaranthine support this work would never have seen the light of day. He confirmed speculation that meticulous oversight and long hours conspire to support creative thoughts despite visions of a future without acid. I am also grateful to the team at Sudler & Hennessey, London, who designed a carefully balanced production schedule and provided valuable logistic and creative support throughout the course of our enterprise. Their artistic and editing input of rare quality and the legacy of their skills as evident in this book attest to their exquisite talent. The amalgam of Sudler & Hennessey's sagacious contributions and the generous support provided by ALTANA Pharma facilitated the consummation of this felicitous endeavor. Alex Modlin provided invaluable pictorial and logistic support and his constant electronic backup saved many tense situations. In particular, he deserves commendation for his extraordinary abilities to identify pictorial material and provide information on a timely basis. All supported the indefatigable Shelley Robinson in her quest to textualize a tangle of history, organotherapy, science and clinical comment into a manuscript of perceivable form.

KEVIN LYE

I regret not having been able to accede to the request that the title of the volume be "The Last Empire of Medicine" or "The British Victory over Ulcer Disease". Although the merits of the claims were self evident, better judgment prevailed! I am particularly obliged to a number of individuals, including Kevin Lye and Sally Gray (London) for their contributions to my current obsession. Each provided much information and great support in the identification of obscure images and disease factors. Truly, they toiled with great effectiveness and good spirit. Josie Dance in London provided invaluable support and much information that could not be located in the colonies.

I believe that prolonged exposure to Gevrey Chambertin fructified the seeds of this endeavor, and that the serenity of the Athenaeum broadened my scientific horizon and honed my thought processes in a fashion that can only be achieved by a Burgundian hepatic saturation. I considered the encounters in London, Edinburgh, Manchester, and Birmingham to have restored the balance of creativity and vivified my mucosa in a fashion consistent with the creative literary process. David Rosin in particular sought to succor me at the Garrick, only to conclude that my acting talents were without merit and my writing barely passable. Only by dint of serious persuasion was I persuaded by Nick Wright not to succumb to the perils of the Tynanian dictum and have therefore abjured from the temptation to "write

SUDLER & HENNESSEY, LONDON

SHELLEY ROBINSON

SALLY GRAY

heresy, pure heresy – rouse tempers, goad, lacerate and raise whirlwinds". Consequently, this book is sadly lacking in rebarbative comment, of which I am particularly fond, believing it to be the one truly definable cause of gastrointestinal dysfunction and mucosal damage.

A great debt is due to Yale University School of Medicine and in particular the History of Medicine Library that provided me with the ideal milieu to pursue these studies. The late Larry Holmes, Chairman of the Department of the History of Medicine, shared his extraordinary wisdom with me. He opened new vistas of thought in educating me of the contributions of numerous figures on the wide stage of medical history. Toby Appel, a librarian possessed of infinite patience and limitless knowledge, was especially helpful in guiding me through difficult areas. My co-author Mark Kidd provided incredible intellectual support and imbued the project with a zeal only possessed by the young. His dramatic and repetitive attempts at determining the effects of short chain carbon fragments on extending the limits of gastroenterological knowledge failed in my estimation; although as might be predicted of a "bosbok" he remains unconvinced of this outcome.

In particular, I am grateful for the sagacious input of my wife Maria, who has over the years claimed to perceive some faint merit in my endeavors and whose patience and amazing tolerance of my idiosyncrasies facilitated pursuit of the elusive concept of a gastroenterological paradise where surgical and intellectual scholarship might be appreciated. There is no doubt in my mind that without her personal support and gentle guidance, neither this nor any of the other texts I have penned would ever have been such labors of love.

Numerous institutions and individuals generously provided me with access to

JOSIE DANCE

material and allowed its usage. These include the Yale University History of Medicine Library; the Hunterian Museum and Library of the Royal College of Surgeons of England; the Royal Society of Medicine; The Royal Society of Pharmacy, the Worshipful Company of Apothecaries; the Royal College of Physicians of England; and the Wellcome Institute for the History of Medicine. Innumerable colleagues, scientific collaborators, and friends have generously allowed me to use information emanating from their labors: *Ars Gratia Artis*.

TOBY APPEL

I am entirely responsible for any errors, oversights, and misinterpretations of either history or scientific data expressed in this text, although George Sachs has constantly reassured me that the likelihood of any individual involved in the study of the ECL cell being associated with such an eventuality is so minimal as to not warrant serious consideration.

Lastly, I wish to acknowledge Caius, Linacre, Vicary, Wren, Lower, Hunter, Prout, Cooper, Sydenham, Moynihan, Lister, and Hurst (to mention only a few) for exciting in me so monstrous a curiosity regarding the evolution of medicine and gastroenterology in Britain. Their extraordinary speculations, marvelous experiments, and clinical interventions altered the entire pattern of medical thought and led to the development of effective treatment of countless patients. A perusal of their life and times provides not only an example of what man may achieve but remains an inspiration to all who practice medicine.

Finally, the most profound acknowledgement is due to the intrepid pioneers of medical science, who in the diverse dissecting rooms, operating suites, and laboratories of London, Edinburgh, Glasgow, Manchester, Birmingham, Guy's, Barts, the Hammersmith, Oxford, and Cambridge so successfully overcame the intellectual obstacles of their times as to vault the boundaries of contemporary scientific and therapeutic limitation. By their exquisite delineation of physiology, bacteriology, pathology, endocrinology, pharmacology, and surgery, they sought to master the mysterious mechanisms of the mucosa, acini, islets, and the genome. Thus, like the intrepid maritime explorers of the past, they voyaged beyond the confines of the organ and its cells to pierce the furthermost reaches of the gastrointestinal tract in their quest to cure the afflicted. *"Qui genus medici ingenio superavit."*

ALEX MODLIN

IRVIN M MODLIN
Madrid, November 3, 2003

CONTENTS

FOREWORD

Scholarship is a word often used these days, often without much thought. Certainly, within the confines of research assessment in our subject, that of medicine, it is often derided, with preference being given to the champions of the experimental method and the randomised clinical trial. But bringing the history of our subject alive, as Irvin Modlin and Mark Kidd have done in this book, is entirely worthy of our admiration and respect.

To analyse the evolution of medicine in Britain, from its early beginnings, through the Middle Ages to the Age of Enlightenment and on to the more modern period which saw the emergence of gastroenterology as a specialty, is to embark on a journey indeed. As a nation, we are peculiarly diffident, certainly about blowing our own trumpets. This book provides us with that platform, to mix a metaphor. It really is quite remarkable the role which this country has had in the development of modern medicine, and in the development of gastroenterology on an international level. Some of our glitterati are of course well recognised, and their memories preserved within our British Society of Gastroenterology's prize and lecture structure – every year sees a new Arthur Hurst, Avery Jones and Basil Morson Lecturer, and fortunate, indeed, are their recipients. But offline, so to speak, other luminaries are honoured, as we recall the achievement of William Prout in discovering the nature of gastric acid each time the Prout Club meets to dine and debate motions of ephemeral delicacy with (usually) flair and discretion. But there are many others, whose distinction we do not commemorate.

Our Society has included in its membership its share of erudite historians – Chris Booth and Hugh Baron spring immediately to mind – and here, in this book, the men and women who did so much to develop our subject are done really proud. The authors have spared no effort in tracking down the most rare and beautiful illustrations, which greatly enhance the value of such an evocative text. As the current President of our Society, I have always, I suppose, been conscious of the continuity, over the years, through which my distinguished predecessors have made their many contributions to the advancement of our subject. But reading through this book, does, I think, give context to the tremendous contribution our Society has made to the origins and emancipation of gastroenterology. I commend it to you – and Irvin and Mark, we are in your debt.

NICK WRIGHT
President, British Society of Gastroenterology
London, November, 2003

PREFACE

JOHN ARDERNE

The early inhabitants of Britain no doubt pondered the source of the groaning and rumbling in their bellies as the cold damp winds howled off the North Sea, threatening to extinguish the small cooking fire and the simmering pot. A stewed rabbit in parsley and some fermented barley did much to dispel the discomfort, but offered little relief from the subsequent gnawing epigastric pain that followed, although it was known that this could be somewhat assuaged by a mouthful of the appalling concoction provided by the local Druid healer. Such was the early state of British gastroenterology before the Norsemen, Romans, clerics, and charlatans crossed the island seas and permeated the land with an amalgam of superstition and medicine that ranged from Byzantium to Batavia in its origins. Given the basic power of abdominal and in particular gastric sensation to evoke either pleasure or discomfort, peace of mind or apprehension, it is little wonder that any aberrations of bodily function that interfered with the acquisition, assimilation, and evacuation of food resulted in disquiet and concern regarding health. It may be said that apart from man's interest in the pleasures of procreation, there is little more powerful than the sensations evoked by food and wine in motivating human response. Indeed, the placation of the cerebral and visceral pleasure centers was regarded from the earliest days of the Romans and Greeks as no less a life requirement than the pursuit of procreative gratification. Both the frescoed walls of Pompeii and their triclinium scenes, as well as the black and ochre kraters of Athens, bear mute and splendid witness to the admiration with which these most civilized of cultures admixed the pleasures of lust, libation, and gustation.

THOMAS LINACRE

Little evidence remains of the early British medicine as practiced by the Druids and the shamans of the Celts, and much of what constituted early practice was derived from the material provided by the successive influx of Celts, Norsemen, Romans, and French as the island kingdom was repeatedly overrun. The chronicles of Bede and his clerical brethren provide some of the earliest information of the amalgam of superstition and clerical obfuscation that represented early British medical doctrine. With the passage of time, folk practice derived from the experience of herbalists mingled with prayer and even magic. Thus rational medicine and prudent practice were often hard to distinguish from alchemy, mysticism, roguery, and charlatanry.

The prudence, honor, and foresight of men such as Caius, Linacre, and Vicary did much to consolidate the basis of sound medical training and ensure respectable medical conduct. With some prodding, a feudal system comprised of patronage and guilds evolved into organized societies, and great universities such as Oxford and Cambridge developed medical programs that enforced adequate training and ensured appropriate performance standards. Royalty became variously involved by endowing hospitals, endorsing

THOMAS VICARY

useful change, and even promoting medicine, as their own interests coincided with that of their medical retainers and the perceived needs of their subjects. In this respect, Henry VIII and Elizabeth I were particularly prominent, while Charles II supported the foundation of the Royal Society. Thus the endeavors of Harvey, Willis, Boyle, Lower, and a host of early physician scientists flourished under the benevolence of a monarchy appreciative of a world of curiosity. Subsequent generations of intellects followed, and Cooper, Bright, Addison, Gull, and Hodgkins, to mention only a few, succeeded Hunter, Sydenham, and Sloane in an age of medicine redolent with intellectual prowess. Such was the potency of British intellectual endeavor at this time that Darwin, Huxley, Faraday, Dalton, and Lister each bestrode the stage strewn with great advances, the likes of which had not been equalled for many centuries.

THOMAS SYDENHAM

The transition of intellectual power from the Church to the universities facilitated the growth of the life of the mind. In addition, the fiduciary success of the Empire further supported the development of medical and surgical progress, as hospitals and scientific laboratories proliferated. British medicine in the 19th century was amongst the most advanced in the world, and there were few that did not seek further education in its halls of learning or at the feet of its masters. The Colleges of Surgery and Medicine exerted international appeal and influence, and hospitals such as Barts, Guy's, St Mary's, and St Thomas' became regarded as Icons of medical and surgical practice.

SIR BERKELEY MOYNIHAN

In the midst of the diverse general type of practice that had evolved at the turn of the 20th century, the advantages of specialization were controversial. However, forward thinking men such as Hurst recognized this need and promulgated first a Gastroenterological club and then a society to fulfil the goals of education, training, and the dissemination of such information. The British Society of Gastroenterology and Endoscopy has, over the course of a century, become internationally recognized for its excellence. Its members have individually and collectively contributed to many of the most important advances in the field, and demonstrated that the great traditions of the past are admirably reflected in a bright and exciting future.

SIR FRANCIS AVERY JONES

IRVIN M MODLIN
Singita, Sabi Sands, December 3, 2003

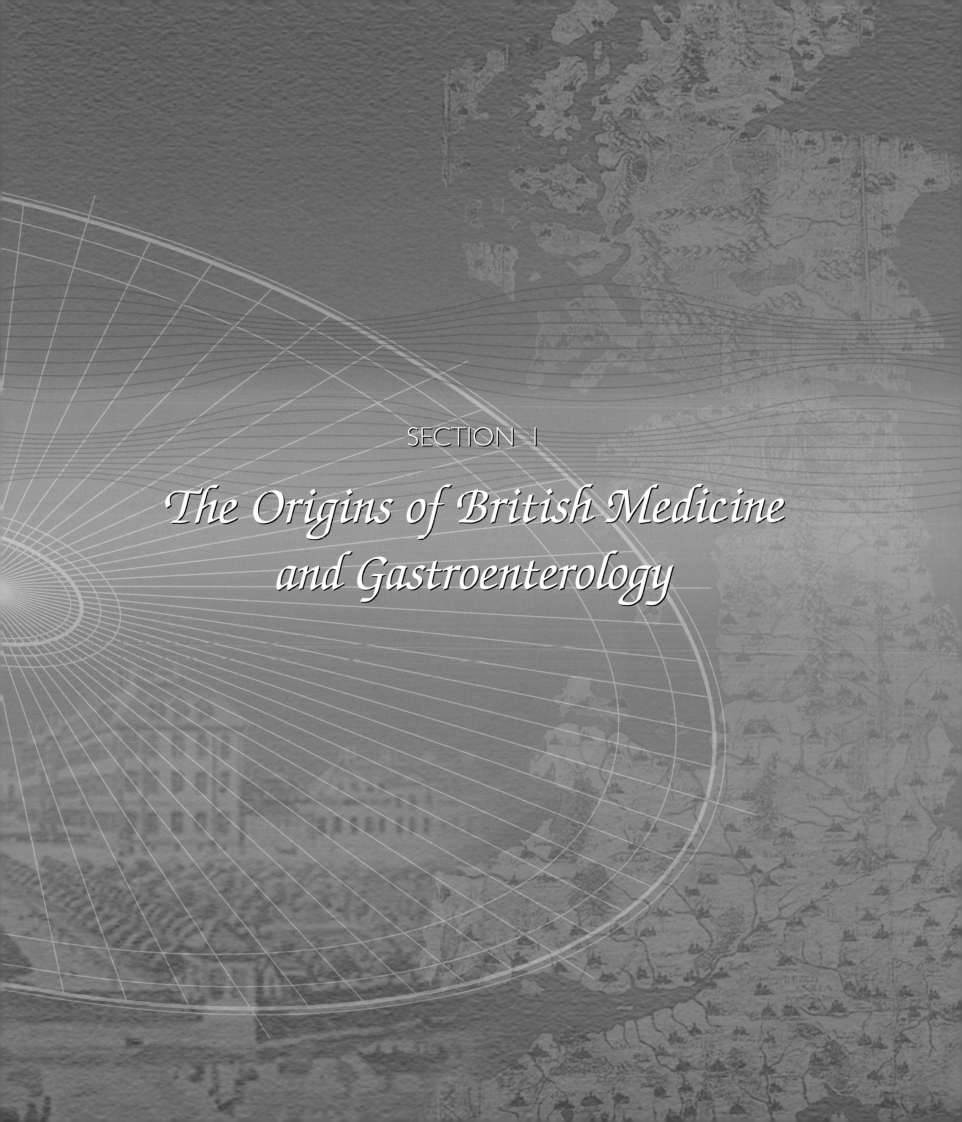

SECTION 1

The Origins of British Medicine and Gastroenterology

THE ORIGINS OF BRITISH MEDICINE AND GASTROENTEROLOGY

INTRODUCTION

The precise origins of medicine in Britain are lost in the mists of time and little early evidence of the practices or even the practitioners remains. As in most early civilizations, it may be assumed that much of the initial medical practice was based upon superstition, magic, and the concept of divine influence on the initiation and cure of disease. Indeed, the remnants of the Druids and the early priests still linger in lonely and windswept corners of the land and bear mute testimony to the unique and mystical rites of long forgotten and ill understood practices. The fact that Britain was separated from Europe meant that while some medical and religious customs were inherent to an island people, they were also subject to intermittent influxes of novel concepts and different practices, as marauders or invaders each left their cultural legacy on the indigenous inhabitants. In this respect, Britain was the subject of intermittent waves of European, Celtic, and Scandinavian migrations, as traders, nomads, and even aggressors respectively inflicted themselves on the populace. The final arrival of the Roman legions bearing their own brand of deities and an overlay of Greek medicine further complicated the melange of medicine and produced a complex pot-pourri of interwoven medical lore. Finally, superimposed upon this diverse and motley medical fabric, the church layered its own diffuse and variegated beliefs, ensuring that the laity recognized that sin was disease and cure no more than salvation that could only be proffered by priests and a declaration of complete fealty to the savior and ultimate deity.

An early map of Britain and the surrounding seas indicates the isolation faced by the original inhabitants.

Thus, in the earliest of times, it might be said that health was the accepted mode of life and illness an aberration that was not only ill understood but also considered to be due to divine providence, fate, or the work of malign influences resident in the stars or woods, or strange humors that emanated from fens and marshes. Obvious causes such as insect or animal bites could be understood, but mysterious afflictions which induced burning temperatures, shaking, chills, and loss of appetite and weight were less comprehensible. The relationship between a gored thigh and demise was obvious, as were the results of eating food that produced abdominal pain, vomiting, and diarrhea. The nature of such events was relatively easily discerned, but occasions where the appetite inexplicably faded, cutaneous sores appeared as muscles wasted and masses materialized were frightening and required help and advice from those skilled in the arts of illness. As such, the earliest medical practitioners of any sort would almost certainly have been those designated as priests or magicians and skilled in the arts of herbal remedy. How they acquired such knowledge or became specifically interested in disease is difficult to ascertain, but certainly the power to heal must have provided considerable influence and authority. Possibly, a nurturing personality or a random event whereby advice resulted in cure led to a reputation, which then became handed down from generation to generation.

While curiosity regarding the use of certain agents or plants may have initiated a skill in early shamanism or herbalism, it is possible that the healing properties of herbs may have initially been noted through observation of animals. Subsequently, primitive experiments with roots, leaves, and applied ointments led to the development of infusions, decoctions, and ointments. The superimposition of such agents upon magic or religious rituals would have culminated in the acceptance by a group that a certain individual was the possessor of unique skills that might represent both his expertise as well as the notion that a divine or spiritual power was in some way connected to the healer. The herbalist or spiritualist among primitive tribes would accumulate information and experience and note that their skill and service not only had a material value, which enabled them to live in their community by providing a service not involved with manual labor, but also conferred a form of divine or mystical authority. To further amplify their position within primitive society, a healer or priest could then conjure an aura of mystery and magic, and maintain the secret of their skill within a family, further ensuring that their status might be perpetuated. By further perpetuating theories of supernatural power and its relationship to disease, they were able to amplify their social standing by suggesting skills of such power that they were able to protect their fellow beings from the malign influences of demons and gods. Thus, the early uses of therapeutic agents were surrounded with the practice not only of primitive medicine but also quasi-religious and supernatural skills involving incantations, exorcism, superstitions, and the development of a priest craft. The subsequent extrapolation of such behavior fed on the credulity and anxieties of humans who were ill-led to the fakery, impostures, and quackery that have been constant companions of the healing art since its inception.

A Druid (*right*) invoking the mysteries of the secret of the stones within the magical stone ring of Stonehenge (*left*). His staff is not dissimilar to the latter-day caduceus, an emblem of his knowledge that was indicative not only of his authority but also his ability to provide magic and healing power.

The concept of therapy cannot be considered without taking into account early man's notion of health and disease. This in itself has inherent difficulties, since it is not truly possible to assess what a person many millennia removed from our civilization may have imagined under circumstances where his feeling of well-being became altered. Considerations for the cause of the problem must have ranged from the malign influences of his tribe to the designs of an enemy or ingestion of poor food, and possibly even the influence of stars, planets, or supernatural beings that inhabited the forests and mountains of his environment. Thus, a primitive man's understanding of the human body is unintelligible unless we consider the preconceptions that may have preoccupied the primitive mind. All undeveloped and primitive races possessed what to them must have represented complete "explanations" of the world in which they lived. Such elucidations, like modern scientific rationalizations, consisted in part of "laws" which would, according to the custom of a particular group, be regarded as invariable. As might be predicted, the tenets which primitive man devolved from contemplation of his life and times were somewhat more inaccurate than represented by current scientific doctrine, and unlike contemporary scientific imperatives, these explanatory principles were not explicitly stated or formulated in such a fashion as to be normative for the doctrines or beliefs of the time.

For the most part, it has been customary to regard the class of data which primordial peoples developed as an explanation of their world as falling within the category of magic. Within this context, two fundamental principles (the law of contagion and the law of similarity) underlying magical ideas require consideration as regards concepts of health and disease. The concept of contagion states that objects, which at one time have been in continuity or juxtaposition, continue to exert an effect one upon the other, no matter how distantly they may ultimately come to be removed. Thus, if a primal man wounded an enemy, he supposed that he might later exercise an influence over the progress of the healing of the wound by subjecting the weapon that inflicted the injury to various forms of treatment. Thus, heating the blade of the weapon in a fire would be presumed to result in the wound becoming hot and inflamed. This law of contagion, although it had little or nothing to do with the science of bacteriology, directed mankind into what at this time might at initial enquiry appear to be a consideration of hygienic

pursuits. In fact, observation of primitive tribes reveals that individuals are obsessive about the disposal of their excrement, nail parings, and particles of uneaten food. This does not reflect a preoccupation with hygienic principles, rather a belief that such preemptive activity will obviate ill disposed individuals from subjecting man to harm by magically manipulating materials that were once in contact with him.

The law of similarity states that objects or circumstances which bear some apparent similarity, whether in form, shape, color, or sequence of events, are considered by the primitive mind to be fundamentally related. Thus, certain primitive tribes, for instance, have a belief that a yellow bird is useful in the treatment of jaundice, and being attracted by the similarity of color, capture birds with yellow feathers or eyes. After reciting appropriate incantations over them, they are released in the belief that the bird acquires and carries away with it the agent of the affliction or "illness principle". In the canon of pharmacology, this set of "principles" subsequently became adopted under the names of the "doctrine of signatures" and *"similia similibus curantur"*. A further but alternative extrapolation of this concept led to the belief that objects that possessed certain characteristics directly opposite could be considered to exhibit a sympathetic relationship with one another.

In order to further protect himself from an often hostile and inexplicable reality, primordial man almost of necessity developed an alternative set of explanations to comprehend the phenomena of the external world and within himself a novel rationale that countermanded the theme of invariability implicit in magical formulae. Such enlightenment was based upon the necessity and assumption that under certain circumstances, natural laws could be offset by the influences of supernatural or spiritual power.

During the Neolithic period, ancestor worship was a central feature of society and a great emphasis was placed on the burial of the dead. Magnificent tombs were therefore built as "houses" for the dead. These usually comprised stone chambers with long entry passages enclosed in a protective mound. The latter preserved and facilitated the subsequent access to tombs for religious purposes.

It is likely that the concept of a spirit was initiated by the fundamental observation of the stark differences between life and death, whereby the deceased were cold, pale, bloodless, and, above all, motionless. In fact, motion and life came to be identified as so inseparable that many primitive cultures even to this time are accustomed to regard anything that moves as "more or less alive". Primitive man considered this ineffable "something" which brought about movement during life and, on departing, left the corpse motionless as an entity capable of traversing space. Despite it being unseen and unheard, it was considered pervasive and capable of exerting an influence that might be good or evil depending upon extant circumstances. This concept of a disembodied life principle forms the basis of the primitive idea of spirit that was subsequently extrapolated by prescient philosophers, including Descartes and Pascal, into the concept of the soul. Since they were disembodied, such spirits were not considered subject to the limitations of space, time, or the travails of the flesh, and were thus capable of exerting an influence beyond the human sphere. It was divined that a mortal might avail himself of such power by securing the offices of a spirit to intercede on his behalf, and in such a fashion, set aside natural law or the fate of the flesh.

In this respect, the concept of the vampire is of particular interest in contemplating the principle to which therapy might be applied. Thus, the characteristics of cold and pallor, which are associated with death, are direct reflections of bloodlessness, and primitive man noted early that extensive hemorrhage was incompatible with life. From this observation arose an inkling that the life principle in the living might reside within the blood and that assimilation of the blood of another might vitiate the loss of spirit associated with bleeding and death. Further experience with regard to the dramatic loss of blood (and life) in the event of wounds to the heart led to the development of a reasonable belief that the life principle might reside either in the blood or the heart, or even in both. Indeed, the dramatic importance directed at the excision of the heart as undertaken by the Mayans further supports the early notions of the "spirit" as being a heart–blood related entity. Similarly, the realization of the massive blood content of the liver led to some early magico-medical writings regarding the seat of life as residing in the liver, while also conferring upon the heart various functions consistent with a role in the mentation process.

Torture and human sacrifice were fundamental religious rituals of Mayan and Aztec societies. They were believed to guarantee fertility, demonstrate piety, and propitiate the gods, and if such practices were neglected, cosmic disorder and chaos were thought to result. The drawing of human blood was thought to nourish supernatural beings and was thus necessary to achieve and maintain contact with them. The central role of the heart was well recognized and therefore considered the ultimate gift to the gods.

Such primitive theories of the phenomena of life and disease provided minimal opportunity to embrace a deeper understanding of the mysteries of bodily function, let alone the concepts of miasma and pathology. However, with the passage of time, the failure of the primitive scheme of explanations in the face of more complex forms of practical life mandated a more rational consideration of details, which had been previously neglected. Initially, attention was directed to structure and early anatomical concepts led to a basic understanding of the fabric of life upon which was slowly grafted a vague appreciation of function. Indeed, the earliest cryptic pictures drawn during the upper Paleolithic epoch by the Cro-Magnon man indicate that he was not completely without some factual anatomical and physiological knowledge. Albeit that the cavern walls predominantly reflected magical concepts, presumably superimposed upon this framework of practical topographical anatomy, embodied in the designs is an obvious understanding of structure and function. Nevertheless, prior to the Greek era, only the vaguest references reveal any evidence of anatomical information and despite their apparent sophistication, the Egyptians exhibited a profoundly limited grasp of human design, preferring to devote themselves to magic and the attainment of a healthy afterlife.

Although certain of the ancient papyri make superficial references to anatomical structure, prior to the discovery of Babylo-Assyrian texts dating back to 7000 BC in the ruins of the palace of Ashurbanipal at Nineveh, few writings reflecting ancient medical practices can be identified. This collection, unlike older records, is not the remnants of a mere legal repository, but actually represents a library in the more modern sense of the word and from them some insight into ancient medicine may be gained. The *Code of Hammurabi*, which is believed to be based upon a still older source and is a legal document, makes it clear that a definite medical class existed in the valleys of the Tigris and Euphrates at a much earlier period than any medical texts would indicate themselves. The material relates to the practice of medicine and describes the physician or "Asu" who was the representative of the healing god Ea, and thus, in a sense, a vaguely priestly individual. Of note even this early in history is the fact that the physician was specifically distinguished from the surgeon and veterinarian, and a separation was established between magical and religious procedures, as well as between these and objective practices in medicine.

Furthermore, the concepts of therapy are defined not only in terms of efficacy but also as they relate to therapy, which might be deemed to have been inappropriate or wrong, or to have failed. Thus, definite penalties were laid down for the practice of witchcraft and physicians, necromancers, and priests were also proscribed for malpractice. Although an initial consideration of the *Code of Hammurabi* might allow for the belief that a very advanced state of medicine existed in Babylonia, subsequent records indicate that this is an illusion. The concept behind the disease in the majority of old Babylo-Assyrian texts represents a transmogrification or modified conception of possession by spirits or devils, of which the Babylonian mythology possessed an overabundant supply. Indeed, suffering was considered by the ancient Babylo-Assyrians as the result of wrongdoing much in the same fashion as is held by contemporary Buddhists. In the face of this ideology, it was rational for a sick man to attempt to placate an imaginary, irate deity rather than to seek out a physician, and it was only in isolated circumstances that the medicine of this civilization attained objectivity.

The ancient Assyrian King Sargon, standing before the sacred tree (modified from Saint-Elme Gautier) paying homage to the divinity of life, holds the lotus and acknowledges this and the date tree as icons of fertility and knowledge. The Assyrians had an advanced legal culture and the medical component of these laws held the physician responsible for therapeutic outcome. The price of malpractice was high and could even lead to the loss of a limb or an eye for the caregiver ("*lex talionis*").

Birds, animals, and celestial objects such as the moon, sun, and stars were part of a complex system of predicting life outcomes and prognosticating the future in the ancient kingdoms of the Middle East. In Egypt, medicine and magic were intimately interwoven, yet common sense and clinical acumen were evident, especially among the priestly class. The records of Egyptian medical practice provide evidence of both sagacity and effective therapeutic intervention.

Although the Babylonians made no distinction between arteries and veins, they did distinguish between venous blood (blood of the night) and arterial blood (blood of the day). This confusion of arteries with veins was based upon the failure to understand the nature of the circulation of the blood, but allowed for some consideration of the blood as a substance that might harbor the agents of ill health. The Greeks were inconclusive in their understanding of the blood and its conduits. As a result, arteries were incompletely differentiated from veins, since they noted that some arteries were normally empty of blood after death; thus a precise distinction between arteries and veins was not extant in ancient times. Bleeding to liberate "evil spirits" was not widely practiced and the Egyptians in particular believed that the majority of disease arose in the bowels from the "dirt" contained therein. In consequence, much of their medical practice was "anocentric" and emphasized the use of enemas to administer cleansing agents or purgatives to eliminate disease.

Apart from such notions in the Nile Valley, the inhabitants of the valleys of the Tigris and Euphrates were aware that diseases also afflicted specific organs (lungs, liver) and used this knowledge to seek understanding as well as to provide portents for the future. This notion was elaborated upon by the Babylonians, who supposed that certain animals (sheep) possessed a knowledge of the future denied to humans and that this understanding was reflected in the shape of their liver. As a result of this quasi magical-religious medical association, priests developed complex clay models of the liver that bore special designations for the three main lobes and the associated major anatomical structures. The *"fossa venae umbilicalis"* was designated "river of the liver" and the two appendages attached to the upper lobe – the *"processus pyramidalis"* and the *"processus papillaris"* – were respectively described as the "finger of the liver" and the "offshoot," while the depression separating the two lobes from the *"lobus caudatus"* was referred to as the "crucible" of the liver. In addition, the gallbladder, cystic and hepatic ducts, and the *"ductus choledochus"* were all specifically mentioned and each structure or aberration thereof (stones, lumps, scars) was accorded a prognostic value for the health of the patient being considered or the future, if prophecy was the intent of the divination. At a much later time, it became the custom to offer to the various deities models of organs or parts of the body which were supposed to be diseased. These models were called votive offerings or *"anathemata"* and the concept of offering them to the gods represented an expression of the "law of similarity" in magic.

The earliest evidence of a developed medical system in Egypt, as in Babylonia, is indirect and when apparent, as in inscriptions, stele, or papyri, offers definite proof that a system was present in an undeveloped form long before the time of the record. Thus, the notations of the Ebers papyrus presuppose the existence of a line of thought which must have existed for a substantial prior period of time. As in the case of the Mesopotamian civilization, the Egyptian priestly class was not only of importance politically and economically, but also ecclesiastically. Despite the fact that bodily suffering was considered the result of transgression of sacred law and that to a certain extent the superimposition of Egyptian theology interfered with objective medicine, useful medical remedies and concepts are proposed in the Ebers papyrus. A major issue however was the Egyptian restriction against profaning the body, based upon the assumption that unless its form was carefully preserved until the time of resurrection, the spirit would be incapable of incorporation and would become lost in the void. The Egyptians were especially worried about desecration of the body, since falling prey to animals or the depredations of worms would result in the body becoming utterly lost to its former spirit. As a result of this belief, an elaborate process of preserving the dead – mummification – became a mainstay of medical and theological practice. Thus, the specific prohibition against profaning the dead as well as a philosophy which stated that suffering and consequently disease were due to the intervention of a deity led to an avoidance of the opportunity to view and comment upon anatomy and disease.

In 1872, George Ebers (*bottom right*) discovered in Thebes a papyrus (*background*) that provided vivid insight regarding the basis of Egyptian medical practice. Despite their apparent religio-political sophistication, the Egyptians however exhibited a profoundly limited grasp of human design, preferring to devote themselves to magic and the attainment of a healthy afterlife. Thus, Egyptians believed that the best one might do for the living was prepare them for a wonderful afterlife, as there was little therapy available for disease and outcome was believed to be in the hands of the gods. A talisman or herbal remedy or enema combined with prayer was the best that a patient could expect.

The liver was regarded in many ancient cultures as a source from which divine prognostication might be derived. Thus, augurs (*top right*) would sacrifice animals and inspect entrails for messages that might allow prediction of the future. Hepatic anatomy was well known to the ancient Babylonians and numerous clay tablets and models have survived to attest to the importance to which ancient civilizations of the Middle East ascribed "hepatoscopy" as a form of prophecy (*left*).

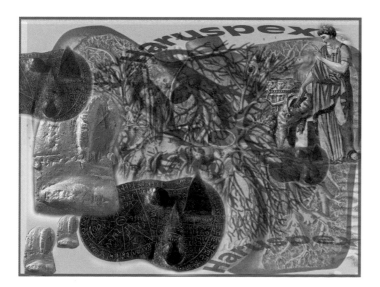

Although the Babylonians were concerned about the reunion between body and spirit, the concept never attained the obsessional level encountered in the land of the Pharaohs. Medication was modest and mostly represented by herbal infusions, complex recipes of honey, wine, and grains, while administration was for the most part *per anus*, although *per os* was possible if the mixture were palatable. Direct physical intervention was usually restricted to repair of broken bones, reduction of dislocations, and removal of arrows and javelins. Among the Babylonians, the surgeon was a recognized but ignorant craftsman, although in Egypt, despite the fact that his function was somewhat better regarded, religious law nevertheless restricted his practice to mostly reparative and superficial manipulations.

Since magical ideas obey the laws of similarity and contagion, it might be predicted that the therapeutic efforts of primitive man would follow such principles. Indeed, primitive pharmacology exhibits numerous examples whereby the law of similarity makes itself apparent. Thus, a medicine to turn gray hair black may be produced by stewing birds such as the raven, which has intensely

Early medicine was a complex admixture of magic, superstition, and religion. The belief that a cure for the ailment of a particular disease could be provided by a magical property that resided in the afflicted organ led to the development of mystical notions that later evolved into the "laws of similarity". Procreation was regarded as the cure for all illness – a notion that has persisted from time immemorial.

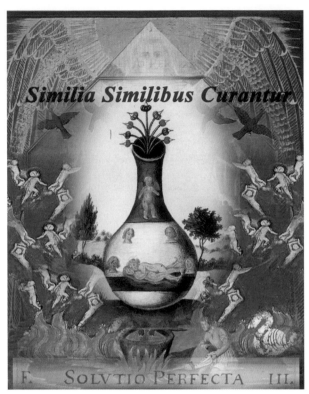

Classical ancient medical literature abounds with descriptions of medical matters. Although life in the less civilized areas such as Gaul or Britain often ended in violent death by the sword, the ruins of military camps and cities such as Pompeii have yielded a wide variety of relatively sophisticated medical instruments. These were an important part of any Roman physician's armamentarium and underscored the differences in the art between the conqueror and the conquered.

black feathers. In a similar fashion, the extrapolation of this process of reasoning allowed for the belief that parts of plants which resembled organs or portions of the body could be considered to exert an influence over them. Indeed, the subsequent amplification of notions such as this became explicit in the development of the medieval doctrine of signatures, and the current usage of an agent such as ginseng is a modern example of its continued persistence. The antithesis of the theory of cure by the application of the law of similarity (*similia similibus curantur*) also suggested itself, and in this fashion, concepts such as the utility of cold remedies for febrile conditions developed. The application of the law of contagion (objects once in juxtaposition continue to exert some mystical power over one another in perpetuity) is also frequently exemplified in medical systems. Thus, so-called moonstones, which were believed to have been formed in the earth under the influence of the moon, were long utilized to treat insanity, at that time held to be consequent upon the malign effects of prolonged lunar exposure ("lunatic").

Despite such arcane notions, primitive pharmacological ideology did not solely reflect theory and some concepts were based upon either observation or personal experience. Thus, abdominal symptoms could be related to the consumption of specific fruits which were then avoided. Similarly, the observation that animals when ill consumed certain herbs or berries led to the adoption of a similar practice in humans in the hope of effecting a cure. In some circumstances, a misinterpretation of an affliction allowed for the development of a legitimate confusion between magic and disease. Thus, a common primitive concept of the intrusion of an irate deity into the body was that evil spirits would be sent to torment the patient and would result in the gnawing pains that accompany many diseases. Given the prevalence of the filth and vermin which were a constant feature of primitive existence and the notable presence of maggots in many putrescent diseases, early physicians concluded that the early pain of disease was as a result of malignant spirits which were now, in the form of worms, working their way out of the part of the body they had so long tormented. Thus, much of magic cures could be supported not only by prayers and potions designed to rid the body of spirits but also by the dramatic demonstration of parasites being passed *per anus* or being extracted from cutaneous sores. As might be expected, many complex early pharmacological interventions redounded with highly developed religious incantations, which were deeply cognizant of demonology and firmly founded upon the belief that the suffering incident upon disease was the result of personal malfeasance. In particular, Babylo-Assyrian remedies were usually accompanied by complex incantations intended as prayers to the putative divinities involved, and in this fashion, the two different concepts of etiology and "*therapeusis*" could be melded into a single beneficial procedure.

The evolution of medical care and the practice of physicians throughout English history demonstrate many of the different facets that are common to diverse medical cultures throughout Europe. In addition, there exists evidence of innumerable examples of diagnosis and treatment clearly analogous to medical care in other regions and times. The warp and woof of history sometimes facilitated transmission of ideas almost unmodified and at other times produced exotic alterations or cultural adaptations reflecting either the passage of time or distance or permutations induced by intermingling with local practices and beliefs. An island may be regarded as isolated or susceptible to cultural wave action depending on the tides of fate and fortune and the caliber of the invaders or the susceptibility of the inhabitants. This book seeks to document aspects of the development of medicine as it pertains to the British and in particular, to focus upon their contributions to the field of gastroenterology and gastrointestinal surgery.

In an attempt to protect against poisoning and disease, arcane incantations, mythical animals, amulets, and exotic substances were sought from the farthest ends of the earth. Much disease was, however, felt to be caused by evil spirits naturally present in certain animals or by the influence of malignant individuals on such vermin or beasts. The denizens of a fevered imagination were often conjured into a pseudo reality where demonic possession and illness became one and the same. Wine in particular was recognized to have special properties.

2 ANGLO-SAXON ENGLISH MEDICINE

In general, Anglo-Saxon medicine belongs to the Dark Ages and its overall description demonstrates the prevalent ignorance with regard to medicine as well as the futility of most of the measures prescribed. Thus, the spirit of curiosity coupled with enquiry, which had prevailed in more classical times, had given way to barren formulae. Most leeches were content to copy dead material without questioning its value or its authority, and there were few individuals who by pondering and questioning were able to lead mankind through the accumulated rubbish of unscientific ages to knowledge. Both the magic and the medicine of the Anglo-Saxons were largely derived from the works of Pliny and from late classical writers such as Marcellus Empiricus and Celsus. In consideration of magic, Pliny noted sagaciously that "irrespective of the fact that it first originated in medicine, no one entertains a doubt that under the plausible disguise of promoting health, it insinuated itself among mankind as a higher and more holy branch of medical art". He further commented that "in the next place, with promises most seductive and most flattering, it added all the resources of religion, a subject upon which, at the present day, man is still entirely in the dark". There is little doubt that Anglo-Saxon medicine, whether Church or lay, was steeped in superstitious and magical practices that had for the most part originated with the teachings of the Romans and the Greeks, but to a certain extent reflected native Teutonic and Druidic material. Thus, in the earliest of times, magic became intimately associated with most branches of medicine, thereby ousting the healing art itself, and the magical attributes of objects then used for effecting cures were those which had most value in the eyes of the Anglo-Saxons. Although certain diseases such as insanity lent themselves more than others to treatment by means of magic, acute illness and obstetrics were for the most part not amenable to superstition, religious intervention, or herbal remedies. Under such circumstances, a patient could do little but place himself in the hands of a hopefully divine providence.

THE VENERABLE BEDE AND RELICS

The Anglo-Saxon period is generally regarded as stretching from the mid 5th to the mid 11th century, but the precise details of the era vary considerably during these 600 years, since few records remain. During the earlier period, the Venerable Bede is almost the only authority, but fortunately, he provided quite detailed information on cures effected in his time. Since the manuscripts that contain prescriptions which have survived date mostly from the 10th and 11th centuries, knowledge of later Anglo-Saxon medical practice is more complete than for the earlier periods.

The works of the Venerable Bede (*left*) overall fall into a number of broad groups comprising grammatical and "scientific" scriptural commentary, and historical and biographical texts. Although his earliest works include treatises on spelling, hymns, figures of speech, verse, and epigrams, his first treatise on chronology, *De temporibus* (*On Times*), with a brief chronicle attached, was written in 703 AD and was particularly concerned with the reckoning of Easter. Subsequently, in 725 AD, he completed a greatly amplified version, *De temporum ratione* (*On the Reckoning of Time*), with a much longer chronicle. In 731/732 AD, Bede completed his *Historia ecclesiastica*, which was divided into five books and recorded events in Britain from the raids by Julius Caesar (55–54 BC) to the arrival in Kent (597 AD) of Saint Augustine.

The art of curing the sick as well as the duty of caring for them was almost entirely in the hands of the Church in Anglo-Saxon times. Based upon the report of Bede, the medical manuscripts of Hippocrates, Galen, and certainly Isidore of Seville (who derived much from them) were among those which Benedict Biscop brought with him from Rome to enrich his two monasteries of Monkwearmouth and Jarrow. The similar curiosity and commitment of other priests such as Saint Wilfrid had ensured that other texts had found their way to England and been stored in different monasteries. As a consequence of such acquisitions, the Church was the possessor of the book – knowledge of contemporary medicine – and predictably exercised its power and authority over the practice of medicine. Nevertheless, the common folk possessed the practical knowledge of herbal and other remedies, which had been handed down verbally from one generation to another.

In its capacity as the arbiter of medical knowledge, the Church thus provided official sanction for medical practice, and in so doing, rendered it effective in the eyes of the patients, both lay and clerical. Thus, its prayers were requisitioned for the sick, its blessing was attached to prescriptions, its relics were used as media for cures, and wells had to be blessed by the Church before their water could be used for healing purposes.

Church policy inculcated the population that disease was a punishment incurred as the result of sin and that only the Church might sanction the forgiveness of sin after due repentance. Since the latter state could only be provided by the clerics, it became axiomatic that the Church was capable of healing and curing disease. A typical description of such an illness and cure is detailed in the anonymous *Life of St Cuthbert*: "There came some women bearing a certain youth who lay on a litter; they carried him to… the holy bishop… adjuring him in the name of our Lord Jesus Christ that he would bless him with his holy relics and would utter a prayer for him to the Lord, beseeching God's pardon for the sins by which he was bound and on account of which he endured punishment. So the bishop… prayed… and blessing the boy, he drove away the disease and restored him to health." It is of interest to note that the medical aspect of the tale is of minimal importance (the disease from which the youth was suffering is not specified) and the primary motive of the author is simply to portray the power and holiness of the saint.

As disease was regarded as a supernatural visitation, supernatural means were naturally used to avert and cure it. Thus it was the obligate responsibility of a saint, following in the footsteps of Christ himself, to cure the sick. Indeed, the texts of Bede, Eddius Stephanus, and others amply demonstrate that the Anglo-Saxon saints nobly did their share in this work. As might be predicted, the most successful cures were probably those of functional disorders and were accomplished by means of faith and suggestion.

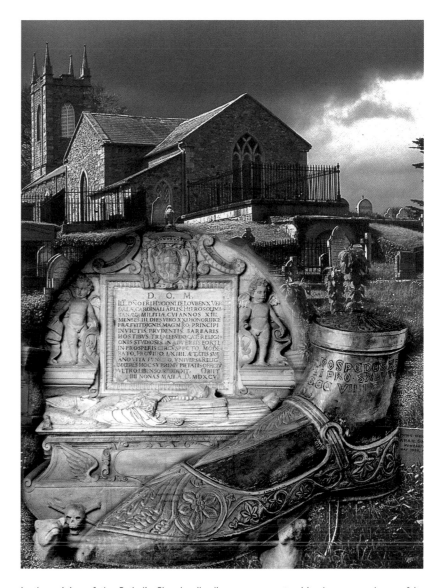

In the opinion of the Catholic Church, all relics possess great spiritual power, and one of its fundamental teachings has been that "where the relics are, there is the saint". The remains of the British martyr Saint Edward (*left*), son of King Edgar the Peaceable, who succeeded to the throne as King of England in 975 AD, can be found at Brookwood Church. Theodoric Paulus stated: "St Edward was a young man of great devotion and excellent conduct; he was wholly Catholic, good and of holy life; moreover, above all things he loved God and the Church; he was generous to the poor, a haven to the good, a champion of the Faith of Christ, a vessel full of every virtuous grace." Edward was an earnest supporter of the monastics in the life of the Church, as his father had been before him. But this aroused the displeasure of the powerful secular party within the Church, and, as so often happens in (Church) life, that displeasure found allies with ambition and jealousy, and the young King was brutally murdered at Corfe in Dorset in 979 AD.

The usual instruments employed by the Church for curative purposes were relics, although their success was largely dependent on the amount of faith possessed by each patient. In all likelihood, the more belief, the more effective the potency of the relic. Thus, Bede recounted the case of a saintly-minded priest who recovered from a long illness after communion with the spirit of Saint Cuthbert at the tomb of the latter. The supplicant claimed after prayer "to have received throughout his body such a great power from the Saint's incorrupt body that he rose from his prayer without exertion and returned to the guest-house without the aid of his attendant or of his staff".

With the passage of time, the Anglo-Saxon concept of healing by means of relics attained a more organized form, as techniques evolved both for the preservation of the relics themselves (that is, the bodies of saints) and also for extracting "virtue" from them so that they might be used for healing purposes. Eddius Stephanus, speaking of the death of Saint Wilfrid at Ripon, commented on the practice as follows: "They put up a tent outside the monastery, bathed the holy body, and emptied the bath on to the ground in the same place. The monks who inhabited the monastery thereafter erected a wooden cross on the site, and the Lord used to perform many marvels there." It was accepted that the earth, hallowed by the water in which the body of the revered saint had been washed, had become endowed with healing "virtue" and thus became the means for future cures. A similar tale was also recounted by Bede regarding the death of Saint Oswald, to the extent that "so many took up the dust of the very place where the body fell, and putting it into water did much good with it to their friends who were sick. This custom came so much into use that, the earth being carried away by degrees, there remained a hole as deep as the height of a man".

As a result of this firm belief in the power of particular holy sites, many places in England, such as the shrines of Saint Alban at St Albans and Saint Swithin, assumed a Lourdes-like role in the healing of the afflicted. Apart from the management of functional disorders, the Church was particularly involved with intervening in the most serious of all "illnesses," namely that of possession by the devil. While psychosomatic complaints were especially amenable to treatment by means at the disposal of the Church, it was in the therapeutic application of exorcism that it had no peers. The duty of expelling "devils" from those possessed by them was assigned to one of the seven orders of priests and a specific series of prayers was devised to assure the success of the exorcism. If clerical intervention was of no avail and the devil was "obstinate," more drastic and sometimes quite novel measures were taken. Thus, a prescription in the third leechbook (§ xl) describes with assurance: "If a man be *monaj-seoc*, take the skin of a porpoise, make it into a whip, beat the man with it: he will soon be well."

In the earlier part of the Anglo-Saxon period, relics were resorted to if exorcism was of no avail and Bede even describes a cure effected by the divine power of Saint Oswald in dealing with what was most likely a grand mal seizure: "There came a guest to Bardney Abbey who was

wont often in the night to be of a sudden grievously tormented with an evil spirit. He was hospitably received, and after supper lay down on a couch. Then he was suddenly seized by a devil and began to shout and grind his teeth, and to foam at the mouth, and he began to twist his limbs with all sorts of movements. None being able to hold or bind him, a servant ran and… acquainted the abbess. She… calling a priest, desired he would go with her to the sufferer… The priest chanted and recited exorcisms and did all that he could to allay the fury of the wretched man; but he produced no effect in spite of all his exertions. The abbess then sent a servant for some of the dust on which had been spilt the water in which Saint Oswald's bones had been washed, and as soon as it arrived in the room, he was suddenly silent and laid down his head as if released for sleep, stretching out all his limbs at 'rest'."

Despite the interest of the Church in many different aspects of disease, it vehemently refrained from the practice of surgery based upon the age-old injunction of "*sanguine abhorret Ecclesia*". This issue of the separation of the Church from the practice of surgery is specifically borne out by Bede in recounting the management of the illness of Saint Etheldrida, where the medicus Cynifrid was summoned by the ecclesiastics. Cynifrid is described as having successfully performed the operation on the Saint, since the ecclesiastics themselves could not undertake this and he must therefore have been a layman.

The names of at least four leeches – in addition to Cynifrid – who practiced in Anglo-Saxon times are known, of which the most distinguished was Baldwin of Chartres, who became Royal Physician to Edward the Confessor. One of his most memorable cures is recorded as that of Leofstan, Abbot of Bury, whose paralysis he successfully treated. The others are Bald, the owner of the first two leechbooks, whose name occurs in the colophon of the second; Oxa, who prescribed a recipe for the disease called "*jebr-ddl*" in the first leechbook; and Dun, who prescribed for lung disease in the second leechbook. However, whether the last three were clerics or laymen is not entirely certain. Of note is the use of the word "*lcece feoh-a*" ("physician's fee") suggesting the beginning of the craft, if not yet the profession, of medicine.

The leechbooks (*background*) were regarded as the vade mecum of medieval life. They were consulted in order to identify what kind of bloodletting was necessary (if any), whether the patient should rest or exercise more, if a change of diet were in order, or what medication or herbal remedies were necessary for treatment. It is of interest that "although arthritis and rheumatism were common disabilities, herbals and leechbooks prescribed more remedies for conditions affecting the eyes than for any other single complaint". The gut was almost *terra incognita* in terms of rational therapy, bleeding, purges, and vermifuges being the order of the day.

The wamb and humors

In the prescientific age of leechdom, two immense problems faced the leeches. Firstly, they were utterly ignorant of causation and secondly, they had no knowledge of the appropriate methods of treatment. In fact, the Anglo-Saxon derivation of etiology reflected classical and post-classical sources, native Teutonic sources, and what little could be gained from the body of Church medicine. Thus, a perusal of manuscripts of the time reveals that the "philosophical basis" of the medicine of the Dark Ages was the doctrine of "the four elements and the four humors." During the Dark Ages, physicians and patients alike accepted that there was a close relation between the external and the internal world – the macrocosm and the microcosm – and so they discerned a parallel between the four ages of man and the four seasons; between the humors of the body and the solstices and equinoxes; between the four elements and the four cardinal points. Thus, the Anglo-Saxons retained among their ideas of the constitution of the human body the Hippocratic doctrine of the four humors: blood, phlegm, black bile ("*cholera nigra*"), and yellow (or red) bile ("*cholera rubra*"). The predominance of any of these influenced a man's temperament; that of the first-named inclined him to be sanguine in his nature, that of the second to be phlegmatic, that of the third to be melancholic, and that of the fourth to be choleric. Combined with the four humors, two and two in each case, were Aristotle's four fundamental qualities: the hot, the cold, the wet, and the dry. Physiology and even diet were considered to be governed by such formulae; thus digestion involved the combined operation of the hot and the wet.

The second leechbook deals with "the various nature of the *wamb* (stomach) and its imperfection, how a man may recognize it". It deals with the *wamb* when it is hot, cold, or moist. The first condition digests food well; the third has a good appetite for meat, but not a good digestion; but a cold wamb was considered capable of engendering disease of the brain ("*breegenes-dill*") and madness. The Hunter manuscript (written shortly after the close of the Anglo-Saxon period) in Durham Cathedral Library comments in detail on the practice of medicine as governed by these philosophical principles. Of particular interest is an elaborate diagram of eight intersecting arcs within a circle, designed to show the correspondence of the elements, seasons, humors, and the four ages of man.

Singer was of the opinion that "Native Teutonic medicine" could be distinguished from imported elements by the presence of four characteristic elements. These were a) the doctrine of *specific venoms*, b) the doctrine of *the nines*, c) the doctrine of *the worm* as the cause of disease, and d) the doctrine of *the elf-shot*. Evidence for this proposal can be found in the 'Lay of the Nine Healing Herbs' in the *Lacnunga*, where the first three doctrines may be found together. The verses recount how Woden (a non-classical icon and therefore indicative of the origin of the poem) destroyed the serpent, and how the "Nine Diseases" arose from the nine fragments into which its body was severed.

Elf-shot and worms

In Anglo-Saxon times, worms were considered a predominant source of many diseases. Apart from intestinal worms, of which innumerable varieties are described in recipes, "*wyrm*" is often referred to as the cause of disease in the hand, the eye, the ear, or the teeth. As might be predicted, the leechbooks contained numerous remedies directed against specific worm-induced diseases. Thus, a collection of remedies in the first leechbook describes the management of tooth disease as follows: "…if a worm eat the teeth a candle should be made of acorn meal and henbane-seed and wax, and lighted… let it smoke into the mouth; place a black cloth underneath: then the worms will fall on to it."

Although an important component of early Anglo-Saxon medicine, the doctrine of the elf-shot is also one of the chief characteristics of Finnish magic. The English attributed the sudden attack of disease to having been struck by the arrows of elves, since the elves were believed to exhibit a predilection for shooting their arrows at domestic animals. In contrast, infection was considered to be caused by "flying venom". Considerable attention was directed to the consideration of various charms for horses that were deemed to have been "elf-shot". Thus, the *Lacnunga* suggests the following remedy: "If a horse or other beast be shot (*gescoten*), take seed of dock and Irish wax, let a mass-priest sing twelve masses over them, and put holy water on them, and put it on the horse or cattle."

In early times, one of the few objective and frightening indications of disease was the observation of parasites such as worms or their ova. The identification of such noxious creatures led religious authorities who were particularly interested in medicine to suggest that suffering was associated with personal malfeasance and that the loathsome denizens identified in the stool were manifestations of possession of the body by evil forces.

The word "*stice*" has been translated as "stitch" when used for a disease which was caused by the shots of elves or of witches, but since *stice* also means "puncture," it has been proposed that the nomenclature refers to the hole made in the victim by the elf-shot. The second leechbook provides at least two different remedies for disease, depending upon whether it could be established if the elf-shot had penetrated the skin or not. Elsewhere in the text, it is noted that "the white stone" is powerful against *stice* and against flying venom, and against all unknown maladies, whether caused by supernatural agencies or by witchcraft. Further consideration of the subject of disease causation refers to the effects of witches and the disease they caused by their discharge of "little spears," which were regarded as responsible for "*fcer-stice*" or the maladies associated with "sudden puncture". The doctrine of elf-shot as a cause of disease resembles closely the classical theory that considered pestilence as caused by the arrows of irate gods, especially of Apollo. An alternative Anglo-Saxon theory of the cause of pestilence was also derived from the classical medical theories originally propounded by Galen, who described pestilence as "a disease which attacks all, or the greater number, arising from corruption of the air with the result that great numbers perish". Bede refers to pestilence as being "produced from the air when it has become corrupted" and in so doing, probably derived his idea from Galen, although it is more likely that he learned it through the intermediary source of Isidore of Seville, with whose writings he is known to have been familiar.

With the advent of Christianity, the previous notions of elf-induced heathen disease were transmogrified to a demonic causation, and therefore diseases attributed to such agents were considered to reflect demoniacal possession. To embrace this shift in medical logic, the charms were therefore appropriately modified, and to ensure protection "against elf-disease," it became necessary to dip the herbs in hallowed water, lay them under the altar, sing psalms and masses over them, and perform other suitably Christian rituals. In many instances, the older heathen rites were undertaken prior to the administration of the more acceptable Christian drink or salve!

BLOOD AND THE BASIS OF DISEASE

A particular difficulty in the Anglo-Saxon conceptualization of disease lay with the concept that the disease itself was regarded as having volition and personality that could be affected by an external agency. Thus Bede recounts the tale of a young boy at Bardney who was suffering from an illness. One of the monks instructed him to "go into the church, and get close to St Oswald's tomb". Having complied with the instructions, it was noted that "the disease durst not affect him as he sat by the saint's tomb, but fled so absolutely, that he felt it no more". Although it is difficult to distinguish this description from the concept of demonic possession, the Church formulated various theories detailing the manner in which a devil might find entrance into a man. Such proposals included inhalation during breathing, surreptitious entrance while sleeping, or even ingestion during the eating of food. Jacques de Vitry, in Exempla, illustrated this last possibility as follows: "Saint Gregory tells of a nun who ate a lettuce without making the sign of the cross, and swallowed a devil. When a holy man tried to exorcise him, the devil said: 'What fault is it of mine? I was sitting on the lettuce, and she did not cross herself, and so ate me too'."

Since the cause of disease was in general unknown, it follows that the Anglo-Saxons were very weak with regards to diagnosis. They had no specific knowledge of the internal organs of the body or of their diseases, and in desperation, considered blood to be the ultimate causation of all illness, or at least to be related to it. The concept of bleeding for cure therefore became a central component of therapy and was employed "nearly always, nearly everywhere, and nearly for everything". Since at this time there existed no concept of the circulation, it was axiomatic that blood was considered stationary. Thus, the particular vein from which blood was to be taken was therefore of critical relevance to disease management and certain veins were identified as likely to cure certain diseases.

Erasistratus of Chios (fl circa 250 BC) was a Greek anatomist and physician of the Alexandrian medical school or sect and is considered the founder of physiology. Although regarded especially for his studies of the circulatory and nervous systems, Erasistratus noted the difference between sensory and motor nerves, but considered that the nerves were hollow tubes containing fluid. His highly advanced concept of the circulatory system alleged that air entered the lungs and heart and was carried through the body in the arteries, and that the veins carried blood from the heart to the various parts of the body. Erasistratus was the first major exponent of pneumatism about 300 BC (though the concept had been suggested earlier by other commentators), which was based on the premise that life is associated with a subtle vapor called the pneuma.

It is reputed that the theory that excess of blood was the chief cause of disease originated with Erasistratus of Chios in the 3rd century before Christ. The logical conclusion that the diminution of the local supply by bloodletting was therefore the logical treatment of disease at a specific location seemed clearly apparent, although not used by his school. Nevertheless, bloodletting, or venesection, as the technique became known, was the most popular therapy both in his time and in the succeeding Dark Ages, and persisted for many centuries thereafter as a crucial adjunct to any form of medical management. Unfortunately, it was often applied without due consideration of a patient's condition, and according to detailed and archaic prescribed formulae rather than according to reason, with the result that many who might well have survived without this intervention perished.

The therapeutic basis of bloodletting seems to have been connected with the doctrine of the humors; thus an evil humor could be eliminated from the system as the blood carried it away. A corollary of this notion was the belief that bloodletting had to be employed at intervals so as to draw off the evil humor as it accumulated, thus keeping the body in a healthy condition. Bede, in his *De minutione sanguinis, sive de phlebotomia*, begins by noting that the best time for bloodletting is from March 25 to May 26, "because then the blood is undergoing increase". The greater part of his tract deals with the parts of the body from which blood should be drawn for pains in various places and specifies which days of the moon are dangerous in each month. In the last paragraph, however, Bede points out that phlebotomy may be practiced at all times, "*si necessitas urget*" ("if the need is urgent").

Baths, purgatives, and emetics

Although the use of naturally occurring springs and thermal vents reflects Druidic custom, the formal use of baths for medicinal purposes was derived by the Anglo-Saxons from the Romans. Bede commented upon the subject, noting that Britain "has both salt and hot springs, and from them flow rivers which furnish hot baths, proper for all ages and sexes, and arranged accordingly". While considered of great beneficial value for the cure of sundry illnesses, baths often encouraged dissolute behavior and it is likely that a certain amount of infective disease transmission occurred under what were presumed to be salubrious conditions. Certainly, the Anglo-Saxons lacked the architectural skill of the Romans and failed to construct complex edifices for bathing, relying more on natural formations.

The baths of the emperor Caracalla (188–217 AD) (*background*) were huge, with the central mass of the building measuring 390ft wide by 740ft long. The largest room was the vaulted tepidarium, which measured 82ft by 170ft and was 125ft in height. The complex was extraordinary both in size and opulence, accommodating some 1,600 bathers as well as other activities such as sports and theatricals. The ancient Romans were well aware of the importance of cleanliness and considered the ritual of the daily bath to be an important component of societal behavior, since it vivified the body and fructified thought. It also served to provide a communal environment within which both the corpus and the libido might be cleansed in accordance with the moral norms of the times.

In addition, they developed other somewhat less rational means than baths for producing warmth for the benefit of the sick and infirm. Thus, the second leechbook prescribes as a remedy for the patient who has a "stomach which is of a cold or moist nature" that it is "helpful to him that a fat child should sleep by him, so that he should always put him near his stomach". It is of little surprise that the same proposal had also been described by both Oribasius and Paul of Egina. Its origins in antiquity may be further noted by the fact that the *First Book of Kings* opens with a passage in which the elderly King David is treated in his old age in a similar way.

Much as bloodletting was thought to remove noxious elements from the body, so emesis and bowel evacuation were considered important. In custom with many medicinal practice and remedies of the times, emetics and purgatives are therefore widely detailed in Anglo-Saxon recipes and the phrase "drink a strong drink that will run up and down" denotes recognition that the ideal remedy would be one effective for both purposes simultaneously. Cauterization was also used as a remedy not only in connection with wounds but also when it might appear to have had no practical utility. An 11th century manuscript in the Sloane collection in the British Museum contains a primitive descriptive anatomical atlas indicating where the cautery was to be applied to ensure maximum efficacy.

The ancient art of cupping was practiced to draw off secretions as well as blood and the techniques are well described in the leechbooks. Thus, the management of a swollen liver detailed in the second leechbook describes how the secretion should be drawn off at intervals using either "glass or horn". Since techniques for the manufacture of the former were scarce and the product expensive, the horn of an animal was generally preferred.

Animal and herbal remedies

As might be predicted in a society that had evolved from Druidic practices and then been exposed to Roman medical practice, the number of animal remedies employed were few compared with the number of herbal remedies. The *Medicina de quadrupedibus* of Sextus Placitus, of which the vernacular Anglo-Saxon version is printed in the first volume of Cockayne's *Leechdoms*, is arranged using an index based upon the animals from which the remedies were derived and not the diseases which were to be cured. As such, it was of limited value to the practitioner seeking a ready therapeutic recommendation. In order to facilitate administration of the various parts of an animal that might be ingested or applied *a salve*, detailed instructions were provided regarding appropriate admixture with oil, wine, vinegar, or honey, so as to dissolve them or to make them into an ointment. Nevertheless, despite the complex and arcane methods employed, little could have been done to adequately disguise the ingredients. Although such therapeutic mixtures of dog tongue, rabbit ear, sheep intestine, and horse penis might be considered offensive by current standards, it is likely that culinary customs of the time were such that they excited less offense than might be anticipated. Nevertheless, in some circumstances, the inability of the patient to tolerate oral intake of a vile concoction necessitated the use of the clyster mode of administration. Indeed, many of the remedies described would probably have been more useful as emetics than as medicine!

By far the largest number of the remedies prescribed was herbal in nature and although precise details are provided in all three volumes of Cockayne's work, the first volume, the *Anglo-Saxon Herbal*, deals especially with them. Innumerable varieties of plants are described and each species is illustrated in bright colors in the manuscript, while the text details the various uses (useful and otherwise) to which each should be put. In addition, considerable information is provided in regard to the diverse magical rites to be performed when gathering or administering to ensure maximal efficacy. It is likely that the numerous green herbs used may well have been beneficial because of their antiscorbutic properties; and since they were employed in the early spring, they may have helped to correct the winter-induced alteration of the blood with which the early Anglo-Saxons were prone to suffer after a long winter's diet in which salt meat and dried peas predominated.

English medicine at the end of the first millennium represented a conglomeration of diverse influences, ranging from Celtic, Norse, Norman, and Druidic to Roman and even Byzantine. It was characterized by a melange of Anglo-Saxon herbals tainted with Druidic superstition and even some Arab culture derived from the University of Paris. The physicians were known as leeches in recognition of the universal remedy they provided in the prescription of bloodletting!

THE EVOLUTION OF MEDICINE IN ENGLAND

The advance of medical progress in England was somewhat different to that experienced on the Continent of Europe, since its insular location diminished the stresses and strains engendered by the advent of Humanism and the Renaissance. As such, the British were for much of the time little more than spectators of the passing show rather than actual participants in the epic events that encompassed the times. Nonetheless, the news of these exciting European changes permeated the fabric of English society and many curious young Englishmen attracted to the new knowledge found the concept of an Italian education irresistible. As a result, they ventured abroad, particularly to the Italian universities of Padua, Bologna, and Florence, before returning to England to transplant and foster the "new learning" in their homeland. A prominent individual among these was Thomas Linacre, who, because of his lifelong service and dedication to the cause of Humanism, subsequently earned the sobriquet of the "Restorer of Learning" in England.

Thomas Linacre

Thomas Linacre was born at Canterbury in 1460 and at the age of 20, went to Oxford, becoming a Fellow of All Souls College in 1484 and thereafter devoting himself to the study of Greek. In 1488, his former teacher at Canterbury William Selling was appointed Ambassador to Rome and Linacre elected to accompany him to Italy. Seizing upon the opportunity to advance his

knowledge and sophistication, Linacre then studied with the poet Angelo Poliziano and with the great Greek scholar Demetrios Chalcondylas at Florence before then proceeding to Padua, where he took his degree in medicine. On his return to England, he once again settled in Oxford, where he taught Greek and practiced medicine.

Not long thereafter in about 1500, he was summoned to court and became Tutor and Physician to Prince Arthur. On the accession of Henry VIII, Linacre was appointed Physician both to the King and to the great in both Church and State. As might have been predicted, such responsibilities resulted in great demands on his time and in 1509, Linacre was ordained as a priest, not so much because of a desire to serve in a religious capacity but, as he confided to his friend the Archbishop of Canterbury, with the view to obtain the necessary leisure for his literary work.

Thomas Linacre (*right*) was not only a cleric and an astute medical politician and visionary, but also the Royal Physician of Henry VIII (*background*). He used his influence with the sovereign to transform English medicine and became the founder of the Royal College of Physicians of London. A driven man of great honor and intellectual rigor, his lasting contributions to medicine include some of the greatest translations of Galen's works from Greek into Latin. Indeed, no less an authority than Erasmus opined that Linacre's Latin was of better quality than Galen's Greek! Linacre himself published his experiences in a series of texts entitled *Methodus Medendi*, *De Sanitate Tuenda*, *De Symptomatum Differentiis et Causis*, and *De Pulsum Usu*.

There is abundant evidence that Linacre was not only a skillful physician but also a great scholar, and his most important literary labors included his translations of Galen from Greek into Latin. Indeed, such was his level of scholarship that even during his lifetime there existed controversy as to whether he was a more formidable Latin or Greek scholar. Johnson, in his usual witty fashion, remarked: "By his endeavors Galen speaks better Latin in the translation than he did Greek in the original." As a consequence of his great scholarship, numerous writings, and contagious enthusiasm in the teaching of the classical authors, Linacre almost single-handedly became a major force in the spread of Humanism in England.

Apart from being the talisman of the intellectual revolution in England, it is certain that the greatest service of Linacre to English medicine was his initiative to establish a Royal College of Physicians of London after the model of similar institutions in Italy. Prior to his arrival in London, the entire city teemed with medical quacks and impostors, and the whole system of licensing qualified practitioners was unsatisfactory, being permeated with dishonesty, patronage, and unscrupulous persons. In 1511, as a result of such widespread dissatisfaction and concern, Henry VIII, noting that physic and surgery were practiced by unskilled persons such as smiths, weavers, and women, persuaded Parliament to pass a law enabling the bishops the power to license physicians and punish irregular practitioners. In order to facilitate this process, each bishop was entitled to appoint a board of examiners to determine and render consistent the qualifications of physicians and surgeons. In fact, this system was considered so effective in comparison with the previous chaos that licensing by the bishops thereafter continued unchallenged until the end of the 18th century. In order to further codify and uphold the level of professional practice, Linacre in addition proposed that a college be established which would license practitioners only after they had passed the prescribed examinations, with the exception of graduates of Oxford and Cambridge. As a result of the joint advice provided by

Linacre and Cardinal Thomas Wolsey, Henry VIII established the Royal College of Physicians in 1518, and Linacre became its first President, holding this esteemed office until his death in 1524. As a mark of his unique contributions, Linacre was buried in St Paul's Cathedral, although his tomb remained unmarked by any memorial until John Caius, who was President of the College in 1557, erected a monument at his own expense. Sad to say this memorial perished along with the Cathedral in the great London fire of 1666.

John Caius

John Caius was born in 1510 and graduated at Gonville Hall, Cambridge, in 1532. Although he had initially planned to enter the Church, his disdain for the Reformation movement that was then sweeping the country led him away from orders and instead he turned to medicine and entered the University of Padua. As a student in this salubrious institution, he became a pupil of Montanus and lived in the same house as Andreas Vesalius. Despite their close proximity, the young Flemish anatomist appears to have little influenced Caius, for he remained a convinced Galenist and in subsequent years, never referred to his former association with Vesalius. In 1540, Caius, known as Joannes Gavius Brittanus, was appointed "Professor of Dialectics" and lectured in Greek for a year before graduating from Padua in 1541. The Paduan education, with its firm advocacy of Galenism, was well accepted by Caius, who continued his championship of Galenic medicine by publishing in 1544 *De Medendi Methodo* (*Concerning the method of healing*).

On his return to England, he practiced in a number of locations, including Cambridge, Norwich, and finally Shrewsbury, where he was witness to a major epidemic of the sweating

John Caius (1510–1573) was respectively Physician to Edward VI, Queen Mary, and Elizabeth I. He was one of the co-founders of Gonville and Caius Colleges in Cambridge and as such participated vigorously in the advance of early medical education. Despite his staunch adherence to the Catholic faith, he was on nine occasions elected to the presidency of the Royal College of Physicians. Despite his high standing in certain circles, he was nonetheless accused of atheism and of secretly keeping a collection of ornaments and vestments for Catholic use. The latter were found and burned in the College court!

sickness. Much enlightened by this harrowing experience, he subsequently described this epidemic in an important text. This most original work, published in London in 1552, remains the classic description of the disease and was entitled *A Boke or Counseill against the Disease commonly called the Sweate or Sweatyng Sicknesse*. Having gained experience in his former positions and supported by the reputation garnered from his text, Caius, in 1552, then settled in London where he soon attained professional eminence and became Physician successively to Edward VI, Queen Mary, and Elizabeth I. The latter however subsequently dismissed him from her service because of rumors of his adherence to the Roman Catholic faith.

In 1555, Caius was first appointed President of the Royal College of Physicians – an honor that would fall to him on a further nine occasions. Feted by royalty and swamped by patients and honors, Caius as a profoundly wealthy alumnus during this period provided a substantial sum to his former college in Cambridge, which was rebuilt and renamed Gonville and Caius College. In 1574, deeply concerned by a book that had been penned by an Oxonian claiming that Oxford was older than Cambridge, he in response wrote a book, *De Antiquitate Cantebrigiensis Academiae*, asserting that Cambridge had been founded by Cantaber in 394 BC and was 1,267 years older than Oxford. In 1558, Caius assumed the title of Master of Gonville and Caius College, but reports indicate that he quarreled relentlessly with both Fellows and students. A search of his rooms by the rival faction led to the discovery of "muche popishe trumpery" and culminated in some embarrassing and difficult political moments.

Perhaps in response to his disgruntlement with academic matters of the time, he thereafter wrote a book on English dogs for Gesner, whose death occurred during its preparation. Nevertheless, the text was published in 1570 as *De Canibus Britannicis* and represented a notable contribution to natural history. Caius died in 1573, having, as it is said, predicted the exact day of his death. He was buried in the Chapel of Gonville and Caius College, where his tomb may still be seen bearing to this day its laconic epitaph *"Fui Caius"* ("I was Caius").

Arderne was a sound practical surgeon who employed methods the principles of whose practice were, according to Power, "not very different from those of the modern aseptic surgeon". His teachings emphasized that wounds should heal without suppuration, that irritating solutions should not be used on wounds, and that dressings should be changed as infrequently as possible. In the best traditions of surgery, it was reported that he "operated boldly" and indeed, the operation that he described for fistula in ano, namely dividing the fistula from end to end, after falling into disuse for nearly 500 years, is now widely utilized as the standard of care.

SURGERY IN ENGLAND

The history of surgery in England has many points of resemblance to that of France. John of Gaddesden and Gilbertus Anglicus were both physicians and surgeons. John Arderne was, by contrast, primarily a surgeon and has often been called the "Father of English surgery".

John Arderne

John Arderne was born in 1307, practiced first in Wiltshire, then in Newark, and finally in London. Nothing authentic is known of his early education or training, except that he was an army surgeon in the service of Henry Plantagenet, Earl of Derby, and later, first Duke of Lancaster, and served in the Hundred Years War with France. Arderne was almost certainly well educated, since his practice was primarily among the nobility, wealthy landowners, and the higher clergy. A mark of his education was that he wrote not only extensively but also in Latin, and his manuscripts appeared in separate treatises, which were collected after his death. A number of these manuscripts have been preserved and have been published in translation as an illustrated manuscript of his collected works by Sir D' Arcy Power. *De Arte Phisicali et de Cirurgia*, copied around 1412, is still preserved and maintained in the Royal Library at Stockholm. Surprisingly for so erudite an individual, most of his writings were never printed, the sole exception apparently being an abridgment of the *Treatises of Fistula*, published in 1588.

Early English medicine, particularly as practiced by John Arderne (*top left*), focused heavily on the management of anorectal disease. In his text *Treatises of Fistula in Ano: Hemorrhoids and Clysters*, he provided considerable detail on the agents and techniques he utilized in the management of this vexatious problem. His work provides good evidence of his great clinical insight and his early mastery of the basic principles of anorectal pathology and its care.

In respect of remuneration for his special services, the surgical fee required by Arderne for the cure of a fistula was 40 pounds in advance, a suit of clothes, and 100 shillings annually as long as the patient lived! Given the fact that a common laborer of Arderne's time was paid about a penny a day, his fee might be regarded as reasonable remuneration. If Arderne were to reside in New Haven at this time where the minimum wage for a day laborer at Yale is about US $50 a day, Arderne by comparison would have received $75,000 for a single operation, plus $30,000 a year as long as the patient lived.

The Hundred Years War (1337–1453) and the War of the Roses (1453–1497) created a great demand for military surgeons. These wars were expensive, since the soldiers were well paid and represented a large financial investment as their lives and health had a monetary value. Such circumstances led to surgeons becoming important assets in that they were capable of securing the investment in the soldier and keeping him healthy and able to fight for as long as possible. Although initially such army surgeons were not united in any army corps and served individual commanders or noblemen, in 1369, they amalgamated themselves into a society – the Military Guild. The terms of service were not lax and apprentices were required to serve six years before being examined by the Masters of the Guild with a view to becoming independent practitioners. Although success led to admission to membership, failure resulted not only in a further service for yet another six years, but permanent exclusion if they once again failed the repeat second examination.

Surgeons who looked after the general population in various cities followed much the same practice as other practitioners of trades such as weavers, greengrocers, goldsmiths, and merchants and just before 1300, British barber-surgeons too began to form guilds. These guilds of barber-surgeons took in apprentices, taught them by lectures, dissections, and practical demonstrations, examined them at the end of their studies, and licensed them to practice in the city where the guild had its seat. A legal statute enacted in 1313 compelled everyone to belong to a guild; if his own craft did not have a place for him, it was mandated that room must be made for him in another. As a result, barber-surgeons were to be found in various guilds, while the barber-surgeon guilds sometimes included silk weavers, cap makers, chandlers, and rope makers. In 1462, the guild was incorporated and thereafter became known as a company. As might be predicted given the widespread need for surgical expertise in a society where all illness was treated by surgical venesection, the barber-surgeons grew rapidly in numbers and became the most numerous of all the 39 "livery" companies – those wearing a distinctive livery or dress. Thus in 1537, the Barbers had 185 members, while the Skinners had 151, the Haberdashers 120, the Fishmongers 109, and the Merchant Tailors 96. Such was the effectiveness and functionality of this method of securing a labor group that the guilds eventually evolved into legal corporations, which included nearly all British surgeons for the subsequent 400 years.

In 1511, an Act of Parliament was passed which provided the bishops with the power to license practitioners and to punish offenders. Then in 1518, Henry VIII, at the instigation of Linacre, founded the Royal College of Physicians, which had the power to examine candidates and license them if they passed the examination. Thus, in London at that time there existed several regulatory bodies deemed capable of licensing: the Universities, the Bishop, the Guild of Military Surgeons, the Company of Barber-Surgeons, and the Royal College of Physicians. Some of this confusion and redundancy was decreased in 1540 when the two surgical guilds were united by an Act of Parliament to form the United Company of Barbers and of Surgeons (Barber-Surgeons' Company). An important component of this Act was embodied in the declaration that the surgeons should not barber and the barbers should not practice surgery, although united in the same legal corporation.

Thomas Vicary

An outstanding surgeon of this period was Thomas Vicary, born circa 1495. Although originally a simple practitioner at Maidstone, he relinquished his country practice and moved to London, where following admission to the Barber-Surgeons' Company, he became Senior Warden in 1528 and was appointed Surgeon to Henry VIII. Such was his surgical and certainly his political expertise that in 1535, he became Chief Surgeon to the King and was in addition granted some abbey lands that had recently been confiscated. Given his professional skills and obvious royal patronage, in 1541, Vicary was elected Master of the Barbers-Surgeons' Company.

Thomas Vicary (*bottom right*) from an etching after the picture by Hans Holbein. Vicary was a surgeon of great clinical renown and considerable political clout. As a leading member of the Fellowship of Surgeons, he had become Surgeon to Henry VIII and subsequently held this position during the reigns of Edward IV, Queen Mary, and Elizabeth I. Vicary was in part responsible and undoubtedly influential through his royal connections in cementing the bond between the large, established Company of Barbers and the small Fellowship of Surgeons, and was appointed the first Master of the Barber-Surgeons' Company after its founding in 1540. His first book, *A Profitable Treatise of the Anatomy of Man's Body*, published in 1548, was little more than a compilation, for he was not an original writer and was a pre-Vesalian anatomist, but his writings provide a reasonable picture of the medical practice of his time. Although often considered as the first Lecturer in Anatomy at the Barber-Surgeons' Hall, this accolade properly belongs to John Caius.

THOˢ VICA[...]

Under his stewardship, the new united Company upheld its responsibilities seriously, especially its accountability for educating its apprentices, who on an annual basis usually numbered about 1,000. The Act of 1540, which gave birth to the Barber-Surgeons' Company, specified that "four persons condemned adjudged and put to death for felony" should be delivered yearly to the Company "for anatomies". Having secured a supply of bodies guaranteed by law, the Company appointed a reader of anatomy and four demonstrators to conduct the dissections, thus ensuring that there would be both teachers and teaching material. Vicary was probably the first reader, and the book published in 1548 with the title *A breefe Treatise of the Anatomie of man's body Compyled by me Thomas Vycarie Esquire, and Sergeant Chirurgion to King Henry the eyght* was probably the text from which he lectured. However, it was regarded by contemporary historians as "a worthless treatise on anatomy based upon the teaching of Lanfranc and Henri de Monde". Overall, Vicary's writings were relatively few and unimportant, but his influence, reputation, and prestige during his lifetime were enormous, and he employed them with good effect in ensuring the advancement of surgery.

The reputation of Italian anatomy was however growing in England, and in 1543, Caius, aged 36, who had just returned from Italy where he had known both Vesalius and Realdo Colombo, was appointed Reader in Anatomy, a post he held for nearly 20 years until 1563. The effectiveness with which he carried out this responsibility given his scholarly background and excellence in anatomy led to the determination that the reader would thereafter always be a university graduate.

In 1537, St Bartholomew's Hospital, a Church institution, was separated from the Priory and its revenues seized by Henry VIII, who at that time was confiscating the property of the Roman Catholic Church and diverting its revenues to the State. As a result of this draconian decision, the citizens of London and of many English cities were faced with the tragedy of ill patients dumped onto the streets with no provision for their treatment. The crushing edict resulted in the bed capacity of St Bartholomew's Hospital being reduced to two or three beds for almost seven years before the King relented and refounded the hospital under the direction of his own surgeon, Vicary. Appointed as Resident Surgical Governor, a position he held until his death in 1562, Vicary played a substantial role in reconstituting one of the great medical institutions of the nation.

Thomas Gale

Thomas Gale, a distinguished contemporary of Vicary, was born in London in 1507, learned surgery as an apprentice, joined the army of Henry VIII taking part in the battle of Montreuil, and later served with the English contingent in the army of Philip II at the siege of St Quentin in 1557. On his return to London, he rose rapidly in his profession, became Master of the Barber-Surgeons' Company in 1561, and died in 1587. Gale was an excellent clinical surgeon and in addition taught surgery in the curriculum of the Company and wrote the first complete work on surgery in the English language, *An Enchiridion of Chirurgerie*, published in 1563. A prolific writer, in the same year he published *An Institution of a Chirurgion, An Antidotarle,* and *An excellent Treatise of wounds made with Gonneshot, in which is confuted bothe the grose errour of Jerome Brunswicke, John Vigo, Alfonse Ferrius, and others: in that they make the wounde venemous, whiche commeth through the common pouder and shotte etc*. Despite the lengthy title of the latter, the message was clear and correct. Gale was clearly of the opinion that such wounds were not poisoned and should be treated simply without the use of complex medications and styptics that were more than likely to result in infection and gangrene. Since Gale failed to mention Ambroise Paré, who held similar views, it has always been assumed that he was unfamiliar with Paré's work, which had been published 18 years previously in 1545.

The clinical surgeon Thomas Gale was a prolific writer and judging by the demeanor of his portrait, a much-regarded figure. He is best remembered for having produced one of the earliest complete works on surgery in the English language, *An Enchiridion of Chirurgerie*, published in 1563.

John Halle

John Halle was born in Maidstone in 1529 and although he died a relatively young man in 1568, had during his brief life participated in Sir Thomas Wyatt's rebellion, been imprisoned, and translated Lanfranchi's *Chirurgia parva* into English in 1565. A gifted individual both articulate and opinionated, he also wrote *A Very frutefull and necessary briefe worke of anatomie* as well as *An Historical Expostulation against the Beastly Abuses bothe of Chyruigie and Physycke in our time,* and *The Courte of Vertue*, containing tunes to which the Scriptures could be sung. Although prolific and clever, a careful appraisal of Halle's translation of Lanfranchi reveals that much liberty was taken with the text, and his anatomy is a mere compilation of medieval learning with apparently no knowledge of the *Fabrica* of Vesalius that had been published 22 years previously. Despite such shortcomings, Halle was of considerable service to surgery, since he declaimed widely that surgeons must be educated men and should have skill in physic as well as in surgery, while insisting vehemently that quacks must be tracked down and exposed.

William Clowes

William Clowes is one of the most colorful figures in the history of British surgery. Clowes was born in 1544, learned surgery as an apprentice to George Keble, and served as an army surgeon in the unsuccessful campaign of Ambrose Dudley, Earl of Warwick, against the French, where he not only gained excellent experience in military surgery but also began his lifelong friendship with John Banister. After serving several further years in the navy, he settled in London about 1569 and soon thereafter was admitted to the Barber-Surgeons' Company before, in 1575, being appointed to the surgical staff of St Bartholomew's Hospital. In 1585, he once again took up a military position and served as surgeon to the army of the Earl of Leicester, which had been shipped to Holland to support the Dutch against the Spaniards. In 1588, Clowes served in the navy under Sir Francis Drake and was present during the massive defeat inflicted upon the great Spanish Armada under the leadership of the Duke de Medina Sedona. As a consequence of his widespread popularity and skill, Clowes had a large practice in London, where he was highly respected both as a patriot and a physician. Sadly, he died of the plague at his country home in Essex in 1604 during a severe epidemic.

Despite all his military activities, Clowes still had the time to write and published five books, all of which were well received and held in high regard. These were: *A short profitable treatise touching the cure of the disease called morbus gallicus by inunctions* (1575); *De morbo gallico* (1579); *A briefe and necessary treatise touching the cure of the disease now usually called lues venerea* (1585); *A Prooved Practise for all young chirurgians, concerning Burnings with Gunpowder and Wounds etc* (1588); and *A right Frutefull and Approved Treatise for the Artificial Cure of Struma or Evill, cured by the Kinges and Queenes of England* (1602). Indeed, he was an excellent and interesting writer, never obscure, and always able to provide shrewd observations and sensible conclusions. *A Prooved Practise for all young chirurgians, concerning Burnings with Gunpowder and Wounds etc* was so successful that it went through four editions, proving to be the most popular of Clowes' contributions and detailing his disagreement with the notion that gunshot wounds were poisonous, while providing his suggestions for the best methods of treatment to be employed.

William Clowes (1544–1604) (*bottom left*), Surgeon to Elizabeth I and James I, was also heavily involved in naval medicine and, indeed, served under Sir Francis Drake (*top right*) against the Spanish Armada. This engagement proved to be the apogee of his military career, since he had previously served in the disastrous invasion of Normandy with the ill-fated army of Ambrose Dudley, Earl of Warwick. Of the latter event, Clowes reported little apart from that he had learned that fingers were the best of instruments, and that scabbards made good splints!

John Banister

John Banister (1533–1610), as so many surgeons of his time, began his career as an army surgeon in the employment of the Earl of Warwick. Following this, he studied in Oxford, received the degree of bachelor of medicine in 1573, and settled in Nottingham, where he attained a substantial reputation as a physician and surgeon. In 1588, he moved to London in obedience to a letter from Elizabeth I, becoming licensed in 1593–1594 by the Royal College of Physicians to practice medicine as well as surgery. Although Banister was a voluminous writer, he was rather a compiler and translator than an original thinker and his most popular works included *The historie of man sucked from the sappe of the most approved anathomistes in this present age* (1578) and *The workes of that famous chyrurgian Mr John Banester* (1633). In addition to his clinical practice and writing, Banister aspired to become an educator of repute and he taught anatomy at the Barber-Surgeons' Hall in 1581. The rendition of his services to the Company became the subject of an important painting, which is preserved in the Wellcome Historical Medical Museum in London.

Banister was a rare breed, being both a learned physician and a practical surgeon, a combination excessively rare at that period. Although he apparently tried to further a reunion of medicine and surgery, this proved as fruitless then as it has been in the succeeding four centuries! Surgery in England, as Power remarked, "had always been subservient to physic, and in this subordinate position, it was destined to remain until our own times". Thus, physicians were burdened with the weight of tradition and their training was largely theoretical and imparted by lectures. The surgeon was considered to be an essentially practical man, capable of treating wounds and injuries as they occurred, but regarded as unfettered by any significant knowledge of the general principles of medicine. Although thoughtful surgical individuals such as Gale, Clowes, and Banister suggested that all surgeons should be examined in physic as well as in surgery, little notice was taken of this excellent advice, and the discipline remained one of manual skill rarely contaminated by intellectual endeavor. In this respect, surgical books would for centuries thereafter remain largely records of individual cases, with little or no attempt being made to either generalize the subject or to establish broad surgical principles applicable to a wide range of disease processes.

Torn from the Root, that wicked Tongue,
Which daily swore and curst!
Those Eyeballs from their Sockets wrung,

His Heart, expos'd to prying Eyes,
To Pity has no Claim;

John Banister (1533–1610) (*bottom left*) was an eminent physician and regarded as a master of the art of anatomy. Unfortunately, not all shared the views of the surgeons in regard to their "art". William Hogarth in particular lampooned the topic in his print 'The Reward of Cruelty' (*background*). The surgeon John Freke (1688–1757) (of St Bartholomew's Hospital) is pictured in the president's chair and the executed malefactor Tom Nero is depicted being subjected to vivisection – a fate worse than death. It was believed that dismemberment would deny the possibility of resurrection at The Day of Judgment. Hogarth and his supporters considered the surgeons to be perpetrators of callousness and brutality, as exemplified by the gouging out of the right eye, the evisceration, and the dog being fed a portion of the body.

4 | OXFORD AND CAMBRIDGE

The development of medicine in a country has always been based upon an amalgam comprising in various proportions of folklore, local customs, the Church, schools of learning, and the influence of either foreign invaders or travelers. In this respect, the insular nature of Britain somewhat altered the mix. Certainly, great universities have always had a role in the establishment of formal medical structures in society. Thus, the cornerstone institutions of England bear some comment. Although popular legend would have it that the University of Oxford was founded by King Alfred the Great, it was actually established by English students who migrated from Paris about 1167. This relocation back to the homeland occurred during the quarrel between Henry II and Thomas Becket, who was supported by the French King. To counter this French meddling, Henry ordered that all English students in Paris who were in holy orders should return to England "under pain of losing their benefices". This migration was followed by the establishment of a *Studium Generale*, or Great School, at Oxford, since most of the students returned as "they loved their revenues." Thus, Oxford was a daughter of the University of Paris and, like Paris, was a university of masters. Indeed, in its formative years, Oxford was directly modeled upon Paris in almost every way and the students and masters, as at Paris, were clerics, wearing the tonsure and clerical garb, and the courses of instruction were modeled upon those of Paris. The origins of Cambridge University were much less complex and the institution was founded by a migration of students from Oxford about 1229, following a riot between the students and the citizens of

Oxford. During the Middle Ages, although Oxford became a great center of classical learning, it never achieved a reputation as a medical center anywhere near equal to the European universities of Paris, Montpellier, Padua, and later Leiden. Despite this lack of prominence in the field of medicine, it did, however, produce several well-known scholars, whose investigations included medical and allied subjects and whose reputation became worldwide.

Thomas Becket (1118–1170), Archbishop of Canterbury and initially a great friend of Henry II, was murdered by a group of knights after he came into conflict with the King over the relationship between the Church and the State. Although he was canonized in 1173, Henry VIII subsequently ordered the shrine to be demolished.

Michael Scot

Michael Scot (circa 1175–1223) was a somewhat legendary figure in the history of medieval science, although very little is known of the details of his life. It is known that he studied in Oxford and in Paris and, after his ordination, held various benefices in Italy, but refused appointment as Archbishop of Cashel in Ireland since he could not speak the language of the natives. A man of considerable gifts, he also learned Arabic at Palermo and Toledo, and was thereafter attached to the court of Frederick II of Sicily as a savant. In the capacity of resident scholar he, at the request of the Emperor, superintended a translation of Aristotle from Arabic into Latin. A prodigious writer, Scot compiled numerous arcane texts on alchemy, astrology, physiognomy, and astrological medicine. Given the hazy interface between philosophy, medicine, and alchemy, he acquired a great reputation as a magician and much speculation surrounded his life. Although he was supposed to have died in Scotland, it is more likely that, having spent most of his life in the service of Frederick II, he died in Italy. Nevertheless, his reputation was especially great in Scotland, where, as Sir Walter Scott related: "In the south of Scotland any work of great labor and antiquity is ascribed either to the agency of Auld Michael, of Sir William Wallace, or of the devil."

Bartholomaeus Anglicus

Bartholomaeus Anglicus was an English Franciscan who studied at Oxford, then became a lecturer at Paris (circa 1220), before a decade later relocating to Magdeburg to lecture at the request of the General of the Franciscan Order. About 1250, he composed the text *De proprietatibus rerum* (*Concerning the Properties of Things*), a general encyclopedia which achieved widespread popularity during the Middle Ages. Such was the acceptance of this work that 12 Latin editions, eight French editions, one Dutch edition, two Spanish editions, and three English editions were finally produced. Bartholomaeus was understated about its importance and referred to it as a "simple and rude" compilation, not intended for advanced students. Nevertheless, despite his protestations of minimalism, the range was vast and covered diverse subjects, including demons, psychology, physiology, optics, domestic science, medicine, poisons, astronomy, astrology, air and birds, water and fish, animals, geography, and magic. The section on medicine was no less than 70 chapters in length and quoted Constantine, the African, on nearly every page. Apparently widely read and familiar with a broad range of materials, Bartholomaeus also referred frequently to Avicenna, Averroes, Egidius, Galen, Haly Abbas, Hippocrates, Rhazes, and Ruphos.

As might be predicted, his views on anatomy and physiology were characteristic of the medieval period and like many of his contemporaries, he assigned a certain intellectual function to each organ. Thus he regarded the brain as the home of the senses: "In the anterior cell or ventricle, imagination is formed; in the median, reason; in the posterior, memory and recollection... Madness is infection of the foremost cell of the head with privation of imagination, like as melancholy is the infection of the middle cell of the head with privation of reason." Some other ideas regarding the abdomen were equally imaginative. Thus the spleen "is the source of laughter, by the gall we are wroth, by the heart we are wise, by the brain we feel, by the liver we love". In regard to the vascular system, he accepted the explanations of Constantine as fully satisfactory: "The veins arise from the liver, just as the arteries from the heart and the nerves from the brain." Similarly, he followed the functional interpretations proposed by Constantine and believed that the veins "bring blood from the liver to nourish the members of the entire body... The arteries receive and take care of the spirits."

Despite the modest claim of Bartholomaeus (surely based upon his Franciscan background) that his work was devoid of originality, the text

actually was not only a remarkable compendium of knowledge but through his personal remarks, served to provide an excellent and detailed picture of medieval life. Of particular medical note is the fact that the French translation, published at Lyon in 1482, contains the first illustration of a dissection in any printed book. Similarly, the English translation that was published in London in 1495 presents the first picture of a dissection to appear in an English printed book.

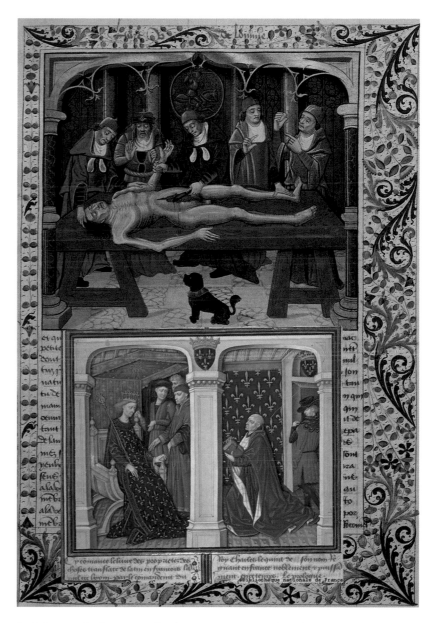

Bartholomaeus Anglicus was a Franciscan encyclopedist and theologian of the 13th century. An Englishman by birth, he became Professor of Theology at the University of Paris, when, in 1224, he entered the newly established Order of St Francis in company. About 1250, he authored *De proprietatibus rerum*, a medieval encyclopedia of natural history. He continued his lectures in the claustral school until 1231, when he was sent to Magdeburg in Germany. He was succeeded by his illustrious countryman Alexander of Hales, who, by being a member of the University, raised the private school of the Franciscans to the dignity of a School of the University.

Roger Bacon

Roger Bacon (circa 1214–1292), a member of the Franciscan order, was born near Ilchester and studied at Oxford, where he took his master of arts. Thereafter, he moved to Paris, where he also received a master of arts, remaining several years lecturing on Aristotle and writing on theology, mathematics, optics, and geography. After his return to England, his attacks on the Franciscans, Dominicans, and secular priests resulted in a condemnation of his works and to a prolonged imprisonment from 1277 to 1292. He was released from prison only a short time before his death.

Given his intellectual skills and versatility, his interests were legend and his contributions diverse. Bacon has been variously described as the inventor of the magnetic compass, gunpowder, lenses for reading, and even flying machines. Some scholars have even interpreted his writings to have predicted

the discovery of America! In fact, the magnetic compass was already well known in Bacon's time, and gunpowder, as Bacon himself notes in *Opus Tertium* (1267), was already in common use in toy explosives for children. Similarly, Robert Grosseteste (1175–1253), Bishop of Lincoln, was familiar with magnifying lenses, which were a new discovery in his day. Bacon's writings on flying machines discuss the possibility only of their construction, and his suggestions regarding the probability of another continent first appeared in a work published in 1487 and first seen by Sir Christopher Columbus after his return from America in 1492.

Despite his great reputation, a careful perusal of the work of Bacon reveals that the claims that have been attributed to him were more those of his followers than Bacon himself. Thorndike noted: "...one finds a different interpretation may be put upon many a passage and realizes that, even in his most boastful moments, Roger himself never made such claims to astounding originality as some modern writers have made for him." In essence, Bacon was essentially a child of his century, credulous, even superstitious, and yet his *Opus Maius* remains one of the most remarkable books of the 13th century, although it was not printed until 1733. Nevertheless, such was his ultimate reputation that he was referred to by his successors and posterity as "Doctor Mirabilis".

Roger Bacon (circa 1214–1292), also known as "Doctor Mirabilis," studied geometry, arithmetic, music, and astronomy as a young man and received a degree from the University of Paris around 1241. After taking his degree, he lectured at Paris on Aristotle's ideas, but at this stage, he showed little interest in science. His interest in mathematics and science was acquired at Oxford, to which he returned in 1247. He was much influenced by Robert Grosseteste and worked for most of his life on languages, mathematics, optics, and sciences. In particular, he concentrated on studying these topics at Oxford between his arrival in 1247 and 1257. It is probable that Bacon's most important mathematical contribution was the application of geometry to optics. In 1257, perhaps largely due to ill health, Bacon left the University of Oxford and entered the Order of Friars Minor, where he continued his interest in the sciences. His emphasis on empiricism has led him to become regarded as one of the earliest advocates of the modern scientific method, although he remained a faithful scholar of Catholicism even though ultimately imprisoned by the authorities for his views.

John of Gaddesden

John of Gaddesden was born about 1280 and became probably the best-known English physician of the Middle Ages. He apparently went to Oxford for grammar school and thereafter studied arts, medicine, and theology, taking his degree in all three subjects. Each student of this period was required to have a copy of Galen's *Tegni*, the *Aphorisms* of Hippocrates and *Regimen of Acute Diseases*, *The Book of Fevers* by Isaac, and *The Antidotarium* of Nicholas. Indeed, such was the reliance upon printed material and the nature of the curriculum that it has been remarked that "the fourteenth century English physician could enter upon practice without any other knowledge than that derived from books". After he had been awarded his degree, Gaddesden began to lecture at Merton College and in about 1314, wrote a superb text, *Rosa Anglica*, which was first printed at Pavia in 1492. Indeed, Gaddesden's book was the first medical work by an English author to be printed.

Although Gaddesden himself was highly enamored of his own work – "As the rose overtops all flowers so this book overtops all treatises on the practice of medicine" – not all his colleagues shared his enthusiasm. In fact, the comment of the contemporary French medical authority Guy de Chauliac is remarkably different in its assessment: "Finally there arose an insipid Rosa Anglica which was sent me and seen. I had believed to find in it a fragrant odor, but I found the fables of the Spaniard, of Gilbert and of Theodoric." It would seem that the Frenchman was somewhat less than admiring of the originality of the text of Gaddesden and more mindful of its origins than the author.

Rosa Anglica may be regarded as a characteristic product of scholastic medicine in that the author, an educated cleric, exhibits great scorn for lay practitioners and barbers, although he does not scruple to charge them high prices for his prescriptions. The text however provides good evidence that Gaddesden was a well-read man, since it quotes 34 authorities, including 12 Arabic physicians and six Greeks. In this respect, the book attests to the fact that Arabic medicine had penetrated even to England, where, a half century later, Geoffrey Chaucer, in *The Canterbury Tales*, describing the works the learned doctor in "*physik*" knew, mentions six Arabians, four Arabists, and five Greeks.

Some critics have derided the *Rosa Anglica* and described it as little more than a "farrago of nonsense," but this is a somewhat unfair description, since although it contained a fair amount of nonsense, as did most books of that period, it also evinced evidence of some sound common sense. Thus Gaddesden advised consumptives to live in a dry, clear atmosphere at a high elevation and drink much milk. Similarly, he treated hydrops (edema) with complicated prescriptions, which included diuretics, but, as this prescription was costly, he advised poor patients to drink their own urine every morning. In addition, he advised that, in dropsy, the patient ate bread containing a "small quantity of salt" and cautioned against bread which "is not healthy because it is too salty". Although it is unlikely that Gaddesden knew that urea in urine was a diuretic or that he appreciated the clinical relevance of salt-free diets in renal disease, he was obviously an astute enough clinician to have recognized the value of these two methods of treatment. On the contrary to such reasonable practice, as an adherent to the doctrine of signatures, he treated "the most noble son of the King of England" suffering from smallpox by placing him in a red room and covering him with a scarlet coverlet! In Gaddesden's description of diabetes, it is intriguing to note that the disease is called in English "*candepisse*" – "*cande*" being the word employed by Gaddesden for syrup. However, this appears to have been a misprint, and the original manuscript reads "*chaude pisse*". Apart from his books and clinical skills, Malgaigne considered that Gaddesden may have been the first to employ forceps for the extraction of stones in the bladder.

Nevertheless, despite his scholarly productivity and effectiveness, the overall assessment of Gaddesden by scholars of the history of medicine has not been generous. Thus, Cholmeley summed him up as "a man of good education and as regards his medical education, one who was acquainted with the writings of his predecessors. More than this, he must have been an accurate clinical observer. Of anatomy he naturally knew next to nothing, and of physiology even less." Unfortunately, the mists of time closed around Gaddesden and little is known of his later life, except that he later became a canon of St Paul's Cathedral in the period around 1333.

The crowning of Edward III, son of King Edward II of England. His physician, John of Gaddesden (1280–1361), a doctor of physic appointed to Edward II, was a staunch advocate of the doctrine of signatures and achieved considerable fame for saving the young Prince from smallpox. When the young Prince appeared about to die from the disease, he achieved a miraculous cure by draping the entire sick room in red. With typical love of imagery popular among medieval writers, Gaddesden derived the title of his book from the fact that, as a rose has five petals, so his book had five parts, dealing with fevers, hygiene, injuries, diet, and drugs. Gaddesden is mentioned by Geoffrey Chaucer in the prologue to *The Canterbury Tales* as one of the authorities known to the doctor of "*physik*":

Well knew he the old Esculapius

And Deiscorides, and eek Rufus...

Avervois, Damascien, and Constantyn:

Bernard, and Gatesden, and Gilbertyn.

5 THE DARK AGE – MAGIC AND MEDICINE

The practice of the healing art during the centuries that intervened between the fall of Greek science and the rise of the experimental method is a difficult topic, since the material relating to this is as sparse as the sources of information are meager. The history of the evolution of medicine in this stretch of time is sharply delineated into two components by the arrival in the West of Arabic learning, an event that would prove to be of considerable importance for the subsequent development of the human intellect. Arabic knowledge constituted the remnant of Greek science that had resided in the Moslem world since the fall of Greece and thereafter slowly entered the Occident at times which varied in different countries but which may roughly be regarded as the 12th century. This section focuses mostly on pre-Arabian material and is generally regarded as the Dark Age medicine and as far as English medicine may be regarded, this stretched into as late as the 13th century. Thereafter, most medical material other than pure folk medicine exhibited evidence of Arabian influence.

The history of the magical and medical practice of Early England has survived in a fragmentary state, mostly as manuscripts and folklore, of which the former constitutes the best record. Nevertheless, these documents were produced by a barbarian people among whom the Latin culture was diffusing itself from the shattered fragments of the Roman Empire and are therefore often of only modest value. As might be supposed from the times, the main means in the spread of southern culture among the English was the Church and its instrument – the art of writing. Unfortunately, clerical writing tended to evolve as the material exhibited more and more of an ecclesiastical tone and less of the original magic of medicine. Thus, the primary nature of the medicinal practice recounted would fade as different renditions were penned and church doctrine permeated medical views.

Thus, the 8th-century writer the Venerable Bede produced almost purely ecclesiastical material, bearing hardly a trace of the heathenism of his father or grandfather and almost without any indication that the imported culture was a new thing in his part of the world. Indeed, there is hardly any mention of a heathen god or hero and practically no word of native magic. As such, the works of Bede could have been the product of a foreign missionary rather than an Englishman, since they lack information as to native customs and relate little of native medicine while providing numerous medical references.

Alternatively, manuscripts such as *Beowulf* or the *Lacnunga*, while not earlier than the 11th century, are replete with more primitive material. Although the *Lacnunga* is of a relatively late date, it is probably the best source of the primitive medicine of Britain untouched by Christian influence. Its compiler was comfortable with using the names of the northern gods in the weaving of his spells, and purely heathen paragraphs alternate with charms mentioning the sacred personages of Christian tradition.

As the Roman grip on Europe waned and Christianity supervened, the practice of medicine evolved into a strange admixture of pagan beliefs, magical invocations, and monastic injunctions against sin and its divine penalty of illness. The promulgation by the Church of the concept that disease was a product of sin and that cure might only be achieved by prayer and purification further accentuated the decline of rational thought. As a result, scientific enquiry waned and ritual and dogma became the accepted medical modus operandi.

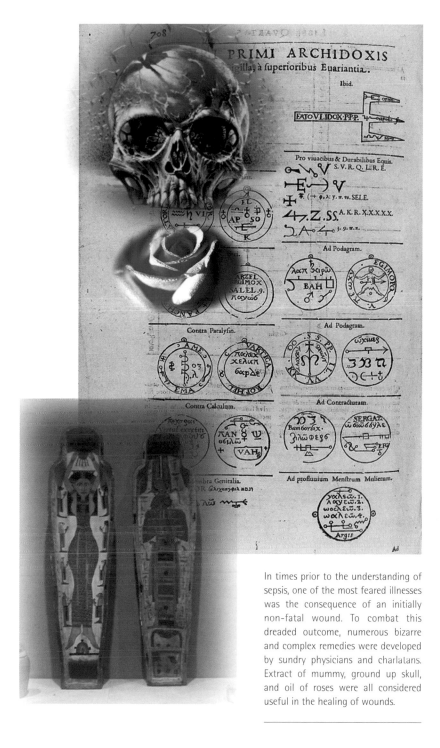

In times prior to the understanding of sepsis, one of the most feared illnesses was the consequence of an initially non-fatal wound. To combat this dreaded outcome, numerous bizarre and complex remedies were developed by sundry physicians and charlatans. Extract of mummy, ground up skull, and oil of roses were all considered useful in the healing of wounds.

As a youth, he was wild and on one occasion, while penniless near Oxford, he obtained a week's lodging by pretending to charm away an ague from his landlady's daughter using a few words of Greek scribbled on a scrap of parchment and bound to the girl's wrist. Many years thereafter, an old woman was brought before him charged with sorcery in that she professed to cure ague by the application of a magic parchment. On examining the fragment, Justice Holt found it to be the very piece with which he had worked his miraculous cure many years before, since his own Greek words were still legible. His lordship confessed and the woman, who was acquitted, was one of the last to be tried for witchcraft in Britain.

In the past, Early English magic and medicine was investigated primarily by philologists, interested in the material as literature in the Anglo-Saxon language but paying less attention to the nature and affinities of its magical elements. More recent analyses of the subject have viewed magic and medicine as a whole and have focused more on the cultural factors that comprised the interface, setting aside the semantics and nuances of its transcription. This has facilitated the derivation of a better picture of the attitude of the inhabitants of the country towards the healing art before the arrival of that scholastic method and Arabian learning which engendered nearly as great a mental revolution in the 13th century as the experimental method and scientific attitude did in the 17th century.

Although the nature of the medico-magical material is critical, it is worth considering the people for whom it was written and by whom it was used. Most documents from the Dark or Middle Ages were written by clerics, and it is certain that the most beautiful of the Early English medical manuscripts, including all the illuminated specimens, were prepared in monasteries. The texts of these illuminated manuscripts are however copies, or at best, little but translations, and the documents from which they originated were hardly, if at all, clericized or even Christianized. Moreover, the content of certain works such as the *Leechbook* of Bald and the *Lacnunga* clearly indicate that the scribe himself must have been a layman, and there is adequate evidence that as early as the 7th century, there existed lay physicians in England who were freely consulted by prominent ecclesiastics. Of the status and character of these leeches little is known, although they probably closely resembled the hereditary physicians of the Welsh and Gaelic peoples. In the illuminated Early English manuscripts, although there are a number of pictures of leeches, they are never represented as tonsured and it appears that the medical writings are less clericized than most Early English material.

The Anglo-Saxon medico-magical writings form a very composite mass in which a great variety of elements may be distinguished, including Greek Medicine filtered through Latin (true Dark Age medicine), ecclesiastical elements, Salernitan texts, native Teutonic magic and Herb Lore, Celtic magic, a composite mass of Herb Lore from southern Italy, Byzantine magic and theurgy, and even pagan Roman spells.

Nearly all early medicine contains much magic and certainly among the North European barbarians, this was essentially syncretic. Indeed, of all forms of cultural influence, it is probably magic that passes most easily and most rapidly from people to people, thus any object or process or person, held in esteem by a superior class, may easily acquire magical powers among those of lower culture. Thus, Quintus Serenus Sammonicus, a Latin physician of the 3rd century, advised that placing the fourth book of Homer's *Iliad* under the head of a patient was the best remedy for quartan ague! An even more absurd instance of the ease and rapidity of the passage of exotic magical formulae is narrated in regards to Justice Holt (1642–1710).

Medicine reached the barbarian peoples of the West at a time when the scientific system of Greece was in complete decay, and since it came through Latin channels, it was merely copied or traditional and possessed little of the living characteristics so associated with the Hippocratic and Galenic works. Although mostly of marginal quality, it enabled an estimate to be derived of which Greek medical books were available to scholars of the later Empire and the influence of Greek sources on Early English literature to be defined. A review of Cassiodorus (490–585 AD) and others indicates that during the Gothic domination of Italy there was an active process of translation of Greek medical works into Latin. Thus, by the examination of manuscripts and review of ancient library catalogues, a good idea of the material available for distribution among the barbarians of the North and West between the 7th and 11th centuries can be formed. This process is facilitated by the fact that characteristic Dark Age medicine is singularly constant in character, whether it comes from southern Italy, Rhineland, Gaul, or Switzerland. This system of monkish medicine was practiced in its entirety in each center, for instance, at the Anglo-Saxon settlement of St Gall, where a 9th-century plan of a hospital and physic garden projected there can be studied.

The School of Medicine of Salerno (1000 AD), initially under the influence of Cassiodorus and later Nicholas, promulgated a code of health that became widely accepted. Its practitioners and graduates were for centuries regarded as the preeminent physicians of Europe, and the name Salerno grew in stature to the point that it came to epitomize the art of medicine.

The medical writings of the Dark Age that are classical in origin may be classed under three headings: 'Translations of Greek works into Latin'; 'Works written primarily in Latin'; and '*The Natural History* (*Historia Naturalis*) of Pliny the Elder and of his abstractor Plinius Valerianus' – which were available in England at an early date. Indeed, from Bede and Alcuin onward, Pliny, together with Isidore of Seville (560–636 AD), provided the basis of such natural knowledge as was possessed by English writers. Indeed, Pliny was probably the most widely read of any non-ecclesiastical writer throughout the Dark Ages.

Gaius Plinius Cecilius Secundus (23–79 AD), known as Pliny the Elder, a Roman scholar, encyclopedist, and nationalist, was born in Novum Comum (Como) in Gallia Cisalpine. He completed his studies in Rome, where he received education in literature, oratory, and law, as well as a subsequent extensive military training. The first sentence in the preface to Pliny's *The Natural History* (*Historia Naturalis*) (*center*) states: "Happy were they in times past reputed (and not unworthily) who had that gracious and heavenly gift, *aut facere scribenda, aut scribere legenda*: that is 'either to do such things as deserved to be written, or to write that which was worth the reading'." In his encyclopedic tract comprising 37 books, which was dedicated to the Emperor Titus, Pliny described the full complexity of the world in all its aspects. His views on botany occur in Book XVI, while Books XX–XXV and XXVII detail what was then known about medicinal drugs obtained from plants.

THE BASIS OF EARLY MEDICINE

Manuscripts written in England before the Arabian revival contain numerous quotations from all of these works. Indeed, they form the groundwork of early English medicine and the practice derived from these works forms a fairly definite and easily traced system. Its philosophical basis is the doctrine of the four elements and the four humors, a view that is amply illustrated in English manuscripts. In the medical belief of the Dark Ages, there was a close relation between the external and the internal world, the macrocosm and the microcosm. Thus, a parallel was discerned between the four ages of man and the four seasons, between the humors of the body and the solstices and equinoxes, between the four elements and the four cardinal points, and so on. Such a scheme is elaborated in a diagram drawn up by Byrhtferth of Ramsey (circa 1000 AD), the commentator of Bede. This diagram is remarkable for associating the initials of the four cardinal points (Arcton, Dysis, Anatole, Mesembrios) with the letters of the name "ADAM," to whom in the text the term "protoplast" is attached. The occurrence of this word is itself of interest, since it is of liturgical origin and is found in the so-called *Sacramentarium Leonianum* (8th century), but is not encountered in liturgies of later Roman origin. It is therefore probable that the scheme that Byrhtferth delineated was accepted in England sometime prior to the 8th century.

The Sphere of Pythagoras

Of more interest is a small 9th century fragment consisting of three paragraphs or sentences in a manuscript that is probably the earliest medical text written by an English hand, although the document itself is in the midst of an Hisperic text and exhibits Irish influence. All three paragraphs of this short text are derived from medical works known to have been in circulation during the Dark Ages and forming part of the characteristic medical system of that period. This manuscript was written at Echternach, a monastery founded by the Englishman Willibrord, the apostle of the Frisians (657–738 AD). The first paragraph discusses the magical device known as the sphere of Pythagoras, which was probably of Egyptian origin, but had spread to Europe through Greek intermediaries as follows: "The device of the sphere of the philosopher Pythagoras, which Apollonius described for the discovery of anything concerning the sick. Thou shouldst determine the day of the week and of the moon (on which he fell sick) and (the numerical value) of his name according to the letters written below. Add them together and divide by thirty and consider the remainder. Examine what is written below, 'and if it fall in the upper part he will live and do well; if below, he will die'."

Pythagoras (fl 530 BC) originated in Samos and founded at Kroton (southern Italy) a society which was at once a religious community and a scientific school. The group excited jealousy and mistrust, and caused much controversy. Since he wrote nothing, it is difficult to determine how much of the doctrine we know as Pythagorean is due to the founder of the society and how much is due to later development. Thus, sometimes Pythagoras is represented as a man of science, and sometimes as a preacher of mystic doctrines. Ultimately, he achieved fame as a philosopher, mathematician, and founder of the Pythagorean brotherhood that broadly grappled with the concepts of seeking truth and defining knowledge.

These devices are often discussed in the Anglo-Saxon manuscripts, since the leechbooks, whether written in monasteries or not, were in essence products of the laity. However, the earliest English specimens of magic spheres of Petosiris are nearly all in liturgical books and associated with bloodletting calendars. Thus the earliest after that of the *Echternach* manuscript is in the *Leofric Missal* written for the Bishop of Exeter in 970 AD, where the device is attached to a venesection text and an apparatus for fixing the date of Church festivals. It is thus probable that the magic sphere was employed in monasteries for determining whether venesection might be used, since bleeding was periodically performed there both as a regimen of health and as an aid to withstanding the lusts of the flesh. Similarly, such missals, though diminutive specimens, were provided with wide overlapping leather flaps so that the volume could be wrapped in them and carried safely through the wet for use in visiting the sick and aiding the priest in deciding whether to administer extreme unction.

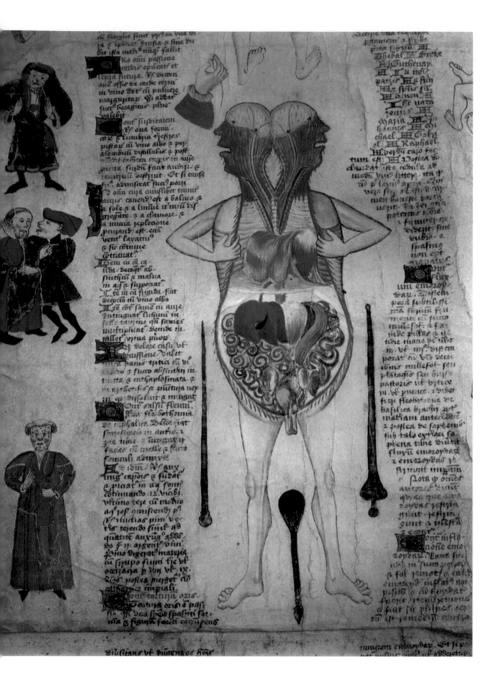

A medieval depiction of specific sites on the body where medical and surgical intervention could be applied to engender cures for disease. Some have obvious rationale, while others reflect erroneous concepts or longstanding superstitions.

commented: "You did very ill and unskilfully to bleed her on that day, for I remember that Archbishop Theodore of blessed memory said that bleeding at that time was very dangerous when the light of the moon and the tide of the ocean is increasing." Nevertheless, the blessing and touch of the good bishop restored her to health and thus was abscess and sepsis dispelled in the Dark Ages of medicine!

The "blessed Theodore" referred to by Bishop John was a Greek ecclesiastic who had come to England as Archbishop of Canterbury in 668 AD and the doctrine he espoused, which connected bleeding with the tides and the moon, was a commonplace of Greek medicine and had also been adopted at Rome. This doctrine is also mentioned in the pseudo Hippocratic *Epistle of Maecenas*, although the putative relation of the condition of the blood to the tides and moon is extensively dealt with in several works of the Galenic corpus, especially in the *Regimen in Acute Diseases* and the spurious treatise *On crises*, from which Theodore more probably derived it. It is noteworthy that in the very early Celtic Calendar of Coligny, the first half of the lunar month, that is to say, the period of the waxing moon, is also considered to be an unlucky date.

Salernitan texts

Salernitan texts, much like ecclesiastical elements, have been carefully documented and therefore their contents are well known. Nevertheless, the early history of the medical school of Salerno is still indefinite, although surviving early southern Italian documents suggest that knowledge of Greek medicine was widely diffused in what was once Magna Grecia in the 7th and 8th centuries, and information from Cassiodorus suggests that this influence might date back as far as the 6th century. By the 9th or 10th century, this diffused medical knowledge to be assimilated at several centers, of which Monte Cassino and Salerno rose to epitomize this phase of medical knowledge. Although at the monastery of Monte Cassino the process progressed little further than copying and translating, at Salerno, a definite lay medical school was established with such success that by the 11th century, a substantial amount of genuine observation and investigation was in progress. Indeed, the editing and referencing of the great monument of that school, the *Breslau codex*, which contained 35 separate medical treatises, has enabled the detection of Salernitan influence almost wherever it occurs in early Western medicine. Thus, one of the primary medical treatises in the Anglo-Saxon language, the so-called *Peri didaxeon*, is in fact mainly a translation of the works of the Salernitan writers of the 11th century, while Latin medical works written in England in the early 12th century are of the same origin. Indeed, such was the influence of the Salernitan school that as well as extending through the Dark Ages, it formed the basis not only of much modern English folk medicine but also of some of the practice of the modern herbalist.

Ecclesiastical elements

Ecclesiastical elements are found throughout Anglo-Saxon medicine and magic and paternosters accompanied every conceivable medical process. Such elements, although perhaps the least interesting of the factors in Anglo-Saxon medicine, are easily recognized and still survive in folklore. One instance documented in Bede's *Ecclesiastical History of the English People* (written 731 AD) is however worthy of notice. It relates the management strategy and thoughts of John of Beverley, Bishop of Hexham, on arriving at a monastery where a nun was seriously ill following venesection. The incident had begun with violent pain at the bleeding site, followed by local swelling and collapse to the point of demise: "The abbess begged the bishop that he would give her his blessing and touch her, for this she believed might aid her." The bishop then asked when the maiden had been bled, and on being told that it was on the fourth day of the moon,

A miniature illumination (circa 1300) from the manuscript *Cirurgia* by Roger von Salerno depicting doctors with patients with a variety of ailments, from stomach abscesses to broken ribs.

Teutonic magic and Woden

The influence of native Teutonic magical material can be distinguished from imported elements of classical, ecclesiastical, or Salernitan origin by the presence of four characteristic elements: the doctrine of specific venoms, the doctrine of the nines, the doctrine of the worm as the cause of disease, and lastly the doctrine of the elf-shot. Although such material is generically referred to as "native Teutonic," it is probably better considered as Indo-Germanic, since these doctrines were common to all Indo-Germanic peoples and even encountered in the Vedas. The presence of these four doctrines in passages of English origin without classical or Celtic elements, and especially in association with references to Teutonic gods or customs, suggests that the material was transferred with the Anglo-Saxon tribes from their Continental home. Perhaps the best specimen of the native Teutonic magic is the *Lay of the Nine Healing Herbs*, which contains three of the four elements of Teutonic folk medicine, namely the doctrines of specific venoms, of the nines, and of the worm, though the fourth doctrine, the elf-shot, is not mentioned:

Then took Woden nine magic twigs,

Smote then that serpent that in nine bits she flew apart.

Now these nine herbs avail against nine spirits of evil,

Against nine venoms and against nine winged onsets,

Gainst the red venom, gainst the white venom, gainst the purple venom,

Gainst the yellow venom, gainst the green venom,

Gainst the livid venom, gainst the blue venom,

Gainst the brown venom, gainst the crimson venom,

Gainst worm blister, gainst water blister,

Gainst thorn blister, gainst thistle blister,

Gainst ice blister, gainst venom blister…

If any venom Flying from the east, or any from south,

Or any from north or any from west come nigh, over the world of men.

I alone know the running streams and the nine serpents.

Now behold. All weeds must now fail among herbs.

Seas must dissolve, all salt water, when I this venom from thee blow.

The opening verses recount how Woden, in warring with the serpent or worm, caused disease to arise from the fragments into which he smote the reptile, and indeed, Woden destroying the worm is a well-known Teutonic myth. In the mythical cycle, Woden was primarily the dispenser of victory, but he was also the bringer of many other forms of good luck and especially of good health. This part of the poem thus resolves itself into a charm of the well-known type, which consists in the relation of a few words, usually of verse, of the story of a cure performed by some sacred personage.

Given the repeated incursions of the Norse into British territory, the amount of Nordic mythology and superstition interwoven into Saxon medicine was predictable. The cyclical wars and the beliefs of the sea warriors were captured in the image of the Ouroboros (*bottom*) and their Pantheon of Deities. They were also well known to William Shakespeare, who in *King Lear* penned: "The gods are just, and of our pleasant vices make instruments to plague us; the dark and vicious place where thee he got, cost him his eyes. Thou hast spoken right, 't is true. The wheel is come full circle; I am here."

A good example of such a charm invoking Woden is to be found in a 10th-century Old High German manuscript at Merseburg Cathedral in Saxony: "Phol (Balder) and Woden fared to a wood; there was Balder's foal's foot sprained. Then charmed Woden, as well he knew how for bone sprain for blood sprain for limb sprain. Bone to bone blood to blood, limb to limbs as though they were glued."

It is of interest that this precise charm is still used for sprains in the Northern Highlands, where perhaps the Norsemen brought it, although in the Gaelic form, Christ has taken the place of Woden. The same charm is known also from other Indo-Germanic sources, as, for instance, the *Atharva Veda*. The Romans identified Woden with the god Mercury since he too was responsible for diseases and their cure. It was also believed that he influenced the casting of lots as a means of bringing good luck. This is in specific reference to the word "tan" in the *Lay of the Nine Healing Herbs*, which is translated as the twig specifically used in the casting of lots. The Roman historian Tacitus, in his commentary on the tribes of Germany, noted that "no people practice more diligently Augury and Divination by lot". The use of the lots is simple and the ancient practice may be best described as follows: "A little bough is cut from a fruit bearing tree and cut into slips; these are distinguished by runes (notis quibusdam), and thrown casually and at random over a white cloth." From the twig for casting lots, "tan" came to mean the lot itself. The nine twigs that Woden was believed to hold were the twigs of fate, which were thought to bring a "better lot" to the sick man on recitation of the magic song. Following the introduction of Woden and his magic twigs, a description of their powers usually followed as a means of establishing the potency of the charm. The nine poisons or flying things are enumerated, and the nine diseases that they produce. Indeed, this nine-fold nightmare may be followed at large throughout Teutonic magic. After the nine venoms and the nine diseases, the poem addresses the four quarters of heaven from which the four winds or "blasts" carry disease, although this use of four refers to the division of the winds according to the four cardinal points of Indo-Germanic origin that were developed independently of classical influence.

Thus, the method of description of these winds is in contrast to the usual Greek and Latin system, which provided specific names to designate the various prevalent winds, a method more applicable to the regular Mediterranean climate, with its periodic recurrence of winds from definite directions. On the contrary, the earliest Anglo-Saxon glosses from the 8th century onward contain the Greek names of winds that were most likely derived from Plinius Valerianus and equated with the suitable geographical direction in terms of cardinal points. In this respect, the custom of uttering a charm against disease successively to the four cardinal points is also of Indo-Germanic origin and is found in the *Atharva Veda*, although it occurs repetitively in Anglo-Saxon literature and is applied with both Christian and pagan invocations.

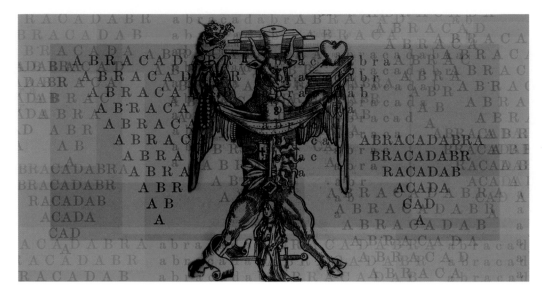

The "Abracadabra" mantra as originally intoned by Quintus Samonicus (Roman physician of the Emperor Severus, 208 AD) was probably little more than Roman plagiarism of an ancient Hebrew injunction "*Abrai, seda, brai*".

Demonic influence

This English doctrine of disease was also shared with the Continental Teutons and with the Celts, although the Teutonic peoples did not harbor the belief in possession by demons, which was so characteristic of the Near East where Christianity arose. Thus, the Teutons considered much disease to be caused by the action of supernatural beings, elves, or witches, whose shafts fired at the sufferer produced his torments rather than actual possession itself. Thus, Anglo-Saxon and even Middle English literature is replete with the notion of disease caused by the arrows of mischievous supernatural beings (the doctrine of the elf-shot). The Anglo-Saxon tribes believed such malicious elves to be ubiquitous, especially in the wild, uncultivated wastes where they contrived to shoot their envenomed darts at the innocent passerby. Such creatures were variously believed to inhabit marshes and waterlogged land or land near water – water elves – and were considered akin to the nixies of Celtic mythology. Such beings were regarded as personifications of the deadly powers of their environment, such as the noxious nature of marshes and fens. Thus, water elves were considered to cause the "dropsy" that might result from passage through a marshy wasteland. Dealing with them was an interesting problem. Some considered that one might bury the elf in the earth in order to prevent his attacks. Thus, the ancient Danish folk medicine remedy of curing a whitlow by thrusting the finger into the ground or lightly covering a sick child with earth are relics of such practice. In Holland, a man struck by lightning – a form of elf-shot – was interred up to the neck to extract the evil, while the Romans, as attested to by Varro, were even more concerned with the protection of the earth. Thus, the Roman charm for gout or pain in the feet required the sufferer to bow to the earth, to spit upon it, and to say thrice nine times the following charm: "*Terra pestem teneto. Salus hic maneto*" ("O earth, bear thou the pain. Health in my feet remain").

Pagan Roman spells

Lastly, it is interesting to observe that the Latin herbal, being copied ultimately from Pagan Roman sources, contained certain Pagan Roman spells, which are known to occur also in certain early Continental manuscripts, of which the earliest dates from the 7th century. It is very remarkable that these should have survived in their full and unexpurgated heathenism in herbals of 12th- and even 13th-century English workmanship. Perhaps the inclusion of an early example of a translation of one such conjuration may best demonstrate how even despite the passage of more than 1,000 years, there is so very little distance between our dreams and those of our early forebears:

Earth, divine goddess, Mother Nature, who generatest all things and bringest forth anew the sun which thou hast given to the nations; Guardian of sky and sea and of all gods and powers; through thy power all nature falls silent and then sinks in sleep. And again thou bringest back the light and chasest away night, and yet again thou coverest us most securely with thy shades. Thou dost contain chaos infinite, yea and winds and showers and storms. Thou sendest them out when thou wilt and causest the seas to roar; thou chasest away the sun and arousest the storm. Again when thou wilt thou sendest forth the joyous day and givest the nourishment of life with thy eternal surety. And when the soul departs to thee we return. Thou indeed art duly called great Mother of the gods; thou conquerest by thy divine name. Thou art the source of the strength of nations and of gods, without thee nothing can be brought to perfection or be born; thou art great, queen of the gods. Goddess, I adore thee as divine; I call upon thy name; be pleased to grant that which I ask thee, so shall I give thanks to thee, goddess, with due faith.

Animals, both real and fantastic, occupied an important place in medieval art and thought, and artists readily employed animal motifs, along with foliate designs, as part of their decorative vocabulary. In this picture, medieval medical practitioners scour their texts to try and identify the underlying reasons for these animal behaviors.

A much-venerated component of the Greco-Roman tradition was a number of different festivals dedicated to various gods. These most probably originated as rites of fertility and as such involved dramatic demonstrations of power, displays of wealth, and evidence of sexual potency, including prodigious feats of numeric conquest and endurance.

The doctrine of the elf-shot was, however, a view of disease that did not long retain its purity of form, since the shafts of the elves were easily confounded with the "flying venoms". In addition, the attacks of elves were comparable to the constant assaults of demons and possession by them, which was so large a part of Christian asceticism. Thus, in later Anglo-Saxon material, a fusion of the ideas of demoniacal possession with the attacks of elves, witches, and other beings of the Teutonic mythology and with the effects of flying venoms becomes apparent as humans become possessed by demons rather than merely elf-shot. Elf-based disease slowly became consigned to animals, as humans became regarded as worthy of more serious malign considerations. Thus, attacks on the bovine species produced numerous reports of elf-shot cattle which serious self-respecting demons might be expected to regard as providing poor material for their attention. Accordingly, there are numerous such references: "If a horse be shot. Take then a knife of which the handle is horn of a roan ox and on which are three brass nails. Inscribe then Christ's cross on the forehead of the horse so that it bleeds, then inscribe Christ's cross on the back... Take then the left ear and prick it through silently... Take then a staff, smite (the horse) on the back, then is the horse whole... Whatever the elf, this has power as a remedy." The process of pricking seems to have been especially efficacious for elf-shot cattle, and is constantly described, possibly as the animal equivalent of venesection.

6 LEECHCRAFT

In the early 19th century, British physicians accepted the use of leeches as an ancient and honorable part of their professional heritage, and recognized the beneficial consequences for physicians and patients alike. At that time, diseases were generally conceived of as collections of morbid symptoms, thus local inflammation was typically defined as a combination of swelling, heat, redness, and pain and regarded as indicative of an excessive quantity of blood in the affected area. It was naturally considered that such situations could be relieved, if only temporarily, by abstraction of blood from the inflamed site. In this respect, leeches were deemed especially useful in areas inaccessible to other methods of local bloodletting, such as around and within the nose and ears, inside the mouth, and in the rectum and vagina. They were also used as a method of general bloodletting – for example, in a patient too weak or otherwise unable to withstand venesection. The usual principle, however, was to place them as near as possible to the focus of the morbid process; thus, in the management of headache, they were placed on the temples; for gastrointestinal inflammation, on the epigastrium; for bladder troubles, on the shaved pubis; and for menstrual disorders, on the thighs, the groin, and the vulva.

HIRUDICULTURE

At the beginning of the 19th century, leeches were generally harvested "by the children of the poorer peasantry," who simply waded and splashed in the water and collected the leeches that became attached to their legs. By the 1830s, things had changed dramatically, such that in 1836, John Pereira wrote: "The consumption of leeches must be enormous." He pointed out that, collectively, the four largest London dealers imported, on average, 600,000 leeches monthly, or 7,200,000 a year. Most of these imports came from France, Germany, Silesia, and Poland. By the middle of the century, there were improved techniques for harvesting leeches; this was accomplished by drawing nets with bait (usually the liver of a recently slaughtered animal) through the water. However, the harvesting in vast numbers meant that leeches soon ceased to exist in whole areas of England and it seemed likely that, within a decade, leeches would be extinct in Western Europe. In England, a tax was levied on imported leeches for the purpose of fostering domestic production and thereby making the country "independent of nations with which we might be at war".

The decline in the natural supply of leeches led to the development of leech farms and to the pursuit of hiruditure. Anxious to ensure their own supply, medical faculties, hospitals, and some governmental units established their own large reservoirs in which leeches could be cultivated and farmers began growing leeches commercially. The main problem in hiruditure was supplying an adequate quantity of blood to enable leeches to breed and grow rapidly. At first, this was achieved by driving into the swamps wretched, lame, and worn-out horses; however, these unfortunate animals perished far too quickly for the leech growers' account. As a result, they devised an alternative strategy and found it more economical to feed the leeches on cows: "The heavy, dull animal, haggard, frightened, and yet resigned to its fate, bears the onslaught of the leeches, which are attached like bunches of grapes to its belly and legs, with a sort of stupid surprise." It was reported that "a breeder who has four hectares of marshes, drives into them every year upwards of 200 cows and many dozens of donkeys for the nourishment of 800,000 leeches".

Through the 1830s, improved techniques for conserving and shipping leeches expanded the opportunities for trade. In January 1841, a sea captain bought 20,000 leeches in Madras, India. They were kept in earthenware tubs on the deck of his ship and received no special care. When the ship reached the Cape of Good Hope, the captain sold the surviving leeches for a profit of more than £100 sterling. In the late 1840s, leeches were regularly imported into western Europe by land and sea from Turkey and Egypt, and in the 1860s, vast numbers of leeches were exported from Australia to Europe and to America. In 1867, the Murray River Fishing Company of Sydney, Australia, reported that 2,000,000 to 3,000,000 leeches would pass through their hands that season.

For many years, cupping and leeching were closely related and it was not surprising that the cupping machine invented by Demours was called an "artificial leech". Leeches are extensile aquatic creatures, members of the Hirudinea division of *Chaetopod* worms that can contract their body from a plump pear-shaped form to a long, thin, worm-like shape.

The two varieties that have been used in medicine are the horseleech and the species known as *Hirudo medicinalis*. They possess chitinous jaws capable of producing a triangular or triradiate bite through which they can suck blood into a vast, expanding stomach that can fill the whole body. Of particular relevance

Leeching was a most popular medieval therapeutic strategy, particularly because it required little skill. Leeches were also popular because they could be used in places where phlebotomy and cupping could not, such as internal membranes, and were thus often also applied inside the nose, ear, eyes, mouth, anus, and vagina. Surprisingly, leeches have to a degree returned to fashion for medical use. The anticoagulant secreted into the wound diminishes scar formation and promotes healing.

is the oral injection of an anticoagulant hirudin into the wound to prevent coagulation, with the result that when the leech is fully gorged and has fallen off, the blood continues to flow freely.

The history of leeching does not appear to extend as far back in medical practice as that of cupping and indeed, the majority of ancient authorities, including Hippocrates, being the most notable, make no reference to the subject. Nicander of Colophon in Ionia, a hereditary priest of Apollo during the 2nd century BC, was the first writer to mention the therapeutic use of the leech. Similarly, Themison, the Roman physician, who flourished in the beginning of the Christian era, advised the application of a cupping glass after the leech had fallen off the patient, while Antyllus used leeches if the patient feared the lancet or if the area to be treated was too rough for cups. If the hands or feet were the

points for application, they were immersed in the water in which the leeches were kept. Pliny's great book on natural history (*Historia Naturalis*) contained a short chapter on the subject:

In cases where it is desired to let blood, the kind of leech used is known by the name of sanguisuga. These leeches are used as an alternative to cupping glasses, their effect being to relieve the body of superfluous blood. Still, however, there is this inconvenience attending them. When they have been once applied they create a necessity for having recourse to the same treatment at about the same period in every succeeding year. Many physicians have been of the opinion that leeches may be successfully applied in cases of gout. Leeches are apt to leave their head buried in the flesh; the consequence of which is an incurable wound which has caused death in many cases, such as that, for instance, of Messalinus, a patrician of consular rank, after an application of leeches to his knee. When this is the case, that which was intended as a remedy is turned to an active poison, a result which is to be apprehended, using red leeches particularly. Hence it is that when these last are employed it is a practice to snip them with a pair of scissors while sucking. The consequence is the blood oozes forth through a syphon as it were, and the head, gradually contracting as the animal dies, is not left behind in the wound.

Galen paid little attention to the bloodsucking abilities of the leech, but was particularly concerned with what should be done if a leech were swallowed, an emergency which is constantly referred to during the succeeding 1,500 years:

Some people advise a draught of urine, others of snow to detach a leech that has been swallowed. But Asclepiades taught that we should wash it out and insert a soft sponge dipped in cold water into the throat and extract the leech when it seized upon the sponge and then he used to give the juice of a lentil. He advised the covering of the outside of the neck with cold water. Appolonius Mys administered a drench of extremely bitter vinegar mixed with urine. He also used a lump of edible snow with edible and drinkable purges in order to detach the leeches, for he states that they are often expelled together with what is ejected from the bowels.

Galen did however provide details of the best method of applying a leech. He advised the snipping off of its tail to increase the flow of blood and he applied cups after the leech had been detached. If the bleeding continued for too long, he applied burnt galls and heated pitch. He regarded leeches as a simple substitute for cupping, for they took only the superficial blood from the skin and flesh. Avicenna gave details of the best types of leech and warned against using leeches with large heads of black or green color, leeches with down on them, or with streaks of bright color. All these were poisonous and gave rise to inflammation, hemorrhage, fever, syncope, paralysis, and intractable ulcers. Nor was it wise to employ leeches whose excrement was black or muddy and whose movements immediately darkened the water and rendered it offensive. He detailed the procedure of their application as follows:

Leeches should be kept a day before applying them. They should be squeezed to make them eject the contents of their stomachs. If feasible, they should be given a little lamb's blood by way of nourishment. The slime and debris should be cleansed from their bodies with a sponge. The place of application must be shaved, washed, and rubbed until it is red. Dry carefully and moisten with sugar-water or milk or scratch with a needle until blood appears. To ensure that they will not crawl into the gullet, nose or anus, one must draw a thread through the tail end from above down, not from side to side, otherwise one would injure the large blood vessels of the animal. When leeches are full and you wish them to come off, sprinkle a little salt over them or pepper or snuff or ashes or nitre or burnt bristles or burnt sponge or wool. They will then fall off. The place should then be sucked by cupping it in order to extract some of the blood at the spot and thereby get rid of the toxic substances left in the wound. Do not leave the patient until the bleeding has quite stopped. If it is a child, watch it in the following night.

The collection of leeches from swamps and ponds was a source of considerable revenue for local populations.

Henri de Mondeville advised the use of leeches for most kinds of skin diseases, delirium, madness, melancholy, for all tumors that had difficulty in coming to a head, and for all conditions suitable for cupping. He thought the best type of leech was small, thin, and slender, like a rat's tail, having a small head, a red belly, a dull blue-green back marked with a small number of yellow lines, and caught from clear stony water containing many frogs, and that they were especially beneficial if applied around the joints of the hands in scabies, around the anus (in particular), and on the heel and sole of the foot for madness: "When leeches swell they can be held up with spoons so that they will not fall off. To remove a leech, thread a horse-hair between the head of the leech and the patient's skin."

Leeches were advised for temporal headaches arranged in groups of 10 or 12 in a circular manner on each temple. For retention of the menses, four leeches fastened by a thread were applied as closely as possible to the uterus. There was no disease that would not benefit from their application to the vessels of the anus, particularly cases of epistaxis, hemoptysis, and hematemesis, and in extreme circumstances, they were also of use in treating obesity.

Great value was laid on the snipping off of the tail. By this means, one leech answered the purpose of several, for it continued to draw blood as before, which flowed drop by drop from its wounded extremity. There was surprisingly little added to the subject of leeching in the 16th, 17th, or 18th centuries, and it remained an extremely popular therapeutic measure, such that in 1775, Richard Mead wrote that leeches were often of vast service in delirium, and he used them in fevers if the patient was too weak to bleed. Similarly, Lettsom in 1815 described the case of a patient who had suddenly become delirious and unconscious. Lettsom shaved his head and applied cold applications before resorting to cupping and leeching. When these failed, he tried cathartics and finally blisters, but despite his ministrations, the fever increased for a further four days before recovery!

In France it was said that the use of leeches to treat children was of national importance, for it increased the population by cutting down the infant mortality. Gallic leeching was widespread and the demand for the creatures so enormous that they were imported from Eastern Europe to meet the demand. A particular utility was in the treatment of colic, where as many as 50 leeches were applied to the abdomen simultaneously.

Leeches were affixed by inverting a wine glass containing as many as were required over the intended area. To increase efficacy, tail snipping was practiced, whereby the ingested blood was lost with the result that the leech continued to suck "ad infinitum". An alternative practice was to rub salt or vinegar on their mouths so the engorged leeches vomited the ingested blood and could then be induced to bite four or five times more. At the end, on being put into clear water, they were as lively as when they were first employed. A truly cost-effective remedial agent – endlessly reusable!

Leeching had become a substantial trade that centered on France. Five kinds of *Hirudo medicinalis* leeches were described according to their size, varying from "thin" to "enormous". They were called after their color or their country of origin – grey, green, blonde, dark, Hungarian, Syrian, Turkish – all. Their weights were a most important factor. In general, 1,000 small leeches weighed from 325–500g, while 1,000 large leeches weighed nearly 10 times as much. The largest were found in the Bordeaux area and weighed as much as 33g each and measured 25cm in length. It was calculated that a leech weighing three drachms sucked three drachms and one scruple of blood, and a further three and a half drachms escaped from the wound; a leech weighing half a drachm sucked half a drachm of blood with a little oozing and 24 large leeches could take 20oz, whereas 24 small leeches removed only 3oz of blood. Thus, leech size was an important therapeutic variable!

At the start of the 19th century, France could support herself with homegrown leeches, but with excessive usage, supplies diminished and once the resources of Spain and Portugal had been exhausted, Italy and Bohemia were used.

By the middle of the century, the vast marshes of Hungary were beginning to fail and Poland, Russia, Syria, and Turkey were utilized for further supplies. Between 1827 and 1844, an average 27 million leeches were imported into France annually at a cost of 830,000 francs. Transportation was a problem, since even if sent in barrels, stone jars, leather, or close-woven bags dipped frequently in water, it was inadvisable to put too great a weight together, otherwise the animals crushed one another. Imaginative strategies were devised and the leeches were sent from Budapest to Paris in large numbers in bags laid on hammocks stretched across a wagon drawn by relays of post-horses. Often, leeches made a journey of six or eight days dry, but in hot weather, it was advisable to moisten them once daily and it became apparent that spring and autumn were the best seasons. Strasbourg was a large collection center, and there they were emptied into zinc baths until the time came to repack them for transport to Paris. At one period, 60–80,000 leeches were sent on this journey daily.

As a result of this huge demand, the prices began to rise such that in 1806, 1,000 leeches cost 12–15 francs, in 1815, 30–36 francs, and by 1821, the apogee of 150–280 francs was reached before a 20-year market plateau developed. A million and a half leeches were sent to England and America in 1823, and the next year England alone received five million. In 1846, the price of a single leech in London had ranged from one shilling and twopence to one shilling and sixpence. In 1804, Wilkinson reported that leeches in the Covent Garden market were eight or nine shillings a dozen, whereas 12 years earlier, they had been three shillings for 100. In a hospital near Nottingham, probably typical of English hospitals generally, the demand for leeches peaked in the 1830s and then fell over the next two decades; by the mid 1850s, annual expenditures for leeches were less than one twentieth what they had been two decades earlier. By 1879, one of London's major importers, a company that had formerly sold more than 30,000 leeches a week, was selling only one tenth as many, "most of which go to Scotland". Whatever therapeutic benefits they may have offered, the advent of more modern medical practice led to leeches almost completely disappearing from the therapeutic armamentarium by the beginning of the 20th century.

Most therapy of the 19th century was permeated by the belief that disease reflected some noxious property present in the blood. Venesection as a means of therapy was widely accepted and vied with the use of leeches for primacy in efficacy. In France, the use of leeches to remove blood from ill persons was so prevalent that demand exceeded supply to the extent that leeches became a huge import commodity during the early part of the 19th century. Such was the presumed widespread benefit of leech therapy that even esophagitis was deemed amenable to leech application.

7 ELIZABETHAN MEDICINE

The last Tudor monarch, Elizabeth I, has been quoted as saying: "I know I have the body of a weak and feeble woman, but I have the heart and stomach of a king, and of a king of England too." Her reign was during one of the more constructive periods in English history and literature bloomed through the works of Edmund Spenser, Christopher Marlowe and William Shakespeare, while Sir Francis Drake and Sir Walter Raleigh were instrumental in expanding English influence in the New World. Similarly, the Queen's own religious compromise laid many fears to rest and enabled rational enquiry to flourish. In addition, fashion and education came to the fore because of Elizabeth's penchant for knowledge, courtly behavior, and extravagant dress.

Elizabeth I resembled her father Henry VIII in that she was a strong supporter of the progress of medicine and surgery and sciences during her reign. Her wise and trusted advisor Francis Bacon noted that she possessed "a love and reverence towards learning" and bestowed much favor on physicians and surgeons, although she was reluctant to grant dignities and rewards for their services. In her time, there were three classes of medical practitioners: the physicians, who were in the process of transitioning from their previous roles as ecclesiastics; the surgeons, who had recently upgraded their performance from being barbers; and the apothecaries, who were in the process of dissociating themselves from the grocers.

In 1511, Henry VIII, acting on the advice of Thomas Linacre, passed an Act that provided that no one should practice medicine within the City of London unless he had been examined, approved, and admitted by the Bishop of London and the Dean of St Paul's Cathedral. In medicine, the doctors were examined by four doctors of physic; for surgery, by other expert persons in that faculty. Outside London and its precincts, the examinations were to be by the Bishop of the Diocese, or his Vicar-General, with such expert persons as he might think convenient. The medical graduates of Oxford and Cambridge were deemed of such excellence as to be exempt from such examinations.

THE ROYAL COLLEGE OF PHYSICIANS

In 1518, Henry VIII, at the advice of his physician Linacre, who had realized the need for the reorganization of the medical profession in England and had advocated the Act of 1511, founded the Royal College of Physicians by Letters Patent confirmed by Statute 14. The original founders of the College with two other physicians were named elects and were mandated to annually appoint from among themselves a president. As a result of this decision, no person without dispensation, except a medical graduate of Oxford or Cambridge, was permitted to practice physic throughout England unless he had been examined and approved by the president and three of the elects. The concept held that it "was expedient and necessary to provide that no person be suffered to exercise and practice physic, but only those persons that be profound, sad and discreet, groundedly learned and deeply studied in physic".

In 1569, Elizabeth I (*top right*) provided a Grant of Arms (*background*) to the Barber-Surgeons' Company. The original coat of arms of 1561 contained the shield of the barbers with a helmet surmounted by a gold "opinicus" (a monster with the forelegs of a lion, head, neck and wings of an eagle, and the tail of a camel). The motto "*De Prescientia Dei*" is flanked by two lynxes (with crown and chain argent) that were added as supporters in 1565.

From its inauguration, the Royal College of Physicians held examinations for the licentiateship and deemed acceptable as candidates graduates or those who had been pupils of a qualified physician. Individuals who wished to practice in London and the suburbs were closely scrutinized by the censors, and when admitted as licentiates, were designated as "candidates" and were eligible for the Fellowship of the College, if of good repute, after a probationary period. For those who sought to practice elsewhere in the country, obtaining a license was far less onerous. William Shakespeare, in *All's Well that Ends Well*, referred to the Royal College of Physicians as the "congregated college" and considered it to be an advance; in particular, that its initiation of a formal medical education was a remarkable improvement on the previous state of disarray.

The Royal College of Physicians (*background: Warwick Lane*) is not only the oldest medical institution in England but also among the most active of all medical professional organizations. John Lumley, Lord Lumley (*top right*), the High Steward of the University of Oxford and a distinguished patron of literature, provided many of the books that made up the original College library collection.

Since a previous Act of Parliament which united the Company of Barbers with the Guild of Surgeons had especially empowered the masters of the united Company "to take yearly the bodies of four malefactors" who had been condemned to death for felony for their "further and better knowledge, instruction, insight, learning, and experience in the science and faculty of surgery," the College obtained a comparable agreement. Thus Elizabeth I, following this precedent, granted a similar permission to the College in 1565 to take up to four bodies a year for dissection of persons executed in London, Middlesex, or any county within 16 miles. The Fellows, under penalty of a fine, were then required to give in turn a public demonstration and anatomical lectures. In 1581, John Lumley, Lord Lumley, together with Richard Caldwell, MD Oxon, FRCP, founded the Lumleian Surgery Lecture, whereupon the College decreed that "one hundred pounds should be set aside to build the College rooms more ample and spacious for the better celebration of this most solemn lecture". Two years later, it was ordered on March 13, 1583, that a "capacious theatre should be added to the College thus enlarged". The College had up until that time met in a mansion, the Stonehouse in Knight Rider Street, that had been provided for them as a gift by the College's first President Thomas Linacre.

The Queen's interest in the College was sometimes not only with matters of administrative importance but also related to personal issues. Of particular interest is a letter of August 11, 1602, signed J Stanhope and Ro: Cecyll, sent "to our very loving Friends Mr Dr Forster, President of the Physicians in London, and to the rest of the Electors," requesting that George Turner, MD, FRCP, whose appointment as an elect had come under negative scrutiny "because of his backwardness in religion," be appointed an elect. The Queen was insistent that he might not be so disgraced, and Dr Turner was duly appointed an elect on August 12, subsequently becoming Treasurer in 1609. It is noteworthy that after his death, his wife acquired an infamous reputation for poisoning Sir Thomas Overbury in the Tower at the instigation of the Countess of Essex in 1613, and was hanged.

Military physicians

Since the health of those entrusted with ensuring the safety of the country was paramount, the Royal College of Physicians, at the request of Elizabeth, selected from their Fellows physicians, a number to be in attendance on admirals and generals during their campaigns. Thus, Thomas Muffett, MD Basle et Cantab, accompanied the Earl of Essex on his expedition to Normandy, while Roger Marbeck, MD Oxon, the Provost of Oriel, the first Registrar of the College, and Physician to the Queen, accompanied the Lord High Admiral, Lord Howard of Effingham, in an expedition against Cadiz in 1596. Marbeck subsequently wrote *A briefe and true Discourse of the late honourable voyage into Spaine, &c*, the manuscript of which still resides in the British Museum. Similarly, in 1597, Dr Henry Atkins was chosen as Physician to the Earl of Essex on what proved to be a disastrous "Islands Voyage" to the Azores. Having embarked at Plymouth with the fleet, he became so seasick, "*ex jactitatione maris*," that it became necessary to relieve him of his post and replace him with Thomas Moundeford, MD Cantab, who subsequently became President of the College. Dr Atkins recovered from his maritime misadventure adequately to later be appointed Physician to James I, and respectfully declined the first baronet's patent on the institution of that order in 1611, dying a very wealthy man in 1635.

Another surgeon who achieved considerable prominence in respect of his military service was Hippocrates d'Otthen, MD Montpellier et Oxon, who was the son of the Emperor's physician. Elizabeth had invited the elder d'Otthen to England, and as a result, both he and his son entered the service of the British Crown. Hippocrates became Physician to the Earl of Leicester for many years, both at home and in the wars in the Low Countries, and the Queen and the State were particularly appreciative of his efforts. After the Earl of Leicester's death, the Queen ordered Hippocrates to become Physician to the Earl of Essex, who he then served in the wars in France and in the Cadiz expedition. Thereafter, he became Physician to Lord Mountjoy in Ireland, and finally, James I appointed him as Physician to the Earl of Hertford, his Majesty's Ambassador to the Archduke of Austria and Burgundy. Presumably exhausted from such extensive and peripatetic service, Dr d'Otthen died in 1611!

EDUCATION AND PRACTICE

The physician in Tudor times was a well-educated man, since the courses at the universities were lengthy ones and conducted by Regius Professors of Physic at Oxford and Cambridge who had been appointed by Henry VIII in 1546. The examinations were rigorous and it was incumbent upon both pupil and teacher to uphold the standards that had been set by the Royal College of Physicians and ratified by the Crown. Dedication and commitment were essential, since the MD at Oxford took 14 years to obtain and the Statutes demanded the initial arts course to the MA degree. The initial arts course required the acquisition of a sound knowledge of Greek, a thorough acquaintance with Latin, and some learning in dialectics and physics, followed by a medical faculty course of seven years. It was mandated that a student dispute twice, respond once, and see two anatomies before he could obtain a BA degree. Under special circumstances, a dispensation might be obtained allowing the faculty course to begin at the BA stage, thus shortening the course to the MD stage by about two years. This enabled the student to obtain the license to practice and the license to give "cursory" lectures to his juniors, thus becoming a pupil teacher or demonstrator. The full course still demanded 14 years from matriculation, and according to the Statutes of 1549, the candidate was required to perform two anatomies and effect at least three cures before he was admitted to the MD. Similar regulations were in force at Cambridge, but in both institutions, provision for clinical study both in physic and in chirurgery was sadly lacking. Indeed, in order to obtain adequate experience, those students possessed of higher qualities, such as John Caius and William Harvey, traveled to the Continental schools (Padua, Bologna, and Montpellier) or gained experience as military physicians. The primary source of almost all contemporary medical teaching was based on the doctrines of Galen and any significant departure from this body of information was regarded as little less than professional heresy. Thus John Geynes, MD Oxon, in 1559, was cited before the College for impugning the infallibility of Galen, and only on his acknowledgment of error, and the provision of a humble recantation signed with his own hand, was he received into the College (FRCP 1560), where he subsequently became Censor and Elect before perishing of plague in 1563.

As might be expected given the Galenic dogma of the day, the theory of the humors, which persisted almost into the 18th century, dominated diagnostic and therapeutic considerations and the entire practice of physic. The four humors or fluids were believed to comprise the human constitution – blood, phlegm, cholera (yellow bile), and melancholy (black bile). The predominant humors determined the temperament as sanguine, phlegmatic, choleric, or melancholic. In health, the proportions of the four humors were balanced, but during conditions of excess or morbid events, they became unbalanced and ill health resulted. In order to rectify such an imbalance, it was necessary to institute a regimen that involved either purging or depleting the excess of humor by bleeding or cupping, or diminishing the bile by means of drugs. Such interventions were themselves each governed by strict rules, thus bleeding could only be done in the appropriate month, as Dr Owen reported when attending Princess Elizabeth in 1554.

The Hippocratic and Galenic consideration of the four humors was dominant during the height of Roman medicine and continued well into the Middle Ages. To further increase the efficacy of such prognostications, they were often augmented by the introduction of astrological signs and gender. The four figures represent the seasons of the wheel of 12 months in which the microcosmic equivalents are the four "humors". Thus, autumn was black gall (Melancholia – Earth) summer yellow gall (Cholera – Fire), spring to the sanguine (Air), and winter to the phlegmatic (Water). To each fluid was attributed a specific personality characteristic that exerted its effect upon the corpus. Thus, blood was associated with a sanguine personality (laughter, music, and a passionate disposition), while a phlegmatic personality was sluggish and dull. Yellow bile represented an individual quick to anger or choleric (cholera meaning yellow, as in yellow fever). Lastly, black bile represented a melancholic or depressed personality (melan meaning black). The human temperament was thought of as a blend of different humors and temperatures as well as degrees of dryness and moisture. Thus, disease and health became considered as a quotient of different components that required a perfect balance to maintain a state of health.

Astrology also had its enthusiastic votaries, and although Nicolaus Copernicus in 1543 had made the Ptolemaic system of astronomy obsolete by his great work, *De revolutionibus Orbium Coelestium* (*On the Revolutions of the Celestial Spheres*), a mass of folklore and superstition clung about the heavenly bodies. Thus, some physicians cast horoscopes of their patients and diagnosed their complaints on them, and used such information to promulgate even more fanciful therapy – for example, it was believed that Leo ruled all diseases in the ribs and sides and trembling or passion of the heart. Indeed, it was regarded as quite acceptable to practice in such a fashion and Thomas Twine, MD Cantab, MB Oxon, who died in 1613, commenting on Wood noted, "he was the friend of Dee and Allen, and was no less eminent in his time as an astrologer than a physician".

Sir Theodore Turquet de Mayerne (1573–1655) (*top left*) of Geneva studied medicine at Montpellier in France before becoming a teacher and physician in Paris. As a result of his liberal usage of mercury and antimony, he was vilified by the Paris faculty and finally fled to England, where he became Royal Physician to both James I and Charles I. Although sundry alchemicals were in widespread use, the introduction of the *Pharmacopoeia Londinensis* (*center*) under the auspices of the London Society of Apothecaries (*bottom right*) and with the help of de Mayerne provided a better guideline for the medical use of drugs.

Nicolaus Copernicus (1473–1543), the Polish astronomer, achieved immortality for the development of the heliocentric, or sun-centered, astronomical theory. This premised that the sun was at rest near the center of the universe, and that the earth, spinning on its axis once daily, revolved annually around the sun. His treatise *De revolutionibus Orbium Coelestium* (*On the Revolutions of the Celestial Spheres*) marks the beginning of modern astronomy and inaugurated what became known as the "Copernican Revolution," which inspired Kepler, Galileo, and Newton in their work. The Church initially fought bitterly to suppress any consideration of such information, since it threatened the current mandates of theological dogma.

In 1585, the College entrusted a committee of six Fellows to draft and publish a uniform *Pharmacopoeia*. By the next year, 1589, Robert Preest, MD Cantab, was associated with Drs Atslow, Browne, and Farmery in the preparation of the definitive formulae of syrups, juleps, and decoctions for the *Pharmacopoeia*. However, the first *British Pharmacopoeia* did not appear until 1618, when it was produced with an introduction by Sir Theodore Turquet de Mayerne by a new committee of eight Fellows, of whom Harvey was one.

In Elizabethan times, much as now indeed, polypharmacy was regarded as appropriate treatment, although many of the drugs and preparations were decidedly unpleasant and based on folklore rather than rational or logical considerations. In the Letters Patent constituting the Royal College of Physicians, there was included a provision assigning to four persons named by the College the duty of "the correction and government of physic and its professors together with the examination of all medicines and the powers of punishing offenders by fine and imprisonment". This duty, confirmed by Statute in 1522, was discharged by the College for 340 years until 1858 and as such, the College visitors were empowered by Statute to destroy any defective drugs in the apothecaries' shops and thus constituted the forerunners of the inspectors and analysts that were appointed under the Sale of Food and Drugs Act of 1875.

As a result of such innovations and foresight, the reign of Elizabeth I witnessed the initiation of scientific therapeutics by the College as can be attested to by viewing commentaries in the British Museum, respectively provided by Dr Hans Sloane and by Dr John Hall. The latter physician was Shakespeare's son-in-law from Stratford-upon-Avon, "where he was very famous," and affords evidence of the complicated prescriptions of the time.

The physician's fee was one angel (10 shillings) a visit and as a result, many doctors became wealthy and acquired estates from the benefit of their professional labors. Of note is the fact that the dividing line between physician and surgeons was not clearly drawn under the Tudors, although by the Physicians' Act of 1540, medicine was defined as comprehending surgery, and thus gave the physicians the right to practice surgery when and where they liked. As a rule, however, the physician did not undertake surgery, and arranged with a "chirurgeon" and an apothecary to be in their service. In Ben Jonson's play *The Magnetic Lady*, inspired by Gilbert's *De Magnete*, Dr Rut is attended by an apothecary, Tim Item.

As regards obstetrics, midwifery was chiefly in the hands of midwives – untrained, often dirty, but made "handy" by experience. Officers appointed by the Archbishop of Canterbury and the Bishop of London licensed such women after the "abilities and honesty of the lives and conversations of the candidate" had been testified to under oath by responsible persons. As might have been predicted, however, the maternal mortality was high, chiefly through puerperal sepsis. Some physicians practiced obstetrics, and Dr George Owen is said to have delivered Queen Jane of Edward VI by cesarean section. In 1569, the Chamberlains, a family of Huguenot refugees who had held secret for many years the great invention of the obstetric forceps, came to England and matters improved somewhat.

England: Dr Chamberlain (*top right*) perfected one of the earliest obstetric forceps (*bottom and center*). As accomplished as they were as "accouchers" the Chamberlain family were, in addition, remarkably successful entrepreneurs. Having concealed the secret of their forceps design for a generation, they also developed an anodyne necklace (*top left*) of "impeachable" medicinal virtue.

Dr John Hall, William Shakespeare's son-in-law, was an eminently successful Stratford physician of the early 17th century. His surviving medical case notes for the years 1611–1635 describe how he treated 155 patients of all classes, from aristocrat to pauper, the majority within a 15-mile radius of Stratford. He recorded symptoms, medications, and the outcomes of his attentions, providing a rare picture of provincial medical practice in Stuart England as well as interesting details on persons close to Shakespeare. His patients included the actor Michael Drayton (*top*), the Stratford schoolmaster John Trapp (*center*), and Spencer Compton, Earl of Northampton.

SELECT OBSERVATIONS ON English Bodies OF Eminent Persons in desperate DISEASES.

First written in Latin by Mr. *John Hall*, Physician : After Englished by JAMES COOK, Author of the *Marrow of Chirurgery*.

To which is now added, an hundred like *Counsels* and *Advices*, for several Honourable Persons : By the same Author.

In the Close is added, Directions for drinking of the *Bath-Water*, and *Ars Cosmetica*, or Beautifying Art : By H. *Stubbs*, Physician at *Warwick*.

LONDON, Printed by *J. D.* for *Benjamin Shirley*, under the Dial of St. Dunstan's Church in Fleet-street, 1679.

POLITICS AND MEDICINE

The responsibility of being a physician to politicians and aristocrats was a mixed blessing, carrying with it both kudos and great risk. The failure to effect a cure might lead to a dramatic perception of public failure, or even worse, the concept that foul play was involved. Thus, a knowledge of drugs might be invoked by unscrupulous politicians in order to remove their rivals from the scene, and some powerful but immoral power brokers such as Leicester maintained individuals specifically for such purposes. Thus Dr Julio, an Italian physician and astrologer, who was in the employ of Leicester, was affirmed to be a skilful producer of poisons, which he applied with such frequency that the Jesuit Parsons ironically extolled "the marvelous good luck of Queen Elizabeth's favorite in the opportune deaths of those who stood in the way of his wishes". In Elias Ashmole's *Antiquities of Berkshire*, there is record of another of Leicester's physicians, Walter Baily, MD Oxon, FRCP, a

Fellow of New College, Oxford, and Regius Professor of Physic at the University, who was a much more honorable character than Dr Julio. It is recorded that before "the moon, sweet regent of the sky, silvered the walls of Cumnor Hall" on a night of tragedy, Leicester (then Lord Robert Dudley) sent his henchmen Anthony Forster and Varney to Dr Baily demanding a potion for his first wife, the ill-fated Amy Robsart. Baily, being a person of considerable integrity, declined: "The doctor upon just cause and consideration did suspect (their design), seeing their great importunity, and the small need the lady had of physic, and therefore he peremptorily denied their request; misdoubting (as he afterwards reported) lest, if they had poisoned her under the name of his potion, he might after have been hanged for a colour of their sin." Baily subsequently became Physician to Elizabeth, and Ashmole reports, as one might have predicted, that the nefarious Leicester endeavored, unsuccessfully, to displace him from the Queen's favor.

A somewhat less fortunate outcome than that of Dr Baily in the web of politics was the fate of Roderigo Lopus, or Lopez, FRCP, the Jewish Physician to the Queen. As early as 1567, Lopez was Physician at St Bartholomew's Hospital and resident medical officer, where he was supported with "a salary of forty shillings a year, which with his house and a certain allowance of billetts and coales". As an individual of considerable medical skill, he was highly regarded by the Queen and she had granted him a monopoly for the importation of aniseed and sumach, thus considerably augmenting his income and prestige. Unfortunately, his inclination to dabble in politics proved his undoing, since he was accused by Robert Devereux, Earl of Essex, of having received a bribe from Philip II of Spain to introduce poison into the medicine of the Queen. Although Elizabeth initially declined to the charge, Essex produced witnesses and letters, and Lopez, protesting his innocence of all charges except correspondence with Philip, was sent to the Tower, tried, and hanged in 1594. Even at this juncture, the Queen appears to have

doubted the justice of the verdict, since she delayed signing the death warrant, and by a rare exercise of her prerogative, she allowed the Lopez family to retain much of the doctor's property.

A similar propensity for meddling in politics was provided by James Good and Edward Atslow, two Fellows of the College who were involved in plots that made the custody of Mary Queen of Scots a constant anxiety to Elizabeth and her ministers. Good, MD, Oxon, Censor and Elect, was imprisoned in 1573 for holding secret correspondence by letters with the Scottish Queen and Atslow, MD, Oxon, Fellow of New College, also Censor and Elect, was a zealous Catholic, who in 1570 visited Queen Mary at Tutbury. Years later in 1579 he was arrested on a charge of conspiring with the Earls of Arundel, Northumberland, and others, but released before, in 1585, being imprisoned and tortured for designing means for Mary's escape. Thomas Morgan, in reporting to Mary, related, "Dr Atslow was racked twice, almost to death, in the Tower, about the Earl of Arundell his matters, and intention to depart England," before being released, only to die in 1594.

In addition to their medical duties, physicians occasionally acted as ambassadors, thus, after Richard Chancellor had discovered the kingdom of Moscovia, or Russia, in 1553, and was received by Ivan the Terrible, three physicians were sent to Moscow in a diplomatic as well as a professional capacity. These were Ralph Standish, MD, Cantab, in May, 1557; Robert Jacob, MD, Basel, in 1581, and Mark Ridley, MD, Cantab, in 1594. Dr Jacob was held in high esteem by Elizabeth and was sent by her to the Tsarina "as being well skilled in female complaints". Jacob clearly relished his role and amplified it into that of marriage broker, recommending Lady Mary Hastings to Ivan as his seventh wife. Fortunately, the Tsar died before the negotiations were concluded. Dr Ridley was sent as Chief Physician to Tsar Boris Godunoff in 1594 by Lord Burghley, but was recalled by Elizabeth after the death of his royal patient, although no dereliction of duty was alleged.

On rare occasions, physicians were employed as secret agents for the government, and one, Dr Thomas D'Oylie, a Fellow of Magdalen College, Oxford, and afterwards Physician at St Bartholomew's Hospital, in a letter to the Earl of Leicester, narrated the consequences of such employment. Having been captured on the Earl of Oxford's ship by two French men-of-war in 1585 off Dunkirk, "he was stripped naked, put in the common jail," before being eventually ransomed for 500 guilders. He added: "I escaped well because they found nothing in my chest but four physic and astronomic books. All letters and notes for your Honour's business I drained out of a porthole when they entered the ship."

An old print of Roderigo Lopus, or Lopez (1525–1594) (*background*), Physician at St Bartholomew's Hospital, who conspired to poison Elizabeth I (*left*). Lopez was a Portuguese-born Jew who studied medicine in Spain before escaping the Inquisition and coming to London in 1559. Already in his thirties, in England he rose to be a society physician, well known to the high and mighty of his day. In 1586, Lopez, at the peak of his profession, was appointed Body Physician to the Queen and became highly regarded by her. His ethnic and Spanish background as well as his involvement in espionage for the government placed him under suspicion. Finally, a cabal of the aristocracy after a less than balanced trial convicted him of attempting to poison the Queen and he was executed.

THE LIFE OF THE MIND

There is ample evidence that physicians of Tudor times were erudite and learned men, indeed, most had been Fellows of colleges at Oxford or Cambridge and many regarded Linacre and John Clement, who taught Latin and Greek and wrote classical studies, as ideal role models.

John Caius

John Caius, MD, Cantab, PRCP, was, prior to his adoption of medicine as a primary interest, Professor of Greek at Padua and assimilated a large collection of correct editions of Celsus and Galen during his sojourn in Italy. In addition, Caius was a correspondent of Gesner, who in the preface to his *Icones Animalium*, referred to him as an individual of consummate erudition, judgment, fidelity, and diligence; and in an epistle to Elizabeth I, termed him "the most learned physician of his age". In return for such fulsome praise, Caius supplied Gesner with information on rare animals and plants, and composed a treatise on British dogs, published in 1570. During his stay in Padua, Caius was the pupil and friend of Andreas Vesalius, and as a result, upon his return to England was the first to introduce the study of practical anatomy into this country, and the first publicly to teach it in the Hall of the Barber-Surgeons in 1546 and at Cambridge in 1557. In 1552, he published his account of the sweating sickness in English, which he afterwards improved and translated into Latin. He was Physician successively to Edward VI, Queen Mary, and Elizabeth I, and co-founder of Gonville and Caius College, of which in 1559 he became Master. Unfortunately, his Roman Catholic beliefs led to conflict with his Protestant Fellows, who burned his mass vestments, and he resigned his mastership in 1573. From 1555 to 1560, he was President of the Royal College of Physicians and again in 1562 and 1563, and died, as he had predicted, on July 29, 1573, aged 63.

William Harvey (1578–1657) (*right*) completed his medical education at the University of Padua. His personal stamma (*background*) on the wall of the Medical School indicates his English origins (Anglia). Harvey became widely regarded as "the greatest physiologist the world has seen". His extraordinary discovery of the circulation was reserved for the reign of Charles I (*top*) and he himself remained a lifelong ardent royalist, despite the depredations this belief brought upon his career.

William Gilbert (1540–1603) (*bottom right*), MD, Cantab, was one of the greatest of the Elizabethan scientists. He was Fellow of St John's College and Physician to Elizabeth I as well as President of the Royal College of Physicians in 1600. Gilbert was responsible for the establishment of the sciences of magnetism and electricity, and indeed his contributions may be regarded as hallmarks in the dawn of scientific experiment. Elizabeth I was much enamored of his work and regarded him as a sage counselor, bestowing a sizeable pension on him to assist in his experiments, which were published as *De Magnete* in 1600. As one of her favorite and most trusted physicians, Gilbert attended the Queen in her last illness.

Botanist physicians

William Turner (died 1568) was an MD and Dean of Wells, and despite being a physician, achieved the honorific of being regarded as the "Father of English botany". His elegant and detailed scientific study of plants was published as a herbal in 1548, and for a century thereafter, was regarded as the definitive text on the subject. Another medical botanist was William Bullein, MD, (died 1576), who wrote the earliest of English herbals, *The Booke of Simples*. Thomas Penny, MD, FRCP (died 1589), was a worthy successor to Turner and supplied rare plants to Gesner, Camerarius, and Crusius, becoming so well known that no less an authority than John Gerard referred to him as "a second Dioscorides for his singular knowledge of plants". Gerard (1545–1612), became Curator of the botanic garden which the Royal College of Physicians made in 1587, and was in addition to his botanical skills a barber-surgeon and Master of the Company in 1607.

John Tradescant (*bottom right*), an esteemed botanist and medicinal herbalist of England, cultivated the plum in 18th century London. As the son of Charles I's naturalist and gardener (*top left: Tradescant senior*), he added to his father's collection of natural history objects. The remains of their original garden still exist in Lambeth and are directly opposite the Royal Society of Pharmacy.

THE SCIONS OF THE SURGEONS

In 1540, Henry VIII, at the instigation of Thomas Vicary, his Sergeant-Surgeon, united the barbers and the surgeons in the formation of the Barber-Surgeons' Company. Vicary maintained his royal influence, subsequently becoming Surgeon to Edward VI, Queen Mary, and Elizabeth I before dying in 1562. It may well be said that his promotion of this union was principally responsible for elevating surgery to the dignity of a profession, thus providing it with corporate and municipal privileges.

In addition, he ensured that the Company established a high standard of education and qualification, and promoted the teaching of anatomy and surgery with the result that operative surgery was transformed from a barbarous unlicensed melee to that of professional status, where dexterity and resourcefulness were acknowledged to be of import. Nevertheless, surgeons were not allowed to administer "inward remedies" except by special permission of the Royal College of Physicians, a restriction successfully maintained by Caius before the Lord Mayor and the Queen's Commissioners. In 1593–1594, for instance, the eminent surgeon John Banister (1540–1610), in response to a direct request from Elizabeth, received a limited license to practice medicine from the College.

The most famous surgeons of the Queen's reign were Vicary and Richard Ferris, who were both Sergeant-Surgeons to the Queen. Of particular importance were also Thomas Gale (1507–1587), author of *Certaine Workes of Chirurgerie*, in which he advocated conservative surgery.

Apart from the generalist concept of science and surgery, there was some consideration of specialization, and in this respect, ophthalmology began as a specialty during the reign of Elizabeth I. Thus in 1561, the Royal College of Physicians granted a faculty to John Luke to treat diseases of the eye, although he was forbidden to provide any treatment that was not strictly limited to the use of external means. Dr Baily's tract, *A briefe Treatise concerning the Preservation of the Eyesight*, was first published in 1586 and went through seven editions. Richard Banister, "Mr in Chyrurgery, Oculist and Practitioner in Physic," whom Sorsby termed "the first authentic voice in British ophthalmology," qualified in 1602, but did not publish his *Breviary of the Eyes* until 1622.

In addition to medicine and science, two Fellows of the College became headmasters of two great public schools. Thus Christopher Johnson, MD, Oxon, a Wykehamist and Fellow of New College, was "a most excellent Latin poet, philosopher, and physician," and in 1560, became Headmaster of Winchester, spending his leisure in his beloved study of physic, "but not to the neglect of his school". Clearly dissatisfied with the meager wages of a teacher, he subsequently resigned his headmastership to practice in London, becoming an Elect and Treasurer of the College, dying in 1597. Similarly, Reuben Sherewood, MD, Cantab, Etonian and Fellow of King's College, was initially Headmaster of Eton in 1571 before moving to Bath, where he practiced successfully until his death in 1598.

Another physician who achieved fame outside of medicine in the reign of Elizabeth I was Thomas Campion, MD, (1567–1619), who became a celebrated musician and poet such that his first collection of English poems, *A Book of Airs*, was received with considerable acclaim in 1601.

Commemoration of the Act of Union between the Company of Barbers and the Guild of Surgeons in 1540. Stipple by WP Sherlock after the picture at Barbers' Hall.

William Clowes (1544–1604), Surgeon to Elizabeth I and at St Bartholomew's Hospital, served first as an army surgeon in the Earl of Warwick's army at Le Havre in 1563, then in the Low Countries with Leicester in 1585, and later as a naval surgeon in the victory over the Spanish Armada. He first wrote *De Morbo Gallico* (1579), the text of which is in English, and thereafter published books on affections of the skin, wherein he affirmed the efficacy of the "Royal Touch" for cases not responding to ordinary treatment. In addition, he recorded numerous interesting cases in his *Prooved Practice for all young Chirurgians*. George Baker (1540–1610) was another royal surgeon of repute who despite being a scholarly man, in 1577 came to fisticuffs in the fields with Clowes and both surgeons were admonished by the Barber-Surgeons' Company for this reprehensible conduct. Yet another surgeon of note was John Woodall, medical officer in the army of "brave Lord Willoughby" in the Low Countries in 1591, who published *The Surgeon's Mate* (1617), which became regarded as an important manual of practical surgery.

The frontispiece of *The Surgeon's Mate* by John Woodall (1639).

Arris and Gale

In 1493, the Company of Barbers and the Fellowship of Surgeons entered into an agreement, which acknowledged their respective guilds and responsibilities. This facilitated to some degree their interaction, since before this time, the two separate entities had both attempted to regulate the practice of surgery in the City of London. The Company had from the earliest times regarded their obligations for the training of surgeons with seriousness. In 1540, the complete union of the Company of Barbers and the Fellowship of Surgeons thus consolidated many of the objectives of both groups. In particular, training and accreditation of surgeons were important issues. The 1540 Act of Henry VIII which united the two bodies clearly indicates that one of its aims was to improve the standards of surgical practice. Thus, after the union, the Company diligently undertook such responsibilities in formalizing the anatomical lectures and demonstrations which had hitherto been conducted in a somewhat casual fashion. The Act had provided the Company with the annual right to the bodies of four malefactors "condemned, adjudged and put to death for felony by the due order of the King's law of the realm for anatomies".

John Banister delivering an anatomical lecture at the Barber-Surgeons' Hall in 1581. The two anatomical masters stand beside him, one holding a scalpel, the other a probe. On the opposite side of the table are the two stewards wearing their white protective sleeves. Banister is depicted teaching from the octavo second edition of *De Re Anatomica* (Paris, 1562) by Realdo Colombo.

The "anatomies" thus took place four times per year, with three lectures (the visceral, the muscular, and the osteological) being delivered by a reader on each occasion, whose fees were respectively £6, £4, and £2. The reader was quite often a physician, since not many surgeons were deemed capable of undertaking the task. The rules which governed the precise conduct of such lectures were complex, and strict adherence was required, else a fine was levied against the miscreant. In particular, serious strictures existed against the conduct of "private" anatomies by members of the Company at any site other than the hall designated for the prescribed lecture. Thus, the choice of the anatomical readers, conduct of the anatomy lecture, and the specific site of the anatomical theatre formed an integral component of the training structure of the Company.

The importance of such lectures was emphasized by instructions of the Company that attendance by surgeon members was held to be compulsory for a minimum of one day of each of the three-day lectures.

On October 27, 1645, Mr Edward Arris donated £250 to the Barber-Surgeons' Company to support the institution of such a course of lectures in anatomy, more specifically dealing with the human musculature. Some 10 years later, on August 13, 1655, Mr John Gale in his will provided further support of £16 per annum to be used for the lectures in osteology. Nominations were usually submitted at four-yearly intervals for the reader of the osteology lecture (Gale's foundation). However, elsewhere in the minutes of the Company, it is often referred to as an anatomy lecture called "Gale's anatomy". Almost 100 years later, when the Company and Fellowship separated in 1745, it was agreed that the Arris and Gale lecture funds were to pass to the Company of Surgeons, and in 1800, they were vested in the Royal College on its formation. In 1810, the two series of lectures were combined and Sir William Blizard of the London Hospital delivered the first Arris and Gale Lecture in that very year. Although the lectures were suspended for the following three years, they were subsequently reintroduced and have been given almost without interruption up until this time. The list of those privileged to present the lectures virtually enshrines the development of clinical surgery through the 19th century and thereafter surgical science of the 20th century.

Edward Arris

Edward Arris was born in London in 1591 and admitted to the freedom of the Company by patrimony on January 21, 1617. He had studied his art with his father and was admitted to the livery on October 9, 1627. Subsequently, on April 30, 1629, he was granted a diploma to practice surgery. In 1632, he was chosen

The coat of arms of Alderman Edward Arris: argent on a cross gule, five fleurs-de-lys or.

Steward and the next year Master of the Anatomy. Some eight years later, on April 23, 1640, he was elected as an assistant, and served the office of Warden in 1642. Within six years, he was appointed as one of the examiners of surgeons, on February 10, 1648, and finally elected as Master of the Company in 1651. At the age of 71, on July 3, 1663, Mr Arris was nominated by the Court of Alderman, of the Bridge of Ward Without (loco Richard Evans), and subsequently sworn in on July 28. It seems likely that this civil office was not of considerable interest and imposed some arduous tasks, since shortly thereafter he applied to be discharged from this onerous responsibility. As a result of this matter being successfully negotiated, he was obliged to pay a fine of £300 to the City.

In 1645, Arris, with considerable subtlety and modesty, anonymously founded an anatomy lecture, which has lived on to this day as the oldest endowed lecture of the College. It is noted in the *Annals* of the Barber-Surgeons for October 27, 1645: "This day Mr Edward Arris acquainting this Court that a person a friend of his (who desired his name to be as yet concealed) through his greater desire of the increase of the knowledge of Chirurgery did by him freely offered to give unto this Corporation for ever the sum of £250 to the end and upon Condition that a humane Body be once in every yeare hereafter publiquely dissected and six Lectures thereupon read in this Hall if it may be had with Conveniency and the Charges to be borne by this Company…"

Apart from the verbal memorials that attest to Arris, the Barber Company possesses a fine portrait depicting him as the surgeon demonstrator in an anatomy lecture. No doubt his interest in this subject was to a large part responsible for his subsequent generosity. It was the custom of the Company to exhibit pictures of the "forty one philosophers" who were former masters of anatomy and examiners of surgeons. Their portraits were placed in the "Table of Anatomy," which was a large composite of effigies. New faces were placed on old shoulders by "blotting out" such "faces" as had retired or been removed for misconduct. Thus, on August 9, 1647, it is recorded: "This Court takeing into consideracon the greate benefitt and proffitt That have accrewed to this House by Mr Edward Arris a loveing Brother of this Company This Court doth order That his picture be sett up in the Blanck Table in the Hall next the Anathomy Table at the charge of this Hows". Some 10 days later, Arris negated this suggestion: "Upon the earnest request of Mr Edward Arris to this Court That his Picture be nott sett up in the Hall according to the Order of the last Court of Assistants. This Court to satisfy Mr Arris modest request therein doth order that that order be annulled and not put in execucon." Despite his protestations, Mr Arris' portrait was painted and placed in the Hall. Sadly, however, it was lost in the war, although a second painting was fortunate enough to survive unscathed. In this painting, Arris is the model for the surgeon demonstrator, depicted with the Anatomical Reader Sir Charles Scarborough (1616–1694). They are portrayed during the course of an anatomy lecture.

The portrait of Sir Charles Scarborough and Edward Arris painted by Robert Greenbury. Scarborough was Physician to Charles II, whom he attended on his last illness, and to James II and William III. He was elected Anatomical Reader on October 12, 1649, to revive the periodical lectures, which had then lapsed. The coat of arms of Arris are depicted on the wall behind him. Of interest is Greenbury's composition of the portrait, whereby the arm of the dissected corpse provides the link from Scarborough to Arris. The hands of Scarborough in an elegant fashion define the point he is making, while Arris with an intent and focused gaze provides gravity and lends authority to Scarborough's knowledge. The hands of Arris gently hold and delineate the musculature of the forearm, as if defining his commitment to the subject of anatomy. This painting, together with that of Henry VIII by Hans Holbein, survived the war in the National Library of Wales at Aberystwyth, due to the foresight of Sir Lionel Denny, the Master of the Barber-Surgeon's Company, who arranged for their storage.

Arris died on May 28, 1676, at the age of 85, having sired 23 children, of whom only two, both boys, reached adulthood. Both Robert and Thomas Arris, his sons, followed in his footsteps as doctors, Robert becoming a surgeon, who was admitted to the freedom on January 21, 1651, and Thomas, who became not only an MD but also an MP for St Albans, Hertfordshire. The latter misguidedly sought to interfere with his father's benefaction to the Company. Edward Arris was buried in the Church of the Holy Sepulcher in the same grave as his father, his mother, and his wife. In his last will and testament of May 20, 1676, he bequeathed his property to his only surviving son Thomas Arris MID, MP, and his children.

In St Sepulchre's Church, the tablet commemorating the alderman bears this inscription:

Edward Arris Esqr gave to the Company of Chirurgeons 30L for an Anatomy Lecture & to the Hospital of St Bartholomew 24L both yeerly for ever to Christ's Church Hospital 100L & 50L towards rebuilding of this Church and several large gifts to the poor of this Parish wherein he was born, and all these in his life time hee deceased the 28th of May 1676 aged 85 & lyeth buried by his wife.

John Gale

Much less is known of John Gale, who was son of William Gale, a Master of the Company in 1595 and 1610. Unfortunately, Gale passed away on November 19, 1610, in mid-office and was succeeded by Mr John Peck, who had been a Master of the Company in 1605. Little is known of Gale's life except that he is buried in the churchyard at Monken Hadley, where the brass inscription on the floor of the north side of the altar reads as follows:

Blessed are they y` concydereth ye poore & needie. Here lyeth the bodye of William Gale Citizen & Barber Chyrurgion of London who dyed the XIX daye of November 1610. Then being ye second tyme Master of his Company, he had two wives, Elizabeth & Susan & had issue by Elizabeth V sones and eight daughters and was LX and X yeares of age or thereabouts at ye time of his death.

There were formerly brasses of effigies of Gale and his two wives but they have since been removed. His son, John Gale, was a surgeon of Bushey who, on August 13, 1655, in his will bequeathed to the Company £16 per annum to be used for a lecture in osteology. The money was to be derived from income payable out of certain houses on Snow Hill in the parish of St Sepulchre and to be utilized for the founding of a lecture in the name of "Gale's anatomy". One may assume that he followed in his father's footsteps and held his association with the Company in esteem, particularly because his father had twice acceded to the mastership.

Gale died on January 5, 1655, and is buried at St James' Parish Church, Bushey, where the inscription on his grave reads:

Here in hope of a happy resurrection through Christ, lies the body of John Gale, Esq who was father to Mary Gale, by his second wife Jane, and sister to Mrs Elizabeth Terry, both which are here interned next unto him; he lived to the age of 70 years, and peaceably departed this life January 5th, 1655.

The Church of St James, in Bushey, Hertfordshire, where John Gale and his family are interred.

THE APOTHECARY

The apothecaries belonged to the Grocers' Company, where they received their technical training as apprentices primarily in the art of compounding and dispensing, although they also assisted physicians in applying certain forms of treatment.

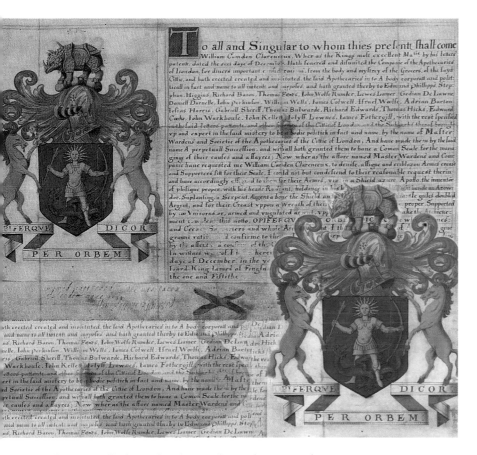

Sir Thomas More (1475–1535) was born in Milk Street, London, son of Sir John More, a prominent judge, and educated at St Anthony's School in London. As a youth, he served as a page in the household of Archbishop Morton, who predicted he would be a "marvellous man". More studied Greek and Latin literature at Oxford under Thomas Linacre and William Grocyn, where he also wrote comedies. In 1494, he returned to London to study law, was admitted to Lincoln's Inn in 1496, and became a barrister in 1501. During his life he was variously a knight, Counselor to Henry VIII, the Lord Chancellor of England, and the author of *Utopia* – the fictitious travels of Raphael Hythlodaye lost on his way to the Americas. He ultimately perished a martyr, executed at Tower Hill on July 6, 1535, because of his objections to the religious politics of Henry VIII. His final words on the scaffold were: "The King's good servant, but God's First." More was beatified in 1886 and canonized by the Catholic Church as a saint by Pope Pius XI in 1935.

The patent (*background*) and coat of arms (*bottom right*) of the Society of Apothecaries. The attributes and powers attributed to himself by Apollo were subsequently incorporated into the coat of arms and are described in Burke's *Encyclopedia of Heraldry* in 1851 as follows: "In shield, Apollo, the inventor of physic, with his head radiate, holding in his left hand a bow and his right a serpent. About the shield a helm, there upon a mantle and for the crest upon a wreath of their colors, a rhinoceros, supported by two unique wands, armed and ungulate." Upon a compartment to make the achievement complete, this motto, "*Opiferque per orbem dicor*" – the Latin quotation for the newly incorporated Society of Apothecaries – was chosen and inserted by William Camden, the famous antiquary and "Clarenseux King at Arms" in the reign of James I.

William Bullein, in *The Booke of Compoundes and the Apothecaries Rules*, was careful to remind the apothecary "that he doe remember his office is onely to be the Physician's Cooke". Although often portrayed as impecunious and unkempt, as in Shakespeare's half-starved character in *Romeo and Juliet*, the apothecaries were, as a rule, a prosperous and reputable set of men. They were well organized, and in 1616, agitated successfully to be regarded as a professional corporation receiving an independent Charter to this effect from James I. Despite such apparent autonomy, however, the Royal College of Physicians still retained the authority to evaluate the stores of the apothecaries to ensure that the public were protected from administration of, or exposure to, any "evil and fawty stuffe".

PUBLIC HEALTH

Given the lack of knowledge of disease vectors and the nature of communicable disease, it is little surprise that there existed little in the way of sanitation and sewage disposal was either primitive or unavailable. Preventive medicine was thus in its infancy, although Sir Thomas More, saint and martyr, Sir John Elyot, and Andrew Boorde in the reign of Henry VIII had grasped its fundamental principles and those of hygiene, nutrition, and education, and had set forth their application in their writings. These men were advanced in their conception of such problems and More, apart from his numerous other gifts, was an enlightened public health reformer, as can be judged from a perusal of his text *Utopia*. As Commissioner of Sewers, he improved water supplies, and his plague edicts were embodied in the plague orders of 1543, which were adopted in the Elizabethan regulations. The Corporation of London drafted numerous orders relating to infectious diseases, scavenging, and sanitation, and thus Tudor England provided the basis for the establishment of the beginnings of an organized and permanent public health administration.

Despite the evolution of pharmacology, quackery and charlatanry were established professions and numerous individuals enriched themselves on the gullibility of the average medieval patient and the lack of remedies of proven efficacy.

CHARLATANS, QUACKS, AND EMPIRICS

Elizabeth I was, like her father, an amateur of medicine and fond of presiding at the disputations in the Physic Act at her visits to Oxford and Cambridge. Despite the fact that she had illustrious physicians and surgeons at her command, sometimes she chose to place great faith in the ministrations of untrained quacks such as Margaret Kenwix, or exotic mystics such as John Dee. Indeed, her eccentricities in this area often placed her and her advisors at loggerheads with the Royal College of Physicians. On one occasion, the Queen presided at a disputation, while her physician Dr Walter Baily opposed the questions whether

any inconvenience whatever might ensue" rather than stop Kenwix from practice. The other two cases concerned two charlatans variously referred to as Not and Buck, who medically attended Walsingham. In the latter instances, the College proved inflexible and remonstrated, whereupon Walsingham promised that he "would in future cease to act in any way contrary to the benefit and dignity of the College".

In terms of individual practice, the Royal College of Physicians was rigorous in areas that were not necessarily objectionable. Thus, they strongly abjured the longstanding practice of diagnosis by "water-casting" (inspection of a patient's urine) by physicians and wise women. In this respect they may have erred, since clearly there was much medical information to be gained from the objective study of the urine.

slowly digested foods were preferable to those easily digested and whether life could be prolonged by medical art. The dissertations lasted for five hours, and the Queen "gave very attent care unto them and tarried to the full end thereof". Herbert R Spencer, in his commentary on Elizabethan and Shakespearean medicine, remarked: "We cannot be surprised therefore that the Queen refused to take medicine when she was on her deathbed."

In spite of the oversight and regulations of the College and the Barber-Surgeons' Company, quacks and empirics flourished and had influential clients who strongly and often misguidedly supported their malpractice. Thus, none less a personage than the eminent Sir Francis Walsingham

attempted on three occasions to prevent the College from restraining quackery. In the first case, Walsingham ventured so far as to threaten the College with penalties if they did not comply with the request to desist from the censorship of Kenwix, a herbalist, patronized by the Queen. The College courageously replied that it was "willing and content to abide

Uroscopy or urinoscopy was the practice of diagnosing disease through the examination of urine. It was one of the earliest methods used by "modern" physicians and can be traced back to before the 2nd century and Galen. Together with astrology and alchemy, it played an important role in medieval medicine. As with most superstitions and beliefs, there is some truth in its diagnostic utility and certain diseases could readily be differentiated by gross examination of the urine, although some of the derivations strained credibility.

Elizabeth in particular possessed great belief in the enigmatic mathematician and astrologer John Dee (1527–1608). "Dr Dee" (he had, possibly, an LLD) was a graduate of St John's College, Cambridge, and one of the original Fellows of Trinity College, Cambridge. Such was his intellectual curiosity that as a student and traveler, he even visited as far afield as St Helena and later in life advanced to the post of Warden of Manchester College (1595–1604).

Despite being offered high ecclesiastical preferment, he declined, choosing rather to practice as an alchemist, searcher for the philosopher's stone, the elixir of life, and held himself up as a professor of occult mysteries. Indeed, such was his reputation that the Queen deigned to become his pupil in 1564 and frequently consulted him on items as varied as her health, the comet of 1577, and her amorous inclinations. Also, mostly for interaction with her subjects, was her decision to visit him twice at his house at Mortlake to see his library. Clearly the friendship and regard was

substantial, since in 1571, when Dee was seriously ill, she sent two of her personal physicians, Dr Atslow and Mr Balthorp, to see him, as well as Lord Sidney with "divers rarities to eat". In October 1578, by the Queen's command, Dr Dee conferred with Dr Bayley "concerning her majesty's grievous pangs and pains caused by toothache and the rheum". Given the Royal request and the fact that Dr Dee was of course a very exceptional empiric, it seems that the objections of the College were waived and no doubt Dr Bayley felt ethically justified in meeting him.

DEATH AND DISEASES

Given the lack of understanding of infection, the lack of sanitation, the parlous state of drinking water, and the limited availability of medicinal therapy and surgery there was much disease and a high morbidity and mortality in the England of Elizabeth I. A great source of documentation is provided by the plays of Shakespeare and Ben Jonson, which contain many allusions to the prevalent maladies. Thus Thersites in *Troilus and Cressida* mentions 15 diseases under popular names: "Now, the rotten diseases of the south [syphilis], the guts-griping [colic], ruptures [hernias] catarrhs, loads o' gravel i' the back [stone in the kidneys], lethargies [apoplectic strokes], cold palsies [paralysis of the limbs], raw eyes [chronic inflammation of the eyelids], dirt-rotten livers [hepatic affections or so ascribed], wheezing lungs [asthma], bladders full of imposthume [chronic cystitis], sciaticas, lime-kilns i' the palm [psoriasis of the palm], incurable bone-ache, and the rivelled fee-simple of the tetter [some skin disease], take and take again such preposterous discoveries!"

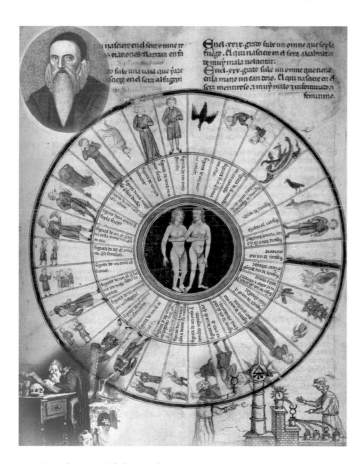

John Dee (1527–1608) (*top left*), the scholar and astrologer, engraved by W Sherlock from a picture in the Ashmolean Museum, Oxford. A melange of astrology, the zodiac, and notions of internal balance dominated early concepts of physiology, and Dee was adept at providing a mixture of science and mysticism in the process of caring for his patients. As such, the use of astrological maps (*background*), as well as scriptures, mythology, and alchemy, were woven together in an arcane fabric of magic and medicine by which diseases could be identified, contained, and cured.

William Shakespeare (*top left and center*) was unarguably the greatest English dramatist and as such documented with extraordinary perspicuity the character of the time in which he lived. His contemporary Ben Johnson (1572–1637) (*top right*) was also a poet and actor, and friend – Shakespeare himself acted in one of Johnson's early plays, *Every man in his humor* (1598). Johnson wrote of Shakespeare: "I loved the man, and do honor his memory (on this side idolatry) as much as any. He was, indeed, honest, and of an open and free nature; had an excellent fancy, brave notions, and gentle expressions, wherein he flowed with that facility that sometime it was necessary he should be stopped. 'Sufflaminandus erat,' as Augustus said of Haterius. His wit was in his own power; would the rule of it had been so too."

"Surfeits" due to immoderate eating and drinking often occurred and gout and bladderstone prevailed among the well-to-do. Cutters for stone achieved legendary prominence and perineal lithotomy was a much-valued procedure amongst itinerant physicians. Scurvy was prevalent, both due to the lack of green vegetables as well as the constant boiling of most foods, until William Butler (1535–1618), a Cambridge physician, put scurvy grass and other herbs into the beer. Scabies was so common that it was called "the English itch" and the variety of medications and concoctions for this problem were innumerable. Syphilis was a deadly scourge that was regarded as a legacy of the French and Spanish and was treated with a variety of remedies, including mercury, sweating, bleeding, and a variety of irritants. Leprosy (the term also included several skin diseases) was nearly abolished, but still lingered on, and such unfortunates were considered victims of their own sins or shunned as bearers of a "dreaded lurgy". There was much indigenous malaria, especially in the Fen districts, and a variety of illnesses related to fever, relapsing weakness, fatigue, and anemia were undoubtedly due to the sequelae of chronic infection.

Measles was often confounded with smallpox and these two diseases in addition to pulmonary tuberculosis exacted a heavy toll on the populace. Royalty were not immune and the racking cough and active tuberculosis of Edward VI were dramatically accentuated by the attack of measles and smallpox from which he suffered in April 1552. Similarly, Elizabeth I was plagued by intermittent illnesses and as a princess in 1553, she experienced severe puffiness of the face and leg swelling, having probably suffered from scarlet fever followed by acute nephritis. As Queen in October 1562, she had a dangerous attack of smallpox, and in a letter from De Quadra to the Duchess of Parma, he noted, "she was all but gone". In her convalescence, the Queen was concerned with the pockmarks on her face and anxious lest these might result in disfigurement. A decade later in October 1572, she suffered another severe attack, although this may have been chicken pox.

Rheumatic complaints, attributed to the fogs and damp of England, were prevalent and although some were surely due to rheumatic fever, the majority were probably chronic rheumatism and early onset osteoarthropathy. Mary Queen of Scots suffered much from the chronic arthritic form during her captivity in England and was permitted to take the baths at Buxton, which belonged to her gaoler, the Earl of Shrewsbury. Dr Jones was the resident physician and was responsible for much laudatory comment and claims regarding the value of such therapy, thereby considerably enhancing the fame of the watering place. Water treatments were considered most efficacious and spa treatment also began at Harrogate under the auspices of Timothy Bright, MD, Cantab, who not only wrote an erudite treatise on *Melancholia*, a book on hygiene, but also was responsible for the invention of modern shorthand.

An early page from an illuminated manuscript depicting a monk scratching and searching for the scabies parasite. A variety of ill understood diseases were generically referred to as the "itching disease". The lack of sanitation, poor food hygiene, infestation with rodents, and the generally poor living conditions provided a veritable cornucopia of parasitic diseases.

The medieval use of baths was for the most part utilitarian and health related, although they served an important social function in terms of serving as a common meeting place. As might be predicted, however, bathhouses also served as centers of sensual delight, and although ablutions were primarily designed for cleanliness, the use of the environment for social activity promoted the spread of venereal disease. Indeed, the repressed fantasies of later societies created exotic and sensual visions of the bath and its erotic possibilities that became a favorite subject of painters and their patrons. Later, in Victorian society, the use of imagery based upon classical history often served as an adequate pretext for the legitimization of sexual material regarded as taboo in everyday life.

Numerous other dangerous maladies assailed the English population of the time and included a devastating epidemic of influenza in 1557–1558, as well as the sweating sickness, which Creighton and Michael Foster identified as the "Picardy sweat". The fifth and last epidemic, well described by Caius, was in 1551, although plague had remained endemic in England since 1349, when the Black Death destroyed two million people, half the existing population. Given the conditions of the time, the City of London was rarely free from plague and there were serious outbreaks in 1582 and 1603. So great was the prevalence as well as the concern with the situation that The Privy Council, when ordering precautions against the spread of the disease, considered that London should have a special plague hospital.

Unfortunately, there were few hospitals, since despite the advice of More, Henry VIII had abolished the monastic hospitals and the only metropolitan hospitals which survived, through the wisdom and persistence of the citizens of London, were the five Royal Hospitals – St Bartholomew's Hospital, St Thomas' Hospital, Christ's Hospital (founded in the buildings of the Grey Friars), Bethlehem Hospital for the insane, and Bridewell, a prison hospital.

As a result of the avid meanderings of the privateers and the fleets that preyed upon the Spanish possessions of the New World, numerous novel diseases were encountered. These included "*calenture*" (heatstroke), "*Jas espinas*" (prickly heat), "*camaras de sangre*" (tropical dysentery, from which Sir Francis Drake died in 1595), and "*tabardillo*" (yellow fever). Many of these disease were studied by English ship surgeons and first described by George Waleson in 1598 in the first English treatise on tropical medicine entitled *The Cures of the Diseased in remote Regions: Preventing Mortalitie incident in Forraine Attempts of the English Nation.*

The word "plague" is a derivative of the Latin "*plaga*" meaning "a strike or blow that wounds". In the Middle Ages, while individual illnesses were difficult to cure, communicable diseases were catastrophes for the entire population. The advent of the plague resulted in the obliteration of entire cities and towns. Given the fact that a bacterial cause and insect or rodent vectors were not understood, the flight of individuals seeking safety with neighbors or relatives actually accentuated the problem. The use of strange garb (*top*) by plague doctors probably helped any exodus.

Sir Francis Drake, a navigator and privateer, was one of the greatest English sea captains of all time. Although revered as a hero for his role in defeating the Spanish Armada (*bottom left*), he was despised as an upstart by the old nobility. Drake epitomized the self-made Elizabethan privateer, rapacious in the hunt for treasure (especially Spanish) but daring and visionary in exploration. In the *Golden Hind* he became the first Englishman to circumnavigate the globe, and even claimed a portion of California for Elizabeth I along the way. His attack on Cadiz and his devastating raids on the Spanish Main earned him the fear and the grudging respect of the Spaniards, who referred to him as "*El Draque*" ("The Dragon"). A premature death from dysentery led to a sea burial in Nombre de Dios Bay, although this site is a source of controversy.

8 | THE ROYAL SOCIETY

Although the Royal Society had been formed with the approval of Charles II in 1660, it unquestionably began even earlier, about 1645, when a group of doctors and scientists in London formed a society they called the "Invisible College," which met in their lodgings or at Gresham College. Several of the members subsequently moved to Oxford and continued these meetings there. Thomas Sprat, whose *History of the Royal Society* appeared in 1667, noted: "It was therefore, some space after the end of the Civil Wars at Oxford, in Dr Wilkins' Lodgings, in Wadham College, which was then the place of Resort for Vertuous, and Learned Men, that the first meetings were made, which laid the foundation of all this that follow'd. The most constant attendants were Dr Seth Ward, later Lord Bishop of Exeter, Mr Boyle, Dr Wilkins, Sir William Petty, Mr Mathew Wren, Dr Wallis, Dr Goddard, Dr Willis, Dr Bathurst, Dr Christopher Wren, and Mr Rook." By 1667, the Royal Society was well enough established and in communication with other European scientists such that it invited Malpighi to become a corresponding member.

At this period, although Oxford was under Puritan rule, this list of names indicates that it was far from being the place of "Puritan desolation" that the royalists claimed. Dr Wilkins, the Warden of Wadham, was a man of vast attainments, at that time a Presbyterian minister and soon afterwards brother-in-law of Oliver Cromwell – as versatile in science as he was fickle in politics, since later, under the Restoration, he gained Royal favor and became Bishop of Chester. Sir William Petty was a brilliant man of science; Seth Ward, an outstanding astronomer; Dr Wallis, one of the greatest of English mathematicians; Sir Christopher Wren, the famous architect; Dr Goddard was physician to Oliver Cromwell, a Fellow of the Royal College of Physicians, and later Professor of Physic at Gresham College; Dr Willis was secretly an Anglican and a royalist, later one of the outstanding physicians of his time; while Robert Boyle would emerge as one of the great names in the history of science.

Sprat reported: "Their meetings were as frequent as their affairs permitted: their proceedings rather by action, than discourse; chiefly attending some particular Trials, in Chymistry, or Mechanicks: they had no Rules nor Method fix'd: their intention was more, to communicate to each other, their discoveries." These meetings continued for several years until 1658, when the group disbanded, but, as the greater number of the members moved to London, they met again regularly at Gresham College. Unfortunately, the activities of the Society were once again disrupted by the wars of that year, when Sprat says, "the place of their meeting was made a Quarter for Soldiers". After the Restoration of Charles II, the Society was formally incorporated in 1662.

Charles II portrayed as a royal with scientific interests and a penchant for patronage. Samuel Pepys wrote that at Whitehall, Charles had his "little elaboratory, under his closet, a pretty place, and was working there but a day or two before his death, his illness disinclining him for his wonted exercise". It appears that the King took a curious interest in anatomy; on May 11, 1663, Pierce, the surgeon, reported to Pepys "that the other day Dr Clerke and he did dissect two bodies, a man and a woman before the King with which the King was highly pleased". Pepys also records on February 17, 1662/3, on the authority of Edward Pickering, another story of a dissection in the royal closet by the King's own hands.

THE OXFORD PHYSIOLOGISTS

The beginning of the Royal Society as a group of young scholars in London and later at Oxford who were interested in natural science provided evidence of a novel intellectual development in an institution that had previously been more focused on humanities than natural science. This primary impetus was initially provided by an informal group now remembered as the Oxford physiologists, mostly members of the Royal Society that met in Dr Wilkins' lodgings in Wadham College.

Robert Boyle

One of the leaders of this group was the Honorable Robert Boyle, seventh son and fourteenth child of Richard Boyle, first Earl of Cork, who had originally been transferred to Ireland as a clerk in the service of Elizabeth I and thereafter became the most wealthy and powerful landholder in Ireland. Robert Boyle initially went to school at Eton, where he was recognized as a brilliant student. Although created "Doctor of Physick" at Oxford in 1665, he never attended a university, but instead studied and traveled with a tutor, thus becoming a good classical scholar and learning French, German, and Italian. After spending some time on the Continent, he returned to London, where he became associated with the "Invisible College" and began to undertake scientific experiments. Although he subsequently moved to Oxford for political reasons, he was not connected with any college and after a relatively short period of time, returned to London and became one of the incorporators of the Royal Society in 1662.

The concept of amplifying health by utilizing a direct route was promulgated by the wealthy Irish intellect Robert Boyle (*left and bottom*). His thoughts were embodied in a unique remedy referred to in his text on the subject, *The Spirit of Human Blood* (*right*). It was, as might have been predicted, an uncommon therapy, for blood was a commodity not freely available and "healthy" blood was in especially short supply, "being drawn from persons that parted with it out of custom or for prevention". To be safe and efficacious, it was essential that the blood was obtained from healthy individuals, since that acquired from persons of dubious health was clearly unlikely to be salubrious. The blood was dried, put in a retort, and heated on a sand bath, and the material distilled such that the spirit (spirit in this context was interpreted as the volatile salt of human blood) was preserved. Boyle regarded it as an alkaline material similar to that obtained by distillation of hartshorn, urine, or sal ammoniac; rather a disappointing substance compared with its name.

In 1658, while Boyle was in Oxford, he became intrigued by the work of Otto von Guericke, who had invented an air pump eight years previously and secured the services of an impecunious chorister of Christ Church, Robert Hooke, to assist him in the construction of an air pump. As a result of these studies, Boyle in 1660 published his first scientific book, *The Spring and Weight of the Air*, in which he had formulated what has since become known as Boyle's law – "that, at a stated temperature, a given mass of gas varies in volume inversely as the pressure".

Boyle also noted that birds and mice, placed in a chamber, die promptly when the air is removed by an air pump and remarked, "We may suppose that there is in the Air a little vital Quintessence… which serves to the refreshment and restauration of our vital Spirits" and added that this theory which had previously been advanced by Paracelsus, "should not be barely asserted but explicated and prov'd". A brilliant scientist and a prolific writer, his text *Sceptical Chymist*, published in 1661, was followed by a work entitled *Origine of Formes and Qualities* (1666). His prescience was such that he early on became convinced of the atomic structure of matter and in his final work, *General History of the Air*, published shortly after his death, he enunciated the modern kinetic theory of gases – that a gas is a collection of freely and independently moving molecules.

At his death in 1692, Boyle had authored 42 books, of which 30 were scientific treatises and the remainder theological and philosophical tracts. In terms of his scientific contributions, he addressed almost all phases of knowledge except astronomy, having written and studied respiration, combustion, the chemical nature of the blood and wine, magnetism, and electricity.

Robert Hooke (1635–1703)

Robert Hooke began his scientific career as assistant to Boyle, and was one of the early members of the Royal Society before attaining the position of Curator, which he held until his death. In 1667, he performed a memorable experiment on artificial respiration before the members of the Society and demonstrated that the essential factor necessary to maintain cardiac function and life was a supply of fresh air. Although artificial respiration had been described by Andreas Vesalius, he had failed to recognize the significance of the air in maintaining life. Thus Vesalius had observed that when the lungs were inflated through the trachea, the heart continued to beat strongly; but when the inflation ceased, the beat of the heart and arteries became "undulating, crawling, wormlike, the movement of the pulse was not seen". He had carefully noted that such changes disappeared as soon as the lungs were inflated. Hooke modified the experiment by puncturing the lungs in numerous places while continuing to pass air into them through the trachea. Although the lungs remained motionless in this experiment, the heart continued beating strongly as long as fresh air was supplied. In this fashion, Hooke demonstrated that the movements of the lungs, so long considered essential to respiration, were only an incidental factor.

In addition to his respiratory studies, Hooke was also an early and enthusiastic worker with the microscope. His text *Micrographia*, published in 1665, provided superb examples, with numerous fine plates showing the histology of vegetable structures and aspects of microscopic details of creatures. It is considered that Hooke was the first writer to employ the term "cell" in the context of structure, although there was considerable controversy as to his primacy in the use of the microscope and a number of other areas of his scientific endeavor. Hooke did however note in the preface of his book that the first microscopic drawings with which he was familiar were those of Wren and that he began his work "with much Reluctancy, because I was to follow the Footsteps of so eminent a Person as Dr Wren". He failed to comment upon the earlier work of Anthony van Leeuwenhoek, who some time earlier provided the Royal Society with much material, as well as examples of his original microscope designs.

Sir Christopher Wren (1632–1723)

Sir Christopher Wren, born in 1632, was the son of the Dean of Windsor and was admitted to Wadham College at the early age of 14, receiving his Bachelor's degree in 1650 and his Master's degree in 1653. In 1660, at the age of 28, he was appointed Savilian Professor of Astronomy at Oxford. While a student at Oxford, Wren belonged to the "Invisible College" and both witnessed and carried out a large number of mechanical, astronomical, physical, and physiological experiments. A good

Robert Hooke (1635–1703) was able to gain wide prominence for his microscopic analysis of diverse plants, insects, and human structure. No portrait survives of Hooke and his name remains obscure, due in part to the enmity of his famous, influential, and extremely vindictive colleague, Sir Isaac Newton. Nevertheless, Hooke was perhaps the single greatest experimental scientist of the 17th century and his interests knew no bounds, ranging from physics and astronomy, to chemistry, biology, and geology, to architecture and naval technology. Hooke collaborated or corresponded with scientists as diverse as Christian Huygens, Anthony van Leeuwenhoek, Sir Christopher Wren, Robert Boyle, and Newton. Hooke's reputation in the history of biology largely rests on his book *Micrographia* (*bottom left*), published in 1665. Having devised the compound microscope and illumination system, one of the best such microscopes of his time, he used it in his demonstrations at the Royal Society's meetings to demonstrate the microscopic structure of life.

friend of Thomas Willis, he assisted the latter in the preparation of *Cerebri Anatome* and, in 1656, undertook the first experiment of intravenous infusion, injecting wine, ale, opium, scam, and other substances into the veins of a dog and studying their effects. This experiment formed the basis of the concept of blood transfusion that was subsequently successfully performed by Richard Lower. Although Wren was advanced in his thoughts regarding the possibility intravenous medication, the procedure had been first described by Johann Daniel Major, Professor at Kiel, in a text entitled *Prodromus inventae a se Chirurgiae Infusoriae* (Leipzig, 1664). In addition to his scientific work, Wren explored the concept of splenic function and successfully demonstrated that the organ could be removed from a dog without affecting the health of the animal. As might have been predicted from an individual of such scientific brilliance, he was an early member of the Royal Society and rose to become its President in 1680.

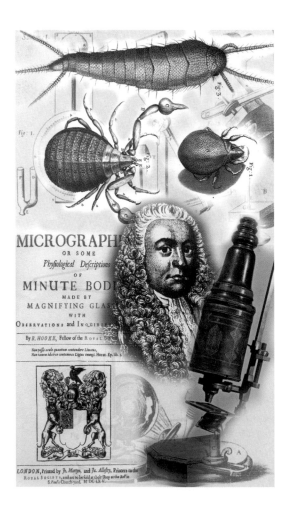

Sir Christopher Wren, as President of the Royal Society, had trained as an astronomer and even dabbled in medicine before recognizing that his future lay in architecture. One is left to ponder what a mind that conceived of St Paul's Cathedral might have achieved if directed to medical science! Buried under a simple, unadorned, black marble slab in the Cathedral that he had spent 35 years building, the plaque reads "*Lector, si monumentum requiris, circumspice*" ("Reader, if you seek a monument, look around you").

Notwithstanding his mathematical, medical, and scientific skills, Wren was in addition a gifted architect and in 1666, after the great fire of London, was appointed "Surveyor-General and principal Architect for rebuilding the whole City: the Cathedral Church of St Paul and all the parochial Churches". In addition to designing the new St Paul's Cathedral, he designed 51 parish churches. Unfortunately, his magnum opus as the architect of so extraordinary an edifice to some extent obscured his contributions to the subjects of mathematics, physics, meteorology, and physiology. He died in 1723 at the advanced age of 91 and was buried in St Paul's Cathedral, honored with the unique and subtle epitaph "*Lector, si monumentum requiris, circumspice*" ("Reader, if you seek a monument, look around you").

Richard Lower (1631–1691)

Richard Lower, another member of the distinguished group of Oxford scientific thinkers, was born near Bodmin, Cornwall, and in 1649 entered Christ Church College, Oxford. There, he became assistant to Willis, who was working on the structure of the brain. Willis, in his celebrated book *Cerebri Anatome*, which appeared in 1664, gracefully acknowledged the assistance of Lower, referring to him as "a physician most learned and an anatomist of the greatest skill" adding, "with him as companion and collaborator hardly a day passed without some anatomical experiment".

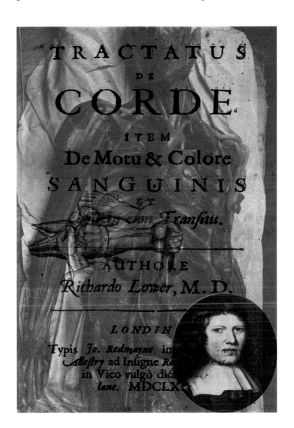

Richard Lower (1631–1691) (*bottom right*) of Cornwall and subsequently Oxford was the first to perform the successful transfusion of blood from one animal to another and repeated the procedure on one Arthur Conga in the presence of the Royal Society. Since adequate venous access was a problem, he used a primitive syringe comprising a bladder and a hollow metal tube to infuse the agent into a vein.

In February 1665, the same year he received his medical degree, Lower performed what proved to be one of the most memorable experiments of the time by transfusing blood from one animal to another. Two years later, he was elected a Fellow of the Royal Society, and had the opportunity to demonstrate his method to the Society in London. Samuel Pepys, the diarist, reported that Lower transfused "a poor and debauched man" with the blood of a sheep. As a consequence of the recognition afforded him by his original studies, Lower soon thereafter moved permanently to London, probably at the instigation of his friend and patron Willis, who had left Oxford for the city in 1666 and soon developed a large practice.

Given his admirable personality and his obvious medical skills, Lower soon acquired a large practice in London and in 1669 published his text *Tractatus de Corde*, one of the classics of medicine. This work provided a far more accurate description of the anatomy of the heart than any preceding work, and was useful in that it also dealt with aspects of physiology and pathology. The text accurately described one of the first known examples of adherent pericardium, and discussed in detail the physiology of the heart and of respiration, as well as Lower's novel method of blood transfusion. Apart from independent observations on the work of the heart and on the velocity of the blood flow, Lower concluded that the red color of arterial blood was due solely to the absorption by the blood of "the nitrous spirit of the air" ("*spiritus aeris nitrosus*") when exposed to the air in the lungs.

When his former mentor Willis died in 1675, "Lower was esteemed the most noted physician in Westminster and London, and no man's name was more cried up at court than his". Unfortunately, this well deserved reputation soon diminished, since in 1678, Lower became embroiled in the reverberations of the so-called Popish Plot, and as a result of his activities in relation to the Whig cause, lost most of his practice. At his death some 10 years later, his influence and popularity had much decreased as a consequence of his political views.

John Mayow (1643–1679)

John Mayow was born in London, entered Wadham College, Oxford, at the age of 15, and two years later was appointed Fellow of All Soul's. At Oxford, he found himself in the very distinguished company of Willis, Boyle, Wren, Lower, and Hooke, and became interested in the problems this group was trying to solve. Mayow graduated in law, yet according to Anthony A Wood, "he studied Physic, and became noted for his Practice therein, especially in the Summer-time, in the City of Bath". It seems fairly certain that he studied medicine under the tutelage of Lower and witnessed many of his experiments. Mayow subsequently moved to London, was admitted as a Fellow of the Royal Society in 1678, and tragically died only a year later at the early age of 35. Despite his premature demise, he produced two excellent books on which his reputation rests, *Tractatus Duo... De Respiratione: Alter De Rachitide* (1668) and *Tractatus Quinque Medico-Physici Quorum primus agit de Sal Nitro, et Spiritu Nitro-Aereo* (Oxford, 1674).

John Mayow (1643–1679) (*top right*), although initially trained in law at Oxford (1670), made medicine his profession. He became best known as a chemist and physiologist who, approximately 100 years before Joseph Priestley and Antoine-Laurent Lavoisier, identified "*spiritus nitro-aereus*" (oxygen) as a distinct atmospheric entity.

Although Mayow achieved little prominence during his life, a reconsideration of his work has led to a substantial reassessment of his contributions. Thus, his discussion of "nitro-aerial particles" and his recognition that these were a particular constituent of the air that "also supports combustion and is contained in nitre" is a fundamental observation. Furthermore, his nomenclature that described this substance as a "nitro-aerial spirit" suggests that he had in reality discovered oxygen, although a further century would elapse before Joseph Priestley would once again rediscover it. Nevertheless, not all scholars have supported this interpretation of Mayow's work and it has been concluded that others made many of the discoveries attributed to Mayow. Thus, he was not the first to suggest the existence in the air of a vital substance also present in nitre and nitric acid, he was not the first to call this nitro-aerial spirit, and Patterson even went so far as to label *Tractatus Quinque* as little more than "a mass of speculation almost entirely unsupported by any kind of evidence; and where there is evidence, very little of it was supplied by Mayow". However, Mayow, as Fulton noted, did devise one original ingenious experiment in which he placed an animal in a vessel over water and demonstrated that the air gradually diminished as a result of the animal's breathing, with the result that the water was gradually drawn up into the vessel. Mayow then applied the term "*spiritus nitro-aereus*" to describe the portion of the air that the animal absorbs during respiration. Fulton concluded: "This experiment is entirely original with Mayow, and, while his views were closely similar to those of Boyle and were perhaps derived largely from him, this particular experiment is of great importance historically." Despite the controversy surrounding the magnitude of his contributions or whether his work was original or copied from others, Mayow did cause further comment and experimentation with his theory that "nitro-aerial particles" were necessary for life.

Francis Glisson (1597–1677)

Francis Glisson was another example of the superior minds that were attracted to the company of the "Invisible College" in London and in so doing, became one of the early members of the Royal Society. Glisson studied at Gonville and Caius College, Cambridge, and received his medical degree in 1634, before being appointed in 1636 Regius Professor of Medicine. Although he held the position until his death, he apparently never delivered any lectures in Cambridge and went there only occasionally for University examinations of candidates. It has been surmised that his strong Presbyterian leanings made his prolonged presence in the overtly royalist atmosphere of the University somewhat uncongenial, and as a result, he spent most of his professional life in London, where he was active at the Royal College of Physicians and its President for three terms. Glisson was a philosopher, anatomist, physiologist, pathologist, orthopedic surgeon, and clinician. Although his first work, *De Rachitide, seu Morbo Puerili*, published in 1650, has been described as the first monograph on rickets by an English author, it was in actuality preceded by a treatise of Daniel Whistler on this subject. Nevertheless, it was however Glisson's excellent account that

focused considerable attention towards this disease. His second work, *Anatomia hepatis*, published in 1654, was the best account of the anatomy of the liver up to that time, and his description of the fibrous sheath enveloping the portal vein, hepatic artery, and duct was so accurate and original that this structure is still known as "Glisson's capsule".

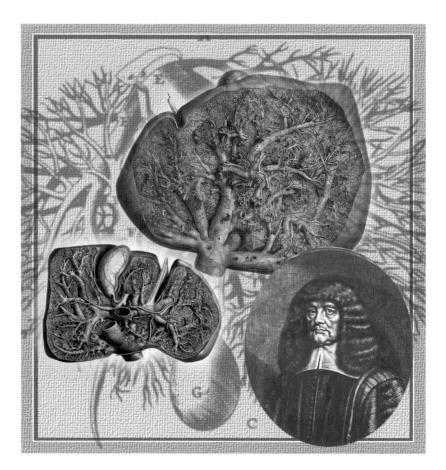

Francis Glisson (1597–1677) (*bottom right*) was one of the most important representatives of medicine in the 17th century and given the preoccupation with the role of the liver in life, focused his interest on the organ. In his book *Anatomia hepatis* (1654), he provided the first description of the capsule of the liver and described its blood supply more accurately than any text that had been previously published. Thenceforward, his name has been inseparably connected with the capsule, under the designation "Glisson's capsule". In addition, he provided a description of the sphincter of the bile duct, but this was glossed over by Oddi more than two centuries later. In its time, the *Anatomia hepatis* was the most important treatise on the physiology of the digestive system.

The third work published in 1672 by Glisson at the age of 75, *Tractatus de Natura Substantiae Energetica*, is noteworthy for its introduction of the concept of irritability, which he regarded as a property of living tissue. This concept was revived a century later by Albrecht von Haller and subsequently became fundamental to the development of physiology. His last work, *De Ventriculo et Intestinis*, appeared in 1677, the year of his death, and dealt further with the idea of irritability. Of particular interest in this text is the description of the famous experiment in which Glisson placed an arm in a large glass tube filled with water and demonstrated that muscles do not increase in bulk when they contract since the water does not rise in the tube and overflow.

Thomas Willis (1621–1675)

Thomas Willis was the elder member and patron of the Oxford group, having entered Christ Church College, Oxford, at the age of 15 and received the degree of Bachelor of Medicine in 1646. An ardent royalist, he served in the army of Charles I, and with the defeat of the royalists, began practicing in Oxford, taking a house where he set aside one room in which religious services according to Anglican rites were regularly held. At Oxford, he was one of the small group which met in Wadham College and later became transmogrified as the Royal Society. After the Restoration, he was appointed Sedlian Professor of Natural Philosophy and in 1664, published his *Cerebri Anatome*, the success of which was due in no small measure to the anatomical research of Lower and the illustrations provided by Wren. This work subsequently became a classic, and the original commentary upon the vasculature of the brain led to the introduction of the term "circle of Willis," which has subsequently become an accepted eponym in anatomical nomenclature.

In 1666, on the invitation of the Archbishop of Canterbury, Willis moved to London, where Wood recorded that "in a very short time, he became so noted, and so infinitely resorted to, for his practice, that never any Physician before went beyond him, or got more Money yearly than he". Such was his renown that he not only became a Fellow of the Royal Society and of the Royal College of Physicians, but also was frequently summoned to treat members of the Royal family. The esteem in which he was held culminated in his burial at Westminster Abbey in 1675.

Willis was a follower of the Iatrochemical School and speculated so much on fermentations that some scholars have criticized that "instead of busying himself in observation and experiment, he was exercised in framing theories". Although his text *Pharmaceutica Rationale* enjoyed a great reputation in its time, Sir William Osler was somewhat critical of its content, remarking: "It is as dead as Willis. It gives me a shudder to think of the constitution our ancestors had, and of how they withstood the assaults of the apothecary."

However, filled as he was with the arcane and undigested theories of fermentation, Willis was a keen observer and his description of influenza and the epidemics of typhus and typhoid, which raged in the Royal and Parliamentary armies, are classics of their time. As a diagnostician and clinician, he had few equals and his report regarding the taste of diabetic urine – "wonderfully sweet as if it were imbued with Honey or Sugar" – was the first in Europe. In addition to his cerebral commentary, he also noted the constriction of the bronchioles in asthma and provided the earliest clearly recognizable descriptions of cardiospasm (achalasia), myasthenia gravis, and hyperacusis.

Thomas Sydenham (1624–1689)

Thomas Sydenham, who was born at Wynford Eagle in 1624, was a very different type of physician. He entered Oxford in 1642 but stayed only a short time before leaving to fight in the Army of the Parliament against the King. After the victory of Oliver Cromwell, he returned to Oxford, then under Puritan rule, and entered Wadham College, where a year later in 1649 he was created Bachelor of Medicine by command of the Earl of Pembroke and appointed a Fellow of All Souls' College, probably in place of an expelled royalist.

Although the "Invisible College" was at that time holding its meetings in Oxford, there is no evidence that Sydenham had any contact with them, and indeed, his later writings reveal that he had no sympathy or interest in anatomical and physiological experiments. He did however subsequently in London become a close friend of Boyle, although this may more have reflected their advanced social status. In about 1656, Sydenham married, took a house in London, and settled down to practice, but three years later, moved briefly to Montpellier, where he studied further with the noted physician Barbeyrac.

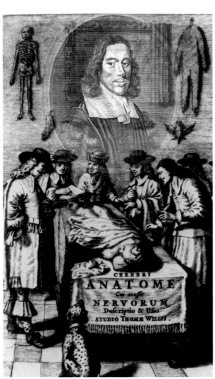

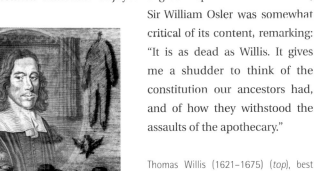

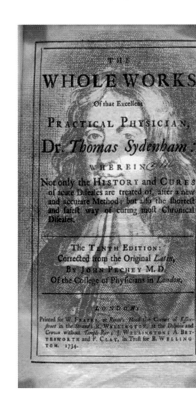

Thomas Willis (1621–1675) (top), best known for his contributions to cerebral vascular anatomy, was also the first to describe a number of diseases, and several anatomical parts now bear his name. He coined the terms "thalamus opticus," "nucleus lentiformis," and "corpus striatum" and was one of the original founders of the philosophical "Clubb" that subsequently became the "Royal Society of London for the Promotion of Natural Knowledge". Interestingly, he is also remembered for resuscitating a young woman who had been hanged and then brought to him for dissection!

In the latter half of the 17th century, internal medicine took an entirely new turn in the work of one of its greatest figures, Thomas Sydenham (1624–1689), also referred to as the "English Hippocrates" and the "Father of English medicine". He revived the Hippocratic methods of observations and experience, was one of the principal founders of epidemiology, and his clinical reputation rests upon his first-hand accounts of gout, malarial fever, scarlatina, measles, dysentery, hysteria, and numerous other diseases. He also introduced cinchona bark into England, and rightly praised opium in a medical world that often had little to offer in the way of cure.

Sydenham's progress in London was at first very slow, since in 1660, Charles II ascended the throne and feelings were not supportive of those who had supported Cromwell. Thus physicians such as Sydenham, who himself had served in that army and whose brother, Colonel William Sydenham, had been a well-known commander, could expect neither preferment at Court nor practice among the royalists and "upper circles". It is noteworthy that only in 1663 did Sydenham pass the examinations of the Royal College of Physicians and become a Licentiate, since prior to this time he had practiced without a license, as many probably did during the troubled times of the civil wars and the Commonwealth. Indeed, Sydenham never attained the rank of Fellow, since he did not possess a medical degree until 1767, long after his fame had been established.

The first book, *Methodus Curandi Febres* (it dealt with the currently popular topic of fevers), written by Sydenham was dedicated to Boyle and published in 1666. It provided strong support for the practice of a cooling regime in fevers and was very favorably received both in England and on the Continent. Subsequently, in 1676, when reconfigured as *Observationes Medicae*, it contained many excellent descriptions of disease, including scarlet fever, measles, and influenza. Four years later, in 1680, Sydenham produced *Epistolae Responsoriae* and in 1682, the wonderful text *Dissertio Epistolaris*. Seemingly inexhaustible in both energy and knowledge, in 1683, he published *Tractatus de Podagra et Hydrope*, in which he described in detail his tribulations with his own gout. The text is noteworthy in that it contains a masterful description of an attack of acute gout and the oft-quoted remark: "Gout, unlike any other disease, kills more rich men than poor, more wise than simple." The tract on dropsy was much less important and it is apparent from a perusal of the work that Sydenham failed to understand the cause of dropsy, since he was apparently either unfamiliar with William Harvey's theory of the circulation or had decided not to recognize his contributions, being mindful of the royalist sympathies of the latter. Indeed, nowhere in the works of Sydenham is there any mention of the observations of his great contemporary Harvey and one might assume that either Sydenham was quite unaware of Harvey's discovery, which seems unlikely, or that he chose to ignore it.

Sydenham continued to write, enlarging his works and supervising new editions, with the result that his fame was enhanced while his practice amplified to the point that at his death in 1689, he had become widely accepted as one of the greatest physicians of his time. He prided himself on being a practical physician and not a theorist, and was not only quite uninterested in the newer developments in anatomy, physiology, and chemistry, but at times, directly hostile to them. Thus, when the young Hans Sloane, after studying on the Continent, came to Sydenham with a letter of introduction, Sydenham is said to have remarked: "This is all very fine, but it won't do. Anatomy. Botany. Nonsense! Sir, I know an old woman in Covent Garden who understands botany better, and as for anatomy, my butcher can dissect a joint full as well; no, young man, all this is stuff: you must go to the bedside, it is there alone you can learn disease."

While rich in its expression and delightful in its recount, the story is not in itself utterly improbable, since Sydenham believed fervently and taught constantly that medicine could be learned only at the bedside. He adumbrated endlessly that disease should be studied as any other natural phenomena and its symptoms minutely noted and documented. Indeed, he wrote descriptions of disease unrivaled since the time of Hippocrates, and much like Hippocrates,

possessed great faith in the healing powers of nature. Sydenham was a great admirer of the sage of Kos and so regularly referred to the precepts of Hippocrates that after his death he became referred to as the "English Hippocrates". As such, a guiding principle of his practice was the aphorism, "What is useful is good". Thus he rapidly accepted the efficacy of the Jesuit's powder (quinine) in fevers and employed it widely, although many of his colleagues bitterly fought this innovation. Such was his prescience that he regarded fever as Nature's method of neutralizing the injurious matter causing disease and in this respect, predated observations of two centuries later that documented the temperature sensitivity of bacterial organisms.

Although primarily focused on religious conversion, many priests were well-versed in cartography, medicine, and philosophy, and in their travels accessed not only novel diseases in exotic and far off lands but also the local remedies. The Jesuit fraternity was instrumental in identifying the medicinal use of cinchona (*top*) and introducing it into Europe, and as a result, certain species of Peruvian bark were referred to as "Jesuits' bark".

Richard Wiseman (1622–1676)

The remarkable period in the history of English medicine that produced Harvey, the Oxford group of physiologists, and the clinicians Willis and Sydenham also produced one of the outstanding British surgeons, Richard Wiseman, who was born in 1622. Although nothing is known of his parentage or early education, he was apprenticed to Richard Smith at the Barber-Surgeons' Hall at the age of 14, and after serving an apprenticeship of seven years, entered the Dutch navy as a surgeon. Since the Dutch were engaged in a fierce war with Spain, Wiseman saw much active service before returning to England during the Civil War, where he served with the Royalist army. After the rout at Truro, he accompanied Prince Charles, later Charles II, to Jersey, France, Holland, and Scotland, and was finally captured at the battle of Worcester. Given his reputation, he was finally released and permitted to move to London, where he was at once admitted to the Barbers-Surgeons' Company, and began practice. Unfortunately, his political sympathies were not well controlled and in 1654, he was once again arrested, this time for assisting in the escape of a prisoner from the Tower. After his release, he then served for three years in the Spanish navy, during which service

he spent much time in the tropics before returning to London, where he was appointed Surgeon in Ordinary to the King after the Restoration and chosen Master of the Barber-Surgeons' Company in 1665. The ascension of Charles II proved felicitous to his career and in 1672, he was promoted to the position of Principal Surgeon and Sergeant Surgeon, thus further amplifying his already successful practice, although his meteoric rise was dramatically terminated by his sudden and unexpected demise at Bath in 1676.

Wiseman's *Severall Chirurgicall Treatises*, first published in 1676, represented a landmark in the history of British surgery. It was primarily written for better-educated surgeons, not as a compendium of surgical practice but rather as a series of treatises on surgical topics based on the unique experience of the author. The treatises are eight in number and deal with the following: "of Tumors; of Ulcers; of diseases of the Anus; of the King's Evil; of Wounds; of Gunshot Wounds; of Fractures and Luxations; and, of the Lues Venerea." As Sir D'Arcy Power noted: "All are written in such pure English that it is a pleasant literary exercise to read them for their style alone."

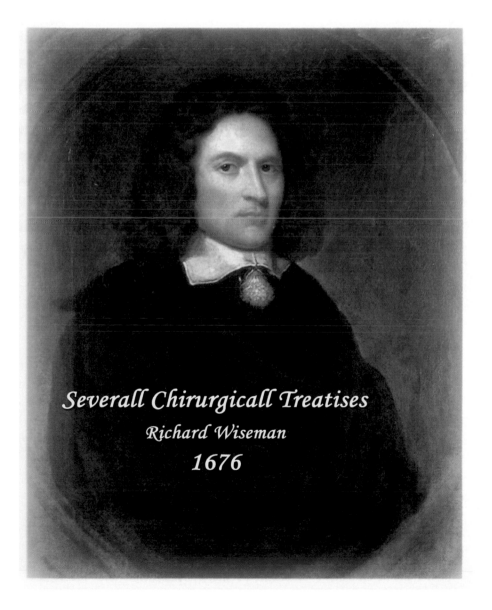

Severall Chirurgicall Treatises
Richard Wiseman
1676

Wiseman was an ardent royalist, and despite his apparent intelligence and erudition, was a firm believer in the efficacy of the "King's Touch". He provided an excellent description of scrofula – the "King's Evil" – its complications, and treatment, but noted, deprecatingly, that what he wrote "will do little more than show the weakness of our ability, when compared with his Majesty's, who cureth more in any one year, than all the Chirurgeons of London have done in an age". As a physician in the navy of the King of Spain, he saw much "*Lues Venerea*," noting with disappointment, "our Mariners as soon as their pockets were full of money would be getting ashore to the Negroes, and other common Women, that usually attended their Landing". As was the custom of the time, Wiseman treated the sufferers with bleeding, purgation, and especially with "Salivation, without which few great Cures are done in this Disease... The methods of Salivating are divers, but all by Mercury".

Wiseman was on excellent terms with physicians and rarely treated a patient unless sent to him by a medical man. As such, he represents the transition from the period when the surgeon learned his craft from the rough school of war, to a period when the surgeon saw his patients with the physician in civil practice as a colleague, and employed gentler and more refined methods as opposed to the cruder skills of the barbers and military surgeons.

Richard Wiseman (1622–1676) was a Sergeant Surgeon to Charles II and was present at many of the battles of the Civil War. He described the war wounds as follows: "Wounds made by gun-shot are the most complicated sort of wounds that can be inflicted: For they are not only solution of continuity, but have joined with them contusion. Attrition, and dilaceration, in a high and vehement kind. To this we may add all sorts of fractures and accidents, as haemorrhagia, inflammation, erysipelas, gangrene, and sphacelus; besides the extraneous bodies which are violently carried into the wound, and multiply indications." In addition to his interest in military medicine, he was also the first person to treat leg ulcers with stockings, which were made of leather laces.

The power of the Papacy was immense in a society that had been preconditioned to believe in the supremacy of divine power. The Pope himself possessed influence that rivaled that of kings, since his troops were the bishops and vicars who controlled the common people. A ruler would therefore do well to support the Church and the Pope, for it was difficult to disagree with God's earthly representative. In this fashion, Catholicism utilized both divine and secular authority to promote the authority and influence of the Church.

ENGLISH MEDICINE BEFORE THE COLLEGES

Although the status of medical practice in medieval time has for the most part been portrayed as ineffective, overpriced, and riddled with superstition, the early physicians exhibited an impressive range of academic accomplishments and exerted considerable influence in political, religious, and cultural affairs. For the most part, this was accomplished by medical persons adopting a position closely aligned with religion. In an age where the overwhelming authority of the Church colored the lives of all and theology was regarded as the dominant intellectual force as well as bearing divine sanction, the positioning of physicians under a clerical umbrella was sound strategy. Thus, in an age when life was generally painful as well as short and a high mortality the lot of all, a divine affiliation was a prudent posture. What might today be regarded as an apparent paradox was therefore no more than sound medical and political

strategy. Thus the practitioner, who was often also a priest, dealt with spiritual as well as earthly diseases, exploring the darkest recesses of the divine souls of his flock while examining their earthly bodies. As such, he fulfilled the role of a spiritual confidant, worldly sage, and mentor, offering advice on all aspects of both the human and sacred condition of his ward. The absolute belief that physical suffering was a manifestation of sin enabled confession to become a large component of therapy, and hence the talking cure long predated the practice of Sigmund Freud in Vienna. The entire doctrine and practice of medicine and surgery was established as a component of canon law and regulated by Church authority, since the maintenance of a healthy temporal body was little more than a facet of the quest of mankind for eternal salvation.

Sigmund Freud (*center*) and the legendary couch in his "transplanted" study at Maresfield Gardens, London. Despite having been evicted from Vienna by the Nazis, Freud's teachings generated a widespread interest in psychoanalysis. Perhaps Freud's narrative approach – the analysand was given the power to talk – has roots in the earlier "confessions" of the Church (*bottom left and right*). Above his couch hung the picture of his teacher Jean Martin Charcot (of biliary triad fame), from whom he had first learned the concept of hysteria.

In a society dominated by pomp and circumstance and preoccupied with the external manifestations of wealth and status, the late medieval English physician sort to portray both an image of sartorial elegance and intellectual demeanor. Despite a traditional role that supported a modest and sober style of dress consistent with his professional gravitas and discretion, the times produced an uncomfortable conflict, as men of erudition and influence sought to publicize their accomplishments. The adoption of a classic style encumbered by heavy gold chains, fur-trimmed robes lined with silk, and the glitter of costly gems not only defined a physician as a person of consequence, but provided evidence of a role close to that of the highest ranks of the Church and the aristocracy. Indeed, such was the level of esteem in which some physicians were held that medical advisors to royalty were remunerated at a level commensurate with that of a junior minister of state. In addition, and of particular relevance to both religious and secular events, was the opportunity to exercise considerable authority in the public sphere, especially if the monarch was old or sick. This facet of medical influence in some circumstances reached a point that on occasion, a royal physician might even undertake an active lead in the formulation of government policy. Thus, not only worldly affluence but also substantial political influence lay within the grasp of the successful practitioner and enabled him to exert an effect on society that has rarely been achieved in recent times.

Since the medieval physician plumbed the recesses of the soul as well as the body, often being more familiar with his patients' spiritual health and psychological anxieties than he was with their physiological infirmities, a symbiotic physician–patient relationship was a major feature of medicine. Indeed, at a time when viable alternatives to preventive medicine were virtually non-existent, the physician exerted extraordinary influence that was further supported by his relationship to the overwhelming authority of the Church, which impinged upon almost every aspect of human life. Thus, the difference between 15th century medicine and that of the 21st reflects to a great degree not only advances in science but also the role of religion in medicine. Medicine of this earlier period has often been harshly characterized as ineffectual and overpriced, its practitioners powerless in the face of disability and disease as well as befuddled by superstition and dogma. Indeed, many have painted a depressing picture of medicine in the Middle Ages that was shared by patients and practitioners alike. Thus patients were abusive and litigious, while cartoonists and satirists ridiculed the medical profession's fatal combination of ignorance, rapacity, and hubris with venom and vituperation rarely encountered in contemporary media.

Despite such examples of criticism, theirs was only one of many contemporary responses to the attempts of the physician to exercise his art and is far less harsh when viewed within the appropriate social and cultural context of the time. To most observers, the physician was neither a cynical opportunist nor a charlatan, but a dedicated mediator between life and death, whose advice, when properly followed, might not only deliver physical and spiritual health, but also bore with it the hope of redemption.

A portrait of a richly attired physician, made wealthy by the success of his practice and secure in the richness of his knowledge and the place afforded to him by society.

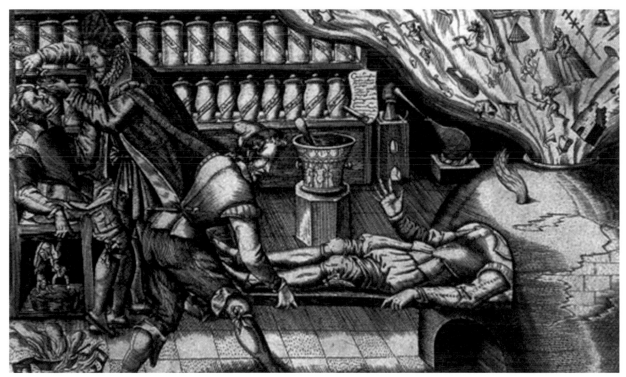

A cartoon variously depicting a physician (an alchemist) curing a man of fantastical thoughts by heating him in an oven or demonstrating how much nonsense was in the mind of man.

Piety, peculation, and professionalism

Although neither Oxford nor Cambridge produced more than a handful of fully qualified physicians at any one time before the 16th century, the communal standing of a physician was bolstered by his membership of a narrow academic and social elite. Indeed, only 94 individuals graduated in medicine from Oxford University between 1300 and 1500, and a mere 59 from Cambridge. This may represent the fact that many students succumbed early to a desire for prosperity, and departed into practice prior to acquiring a degree. Although there were early attempts in the 1420s to establish a professional collegiate structure similar to that evident in other parts of Europe, these were failed since the two English Faculties of Medicine were feeble, conformist, and geographically remote from the main city centers of power and the Court. Given the circumstances, the majority of talented graduates opted for lucrative employment at Court or in the retinues of lords and prelates, rather than the pursuit of an academic career. Furthermore, since most aspiring physicians possessed holy orders, they could be rewarded with profitable livings – usually held *in absentia* – and ascended rapidly up the ecclesiastical ladder.

The warring Lancastrian King Henry V (1387–1422) (*left*) secured much of northern France for England. His much vaunted prowess was recounted as follows: "This Henry was a king, of life without spot, a prince whom all men loved, and of none disdained, a captain against whom fortune never frowned, nor mischance once spurned, whose people him so severe a justicer both loved and obeyed (and so humane withal) that he left no offence unpunished, nor friendship unrewarded; a terror to rebels, and suppressor of sedition, his virtues notable, his qualities most praiseworthy." His son, Henry VI (1421–1471) (*right*), who never saw his father, spent his life attempting to retain both of his crowns (England and France), and precipitated the War of the Roses that was only terminated by his murder. Interestingly, he suffered from a mental illness that it is claimed he inherited from his mother's Valois blood.

Examples of individuals that prospered under such an arrangement included Nicholas Colnet, Physician to Henry V and one of the most successful pluralists in Lancastrian England; Gilbert Kymer, who treated Henry's brother and became Chancellor of Oxford University; and John Arundel, whose promotion to the bishopric of Chichester in 1458 represented due recompense in lieu of many years of loyal service to the ailing Henry VI. Similarly, many physicians such as Thomas Moscroff, who was retained by Edward Stafford, Duke of Buckingham (the richest peer in early 16th century England) while still studying medicine at Oxford, occupied a prominent position in the retinues of the aristocracy. It is of interest that in addition to acting as Buckingham's "*cownsellour in fysyke*," Moscroff also supervised the health of his finances, worked as a legal advisor and secretary, and officiated in the ducal chapel.

Lay physicians were no less involved in religion and sought to equal if not exceed their clerical colleagues in personal piety. In this respect, a fine example is provided by Sir William Buttes, who was regarded as an individual of formidable learning and consequently established himself as the favorite medical advisor of Henry VIII. For his services to the Crown, he was rewarded with a knighthood and used his position to successfully exploit Henry's dependence upon him to further the English Reformation. Examination of his activities reveals Buttes to have been a shrewd psychologist, and he is reported to have been constantly armed "with some pleasant conceits to refresh and solace the king's mind". Such was his skill that he demonstrated consummate dexterity in dealing with a notably intransigent patient in a fashion that enabled his views to directly influence the policies of the monarch. Although he chose to exert his influence in the support of the Protestant rather than the Catholic cause, his stratagems differed little from those of earlier generations of royal physicians, who appealed to the consciences as well as the more material instincts of their patients. In this respect, the *Book of Martyrs* by John Foxe provides a memorable vignette of Buttes' sway, and documents how, in 1543, he used his influence "pleasantly and merrily" with the King on behalf of an evangelical preacher, who then risked the stake for making outspoken attacks on traditional religion. Indeed, it is a substantial testimony to the strength of their relationship that the persecution of Protestants by Henry only attained real effectiveness two years after the death of Buttes, when a rival faction regained the political initiative.

The Lateran Council

The Fourth Lateran Council, the Twelfth Ecumenical Council (1215), was generally considered the greatest council before Trent and was years in preparation. Pope Innocent III desired the widest possible representation, and more than 400 bishops, 800 abbots and priors, envoys of many European kings, and personal representatives of Frederick II (confirmed by the Council as Emperor of the West) took part. The purpose of the Council was twofold: reformation of the Church and the recovery of the Holy Land. Many of the decrees that were developed touching on Church reform and organization remained in effect for centuries. The Council ruled on such vexing problems as the use of Church property, tithes, judicial procedures, and patriarchal precedence.

The Council of Trent. This Nineteenth Ecumenical Council of the Roman Catholic Church (1545–1563) was of critical relevance both for its adoption of a number of sweeping decrees on self-reform and for its enunciation of dogmatic definitions that clarified virtually every doctrine contested by the Protestants. Despite internal strife, external dangers, and two lengthy interruptions, it played a vital role in revitalizing the Roman Catholic Church.

In addition, it ordered Jews and Saracens to wear distinctive dress and obliged Catholics to make a yearly confession and to receive communion during the Easter season. The Council sanctioned the word "transubstantiation" as a correct expression of Eucharistic doctrine and vigorously condemned the teachings of the Cathari and Waldenses. Pope Innocent also ordered a four-year truce among Christian rulers so that a new crusade could be launched, and in so doing, initiated yet another violent and misguided purgation of European aggression. In essence, this assembly represented one of the most significant events that altered the history of medieval medicine and generated a radical impact on future developments, since the recommendations of the Council were strictly observed throughout the whole of western Christendom. Of particular relevance to those involved in the practice of medicine were two rulings, the first relating to the confessional and the second to the concept of the pollution of the blood.

The talking cure

The basis of this concept, which embodied the function of the confessional, was enshrined in two rulings passed at the meeting of the Fourth Lateran Council of 1215. The first ruling directly considered the topic of confession and dealt with the intimate connection that, in a pre-Cartesian world, was perceived to exist between the body and the soul. This declaration embodied the concept "that the sick should provide for the soul before the body" and decreed that the priest, who was also referred to as the "physician of the soul,"

should confess and absolve the patient before treatment began. This stipulation was based upon the premise that since all bodily disease originated in sin, the only possibility of a cure rested in the renunciation of guilt or the expurgation of sin.

However, in order to conduct such an important practice, the physician had first to heal himself, and on entering the confessional, was faced with a multitude of questions in regard to his own conduct. These included the necessity to satisfy the clerical authorities that he had always ensured that the spiritual and temporal affairs of his patients were in order, that he had refrained from the sin of exposing human life to risk in the interests of crude material gain, and that he had always demonstrated compassion to the needy. Although Christ was often considered or portrayed as a physician, it was apparent to all that apostolic poverty was rarely evident in a profession that exhibited such fascination with outward appearances.

"Christ the Physician". Given the helplessness of physicians when faced with disease, the portrayal of Christ as a healer had great appeal. It was assumed that divine skill applied to ill health would produce recovery and that doctors lacked such abilities since they were not true believers. The portrayal of the flask of urine indicates a latter-day (16th century) focus on urinoscopy as a diagnostic and prognostic tool. In the background, a motley collection of patients is ministered to in the presence of divine healing power. After a millennium of support and tolerance for pantheism, the advent of monotheism was initially unsettling for Rome. Although not unfamiliar with the concept after their subjugation of Judea, Christianity was looked upon with some degree of reserve and even with intermittent acute persecution. The acceptance by the Emperor Constantine of Christianity as the religion of the Eastern Empire brought the creed a measure of acceptability.

Although this injunction was regarded as fundamental to the faith, in practice, it proved hard to enforce and was even considered by some practitioners to lay the basis for harmful psychological effects and even to interfere with the timely initiation of care. Indeed, the 14th century French surgeon Henri de Mondeville, who rose to prominence in the service of Philip the Fair, deplored the prospect of disagreeable bickering between surgeons and priests, while patients in urgent need of medical attention expired for want of care. De Mondeville clearly recognized a conflict of professional interest and potential problem in the delivery of medical care, although many of his colleagues actually joined with their patients in seeking confession and absolution before wielding the knife. The situation was however commonplace, since by the early 13th century, most surgeons were invariably laymen or clergy in lower orders and the overwhelming majority of English university physicians had been ordained as priests and were thus able to administer the sacraments as well. Thus, the confessor and the physician were often one and the same person, and diagnosis and treatment of the diseases of the soul consequently became intimately linked with, if not inseparable from, the care of the body.

The precise nature of verbal process, which was often medically based, that constituted the confession provides important information as to the mechanism by which the experience was thought to function. Indeed, in this respect, the inclusion of medical terminology was consonant with numerous other areas of medieval religious activity. In the *Livre de Seyntz Medicines* (*Book of Sacred Medicines*, 1354), that belonged to Henry of Grosmont, Duke of Lancaster – a long, sustained meditation composed during the aftermath of the first outbreak of plague in England – a comparison is drawn between the slow process of spiritual healing and the conquest of sin with the struggle of a physician against disease. Since many English noblemen were highly sophisticated, well-educated men who relished the society of learned and eloquent physicians, the narrative provides good evidence of the exposure of Lancaster to medical knowledge. Thus, the remedies suggested by Lancaster offer direct analogies: the theriac of a good sermon, the ointment of Christ's blood, the salve of the Virgin's kiss, the amputation of penance, and the "*gratia Dei*" ("grace of God") applied to a festering mouth after cleansing by confession. The latter metaphor is in itself quite revealing, since the name "*gratia Dei*" was linked to one of the most common ointments for wounds and sores that were subsequently produced in the later Middle Ages.

By use of special prognosticatory skills utilizing either urinoscopy or astrology to determine how long the patient might survive, the qualified "*medicus*" was able to protect against the terrors of "*mortua improvisa*" ("sudden death") by providing as a substitute for limited medicinal intervention all the solace of organized religion. While this might currently be considered of relatively little importance, at a time when dying unconfessed without the protective rituals of the Church doomed a soul to lengthy sojourn in purgatory, or even eternal damnation in hell, spiritual health was regarded as a necessity and urgent priority. Despite such awareness, the medieval populace generally recognized with grim inevitability that "there is no medicine for death," and thus had very different expectations of their medical practitioners, who routinely managed the transition from one world to the next. A good example of this is provided by the classic account of the assiduous physician, a Dominican theologian John de St Giles, who presided over the deathbed of Bishop Robert Grosseteste (died 1253). Abrogating his usual role as a medical "persona" he attended the dying bishop "as a constant companion... offering consolation of both body and soul," thus serving the spiritual needs of his patient and enabling him to achieve the "good end" so solemnly desired by the medieval Christian.

The priest as a curative agent was embodied in the concept of illness as a consequence of sin and absolution – cure or death being the salvation. In the Catholic Church, in addition to the prayers recited for the sick and dying, the last sacrament was the Eucharist (communion) in the form of Viaticum. If a priest were available, he would hear the patient's confession, give the sacrament of the sick, and offer communion, thus facilitating the final cure – death. In this fashion, priests were regarded as physicians of both the body and the soul, providing comfort for mortal suffering and salvation for eternal cure (rest).

The pollution of blood

The second important ruling of the Lateran Council of 1215 related specifically to the future prohibition placed on the shedding of blood or the use of cautery by clergy of the order of sub-deacon or above. Prior to this time, medicine and surgery had often been practiced together by distinguished ecclesiastics, such as Abbot Baldwin of Bury St Edmunds (died 1097), whose skill was held in such veneration that he had attended to the health of both Edward the Confessor and William the Conqueror.

The Lateran Council determined that blood was regarded as capable of pollution and that men of God, especially in the newly reformed Church of Pope Innocent III, should not have hands tainted with the bodily fluids of their patients while celebrating the Eucharist. Such allusions to the transmission of impurities from patients had long been part of clerical concerns and as early as 1109, Abbot Faritius of Abingdon had been sadly disillusioned when his ambition to become Archbishop of Canterbury had been thwarted by the assertion that "a man who spent his time examining the urine of women" was unworthy of such an office. It has, however, also been rumored that his unctuous affability and extreme personal charm, which had been deployed to such exceptional effect upon his aristocratic female patients, may also have diminished the enthusiasm of his peers in supporting him for such high office.

A similar concern in terms of the spilling of blood was enshrined in the performance of surgery, since demise under such circumstances often engendered accusations of manslaughter. Indeed, the possibility of accidental homicide was formidable given the lack of knowledge in regard to antisepsis, the absence of anesthesia, blood transfusion, or any form of antibiotics. A further issue was related to snobbery and the hierarchy of the Church in that senior clergy sought to separate themselves from the practice of what was essentially a craft rather than an art, and to be identified more positively with a higher or more intellectual avocation. Since the majority of health care available in medieval England was in the hands of apothecaries, empirics, unlettered women, and other assorted irregulars, the establishment of well-defined boundaries had obvious advantages in demarcating those empowered with a higher calling from a motley array of individuals seeking to provide a medical service for fees. In addition to this internal desire for separation from the lower medical masses, the rise of the universities, with their burgeoning faculties of medicine, provided a powerful incentive towards the specialist and essentially theoretical study of medicine by senior clergy. Furthermore, in England, unlike France and Italy, no significant attempt was made during the Middle Ages to integrate the surgeon into an academic program of training by offering anatomy classes or even occasional dissections, and thus this group drifted further into the outskirts of "acceptable" medicine and became more regarded as artisans than practitioners of a refined and educated art.

The health care of both Edward the Confessor (*background*) and William the Conqueror (*bottom right*) was undertaken by Abbot Baldwin of Bury St Edmunds. Despite being a weak but violent man, Edward's greatest achievement was the construction of a new cathedral, where virtually all English monarchs from William the Conqueror onward would be crowned. Since it was decided that the minster should not be built in London, a place was identified to the west of the city ("Westminster"). When the new church was consecrated at Christmas, 1065, Edward could not attend due to illness. William defeated Edward's son Harold and the subsequent Norman Conquest, according to scholars: "...raised the English to that level of culture which the continental people had already reached and left it for the Plantagenets of Anjou to make England in her turn 'a leader among nations.'"

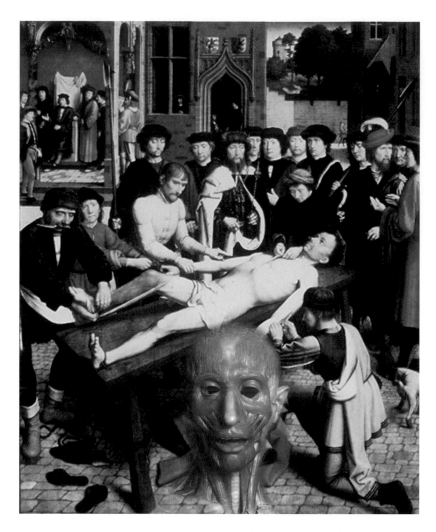

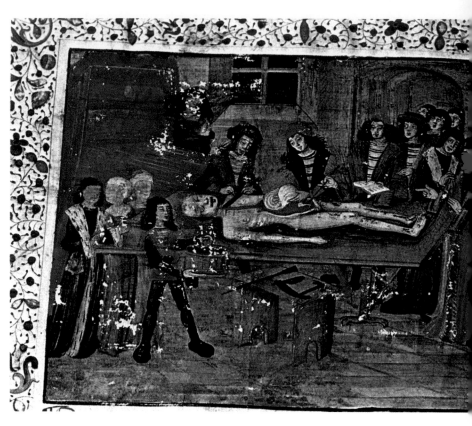

Whilst the beautiful paintings of the great anatomists and their elegantly attired colleagues invoke a sense of an intellectual salon, such was not the case. The absence of preservatives, refrigeration, and disinfectants rendered putrefaction, malodor, and decay dominant themes in the world of anatomical dissection. It required considerable intellectual curiosity and a strong stomach to learn anatomy in the days of yore.

'The Flaying of the Corrupt Judge Sisamnes' by Gerard David (1498). This medieval depiction of a man being flayed, although focused on the nature of crime and retribution, attests to the skill of the barber-surgeons, who were employed to undertake this early form of punitive surgery. The painting recounts a Persian story as related by the Greek historian Herodotus, whereby Sisamnes, a judge under King Cambyses, accepted a bribe and issued an unjust verdict. The King immediately had him arrested and flayed alive, after which his skin was used to cover the seat from which his son would henceforth sit in judgment.

As a consequence of these reasons, the ruling of the Fourth Lateran Council had profound ramifications for English medical and surgical practice. Surgery passed almost exclusively into the hands of laymen trained in artisan guilds or members of the lower clergy and became regarded as an "*ars mechanica*" comparable to a practical, hands-on activity, like stone masonry or carpentry. Thus to surgeons fell the unsavory, bloody, or dangerous tasks of amputation, stone cutting, abscess drainage, and the like, but also the intimate aspects of prophylactic humoral therapy, such as the administration of laxatives, clysters, suppositories, baths, phlebotomy, and cupping. In addition to such unflattering tasks, the surgeon was also responsible for embalming the royal dead, which although it indubitably provided him with a better grasp of human anatomy, set him even further apart from his more academic colleagues. As a result of such practice patterns, the dichotomy became reflected in the respective garb, rank, and remuneration of the two types of practitioner and further defined their differences. Although royal surgeons were often erudite men, well versed in medical theory, they rarely enjoyed the social or intellectual prestige of their senior associates, given the defining traditions that delineated the social hierarchy of the time.

The benefits of virtue and learning

Although in England, "*Physic*" was regarded as an increasingly esoteric subject, studied from a syllabus that, from the European Humanist perspective, appeared not only to be outdated but also hopelessly obfuscated by scholastic accretions, the subject was still held in high regard. Staunch advocates of this system maintained that the first aphorism of Hippocrates, "*ars longa, vita brevis*" ("art is long, life is short") unquestionably justified a protracted training established on the foundations of a liberal arts program. For purists of this type, the "*trivium*" (grammar, rhetoric, and logic) and "*quadrivium*" (mathematics, music, geometry, and astronomy) constituted a mandatory preparation for a medical career, especially one to be pursued in high places, where learning, wit, and an easy social manner carried a high premium. Thus, it is no surprise that the eminent English physician John of Gaddesden began his *Rosa Medicina* of circa 1230 by advising his readers that "one ought not to enter into the halls of princes without a knowledge of books". Since some royal physicians, such as

John Somerset (died circa 1454), were masters of grammar as well as medicine, it followed logically that they would teach as well as heal their patients. And indeed, the two activities were deemed synonymous, to the extent that Somerset, when first employed at the court of the infant Henry VI, functioned in the dual capacity of pedagogue and physician. Such was his level of erudition as a graduate of both Oxford and Cambridge and his subsequent royal influence that he played a major role in implementing, and perhaps even formulating, Henry's two most cherished educational projects: the founding of Eton College and of King's College, Cambridge. It is noteworthy that this early tuition provided such enduring effect that Henry considered these projects vital for "the health of his immortal soul". Thus, physicians exerted a broader influence than that on health-related matters alone and wider issues of statecraft as much as medicine were at stake, since the well-being of princes, and thus of the people they governed, depended upon a subtle combination of learning, virtue, and physical fitness, which men such as Somerset were trained to promote.

providing advice as a dietician, confidant, and mentor rather than an interventionalist. The evolution of the physician into this role was predictable given the enormous risks of surgery and the likelihood of death or debilitating illness as a result of even quite minor complaints, given the absence of adequate medications. Logic thus dictated that the assumption of a care provider role focused on preventive medicine would be of far more clinical relevance. Indeed, this style of medical care accorded well with the all-pervasive classical Greek tradition as disseminated by Christian translators and teachers, which in the later Middle Ages had been transmogrified into the popular and widespread doctrine embodied in the "*regimina sanitatis*" or manuals defining the requirements to ensure a healthy life. Much of this information actually derived from the medical components of the *Secreta Secretorum* (*Secret of Secrets*), a text of Arab origin that comprised exhortatory, albeit entirely fictitious, letters supposedly sent by Aristotle to his pupil Alexander the Great on the conduct and lifestyle befitting a successful – and therefore healthy – prince.

Medical knowledge was influenced by factors outside of medicine. In particular, the growth of commerce, the new learning of the Renaissance, Johann Gutenberg's invention of a printing press using movable type, and a substantial explosion of literacy widened the circle of book collectors to include wealthy merchants whose libraries contained herbals, books of law, medicine, and books of hours and other devotional works. Italian Humanists such as Francesco Petrarch and Giovanni Boccaccio searched for and copied manuscripts of classical writings to establish their scholarly libraries, while scholars such as Niccolo Niccoli (Librarian to Cosimo de Medici) and Gian Francesco Poggio Bracciolini shared this enthusiasm for the classics. Individuals such as Diane de Poitiers and Jean Grolier made notable collections of books outside Italy, although Florence remained the center of the rising book trade.

The wisdom of the Greeks of Alexandria transmuted through the schools of Padua, Montpellier, Paris, and Leiden has moved science ever closer to the understanding of the secrets of the body. Sadly, however, there remain many critical issues, which at this time defy resolution. Suffice to say, however, that the love of knowledge and the desire to satisfy intellectual curiosity appear to be as strong now as they were when Nikodemos the Anthonite penned his reflections on Ecclesiastical truth (*inset*). Although the *Orthodoxia* (*bottom right*) will continue to burden those who seek to gaze beyond the horizon, the temple of knowledge (*center*), like the museum in the text *Meibonius* by Diogenes Laertius (Amsterdam, 1698), will always be open to those possessed of enquiring minds.

Corpore sano

Despite the fact that medieval physicians had studied many subjects beside medicine and were well versed in liberal arts, they also had considerable experience in dealing with the sick. Indeed, they possessed much practical expertise, although they exercised their art in a fashion that differed from current practice in that their overall function was more as a general support person

In fact, a perusal of the material reveals that the rather tendentious advice provided by the writer in regard to sexual abstinence and the virtues of moderation are most unlikely to have appealed in any way to Alexander. Nevertheless, the leadership of the medieval Church warmly accepted the admonitions regarding chastity and denial of pleasure. The unforgettable and terrifying results of the plague were widely viewed as a judgment emanating from God upon sinners. Given the utter paucity of any useful medical intervention, the populace sought with fervor any spiritual and medical advice literature that might provide consolation. As a result, mass-produced "*regimina*" circulated widely in the vernacular, while the wealthy had their own custom-made manuals designed after protracted and no doubt expensive consultations with a personal physician. A good example of personal regimen was the Latin manual produced in 1424 by Gilbert Kymer as a guide for his patron, Humphrey, Duke of Gloucester, which offered a salutary caution against the physical and moral dangers of excessive sexual activity. Its frank tone and the nature of its comments provide a clear indication of the intimacy of Kymer's relations with the Duke, whose unrestrained hedonism clearly concerned him as both physician and priest.

Although medieval therapeutics was a complex melange of medicine, herbalism, superstition, and even astrology, the overall principles focused on maintaining the four bodily humors in a state of balance. It was widely held that good health could only be maintained by the careful balance and regulation of six external factors known as non-naturals. In this respect, the physician was the primary advocate of that "*mesure and attemperaunce*" utilized so frequently by authors of political and moral advice literature for princes, while the good ruler was always framed as a Christ-like model of perfect equilibrium.

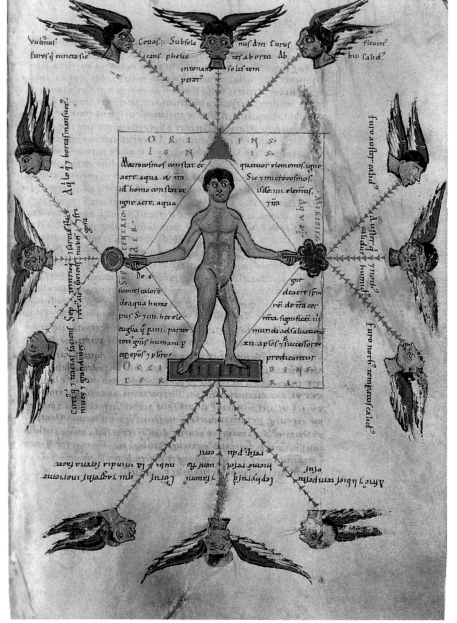

A medieval depiction of the four humors demonstrating an association with the cardinal points of a compass.

Indeed, a fine example of this concept was presented by consideration of the expulsion of Adam from Paradise after the Fall. The consequence of the loss of humoral equipoise was of one of the devastating penalties of Original Sin and the subsequent humoral imbalance led to the forfeit of eternal life. Since it was believed that the vast majority of humors were considered to be generated by the ingestion of food and drink through the process of coction (the gastric cooking process), the diet remained the most important and most easily managed of the non-naturals. As a result, it became regarded as one of the most important tools in medicine and was the first line of therapeutic intervention. Nevertheless, the practice of sexual restraint and the avoidance of gluttony alone were not sufficient, since to maintain absolute balance, the entire life of an individual, including exercise, sleep, bowel habits, and anxiety, required diligent attention. The preservation of this delicate balance was to a large extent the task of the physician, who by dint of constant interaction and consultation with the patient, supported his client in achieving the most desirable balance. Given the need for such delicate attention, a physician was expected to maintain close proximity to his patient to ensure adequate medical and spiritual guidance. As a result, the relationship between doctor and patient achieved a unique proximity and it is likely that under such circumstances, physicians exerted considerable personal influence.

Christianity and medicine

As a direct consequence of the close relationship between medicine and the clergy, the association in the public mind between medicine and Christ was ubiquitous and all pervasive. Thus sermons, texts, statues, iconography, and funerary monuments all served as vehicles to further this domain of medical and clerical healing. The concept of physical and spiritual health and healing pervaded all aspects of the discourse of the social and intellectual elite, and enhanced the status of those whose vocation embodied aspects of both the regal and much of the divine.

The "*regimen sanitatis*" was utilized as the basis for many of the theoretical concepts and actual practices of the late medieval preachers, who in their sermons powerfully reinforced the image of the "good physician," following in the steps of Christus Medicus. Surprisingly, the clerics did not espouse the limitations of earthly practitioners as fragile and limited, but strongly supported such individuals as following in the steps of Christ as a physician – a concept initially formulated by Saint Augustine of Hippo (died 430 AD) – who had placed much store on the Deity drinking the bitter medicine of the Passion to reassure his anxious patients. This notion was widely promulgated and led to a wide range of medical metaphors. Although such positive admonitions were more the rule than the exception, intermittently preachers would attack the greed and lack of compassion exhibited by successful physicians. On other occasions, the clergy would assume the specialist terminology of the university-trained physician in an attempt to cajole their parishioners towards moral improvement. Thus admonitions of this kind might include exhortations such as: "Christ, the most sovereign leech, had, after all, devised a regimen for each of his patients, who by following it might purge their diseased soul of the corruption of sin."

As might be predicted, physicians of note such as Kymer, who had successfully guided many patients towards their divine reward, adopted such clerical assessments with appropriate modifications as deemed necessary by their individual persona. In keeping with his status as Dean of Salisbury Cathedral, Kymer was interred adjacent to the relics' altar as an appropriate reflection of his position as earthly and spiritual physician to no less than two kings and a royal duke. His earthly rewards from a practice paid of considerable magnitude were devoted to the glazing of a Cathedral window, which not unexpectedly bore his image and an appropriately phrased invocation. The sumptuously colored and configured window depicted Kymer entreating the Summus Medicus, through the healing saints, to administer medicine to his soul so that he might enjoy the everlasting health of heaven.

Given the central role of the Church in managing the lives of its clients, the central issue of health was a dominant concern. It was therefore accepted policy to portray the founder not only as a divine being but one closely involved in ministering to the health of his earthly wards. Christ was therefore often portrayed as a physician caring for the physical as well as spiritual well-being of the ill and afflicted.

9 MEDICINE AND ROYALTY

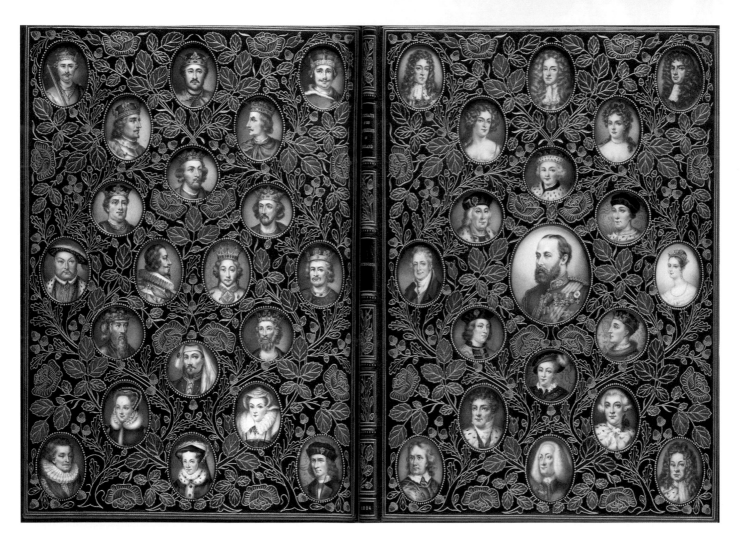

A book cover montage depicting the kings and queens of England. To a greater or lesser degree, many were involved with the delivery of health care to their subjects, although some were personally responsible for dramatic political and personal decisions regarding life and death.

There has existed a close relationship between the Crown and the profession of medicine, and in the long roll of sovereigns, there are many who demonstrated clearly their interest in its advancement. Initially, this was defined by a personal relationship, as in patronage or in the practice of the Royal Touch. Subsequently, corporate medicine in England was validated by Royal Charters and indeed over the last five centuries, physicians, surgeons, general practitioners, public health, hospitals, and nursing have all at some period profited by the active interest and encouragement of a sovereign and their association with the Healing Art.

THE FOUNDATION OF HOSPITALS

From Saxon times throughout the Middle Ages, various sovereigns were active in founding hospitals, lazar-houses, and homes for the destitute. As early as the 10th century, Athelstan assisted the saintly work of the canons of the Minster at York by founding St Peter's Hospital in that city. Similarly, the Hospital of St Giles in Holborn was founded by Queen Maud, consort of Henry I, some time before 1118, while the Leper-hospital of St Bartholomew in Oxford was founded by Henry in 1126; by the year 1135, Henry had founded four other institutions in Colchester, Cirencester, Lincoln, and Newcastle-upon-Tyne.

A medieval depiction of a patient infected with leprosy. The early understanding of the disease was somewhat confused, but since Biblical times, all were aware of its potential severity. It was known to be highly contagious, thought to be associated with sexual contact, and even believed to be hereditary. Infection by the devil (*bottom*) or evil spirits was considered the commonest etiology until Gerhard Henrik Armauer Hansen (1841–1912) identified the causal bacteria of leprosy (*Mycobacterium leprae*) in 1873. Nevertheless, in 1898, the British Government of India perpetrated a cruel "Leper Act" which required "lepers" to be treated like animals and to suffer compulsory segregation in asylums or "Leper Colonies". Although Gerhard Domagk, a German chemist, had in 1908 successfully produced the parent chemical of the sulphone family of drugs, which evolved into diamino diphenyl sulphone (Dapsone or DDS), only in 1941 was this toxic agent successfully used on humans by the American physician Guy Faget. His son Max was to become a principal lifesaver himself and designed the capsule ejection systems for the manned NASA spacecraft.

In 1165, Malcolm IV of Scotland, who was also Earl of Huntingdon, established the leper-house of St Margaret at Huntingdon and it was annexed to a Cambridge college in 1462. Since the Hospital of St Leonard at York had fallen into disrepair, King Stephen once again established it in 1135, and soon thereafter his wife, Matilda, founded St Katharine's in London. King John was regarded as an outstanding patron of lepers, and is reported to have founded hospitals near Bristol, Lancaster, and Newbury. During the whole of the 12th century and during the 13th century, the sovereigns of England continued to take an active interest in this saintly work, though the need for leper-hospitals as such gradually diminished, such that by the time of Edward III, the leper-hospitals at Oxford and elsewhere contained no lepers, and in 1434, new statutes had to be drafted for the great leper-hospital at Durham, since in that area there were almost no lepers. One of the last of these houses of succor to be erected was the Hospital of St John the Baptist in Cheapside, which was founded by Henry VII in 1505.

Although the dissolution of the monasteries by Henry VIII led to great social changes in the community, his Act also resulted in the rise of the major London hospitals. Unfortunately, the initial abolition of the infirmaries, hospitals, and almshouses related to the monasteries resulted in a great increase in the numbers of beggars and vagrants in the streets. While the earliest of the great London hospitals, St Bartholomew's, was from the time of its foundation in 1123 used for the treatment of the sick, it is not commonly realized that the hospital originally came into being through the generosity of Henry I. As the legend is told, this event was initiated by a vision of Rahere, an Augustinian monk who had traveled from England to Rome.

The mausoleum of Rahere in the Chapel of St Bartholomew's. Rahere established a hospital for the poor and sick of London in 1123 after receiving a vision while feverish and near death in Rome. Thus, Italian malaria may be credited with inspiring the establishment of one of the early bastions of intellectual medical thought. This facility evolved into what is now the Royal and Ancient Hospital of St Bartholomew's.

On arrival, he experienced a revelation in which Saint Bartholomew the Apostle instructed him to found at Smithfield a tabernacle of the Lamb, a temple of the Holy Ghost. A minor obstacle to this dream was posed by the fact that on his return, it became apparent that the chosen site belonged to the King. Undismayed and obviously supported by the ethereal presence of Saint Bartholomew, Rahere was successful in his supplication and thereafter built a priory and its attached hospital. According to Sir D'Arcy Power, the hospital "was designed to give help to the needy, orphans, outcasts, and poor of the district, as well as to afford relief to every kind of sick person and homeless wanderer. The sick poor were to be tended until they recovered, women with child until they were delivered, and if the mother died in hospital the child was to be maintained until the age of seven years." There is no doubt that St Bartholomew's was concerned with the treatment of the sick from its very foundation and that in two successive years, 1223 and 1224, Henry III made a gift to the hospital of an oak tree from Windsor Forest to heat the hospital and thus comfort the suffering. Despite such early royal munificence on the dissolution of the monasteries, Henry VIII seized the revenues of St Bartholomew's

Priory for himself, despite the petitions of the citizens for the continuance of the hospital. Eventually, Henry was persuaded of the error of his ways and relented, such that in 1544, 1546, and 1547, he granted three Charters to the hospital. These essentially reconstituted the institution for its original purpose, and the hospital is currently administered under these Charters, especially that of 1546.

EDWARD VI AND THE ROYAL HOSPITALS

In the early days of the reign of Edward VI, the streets of London were swarming with the poor and destitute, with rogues, and with loose women. Richard Grafton, who had printed the *Book of Common Prayer* in 1549 and 1552, was much concerned, and he interested Nicholas Ridley, the Bishop of London, in the matter such that in February or March 1552, when Ridley preached before the King at Whitehall, he used the opportunity to broach the matter. This famous sermon dealt with the necessity of caring for the poor and as soon as it was completed, Edward sent of his own accord for Ridley and asked what steps should be taken to resolve the matter. The Bishop was astonished at the King's knowledge of the problem, and suggested that his sovereign should address a letter to the Lord Mayor, Sir Richard Dobb, asking him to advise appropriate action. Without delay, Edward wrote the suggested letter, and having signed, asked Ridley to deliver it by his own hand to the Lord Mayor. As a result of this action, a part of the difficulties were overcome. This event was much like the change in social life produced by Henry VIII's dissolution of the monasteries, which had always had as part of their function the succoring of the needy, the crippled, and the sick. A similar form of persuasion led to the restoration of St Bartholomew's Hospital to its original purpose, and in a like fashion, the citizens of London acquired the Hospital of St Mary of Bethlehem for the care of the insane.

An 18th century map of London with insets of some of the great medical institutions: St George's (*top left*), St Luke's (*top right*), Greenwich (*center*), Chelsea (*bottom right*), and Newgate (*bottom left*).

The development of a personal friendship and close ideological relationship between the Bishop of London (*left*) and Edward VI (*right*) led to the development of a number of hospices for the poor and destitute.

At that time, the area later occupied by Christ's Hospital was covered with the semi-ruined buildings of a dissolved convent of the Grey Friars, into which "rogues and disorderly women crept at night to sleep". This ancient hospital had been surrendered to Henry VIII in 1540, and during most of the reign of Edward VI, was owned by Sir John Gate and had become virtually derelict. As a result of the legislation, the City now proposed to take over this building for the reception of fatherless and pauper children as well as St Thomas' Hospital for the treatment of the sick and infirm. It has long been theorized that Henry had actually intended to re-establish these as hospitals, as in the case of St Bartholomew's Hospital; however, his untimely death obviated this possibility. Although the proposed action of the City Fathers would deal in part with the social problem of the City, there remained the most difficult problem of the reformation and employment of tramps, rogues, and dissolute women. They therefore proposed to supplicate the King for the royal palace of Bridewell. A deputation waited on Edward in May or June 1552, and after it had presented its report, Ridley, on his bended knees, presented a personal supplication for Bridewell. Edward presumably gave his permission for the citizens to continue with their scheme for Christ's and St Thomas' – already owned by them – since in November 1552, Christ's Hospital received 380 children, and at the same time, 200 sick and aged persons were admitted to St Thomas' Hospital. But since Bridewell was not the personal property of the King and also belonged to his successors, he indicated that it was first necessary to consult his Council.

Within six months of this discussion, in January 1553, Edward began to show the early signs of pulmonary tuberculosis and sought to finalize the matter. Thus, on April 10, the Lord Mayor was summoned to the Court at Whitehall, and there, in the words of Stow, "the King's majesty gave to him, to the commonality and citizens, for to be a work-house for the poor and idle persons of the city of London, his place of Bridewell". One day later, the King departed to Greenwich, whence he never returned to London. Fortunately, the Charter which the King had personally inaugurated could now be completed by his Council's officers, and thus, on June 12, Edward executed an indenture with the City of London, whereby he consented to be named the founder and patron of the three new hospitals, and the appointment of governors and other officials for the three hospitals was authorized. On June 26, the Royal Charter of King Edward VI of the Hospitals of Christ, Bridewell, and St Thomas the Apostle was granted and formally signed by Cotton, who was at that time controller of the royal household. Sadly, the condition of the King had become desperate, and on July 6 – 10 days after the granting of the Charter – he passed away.

A translation of the Charter can be read in Parsons' *History of St Thomas' Hospital* and from the wording, it is quite clear that Edward intended the provisions to apply jointly to these three hospitals, thereafter to be called the "Royal Hospitals". It clearly stated that the governors should be body corporate and politic, and that the governors and their successors should have a common seal.

At Bridewell, a picture exists which is supposed to represent the granting of this Charter by Edward. Although it was formerly attributed to Holbein the Younger, it was later realized that he died 10 years before the event depicted and therefore the most probable attribution was to the court painter William Scrottes, who was born in the Low Countries. Although the style is consistent with the fact that it is obviously a contemporary work, it is curious that there existed no record of it whatsoever until 1751, when the governors thanked Mr George Vertue for his engraving of the picture.

A symbolic representation of the grant of the Charter of the three Royal Hospitals – St Thomas', Christ's, and Bridewell – by Edward VI to the Corporation of London, on June 26, 1533. This painting by William Scrottes has great merit, although Scrottes took artistic license in turning the sickly King into a pompous youngster, and in making the other characters appear older. The painting has remained at Bridewell and has always been associated with that institution. Although some have debated the authenticity of the event, the King is not reading from a document but rather presenting to the Lord Mayor a certificate which, given the enormous attached seal, could only be a Charter. (Courtesy of Christ's Hospital.)

In the year 1555, the Hospital of St Mary of Bethlehem became a Royal Hospital, and two years later, St Bartholomew's Hospital was added, so that the final number became five. The establishment of the great provincial and London hospitals in the 18th century reflected a wave of philanthropy, which spread over the country at that time, and while important in maintaining the momentum, royal patronage played only an indirect part in their foundation.

PERSONAL INTEREST OF THE SOVEREIGN IN MEDICINE

During the Renaissance, it was well accepted that a reasonable amount of medical knowledge was a requisite part of the educational equipment of any gentleman; indeed, Henry VIII provided an excellent example of the case in point. Apart from his practical interest in physicians and surgeons, he dabbled in pharmacy and treated the illnesses of his friends. In support of this there exists in the British Museum a manuscript, the *Diary of Dr Butts*, which is in effect a pharmacopoeia of plasters, liniments, and cataplasms drawn up by Butts and three other famous physicians of the time. Of interest is not only the fact that many of these medicaments were devised for the treatment of Henry's ulcers, but also that included among them is a prescription entitled "The King's Majesty's own Plaster," which was described as a plaster devised by the King to heal ulcers.

As might be expected of a royal remedy, it consisted not only of guaiacum wood but also pearls! Other formulae are described as having been "devised by the King at Greenwich and made at Westminster" and were recorded as having been designed for "the treatment of excoriations and swelling of the ankles, and also to prevent inflammations and to remove itching". Clearly, Henry's daughter inherited this interest, since it is reported that Elizabeth I also dabbled in prescribing and sent a formula of her own devising for a "cephalico-cardiac medicine" to Rudolf II, the Holy Roman Emperor. Such was her knowledge of the subject that she was also credited with having selected the doctors and pharmacists for Ivan the Terrible of Russia!

Thomas Geminus – surgeon and anatomist

More important than pharmacy and medication for the scientific advancement of medicine was the interest that both these sovereigns devoted to anatomy. The *Fabrica* and the *Epitome* of Andreas Vesalius were published at Basle in 1543 and two years later, there appeared in London a folio work entitled *Compendiosa totius Anatomie delineatio, aere exarata per Thomam Geminum.* Little is known of Thomas Geminus except that he was a foreigner who came to England in 1540 from the village of Lys-les-Lannoy, about 15 miles from Lille, in French Flanders. Despite some doubts on his actual profession, Geminus was almost certainly a surgeon, and he was probably also a maker of surgical instruments attached to the Court, since he received £10 per annum from the Privy Purse until 1563, when he died. In addition, Geminus was also a skilled engraver and was the first-known line-engraver to work in England, where he made some of the plates for the famous women's book entitled the *Byrth of Mankynde*, and he followed this with his *Anatomy* of 1545.

Andreas Vesalius (1514–1564) (*inset*) and the front page of his seminal work *De Humani Corporis*. Prior to Vesalius, most anatomy reflected information gained from animal dissection (chiefly pigs and apes) or limited information derived from the examination of wounded soldiers or gladiators. Vesalius' work established anatomy as an art based on the human physique and revolutionized 16th century medical thought.

The most important part of this work on anatomy consists, apart from the engraved title page, of 40 engraved plates, which are direct copies of the woodcuts that appeared in the *Fabrica* and the *Epitome*. There is also a short accompanying Latin text, descriptive of the plates, which is considerably shorter than the *Fabrica* text and is not a précis of it. Vesalius was quick to point out that his great work had been plagiarized and he accused "that Englishman" of having copied his illustrations poorly and without skill! Although he might have been justified in complaining about the plagiarism, Vesalius had little cause to be heated over the quality of the Geminus copies, since they are competent engravings, and the fact that they were reprinted four times indicates that they met a need. In the long dedication, Geminus refers to Henry VIII in flattering terms, and the ornate title page bears the Royal Coat of Arms, thereby indicating that the work was published with the knowledge and approval of Henry.

The engraved title page of Thomas Geminus' *Compendiosa totius Anatomie delineatio* (first edition; London, 1545) (*left*). The design bears the Royal Coat of Arms of Henry VIII (*top left*). On the right is the similarly engraved title page of the fifth edition (London, 1559). The plate used is that of the 1545 edition, with the substitution of a portrait – probably the earliest published – of Elizabeth I (*bottom right*) in place of the Royal Coat of Arms of her father. Both father and daughter were to exert profound influence on the development of British medicine.

Seven years after its first appearance, a second edition of Geminus' *Anatomy* was reprinted (1552) and in 1553 and 1557, the third and fourth editions appeared as English translations. Since all these editions bore the Royal Coat of Arms on the engraved title page, the book was therefore also sponsored by Edward VI and Queen Mary. The fifth and last edition, also in English, appeared in 1559, the year after Elizabeth I came to the throne, and in this version, the engraved title page again appears, although the Royal Coat of Arms have now been replaced by an engraved portrait of Elizabeth, which, though not particularly attractive, is one of the few surviving portraits from the early years of her reign.

The Crown and the physicians

At the dawn of the 16th century, neither the physicians nor the surgeons in England were looked upon with the respect which they claimed on the Continent. Many quacks practiced both medicine and surgery, and conditions were such that effective control was difficult until the influence Thomas Linacre effected an amelioration of the situation. As one of the earliest English Humanists, he had spent a lengthy period in Italy before he was summoned from Oxford to undertake the education of Prince Arthur. On the death of the Prince, Linacre, who had by this time become highly respected and popular, as well as being recognized by Prince Henry, departed the Court to practice medicine. On Henry's accession in 1509, Linacre was appointed his Physician, and the King could thus enact many of the ideas which his medical advisor had long harbored regarding the regulation of medical practice. Thus, in 1512, an Act was passed which provided that no one should practice the profession of medicine within the City of London or within a radius of seven miles unless he had passed an examination conducted by the Bishop of London or the Dean of St Paul's. Experts in medicine and surgery carried out the examination, and similar arrangements were made for the provinces, although it was decided that graduates in medicine of Oxford and Cambridge were exempt from this assessment.

In 1518, Henry VIII granted a Foundation Charter to the College of Physicians (*top left*). In 1656, Oliver Cromwell granted a Charter (*bottom left*), followed by Charles II in 1663 (*bottom right*) and James II (*top right*) in 1687. The original Grant of Arms of 1546 (*center*) showed a hand emerging from a cloud "*ffelinge the powllse of an arm*" and contained a "*powme granate golde*". The latter was included because of its alleged power to cure "burning agues". In 1963, a modified design (*bottom*) was introduced, whereby the hand was shown to be feeling the site of the pulse correctly.

Since this measure failed to be as effective as Linacre desired, he thereafter proceeded with a scheme for the establishment of a Royal College of Physicians and on September 23, 1518, the College was constituted by Letters Patent. As it transpired, there existed some ambiguity in the wording, and the constitution of the College was therefore further ratified and confirmed by a statute. The founders were Linacre, John Chambre, and Ferdinand de Victoria, Physicians to the King, together with Nicholas Halsewell, John Francis, and Robert Yarley. By the statute, these six, together with two other named physicians, were appointed elects and were enjoined to annually "appoint a president from among themselves". Linacre was elected the first President of the new College, and he continued to be appointed annually to that office until his death in 1524. Despite the strength of character of Linacre, it is however certain that without the active interest of Henry VIII and of Cardinal Thomas Wolsey, Linacre's plans would not have matured. In addition to supporting Linacre, Henry also furthered the cause of medicine by his foundation of the Regius Chair of Physic at Oxford and at Cambridge.

The Crown and the surgeons

Although the foresight and interest of Henry as regards medicine enabled both the physicians and the surgeons to become separately incorporated during his reign, in each case, the interests of the King were paramount in assuring success. Thus, in the case of the surgeons, Henry had a personal interest, since he was intermittently troubled by a varicose ulcer in the leg. In each case also, a powerful personality was at work – thus Linacre served the physicians well and in a similar vein, Thomas Vicary was a powerful advocate on behalf of the surgeons.

During the 14th century, the craft of surgery was in a chaotic state in London. Indeed, to parody a famous sentence of Lord Macaulay, it may be said that there were barbers and there were surgeons; but while some barbers were surgeons, the surgeons were not barbers! A Fraternity or Guild of Surgeons – a weak and ineffective body with some limited power to control the professional activities of its members, had existed in London from at least 1369. The Guild of Barbers was probably an older body, since its records dated back to 1308. Some of its members were barbers who shaved, drew teeth, and let blood, while other members did minor surgery and work that now would be considered largely that of a general practitioner. As time passed, the Guild of Barbers flourished and was eventually elevated to the dignity of a City Company, the members of which had the right to wear livery and to govern the professional conduct of its members.

In 1493, the surgeons and the barbers entered into a loose alliance, but the position was perceived as unsatisfactory, since there was little possibility of controlling the numerous quacks, cutters for the stone and the cataract, and performers of similarly dangerous operations – which in either event were usually left to them by both the surgeons and the barbers.

In 1518, Henry VIII granted the College of Physicians a foundation Charter (*background*) that was ratified by Parliament on April 15, 1523, and in 1546, a Grant of Arms was made (*top left*). For reasons that are unclear, the document was never finalized and lacked the "H" and the Royal Coat of Arms of Henry (*bottom center*). Although the constitutional rules of the College were initiated as early as 1520, it remained for John Caius in 1563 to produce the first consolidated edition. Later editions such as the 1647 version of the College Statutes contained the College's coat of arms (*bottom right*) and were characterized by a textual richness as embodied in the title page (*center*).

This unsatisfactory state of affairs was well known to Vicary, a young surgeon of great ability who had come to the attention of Henry VIII by temporarily curing his leg ulcer at Canterbury during one of his progresses. As a result, in 1528, Henry appointed him as his personal surgeon and thereafter, in 1530, he was given the reversion to the post of Sergeant-Surgeon, and in 1536, he finally succeeded to this position. Vicary was adept at using the rank and influence afforded to him to influence the King, with the result that in 1540, the two Companies of Surgeons and Barbers were formally united into a new company known as the Masters or Governors of the Mystery and Commonality of the Barbers and Surgeons of London – or in short, the Barber-Surgeons' Company. Vicary was not a master of either company at that time, but such was the extent of his great influence that Holbein, in his famous picture, showed him receiving the Charter of incorporation from the King. This union persisted for just over 200 years until 1745, when the two companies separated, and the Surgeons' Company ultimately became the Royal College of Surgeons of England.

The Crown and the apothecaries

A similar state of affairs existed in respect of the apothecaries, but the royal interest that brought about a consolidation of their affairs was not that of Henry VIII but of James I. The grocers of London had arisen out of a Guild of Pepperers, which was known to exist in the late 12th century. Edward III incorporated the grocers in 1345, and they received a Royal Charter from Henry VI in 1429. Twenty-six years later, they were entrusted with the task of examining the drugs and other *materia medica* sold by the apothecaries. As a result, the apothecaries eventually became members of the Grocers' Company, probably with considerable financial advantage, since the grocers were wealthy and ranked second among the City companies. From the very outset, the alliance between the two parties was uneasy.

The Society of Apothecaries was incorporated by Royal Charter from James I in 1617. The Letters Patent provided the Society with the right to "have, purchase, retain and appoint a certain Hall, or Counsel-House" in the City – Cobham House in Blackfriars was chosen. This was originally a guesthouse of the former Dominican Priory of the Black Friars. The entrance to Apothecaries' Hall from Black Friars Lane (*center*) led to an impressive entrance hall (*background*) featuring the staircase, dating from just after the Great Fire, and a cabinet displaying a selection of apothecaries' drug jars. The coat of arms of this venerable institution (*top right and bottom left*) bears testimony to the role of Apollo the physician and the magical healing powers of the unicorn.

By 1562, the Royal College of Physicians had attempted to obtain control of the apothecaries and to have them taken away from the jurisdiction of the grocers, since they claimed that the apothecaries not only sold *materia medica*, but also provided medical advice and applied the drugs which they advised. This practice later became a bone of contention between the physicians and the apothecaries. But in addition, the physicians had a grievance, since they complained that the apothecaries not only compounded drugs but saw patients, whereas the apothecaries themselves were aggrieved because some physicians not only saw patients but also compounded drugs. In order to resolve this dispute, in 1588, the apothecaries petitioned Elizabeth I for a monopoly in compounding and selling drugs, but were refused. To add insult to injury, the grocers then complained that the apothecaries were having the best of two worlds, since they not only sold drugs but also groceries.

When Elizabeth died and James acceded in 1603, all Charters and monopolies had to be surrendered for inspection, as was the custom on the death of a sovereign. In most instances, the Charters were simply restored as a pro forma matter; however, on this occasion, the Grocers' Company was returned with the instruction that the apothecaries were to form a separate section of the Company. Much encouraged, the apothecaries noted that they had no voice in the government of the Company, and under the stimulus of Gideon De Laune, the Apothecary to James' consort Anne of Denmark, they determined to agitate for complete separation from the grocers. Although de Laune was anxious to have a Bill promoted in Parliament for this purpose, the grocers exhibited great hostility, and he became the only apothecary who maintained his position in the face of the opposition produced by the grocers. It was several years (1614) before the apothecaries of London summoned enough purpose to undertake the next step, when on April 2 of that year, they presented to James a Humble Petition in which they asked to be incorporated by Royal Charter, as in the case of the physicians and the barber-surgeons.

James acted at once and instructed Sir Francis Bacon and Sir Henry Yelverton, the Law Officers of the Crown, to confer with Sir Theodore Turquet de Mayerne and Henry Atkins, the representatives of the apothecaries, and to report. While it was well recognized that Bacon had little regard for physicians in general, he now demonstrated that he was active in the interests of the apothecaries.

The complex political machinations of Gideon De Laune (*bottom right*) supported by the clout and influence of Sir Francis Bacon (*background*) and Sir Theodore Turquet de Mayerne (*left*), led to the establishment of an independent Charter for Apothecaries in 1617.

Thus, he and Yelverton recommended the separation of the apothecaries from the grocers, and suggested that the apothecaries might be more fittingly associated with the physicians. The King replied to his law officers at once, and suggested that the new company should retain the precedence which it had formerly held as a part of the important Grocers' Company. However, both the physicians and the grocers petitioned against the new proposal, since it suited neither; although the position of the apothecaries was internally weakened by the fact that they were as a body not unanimous in the desire to secede from the grocers. Despite this, a Charter was drafted which would have succeeded in making the new company subservient to the physicians except for the intervention of Bacon, who continued to press the case for the apothecaries. Indeed, it was largely due to him that this draft Charter was amended so that when signed on December 6, 1617, it permitted the apothecaries to manage their own affairs. Thus, while the apothecaries had triumphed, the disputes continued, and it was well over 200 years before the position of the apothecaries in relation to the physicians and surgeons was resolved.

The Crown and the Royal Society

The history of the foundation of the Royal Society is a well known but an important component of the relationship between medicine, science, and the monarchy. By the year 1645, a group of men interested in experimental philosophy and such matters had begun to meet in London. The gatherings usually took the form of casual discussions that covered a wide field, including the medical sciences, and occurred at the houses of Robert Boyle and of other members. John Wallis, the recorder of these events, noted that "about the year 1648–9" the company divided and some members went to Oxford while others remained in London. The Oxford Society developed into the Philosophical Society of Oxford, and continued to hold meetings until 1690, when it finally became defunct. The London Society however continued its meetings, usually at Gresham College, until about 1658, when the grave political disturbances towards the end of the Commonwealth made it expedient to discontinue them. Fortunately, the Restoration improved matters vastly, and the meetings at Gresham College were resumed with a new awareness that the Society should be organized on more formal lines. As a consequence of this decision, a memorandum was drawn up to promote a future line of action that would consolidate and validate the group.

The Statutes of the Royal College of Physicians were initiated in 1520 and by 1561, John Caius had ensured that the *Annals* of the group were available (*center*). The Statutes were also published by John Badger in 1693 (*top right*), after he had successfully undertaken the required examination but was nevertheless denied admission. His aim was to publicize the injustice and culminated in an appeal to Parliament to remedy the matter. The golden mace (*foreground*), which recapitulates the design of the Speaker's mace of the House of Commons, was presented to the College by John Lawson, a noted Arabic scholar, in 1693. In 1694, he was elected President! It was designed by the goldsmith Anthony Nelme in accordance with the injunction of Parliament in 1649 that all maces "bee made according to the same forme and patterne".

Fortunately, the times were propitious for such an endeavor, since Charles II had diverse interests, including the possession of a "*chymist*" laboratory and an operator in his palace, while it was rumored that he frequently visited the laboratories of his friends and discussed scientific matters. As a result, early in December 1660, the journal-book of the new Society records that Sir Robert Moray, who had been with Charles during his exile and exerted much influence in Court circles, had brought word from the Court that the King had been acquainted with the design of the members and "he did well approve of it, and would be ready to give encouragement to it". The Society then proceeded to elect Moray President for a month (he was thereafter re-elected) and to limit its membership to 55, and to draw up certain rules regarding elections, officers, and servants.

In addition to Moray, another important member of the infant Society was the diarist John Evelyn, who not only exerted considerable influence at Court, but also had devoted substantial thought to the question of a suitable name for the Society. In November 1661, when Evelyn published his translation of a work by Gabriel Naudé, his dedication to the Earl of Clarendon praised that nobleman for his services "in the promoting and encouraging of the Royal Society". Evelyn had had frequent conversations with the King, and although the name of the Society he proposed may have been suggested by Charles himself, it was certainly approved by him. As a result of this suave diplomacy and flattery, the name was therefore adopted and Charles "was pleased to offer of him selfe to bee enter'd one of the Society".

The diarist John Evelyn (1620–1706) (*bottom left*), apart from writing extensively about medicine and the "Royal Touch," also collected medical material such as the set of four "anatomical tables" – pine boards with dried preparations of the veins, arteries, and nerves of the human body – which had been prepared in Padua in the 1640s and brought back to England by him (*background*). The Restoration of Charles II in 1660 brought Evelyn a long wished-for opportunity to engage in public affairs and he became a founding member of the Royal Society. Although sought by the King for his company and commissioned by him to write, Evelyn never found "the fruitless, vicious and empty conversations" of the Restoration Court congenial. Given his sense of duty, practical knowledge, and sheer capacity for hard work, he was at his best on public commissions and won himself great credit by his indefatigable labors among the prisoners of war and sick and wounded seamen during the Second Dutch War while the country was stricken with the plague.

Given the active support of the King, the matter progressed apace and the Charter of Incorporation passed the Great Seal on July 15, 1662, which thus became the date of foundation of the Royal Society. Charles presented a magnificent mace to the body and this object is still constantly used at every meeting of the Council and of the Society. In the original Charter, the King was described as founder and patron of the Society, but within a few years, two further Charters were granted and Charles further assisted the Society financially by giving it the grant of Chelsea College, which he later repurchased from the Fellows.

Although Charles was the most munificent of its benefactors, the Royal Society has had other royal benefactors, and in 1768, George III financed the Society's expedition to observe the transit of Venus. In 1825, George IV founded two Royal medals, and the grant to provide these has been continued subsequently by succeeding monarchs.

INFECTIOUS DISEASES AND PUBLIC HEALTH

The development of public health measures has been assisted in various ways by the interest of royalty, and indeed, many public health measures can be traced back to the wise reform of the Poor Law by Elizabeth I. A similar important piece of legislation was framed to control the unregulated growth of towns when on July 7, 1580, Elizabeth signed at Nonesuch, near Epsom, a royal proclamation which was designed to check the growth of London beyond the boundaries of the City. This edict was designed to prevent the influx of "landless men" to these areas, and to limit the overcrowding, which was developing in small rooms. Although this could be construed as a potentially wise public health policy maneuver, it also ensured that the cheap labor force of the English country estates did not migrate to the better opportunities available in the cities!

An important measure for the prevention of infectious diseases imported from abroad was the introduction of a quarantine concept that had been developed in Venice, which had been a pioneer in the prevention of plague, which was commonly introduced from the Levant. Indeed, by the end of the 15th century, Venice's sanitary service was imposing in its efficiency, although other areas such as Milan and Marseilles had also practiced quarantine with good results. In England, the practice remained for several generations solely a matter for the Court and was essentially designed to prevent the sovereign from being infected by ambassadors from countries in which plague was rampant. For example, in 1513, when London was afflicted with plague, the Venetian ambassador was excluded from the Court for 40 days whenever a case of plague had occurred in his household. The well-known measures for preventing the spread of plague in London by marking and shutting up infected houses were supposed to have been devised by Henry VIII himself, and were further developed during later plagues, culminating in the plague of 1665.

Even more stringent measures were sometimes adopted by the sovereign to punish those who were supposed to have carried plague. Thus Elizabeth I, who possessed little tolerance, had a gibbet set up at Windsor on which to hang anyone who had carried the plague or who had harbored infected or suspected persons. Charles I also had installed a gibbet at the gate of the Court at Woodstock for a similar purpose.

There is in all the post-Renaissance period perhaps no parallel for the great interest that Edward VII took in the welfare of the tuberculous. Prescient and thoughtful, it is recorded that when he noted at a congress that the emphasis had been laid on preventability of the disease, he asked the simple question: "If preventable, then why not prevented?" In this respect, he foresaw the ever-increasing vigilance that would be necessary to control the spread of tuberculosis.

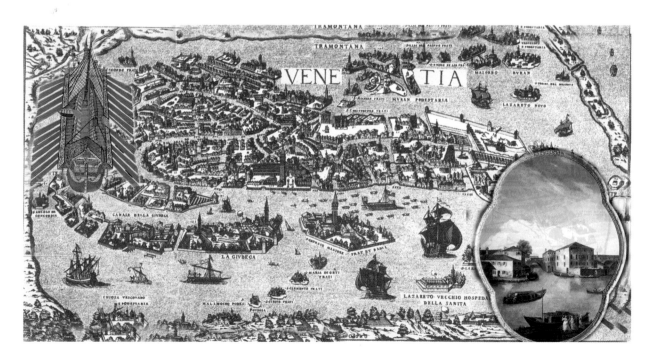

During the 500 years of plague that assaulted Europe, the most oft used method of infection control was isolation. Venice took the lead in measures to check the spread of plague, having appointed three guardians of the public health in the first years of the Black Death (1348). Although patients were quarantined on a number of small islands in the lagoon, this policy did not completely suffice, as the inhabitants of the city never identified that the plague was carried by mercantile traffic and hence the avarice of commerce led to devastating outbreaks of disease. The term "quarantine" derives from the French "quarantaine" meaning a period of 40 days, originally applied to the old sanitary preventive system of detention of ships and men – unloading of cargo in lazarettos and fumigation of susceptible articles – which was practiced at seaports on account of the plague connection with Levantine sea trade.

THE ROYAL TOUCH

'Charles II touching for the King's Evil' – a line engraving by R White – was prefixed to John Browne's *Adeno-choiradelogia* of 1684. The practice of the Royal Healing seems to have reached the height of its popularity during the reign of Charles (*inset*), who is stated on good authority to have during his reign "touched" over 100,000 "strumous" persons. Despite a serious interest in science, Charles' judgment in respect of his own persona as a medical force seems to have been almost delusionary in its intensity.

The fad reached its acme in the reign of Charles II, who touched over 90,000 persons during a 19-year period and is known to have touched as many as 600 men in a single day. The two eminent diarists, Samuel Pepys and Evelyn, described the elaborate religious ceremony when Charles was touching and noted that it was so popular that on one occasion, six or seven patients were crushed to death. James II continued the practice, but William III subsequently refused to participate, although Queen Anne provided the arcane ritual with its last lease of life, since she believed her participation would serve as a means of demonstrating her hereditary right to the throne. Nevertheless, she did not attain the volume achieved by Charles, although in 1712, she is recorded to have touched 200 persons at St James's Palace. It is recorded that one of these was a child aged 30 months who would subsequently become the lexicographer Samuel Johnson. Although Anne may have claimed to cure many patients, she certainly did not succeed in helping the young Johnson, who bore until his death the disfigurement which resulted from scrofula. By the time George I acceded to the throne, the practice of touching had finally disappeared, and such was his disdain for the procedure that he publicly referred any applicants for such ministrations to the exiled Stuarts.

The "King's Evil" was an old, but not yet obsolete, name attached to scrofula, which in the popular estimation was deemed capable of cure by the Royal Touch. The practice of "touching" for the scrofula, or King's Evil, was confined amongst the nations of Europe to the two Royal Houses of England and France. In this depiction, Queen Anne is seen touching the young Samuel Johnson (*right*). Johnson (1709–1784) went on to become one of England's greatest literary figures, but even his death mask demonstrates for posterity the failure of the Queen to erase "the claws of the pox".

The practice of the Royal Touch was exercised by most of the sovereigns of England for over 600 years and reflected the widespread belief that the gift of healing by touching with the hands was supposed to be conferred on the sovereign at his Coronation. The disease treated was nearly always tuberculous cervical adenitis-scrofula, or "the King's Evil" – although other conditions such as blindness were also dealt with in early times. In England, the practice dates from 1066, when Edward the Confessor was reported to have "cured" an affected girl. From the time of Edward I, the practice increased, and it was formalized in a religious ceremony by Henry VII, who altered it such that instead of a providing a dole of one penny to each patient, each was provided with a gold "angel" which was hung round the neck. Elizabeth I regarded her healing duties as a serious responsibility, but James I, who was skeptical regarding the efficacy of the method, had to be persuaded that for political reasons, it was advisable to continue it.

Thomas Guy (1644–1724) (*left*) began his career in 1668 as a bookseller and became immensely wealthy by printing Bibles. He is best remembered for his philanthropic support of public hospitals, building and furnishing three wards of St Thomas' Hospital in 1722. A generous endowment (*center right*) in 1721 resulted in the establishment of Guy's Hospital (*background*) in London.

G uy's Hospital was founded by Thomas Guy, a citizen of London, who made a fortune in the publishing business and in speculation on the stock market. The hospital was built during the last year of his life and was opened on January 6, 1725, 10 days after his death. Although during the first century of its existence it had on its staff a succession of excellent physicians and surgeons, it produced no particularly outstanding figures. However, the beginning of the 19th century was marked by the presence of four remarkable individuals who joined the staff – Richard Bright, Thomas Addison, Thomas Hodgkin, and Sir Astley Paston Cooper. Their contributions to medical science raised Guy's Hospital in London to an eminence equal to that attained by Meath Hospital of Dublin through the work of Robert James Graves and William Stokes. All four men were much like their counterparts at Meath – investigators and teachers and active in establishing and directing a medical school in the hospital to which they had dedicated their professional lives.

Richard Bright (1789–1858)

Richard Bright was the son of a wealthy banker of Bristol, who had spared nothing in providing his son with an excellent education and opportunity to travel. He entered Edinburgh University in 1808, and after studying mathematics, botany, and zoology, entered the medical school, then presided over by Alexander Monro *tertius*. In 1810, after a trip to Iceland where he studied the flora and fauna of the island, he moved to London and served two years as a resident officer in Guy's Hospital, before returning to Edinburgh in 1812, where he took his degree in 1813. The relatively brief dalliance was, as George Thomas Bettany remarked, "a foretaste of the forty years' residence which he practically made within its walls". The following year he went to the Continent, became fluent in French and German, and, in 1815, traveled extensively in Hungary, which was at that stage "*terra incognita*" to most British persons. On his return, he wrote an interesting account of his trip, *Travels from Vienna through Lower Hungary*, which was published at Edinburgh in 1818. The book was an excellent account of the social and economic conditions in Hungary, and was illustrated with numerous full-page sketches by Bright himself, who was an accomplished artist. In these early illustrations, one may note the artistic talent of Bright that enabled him to see clearly and to draw accurately. Such skills would subsequently prove of inestimable value to him in his study of pathological anatomy.

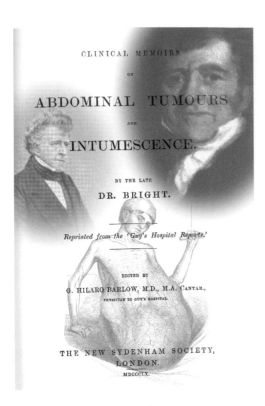

Richard Bright (1789–1858) was the leading medical consultant in London and the most famous of the "great men of Guy's". Although Bright advanced no new theories of disease and did little original classification in pathology, he collected and recorded an extraordinary amount of data from which he was able to draw his conclusions and to base his assumptions. The list of original descriptions attributed to Bright includes those for pancreatic diabetes, unilateral convulsions, laryngeal phthisis, condensation of the lung in whooping cough, and glomerulonephritis (Bright's disease). His interest in the abdomen resulted in the publication of *Clinical Memoirs on Abdominal Tumors and Intumescence* and a graphic description and demonstration of hydatid disease (*bottom*).

In 1820, Bright was appointed Assistant Physician to Guy's Hospital and returned to London, where he resided in Bloomsbury Square in a house that he used as a base for his private practice. For many years, he spent six hours a day in the hospital, studying the patients in the wards and their pathology in the postmortem room. He was a handsome man, possessed of a remarkably even and cheerful disposition, and these qualities, combined with his industry and intelligence, presently attracted a large following. In later years, when his large practice absorbed most of his time, he looked back with nostalgia on the time when he could spend most of his time in the hospital.

Bright's *Reports of Medical Cases*, which was printed at London in 1827, established his fame among his contemporaries and for posterity. In this work, he pointed out the association between diseased kidneys, dropsy, and "albuminous" urine and clearly defined the disease since known by his name. The work was illustrated by striking illustrations in color, and as Bright noted, the "drawings and engravings were executed under my own immediate superintendence". Others before him had noted that, in some cases of dropsy, the urine was scanty and contained albumen, and that certain of these patients showed small, hardened kidneys. Yet, no one prior to him had stressed the association of albuminous urine, sclerosis of the kidneys, and dropsy and grouped them together as a clinical entity, or pointed out the frequency of this syndrome. In addition to recognizing the renal pathology, Bright also noted the frequent association of cardiac hypertrophy in this condition and the increase of urea in the blood.

Besides his *Reports of Medical Cases*, Bright wrote numerous articles – on pancreatic diabetes, acute yellow atrophy of the liver, unilateral convulsions, and "status lymphaticus". The second volume of the *Reports of*

Medical Cases, published in 1831, contains accurate accounts of acute otitis, laryngeal phthisis, cerebral hemorrhage, paralysis, and tetanus, with striking plates of the pathological lesions in typhoid fever, nephritis, acute yellow atrophy, and cerebral lesions. Although Bright was clearly not a great theoretical thinker, he possessed astonishingly good powers of observation, as he literally produced pictures that were as good as photographs of disease for the study of posterity.

During his lifetime, Bright was better known abroad than any British physician of modern times. He died in 1858 at the age of 69, and the postmortem examination revealed an extreme aortic stenosis but normal kidneys, thus refuting the old saw that "he died of his own disease".

Thomas Addison (1793–1860)

Although Thomas Addison was a colleague of Bright at Guy's, he was a man of very different background and temperament, having been born in far less comfortable circumstances near Newcastle in 1793. As a result, he had not enjoyed the advantage of extensive travel, and his personality was unlike the sunny, genial, likeable Bright, being taciturn, unapproachable, and often gruff, hiding an innate shyness under the cloak of gruffness. Addison was initially schooled in Newcastle, becoming such an excellent Latin student that, on transferring to Edinburgh to study medicine, he inscribed his lecture notes in Latin. After receiving a degree in 1815, he began a practice in London and joined Guy's in 1820 for further study. His brilliance soon attracted the attention of the authorities and, in 1824, he was appointed Assistant Physician, later becoming Physician and serving on the staff for 36 years.

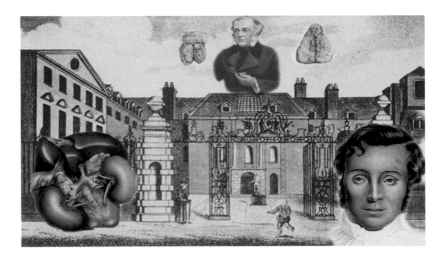

Thomas Addison (1793–1860) (*top and bottom right*) was a brilliant lecturer in pathology and a clinical diagnostician of inimitable skill. Unfortunately, he was possessed of a haughty and almost repellent manner that somewhat diminished his popularity. Sir Samuel Wilks (1824–1911) noted: "The personal power which he possessed was the secret of his position, much superior to what Bright could ever claim, and equal, if not greater, than that of Sir Astley Cooper. In 1849 he described pernicious anemia (20 years before Biermer) as well as a disease of the super renal capsules (melasma suprarenale). The latter publication is now recognized as of epoch making importance since in connection with the physiological work of Claude Bernard it inaugurated the study of the diseases of the 'ductless glands'. A Trousseau of Paris was the first to propose that the suprarenal syndrome be called Addison's disease."

Addison's fame rests chiefly on his description of what he termed "melasma suprarenale" – bronzed skin associated with disease of the suprarenal glands, a syndrome since known as Addison's disease. A brief report of this first appeared in the *Medical Gazette* of March 15, 1849, and was later expanded in his monograph *On the Constitutional and Local Effects of Disease of the Supra-renal Capsules* (London, 1855). This monograph contained some excellent plates of the condition and also described "idiopathic anemia," since known as pernicious anemia or Addisonian anemia. In 1850, Addison published a paper in *Guy's Hospital Reports*, in which he described for the first time "*xanthoma diabeticorum*".

During his lifetime, Addison's reputation did not rest alone upon his discoveries, since his description of suprarenal disease was regarded simply as a curiosity; it also rested upon his skill as a physician and upon his remarkable ability as a teacher. His painstaking examinations and his uncanny diagnoses became a legend, and he was described by a critic as: "A fine, dashing, big, burly, bustling man, proud and pompous as a parish beadle in his robes of office… Every sentence is polished, is powerful; he prefers the grandiloquent. Slow and studied are his opening sentences, studied the regularity of his intonations." Such was his presence and intellectual power that students, although they worshipped him, feared him rather than loved him.

The personal power that he possessed was the essential key to his position and was far superior to that which Bright could ever claim, and equal to, if not greater than, that of the legendary Cooper. As a consequence, Addison was for many years regarded as the leading light of Guy's, so that every Guy's man during the 30 or 40 years of his teaching was a disciple of Addison. Both Sir Samuel Wilks and Bettany recorded that all held "his name in the greatest reverence and regard his authority as the best guide in the practice of the profession".

Thomas Hodgkin (1798–1866)

Thomas Hodgkin, a gentle Quaker born in Tottenham, was another notable member of Guy's group, and, like Bright and Addison, a graduate of Edinburgh, where he took his medical degree in 1823. On his return to London, he became interested in the formation of a medical school at Guy's Hospital and was appointed Curator of the Museum and Demonstrator of Morbid Anatomy. In this capacity, he undertook an enormous amount of work, collecting and assembling specimens as well as making an extensive catalogue, which subsequently formed the basis of his text, *Lectures on the Morbid Anatomy of the Serous and Mucous Membranes* (London, 1836). After serving for 10 years as Lecturer on Pathology, he resigned after his unsuccessful candidature for the post of Assistant Physician, but continued to practice in London. However, being generous by nature and careless in collecting fees, he soon abandoned practice and devoted himself to philanthropy. Assuming the post of personal Physician to Sir Moses Montefiore, he traveled with him extensively in the Orient, where he died at Jaffa in 1866.

The Quaker Thomas Hodgkin (1798–1866) was the most prominent British pathologist of his time and a pioneer in preventive medicine. Such was his skill that there exist four associated eponyms: Hodgkin's disease; Hodgkin's paragranuloma; Hodgkin's sarcoma – a more invasive form of Hodgkin's disease; and the Hodgkin-Key sound – an auscultation phenomenon typical of aorta insufficiency. Despite his unique skills, Benjamin Babington was appointed over him (Babington's sister was Richard Bright's wife!) at Guy's Hospital and Hodgkin resigned and moved to St Thomas' Hospital. As a result of the professional difficulties at Guy's Hospital, and possessed by strong personal religious convictions, he gradually focused more on ethnography and became an Oriental traveller and personal Physician to Sir Moses Montefiore (1784–1885). While traveling in Judea and Samaria, he died and was interred in the Protestant cemetery at Jaffa (Haifa).

Hodgkin's notable work was in the field of pathology. In his *Lectures*, it is apparent that he was one of the first physicians to clearly describe acute appendicitis, and in 1827, he wrote an account of aortic insufficiency with an excellent pathological description, three years before the appearance of Corrigan's classic paper on the subject. In 1832, he published in the *Medical Chirurgical Transactions* an account of the disease since known as Hodgkin's disease, describing seven cases. However, years later, a re-evaluation of the material with the aid of the microscope, which Hodgkin had not employed, demonstrated that only three of these cases were actually Hodgkin's disease.

Sir Astley Paston Cooper (1768–1841)

No account of Guy's Hospital at this period is complete without the name of Sir Astley Paston Cooper, probably the best-known surgeon of his time. Cooper was born in Brooke, near Norwich, in 1768, the son of a clergyman and grandson of a surgeon, and studied at Edinburgh before returning to London, where he studied under John Hunter. In 1789, he was appointed Demonstrator in Anatomy at St Thomas' Hospital and, in 1800, Surgeon to Guy's Hospital, where he remained for the rest of his life. One of his pupils at that time, Benjamin Travers, describing him as the handsomest, most intelligent-looking, and finely formed man he ever saw. Cooper was already at the height of his fame when young Bright first joined the staff.

The bust of Sir Astley Paston Cooper (1768–1841) at Guy's Hospital. Cooper was the doyen of British surgery during the early 19th century, and apart from his sartorial elegance, was recognized as an individual of quixotic intellectual genius. A pupil of John Hunter, he made great strides in surgical technique, most notably in the area of vessel ligation. As a teacher, he stressed practical demonstrations over didacticism and gained the respect and admiration of his students. A Professor of Comparative Anatomy at the Royal College of Surgeons, he was made a Baronet after successfully removing a sebaceous cyst from the scalp of George IV in 1821. In 1828, he became Sergeant-Surgeon to the King, a dignity he retained with the successor, William IV. He is quoted as saying: "If you are too fond of new remedies, first you will not cure your patients; secondly, you will have no patients to cure!"

Sir Astley Paston Cooper (*top right*), using a gastric exhauster (*top left*) that had been developed by F Bush, was able to provide William Prout (1785–1850) (*center*), of Guy's Hospital, with gastric contents. This allowed the latter to generate the first description (1823) of the presence of hydrochloric acid in human gastric juice.

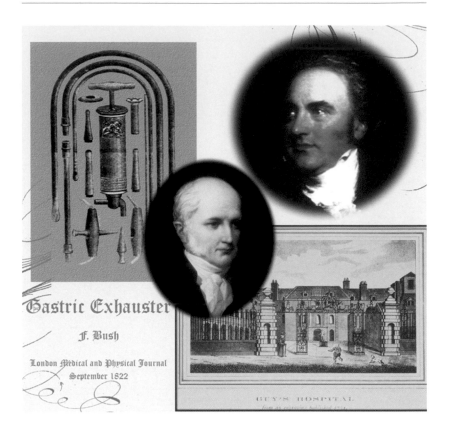

Cooper came into possession of a fortune by marriage and was able to devote himself to study and teaching. So great was his passion for anatomy that he went to the hospital even before breakfast to dissect, and it is said that he dissected every day of his life, even when traveling. Unfortunately, his passion for dissection threw him in close touch with body snatchers or "resurrectionists" so that he became one of their main supporters. Given his wealth, he had no hesitation in spending hundreds of pounds for bodies, and when resurrectionists were caught and imprisoned, he often advanced considerable amounts of money to defend them in court and, if they were convicted, to support them and their families during their imprisonment. This truly bizarre state of affairs reflected the archaic laws of the time, which made it almost impossible to legally obtain a body for dissection.

It is said that few men have worked so hard or so incessantly as Cooper. He rose at six, dissected until eight, breakfasted on two rolls and a cup of tea, saw poor patients until nine, saw private patients or operated until one, then drove to Guy's Hospital and made rounds, and lectured at St Thomas' Hospital at two. Thereafter, he worked in the dissection room for an hour or more, saw his private patients or operated until seven, and then dined and slept briefly before setting out again to either lecture or visit patients until midnight. In addition to this grueling schedule, it should be noted that as he drove from place to place in his carriage, every spare moment was occupied in dictating to one of his assistants.

Cooper was one of the best operators of the day. A close colleague, Mr Chandler, noted: "It is of no consequence what instrument Mr Cooper uses, they are all alike to him, and I verily believe he could operate as easily with an oyster-knife as the best bit of cutlery in Laundy's shop." In 1808, Cooper successfully ligated the common carotid and the external iliac arteries for aneurysms and, in 1817, even the abdominal aorta. A successful operation for a small tumor on the head of George IV was rewarded with a baronetcy. Cooper's books on *Hernia* (1804), *Injuries of the joints* (1822), *Diseases of the Breast* (1829), *Diseases of the Testes* (1830), and *The Anatomy of the Thymus Gland* (1832) were widely regarded as among the authoritative texts of his time. His dissecting and anatomical skills were such that Cooper's fascia (the fascia transversalis) and Cooper's hernia (retroperitoneal hernia) are terms still employed in surgical nomenclature. When he died in 1841, Bettany noted with admirable sincerity and indisputable veracity: "No surgeon, before or since, has filled so large a space in the public eye."

Bowel obstruction due to a hernia is shown. Therapeutic nihilism characterized the management of intestinal obstruction prior to the late 19th century. The condition was uniformly considered to be fatal and treatment focused on the use of opiates, mercury, and terminal expectancy. The repair of strangulated hernias, although undertaken, was associated with major morbidity and mortality due to peritonitis, gangrene, and sepsis. Physicians were thus hesitant to allow surgeons to operate and ignored commentary by luminaries such as Robert Lawson Tait (1845–1899), who complained bitterly to his medical and surgical colleagues: "Is it not better to perform exploration before rather than after death?"

Although science and medicine were advancing in Europe at a considerable pace, there was a not dissimilar amplification in Britain, where outstanding scientists in the fields of chemistry and physics were complemented by a group of distinguished physicians and surgeons. Indeed, the amalgam of these different fields of endeavor would prove vital to the overall advance of medicine.

Sir Humphry Davy (1778–1829) and Michael Faraday (1791–1867)

The son of a poor wood carver, Sir Humphry Davy was early in life apprenticed to a surgeon-apothecary. At the age of 19, he obtained a position at the Medical Pneumatic Institution of Bristol that had been established by Dr Thomas Beddoes to investigate the medicinal properties of various gases. Within a year of his appointment, Davy had discovered that nitrous oxide was safely respirable and would produce great exhilaration. This discovery brought much attention to the young man, with the result that when Benjamin Thompson, Count Rumford, established the Royal Institution, Davy was selected as Lecturer on Chemistry. A few years later, a young man named Michael Faraday, who had originally been apprenticed to a book binder, where he read the scientific books his master bound, enrolled in Davy's class in chemistry, subsequently becoming Davy's assistant and, on the death of Davy, Professor of Chemistry.

The elucidation of scientific problems related to the elucidation of the chemical properties of gases had been considerably facilitated by the work of a number of scientists, including Robert Boyle (1627–1691) and Antoine Laurent Lavoisier (1743–1794). Of particular relevance to anesthesia was the work of Sir Humphry Davy (1778–1829) (*center*), who described the effects of nitrous oxide, and Joseph Priestley (1733–1804) (*bottom left*), who discovered oxygen.

MACFARLAN'S CHLOROFORM and ETHER (KEITH'S)

Clinical experience demonstrates that, for the induction of anesthesia with certainty, safety, and freedom from post operation nausea, Macfarlan's Anæsthetics are any others on the market ever their source of

OUR PRODUCTS
SOLD AT LESS
ONE-THIRD
COST OF
MADE FROM
ETHYLIC ALCOHOL

109, EDINBURGH

32, Bethnal Green Road
LONDON, E.1

Works : Abbeyhill and Northfield, Edinburgh

Davy's studies with gases led in 1816 to the development of the Davy safety lamp, which consisted of an oil lamp covered with wire gauze that absorbed the heat of the flames so that it did not cause an explosion when brought into contact with an inflammable gas. This type of lamp has since been extensively employed in coal mines.

Lenard once remarked: "If Count Rumford's establishment, the Royal Institution had no other result than to provide a working place for Davy and Faraday, this would have brilliantly justified for all time the establishment of the institute." Davy's investigations were mainly in the field of electrochemistry and gases, and in his text, *Researches, Chemical and Philosophical, chiefly concerning Nitrous Oxide*, published in 1799, he described not only the exhilarating effect of the gas but also its anesthetic properties, and suggested its use in surgical operations. Davy, in collaboration with Faraday, also made fundamental investigations on the liquefaction of gases, and in 1831, Faraday gained scientific immortality through his discovery of electromagnetic induction and by the invention of the induction coil. This advance thereafter became immortalized by the adoption of the term "faradic" when referring to an induced current.

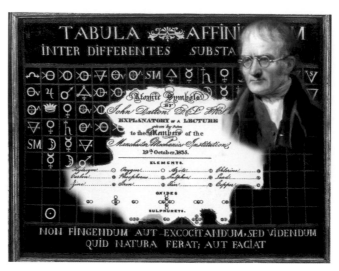

John Dalton (1766–1844) (*top right*) was one of the undisputed leaders in chemical and atomic theory at the turn of the 19th century and developed the atomic theory upon which modern physical science is founded. His most important contribution was the proposal that matter was composed of atoms of differing weights, which combined in simple ratios by weight. This theory was first advanced by Dalton in 1803 (*center*) and has since become a keystone in the evolution of modern physical science. In 1808, Dalton published his text, *A New System of Chemical Philosophy*, which listed the atomic weights of a number of known elements relative to the weight of hydrogen. Although the weights were not entirely accurate, they formed the basis for the establishment of the modern periodic table of the elements.

In 1831, Michael Faraday (*top and bottom left*) elucidated the relationship between electrical and magnetic forces. His work moved beyond the electrostatic production of electricity (*top right and center*) and led to the identification of the principle of electromagnetic induction and the construction of induction coils and transformers (*center*) adequate to produce electrical currents of high voltage.

Among the eminent men of science was also Sir Richard Owen, who studied medicine first at Edinburgh and then at St Bartholomew's Hospital, London, where he came under the influence of John Abernethy, the eminent surgeon. Although Owen originally planned on becoming a surgeon, he finally chose to accept an appointment as Assistant Curator of the Museum of the Royal College of Surgeons, where he spent several years cataloging and studying the Hunterian Collection and in so doing, acquired an unrivaled knowledge of comparative anatomy. He became subsequently Professor at the Royal College, Conservator of the Museum, and, in 1856, Superintendent of the Natural History Department of the British Museum. Owen produced many papers on comparative anatomy, on fossils, on mammals, and on prehistoric animals, and subsequently was regarded as one of the founders of modern comparative anatomy.

Although the thyroid gland has been recognized since earliest times, the parathyroid glands were reputedly the last macroscopic mammalian organs ever described. The observation was initially made in 1850 by Sir Richard Owen (1804–1892) (*inset, top left*) during a postmortem on an Indian rhinoceros which died in the Regent's Park Zoo, London. The specimen of the larynx (*top center*) resides to this day in the Hunterian Museum of the Royal College of Surgeons of England. The rhinoceros (depicted by Albrecht Durer [1471–1528]) achieved almost mythical status during the Middle Ages, as sailors returned from Africa and India with tales of a fabulous beast that was assumed to be the unicorn, given the description of the central horn. That the parathyroid and the rhinoceros should become associated for posterity remains one of the strange quirks of biology and science.

John Dalton (1766–1844) and Sir Richard Owen (1804–1892)

John Dalton, the son of a poor farmer, was himself a farm laborer and then a schoolteacher before undertaking the investigations that led to his fundamental studies on the properties of gases. He also described color blindness and made important contributions to the atomic theory, working out a table of atomic weights. His great merits won increasing appreciation so that, at the time of his death, Dalton, whose formal schooling had ceased at the age of 11, was a DCL of Oxford, an LLD of Edinburgh, a Fellow of the Royal Society, and a member of the Royal Academies of Science of Paris, Berlin, and Munich.

Charles Darwin (1809–1882)

In 1859, Charles Darwin published his seminal text, *On the Origin of Species by Means of Natural Selection*, and in so doing, unleashed one of the great controversies of modern time. Indeed, few books in the history of science have had more influence upon biology, philosophy, religion, and sociology and achieved greater international prominence. Darwin, who was born in Shrewsbury in 1809, the son of a doctor and the grandson of Dr Erasmus Darwin, was a "truant" from both medicine and theology, having studied medicine at Edinburgh and theology at Cambridge. From 1831 to 1836, he served on the brig *HMS Beagle* as a naturalist with a surveying expedition to several Atlantic islands, the coast of South America, and islands in the Pacific and Indian Oceans. During this prolonged voyage, he studied many animals, some still numerous and others recently extinct, and in so doing, established the scientific basis that would fuel his life work. Having read Thomas Malthus' *Essay on Population* in 1838, he became impressed by the concept of life as a struggle for existence, and it occurred to him "that, under these circumstances, favorable variations would tend to be preserved whereas unfavorable ones might be destroyed or lost". He concluded that if such a hypothesis were tenable, such events would culminate in the formation of "new species". Driven by an unshakeable conviction that his hypothesis was correct, Darwin worked constantly on this new theory, collecting data and analyzing it, before finally publishing an essay on the subject. In 1844, he wrote this to his friend, Sir Joseph Hooker, the botanist: "I am almost convinced (quite contrary to the opinion I started with) that species are not (it is like confessing a murder) immutable."

Thereafter, Darwin began a draft of his book and had completed about half when he received from Alfred Russel Wallace an essay, which had been sent to him for his opinion. On reading Wallace's essay, he was startled to find in it a complete summary of his own theory of natural selection. He placed the essay in the hands of Sir Charles Lyell, the geologist, and of Hooker, the botanist, who sent it together with an abstract of Darwin's work to the Linnean Society, which published both together in 1858. Darwin then completed his own work, *On the Origin of Species by Means of Natural Selection*, which was published on November 14, 1859, the entire edition of 1,250 copies being sold out the day of publication. Although the circumstances of the publication after the communication from Wallace led to a controversy regarding their respective claims to priority, a careful study of all the circumstances established the rights of Darwin as the creator of the theory of natural selection and evolution. Darwin's *Origin of Species* demolished, once and for all, the Linnean concept of the fixity of species as well as the various attempted explanations of this assumed fixity. Although the idea of evolution had been previously expressed by Aristotle and by other Greeks, suggested by Sir Francis Bacon, Erasmus Darwin, Johann Wolfgang Goethe, and many others, the systematic and lucid marshalling of facts as delineated by Darwin made it a fundamental concept of biological science, much as Nicolaus Copernicus, three centuries earlier, had made his heliocentric theory the fundamental concept of astronomy.

Darwin's *Descent of Man* published in 1871 fulfilled the prediction he had made in his *Origin of Species* that, through his theory, "light would be thrown on the origin of man and his history". This text essentially terminated the ancient notion that the universe was created for man, a theory that had already been somewhat shaky since Galileo had demonstrated the relative insignificance of the earth in comparison to the immensity of the universe itself.

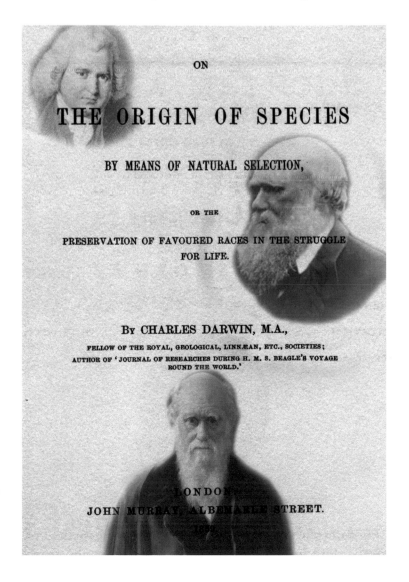

It may be said that the genetic background of Charles Darwin (1809–1882) supported his own theories. His father, Robert Darwin, was a physician and the son of Dr Erasmus Darwin, a poet, philosopher, and naturalist, and a member of the Lunar Society. At 16, Darwin began the study of medicine at Edinburgh University, but repelled by the sight of surgery performed without anesthesia, he departed for Cambridge University to become a clergyman in the Church of England. After receiving his degree, Darwin accepted an invitation to serve as an unpaid naturalist on *HMS Beagle*, which departed on a five-year scientific expedition to the Pacific coast of South America on December 31, 1831. The resulting research formed the basis of his 1859 book, *On the Origin of Species by Means of Natural Selection*. This work, which outlined his theory of evolution, challenged the contemporary beliefs about the creation of life on earth. A subsequent text, *The Descent of Man* (1871), further adumbrated upon his concepts and amplified the theory to the evolution of man from a primitive monkey-like animal. Both books aroused international controversy and many of his scientific contemporaries considered them to be variously offensive, atheistic, and blasphemous, or the product of a feverish and disordered mind. Suffice to say that time has proved Darwin correct and the names of his detractors are for the most part lost in the mists of time, as one might expect based upon the theory of evolution so lucidly propounded. Darwin is thought to have suffered from panic disorder and chronic intestinal problems that have been latterly attributed to Chagas' disease contracted during his travels in South America.

As might have been predicted, the revolutionary concepts of Darwin aroused much bitter opposition among some men of science and particularly among the clergy, many of whom felt that the new theory attacked the fundamental tenets of the Church. Bishop Samuel Wilberforce of the Church of England denounced the *Origin of Species* as "atheistical". Many other Protestant divines followed his example, and even as lofty a personage as Pope Pius IX, in a personal letter, referred to "the aberrations of Darwinism… A system which is repugnant at once to history, to exact science, to observation, and even to reason itself… a tissue of fables". As a result of such violent opposition, Darwin's books were not placed on the Index and the mere mention of his name was itself capable of engendering a major conflagration. Darwin, whose personality was such that he had difficulty with emotional and intellectual tension, declined to be drawn either into controversy or into polemical writing, and lived quietly at Down until his death in 1882 at the age of 74. It is worthy of note that Canon Farrar, one of the noted divines of the Church of England and the famous author of *The Life of Christ*, delivered the funeral sermon on the occasion of his burial in Westminster Abbey.

Thomas Henry Huxley (1825–1895)

While Darwin himself was not fond of controversy, Thomas Henry Huxley thrived on it and devoted much of his energy to a militant championship of the Darwinian hypothesis, on one occasion remarking, "I am Darwin's bulldog". One of the most celebrated occasions of his defense of Darwin was the public debate at Oxford with Bishop Wilberforce, who, after talking for half an hour, turned to his opponent and asked whether it was through his grandfather or grandmother that he claimed his descent from a monkey. Huxley's answer still remains a historical classic of scientific debate and his riposte – that he was not ashamed to have a monkey for his ancestor but would be ashamed to be connected with a man who used his great gifts to obscure the truth – still remains as pertinent now as it was then.

Although Huxley is remembered for his controversies and popular lectures, these were but a small part of his scientific activity. Born in Ealing in 1825, he was the son of an assistant-master in a semi-public school, whom Huxley described as "rather too easy going for this wicked world". His earlier education was rather desultory and Huxley referred to it as "two years of a Pandemonium of a school and after that neither help nor sympathy in any intellectual direction till I reached manhood". During these years, however, he developed a passionate love of reading, particularly scientific books, and at 16, he became assistant to a Dr Chandler, was then apprenticed to his brother-in-law Dr Scott, and thereafter secured a scholarship at the medical school of Charing Cross Hospital, receiving his MB from the University of London in 1845. One year later, he sailed as Assistant Surgeon to *HMS Rattlesnake*, which went out to survey the eastern shores of Australia.

Thomas Henry Huxley (1825–1895) (*right*) was an English biologist and was also one of the strongest of the early proponents of Charles Darwin's theory of natural selection. He was so vociferous in his defense that he earned the nickname "Darwin's bulldog". It was the defeat of the renowned Bishop Samuel Wilberforce during a verbal hors de combat at Oxford that led to the subsequent growth of Darwinian theory in the English establishment. His famous quote during this debate – "I would rather be the offspring of two apes than be a man and afraid to face the truth" – remains one of the great ripostes of the era. The young HG Wells (*left: with a gorilla skeleton*) was a firm adherent to Huxley's viewpoint and a staunch believer in "Darwinism".

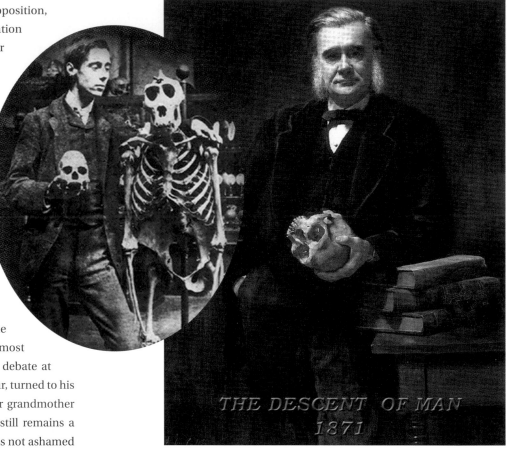

THE DESCENT OF MAN
1871

The voyage of *HMS Rattlesnake* lasted three years and gave Huxley, as the voyage of *HMS Beagle* had previously given Darwin, an opportunity to study a great variety of animal and vegetable life. During the trip, he studied birds, reptiles, mammalia, fish, marine animals and plants, invertebrates, and even geology. His task was especially aided by the use of a microscope that he had brought with him and facilitated his study of both the microscopic appearance as well as the gross appearance of the innumerable specimens. Indeed, so effective were his endeavors that a paper on the *Medusae*, or jellyfish family, sent back to England was published in the *Philosophical Transactions of the Royal Society* and led to his election as a Fellow at the early age of 26.

After his return to England, his fame and reputation grew rapidly, and in 1852, he received the gold medal of the Royal Society, was appointed Professor of Natural History in the Royal School of Mines in 1857, and thereafter selected as Professor of Comparative Anatomy at the Royal Institution. Such was his intellect and skill that in 1862, he was elected Professor of Anatomy at the Royal

College of Surgeons. During this period, he wrote numerous papers and books on comparative anatomy, physiology, biology, and geology, and achieved a wide reputation for his popular lectures on science. Thus, when the *Origin of Species* appeared in 1859, his mind was already well prepared to accept the theory based upon his own extensive observations in similar fields. In fact, Darwin had actually sent an advance copy of the book to Huxley, who knew of the proposed publication but still had some doubts on the validity of the theory. After reading the *Origin of Species*, Huxley informed Darwin that he was "prepared to go to the stake, if requisite" for the doctrine of natural selection and added, "I am sharpening up my claws and beak in readiness for defense of the noble book". Darwin replied: "Like a good Catholic who has received extreme unction, I can now sing '*Nunc dimittis*'." In his *Collected Essays*, Huxley wrote: "It must be admitted that the popularization of science, whether by lectures or by essays has its drawbacks… The 'people who fail' take their revenge by ignoring all the rest of a man's work and glibly labeling him a mere popularizer."

Huxley was also labeled a popularizer by some of his enemies, particularly those that were theological, and was so considered by others unaware of his solid and original contributions to science. His lectures on the origin of the skull in vertebrates, delivered in 1860, demolished the theory that the skull is formed of a series of expanded vertebrae joined together, as had previously been maintained by Owen. His subsequent book, *Manual of the Anatomy of Vertebrated Animals*, published in 1871, passed through 30 editions, and his *Elementary Lessons in Physiology* of 1866 were indubitably masterpieces in their field. The earlier text, *Evidence as to Man's Place in Nature*, published in 1863, written in the charming and lucid style which is characteristic of all his writings, remains one of the best expositions of the ideas of Darwin.

Huxley received an LLD degree from Edinburgh in 1866 and from Cambridge in 1879. In 1833, he was elected President of the Royal Society and in 1885 Oxford, which had seen little of Huxley since his famous duel with Bishop Wilberforce, awarded him a DCL. Huxley was a man of deep convictions, kindly and charitable by nature, and respected alike by friend and foe for his intellectual honesty and uncompromising integrity. From his early youth until his death in 1895 at the age of 70, he believed and taught that "science commits suicide when it adopts a creed".

Sir William Withey Gull (1816–1890)

Thomas Addison, Richard Bright, Thomas Hodgkins, and Sir Astley Paston Cooper, the great men of Guy's Hospital, could not have found a worthier successor than Sir William Withey Gull, a native of Colchester. Gull originally came to London in 1837 at the age of 21, and having obtained a position at Guy's Hospital, became so attached to this institution that he lived within its walls or in adjacent lodgings for the next 15 years. In 1841, he received the degree of MB from London University and, in 1846, that of MD. He taught successively *materia medica*, natural philosophy, physiology, and anatomy at Guy's and, in 1858, became Physician to the Hospital. Gull was elected a Fellow of the Royal Society in 1858 and received the degrees of DCL from Oxford in 1868, LLD from Cambridge in 1880, and LLD from Edinburgh in 1884. In 1871, he attended the Prince of Wales, who was ill of typhoid fever, and, on the recovery of the Prince, he was created a Baronet.

Gull was a brilliant and forceful speaker whose addresses bristled with aphorisms and epigrams. He expressed his own impartial attitude toward medicine by saying: "We have no system to satisfy, no dogmatic opinions to enforce. We have no ignorance to cloak, for we confess it." Gull was in particular a great opponent of the polypharmacy prevalent in his day and remarked: "I do not say no

drugs are useful; but there is not enough discrimination in their use." Based upon his skill and urbane manner, he from very early on developed a large practice and was, without question, the foremost physician of London in his time. At his death in 1890, he left a fortune of 344,000 pounds, a sum previously unprecedented in the history of English medicine.

In addition to being one of the greatest practitioners of his time, Gull was a brilliant and attractive lecturer, who also published a number of excellent papers. As such, he was one of the first to describe the pathological lesions in tabes dorsalis (1856), described intermittent hemoglobinuria (1866), and described, with Henry Gawen Sutton, arteriocapillary fibrosis, since known eponymously, in chronic nephritis. His description of myxedema in 1873 was by far the clearest and best published up to that time.

Sir William Withey Gull (1816–1890) taught or practiced at Guy's Hospital for the majority of his life, where he was a famous and popular teacher, noting that the "road to a clinic goes through the pathological museum and not through the apothecary's shop". In 1872, he was created a Baronet after the successful treatment of the typhoid suffered by the Prince of Wales. As Physician to Queen Victoria and her son, he became wealthier than any English physician before him, although the relationship was somewhat tainted by rumors that the dissections of Jack the Ripper were the work of an unbalanced Royal and a skilled surgeon. Although his description of myxedema (1873) was not the first, he early identified the clinical picture as thyroid-related. Gull noted the involvement of the posterior column in tabes dorsalis (*bottom left*), described intermittent hemoglobinemia (1866), and in 1872, the pathological changes of chronic nephritis. He was one of the pioneers of the use of ricins in the treatment of worm infestation and produced the first description of syringomyelia and steatorrhea due to intestinal lymphoma.

Sir James Paget (1814–1899)

George Thomas Bettany was of the opinion that Sir James Paget was "the foremost surgical philosopher and orator of his day" and towered above his surgical colleagues, as Gull did above his medical colleagues. Paget, like Gull, was brilliant and learned, but he had a great dislike for cleverness and an antipathy towards epigrams and proverbs. "To be brief," he said, "was to be wise; to be epigrammatic was to be clever," and one of his favorite sayings was "as false as most proverbs". His love for brevity was well known and it was said that "he never used two words where one was sufficient".

Sir James Paget (*right*) was among those surgeons who sought to correlate a patient's symptoms with the clinical examination and as such, to develop the concepts of clinical surgery as opposed to purely operative technique. His name is eponymously associated with several conditions, particularly the description in 1876 of five cases of "osteitis deformans" which he believed to be an inflammatory disease process.

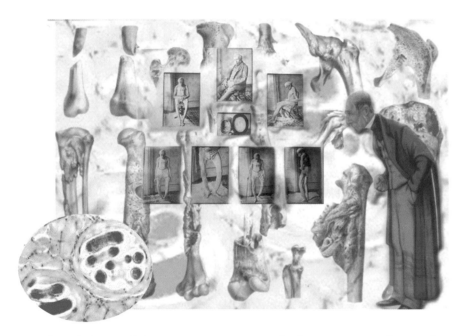

Born in Yarmouth in 1814, Paget was apprenticed to a surgeon at the age of 16 and in 1834, came to London, where he began study at St Bartholomew's Hospital. During his first year's study, he found, while dissecting a subject, some small white specks in the muscles. On examining one of these specks under the microscope, he saw it to consist of a small worm surrounded by a capsule. The specimen was shown to Owen, who named it *Trichina spiralis* and thus to Paget fell the honor as a medical student of being the first to demonstrate trichinosis in man. After passing the examination of the Royal College of Surgeons, he coached pupils, worked as a sub-editor on medical journals, and was appointed Curator of the Pathological Museum in 1837, holding this position for six years. Thereafter, he became a Demonstrator of Morbid Anatomy and later Anatomy until 1847, when he was appointed Professor in the Royal College of Surgeons and, in 1851, elected a Fellow of the Royal Society. In this same year, 15 years after graduation, he began private practice and thus fulfilled the prophecy of Owen, who at the time of his election to the Royal Society had remarked that Paget could be either the first physiologist in Europe or the first surgeon in London whose practice would earn him a baronetcy.

Indeed, Paget's rise in practice was phenomenal but predictable, given his charming persona, dexterous and skillful hands, and learned demeanor gained from 15 years' study in pathology and anatomy. This exceptional combination of talents, both inherited and acquired, enabled him within a few years to earn 10,000 pounds annually. Despite such unmitigated success, Paget never allowed his large practice to dull his scientific interest, and in fact, it seemed to actually increase as his practice grew. Thus his erudition and fortune prospered as his writings became known. Of these, his best known works include *Lectures on Tumors* (1851), *Surgical Pathology* (1863), and *Clinical Lectures and Essays* (1875). His clinical contributions are remembered in the form of two diseases, eczema of the nipple with subsequent mammary carcinoma, which he described in 1874, and the disease of the bones, osteitis deformans, which he first noted in 1876, thereafter describing seven additional cases in 1882. In keeping with Owen's prediction, Paget was created a Baronet in 1871 and appointed Sergeant-Surgeon to Queen Victoria in 1877.

Paget was literally worshipped by his patients and admired and trusted by every member of his profession. He had a great capacity for friendship and apart from his hosts of friends in the English medical life, numbered William Gladstone, Cardinal Newman, John Ruskin, Alfred Lord Tennyson, Robert Browning, George Eliot, John Tyndall, Huxley, Darwin, Rudolf Virchow, and Louis Pasteur among his close friends. He died in 1899 at the age of 85.

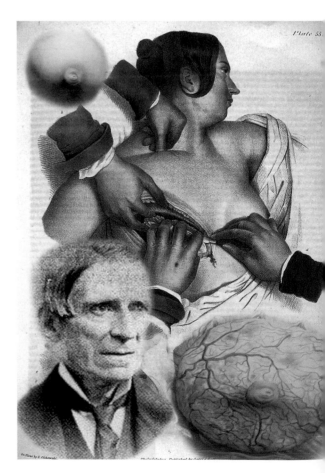

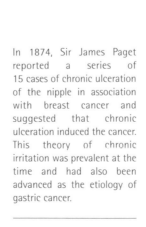

In 1874, Sir James Paget reported a series of 15 cases of chronic ulceration of the nipple in association with breast cancer and suggested that chronic ulceration induced the cancer. This theory of chronic irritation was prevalent at the time and had also been advanced as the etiology of gastric cancer.

Sir James Young Simpson (1811–1870)

Although the bustling metropolis of London seemed to have an especial attraction for young Scotsmen who came down to the City and made their fame and fortune there, such was not the case for Sir James Young Simpson. In this respect, he differed from such leaders of London medicine as William Hunter, John Hunter, Matthew Baillie, Charles Bell, William Smellie, and Robert Liston, all of whom had originated from north of the English border. On the other hand, Simpson, who achieved an international reputation, was born in Scotland, died in Scotland, and lived practically his entire life there.

Born in Bathgate, one of the seven sons of the village baker, at the age of 14, aided by a stipend and financial assistance from an elder brother, he entered Edinburgh University and two years later began the study of medicine, receiving his MD in 1832. Soon after, he was appointed as assistant to John Thompson, Professor of Pathology, as well as becoming an extracurricular teacher of obstetrics. In 1835, he published an article on diseases of the placenta and followed this with noteworthy papers on peritonitis in the fetus (1838), hernia in the fetus (1839), and an exhaustive article on hermaphroditism, which appeared in the *Cyclopedia of Anatomy and Physiology* in 1839. As a result of this productivity and based upon his obvious clinical skills, the following year, at the age of 29, he was elected by a majority of one vote to the post of Professor of Midwifery in the University of Edinburgh.

Simpson took up his new duties with characteristic energy, and his lectures and demonstrations soon achieved widespread popularity, with the consequence that his course on obstetrics rose from the former rank of the dullest course in the curriculum to the most sought after and best attended. As a practitioner, his skill, combined with his charm, tenderness, and sympathetic manner, soon made him the busiest obstetrician in all of Scotland.

ACCOUNT
OF A
NEW ANÆSTHETIC AGENT,
AS A
SUBSTITUTE FOR SULPHURIC ETHER
...
REPUBLISHED BY RUSHTON, CLARK, & CO.,
CHEMISTS AND DRUGGISTS,
110 BROADWAY, AND 10 ASTOR HOUSE.
1848.

Sir James Young Simpson (1811–1870), Professor of Midwifery in the University of Edinburgh, was an early advocate of the use of sulfuric ether to facilitate childbirth. His use of this therapy during the birth of Queen Victoria's child did much to popularize the concept.

William Morton in Boston first administered ether anesthesia on October 16, 1846, and Liston operated under ether anesthesia in London on December 18, 1846. Some months later, on January 19, 1847, Simpson introduced ether into obstetrical practice, but later, because of its disagreeable qualities, particularly its persistent odor and its tendency to cause bronchial irritation, he sought a substitute. This he found in chloroform, the anesthetic properties of which had already been demonstrated by Pierre Flourens, the French physiologist. After some preliminary experiments on himself and on two assistants, Simpson began to use chloroform in obstetrical practice, and on November 10, 1847, he read before the Edinburgh Chirurgical Society a paper describing the employment of chloroform anesthesia in labor.

The Scottish Calvinist clergy opposed Simpson's innovation as unscriptural, since it was written in *Genesis* 111:14: "The Lord God had said to Eve, 'In sorrow thou shalt bring forth children'." However, Simpson was also well versed in Scripture and pointed out that in "the first surgical operation ever performed on man," according to the account in *Genesis*, "the Lord God caused a deep sleep to fall upon Adam; and he slept; and he took one of his ribs, and closed up the flesh instead thereof". For good measure, he pointed out to the Calvinists that John Calvin himself in his *Commentaries* wrote: "It ought to be noted, that Adam was sunk into a profound sleep, in order that he might feel no pain." The controversy continued for several years, but when, in 1853, Queen Victoria received chloroform during the birth of her eighth child, the respectability of chloroform anesthesia in childbirth was assured.

Simpson was created a Baronet in 1866 and the same year, was awarded the degree of LLD by the University of Oxford. In addition to papers on obstetrical subjects, he also made contributions to archeology and to medical history. In 1869, he received the Freedom of the City of Edinburgh, a signal honor not often bestowed.

Such was the much-touted efficacy of anesthetic agents that even Queen Victoria (*center and bottom right*) consented to be anesthetized under the guidance of Sir James Young Simpson for the birth of the Prince of Wales. For years afterwards, it was rumored that the subsequent licentious behavior of the Prince reflected his perinatal exposure to sulfuric ether.

Although the chief claim to fame of Simpson was unquestionably his introduction of chloroform anesthesia in obstetrics, this was not his only achievement. He introduced iron wire sutures, particularly in the operation for vesicovaginal fistula and for hydrocele; the long obstetrical forceps; "acupressure" – the method of arresting hemorrhage by drawing together the edges of the wound with needles inserted into the tissue; and dilatation of the cervix uteri for diagnostic purposes. In addition, he was particularly interested in what he termed "hospitalism" and wrote several papers on this subject. He collected statistics on some 2,000 amputations in hospitals and the same number in country practice, finding that the mortality in these operations was not only much higher in hospitals than in private homes, but that it increased exactly in proportion to the size of the hospital. As a consequence of this observation, he stated: "The man laid on the operating table in one of our surgical hospitals is exposed to more chances of death than the English soldier on the field of Waterloo… Why is this hospitalism so dangerous to the sick?" With undue prescience, he further noted: "There exists, I think, evidence on this question, tending to show that the constitution of the patient in the surgical wards is liable to be endangered sometimes by the influence of morbific contagious materials from the bodies of other inmates."

Despite such remarkable foresight, Simpson, who had embraced the discovery of anesthesia with such enthusiasm, proved to be one of the bitterest opponents of the practice of antisepsis when introduced by Lord Joseph Lister. Indeed, until his death in 1870, he waged an active campaign against what he rather contemptuously called the "carbolic acid treatment". Why Simpson was so opposed to Lister has been a matter for much speculation over many years, although it was thought to reflect the fact that Simpson and Syme, Lister's father-in-law, had been in conflict for years, thus Lister may have inherited some of its aftermath. In addition, it might be that Simpson may have had a certain jealousy towards a new method of treating wounds, which might threaten to supersede the acupressure technique that he had devised. It was remarked by friend and foe alike that although he was a good lover, he was equally a good hater. At his death, it is said that Edinburgh had never witnessed a greater funeral than that of Simpson, a fair tribute to the esteem and love so many had for him. Yet, as Godlee noted: "Few men who could claim so many friends had so many detractors. For the former he was the embodiment of all the virtues; the latter were unable to speak of him with moderation."

ANTISEPSIS AND ASEPSIS

Lister was born in London in 1827, the son of a prosperous Quaker wine merchant. His early education was received in Quaker schools and he became, on the insistence of his father, proficient in French and Latin. At an early stage in his life, he decided to study medicine and, in 1844, entered University College London, a non-sectarian institution, called by some of the most orthodox "the godless college" since students could receive degrees there, in contrast to Oxford and Cambridge, without taking an oath and subscribing to the 39 Articles of the Church of England. Indeed, such was the strength of opinion on this subject, that dissenters from the Established Church were not given degrees from Oxford and Cambridge until 1858.

Lord Joseph Lister (1827–1912) and the microscope that led to his elucidation of the concept of antisepsis. His subsequent introduction of the carbolic spray to operating rooms diminished infection and revolutionized the advance of surgery as much as the development of anesthesia.

In 1847, Lister was graduated Bachelor of Arts and, in 1852, received his MB. As a student, he was much impressed by Thomas Wharton Jones and Edward Sharpey-Shafer, who encouraged him to carry out some investigations, which were published the following year in the *Quarterly Journal of Microscopical Science*. In this first paper, he demonstrated two distinct muscles in the iris – the dilator and the sphincter – which respectively enlarged and diminished the size of the pupil. A second paper described the involuntary muscles of the skin, which elevate the hairs and produce the well-known phenomenon of "goose skin" or horripilation. These papers, which confirmed some previous observations of Rudolf Albert von Kölliker, pleased the celebrated German anatomist and initiated a lifelong friendship between the two.

In 1853, Lister traveled to Edinburgh to visit the clinic of Syme, then considered by many to be the best and most original surgeon in Britain. Impressed by Syme's ability, Lister gladly accepted the post of "Supernumerary Clerk" to him and the following year was appointed resident House Surgeon. The next year, 1855, he applied for and received the position of Lecturer on Surgery at the Royal College of Physicians and Assistant Surgeon to the Royal Infirmary.

Lister continued to assist Syme and developed great respect for his chief, whose skill, judgment, and original mind he constantly praised in his letters home. Such was his appreciation that in addition, he wrote weekly summaries of Syme's lectures to the *Lancet* in 1855. In addition to admiring the father, Lister in 1856 married Syme's daughter Agnes, and thus intensified the personal relationship between pupil and mentor. Lest this be considered opportunism, it should be recognized that at a personal level, this decision was of the utmost seriousness for Lister, since as a Quaker, marriage outside his own persuasion required resignation from membership to the Society of Friends or disownment. Lister resigned from the Society, joined the Episcopal Church, the church of his bride, and ordered his first doorplate to be inscribed "Mr Lister" instead of plain "Joseph Lister" according to Quaker custom. Although his family regretted his action, his father, with characteristic Quaker humility, wrote to his daughter: "I trust we shall be very careful to say nothing in disparagement of those whom we shall probably find on acquaintance to be our superiors."

Lord Joseph Lister (*bottom right*) and the carbolic spray (*left*) which he designed. In the background, an anesthetized patient is shown undergoing treatment of a fracture.

Lister soon became a busy man, taught surgery at the Royal College of Physicians, operated at the Royal Infirmary, and worked in the laboratory, studying particularly inflammation, gangrene, and the coagulation of the blood, and publishing papers on these subjects. In his investigations, he utilized the microscope extensively and illustrated his papers with "camera lucida" drawings. In 1860, at the age of 33, he was appointed Regius Professor of Surgery at the University of Glasgow and, the same year, was elected Fellow of the Royal Society. Lister departed for Glasgow, in the prime of life, full of energy and ambition and intellectually prepared to take full advantage of his opportunities. Although his predecessors in the chair had been doctors with a large general practice, Lister chose to limit his work solely to the practice of surgery.

In Glasgow, he found the same scourges that he had noted in Edinburgh, namely suppuration and gangrene, to haunt the surgical wards. About 1861, he began to teach his classes: "The occurrence of suppuration in a wound under ordinary conditions and its continuance… are determined simply by the influence of decomposition." In particular, he was aware of the fact that simple fractures healed without complications, whereas compound fractures with laceration of

the skin were followed by suppuration and often gangrene and death. He also recognized that inflammation, or even suppuration, was sure to follow any wound made by the surgeon. While this had been true since the beginnings of surgery and even welcomed by some surgeons who spoke of "laudable pus," Lister considered that sepsis was the principal obstacle to any great advance in surgery and that no operation could possibly succeed in the face of this problem. Finally, noting that closed wounds did not suppurate while open ones exposed to the air did, he concluded that suppuration was in some unexplained manner due to contact with the air but that the air alone did not cause suppuration.

In 1865, Lister discussed this problem with Dr Thomas Anderson, Professor of Chemistry, who called his attention to the work of the Frenchman Pasteur on fermentation and putrefaction. This avenue of information provided Lister with the solution to his problem, since he clearly recognized that it was not the air but the germs in the air that produced suppuration. He saw at once that putrefaction was fermentation and that putrefaction could only be avoided by preventing germs from gaining access to wounds. At the Glasgow Royal Infirmary, notorious for the unhealthiness of its wards, he had an unusual opportunity for testing the validity of his theory. His next step was therefore to identify a suitable antiseptic, and, remembering that carbolic acid had been used successfully as an antiseptic in treating the sewage in Carlisle, he chose carbolic acid.

Although Lister employed carbolic acid in the treatment of a compound fracture in March 1865, his first striking success was obtained in May 1866, and is described in a letter to his father. His method was simple – a piece of calico or lint was soaked in crude carbolic acid and then introduced into the wound with forceps, and a piece of lint also soaked in carbolic was placed over the wound, and over this was placed a slightly larger piece of thin block tin or lead to prevent evaporation. After nine months of experience with this method, there had not been a single case of pyemia, erysipelas, or hospital gangrene in Lister's ward, although the other wards of the hospital exhibited their customary high volume of sepsis.

The first papers of Lister describing his method on 11 patients appeared in the *Lancet* between March and July 1867 with the title 'On a New Method of Treating Compound Fractures'. In August of the same year, he read at the annual meeting of the British Medical Association a paper on the same subject, which was

subsequently published. These publications attracted considerable attention, and the news media of the day gave the discovery much publicity. Unfortunately, both the media and Lister were confused between the

A photograph of Lord Joseph Lister (*seated center*) and his surgical colleagues at Edinburgh (circa 1854).

discovery of a novel principle in surgery and the recognition that carbolic acid was an antiseptic. Given its success, it was surprising that the new discovery made little headway and in Glasgow, Edinburgh, London, and Dublin, the senior surgeons opposed the new method. However, on the Continent, it met with better success and in 1867 (the same year that Lister's papers were published), Professor Thiersch of Leipzig introduced the method in his clinic, with the result that over the course of 12 months, hospital gangrene disappeared from his hospital.

In 1869, Lister returned to Edinburgh as Professor of Clinical Surgery, where he remained for nine years. In 1870, his bitter opponent Simpson died, as did Lister's father-in-law Syme, and Lister thereafter by common consent became recognized as the first surgeon in Scotland. During this time, he continued to work on his antiseptic methods, carried out laboratory experiments on putrefaction and fermentation, and began his important studies on ligatures. Noting that infections often came from ligatures, he soaked first silk ligatures and later catgut in carbolic acid before employing them, and found that this method of treatment was successful in the prevention of putrefaction. Such was his concern that microbes might fall upon the wound during an operation that in 1870, he introduced the carbolic spray to purify the atmosphere of the operating field. Although he obstinately clung to this practice for 17 years, he finally admitted that it was probably superfluous.

The science of bacteriology can be credited to Louis Pasteur (1822–1895) (*left*), who was able to demonstrate that the fermentation of wine and the souring of milk were caused by living organisms. His work variously led to the pasteurization of milk, the identification of the root disease of vines, the recognition of silkworm parasites, and the development of vaccines. The clinical application of the observations of Pasteur enabled Lord Joseph Lister (*right*) to develop the concept of antisepsis and helped define the role of microorganisms (*top and bottom center*) in disease.

Despite local opposition in Britain, Lister's ideas were received with great enthusiasm on the Continent. After Thiersch's initial support in 1867, Saxtorph of Copenhagen employed the method in his clinic in 1870 and soon thereafter, Volkmann of Halle introduced the practice in his clinic. Godlee described Volkmann as a brilliant surgeon, a man of great literary and artistic ability, a poet

as well, and a man who "rather welcomed than avoided a conflict". And indeed, Volkmann became Lister's most devoted disciple and, by his addresses and papers, did much to introduce antiseptic surgery throughout Germany. However, other notable figures, including Heinrich Adolf von Bardeleben and Ernst von Bergmann in Berlin, Johannn Nepomuk von Nussbaum in Munich, and Theodore Billroth in Vienna also became active champions of Lister. As a result, when Lister traveled to Germany in 1875, he was welcomed as the surgical hero of the age and his visit transformed into a triumphal tour.

In 1877, after an absence of 25 years, Lister returned to his alma mater as Professor of Clinical Surgery at King's College Hospital, London. Fresh from Edinburgh, where he was an idol of the large classes, who attended his lectures, he found King's College to be a chilling contrast. The students showed little enthusiasm for their new professor and attendance at his classes diminished, since the students soon discovered that, if they aired his views in their examinations, conducted by outside examiners, they were likely to fail. As a result, Godlee reported, "only a few, seldom more than a dozen, came to the lectures, mostly those who had passed in surgery and had no need to think any more about examiners". Despite this surprising reception, Lister occupied the Chair of Surgery at King's College for the following 15 years.

In 1881, the Seventh International Medical Congress met in London, and Virchow, Pasteur, Huxley, and Volkmann delivered the principal addresses. Volkmann, who delivered the address on surgery and was obviously unaware of Lister's reception at King's College, commented, "England may be proud that it was one of her sons whose name is indissolubly bound up with this greatest advance that surgery has ever made". Nevertheless, slowly but surely, the great eminence of Lister was recognized at home as well as abroad, and in 1883, he was created a Baronet while in 1885, he received the Prussian order Pour le Mérite. In 1895, Lister was elected President of the Royal Society and in 1897, elevated to the peerage as Lord Lister. Six years later, in 1903, on the occasion of his coronation, Edward VII instituted a new order, the Order of Merit, appointing Lister as one of its 12 members. Lister died in 1912 and, after an impressive funeral service in Westminster Abbey, was buried at his express wish beside his wife in West Hampstead Cemetery.

During Lister's life, an attempt was made to differentiate sharply between antiseptic surgery and aseptic surgery as advocated by von Bergmann, and thus to minimize the importance of Lister's discovery. Von Bergmann, himself, very graciously repudiated such attempts and remarked: "I have been no heaven-storming pathfinder… I have not placed myself in the rank of a Lister… If I have accomplished anything, it has been in the way of critical repetition and improvement." In the last analysis, it may be said that Lister achieved aseptic surgery by the application of antiseptic methods.

Although the two revolutionary discoveries – anesthesia and antisepsis – that so altered all surgery, including gastrointestinal surgery, were made within the span of 20 years, fate dealt quite differently with the two discoverers. Morton died embittered, discredited by many, and practically penniless, while Lister died a peer of the realm, honored by the world and admired by patients and colleagues alike.

12 THE FOUNDING OF THE GASTROENTEROLOGICAL CLUB

Sir Arthur Hurst (1879–1944) was the first British physician to stimulate interest in the disease and disorders of the alimentary tract, and it was his curiosity, enthusiasm, and the high quality of his original work which laid the foundations for gastroenterology as it exists currently in Britain. As Sir Francis Avery Jones so aptly remarked: "Hitherto the gut had remained invisible, impalpable and except at both ends, inaccessible." Within the lifetime of Hurst, visualization began to be achieved and clinical gastroenterology emerged as a specialty.

Apart from his classic publications, Hurst's weekly clinical meetings at Guy's Hospital attracted a wide audience from home and overseas. As a result of his imagination, dynamic personality, and critical approach, he stimulated increasing interest in the disorders and diseases of the alimentary tract and within the next decade, in every large hospital in the country, one at least of the general physicians began to take a special interest in gastroenterology. In addition, a similar interest had emerged among some surgeons, radiologists, biochemists, and pathologists.

By the time Hurst formed the "Gastroenterological club" in 1937, the basic foundations on which British gastroenterology have since been built had been laid. A selection of his papers, together with a biographical study, were compiled by Thomas Hunt and published in 1977, and each year a specially bound copy is presented to the Sir Arthur Hurst lecturer. During the 1920s and 1930s, Hurst was extremely popular and lectured to medical societies around the country and also at medical conferences in France and America. Thus by the early 1930s, some medical students would be taught at some time by physicians or surgeons who had already acquired a deep interest in gastroenterology. On the whole, however, the majority of medical students still found digestive diseases rather dull and uninteresting, since there were few physical signs and little in the way of diagnostic studies available. Interest was however sharply accelerated after 1934 with the introduction of the semiflexible Wolf-Schindler gastroscope from Germany, and after John Ryle had generated considerable enthusiasm with the publication of his text *The Natural History of Disease*. His studies on duodenal ulcer, gastric secretion, and pain were in the best scientific traditions. Further academic influence emanated from John McNee, who was the first to study liver disease scientifically and was followed later by Harold Himsworth at University College Hospital, London.

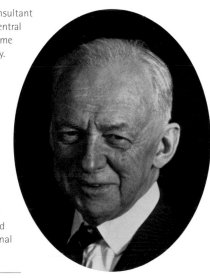

Sir Francis Avery Jones (1910–1998), Consultant Physician and Gastroenterologist at the Central Middlesex Hospital and St Mark's Hospital, became the doyen of latter-day British gastroenterology. While at Barts, he developed a major interest in peptic ulcer and its complications, especially hemorrhage. This subsequently led to his establishment of a gastrointestinal group at the Central Middlesex Hospital, where he built up one of the first British clinical and research units in that specialty. Present at the inauguration of the British Society of Gastroenterology in 1937, he helped found the journal *Gut* in 1960 and became one of its early editors. In 1966, he was elected President of the Society and subsequently became its archivist and a highly regarded spokesperson on public and professional gastroenterological issues.

John Ryle (1889–1950), while the Regius Professor of Medicine at Cambridge, became persuaded that medical schools should adopt a broader population-based perspective in addition to the purely clinical emphasis that prevailed. When the Nuffield Trust established a chair and an Institute of Social Medicine at Oxford University, Ryle relocated geographically and intellectually to become the first Professor of Social Medicine at Oxford. Thereafter, he initiated important studies of the distribution of health services and of disease, producing several books, many of which became classics in the field. His ethos is best summarized as follows: "There is no disease of which a fuller or additional description does not remain to be written; there is no symptom as yet adequately explored."

The Natural History of Disease

JOHN A RYLE

At the Royal Free Hospital, Sir Daniel Davies added a new dimension to gastroenterology by his emphasis on the need to consider the patient in his emotional and environmental setting, and demonstrated the value of establishing full rapport with the patient, particularly in the management of gastric and duodenal ulcer. In Birmingham, Lionel Hardy established a great clinical reputation in addition to delivering the Croonian Lecture on 'Order and disorder in the colon' prior to becoming the first Secretary of the Gastroenterological club, the forerunner of the British Society of Gastroenterology. The educational basis of gastroenterology was strongly supported in the London Medical Schools, where a number of outstanding teachers, including Sir Arthur Hurst, Dr Arthur Douthwaite, and Dr G Lintott (Guy's), Dr Geoffrey Evans, Dr E Cullinan, and Professor Leslie Witts (Barts), Dr Izod Bennett and Dr George Hadley (Middlesex), Dr Thomas Hunt (St Mary's), Mr Harold Edwards (King's), Sir Daniel Davies and Dr Percy Thompson Hancock (Royal Free), Sir Henry Tidy (St Thomas'), Sir Adolphe Abrahams (Westminster), Dr Charles Newman (Postgraduate Medical School), and Dr Maurice Shaw (West London), were prominent exponents of different aspects of the diagnosis and therapy of individual areas of the gut.

of the smaller, proximally illuminated Lloyd-Davies sigmoidoscope proved to be an important step forward in facilitating a view of the nether regions.

In addition to pathologists, radiologists, physicians, and surgeons, Hurst recognized that gastroenterology owed much to the work of British physiologists, including Sir William Bayliss and Ernest Henry Starling, who in 1920 demonstrated the existence of chemical messengers. The identification of secretin by them and the discovery of gastrin by John Sidney Edkins led to the establishment of endocrinology and the understanding that apart from neural regulation, the gut was subject to complex endocrine modulation.

Sir Adolphe Abrahams (1883–1963) (*center*), born in Cape Town, South Africa (*background*), was a multi-talented gastroenterologist educated at Emmanuel College, Cambridge. His strong interest in athletics reflected the family propensity for sport and he wrote a number of books on the subject (*The Human Machine*) as well as texts on duodenal ulcer and colitis. One brother, Sidney Abrahams (1885–1957), competed in the 1906 and 1912 Olympics, and the other, the inimitable Harold Maurice Abrahams, won the gold medal at the 1924 Paris Olympics in the 100-meter sprint. The film *Chariots of Fire* (*top left*) memorialized the latter event, and in so doing, highlighted the controversy surrounding the use of professional coaches.

Interest in surgery of the gut had also amplified considerably since Sir Berkeley Moynihan had popularized gastroenterostomy for the treatment of duodenal ulcer and rendered gastrointestinal surgery a safer venture than it had been previously considered. Similarly, Charles Illingworth's unit in Glasgow had produced many important studies, particularly in relation to peptic ulcer, while Sir David Wilkie achieved the honor of being elected the first surgical member of the Gastroenterological club. Harold Edwards, Director of the Surgical Department at King's College Hospital, exerted a particularly effective influence in relation to the management of diverticular disease, and in supporting the early use of the semiflexible gastroscope. In this respect, he was especially fortunate in that the pathologist Dr H Magnus undertook much novel study of gastric histology. At the time that the club was just beginning, Norman Tanner had begun his pioneering work in the field of gastric surgery as clinicians struggled to manage the gastric neoplasia and the complications of peptic ulcer disease. Although Salmon and the establishment of St Mark's Hospital in London in 1835 had initiated specialization in surgery of the colon and rectum, by the turn of the 19th century, it had already achieved national and international recognition, particularly for the progress in surgery for cancer of the colon and rectum. The advances engendered by Sir HE Lockhart-Mummery, Basil Morson, and Miles in surgery and pathology had been predated by the work of Dr Cuthbert Dukes, whose classification of the stages of colonic neoplasia represented a fundamental advance. Similarly, the introduction

THE ATHENAEUM AND THE LANGHAM

Hurst was well versed in the importance of friendship in professional life and had been an original member of the Association of Physicians, founded by Sir William Osler in 1907, as well as the "Medical pilgrims" – a traveling club – as a member of which he had visited Paris, Berlin, and Rome. Cognizant of the need to provide a framework within which the second generation of "gastroenterologically" trained general physicians might function, Hurst by the early 1930s had already established the practice of dining regularly with like-minded friends at his club the Athenaeum or inviting them to speak at Guy's.

The Athenaeum club in London, also known as Wisdom's House, designed in the Greek style by Decimus Burton, was the site at which Sir Arthur Hurst and his colleagues conceived the notion of a "Gastroenterological club". The Athenaeum was founded by John Wilson Crocker, Secretary of the Admiralty and Editor of James Boswell's *Life of Johnson* in 1824. At the time of its inception, it was described as "an association of individuals known for their scientific and literary attainments, artists of eminence in any class of the fine arts and noblemen and gentlemen distinguished as liberal patrons of science, literature or the arts". Michael Faraday was Secretary of the first committee, with Sir Humphrey Davy in the Chair. Of the original list of members, eight subsequently became Prime Minister and at one time in the late 19th century, the waiting list for admission was 16 years!

In 1936, he decided that a more formal arrangement might be beneficial and he considered the possibility of establishing a Gastroenterological club. With this in mind, he invited a few friends to dine with him at his club and to discuss whether such a project was both worthwhile and feasible. At the initial informal discussion, it was decided that the council should consist of Hardy, Hunt, Tidy, and Witts, with Hurst as Chairman. The club would have 40 members and it was agreed that the first meeting should take place in November 1937. Thirty-six members together with seven guests attended this historic gathering at the Langham Hotel, and after a fine meal, a business meeting was convened. As the progenitor of the idea, Hurst set out his ideas in forming the club and suggested that the first rule should read: "The objects shall be the advancement of Gastroenterology and the promotion of friendship amongst those who have a special interest in disorders of the alimentary tract." The issue of membership was broached by Sir Robert Hutchison, who opined that it was desirable that surgeons be admitted to the membership and it was thereafter resolved that the membership should include one radiologist (AE Barclay), one pathologist (MJ Stewart), one biochemist (EC Dodds), and a surgeon of similar standing, namely Sir David Wilkie.

This discussion, which would subsequently establish the pattern of membership for the future British Society of Gastroenterology, was thus set at the inaugural meeting. On the Friday afternoon, the meeting opened with a discussion on the technique and value of gastroscopy by Stanley J Hartfall, and

this was followed by a discussion of alkalosis opened by Ryle and Dodds. On the Saturday morning, Ernest Bulmer spoke on the technique of X-ray examinations of the small intestine using radiographs illustrating normal appearance, and regional ileitis. SW Patterson, who was deputizing for Sir Ernest Spriggs, spoke of experiences of small bowel disorders seen at Ruthin Castle, and Barclay showed films illustrating the importance of negative pressure in the mechanism of swallowing, as seen in hens, rats, and man. GD Hadley, introduced by Ryle, made a valuable communication on the value of blood volume estimations in the assessment of bleeding in gastric hemorrhage and David Smith recounted a remarkable case of hematemesis occurring from the malignant transformation of a gastrojejunal ulcer. Patterson provided a brief communication on the diagnosis and frequency of gastrocolic fistula and in the afternoon session, Hurst discussed the value of ileostomy in the treatment of ulcerative colitis. HA Magnus, introduced by Witts, spoke of the postmortem appearance of the stomach in Addison's anemia and H Treble, introduced by Hurst, described a new clinical syndrome consisting of gastroenteritis with polyneuritis and cardiac hypertrophy due to generalized amyloidosis. WN Mann, introduced by Hurst, drew attention to the falling incidence of hourglass stomach as shown by the postmortem reports at Guy's Hospital and the clinical records of New Lodge Clinic and Ruthin Castle. Finally, EB French, introduced by Hurst, suggested, based upon personal experiences of himself and a few colleagues, that the physical basis of the "morning after" was a disturbance of hepatic function as determined by the laevulose test and associated with a transient achlorhydria.

The potent message and the magnitude of the success generated by this first meeting may best be attested to by the fact that present at this inaugural session was none other than Avery Jones, who attended as the guest of his chief, Professor Witts. His later remark of 1987 of his recollection of that meeting, "Sir Arthur Hurst had made a further fine contribution to gastroenterology in Great Britain," in its usual understated fashion bore witness to what has proved to be a seminal event.

A list of the signatories at the inaugural meeting of the "Gastroenterological club".

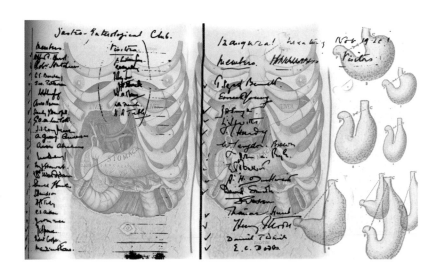

13 BRITISH GASTROENTEROLOGY – THE EARLY YEARS

There is little doubt that the early history and indeed much of the ethos of the British Society of Gastroenterology reflects the life and contributions of Sir Arthur Hurst. Born in 1879, the son of a well-to-do Bradford wool merchant, Hurst died suddenly on August 17, 1944, in Birmingham, at the house of his lifelong friend Lionel Hardy.

Hurst had been blessed in that he had been born during a time that represented a flowering of English intellectualism. Thus a mere 20 years had elapsed since the publication of Charles Darwin's *On the Origin of Species by Means of Natural Selection*, and the world of medicine in his early lifetime saw those advances in fundamental principles associated with some of the great names of the discipline. Thus Ivan Petrovich Pavlov, Theodor Kocher, Elie Metchnikoff, Paul Ehrlich, Lord Joseph Lister, Louis Pasteur, Sir James Mackenzie, Ernest Henry Starling, Sir Charles Scott Sherrington, and Sir Thomas Lewis were all part of the medical scene. Antisepsis had been accepted, anesthesia was widely employed, and in 1896, Ismar Boas in Berlin had established gastroenterology as a separate discipline of medicine. Atomic elements were being discovered and Wilhelm Conrad Roentgen had introduced cathode rays, Elsner a gastroscope, and George Kelling a laparoscope, and physicians had begun to pierce the darkness of the abdominal cavity and change the face of diagnosis.

The 64 years of Hurst's life spanned an extraordinary period of medical progress that began with the discovery of the tubercle bacillus by Robert Koch and ended with the introduction and usage by Sir Alexander Fleming of penicillin in 1944. As a schoolboy aged 16 years, he would have been cognizant of Crooke's tubes and Roentgen's subsequent discovery of X-rays in 1895, and two years later, the founding of the discipline of gastroenterology by Boas in Berlin. He would have just passed his third decade in 1910 when Sir Berkeley Moynihan penned his classic monograph on duodenal ulcer and reached middle age when Rosenheim Henning, Max Nitze, and Rudolph Schindler invented and modified the gastroscope into a usable device. In his sixties, he would have witnessed the establishment of needle biopsy and the elucidation of the true nature of infective hepatitis (1939). Such were the life and times of Sir Arthur Hurst.

Sir Arthur Hurst (*bottom right*) published a detailed account of the movement of the stomach, intestine, and colon in 1908. He had been influenced by the pioneer X-ray studies of Walter Cannon (1871–1945) (*top left*) of Harvard, with whom he worked.

Hurst studied physiology at Oxford in 1899 and 1900 under Gotch and Haldane at the time when Sir Henry Acland had just been succeeded as Regius Professor of Physic by Sir John Burdon-Sanderson. He thereafter qualified from Guy's Hospital in 1905 and subsequently in 1908, at the age of 27, was elected to its staff. Prior to this appointment, he traveled in Germany as a Radcliffe Traveling Fellow of Oxford University and worked both in Munich and (in 1906) in Boston and other cities in America. The opportunity to interact with some of the great medical thinkers of his generation was to prove an important formative experience in the subsequent development of his career.

The early work of Hurst reflected his exposure to Walter Cannon in Boston and began in 1906 when he was among the first physicians in England to use radiography for investigating the alimentary tract. As was the custom of the times, his first subjects were his physiology students at Guy's Hospital, and the reports of his findings on the act of swallowing a bismuth meal mark the beginnings of the use of such radiological techniques in the diagnosis of digestive disorders.

It is worth recalling that at the time (1906) that such studies were undertaken, the common diagnosis for most abdominal disorders was encompassed by the vague term "gastric neurasthenia" and the elements of treatment encompassed static electricity, bitter tonics (condurango), or ingestion of silver nitrate. The subject of "gastroenterology" was a vague conglomeration of symptoms and suppositions, with treatment being almost wholly empirical. Thus the cognoscenti of the abdomen discussed such conditions as gastric myasthenia or atony of the stomach and ptosis of the viscera with aplomb, and surgeons even operated upon these fanciful notions with a view to cure. As regards the consideration of hepatic disease, it was believed that a weak liver was a common disorder and that patients could be "liverish" – thus maintaining an archaic Galenic view of medicine that had persisted for almost two millennia. Popular biliary stimulants included sarsaparilla and dandelion, and the strenuous Weir Mitchell treatment was in great use, with isolation, rest, massage, forced feeding, and electrical stimulation of the skin from an induction coil being widely accepted as rational therapy. When all else failed, bath therapy, country walks, and copious quantities of beef tea were considered mandatory to ensure rapid recovery.

The investigation of the movements of the alimentary tract using the bismuth meal led Hurst to recognize the great variations in size and position in the abdomen of the stomach and colon in normal individuals. The publication of this work in the *British Medical Journal* (1907) was regarded as a landmark in gastroenterology and led to the dismissal of much of the current vague and speculative thinking regarding the nebulous concept of visceroptosis. This important contribution was followed by his book on constipation, and later, after his association with AE Barclay, by a series of investigations on the radiology of the digestive organs.

At the same time as the advances in radiology, considerable progress was being made by scientists such as Sir Michael Foster, Sherrington, John Langley, Sir Henry Hallett Dale, John Sidney Edkins, and Starling in the field of

physiology and chemistry. As a consequence, the concept of chemical pathology was initiated and the investigation of the biochemical basis for disease became a major focus of clinical medicine. Though the interests of Hurst were partly biochemical, such was the breadth of his intellectual curiosity that his clinical activities soon spread to encompass aspects of cardiology and neurology. In collaboration with G Goodhart, he recorded the earliest case of auricular flutter after the development of the electrocardiograph by Lewis in 1910, and as Neurologist to Guy's Hospital, he began to develop a serious interest in the subjects of neurosis and hysteria. Possessed of a curious mind and a keen intellect, he further pursued this area of interest, becoming a regular attendee at the clinics of Joseph Babinski, Joseph Jules Dejerine, and Pierre Marie in Paris. Lest it be considered that he lagged behind in any field of endeavor, it is worth noting that at about the same time (1908), he bought his first motor car, a two-cylinder Wolseley, which was the first consultant's motor car to penetrate into the courtyard of Guy's Hospital, hitherto sacred to only the horse and carriage.

As an Army Major, Sir Arthur Hurst was greatly affected by both World Wars and published his clinical approach to wartime diseases in 1943. He was particularly affected by the men suffering from shell shock during the First World War and developed a treatment that allowed him to "cure" up to 90% of such patients. This entailed moving them to the peace and quiet of the rolling Devonshire countryside, where the men could work on the farm and were encouraged to use their creative energies. These pioneering methods were both humane and sympathetic – the long-term efficacy was not recorded.

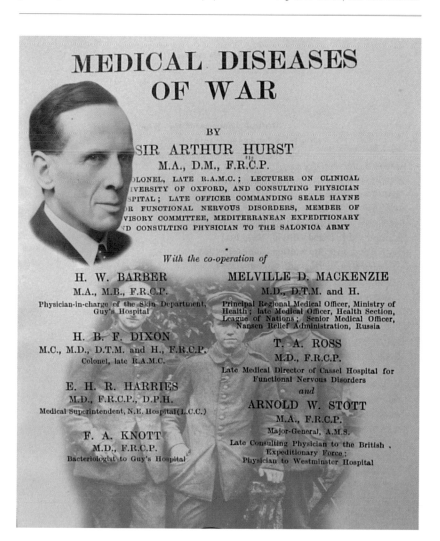

Hardy, who was one of Hurst's closest friends, noted that he was a man who brought warmth and vitality into both his social and professional life, and always felt the importance of linking the two together in friendship and good fellowship. As such, he was an original member of the Association of Physicians founded by Sir William Osler in 1907 and of the Medical Traveling Club formed in 1927. Much in the same fashion as Mackenzie was responsible for initially bringing together those working in cardiology, Hurst undertook a similar role in gastroenterology. Thus in 1936, when Hurst contemplated the possibility of forming a small Gastroenterological club, he invited one or two colleagues to dinner at the Athenaeum club to discuss the project. By 1937, these plans had progressed to the point that he proposed that a council of five be appointed in order to draft detailed plans for the club. As a result of these deliberations, the first meeting attended by 36 members and seven visitors was held at the Royal Society of Medicine in London on November 19 and 20, 1937. Hurst was appointed Chairman and the other members of the first Council were Hardy, Thomas Hunt, Sir Henry Tidy, and Leslie Witts. The order of business was the approval of the draft rules for the club followed by a discussion of the main subject, gastroscopy, which was introduced by Stanley J Hartfall. This was followed by a discussion on alkalosis that was led by John Ryle and EC Dodds. Subsequent to the conclusion of the professional component of the meeting, a dinner was held at the Langham Hotel and thereafter Hurst adumbrated upon his concepts regarding the development of gastroenterology and stated his purpose in forming the club. His proposal of the first rule embodied the credo of the group: "The objects shall be the advancement of gastroenterology and the promotion of friendship amongst those who have a special interest in disorders of the alimentary tract." With his customary eloquence and usual perspicuity, Sir Robert Hutchison thereafter spoke of the desirability of admitting surgeons to membership given their intimate involvement with diseases of the alimentary tract. It is recorded in the minutes that "after discussion it was resolved that as the club (already) numbered one radiologist (AE Barclay), one morbid anatomist (MJ Stewart), and one biochemist (EC Dodds) of eminence, a surgeon occupying a similar standing should be elected, and it was unanimously agreed that Sir David Wilkie should be invited to occupy this position". Thus, from its very inception, the club recognized the critical importance of establishing an interactive relationship between the different disciplines involved in the diagnosis and management of gastrointestinal disease.

In 1938, the second meeting of the club was held at Cambridge under the chairmanship of Ryle, the Regius Professor of Physic at the University. The principal subjects of discussion were quite diverse and included the psychosomatic factors of ulcerative colitis, the deleterious action of aspirin on the gastric mucosa, and the biochemical changes in the blood after gastrointestinal bleeding. In terms of administrative events, it was agreed that Hardy be elected Secretary and indeed this decision proved to be most felicitous, since his ensuing contributions to the club were essential to its subsequent growth and success. An interesting additional decision taken at the Cambridge meeting was that the club should elect a new president every year, as opposed to choosing one who might retain office for three to five years, or longer. This proposal was as a direct result of an initiative raised by Hurst himself, and the ruling was adopted and acted upon except during the period of the Second World War when Hurst acted as unofficial Chairman at two successive wartime meetings.

A celebratory dinner was held at the Langham Hotel following the successful inauguration of the Gastroenterological club on November 20, 1937. Those present included (*clockwise from top left*): Leslie Witts, Sir Arthur Hurst, Thomas Hunt, Sir Henry Tidy, and Lionel Hardy.

Presidents of the British Society of Gastroenterology

	DATE	PRESIDENT		DATE	PRESIDENT		DATE	PRESIDENT
1	1937	A Hurst	22	1962	H Taylor	43	1983	JE Lennard Jones
2	1938	JA Ryle	23	1963	WA Bourne	44	1984	RB McConnell
3	1940–42	A Hurst	24	1964	CE Newman	45	1985	EL Blair
4	1943	H Tidy	25	1965	WM Capper	46	1986	GP Crean
5	1945	T Izod Bennet	26	1966	F Avery Jones	47	1987	J Alexander-Williams
6	1946	A Abrahams	27	1967	I Fitzgerald	48	1988	JJ Misiewicz
7	1947	E Spriggs	28	1968	N Tanner	49	1989	JH Baron
8	1948	TL Hardy	29	1969	HT Howat	50	1990	R Williams
9	1949	G Evans	30	1970	NF Coghill	51	1991	R Shields
10	1950	J McNee	31	1971	AA Harper	52	1992	JR Bennett
11	1951	W MacAdam	32	1972	WI Card	53	1993	M Hobsley
12	1952	AH Douthwaite	33	1973	S Sherlock	54	1994	MS Lowosky
13	1953	LSP Davidson	34	1974	WT Cooke	55	1995	IAD Bouchier
14	1954	SW Patterson	35	1975	SC Truelove	56	1996	PM Smith
15	1955	LJ Witts	36	1976	JC Goligher	57	1997	RH Dowling
16	1956	T Hunt	37	1977	G Watkinson	58	1998	MJS Langman
17	1957	CF Illingworth	38	1978	W Sircus	59	2000	L Turnberg
18	1958	C Dodds	39	1979	CC Booth	60	2001	ATR Axon
19	1959	HW Rodgers	40	1980	BC Morson	61	2002	DP Jewell
20	1960	H Edwards	41	1981	AE Read	62	2003	RN Allan
21	1961	E Bulmer	42	1982	CG Clark	63	2004	NA Wright

Although the activities of the club were somewhat curtailed during the Second World War, the club did manage to hold two meetings. Unfortunately, although a meeting had been arranged for May 10, 1940, it was cancelled owing to the invasion of Holland, but a few members dined together as guests of Hurst at the Athenaeum. Of particular interest was that the Oxford gathering of 1941 engendered considerable debate on the subject of dyspepsia in members of the military forces, thus addressing a lifelong interest of Hurst, namely dyspepsia. The issue was further raised at the subsequent London meeting, where it was suggested that the club might exert its authority in the form of some published statement on the prevention of peptic ulcer recurrences. This matter had arisen based upon the discomfort that Hurst had expressed at his own methods for ensuring ulcer prevention. After some heated discussion, it became apparent to the members that the club was in no reasonable position to issue any balanced advice, since there existed considerable dissent among the members themselves as to what the optimum mode of therapy should be. The Secretary, Hardy, recorded that "although there was no agreement on either fundamentals or details, there was abundant evidence of a healthy individualism and a dislike for any sort of authoritarian regime".

The indefatigable Hurst weathered the war years in fine spirit and his return to work at Oxford was well received by his colleagues, although increasing difficulties with asthma and deafness rendered his task somewhat difficult. Nevertheless, he was energetic, effective, and enthusiastic until August 17, 1944, when he died suddenly in the home of Hardy at Birmingham. As a result, no meeting of the club was held that year and in the following year, 1945, the club recorded a resolution that read as follows: "That the Club records its deep regret at the death of its founder the first Chairman, Sir Arthur Hurst, and desires to place on record its great appreciation of his services to the Club, his many original contributions to gastroenterology and his outstanding qualities as a physician and teacher."

Hardy noted with the kindness of a friend and the scholarship of a professional that although "some of his many original ideas proved incorrect, his brilliant work on achalasia of the cardia, on dyschezia, and on chronic gastritis as a precursor of gastric cancer, represent three examples of his far-sighted conceptions which have been confirmed by the passage of time". Of particular relevance however was his role not only as an intellect but also as a stimulator of medical thought, and as a promoter of international cooperation, research, and friendship. Indeed, these principles were to be embodied and even amplified in the evolution of the club and the Society in its subsequent years.

Following the demise of Hurst, the small club consisting of the 40 original members elected to change its title to that of the "British Society of Gastroenterologists" and altered the existing rules to accommodate this decision. Thus in 1949, the title of "British Society of Gastroenterology" was adopted. In the succeeding years, the Society grew in strength and prestige, and Dr Thomas Hunt, Mr Hermon Taylor, and Dr W Bourne successively followed Dr Hardy as Secretary.

Meetings were held annually in November and "*Gastro-Enterologia*" published the proceedings until 1948, when a proposal to establish a "British Journal of Gastroenterology" was further evaluated by a select committee. As a result of these deliberations, it was considered that the limited number of good gastroenterological papers was such that they might be more effective if published in widely read general medical journals as opposed to a specialized journal read only by a limited number of doctors. Following the adoption of this recommendation, the proposal was decisively outvoted at the annual meeting of the Society, and it was not until a further decade had elapsed that it was once again considered.

The contents of the first edition of *Gut* (*bottom left*) and a 50-year selection of the best scientific and clinical papers published under the auspices of, or inspired by, the interactions of the British Society of Gastroenterology (*background*).

The activities of the society between the years 1950 and 1960 reflected to some extent the altered international face of medicine in a postwar world. Thus, a number of notable events both in the life of the Society and in gastroenterology in general occurred. Firstly, the Society sought to become more visible and as a result, began once again to take a more active part in the international meetings that had begun after the termination of hostilities. Although it had previously been agreed in Paris in 1937 to hold the Third International Congress of Gastroenterology in London in 1940 with Hurst as President and Hunt as Secretary, this meeting had been cancelled due to the military exigencies of the time. Indeed, it was not until 1952, when formal international meetings again became possible, that the British Society was officially represented at the Meeting of the Association of the National European and Mediterranean Societies of Gastroenterology at Bologna. In July 1956, the British Society acted as host in London at the fifth meeting of this Association, which was attended by over 800 visitors and delegates, including many distinguished physicians, surgeons, and others from North America and distant parts of the world. The overall assessment of the outcome of this meeting was that it had attained a high standard and both the scientific and social programmes were considered extremely successful. The proceedings of this congress were edited by Harold Edwards and published by Messrs Karger within a few months of the end of the meeting, and the 800-page volume was regarded as an important addition to the gastroenterological literature of the time. After the London meeting, the World Organization of Gastroenterology was established and held its first meeting in Washington in the United States in 1958, under the Presidency of Dr H Bockus.

In addition to these developments in European and world meetings, the meetings of the British Society itself began to be characterized by an increasing number of novel contributions, as increasing numbers of younger British physicians, surgeons, and research workers began to specialize in gastroenterology.

The volume of new papers, both scientific and clinical, was evident by the wide diversity of subjects discussed at the meetings of the Society.

1948	*Birmingham*, disorders of the small intestine
1949	*London*, gastric acid secretion
1950	*London*, post-gastrectomy syndrome
1951	*Leeds*, hiatus hernia
1952	*London*, hemopoiesis in relation to disorders of the alimentary tract
1955	*Edinburgh*, abdominal visceral blood flow
1956	*Oxford*, carcinoid tumours; anticholinergic drugs; the secretion of mucus, etc
1958	*London*, blood groups
1959	*Belfast*, hormones and the alimentary tract

The format of the Society meeting evolved from that of a club to a multifaceted scientific and educational forum, where not only were many short papers read, but demonstrations, medical exhibitions, and topic forums were introduced, with the result that new contributions increased steadily in number and in complexity. As a consequence of the rapid amplification in information and enthusiasm, more visitors interested in gastroenterology attended, and in 1959, the number of members elected increased from 65 to over 100.

Thus, by 1960, the issue of a specific journal devoted to the subject of gastroenterology once again became a topic of serious debate, as the leadership considered that both the special interests of gastroenterology and the size and authority of the British Society of Gastroenterology justified it. Nevertheless, some individuals were concerned, since British medicine had long mistrusted the concept of narrow specialization, believing that specialists should not lose touch with the main themes of medicine or surgery. Thus it was held to be of importance that a specialist journal that evolved out of the development of general medicine should retain its contact with it. Nevertheless, it was recognized that an advancing discipline requires a special vehicle because the specialty needs it as an essential mode whereby knowledge of an advancing subject can be both focused and accessed by those specifically interested in the particular area. Out of this background was *Gut*, the journal of the British Society of Gastroenterology, born.

SIR ARTHUR HURST (1879–1944)

Sir Arthur Hurst (1879–1944) was born in Bradford, England, and in 1936 established the Gastroenterological club, subsequently the British Society of Gastroenterology. In 1937, at the first meeting, Hurst was elected President and his contributions are currently memorialized in the annual award of the Hurst medal. The original family name was changed from Hertz in response to British sensitivities to Germanic origins.

Sir Arthur Hurst (formerly Hertz) was born on July 23, 1879, in Bradford, where his family had lived since 1841, being exporters of woolen and worsted from the West Riding of Yorkshire. His great-grandfather had been raised in an old Jewish family in Hamburg before immigrating to Leeds, and his grandfather had subsequently moved to Bradford, where his father was born in 1846. Despite its business focus, the family was cultivated and much involved in the artistic and musical life of the Midlands. As a boy, Hurst initially attended Bradford and later the Manchester Grammar School (1896), where he won many prizes and was an enthusiastic rugby, football, and cricket player. In 1897, he went to Magdalen College, Oxford, having won a Science Demy-ship, and in 1901, he took a First Class Honors degree in physiology. In 1901, he became a student at Guy's Hospital, and was awarded gold medals in both clinical medicine and clinical surgery, and took his Oxford BM, BCh, in 1904. As a result of his achievements, in 1905 he was awarded a Radcliffe traveling fellowship that required him to study abroad for not less than 18 months out of three years. Hurst chose to visit France and Germany, and worked with the great neurologists Jean-Martin Charcot, Joseph Jules Dejerine, Joseph Babinski, and Raymond, as well as the gastroenterologist Mathieu. Initially, he traveled to Professor Friedrich Muller in Munich, where he learnt German and interested himself in people, books, and local customs, though it is noted that he failed to develop a taste for Munich beer. After Munich, he went to Strasbourg, and then, in 1906, to Boston, where he met Walter Cannon at Harvard, who was using the new roentgen rays in his physiological studies on cats. This relationship was to fuel Hurst's lasting interest in X-rays, and he became one of the first to use bismuth for the examination of the alimentary tract in man.

From being Demonstrator of Physiology at Guy's Hospital, Hurst was elected in 1907 to the staff at the age of 27 years, without having been a registrar. His first appointment was as Physician in charge of the electrical department, but within a few months, he had started the first neurological outpatient department in an English general hospital and was soon appointed Neurologist. By 1908, he had established himself at Guy's and began to see a few private patients, with the result that he could proudly recall that during that year he made the princely sum of 163 guineas.

In 1912, Hurst married Miss Cushla Reddiford of New Zealand, but their early years together were soon disrupted when, in 1915, he volunteered for service with the RAMC and was posted to Lemnos, the main base for the Gallipoli campaign. Soon thereafter, he was relocated to Thessalonica, where he served until returning to England in July 1916.

Paintings of Sir Arthur Hurst (*left*) and his wife Cushla (nee Reddiford) of New Zealand (*right*). The portrait of Cushla was completed by Laslo in 1919.

At this juncture, mainly due to the wise advice of Sir William Osler and Sir Maurice Craig, Hurst was appointed to the neurological wards at Oxford. His enthusiasm and energy soon led to his persuading the War Office to take over the buildings of Seale Hayne Agricultural College at Newton Abbot for conversion into a special hospital for the treatment of war neuroses. In the following years until the hospital finally closed in 1919, Hurst provided a good example of his astonishing ability to arouse others by collecting a team of colleagues at the hospital and imbuing them with his own fierce enthusiasm and determination. Throughout a long and distinguished career, Hurst was the recipient of numerous honors and accolades apart from the adulation of his patients and students. Thus, at the Royal College of Physicians, he became in turn Goulstonian (1911), Croonian (1920), and Harveian (1939) Lecturer, although he took little part in College affairs or medical administration. In addition, he held many appointments, was awarded many prizes and medical honors, and his fame and professional friendships were international.

It would not be unfair to comment that few physicians have stimulated more young British doctors to think for themselves and to argue about causes than did Hurst. His approach to bedside medicine was basically physiological, and the great reformation that entered internal medicine in the early years of the 20th century and transformed it from structure and pathology to function owes much to his example and perspicuity.

Hurst was in turn a pioneer in the use of X-rays, testmeal analysis, sigmoidoscopy, and gastroscopy. Possessed of a curious mind, he had from his earliest days trained himself to identify causes and as Neurologist at Guy's Hospital, he had particular opportunities for studying the nervous pathways of

sensation and the mechanism of behavior. This early background provided him with insight that subsequently enabled him to become a pioneer in the diagnosis and treatment of the psychoneuroses that had previously been much scorned by the medical profession. Thus, during the First World War, he became a leader in the use of suggestion in treating nervous disorders, and was one of the first to show why such physical labels as "soldier's heart" or "shell shock" should be discarded and recognized as psychological. In the pursuit of this work, he was considerably helped and guided by Sir Charles Sherrington, from whom he had already learnt much; though not in itself completely novel, it enabled Hurst to attain an important role in the development of clinical medicine.

Of particular interest in his personal views, and despite a profound knowledge of medical history, was Hurst's deep distrust of tradition and a determination to erase dogma based on false theory or pure superstition. In this respect, he was responsible for the removal from gastroenterology of a mass of false conceptions, and was often able to substitute factual data, from evidence which could be confirmed, for traditional and often erroneous beliefs. A good example of this can be obtained in his early book on constipation, in which he showed, partly by the use of the bismuth meal and radiographs, which he was the first to employ in man, how wrong were many of the current views on purgation and the mode of action of laxatives, and was able to define the way in which nervous factors influenced the behavior of the bowel. In addition to re-evaluating dogma, he was not reticent in introducing novel concepts; thus, his initiation of the neologism "dyschezia" (suggested by Cooper Perry) to describe how habit and mode of life could lead to "false" constipation provided a fine example of his ability to rethink medical issues.

Sir Arthur Hurst (*seated fourth from left*) was appointed to the staff of Guy's Hospital at the age of 27, and soon thereafter established himself as a general physician with a special interest in gastroenterology. Although particularly interested in ulcer disease, achalasia, and constipation, he wrote definitively on diverse gastrointestinal subjects.

Apart from his intellectual erudition, Hurst was one of the first great clinical scientists and a masterful clinical observer, able to clarify fundamental facts which had either been obscured by traditional theories or not recognized at all. A fine example of this skill was his demonstration that muscular tension (stretching) was the primary cause of true visceral pain, and another his insistence that variations in gastric secretion were not in themselves disease entities but simply physiological variations.

Yet another example of his perspicuity is provided by his clear appreciation of the role of the nervous system in the causation of digestive disorders. Much of this insight was generated initially by a profound interest in the work of Mesmer and the place of suggestion in treatment, and thereafter amplified by his training with Charcot and others that educated him in the topic of "hysteria" and the distinctions between physical and "neurotic" illness. By applying his knowledge in these areas to the subject of gastroenterology, he was instrumental in securing the ultimate abandonment of such diagnoses as "acid dyspepsia" or "hypochlorhydria". Similarly, he demonstrated that "flatulent dyspepsia" was nearly always a misnomer for nervous "air swallowing" or "aerophagy" and that disturbances of gastrointestinal function often were associated with substantial neural input.

Apart from his obvious intellectual skills, Hurst was in addition a fine diagnostician and a superb clinical educator. His sociability, wonderful memory, sense of humor, and his interest in young physicians made him both a popular and inspiring teacher, and he exercised without doubt a powerful influence on the clinical education of many generations of students and registrars. As might be predicted, Hurst did not suffer fools gladly, and at meetings he would sometimes ostentatiously throw down his bulky hearing aid in obvious disapproval. Nevertheless, though he could at times be intolerant, he was not concerned to be proven incorrect and was especially receptive of the ideas of others, particularly if presented in a logical form. In this respect, he exhibited a remarkable flexibility of mind and quite clearly possessed what Dr Johnson had previously called "the itch of disputation". Indeed, his lifelong friend and colleague Lionel Hardy, in writing of him, noted that of the qualities considered essential to genius, "he certainly had three of the most important: curiosity, imagination, and enthusiasm, combined with an immense capacity for hard work".

Despite his manifold skills and gifts, Hurst was throughout his life plagued by asthma and later severe deafness. Despite these hindrances, he persevered and never allowed them to interfere with his personal or professional activities. Indeed, his drive and energy were all the more remarkable, because, as he wrote in 1921, "I suffer from Asthma so I have the advantage which few writers on the subject possess of 30 years' observation on a single case," and he fought a gallant battle with this disability for another 23 years. Although he was rarely completely symptom free, he at first found complete relief during visits to Switzerland – where he was an enthusiastic bobsleigher. It was well known that on many occasions he would disappear from his ward to give himself an injection of adrenaline, with often two or three more necessary during the day to keep himself comfortable. Although he was quick to play down the disability, he wrote extensively and well on the subject, recognizing fully the role that nervous factors played in its causation. With the passage of age, an almost equally distressing degree of deafness afflicted Hurst, but his strength of personality and courage enabled him to maintain a full work schedule with both optimism and humor. As was once remarked of a previous sage of British medicine, Thomas Sydenham, in respect of his gout, "he never betrayed any indecent impatience or unmanly dejection under his distress". Thus, Hurst bore his infirmities with equanimity and was able to accept – and almost ignore – such restrictions as his health imposed, though he forsook cardiology patients early in his career when he could no longer hear clearly through a stethoscope.

A line drawing of Sir Arthur Hurst as a young man (*background*). Despite his scholarly predilection, he possessed an almost indefatigable passion for cars and as such, was the first to introduce a motorized vehicle into the forecourt of the venerable institution of Guy's Hospital.

As might be expected, tiredness was not a condition that he recognized and no day was long enough for the completion of his interests, whether personal or professional. As such, his days were always full, and he devoted the same attention to his hobbies as he did to his writing, teaching, research, and clinical practice. Thus, in 1907, he became the first physician at Guy's Hospital to own a motor car; he loved country walks and was a skilful clay sculptor (a talent learnt at the occupational therapy sessions that he instituted at Seale Hayne), and his paintings and caricatures were considered notable. After his retirement from the staff of Guy's in 1939, he returned to Oxford and continued teaching both there and at Guy's until his death in 1944 at the age of 65 years.

In 1979, the British Society of Gastroenterology celebrated the centenary of the birth of Hurst, the founder of the Society and its first President. In 1935, Hurst had written to Dr Georges Brohee of Brussels, who was making plans to form a "*Society Internationale de Gastro-Enterologie*," saying: "A private Gastroenterological Club has been formed in Great Britain which will meet once a year in various cities the day before the Association of Physicians." At the centenary celebration of his birth, Hardy was with due pride able to note that from this modest proposal had arisen the British Society, which now numbered nearly 1,000 members. What greater legacy could any man hope for than to be remembered in perpetuity for the gifts of his imagination and by the acclamation of his peers.

A collage of the life and times of Sir Arthur Hurst reflecting the diversity of his interests, intellectual activities, and family. Whether as a skier, soldier, scholar, or scion of the family, he sought always to excel.

GASTROENTEROLOGY AS A SPECIALTY

Doctors in Science and Society
Essays of a Clinical Scientist
CHRISTOPHER C BOOTH

The officers of the British Society of Gastroenterology, 2002.

With the increase in numbers of gastroenterologists and the resultant impact on clinical practice, the British Society of Gastroenterology required representation at national level to promote its objectives and ensure an acceptable standard of practice. In order to effect this, links were respectively established with the Royal Colleges and the Department of Health and Social Security (DHSS) in 1960–1961 and in 1976 by the creation of three committees.

THE ROYAL COLLEGES

Although the British Society of Gastroenterology Council first discussed the establishment of gastroenterology as a specialty in July 1964, informal discussions with the Royal College of Physicians of London in regard to the subject continued over a four-year period. In 1968, an official approach was initiated when a letter was sent to the College formally requesting consideration of the matter. The subsequent committee report that provided a brief description of current practice and recommendations for minimum specialist training was accepted by Comitia of the College in April 1970. Two years later, the College established a standing Committee on Gastroenterology, to include three members nominated by the Society.

The matter was fortuitously expedited, since early in 1970, the General Medical Council had first suggested the possibility of specialist registration to identify those who had reached certain standards of training. Not insensitive to this suggestion, the Royal Colleges had responded and arranged meetings to discuss the issues of advanced training and accreditation. As a result of these deliberations, the Joint Committees on Higher Medical Training (JCHMT) and Surgical Training (JCHST) were developed. The Society was represented at a subsequent meeting of the College, at which 16 Specialist Advisory Sub-Committees (SACs) to the JCHMT were set up, one of which was given responsibility for gastroenterology and comprised two members from the JCHMT and four nominated members of the Society. The establishment of this body enabled gastroenterology to become recognized as a medical subspecialty for training purposes and in addition, through the SAC, the Society acquired a majority voice in setting standards both for training posts and accreditation of trainees.

In 1970, an attempt to attain similar recognition for surgeons who devoted all their time to gastroenterological surgery was rejected, although some two decades later, this proposal was accepted with the introduction of the concept of a certificate of higher training.

INTERFACE WITH CENTRAL GOVERNMENT

In 1974, the Council of the British Gastroenterology Society began to explore the possibility of obtaining a direct link with the DHSS through a liaison committee, and a letter signed by four influential members of the Society was sent to the chief medical officer at the DHSS, requesting a meeting to discuss the establishment of a joint liaison committee. The chief medical officer delegated a member of his staff to discuss the matter and as a result, a committee was established that possessed no executive functions but functioned as a forum for free discussion. This forum provided the opportunity to express views without commitment of the parent bodies and maintain records of meetings that were only available to members of the committee and to those whom they represented. The professional representatives were to be three from the Society and two from the Royal College of Physicians Standing Committee. In July 1975, these proposals were accepted by the Council of the Society and the first meeting, attended by four representatives of the DHSS, was held in March 1976. Although a similar working group was proposed for Scotland during 1976, this proposal did not come to fruition.

Christopher C Booth, a distinguished gastroenterologist and President of the British Society of Gastroenterology, represented the embodiment of a latter-day Renaissance scholar. He distinguished himself in numerous areas: as a clinician-scientist contributing seminal observations on mechanisms of intestinal absorption in man; as a leader (*primus inter pares*) of clinical academic medicine in Britain; and thereafter as a consummate medical statesman and a perspicacious medical historian. His personal advocacy of the relevance of clinical science proved pivotal in opening the doors for a new generation of gastroenterologists. The 1987 text *Doctors in Science and Society: Essays of a Clinical Scientist* illuminated his scholarship and thoughtful contributions to the discipline.

The medical specialty of gastroenterology

Recognition of gastroenterology as a medical specialty occurred gradually and tacit recognition by the Royal College of Physicians was expressed by the formation of the Standing Committee and Specialist Advisory Sub-Committee for Higher Medical Training. Recognition by the DHSS was implicit in the acceptance of the Liaison Committee and by its inclusion of gastroenterology among its list of pure specialists, as well as its acceptance that many physicians provided an important clinical service in gastroenterology while retaining responsibility also for acute general medicine. Such advances represented the outcome of years of discussion and investigation of the issue of specialization. Thus, during the 1960s and early 1970s, many members of the Society and its Council pressed for gastroenterology to be "recognized" as a "specialty". The main problem that the Liaison Committee encountered was "how to define a specialist when almost all gastroenterologists also practiced general medicine". By 1975, however, sessions designated for gastroenterology were introduced into the DHSS Manpower Table and 32 whole-time consultant equivalents were present in England and Wales. In order to determine the number of gastroenterologists and define the needs of the population for such care, in 1973, the Training and Education Committee surveyed the matter. In 1981, a second such survey by the Standing Committee recorded 271 physicians with a special interest in gastroenterology in Britain, while the DHSS enquiry into the matter revealed that gastroenterology ranked second after endocrinology as the most common special interest expressed by general physicians.

Resource allocation

As new techniques of investigation and treatment were introduced, so the needs of gastroenterologists for instruments, space, and supporting staff became more obvious and imperative. In June 1975, the Royal College of Physicians Standing Committee prepared an interim report on the 'Organization of a Gastroenterological Service', which was accepted by the College and published with amendments. Based upon this data, the first meeting of the DHSS Liaison Committee resulted in the establishment of a working party to prepare a paper for circulation to planning authorities. Thereafter, during 1976 and 1977, a DHSS representative on this working party visited the gastroenterological units in 13 different hospitals and acquired awareness of the contribution the specialty was making to the NHS. The consensus of the working party, entitled *The provision of a gastroenterological service in a District General Hospital*, was published as a booklet by the British Gastroenterological Society in 1978 and accepted by the Liaison Committee, the Royal College of Physicians Standing Committee, and the Council of the Society. Given the composition of the working party and that the DHSS circulated the document to all regional and community medical officers, a measure of official approval and influence among administrators was provided.

Concurrent with these activities, the British Society for Digestive Endoscopy published a booklet on the development of endoscopy services that was widely distributed to health authorities. Thereafter, a second booklet on the design of endoscopy units was prepared and distributed by the Endoscopy Committee of the Society, and in 1983, the College accepted guidelines for its representatives on consultant appointment committees setting out the facilities desirable for a newly appointed consultant with a special interest in gastroenterology. As a result of this array of reports and publications, planning authorities were made aware of the needs of a gastroenterological service for appropriate accommodation, equipment, and ancillary staff.

Manpower allocation

In recognition of the efficacy of the new specialty and its broad application to the healthcare system, it became apparent that there was a serious shortfall of adequately trained gastroenterologists. The Standing Committee of the Royal College of Physicians realized this need and prepared a report entitled *The need for an increased number of physicians with a special interest in Gastroenterology*, which was accepted by the College and published in 1983. This report defined the steadily increasing workload of medical gastroenterologists because of the improved clinical service they could offer, and advocated a target of one general physician with a special interest in gastroenterology for every 150,000 members of the population. It also described the need for the development of a comparable support system, including clinical assistants and skilled nursing support.

THE BRITISH SOCIETY FOR DIGESTIVE ENDOSCOPY

The British Society for Digestive Endoscopy was established in 1971 with Dr Sidney Truelove (*inset*) as its first President.

who were also elected at this meeting. It was decided that any member of the Society of Gastroenterology wishing to join the Society for Digestive Endoscopy would automatically become a member without the need for sponsorship. Other candidates would need to be sponsored by a member of the Society of Gastroenterology or the Society for Digestive Endoscopy and would be nominated by the Executive Committee.

The British Society for Digestive Endoscopy flourished, and by February 1972, six months after its inception, had 199 ordinary members; 257 by August 1973; and by December 1975, there were 370. Three other categories of membership were added, including honorary members, corporate membership, and associate membership, which was created for nurses and technicians involved in the practice of endoscopy.

In 1971, Dr KFR Schiller organized a meeting on endoscopy at St Peter's Hospital, Chertsey, Surrey, and the possibility of setting up a society for digestive endoscopy was discussed: most European countries already had such national societies. Sidney Truelove was proposed as the first President and Schiller as the Honorary Secretary, and all interested parties were invited to attend an open meeting at the annual meeting of the British Society of Gastroenterology in Newcastle in September 1971. At the inaugural meeting attended by more than 60 doctors, mostly Society members, an overwhelming majority agreed that the "British Society of Digestive Endoscopy be hereby inaugurated," with a provisional set of rules and elected officers. Subsequently, following some correspondence in the medical press, the name was changed to the more accurate "for" rather than "of" endoscopy. The day-to-day running of the British Society for Digestive Endoscopy was placed in the hands of an Executive Committee consisting of the officers and seven ordinary members,

Although initially the interface between the Society for Digestive Endoscopy and the Society of Gastroenterology was somewhat difficult, as the membership of the former grew and endoscopy achieved greater visibility, the relationship between the two Societies fructified. Thus, as early as 1975, by the time of the Oxford meeting, a single program covered the activities of both Societies and this became the pattern for all subsequent meetings. Apart from the two annual national meetings of the two Societies, numerous other smaller meetings with an endoscopic focus were held throughout the country, which further served to amplify the development of endoscopy. These smaller meetings served to interface experienced endoscopists with novice endoscopists and trainees to allow exchange of information on techniques and to teach them basic skills. Such meetings were central to the training program of the Society for Digestive Endoscopy and were held at least once a year over two to three days and included training sessions for technicians and nurses acting as endoscopy assistants.

In 1973, the Society for Digestive Endoscopy provided a *Memorandum on future national needs for fiber optic endoscopy of the gastrointestinal tract* to Sir George Godber, Chief Medical Officer for the DHSS. It was circulated to all regional medical officers and other interested parties, for example, the British Society of Gastroenterology, and all members of the British Society for Digestive Endoscopy. This document proved to have considerable influence on the establishment and development of endoscopy both in Britain and abroad.

In order to honor the memory of pioneers in the field, an Annual Foundation Lecture was created and the initial oration was given at the first annual general meeting in 1972 by Professor Harold Hopkins, a physicist of Reading University. As a specialist in optics and a pioneer in the development of fiberoptics, Hopkins and his colleague N Kapany developed fiber bundles with an inner core of glass of a given refractive index surrounded by a sheath of glass of a lower refractive index. Their successful delineation of the mathematical relationship between the two refractive indices necessary to retain light within the fiber when it was curved provided the scientific basis for the development of endoscopy. In addition to the lecture, an Endoscopy prize was created for members who had made important advances in endoscopy, and in recognition of his primary role in the establishment of the discipline, the prize was eponymously identified with the contributions of Hopkins.

In the mid 1970s, gastroenterology was recognized as a medical specialty and the Royal College of Physicians defined the training requirements by which senior registrars could be classified as accredited gastroenterologists. The subsequent major increase in hospital appointments of physicians trained in gastroenterology was based upon the recognition that general physicians required special expertise, especially in endoscopy. By 1978, the British Society for Digestive Endoscopy had been in existence for a few years and it

became apparent to many of its members, and those of the British Society of Gastroenterology, that there was little compelling need to maintain a separate society for digestive endoscopy. The subsequent ballot of members of the Society for Digestive Endoscopy overwhelmingly (163 to eight) favored a merger and the Executive Committee of the Society and the Council of the Society of Gastroenterology established a working party which comprised PB Cotton (Chairman) and three each from the Society for Digestive Endoscopy (M Atkinson, JR Bennett, and R Cockel) and the Society of Gastroenterology (CC Booth, CG Clark, and M Hobsley) to arrange the details of the merger. This working party produced a document that contained a set of recommendations for the merger, which were considered at an extraordinary general meeting of the British Society for Digestive Endoscopy in March 1979. At the annual business meeting of the two Societies in Guildford in September 1979, both memberships voted in favor. The main changes were that the future full title of the British Society of Gastroenterology would be "The British Society of Gastroenterology, in which is incorporated the former British Society for Digestive Endoscopy". The new President of the incorporated Society became Vice-President (Endoscopy) of the enlarged British Society of Gastroenterology to be supported by an endoscopy committee responsible for endoscopy aspects of the Society's work. Corporate membership was abolished but endoscopy assistant membership was retained.

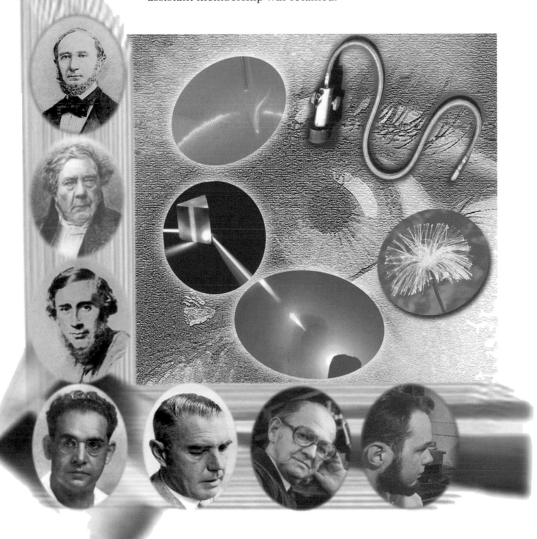

"The Men who Bent the Light" (*from top left to bottom right*): Daniel Colladon of Geneva (1841) was the first to demonstrate light-guiding using jets of cascading water. Jacques Babinet adapted this technique and demonstrated that it could be undertaken in glass rods, but by his death in 1872, had not pursued the issue, even though he had suggested that such a device might be used to "light up the mouth". At the suggestion of Michael Faraday, John Tyndall performed experiments (1853) in London to show the phenomenon of light bending, but omitted to indicate his lack of primacy in the area. While a medical student in Munich (1930), Heinrich Lamm successfully transmitted images through glass fibers. Abraham van Heel, a Dutch physicist, produced the first bundles of clad fibers for image transmission (1952), although a year previously, Holger Moller Hansen of Denmark had applied for a Danish patent on a "flexible picture transport cable". Larry Curtiss of the University of Ann Arbor, Michigan, made the glass clad fibers to be used in the first flexible gastroscope designed by Basil Hirschowitz.

The first publication devoted to diseases of the gut was *Archiv für Verdauungskrankheiten*, initially published in 1885 by Ismar Boas of Berlin. Although the American Gastroenterological Association was founded shortly afterwards in 1897, it was not until 1934 that the *American Journal of Digestive Diseases and Nutrition* appeared. This was replaced in 1943 by *Gastroenterology* as the official journal of the American Gastroenterological Association. Despite the growth of gastroenterology in Britain, *Gut* was not established until almost 20 years later and reflected both the relatively late emergence of gastroenterology as a recognized specialty in Britain compared with elsewhere, and the long established strong tradition of general medicine.

The first mention of a special publication designed to serve the needs of the British Society of Gastroenterology appears in the minutes of the seventh annual meeting in 1946, which record that the motion to establish a journal was defeated by 22 votes to five! The principal reason being that at that time there was insufficient scientific material to justify a separate publication, since it was felt that the *Lancet* and the *Quarterly Journal of Medicine* provided adequate material. Nevertheless, at the same meeting, it was agreed that the proceedings of the annual meeting should be published in *Gastroenterologia* and Mr Harold Edwards and the Secretary (Dr Thomas Hunt) were appointed Editors for the purpose. The following year, Edwards became the British Editor of *Gastroenterologia*, thus strengthening the link with that publication, and the proceedings of the 1947 annual meeting were published in *Gastroenterologia* 1948: 73: 275–98.

In 1954, the editor of the proceedings and the editorial secretary were invited to join the Council as *ex officio* members and a publishing committee was established, but this advance was somewhat diminished by an adverse vote on the provision of a journal. In 1957, Edwards resigned as Editorial Secretary and was succeeded by Sir Francis Avery Jones, who further promoted the concept of a British journal devoted to gastroenterology. Thus a

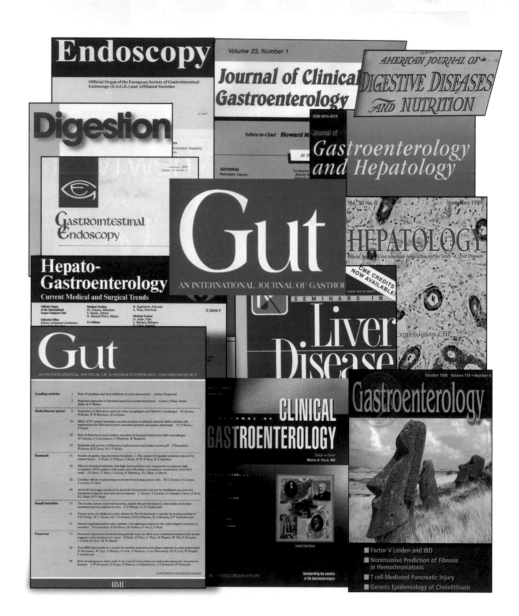

The first journal devoted entirely to the subject of gastroenterology, *Archiv für Verdauungskrankheiten*, was founded and edited by Ismar Boas in Berlin in 1896. Although at the turn of the 19th century only one journal was available, over the next two decades, this would increase to four or five, and by the end of the 20th century, a diverse array of gastrointestinal journals were available. Since the fledgling British Gastroenterological club possessed no formal journal, it published the proceedings of its first scientific meeting in *Gastroenterologia*. The newly established journal *Gut* (*center and bottom left*) first appeared in 1960. Over the next 40 years, this periodical has become an internationally recognized journal and rigorous arbiter of gastroenterological progress.

group including Hugh Clegg, Hunt, Edwards, Morton Gill, and Avery Jones, having convened in the Athenaeum, recommended to the Council that a specialist journal be started. At a meeting held at the Medical Society of London on Friday November 7, 1958, the Council agreed to the foundation of a "British Journal of Gastroenterology" and subsequently proposed that the journal should appear on a quarterly basis. Edwards was appointed as Chairman and Editor and Avery Jones was delegated as Editorial Secretary responsible for the establishment of a broadly based editorial committee. From the outset, it was proposed that the new publication would form part of a series of specialist publications published by the British Medical Association and the current Editor of the *British Medical Journal*, Dr Clegg, was involved in the initial discussions regarding the establishment of the journal. The title was the subject of considerable debate and "British Journal of Gastroenterology," "The Enteron," and "The Abdomen" were all considered. Clegg is credited with proposing the short but succinct and pertinent title, which was, not without opposition, eventually adopted. To quote the minutes of the first meeting of the editorial committee in October 1959: "…the title *Gut* was inclusive, denoted the subject to be covered and was in accord with traditional ideas." It was also established that members of the Society would receive *Gut* at cost price and by July 1961, the editorial secretary was able to report to the Council the increasing circulation of *Gut* and receive their congratulations. It is worthy of note that even at this early date, the circulation was already greater in the United States than in Britain!

early investigation of hematemesis; then followed contributions from Geoffrey Watkinson ('Incidence of peptic ulcer in Leeds'), Richard Doll *et al* ('Distribution of blood groups in peptic ulcer'), RB Welbourn *et al* ('Effect of steroids on gastric secretion'), AM Connell *et al* ('Serotonin and diarrhoea'), Margot Shiner ('Small intestinal biopsy in celiac disease'), TJ Butler ('Pancreatic function'), JM Naish *et al* ('Pseudo-obstruction'), WT Cooke *et al* ('D-xylose test and another paper on the multiple endocrine adenoma syndrome'), and CH Talbot writing on the volvulus of the small intestine. It is to be noted that four of the 11 papers were from the active department at the Central Middlesex Hospital that was under the leadership of Avery Jones, the Editorial Secretary of the journal!

Once launched, *Gut* progressed steadily during its first 27 years of existence, but remained a quarterly until 1963, when bimonthly publication was started, and 12 issues per year were begun in 1969. In 1960, 43 original papers were published and all but two originated in Britain. Contributions totalling 720 from 46 countries were submitted, and 202 appeared in 1986. *Gut* is now distributed to most countries in the world and more recently, additional issues in the form of special supplements have been introduced. Avery Jones remained in the editorial chair until 1970; thereafter it was taken up by Professor Dame Sheila Sherlock, and in 1976 by Christopher C Booth.

The first issue of *Gut* contained a foreword by Edwards, the Editor, followed by a portrait of Sir Arthur Hurst on page two. Opposite this, Hunt provided a preface that linked the early days of British gastroenterology to Hurst's career. The issue contained 11 scientific papers, including the first paper, by GN Chandler *et al*, which dealt with

The Jubilee edition of *Gut* (1987) is shown. The first issue (volume 1, no 1), appeared in March 1960. The initial covers were buff with the introduction of the red coat in 1970. Harold Edwards was the first Editor, and Sir Francis Avery Jones the Editorial Secretary. In his foreword, Edwards made the point that gastroenterology depended on close cooperation between the various medical disciplines and listed some of the problems facing the gastroenterologists of the 1960s: non-ulcer dyspepsia, etiology and treatment of peptic ulcer, inflammatory bowel disease, gastric cancer, and the like. As John Misiewicz perspicaciously noted some three decades later, with the possible exception of the treatment of peptic ulcer, gastroenterologists still face a very similar set of problems.

Jubilee Supplement   BSG 1937–87

Gut

Journal of the British Society of Gastroenterology
Edited by J H Baron

BSG
50th
ANNIVERSARY

Although numerous changes and innovations have been introduced by the successive editors, one of the many bon mots coined by Avery Jones applies to *Gut*: "Whenever I see the word rat in the title, I cross it out." ("Rats" were allowed to survive in the subtitle.) Overall, this quip reflects the strong clinical tradition of the journal, although in more recent times, basic scientists have prevailed. Booth was especially responsible for the introduction of a more stringent peer review system, with all manuscripts being assessed by at least two referees. To further strengthen the process, statisticians and basic scientists were appointed to the editorial committee, as well as pathologists and radiologists.

Sir Arthur Hurst Lecture

In 1966, the Council of the British Society of Gastroenterology, under the Presidency of Sir Francis Avery Jones, recommended that a lecture should be delivered each year in the name of the founder of the Society. The Sir Arthur Hurst Lecture was established in 1967 as the most prestigious honor the Society could bestow and is regarded as a highlight of the annual meeting. A series of distinguished national and international figures have lectured to the Society, including a Nobel Laureate and several presidents of the British Society of Gastroenterology and other national gastroenterological societies. The list of the titles reflects the evolution of gastroenterology.

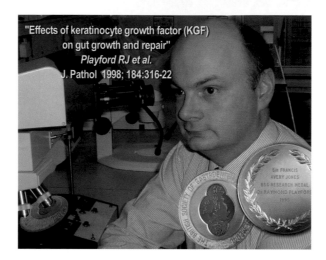

"Effects of keratinocyte growth factor (KGF) on gut growth and repair"
Playford RJ et al.
J. Pathol 1998; 184:316-22

Professor Raymond Playford, the 1995 recipient of the Sir Francis Avery Jones – British Society of Gastroenterology research medal.

British Society of Gastroenterology research medal

In 1976, the British Society of Gastroenterology accepted a recommendation that a research medal should be awarded annually to a researcher who had produced a body of outstanding work on any aspect of gastroenterology. It was required that the majority of the work should have been undertaken in Britain and, with the aim of encouraging young workers, an upper age limit of 35 years, subsequently raised to 40 years, was established. The research medallist was initially required to present a 40-minute lecture on his work at the spring meeting of the Society followed by a 20-minute discussion, although subsequently the discussion period was dropped. The first medal was jointly awarded to Drs Stephen Bloom and Bo Drasar. The choice of medallists has reflected the phases of gastrointestinal research. Thus, while initially physiological and pathophysiological research predominated, later awards reflected a progression into cellular and molecular biological topics.

OXFORD SCIENCE PUBLICATIONS

The biology of epithelial cell populations
Volume 2

Nicholas Wright and Malcolm Alison

The Cell Cycle

The British Society of Gastroenterology research medal awarded to young scientists in the field has recognized the early contributions of individuals who have subsequently made substantial contributions to the discipline. The mysteries of gastrointestinal stem cells (*bottom*) and cellular dynamics (*left*) were examined in a rich, two-volume book, *The biology of epithelial cell populations*, by Malcolm Alison and Nicholas Wright (*inset*), the 1979 recipient of the award.

Date	Sir Arthur Hurst Lecture	Sir Francis Avery Jones – British Society of Gastroenterology research medal
1967	C Code	–
1968	B Creamer	–
1969	RK Crane	–
1970	KJ Isselbacher	–
1971	B Morson	–
1972	MI Grossman	–
1973	IF Lennard Jones	–
1974	IF Hofmann	–
1975	R Williams	–
1976	JC Goligher	–
1977	JS Fordtran	SR Bloom BS Drasar
1978	S Sherlock	DB Silk
1979	BS Blumberg	NA Wright
1980	A Parks	A Ferguson
1981	H Sarles	NW Read
1982	J Black	RM Case
1983	KN Jeejeebhoy	RCN Williamson
1984	LA Turnberg	WDW Rees
1985	J Forte	HC Thomas
1986	KG Wormsley	PJ Ciclitira
1987	Sir CC Booth	MJG Farthing
1988	Sir D Weatherall	DG Thompson
1989	J Holmgren	JM Rhodes
1990	JP Benhamou	A Garner
1991	Sir W Bodmer	I Bjarnson
1992	J Dent	AJM Watson
1993	W Silen	M Kamm
1994	T Starzt	J Jankowski
1995	LW Powell	R Playford
1996	JR Bennett	DH Adams
1997	NA Wright	Y Mahida M Pignatelli
1998	S Moncada	O Aziz
1999	–	S Taylor-Robinson
2000	Sir R Sykes	CP Day
2001	DY Graham	JC Atherton
2002	H Bismuth	S Watson
2003	HJF Hodgson	M Ilyas

Endoscopy Foundation Lecture

At the foundation of an independent British Society for Digestive Endoscopy in 1971, its Council established an annual lectureship to be known as the "Foundation Lecture". It was determined that this award should be to an individual who had been responsible for a major contribution to endoscopy, and Harold Hopkins, who had been instrumental in the development of fiberoptics, was the first recipient. Subsequent to the amalgamation of the British Society for Digestive Endoscopy with the Society of Gastroenterology in 1980, this series of lectures was continued as the Endoscopy Foundation Lectures and a distinguished group of both national and international luminaries have delivered the oration.

Harold Hopkins developed the theoretical basis of fiberoptic technology and received the Nobel Prize for his contributions to the field of optical science.

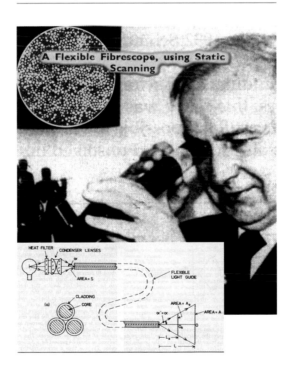

Hopkins Endoscopy prize

Although the British Society for Digestive Endoscopy annually awarded an endoscopy prize to an individual who had made a significant advance in endoscopy, when the two Societies merged, the prize was renamed in honor of Professor Hopkins. The prizewinner is required to deliver a 15-minute paper at a meeting of the Society.

Date	Endoscopy Foundation Lecture	Hopkins Endoscopy prize
1967	–	–
1968	–	–
1969	–	–
1970	–	–
1971	–	–
1972	HH Hopkins	
1973	JF Morrissey	
1974	M Classen	
1975	M Cremer	
1976	CB Williams	–
1977	PB Cotton	M Atkinson
1978	PR Salmon	–
1979	L Safrany	–
1980	GN Tytgat	LR Celestin
1981	A Kerr Grant	HJ O'Connor J Rothwell
1982	AJ Rogers	JDR Rose
1983	DC Auth	J Dawson
1984	J German	–
1985	RH Hunt	–
1986	G Vantrappen	
1987	DG Colin-Jones	TC Northfield
1988	B Hirschowitz	H Barr
1989	BJ Marshall	DG Bell
1990	M Sivak	
1991	CHJ Swan	–
1992	N Soehendra	CP Swain
1993	ATR Axon	–
1994	D Castell	C Choudari
1995	CB Williams	–
1996	T Rosch	BP Saunders CB Williams
1997	PB Cotton	–
1998	AI Morris	GD Bell JF Bladen
1999	–	
2000	MG Bramble	DF Martin
2001	S Chung	GD Bell
2002	B Saunders	CP Swain
2003	T Rosche	

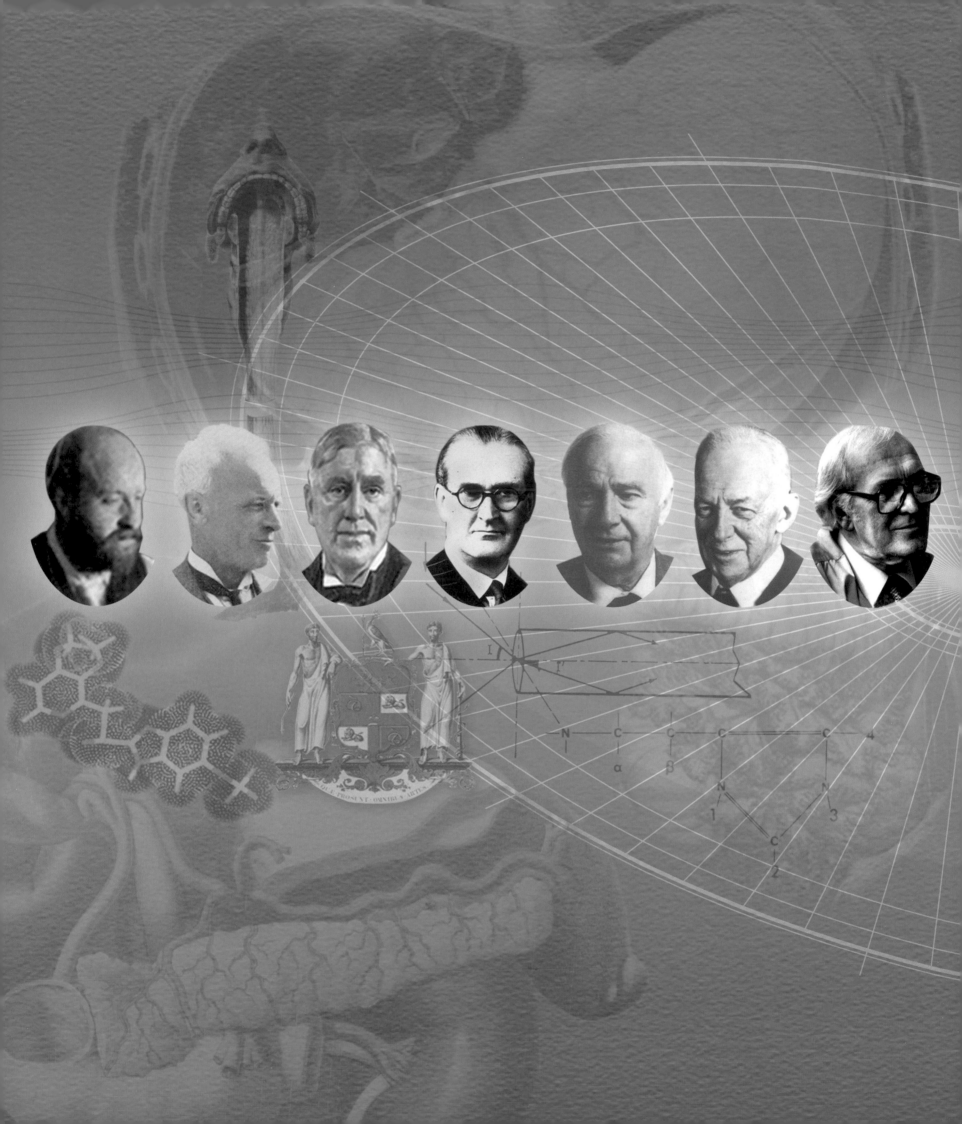

SECTION II

The Evolution of Gastroenterology in Britain

Andreas Vesalius (1513–1564) (*left*), with the aid of the Basel printer J Oporinus (Herbst) (1507–1568), in 1543 produced an exquisite anatomical folio in which the relationship of the stomach and esophagus was delineated. Although Vesalius captured the intimate association of the vagus nerves with the upper digestive tract and demonstrated clearly what would later become known as the angle of His, he failed to comment on the functional nature of the lower esophageal sphincter.

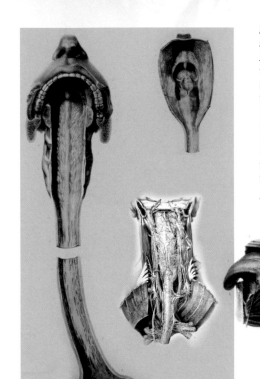

An 1832 illustration of the anatomy of the esophagus by JP Bougery of Paris. Originally trained as a painter by no less a personage than Jean Louis David, the portraitist of Napoleon, Bougery was to find himself unemployed after the defeat of Napoleon and the subsequent loss of patronage. He therefore turned his considerable skills to anatomical illustration.

The esophagus has long languished as an organ not highly regarded by any group and little understood by either laymen or physicians. To some extent, this reflects its course through three different anatomical territories – the neck, mediastinum, and abdomen – and the reluctance of the medical specialists of each group to claim the organ as their own. Even its name is poorly understood and much conjecture exists regarding the origin of the term. Although derived from an old Homeric term for the gullet, the meaning became transmuted to reflect a combination of swallowing and food, thus becoming interpreted as "a tube that conveys food". Aristotle claimed that the name derived from its narrowness and length, and some etymologists have linked the origin of the word to an osier twig, since the old Greek term could also be translated as an "eater of osiers". Whether this reflected the early usage of such flexible branches in the treatment of esophageal obstructions is not known. Although the earliest English usage of the term is recorded in 1398 in a manuscript in the Bodleian collection that refers to "Ysophagus, that is the wey of mete and drinke," by 1541, Guydon stated, "…the Meri otherwise called Ysophgus is ye way of the mete & this Meri commeth out of the throte and thyrleth the mydryfe unto ye bely or stomacke." The word *meri* derived from the Arabic via the translation of the Byzantine Greek manuscripts into Arabic and its later reintroduction back into Europe via the Moorish occupation of the Iberian peninsula. Despite these etymological arguments, the esophagus claimed early medical attention, given the propensity of foreign bodies to obstruct it and the rapid onset of symptoms once ingress of fluids or liquids into the stomach was impaired.

OBSTRUCTION

Blind tubes were initially used for the removal of foreign bodies from the esophagus by either extraction or by forcing them into the stomach. As early as 1493, Johannes Arculanus, Professor at Bologna and Padua, described a short, perforated lead tube for the purpose of clasping foreign bodies such as fish bones. These instruments gave rise to a range of modifications, such as an elaborately carved silver tube with an attachment of small sponges at the lower end. Fabricius Hildanus (1560–1639), who designed the device, described it as: "…a hollow silver bent tube the size of a swan's feather about a foot and a half in length. This tube, which is perforated throughout its length and has a sponge the size of a hazelnut securely attached at its end, is introduced in the esophagus and is utilized with much success in extracting fish bones, small bones, and other foreign objects." Foreign bodies that could not be extracted, however, were dislodged directly into the stomach.

A variety of devices have been used since the earliest times to relieve digestive problems. Peacock feathers were applied to the pharynx to stimulate vomiting, thus relieving gastric distension or expelling ingested poison. Specula (*bottom right*) were thereafter utilized to help visualize the interior of the body – this particular design would remain almost unchanged until the early 20th century. By the 16th century, however, a number of instruments (*bottom left*) had been developed by Arculanus, Hildanus, or Scultetus for the extraction of foreign bodies from the esophagus.

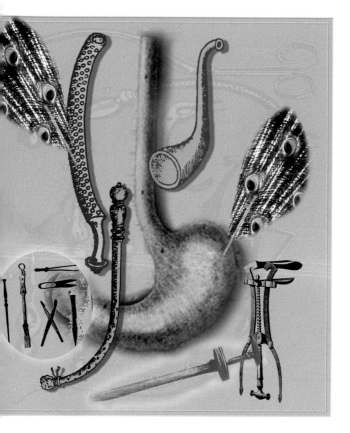

Hieronymus Fabricius ab Aquapendente (1537–1619) of Padua, in addition to advocating the latter course, was also interested in artificial feeding and designed a silver tube covered with the intestine of a sheep, which was introduced through the nose into the stomach. Once in place, the tube was withdrawn and the intestine left in place as a conduit. This device subsequently evolved into catheters of leather that were both easier to introduce as well as greater in length.

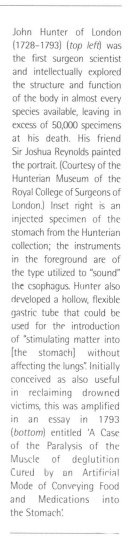

A Case of the Paralysis of the Muscle of deglutition Cured by an Artificial Mode of Conveying Food and Medications into the Stomach

John Hunter

1793

John Hunter of London (1728–1793) (*top left*) was the first surgeon scientist and intellectually explored the structure and function of the body in almost every species available, leaving in excess of 50,000 specimens at his death. His friend Sir Joshua Reynolds painted the portrait. (Courtesy of the Hunterian Museum of the Royal College of Surgeons of London.) Inset right is an injected specimen of the stomach from the Hunterian collection; the instruments in the foreground are of the type utilized to "sound" the esophagus. Hunter also developed a hollow, flexible gastric tube that could be used for the introduction of "stimulating matter into [the stomach] without affecting the lungs". Initially conceived as also useful in reclaiming drowned victims, this was amplified in an essay in 1793 (*bottom*) entitled 'A Case of the Paralysis of the Muscle of deglutition Cured by an Artificial Mode of Conveying Food and Medications into the Stomach'.

John Hunter (1728–1793) of London undertook the next important contribution in this area. Hunter was the first surgeon scientist and intellectually explored the structure and function of the body in almost every species available, leaving in excess of 50,000 specimens at his death. These formed the basis for his collection housed at the Royal College of Surgeons of England. Hunter was extensively interested in the stomach and in particular its acidity, and also wrote a text on digestion in *Observations on Certain Parts of the Animal Oeconomy* (1786). His contributions to the esophagus involve his numerous techniques traversing this organ to enter the stomach. Thus he described the use of a syringe attached to a hollow bougie or flexible catheter of sufficient length such that it might be introduced into the stomach and "convey stimulating matter into it without affecting the lungs". Initially conceived as useful in reclaiming drowned victims, this was amplified in a second essay in 1793, 'A Case of Paralysis of the Muscles of Deglutition cured by an Artificial Mode of Conveying Food and Medicines into the Stomach'.

Hunter also developed a hollow, flexible tube that could be used for the introduction of medicaments as well as food and was used to treat a 50-year-old man with depression, anxiety, and hypochondriasis. The device was introduced by the patient himself to administer flower of mustard and tincture of valerian tube twice daily into his own stomach. The procedure was described as follows: "…a fresh eel skin of rather a small size, drawn over a probang and tied up at the end, where it covered the sponge, and tied again close to the sponge, where it fastened to the whale bone, and a small longitudinal slit was made into it just above this upper ligature. To the other end of the eel skin was fixed a bladder and wooden pipe, similar to what is used in giving a clyster, only the pipe was large enough to let the end of the probang pass into the bladder without feeling up the passage. The probang thus covered was introduced into the stomach and the food and medicines put into the bladder and squeezed down through the eel skin." The long-term compliance and success of the procedure is not recorded!

VISUALIZING THE ESOPHAGUS

While the early pioneers were able to traverse the esophagus, the actual visualization of this organ was accomplished by Adolf Kussmaul (1822–1902) of Freiburg. As early as 1865, Kussmaul had directed his attention to the problem of access to the stomach, initially with the object of effecting decompression in cases of obstruction. Convinced of the clinical relevance of this goal, he initiated a renaissance of the gastric tube at the clinic in Freiburg.

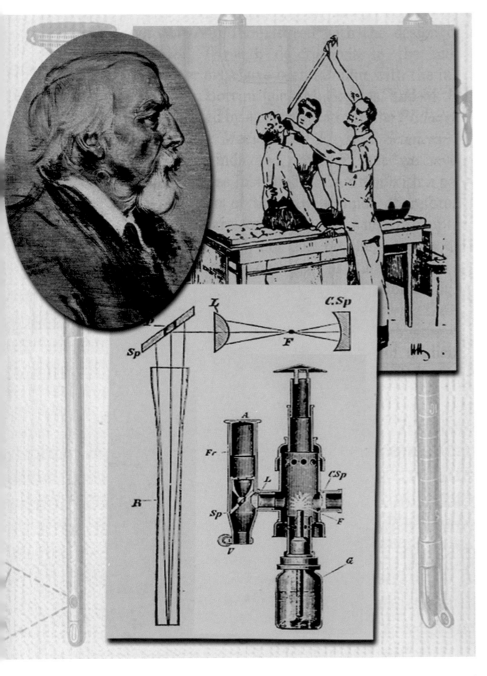

In 1868, Adolf Kussmaul (*top left*) was the first to attempt gastroscopy. The technique he employed to introduce the rigid instrument was based upon that practiced by sword-swallowers (*top right*). The device (*bottom*) was based upon that used previously by Desormeaux of Paris (1865) to study the bladder. A long, rigid speculum was introduced into the stomach and the proximal tube component attached as the light source. The latter was provided by an attached gasogen lamp. Unfortunately, the light was inadequate and Kussmaul could not adequately discern detail.

Initially, Kussmaul had undertaken direct esophagoscopy using a tube-shaped speculum to which he attached the endoscope of Desormeaux for illumination. His concern with patient safety led him to enlist the services of a sword-swallower to help him with the development of a technique that might be safe. After a careful study of a sword-swallower introducing his sword, Kussmaul made a number of design modifications to the original instrument and used two special tubes, each 47cm in length, one round with a diameter of 13mm and the other elliptical. Although the sword-swallower successfully introduced the tube in his usual upright position, the examination was however unsatisfactory, due to both the inadequacy of illumination and the copious amount of fluid obstructing the field of visibility. Although Kussmaul demonstrated the introduction of the tube at the medical section of the Society of Naturalists in Freiburg, and even sent his sword-swallower with the tubes for study at the surgical clinic in Zurich, he failed to publish a report. Difficulties with toleration by patients of the rigid instrument and suboptimal visualization, however, dimmed Kussmaul's initial enthusiasm and sadly for the discipline of endoscopy, despite having identified esophageal pathology on a number of occasions, he failed to further pursue this area in any great detail. Despite this, his experimentation in 1868 laid the foundation for the later work of Johann von Mikulicz-Radecki (1850–1905) of Vienna and Chevalier Jackson (1865–1958) of Philadelphia.

Von Mikulicz-Radecki, the leading pupil and collaborator of Christian Albert Theodore Billroth (1829–1894) in Vienna, was particularly involved in the surgical management of diseases of the gastrointestinal tract.

The development of the open rigid tube by Johann von Mikulicz-Radecki (*top right*) and Fritz Leiter led to the production of an efficient and effective esophagoscope (*bottom left*). The later addition by Leiter of his pan-endoscope was critical in resolving the issue of illumination. It provided a battery-operated universal light source for all endoscopes and was based upon an Edison lamp that provided illumination by reflecting light from a diminutive electric bulb built into the handle. The resolution of the problem posed by inadequate illumination represented a major advance in endoscopy.

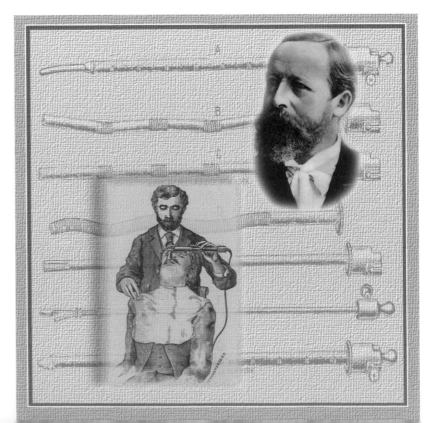

Although the chest cavity was inviolate to surgeons of his time, the esophagus remained a surgical challenge that could not be ignored, particularly since it represented the roadway to the stomach. Initially skeptical of Kussmaul's "endoscopic" approach, von Mikulicz-Radecki undertook the evaluation of the esophagus in 1880 with the help of an elderly woman who had a proclivity for swallowing instruments. He also studied the passage of instruments in cadavers. In this way, von Mikulicz-Radecki was able to determine that apart from a slight resistance at the level of the larynx, the only condition necessary to ensure successful esophagoscopy was that the head of the patient be held firmly in a "sword-swallower's position". Von Mikulicz-Radecki's esophagoscope (which he developed with the help of the instrument-maker Fritz Leiter) had a diameter of 11–13mm and was closed by a knob-like head of a stylet or mandarin that had been placed in the lumen of an instrument prior to its usage. Once the instrument had been successfully introduced to the lower level of the esophagus, the stylet was withdrawn and replaced with a thin flat rod that contained an insulated wiring system and minute conduits utilized for the purpose of cooling the lighting element. At its proximal end, the wire was connected to a Bunsen battery and its terminal end possessed a U-shaped platinum wire that could be brought to incandescence behind a glass window. The light source or "glow bulb" was then cooled by water that flowed in the tiny circuits surrounding the platinum loop. The advantage of this component was that it only occupied a small space within the tube, leaving considerable room for visualization of the lumen of the esophagus.

Using this approach, von Mikulicz-Radecki undertook a series of clinical observations regarding the esophagus. He noted that in a normal organ, the mucosa appeared the same throughout – a uniform, pale red traversed intermittently by tiny blood vessels – and commented that the uniform smoothness of the mucosa produced a glaring effect that made visualization difficult. He also reported some interesting pathological observations and described in detail foreign bodies, cancer, and esophageal compression due to lung disease and aortic aneurysm.

Sir Francis Richard Cruise (1834–1912) (*bottom left*) of Dublin studied at Trinity, Cambridge, learnt to shoot in Connecticut, became a splendid cellist, was appointed Honorary Physician to Edward VII, and was knighted by Queen Victoria. He believed in "the direct exploration of organs for the elucidation of their physiology and pathology" and having graciously acknowledged the contributions of Desormeaux, sought actively to improve the illumination of his device by redesigning the lens and lamp system (*top right*). His original instrument (*bottom right*) as well as a number of other developmental endoscopic devices (*top left and center*) may be viewed at the Royal College of Surgeons of Ireland (*background*).

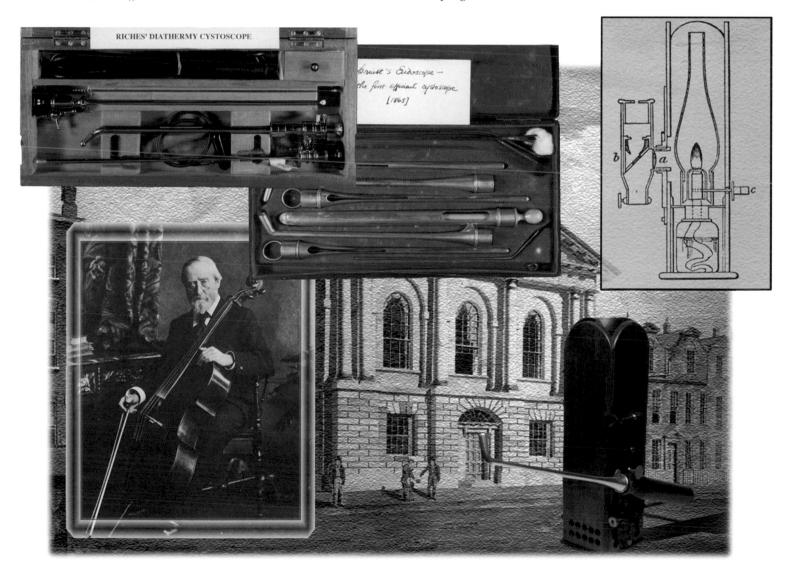

Thereafter, Chevalier Jackson of Philadelphia, an early esophagoscopist of considerable skill, suggested that the stomach could be quite adequately and safely examined utilizing open tubes (1907). Using an open tube devoid of any optical system and differing only from an esophagoscope in its increased length, he became adept at inspection of the stomach. His proposal, however, met with little general acceptance, since it was evident that few possessed the formidable skills necessary to obtain the superlative results that he claimed.

Chevalier Jackson (1865–1958) (*center*), an ear, nose, and throat surgeon of Philadelphia, made important contributions to the subject of endoscopy and the esophagus . Erudite, artistic, sophisticated, and a brilliant surgeon to boot, by 1930 his perspicacity enabled him to consider the concept of gastric juice as one of the causes of inflammation of the lower esophagus. In this respect, he was able to provide strong support for the proposal put forward by Asher Winkelstein (1893–1972) in 1934 that peptic esophagitis was a disease entity worthy of serious consideration.

medical thought. Indeed, the motto "*Simplex Veri Sigillum*" ("Simplicity is the sign of truth") by which Boerhaave lived perhaps most accurately sums up the direction which scientific research took during his tutelage.

Apart from his contributions as a teacher, Boerhaave's most masterful skill was his ability to relate clinical symptomatology to anatomical findings that he subsequently confirmed at postmortem. In this respect, his most significant contribution was made in the description of the ruptured esophagus of his friend and patient Baron Johannes Wassenaar of Rosenbergh, in the neighborhood of Leiden. Wassenaar was a good friend of Boerhaave and occupied the substantial position of Admiral of the Republic and Dikereeve of Rhineland, and Boerhaave, who had previously treated his gout, knew him to be a glutton who took little exercise. On October 29, 1723, at half past midnight, the Admiral's son called Boerhaave from his residence to the home of the Baron, where he found him

ESOPHAGEAL RUPTURE

While impairment to swallowing food constituted a problem, it paled in comparison to the events consequent upon rupture of the esophagus. The classic description of this entity reflects the clinical acumen and erudition of Herman Boerhaave (1668–1738) of Leiden. Undoubtedly the leading physician of the age, Boerhaave was the founder of the "Eclectic school" and it was largely due to his efforts that Leiden achieved considerable fame as a medical center.

Boerhaave, who was particularly interested in teaching and who was in his own right a commanding presence, earned a great reputation as a clinician and bedside teacher. Although he contributed little to clinical medicine outside of his oral instruction, hundreds of students traveled to Leiden from all parts of Europe during his tenure from 1714 to 1738. Included in the list of his pupils are illustrious names such as Haller, Gaub, Cullen, Pringle, van Swieten, and de Haen. Many of these subsequently became leading physicians in their own countries of Sweden, Germany, Austria, and Scotland, and thus further augmented the influence of Boerhaave and the Leiden school of

sitting upright in bed, bent forward, and complaining of acute shortness of breath and pain in his chest. The clinical story as it emerged was that the Baron had some three days previously partaken of a copious dinner together with friends and afterwards, in good health, gone horse riding with his son. Later that evening, the Baron had felt somewhat dyspeptic and as was his habit, had taken three small cupfuls of a gentle emetic. When this failed to produce the required effect, he took four more cupfuls, but on attempting to vomit, had uttered a terrible cry on account of "a violent pain in his chest". Wassenaar described a sensation of "something having broken or torn" and declaring instantly that he was dying, began to pray to God and to resign himself to his will. In the following hours, he took four doses of olive oil (each about 28g) and later drank 6oz of beer. Prior to the arrival of Boerhaave, the patient had been treated by Dr De Bye, but despite the use of clysters and venesection, no improvement had been noted. Boerhaave prescribed a second venesection, soft drinks, and warm compresses, but all to no avail and the following day, the Baron died in great distress.

Herman Boerhaave (1668–1738) (*top right*) was the foremost clinical teacher in Europe and is known for correctly identifying the syndrome of "ruptured esophagus" (later renamed Mallory-Weiss syndrome). Many of his students subsequently became the leaders of medicine in their own countries and thus the Boerhaave school of thought extended throughout Europe. Students were recommended to partake of a tri-part medical curriculum consisting of a preparatory study of the basic natural sciences, followed by advanced study of anatomy and physiology that culminated in observation and instruction at the sick bed and in the autopsy room. The first two components were delivered to students in the lecture hall, while the third was conducted at St Caecilia Hospital. So effective was this system at Leiden that its principles still remain embodied in the curricula of medical schools throughout the world to this day.

Boerhaave, in the presence of Dr De Bye and three other interested gentlemen, undertook the autopsy. The examination of the corpse revealed the presence of subcutaneous emphysema in addition to a large amount of air in the abdominal cavity. When the chest was opened, a tremendous rush of air escaped and Boerhaave was able to identify the rancid odor of the duck meat that had constituted the major content of the Baron's last meal (three days earlier). The lungs had completely collapsed and were floating on liquid that filled the entire chest equally on both sides. During the examination of the left pleural cavity, a finger-sized tear was found in the lower end of the esophagus. Boerhaave's conclusion was that the esophagus, which had been previously healthy, had been spontaneously torn by the violent vomiting induced by the emetic taken by the Baron. He considered the disease, which was previously unknown, to be entirely incurable, yet nevertheless described the symptomatology and anatomical findings with such clarity that the entity today bears his name.

This case history attracted the attention of Norman Barrett (1903–1979) when he was planning the first edition of *Thorax*. Barrett, who made important contributions to the understanding of the esophagus, particularly esophagitis, in which he was particularly interested, was an Australian who had been educated at Eton and Trinity College, Cambridge, before graduating from St Thomas' Hospital in 1928. Thereafter, he became Surgeon at St Thomas' and Brompton Hospitals, President of the Thoracic Surgeons of Great Britain and Ireland (1962), and the Editor of *Thorax* from 1946–1971.

It was during his compilation of the first edition that he found himself short of surgical material and was driven to the conclusion that this deficiency could be best corrected by writing a paper himself. For some reason, he elected to comment on the subject of spontaneous rupture, even though he had never seen a case! In reviewing the published reports, he found that no patient had survived the operative closure of the defect. He was thus able to emphasize the fact that doctors failed to diagnose this condition because they were unaware of its existence and hence the prolonged delay was instrumental in causing sepsis and death. His point was well demonstrated in 1947, when he reported his own experience with the first successful example of survival after operation for closure of an esophageal tear.

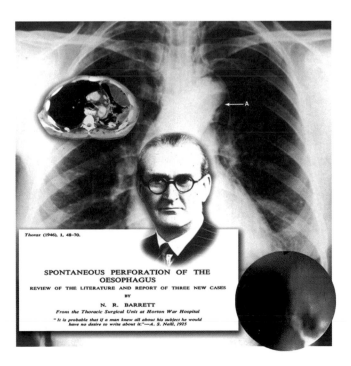

A classic chest X-ray demonstrating juxta-pericardiac free air from an esophageal perforation due to Boerhaave's syndrome (*background*). CT and endoscopic views of a mucosal tear (Mallory-Weiss) that represents an earlier stage in esophageal neural damage prior to final perforation are shown (*top left and bottom right, respectively*). Norman Barrett (1903–1979) (*center*) was the first person to successfully repair the tear in 1946, 220 years after its original description!

ESOPHAGEAL WEB

Although a condition of relatively minor importance, esophageal web is often the source of great diagnostic confusion, particularly when it is associated with unresolved dysphagia. Characterized by iron-deficiency anemia, atrophic changes in the buccal, glossopharyngeal, and esophageal mucous membranes, koilonychia, and dysphagia, the disease has generated considerable eponymous confusion as a variety of physicians were identified as having first described the lesion. In fact, the entity was first described in Britain in 1919 by Adam Brown-Kelly (1865–1941) of Glasgow and Donald Paterson (1893–1939) of Edinburgh. Nevertheless, it subsequently became known by American physicians as the Plummer-Vinson syndrome, although Vinson was adamant that Plummer, though he spoke of the syndrome at an early date, never published his observations. Some, therefore, refer to it as the Plummer-Vinson, Paterson-Kelly syndrome, although the annual reports of the disease are probably of a lower frequency than the number of persons in the eponym.

PHARYNGEAL POUCH

Ludlow described the pharyngeal pouch in 1769, but as a result of a lucid German account over 100 years later, the condition has become eponymously associated with Friedrich von Zenker (1825–1898).

In Britain, Whitehead in 1891 appreciated the necessity for action, but could only suggest doing a gastrostomy for his patient. At the beginning of the 20th century, a series of cases in which excision had been used with considerable success was reported by Butlin in Britain. It was acknowledged, however, that this work was not original, as von Bergmann had performed excision in a case some 10 years earlier. Even in 1891, this condition was considered a pressure diverticulum and subsequent papers generally referred to it as a "pulsion diverticulum". Despite Butlin's successes, there was a high incidence of wound breakdown and fistula formation, and Goldman in Freiburg therefore introduced a two-stage operation to obviate this problem.

In 1950, Negus in Britain published a thoughtful review of the evolution and treatment of the condition, with the result that attention was focused on the etiological importance of the upper esophageal sphincter. This raised the question of whether a myotomy should be part of the operation and also some speculation as to whether the pouch was secondary to upper sphincter spasm engendered by gastroesophageal reflux. The recognized association of pharyngeal pouch and sliding hiatal hernia initially lent some support to this view, but this probably represents little more than a correlatable epiphenomenon.

Ludlow's description (*background*) of the pharyngeal diverticulum or pouch (*top right*) was read by William Hunter (1718–1783) (*bottom left*) in 1769. William was the brother of the more famous John and was better known for his work in obstetrics. In 1867, Friedrich von Zenker (*bottom right*) published his observations on five personal cases and 22 cases from the literature of herniation of the esophageal mucosa (*center*). The condition has become associated with the latter and is now known as Zenker's diverticulum.

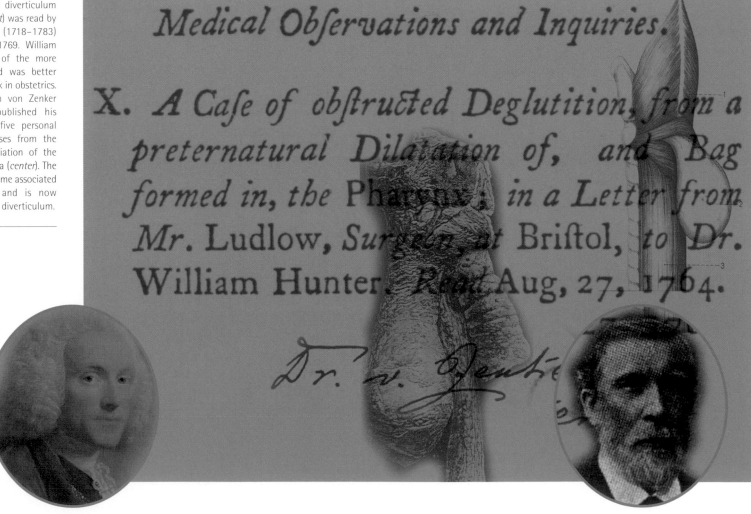

Medical Observations and Inquiries.

X. A Case of obstructed Deglutition, from a preternatural Dilatation of, and Bag formed in, the Pharynx; in a Letter from Mr. Ludlow, Surgeon, at Bristol, to Dr. William Hunter. Read Aug, 27, 1764.

Thomas Willis (1621–1675) (*top left*) achieved immortality for his description of the arterial circle at the base of the brain. His friend Sir Christopher Wren, who initially practiced as a physician before becoming an architect of hospitals and St Paul's Cathedral, undertook the actual drawings of the eponymous circle. Willis was also experienced in the use of esophageal sounds to either remove foreign bodies or dilate strictures. His classic description of 16 years of successful esophageal dilation may well represent the first description of achalasia (*bottom*). Also shown are a variety of 17th century devices utilized for the extraction of foreign bodies from the pharynx and esophagus (*center*).

"*On the convulsive cough and asthma*"
Practice of Physick, Treatise 8, pp 92-96
Thomas Willis, 1684

ACHALASIA AND HELLER

One of the first references to achalasia was in 1675 by Thomas Willis (1621–1675), who not only described the disability but also reported a successful treatment.

Using a sponge on the end of a piece of flexible whalebone, Willis dilated the passage and gave material relief to his patient over many years. This initial therapeutic intervention set the tone for the long-standing controversy that has persisted for decades as to whether luminal dilation or surgical sphincterotomy is the ideal method of treatment.

The main impetus for open operation arose in Germany as a consequence of the work of Ernst Heller (1877–1964), who successfully undertook the first myotomy at the cardia in 1913.

This intervention was based upon Heller's belief that the condition was due to spasm at the lower esophageal sphincter, although this theory was challenged by the work undertaken at Guy's Hospital by Sir Arthur Hurst (1879–1944). Having studied esophageal function with Cannon in Boston, Hurst was convinced that the abnormality represented a failure of relaxation rather than spasm and gave the condition its present name. Although Hurst was particularly interested in ulcer disease, gut symptomatology, and constipation, as well as achalasia, he wrote thoughtfully and definitively on diverse gastrointestinal subjects. In terms of his views on achalasia, Hurst supported dilatation and it was his opinion that was especially responsible for the continued emphasis on the use of his mercury-loaded bougies. Despite this heavy metal approach, results were not perfect, given the blind nature of the technique, and as a result, safer and more effective means of relieving the obstruction were sought.

Ernst Heller (1877–1964) (*bottom*) published a report in 1914 (*background*) on the use of extramucosal esophagomyotomy for the treatment of achalasia of the esophagus. Top left is his original drawing of the operation, compared to the other anastomotic cardioplasties developed in Germany in the first half of the 20th century (*top right and center*). Heller made a complete division of the longitudinal and circular muscle fibers, and did not extend the myotomy into the stomach.

Although this led to the introduction of a surgical procedure that anastomosed the dilated esophagus to the fundus of the stomach, this procedure engendered seriously unsatisfactory results due to the dramatic regurgitation that occurred postoperatively. As a consequence, the Heller procedure, which was well tolerated and had little or no operative mortality in many cases, remained the procedure of choice, even though there remained some dissatisfaction with the results in about 20% of cases. This shortfall provided some encouragement to the advocates of dilatation and stimulated the introduction of alternative methods of "stretching" the area, usually through an esophagoscope.

Aus der Chirurgischen Klinik zu Leipzig (Direktor: Prof. Dr. E. PAYR).

IV.

Extramuköse Cardiaplastik beim chronischen Cardiospasmus mit Dilatation des Oesophagus.

Von
Privatdozent Dr. E. Heller,
Oberarzt der Klinik.
(Hierzu 3 Abbildungen im Texte.)

Im ersten Heft des Archivs für klinische Chirurgie 1913 hat HEY-ROVSKY eine subdiaphragmatische Oesophagogastroanastomose beschrieben, die er bei zwei Fällen der sogenannten „idiopathischen Dilatation der Speiseröhre" mit Erfolg ausgeführt hat. Kurz nach dem Erscheinen dieser Mitteilung an ein Patient mit chronischem Cardiospasmus und starker Dilatation des Oesophagus in die Behandlung der Leipzig Klinik, bei dem mir nach Lage des Falles chirurgisch zur des Leidens geboten erschien. Unter dem HEYROVSKY Erfolge beabsichtigte ich den operativen zu vorzunehmen. Im Verlauf der Operation gewisse Schwierigkeiten der operativen führende theoretische Ueberlegungen, zu ein abweichenden Durchführung der Operation er extramukösen Cardiaplastik. Da reifend bemerken will, im funktionellen Sinne fallen ist, und diese Aenderung des operativ htens nicht unerhebliche praktische Vort Behandlung des Cardiospasmus mit Oeso agenen und ausgeführten operativen Maßnahmen ich mir erlauben, den Fall kurz mitzuteilen.

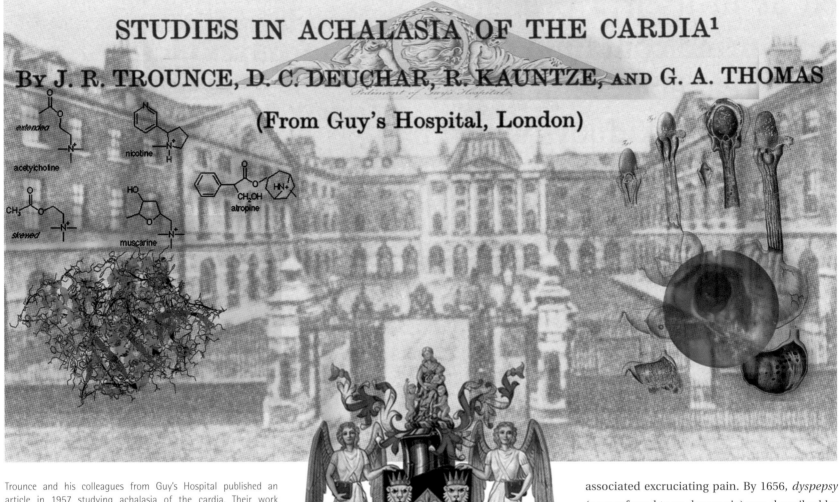

STUDIES IN ACHALASIA OF THE CARDIA[1]

By J. R. TROUNCE, D. C. DEUCHAR, R. KAUNTZE, and G. A. THOMAS

(From Guy's Hospital, London)

Trounce and his colleagues from Guy's Hospital published an article in 1957 studying achalasia of the cardia. Their work demonstrated that the muscle in patients with achalasia behaved pharmacologically as smooth muscle, which also exhibited normal cholinesterase activity (*left*). Despite this pharmacological examination, reflux was thought to be more important in this disease entity.

Although Chagas' disease mimicked achalasia, no parasitic infestation was evident in achalasia patients and the genesis of the problem was unclear until the work of Trounce and his colleagues at Guy's Hospital in 1957 demonstrated the biochemical basis of the abnormality of the esophageal musculature in patients with achalasia.

Nevertheless, many still considered reflux to be more important in this disease entity than any neuromuscular aberration. The efficacy of current therapy with botulinum toxin has rendered this argument specious, and indeed the argument whether surgery is more efficacious now that it is undertaken laparoscopically still continues to fuel the debate between the dilators and the myotomists.

ESOPHAGITIS

History

The history of the subject of esophagitis is mired in the confusion regarding the terminology used to describe its symptomatology as well as by a failure to appreciate the organ as a separate entity from the stomach or the mouth. Despite this, the first description of the disease by Galen was fairly accurate, although somewhat incomplete. Nevertheless, Galen duly noted that although difficulties with swallowing may be due to tumors or paralysis, the esophagus when inflamed hindered swallowing due to the associated excruciating pain. By 1656, *dyspepsy* (now referred to as dyspepsia) was described by Blount as "dyspesie" and by Lovell in 1661 as an "imbecility of the stomach, which is a vice of the concocting faculty and is called apepsy, bradyspepsy, or dispepsy and diaphthora". The recognition that it might be caused by both acid and bile appears to reside in the 1829 notation of Southey, who, in *Epistle in Anniversary*, noted the sensations evoked "by bile, opinions, and dyspepsy sour!" The relationship between the mind, stress, and acid disorders may have been first noted by Lowell, who in the 1848 *Fable for Critics*, opined that an individual had been "brought to death's door of a mental dyspepsy". Similarly, the subject of heartburn, which was initially regarded as a heated and embittered state of mind that was felt but not openly expressed, was described by William Shakespeare in *Richard III* as a "long continued grudge and hearte brennynge betwene the Quenes kinred and the kinges blood".

"A long continued grudge and hearte brennynge betwene the Quenes kindred and the kinges blood"

Richard III (1452–1485), notorious for his suspected role in the 'disappearance' of his nephews, was portrayed by William Shakespeare as a limping hunchback with a deformed arm. It is possible that the Bard utilized artistic license in his portrayal to illustrate the Elizabethan concept of a deformed mind and body. This painting by an unknown hand suggests the last Plantagenet king may not have been as twisted as once thought. Perhaps the last word on this matter should be left to Churchill, who wrote: "No-one in his lifetime seems to have remarked on his deformities, but they are now very familiar to us through Shakespeare's play."

Honkoop published a thesis on inflammation of the gullet in 1774. In 1785, Bleuland, a physician himself, was struck down with the disease and carefully recorded the details of his illness. The first reports of the condition of esophagitis in children originated with Billard, who in 1828 published a statement regarding the ailments of newborn. In 1829, Mondière wrote a thesis describing his own severe personal experiences with esophagitis and in addition, collected much of the extant material on the subject. His laborious compilation represents more industry that discrimination, but the thesis provides a good overview of early 19th century thoughts on the esophagus. Indeed, it is from the work of Mondière that much of the literature sources of esophageal diseases were drawn for the next century. These included Velpeau's *The Esophagus – A Dictionary in Four Volumes*, Follin's essay 'Considerations of Esophageal Disease', and James Copland's *A Dictionary of Practical Medicine*.

In 1835, Graves of Dublin made some observations on the disease, but thereafter confined his attentions to the thyroid, achieving eponymous recognition for his contributions to the subject. In 1878, Knott, also of Dublin, published *The Pathology of the Esophagus* and included in it the cases of esophagitis described by Roche, Bourguet, Broussais, and Paletta, as well as some original illustrations of diseases of the organ. The subject was further illuminated by communications from Hamburger, Padova, Laboulbène, and a number of other distinguished physicians of the time.

An awareness of this problem dates back to 1591, when Percivall described "a sharpnes, sowernes of stomack, hartburning". Thereafter, Swan in 1635 expressed the opinion that "Lettice cooleth a hot stomach called heart-burning". As early as 1607, Topsell noted the potential severity of the disease, commenting upon "the hearts of them that die of the heart-burning disease". Of note was the fact that in 1747, Wesley identified that heart burning was "a sharp gnawing pain at the orifice of the Stomach".

In 1884, Sir Morell Mackenzie (1837–1892) of London defined esophagitis as an "acute idiopathic inflammation of the mucous membranes of the esophagus giving rise to extreme odynphagia and often to aphagia". It was this anglicized description that was utilized to qualify the disease known as esophagitis, which had first been described by Johann Peter Frank (1745–1821) in 1792. Although similar observations had been made previously in 1722 by Boehm, who described an acute pain "which reached down even to the stomach and which was accompanied by hiccup and a constant flow of serum from the mouth," the latter had not defined the condition as accurately.

Johann Peter Frank (1745–1821) was born in Rotalben in the Palatinate of Germany and studied medicine at several German and French universities, receiving a medical degree at Heidelberg before becoming Professor of Surgery at Pavia, Vienna, and Moscow, respectively. Frank is best known for his publication *System of a Complete Medical Policy*, in which he described a comprehensive system of medical care combining preventative and curative medical services. His intellectual capacity to appreciate disease was wide ranging. In this respect, he was the first to accurately describe and define the condition now known as esophagitis.

Sir Morell Mackenzie (1837–1892) (*bottom left*) was regarded as the leading ear, nose, and throat surgeon of London at the end of the 19th century. His definitive text on the subject included substantial information on the esophagus and an erudite chapter on the subject of acute esophagitis and its treatment (*background*). Unfortunately, his medical contributions were somewhat overshadowed by his role in the debacle that led to the tragic demise of the German Emperor (Frederick III of Prussia) from laryngeal cancer.

induced by any attempt to swallow or any movement of the laryngeal muscles. He also noted that such patients developed considerable thirst, but were unable to achieve relief by drinking, since the pain was so severe. In adults, he reported that there was a constant expectoration of frothy saliva and although patients might not always have a fever, they often became delirious. Mackenzie believed the lesion to represent a diffuse catarrhal inflammation of the mucosa of the upper end of the gullet and felt the diagnosis was based upon the history of extreme pain and the absence of pharyngeal inflammation

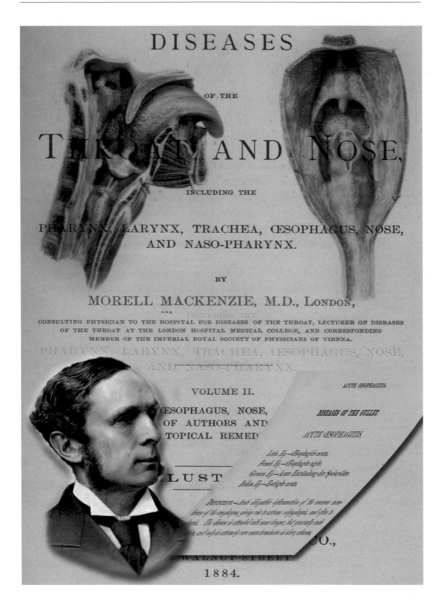

The contributions of Sir Mackenzie

Sir Morell Mackenzie was regarded as the leading ear, nose, and throat surgeon of London at the end of the 19th century. He is also rightfully recognized as the founder of modern laryngoscopy in Britain. Unfortunately, his medical contributions were somewhat overshadowed by his later role in the debacle that led to the demise of the German Emperor (Frederick III of Prussia) from laryngeal cancer.

In the realm of the esophagus, Mackenzie regarded the condition of esophagitis to be of unknown etiology. Nevertheless, he carefully defined the chief symptom as excruciating burning or tearing pain – odynophagia –

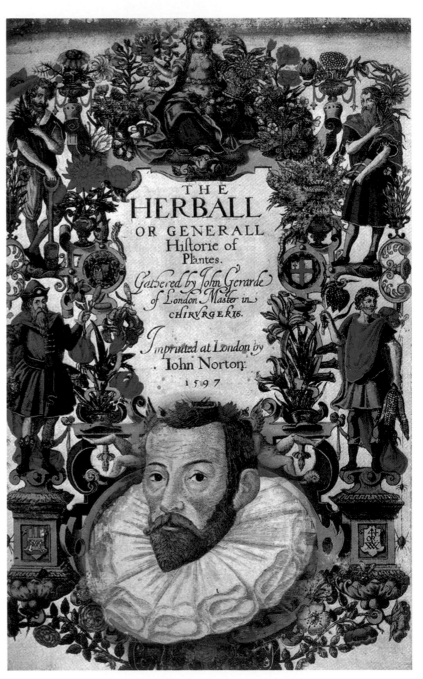

The frontispiece of *The Herball: Or, Generall Historie of Plantes*, written by John Gerard (1545–1612) (*bottom*), a master surgeon of London, in 1597. This encyclopedic tabulation of the known therapeutic strategies of the time included a number of putative remedies for the treatment of the vexatious question of 'Ye dreaded lurgy of Harte Burne'!

on examination! His definitive text on the subject, *Diseases of the Throat and Nose*, which appeared in two volumes in 1880 and 1884, respectively, contained a fascinating and detailed analysis as well as classification of esophagitis, but sometimes failed to accurately distinguish between disease of the lower and upper end of the gullet.

Although Mackenzie's description of esophagitis is very different to that now recognized to represent the contemporary understanding of the disease, his is the first lucid attempt to define the subject. In the 21st century, the term esophagitis is used almost exclusively to refer to an entity involving the lower part of the gullet. Nevertheless, Mackenzie recognized that the inflammatory conditions of the upper part of the gullet were specific and included diphtheria, thrush, tuberculosis, syphilis, actinomycosis, and corrosive damage. Some of the associated non-specific conditions (myalgia, general hyperesthesia) alluded to by Mackenzie are no longer recognized, but as late as 1900, all inflammatory conditions affecting the gullet were still regarded as varieties of esophagitis.

Early treatment of esophagitis

Of particular interest were the treatments proposed in the management of this vexatious condition. It was considered mandatory that the organ be maintained in a state of absolute rest. Thus, feeding was undertaken by nutrient enemata and morphia administered by hypodermic injection to facilitate resolution of inflammation and abolish pain. Poultices were applied along the upper part of the spine, or if the pain was particularly severe, anodyne embrocations such as oleate of morphia or belladonna liniments were rubbed into the back. Mondière, following the French practice of the time, believed in venesection and cupping as well as leech applications (12 to 30 at a time). Counter-irritation by the application of mustard poultices or moxas was also widely recommended. By 1884, Mackenzie was however able to declare that bleeding or even the local abstraction of blood was of little value and that he himself had found counter-irritation to have no effect.

Mackenzie favored derivatives and especially recommended the use of extremely hot *pediluvia*. Bleuland used blisters *loco dolenti* between the shoulders with success and Pagenstecher reported the use of hydrochloride of ammonia to great advantage. This agent had long been a favorite of German and Dutch physicians, and was used as a remedy for many different kinds of disease. Mackenzie was adamant that the passage of bougies was dangerous and should never be attempted, since it was likely to cause rupture of the esophagus. Once convalescence commenced, the patient could be changed from a liquid to a solid diet gradually and if pain returned, immediately returned to a liquid diet once again.

Beetle and insect bites were known to produce pain and inflammation. The use of extracts of blister beetles was considered an excellent method of producing counter irritation and was in certain areas as popular as the fashionable French remedy of using mustard plasters.

Pathology of esophagitis

Despite the attention to the gullet provided by Mackenzie, the disease was not commonly recognized and little was known about it. In 1906, Wilder Tileston (1875–1969), while a pathologist at Harvard University, carefully defined at least 12 different types of ulceration, which included carcinoma, corrosive, foreign bodies, acute infectious diseases, decubitus, aneurysms, catarrhal inflammations associated with diverticulum, tuberculosis, syphilis, varicose, and ulcers due to thrush. Tileston was particularly drawn to the disease that he referred to as "peptic ulcer of the esophagus," which he claimed exactly simulated the behavior and appearance of chronic gastric ulcer. He noted that although a rare entity, it had initially been described by Albers in 1839 and thereafter sporadically noted by pathologists. No less an authority than Karl von Rokitansky (1804–1878) of Vienna concurred that peptic ulcer of the lower esophagus was a real and definable entity, and represented the aftermath of gastric juice in the gullet. Nevertheless, when Tileston reviewed the literature up to 1906, there had only been 44 clear-cut examples of the condition published. The ulcers described were usually single and often associated with chronic peptic ulcer in the stomach or the duodenum. They were large, penetrating lesions sometime 6–8cm in length that lay "above the cardiac sphincter," and although often longitudinal, might also encircle the entire gullet.

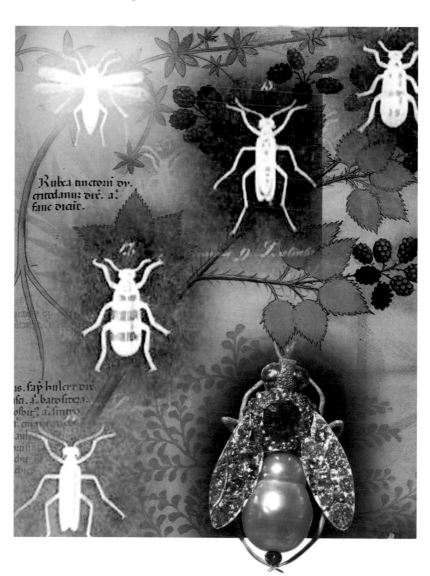

PEPTIC ULCER OF THE ŒSOPHAGUS.

By WILDER TILESTON, M.D.,

ASSISTANT VISITING PHYSICIAN, LONG ISLAND HOSPITAL, BOSTON; CONSULT
MASSACHUSETTS CHARITABLE EYE AND EAR INFIRMARY, BOSTON.

By simple or peptic ulcer of the œsophagus is under
ulcer situated in the lower part of the œsophagus and b
close resemblance to the simple ulcer of the stomach. It i
dition which has received little attention in this country, a
not exc   re, and it has, therefore, seemed worth
repor   three cases, and to give a general dis
of tl

Wilder Tileston (1875–1969) (*bottom left*), while a pathologist at Harvard, was able in 1906 to identify at least 12 potential types of esophageal ulceration. In particular, he noted a disease that simulated the behavior and appearance of chronic gastric ulcer, which he referred to as "peptic ulcer of the esophagus". His seminal manuscript of 1906 reported 41 cases of this rare and novel disease entity. His precise description of the condition accurately noted the typical "overhanging edge" of the healing mucosa (*center*).

inflammation at the lower end of the gullet not previously apparent to clinicians. Thus, by the 1920s, it was apparent that pathologists, clinicians, and endoscopists, while assuming that they were describing the same entity when they referred to peptic ulcer of the esophagus or esophagitis, were each unclear as to the exact nature of the disease process. In 1929, Jackson reported 88 cases in 4,000 consecutive endoscopies, while Stewart and Hartfall in the same year claimed that they were able to identify only one example of esophagitis in 10,000 consecutive autopsies. The subsequent reports of Lyall (1937), Chamberlin (1939), and Dick and Hurst (1942) provided further insight into the nature and occurrence of these lower esophageal lesions. The further substantial contributions by the thoracic surgeon Philip Rowland Allison (1904–1974) of Leeds, England, and his colleague AS Johnstone left little doubt that the authors were confident in their ability to recognize and diagnose "peptic ulcer of the esophagus" or esophagitis.

The patients were elderly and many had no symptoms referable to the esophagus until their admission to the hospital. Death usually occurred from perforation into a large vessel, the pericardium, the mediastinum, or the pleural cavity, although some died of pneumonia. Of interest was the fact that few exhibited symptoms of esophageal obstruction. Tileston further reported that the histology of such ulcers was identical to that of chronic gastric ulcer and that the adjacent mucosa was gastric in type. He assumed it to be "ectopic" since it lined the lower part of the gut in the mediastinum.

The understanding of ulceration of the esophagus and esophagitis itself became further obfuscated with the advent of radiology and esophagoscopy at the turn of the 20th century. The use of these diagnostic tools enabled the identification of a variety of esophageal lesions, particularly ulcers, and

Allison and hiatal hernia

Although diaphragmatic hernia was first described by Ambroise Paré (1510–1590) as early as 1580, historically, the hiatal hernia had hardly been described before the X-ray era, and reflected the classic autopsy technique of that time, in which the esophagus was cut just above the diaphragm and taken out with the heart and the lungs, losing all its connections with its abdominal segment and with the stomach. In 1889, Postempski reported the successful repair of a diaphragmatic hernia by a transthoracic approach and within a year, six further cases had been reported in his clinic. The advent of radiological contrast studies of the gastrointestinal tract led to a better appreciation of the prevalence of hiatal hernias such that Russell Carman (1875–1926) of the Mayo Clinic in 1924 could document 18 cases within a one-year period.

The rarity of the condition may best be considered by the work of Hans Eppinger (1879–1946), who in 1911 summarized the literature on diaphragmatic hernia and reported that of 635 cases of herniation through various portions of the diaphragm, only 11 involved the esophageal hiatus. In 1923, Richards could review 23 observations. By 1925, 30 cases had been seen at the Mayo Clinic. It was therefore only when such a specially adapted technique of examination was introduced by Akerlund that the relative frequent occurrence of this condition was generally recognized. Akerlund reported 30 cases in 1926 and proposed a classification of hiatal hernia, which for many years was regarded as definitive. From then on the number soon became legion. Knothe observed 300 cases at La Charité Hospital in Berlin, representing 8% of all patients subjected to gastrointestinal roentgen examination.

In 1930, Ritvo, a Boston radiologist, published a series of 60 cases, all in adults, and in commenting upon the differential diagnosis, cited cardioesophageal relaxation as a distinct pathological process. Although Ritvo reported epigastric pain, heartburn, nausea, vomiting, and regurgitation as clinical correlates of "esophageal orifice hernia," he failed to postulate gastroesophageal reflux as the cause of these symptoms. Harrington subsequently reported 680 cases of diaphragmatic hernia seen at the Mayo Clinic. From 1930–1946, 984 articles on diaphragmatic hernia were quoted in the *Quarterly Cumulative Index Medicus*. Bernstein himself noted that in the two years prior to his publication, he had identified 38 cases of diaphragmatic hernia in 994 gastric examinations (3.8%). From all these publications, each containing reports of numerous cases, and from his experience, he stated that "hernia of the esophageal hiatus is a very common condition indeed". He concluded that on average, the incidence in relation to the number of patients examined varies from 2 5%.

Before 1940, therefore, all hernias through the diaphragm were generally grouped together and regarded as examples of protrusions of abdominal contents through various orifices. Even the best informed authorities viewed hiatal hernia in this way. Allison, however, supported by Barrett, changed this attitude. These authors focused attention on the idea that symptoms were due mainly to an upset in the physiological function of the area, causing reflux from the stomach. Once this was accepted, tests became necessary to investigate function and measure the degree of reflux. Screening examinations with a barium swallow became important and attention began to be paid to pH studies. A physiological revolution occurred in the mid-1950s with the introduction and development of esophageal manometry. These techniques allowed for measurements of transmucosal potential difference and esophageal pH, and provided better methods for evaluating the need for surgery and assessing the results.

The development of contrast radiology in the first decade of the 20th century (*background*), 70 years before endoscopic identification of esophagitis, enabled radiologists such as Russell Carman (1875–1926) (*top right*) of the Mayo Clinic to identify the presence of a hiatal hernia with increasing frequency. The relationship of this radiological observation to clinical symptomatology became a matter of considerable dispute as surgeons sought to address a much venerated target that had always been their idealized therapeutic domain, namely the repair of a hernia. The fact that such herniation might be associated with reflux and with mucosal disease escaped consideration for decades.

Bernstein, in reviewing the subject of hiatal hernia in 1947, noted some of the causes for the relatively low numbers of diagnoses of the condition: "At autopsy, with all muscles relaxed and the intra-abdominal pressure diminished, this condition may easily be overlooked, and only scattered reports of a few cases were therefore known in the literature of the pre-radiological era. The conventional technique X-ray examination of the stomach with the patient in upright posture usually also fails to visualize these hernias. Examination in recumbent or even Trendelenburg position with application of manual pressure toward the upper abdomen is necessary to produce and demonstrate the condition under the fluoroscope. It is usual for these hernias to disappear as soon as the patient is brought back into upright posture or the increased abdominal pressure is released."

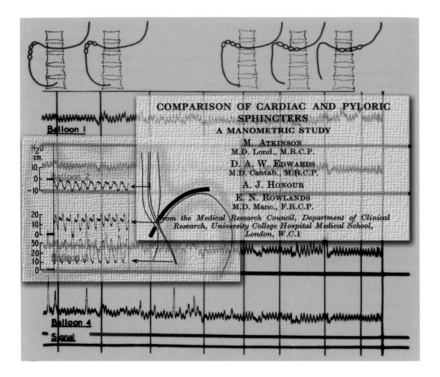

In 1957, M Atkinson and colleagues from the University College London Medical School published their examinations of sphincter pressures (*center*). In the background are the tracings of pressures as a chain of balloons withdrawn in steps from the duodenum to the stomach in a normal subject. No rise in pressure was noted during this traversal. Left are simultaneous tracings in the esophagus, diaphragmatic hernia level, and the fundus. A biphasic inspiratory swing was noted at the level of the diaphragm.

In 1957, in a paper in the *Lancet*, M Atkinson and colleagues from University College London presented their manometric study comparing the cardiac and pyloric sphincters.

This work, conducted with open-ended tubes or miniature balloons which measured pressures in the lumen, demonstrated firstly that a physiological sphincter that relaxed as a function of the swallowing reflex was present at the esophagogastric junction. In contrast, no manometric evidence of a sphincter could be deduced. These advances also raised the question of whether acid found in the esophagus was important in itself or was merely an indicator of the presence of other irritant substances in the gastric juice. Furthermore, the difficulty of relating symptoms to the degree of reflux prompted the search for damaging factors other than acid and pepsin. The work of Capper and Gillison offered an answer to many of these questions, and led to important new investigations on other substances in the stomach that might also be flowing back into the esophagus. Thereafter, the idea that hormones play a major part in the control of the lower esophageal sphincter became one of the most important pharmacological advances.

In his 1946 paper, Allison identified the importance of hiatal hernias in patients with esophageal disease. Thus, when he screened patients with metal clips positioned at the squamo-columnar junction, he found "pouches" of stomach above the cardiac sphincter.

This finding led Allison to develop operations that were designed to improve reflux control at the esophagogastric junction. As such, he was amongst the first to consider that the entity of reflux esophagitis could be managed surgically by appropriate repair of a sliding hiatal hernia. Both he and others studied the anatomy of the area and reviewed previous anatomical descriptions. This led to several surgical modifications designed to make the structures at the hiatus as near to normal as possible. In 1951, Allison reported his results in 204 patients with diaphragmatic hiatal hernia. Interestingly, he only operated on 33 of the patients, all of whom had a sliding hiatal hernia.

In all aspects of the subject, including hiatal hernia in infants and children, surgeons in Britain therefore played a leading part. Despite meticulous surgical technique, analysis of the outcome however demonstrated that a hernia repair alone was inadequate in securing long-term relief from reflux esophagitis. Side by side with the development of operations for hiatal hernia, the anatomy of the diaphragm, the phrenoesophageal ligament, the distribution of the fibers of the phrenic nerves, and the structure and enervation of the right crus of the diaphragm were all studied. Much of this development was British in origin, while the radiographic visualization of esophageal movement and gastric reflux was an especially important component of the Leeds approach propounded by Allison.

From the point of view of surgical technique, the attitude of British surgeons continued to follow Allison in using techniques designed to strengthen the lower esophageal sphincter and make the muscle action of the right crus more normal, but from 1960 there was the alternative operation of fundoplication, which was introduced by Rudolf Nissen (1896–1981).

The Nissen school

The first rational surgical therapy for the condition now ubiquitously referred to under the generic acronym of gastroesophageal reflux disease (GERD) can be attributed to Rudolf Nissen and the technique of fundoplication.

Philip Rowland Allison (1904–1974) (*bottom left*) of Leeds, England, was amongst the first to consider that the entity of reflux esophagitis could be managed surgically by appropriate repair of a sliding hiatal hernia. Despite meticulous surgical technique, analysis of the outcome demonstrated that a hernia repair alone was inadequate in securing long-term relief from reflux esophagitis.

Rudolf Nissen (1896–1981) (*left*) was born in the small town of Neisse in Silesia, the son of the only surgeon in the region. He studied medicine in Breslau, Freiburg, and Marburg, and trained in surgery with Sauerbruch in Munich and in Berlin, where he was Professor of Surgery at La Charité Hospital. In 1933, when Hitler came to power in Germany, Nissen left for Turkey (1933–1939), Boston (1939–1941), and New York (1941–1952). In 1952, he was appointed Professor of Surgery at the University of Basel and remained there until his death in 1981. While Chief of Surgery at the Brooklyn Jewish Hospital in New York, Nissen was regarded as one of the finest surgeons in the city. Einstein, a victim of unrelenting upper abdominal discomfort, sought Nissen's skill in resolving the problem. The demonstration of a hiatal hernia at surgery failed to persuade Nissen to repair it – particularly since the associated aortic aneurysm was more likely the cause of Einstein's symptoms!

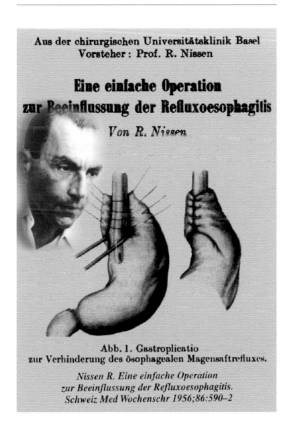

Aus der chirurgischen Universitätsklinik Basel
Vorsteher : Prof. R. Nissen

Eine einfache Operation zur Beeinflussung der Refluxoesophagitis

Von R. Nissen

Abb. 1. Gastroplicatio
zur Verhinderung des ösophagealen Magensaftrefluxes.

Nissen R. Eine einfache Operation zur Beeinflussung der Refluxoesophagitis. Schweiz Med Wochenschr 1956;86:590–2

In his original account of the procedure, Nissen, who was at that time Chairman of the Department of Surgery at the Bürgerspital, Switzerland, treated two patients with chronic reflux disease and termed the operation he employed as a "gastroplication". In the original description of the open fundoplication, two broad folds were wrapped around the esophagus and fixed anterior to the esophagus utilizing four to five sutures. In the course of this operation, major exposure of the esophagogastric junction was required and an incision of the lesser omentum undertaken, often leading to the transection of numerous branches of the vagal nerve, particularly the right trunk.

This inadvertent denervation was responsible postoperatively for considerable gastric motility-related morbid symptomatology. As a result, Nissen and others modified the original fundoplication in order to preserve the vagal branches. The "anterior wall technique" (Rossetti-Nissen total fundoplication) uses the anterior wall of the gastric fundus to create the total wrap, thus obviating the extensive mobilization and division of the short gastric vessels.

A further modification of the original fundoplication procedure, the "short floppy cuff" introduced in 1977 by Donahue and Bombeck, significantly reduced concomitant side effects such as dysphagia and gas bloat symptoms. This technical modification proposed a complete mobilization of the fundus and gastroesophageal junction, a short wrap length (2.0–2.5cm), and preservation of the vagal nerves. In addition to the initial total fundoplication procedures utilized, a partial fundoplication may be performed whereby partial fundal wraps are placed either anterior or posterior to the gastroesophageal junction. A variety of similar procedures have been described and include a posterior, crurally-fixed partial fundoplication (Toupet), or an anterior 180° fundoplication (Dor).

Watson's operation comprises a full mobilization of the lower esophagus and gastroesophageal junction, crural repair, fixation of the esophagus to the crura, and anterior 180° Dor-type fundoplication (the Belsey Mark IV consists of an anterior 270° partial fundoplication, fixed to the undersurface of the diaphragm, and performed through the left chest). In general, it was felt (especially by surgeons) that such procedures had a good outcome and were associated with fewer side effects such as dysphagia and gas bloat. In particular, it was apparent that the partial fundoplications were most useful in patients with evidence of significant esophageal hypomotility. Overall, the wide variety of procedures, their high morbidity, and the absence of rigorous evaluation of the outcome have however generated a sense of restrained enthusiasm for their usage.

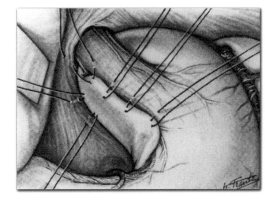

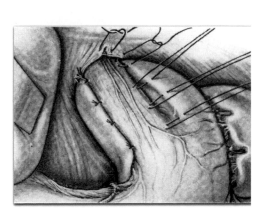

Innumerable modifications of the original gastric fundoplication procedure proposed by Rudolf Nissen have emerged. Whether the variety of permutations and commutations of the techniques proposed represent advances or attest to the fact that no procedure of this kind is adequate remains a source of considerable disagreement amongst both surgeons and gastroenterologists. The Toupet modification (*right*) includes a 240°–270° partial wrap. Top left is a suture of the right hemi-fundus, with the completion below. The Rosetti modification later achieved widespread popularity amongst pediatric surgeons.

Belsey

While it may appear that the discovery by Nissen of the beneficial effect of fundoplication was a serendipitous observation, it nevertheless remains a fact that in undertaking surgery that folded the stomach over an esophagogastric anastomosis to protect it from leaking, he inadvertently also protected the esophagus from the predictable acid reflux associated with resection of the lower esophageal sphincter. On the contrary, the surgical strategy adopted by Ronald Belsey of Bristol reflected the culmination of many years of observations in the Frenchay endoscopy unit and subsequent careful correlation of these findings with the symptomatology of the patient. Using a rigid, 50cm-esophagoscope and examining the sedated but awake patient in the sitting position, Belsey concluded that competency at the cardia depended on its lying well below the diaphragm. Thus, when the gastroesophageal junction was dislocated from its usual relationship with the right crus, the cardia gaped and gastric contents could be detected as rising into the esophagus with deep inspiration.

Belsey described this situation as a "patulous cardia" and proposed that the operative goal should be to fix the gastroesophageal junction 2cm or 3cm below the diaphragm. A series of different surgical strategies were thereafter undertaken in an attempt to maximize the efficacy of this procedure. The Mark I operation was essentially a variant of the Allison approach, while the Mark II and III procedures represented various degrees of fundoplication. These culminated in the crescentic overlay of stomach in the Mark IV procedure as a means of obtaining tissue more substantial than the naked esophagus into which the anchoring sutures could be passed. Of interest is the fact that Belsey's criteria for a good operation included the ability to teach the procedure to others and achieve durable relief from reflux while preserving the other esophageal functions; that is, agreeable swallowing, venting of gas, protection of the airway, and maintenance of the capacity to vomit. The Mark III operation, with three rows of plicating sutures, failed both tests because it was difficult to teach and because the valve was more competent than was acceptable. During the early trial period (1949–1955) with the Mark I, II, and III operations, unsatisfactory results were identified in about a third of the patients and there were also seven postoperative deaths. In contrast, 85% of the 632 patients operated on between 1955 and 1962 had good to excellent results. Belsey delayed formal publication of the Mark IV repair procedure for patients with the isolated condition of patulous cardia for six years before considering it to be of sufficient durability to publish the results, and a full 12 years before the publication of the long-term cumulative results with Skinner. Indeed, the most salient lesson of this classic report was the remarkable restraint exhibited by Belsey in deferring publication until more than two decades had passed and more than 1,000 patients had been treated. Pearson, in a presidential address to the American Association of Thoracic Surgery, quoted Belsey as saying: "The battlefields of surgery are strewn with the remains of promising new operations which perished in the follow-up clinic." The lessons of the publication remain as valid now as they were almost 50 years ago, when gastroesophageal reflux was firmly established as a correctable affliction if the appropriate patient was selected and an experienced surgeon identified. Of particular interest is the recognition that these results were obtained based upon astute observations made decades prior to the availability of cineradiography, manometry, pH studies, and flexible endoscopy.

"Surgical Management of esophageal reflux and hiatal hernia: long-term results with 1030 patients"
J Thorac Cardiovasc Surg 1967; 53: 33–54.
Skinner DB, Belsey RHR

Ronald Belsey (*top left*) of Bristol, England, was a surgeon not only of considerable technical virtuosity but also possessed of an independent and inquiring mind. His thoughtful evaluation, over a period of years, of the nature of the disease of the lower esophageal sphincter led to his development of a series of procedures (Belsey Mark I–IV) designed to obviate the problem of reflux. A number of American surgeons (Skinner, Baue, Ellis) who trained with him at the Frenchay Hospital in Bristol played an important role in disseminating his concepts of fundoplication to the North American surgical community.

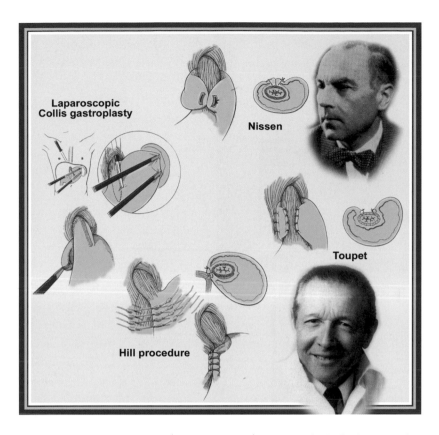

The evolution of antireflux surgery (*clockwise from top*): the Nissen fundoplication, a complete 360° wrap of the gastric fundus posteriorly around the esophagus; the 240°–270° partial wrap of the Toupet fundoplication; the Hill procedure, which included the fixation of the LES in the abdomen and created an angulation in the lower esophagus to prevent reflux; and the Collis gastroplasty. All but the last procedure represent surgical attempts to bolster the sphincter. The Collis gastroplasty was developed to generate a tension-free fundoplication in the setting of a "shortened" esophagus.

Laparoscopy

The introduction of laparoscopic antireflux surgery in 1991 by Geagea, a Lebanese surgeon practicing in Canada, and Dallemagne *et al* in Belgium, had a profound impact on the management strategy of patients with GERD. In much the same fashion as had followed the introduction of laparoscopic cholecystectomy, the novel procedure was widely embraced by surgeons anxious to utilize technical skills to resolve the vexatious problem of GERD. As a result of the perceived advantages of the procedure, surgeons began to undertake laparoscopic fundoplication, often without adequate training and unaware of the appropriate indications. Although the advantages of minimally invasive surgery were evident, initial enthusiasm resulted in failure to initiate prospective randomized trials to critically evaluate the relative merits of the open procedure compared with long-term use of proton pump inhibitors. Nevertheless, early results seemed to confirm all the advantages of the minimally invasive approach (once the learning curve had been negotiated), with early outcomes not significantly different to those reported for the open procedure.

In general, the laparoscopic approach follows the same principles as the open Nissen fundoplication. A particular advantage is the excellent visibility of the gastroesophageal junction at operation and the relatively atraumatic nature of the procedure as compared to a major upper abdominal incision. A short (1–2cm) wrap is advocated to avoid postoperative dysphagia. Other modifications that have been proposed include either division of the short gastric vessels to establish a tension-free fundoplication using a mobile posterior portion of the fundus, or alternatively, non-division with the use of a more anterior portion of the fundus.

BARRETT AND HIS MUCOSA

Norman Barrett believed that the early descriptions of ulcer by Tileston, Stewart, and Lyall differed significantly from those identified by clinicians such as Allison of Leeds. He felt that the former were *rare and of little clinical significance* whereas the latter were *common and important entities*. He further proposed that this confusion had arisen because the pathology of the former had been tacked on to the symptomatology of the latter. Indeed, it was Barrett's opinion that the condition described by Allison in papers in 1946 and 1948 actually represented reflux esophagitis and that this was the best name for the lesion. In the earlier paper, Allison confirmed an association between gastroesophageal reflux, peptic injury to the esophagus, and hiatal hernia.

Norman (Pasty) Barrett (1903–1979) (*left*), originally of Adelaide, Australia, studied in London and was Consultant Surgeon at St Thomas' Hospital (*bottom*). Barrett developed novel concepts relating to the subject of peptic esophagitis and the consideration of a putative condition, which he referred to as a "short esophagus". His reflections on the subject of ectopic gastric mucosa (1957) subsequently spawned a gastroenterological obsession that led to the development of an entirely novel disease entity. Well known for his eccentricity, sailing skills, and idiosyncratic persona, Barrett, if alive today, would certainly regard the pursuit of this illusory biological phenomenon as the medical equivalent of *The Hunting of the Snark* by Lewis Carroll.

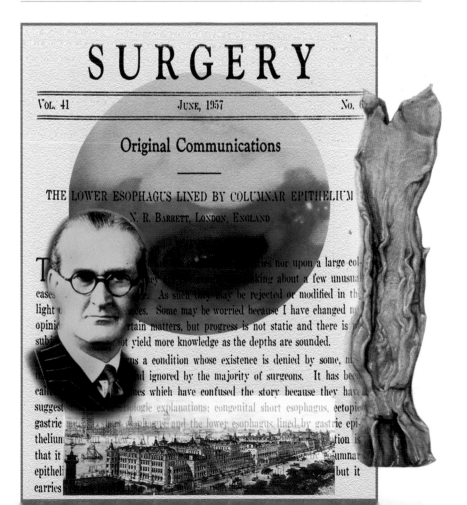

The assessment of the situation at the lower end of the esophagus by Allison was prescient. He was of the opinion that chronic esophageal ulcers could develop into lesions similar to gastric ulcers and noted that the features of the esophageal ulcers that complicate reflux esophagitis are that they are situated in the esophagus and represent digestion of the squamous epithelium. Allison opined that these lesions arose in areas of general acute inflammation and manifested initially as erosions that could either heal or persist depending upon the amount of gastric juice that had access to the gullet. Such areas remained as superficial defects for a considerable period of time in the majority of individuals, but eventually, when the site had become significantly scarred, they burrowed through the muscularis. It was Barrett's initial proposal that the stricture of the esophagus generated by this chronic inflammation had been mistakenly regarded as the esophagus, whereas it was in fact a patch of stomach partially enveloped by peritoneum that had been drawn up by scar tissue into the mediastinum. Barrett therefore concluded that it was the stomach that was the site of the chronic gastric ulcer and that the ulcers that had been described in the lower gullet were in reality gastric and not esophageal, and that they were located below the stricture.

In order to defend his novel and somewhat provocative assertion, Barrett asked two questions. Firstly, what is the esophagus? And secondly, what is meant by "heterotopia" of the gastric mucosa in relation to the esophagus? Barrett regarded the esophagus to be that part of the alimentary canal extending from the pharynx to the stomach lined by squamous epithelium. As regards heterotopia and ectopia, he believed the terms to be interchangeable and to refer to small islets of gastric epithelium found in the esophagus and surrounded on all sides by normal squamous epithelium. He proposed that the alternative scenario, in which gastric mucosa in direct continuity with the rest of the stomach extended up into mediastinum in one sheet, was due to a congenital and pathological condition, which was denoted by the term "short esophagus". His views on the relationship of islets of gastric epithelium to chronic peptic ulcer of the esophagus were novel. In his opinion, such ulcers arose in the esophagus in islets of ectopic gastric mucosa themselves or as a consequence of the secretion of acid into the gullet by such islets.

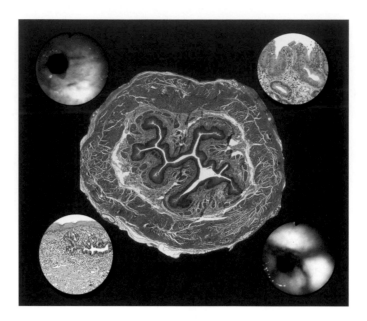

A cross section of a normal esophagus (*center*) surrounded by endoscopic and histological views of Barrett's esophagitis. Endoscopic grade I (*top left*) and II (*bottom right*) are shown with the corresponding histological views of type I (*top right*) and dysplasia of the esophagus (*bottom left*). Given the anatomy of the esophagus and the nonlinearity of the metaplastic mucosa, the biopsy sampling remains the critical issue.

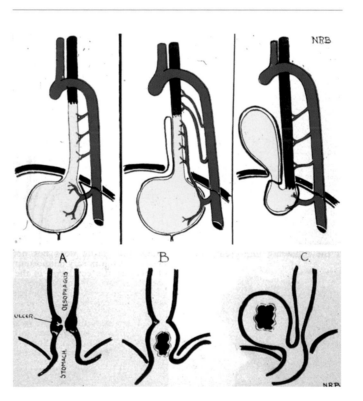

A series of drawings from the early publications of Norman Barrett depicting different esophageal pathology. At the top are diagrams showing the difference between congenital short esophagus (*left*), sliding hiatal hernia (*center*), and paraesophageal hernia (*right*). At the bottom are diagrams illustrating the three types of ulcer that occur in connection with hiatal hernia. On the left is an esophageal ulcer resulting from a sliding hernia, in the center is a gastric ulcer complicating a sliding hiatal hernia, and on the right is a gastric ulcer complicating a paraesophageal hernia.

The history of these ectopic islets of gastric mucosa in the esophagus is actually quite intriguing. Although first described by FA Schmidt in 1805, the observation was overlooked until Schridde in 1904 reported that microscopic ectopic islets were present in 70% of all gullets and always situated in the postcricoid region. In 1927, Taylor of Leeds, examining 900 cases, had identified in six, at the top of the gullet, areas large enough to be visible with the naked eye. Terracol in 1938 reported similar lesions at the top of the gullet, while Rector and Connerly (1941) identified in infants 56 examples at the upper end and seven somewhat lower down. Barrett did not believe that these isolated islets secreted acid or thought that if they did, the volume was of such paucity that it could not cause ulcers. Indeed, he claimed, "nor were there any reports of ulcers associated with such islets". His interpretation of the papers by Tileston, Stewart, and Lyall was that the massive ulceration described by them was in an area of stomach that extended beyond the crura of the diaphragm and that the ulcers were in actual fact chronic gastric ulcers occurring in a pouch of "mediastinal stomach". In contradistinction, Lyall and his colleagues had regarded the ulcers to be in the esophagus and had called the columnar mucosa with which they were associated "heterotopic".

The final conclusion that Barrett arrived at in his provocative but seminal comments on esophagitis was that the word had now become a blunderbuss term and was being used to cover many different pathological lesions. He believed that its usage should always be qualified by the descriptive adjective "reflux esophagitis" and that this condition was common and could produce ulceration of the esophagus and stricture formation. He further believed that this particular lesion was separate to the condition regarded by pathologists as peptic ulcer of the esophagus, which he felt to be an example of a congenital short esophagus. In the latter, there was neither evidence of general inflammation, nor stricture formation, but a part of the stomach extended up into the mediastinum and even into the neck, and it was in this type of stomach that a typical chronic gastric ulcer could form.

Although there is much debate in regard to who first noted reflux esophagitis and what its precise etiology might be, the contributions of Asher Winkelstein (1893–1972) of Mount Sinai have often been overlooked and require consideration. In 1955, in the *Journal of the American Medical Association*, Winkelstein noted: "One cannot avoid the suspicion that the disease in these five cases is possibly a peptic esophagitis, i.e. an esophagitis resulting from the irritant action on the mucosa of free hydrochloric acid and pepsin." Indeed, it was the culmination of Winkelstein's proposal and Allison's later concept of a

chronic reflux of gastric contents that finally assured the place of the term "reflux esophagitis" in the literature. The subsequent arguments as to whether anatomical and mechanical factors such as a hiatal hernia were responsible engendered much discussion.

In 1961, Bernstein and Baker published their acid-based test, which attempted to identify patients with esophagitis by reproducing the symptoms of heartburn. As such, this test (acid or saline infusion) allowed for the determination of whether chest or back pain was due to acid in the esophagus, and indicative of GERD.

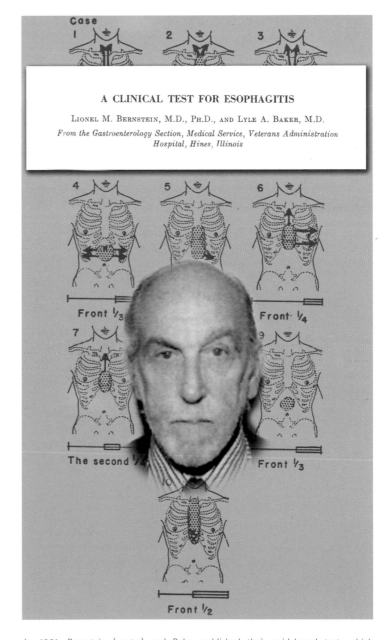

Asher Winkelstein (1893–1972) (*bottom left*), as Chief of Gastroenterology at Mount Sinai Hospital in New York, deserves credit for the initial description of peptic esophagitis. Possessed of a brilliant mind unfettered by dogma, he also was the first to propose the milk drip for the treatment of peptic ulcer disease (*top right*), advocate the use of surgical vagotomy years prior to its introduction by Lester R Dragstedt (1893–1975), and note the relevance of nocturnal acid secretion.

In 1961, Bernstein (*center*) and Baker published their acid-based test, which attempted to identify patients with esophagitis by reproducing the symptoms of heartburn. As such, this test (acid or saline infusion) allowed for the determination of whether chest or back pain (*background*) was due to acid in the esophagus, and indicative of GERD.

Seven years later, in 1968, ED Palmer of New Jersey cast considerable doubt on the relationship between hiatal hernia and esophagitis. In a 22-year prospective study, he reported that many patients with hernia had neither reflux symptoms nor esophagitis, and that many other patients had esophagitis in the absence of a hiatal hernia. At this stage, the role of the lower esophageal sphincter became an area of critical relevance in establishing the primary mechanism of reflux disease.

The further expansion of the gastroesophageal horizon of disease was proposed in 1962 when JH Kennedy implicated reflux symptoms in the production of pulmonary symptomatology and in 1968 when Cherry and Margulies suggested that laryngeal abnormalities might be secondary to gastroesophageal reflux. By 1990, Steven Sontag had demonstrated that more than 80% of asthmatics exhibited reflux and that GERD had assumed almost epidemic proportions. Indeed, epidemiological studies indicated that up to a third of people in developed countries such as Britain and the United States suffered from the disorder.

MEDICAL THERAPY

In the earliest of times, physicians were aware of the complaint of dyspepsia, but were not able to distinguish its exact location. They recognized it as related to the ingestion of food and assumed it to be due to either 'bad' food or disordered digestion. Since the latter was described as *pepsis*, a process that led to what was considered abnormal digestion was referred to as *dyspepsis*, hence the origin of the term "dyspepsia". Indeed, the usage of the term became an almost all-inclusive descriptive for any upper abdominal symptom.

Initially, the well-known Roman practice of postcibal vomiting was practiced to relieve gastric bloating and distention. The reflux-associated sensations that accompanied the regurgitation of fine Falernian wine and other Roman gustatory delicacies no doubt allowed for a fine early appreciation of the symptoms that were associated with esophagitis.

Unfortunately, little rational therapeutic intervention was available for the treatment of gastric disorders and few bothered or were able to distinguish between the esophagus and the stomach as the exact source of the problem. Indeed, up until the late 19th century, the stomach itself was often not clearly recognized as a source of symptoms that were believed to emanate from a variety of digestive organs, including the liver. Thus there existed much confusion between the diagnosis of biliousness and dyspepsia.

From the earliest times, chalk, charcoal, and slop diets had been noted to provide symptomatic relief from dyspepsia. In the 17th century, chalk and pearl juleps were utilized for infant gastric disorders, but little comment was made about adult problems, except by Thomas Sydenham (1624–1689), the Hippocrates of

English medicine, who wrote about gout and dysentery. Throughout the 18th century, there were various descriptions of gastric and intestinal diseases but no specific and logical remedies were recorded. The doctrine of acidity was widespread and prevalent, and the general literature of dyspepsia was substantial. Thus, in 1754, Joseph Black, writing on the subject of carbon dioxide, commented on "*De humore acido a cibo orto*" ("acid and eating"). In 1835 in Paris, Jean Cruveilhier (1791–1873) wrote extensively on the pathology of peptic ulcer and the condition was thus referred to as Cruveilhier's disease. Yet in all these tomes, little specific therapy apart from dietary adjustments or homeopathic remedies was apparent.

Early 20th-century management strategies of esophagitis thus focused chiefly on the avoidance of acid-containing foods or substances containing capsaicin-related compounds, such as peppers and curries. The use of bland diets and milk ingestion was then augmented by the addition of neutralizing compounds and antacids. Loose clothing, loss of weight, and elevation of the head of the bed also achieved considerable popularity, as did a host of proprietary medicines guaranteed to cure reflux, dyspepsia, impotence, and alopecia!

Observationes Medicæ CIRCA MORBORUM ACUTORUM HISTORIAM ET CURATIONEM.

Authore THOMAS SYDENHAM MD

Cicero de Nat. [

Opinionum *Commenta delet* confirmat.

LONDI Typis A. C. Impensis G infigne Capitis Epifcopal D. Pauli. 167

Unfortunately, such regimes led to a significant decline in the quality of life and in addition, to the side effects (diarrhea, milk/alkali syndrome) associated with the use of excessive alkali and cation-containing agents, or severe depression based upon failed expectations. Advances in antisepsis, anesthesia, and surgery led to vain attempts to pexy the stomach, resect the acid-secreting area, and reduce associated hiatal hernias.

The much revered Thomas Sydenham stated with assurance: "...among the remedies which it has pleased almighty god to give to man to relieve his sufferings. None is so universal and so efficacious as opium." Caveat emptor!

ESOPHAGEAL NEOPLASIA

With the advent of antisepsis and anesthesia in the 19th century, larger and more complicated operations could be undertaken with more confidence. This was particularly apparent in surgery of the stomach and esophagus, which for years had been regarded as beyond surgical reach, although isolated efforts had been previously made. Interestingly, as early as 1633, Ambrose Paré had noted that when the esophagus was being sutured, great care should be taken!

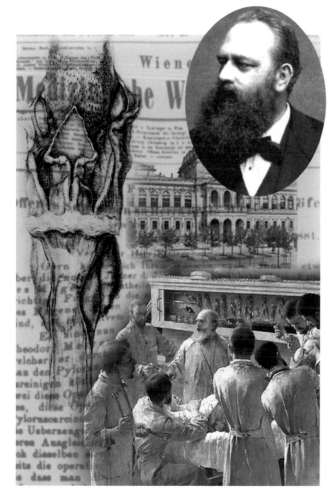

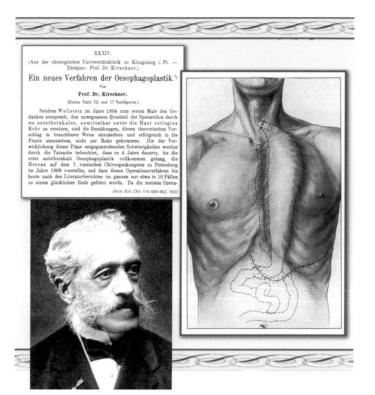

Esophageal replacement was a formidable issue. The development of techniques for the construction of a subcutaneous gastric or small intestinal bypass into the neck (right) alleviated the problem. Although numerous individuals were responsible for the evolution of this procedure, the work of Kirschner (top left) and B von Langenbeck (bottom left) was regarded as pivotal in the development of the operation.

Although Billroth in Vienna had resected the esophagus in 1872, the procedure was rarely undertaken because of its mortality. The commonest problems of the esophagus were posed by strictures due to caustic ingestion in children, which although 'benign', often resulted in death from inanition. In cases of such benign constrictions, a stomach fistula not only permitted the feeding of the patient, but also enabled dilation to be undertaken. In cases where this was not possible, other surgical alternatives were considered, such as the formation of a "gullet in front of the ribcage" – the construction of a tube running under the skin of the ribcage was initially considered, since it obviated the need to open the thoracic cavity, a usually fatal event prior to the work of Sauerbruch. A connection of the stomach with the gullet thus enabled food taken by mouth to bypass the stricture and reach the stomach. Henry Bircher of Switzerland (1894), who extended the work of Victor von Hacker (1852–1933) of Graz, Austria, successfully developed this operation. The latter had undertaken much work in esophageal surgery and had pioneered the concept of connecting the cervical esophagus to the stomach using a skin tube. Subsequently, Cesar Roux of Lausanne improved this procedure by using small intestine placed under the skin of the anterior chest to construct the connection.

Christian Albert Theodore Billroth (1829–1894) (top right) was born in Pomerania of Swedish stock and became renowned as a music critic, scholar, and surgeon. Appointed Professor of Surgery at Vienna in 1867, he became the most distinguished surgeon of his time and attracted to his clinic postgraduate students from all over the world. Many of his trainees became chairmen of surgery at many different European centers and his surgical influence dominated gastrointestinal surgery for almost half a century. Many of the great gastrointestinal surgical advances of the 20th century occurred under his stewardship, including the first esophagectomy (left). In addition, the Vienna General Hospital achieved international status as the greatest teaching center of the time. The picture (bottom right), painted by AF Seligmann, is of the opening of Billroth's new operating room at the Vienna General Hospital in 1890. The operation depicted is that of a neurotomy for trigeminal neuralgia and allows consideration of the possibility of prescience in art.

Carcinoma of the esophagus and cardia

Although the subject of esophageal carcinoma had been well described at the beginning of the 19th century, the first successful resection was only performed in 1913 by the American surgeon Franz Torek (1861–1938). In this procedure, the upper end of the esophagus was terminated in a cervical esophagostomy and the patient fed by a gastrostomy. Many surgeons endeavored to simulate this feat, but not until 1933 did the British surgeon George Grey Turner (1877–1951) at the Hammersmith Hospital record the second success.

George Grey Turner (circa 1937) (1877–1951) was a master surgeon with a particular interest in the esophagus.

Grey Turner used the pull-through or collo-abdominal method, which although a relatively crude approach, offered a chance of survival. In this patient, Grey Turner did not attempt to restore continuity between the cervical esophagus and the stomach at the first procedure, but succeeded in doing so in the ensuing seven months by constructing an antethoracic tube of skin in the upper part and of jejunum in the lower component.

George Grey Turner was one of the first to resect the thoracic esophagus (*center*) and replace it with an antethoracic intestinal tube anastomosis (*top left*). His patient Joseph Wright (59 years of age) is pictured enjoying a meal of poached eggs, bread and butter, tea, and some pears on the 206th day after the first operation.

This successful, albeit prolonged, procedure provided a strong impetus to surgeons and the next substantial advance was provided in 1933 by Ohsawa in Japan. Ohsawa described not only the removal of a cancer but also the restoration of alimentary continuity by an esophagogastrostomy performed at the same operation. Although Ohsawa published his work in 1933, it failed to reach the attention of the Western world, with the result that Adams and Phemister in Chicago reported the same procedure in 1938 in the belief that they had obtained primacy. The first such success in Europe was in 1941 (reported in 1945) by Thompson and in Britain in 1942 by Brock.

The pattern of single-operation esophageal resection was therefore established, but it remained for technical improvements to be made and the results assessed. One important modification was introduced by Ivor Lewis in 1946, whereby resection and anastomosis were undertaken from the right side after the stomach had been mobilized from the left. This was particularly useful for

growths above the cardia but below the pharyngoesophageal junction. When these techniques were fully established, a steady reduction in operative mortality was reported from most surgical centers. As time passed, two things became apparent: the quality of life after esophagogastrostomy or esophagojejunostomy was good (relief of symptoms), but the long-term results were poor, despite all efforts to extend the dissection and remove more esophagus and adjacent tissue. In the ensuing half century, little has changed in terms of long-term outcome, although operative morbidity and mortality have decreased substantially.

Surgeons were therefore driven to reappraise the older technique of esophageal intubation. This had been successfully performed in 1885, with a useful modification reported by HJ Souttar in 1924. Souttar also extended his skills to the endoscope and successfully modified the instrument with a series of angles to facilitate introduction. Although potentially useful, the rigidity of the angulation proved ungainly and a number of perforations, followed by serious criticism, led to its withdrawal from usage. Souttar's method of esophageal intubation, however, required the tube to be pushed down from above. Clearly, it was preferable to do this through the esophagoscope so that laparotomy was avoided and the discomfort to the patient minimized. Despite this, some surgeons preferred to pull the tube through from below, although this is felt by many to be less satisfactory as it requires abdominal surgery.

By 1977, Michael Atkinson and Roger Ferguson in Nottingham had published their fiberoptic endoscopic technique for inoperable esophagogastric neoplasms. They used palliative intubation in 13 patients with inoperable malignant strictures. Although the mortality of this procedure was 8%, the remaining patients appeared to be able to swallow satisfactorily. Three years earlier, in 1974, Price *et al* from Kingston upon Hull had demonstrated a safe method for the dilation of esophageal strictures. The authors used Eder-Puestow dilators that were introduced through the biopsy channel of a fiberoptic esophagoscope. These graded, spindle-shaped bougies were slid over a wire guide, at the end of which was a flexible, metal spring "finger," and facilitated dilation. Although one patient suffered from perforation, the authors demonstrated that this was a safe approach in 27 other elderly patients and suggested it as a viable alternative to massive surgery.

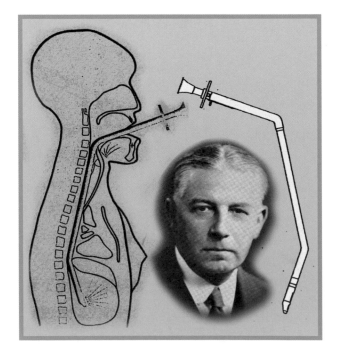

HJ Souttar (*bottom right*) modified the endoscope with a series of angles to facilitate introduction. Although potentially useful, the rigidity of the angulation proved ungainly and a number of perforations, followed by serious criticism, led to its withdrawal from usage.

Carcinoma of the pharyngoesophageal junction

Since surgeons could remove growths at the pharyngoesophageal junction without opening the thoracic cage, surgical efforts in this area began relatively early. Three approaches were tried – namely, intubation, resection, and resection with reconstruction. The Symonds tube, which was utilized in an attempt to bring rapid nonoperative relief, was developed in Britain, whereas physicians in Europe preferred initially to attempt resection. Once successful resection had been accomplished, re-establishment of swallowing included the construction of skin flaps from the neck. A further impetus towards surgical treatment was provided by the work of Trotter in England. Although primarily concerned with pharyngeal cancer, five of the patients he described in his Hunterian Lectures were women with growths in the postcricoid area. For the higher pharyngeal growths, he used skin flap reconstruction, but this was not attempted in the patients with lower growths. Skin tube techniques, either to bridge a local gap or to join the larynx to the stomach, were required for both malignant and nonmalignant disease, but with the operation in several stages, the patient often died from recurrence of the cancer before surgery was complete.

Wookey in Canada undertook further work on the skin tube method, which although promising, failed to gain wide acceptance. Increasingly, it became apparent that a tube of gut should be used if excision and reconstruction were to be attempted. This was initially successfully performed with colon or jejunum, with the gut being brought up in front of the sternum. Goligher and Robin produced a successful and practical technique using the left colon placed in the antethoracic position, and for the most part, this technique replaced other methods where anastomosis to the pharynx was required. In more recent times, a transhiatal technique with a cervical anastomosis of the stomach to the esophagus has become the preferred procedure.

Esophageal replacement

Replacement of the esophagus may be needed because of disease, congenital defects, or trauma, and the efforts to deal with this problem illustrate the general historical development of esophageal surgery. The first methods came from Germany, where Bircher attempted unsuccessfully in 1894 to form an anterior connection by a skin tube. In 1907, however, he recorded a success and his method became fairly widely used around the world. A series of such operations were thereafter undertaken in Birmingham in the decade before the Second World War on women who had strictures from swallowing caustic, either accidentally or with suicidal intent. The operation was somewhat easier in females because of the extra skin and subcutaneous tissue on the front of the chest, and the absence of hair.

The entire concept of esophageal surgery changed dramatically with the introduction of positive pressure respirator procedures. As a consequence, intrathoracic surgery became safe; thus, the successful introduction in Japan in the early 1930s of gastric transposition into the chest heralded a new era in esophageal surgery. Nevertheless, when total replacement of the esophagus was necessary, the anterior route was still favored by many surgeons on account of its general convenience, the easier handling of leaks from suture lines, and the fact that the patient could assist his swallowing manually. Others still considered the Goligher technique (1954) of the left colon replacement optimal, but for practical purposes, it appeared that each technique was as successful as its proponent and none had any particular advantage in terms of dealing with neoplasia, which remained uniformly disappointing for all.

Tylosis

In 1958, Howel-Evans and colleagues of the University of Liverpool identified a new association between tylosis and carcinoma of the esophagus that they had found in two families of Liverpudlians. The demonstration that this was an autosomal-dominant condition and the possibility that the two families were related led to a potentially novel avenue of approach in the elucidation of the disease process. Thus, although tylosis is a rare skin condition (focal nonepidermolytic palmoplantar keratoderma), the genomic mapping of three large kindreds in Britain, the American Midwest, and Germany has enabled the identification of candidate genes implicated in sporadic esophageal cancer. Loss of heterozygosity (LOH) of chromosome 17q appears to be a frequent feature of sporadic esophageal cancer and linkage and haplotype analyses of the British and American families with tylosis and esophageal cancer implicate the tylosis esophageal cancer (TOC) gene locus located at 17q25.

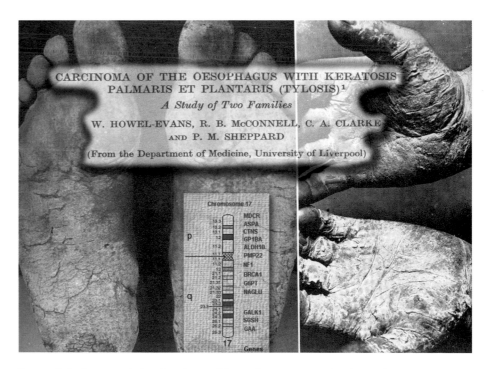

The association between tylosis and carcinoma of the esophagus was recognized in 1958 by Howel-Evans *et al.* Tylosis is a disease that is distinguished by hyperkeratosis of the palmar and plantar surfaces. Genetic transmission is autosomal-dominant and involves a lesion on chromosome 17q25 (*bottom*).

2 STOMACH AND DUODENUM

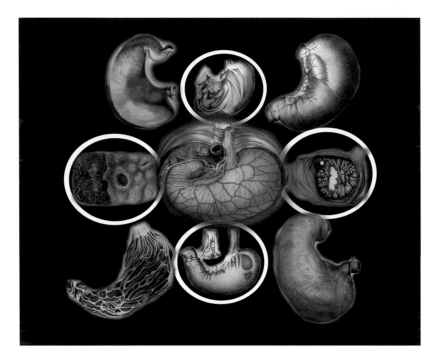

Various anatomical depictions of the stomach by JP Bougery (*center*) and Jean Cruveilhier (*circled*). Depictions by Bougery of the muscles of the outer and inner walls, the gastric folds, and nerve supply to the lesser curvature are placed in the corners of the picture. Cruveilhier's drawings depict gastric pathology and include cancer (*top*), perforated stomach (*right*), ulcer (*bottom*), and blood supply (*left*).

The digestive tract and stomach before Leonardo da Vinci and Andreas Vesalius remained simply an object of ill-understood function and regarded as a mere repository of food, with possibly some spiritual powers. Ancient concepts are best suggested by the terminology employed by William Shakespeare and other dramatists of his time. Thus, in keeping with Greek and Roman usage, the stomach (*ventriculus*) was equated with the belly (*venter*), as noted in the parable about "the belly and the members" in *Coriolanus*, or the episodes of Falstaff and Justice Greedy (Massinger). Indeed, the stomach was most often characterized as being involved with gluttony or drinking by the Elizabethans, whereas the Persian poets such as Saadi noted that an empty belly supported mental and spiritual activity. Later thoughts on the stomach suggested that the entire gastrointestinal tract was associated with pluck and courage ("guts"). However, apart from these literary allusions, little was known about the organ itself.

Andreas Vesalius had beautifully illustrated the anatomy of the organ and depicted its relationship to other intra-abdominal structures, especially the "wandering nerve" or vagus. Understanding of the precise functional significance of this observation would however require almost four centuries before the investigations of Ivan Petrovich Pavlov further defined the functional significance of neural regulation. Descriptions of the coats or layers of the stomach added little to the elucidation of function, and the use of animals or fish as experimental models further obfuscated issues, as the pyloric ceca became confused with elements of the pancreas by Regnier de Graaf and his colleagues. The introduction of microscopy to the study of the stomach reflected the contributions of Anthony van Leeuwenhoek to the improvement of lens design. Godefridus Bidloo and Herman Boerhaave applied his techniques early in the 18th century to the study of gastric glands, and in Bidloo's text are the earliest examples of microscopic anatomy. Subsequently, Camillo Golgi, while working with Giulio Bizzozero in Pavia, demonstrated that these glands considerably alter their morphology as the resting stomach enters the secretory mode.

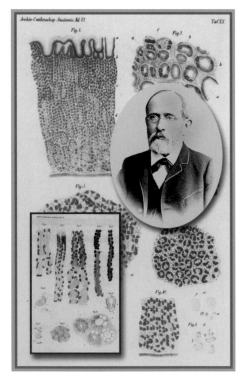

Rudolph Heidenhain, Professor of Physiology at Breslau, was amongst the first to conduct classic research on the structure of the gastric gland and the secretory apparatus of the stomach. Eight years into his tenure, Heidenhain began a systematic study of glands, which would occupy him for almost the next 30 years. His observations led him to the conclusion that the "*Labzellen*" (rennin cells) were distinct from a second type of cell which he termed a "*Hauptzelle*" and which formed the complete lining of the gland. Since he felt the "*Labzellen*" were more peripheral, he therefore renamed them "Belegzellen". These two types of cell are now known as the parietal (Belegzellen) and the chief (Hauptzelle) cell, respectively.

GASTRIC ACID

The early Greeks were not aware of acids in the modern chemical sense, but were able to identify them as bitter-sour liquids. Diocles of Carystos (circa 350 BC) was able to specify sour eruptions, watery spitting, gas, heartburn, and epigastric hunger pains radiating to the back (with occasional splashing noises and vomiting) as symptoms of illness originating in the stomach. Approximately 300 years later, Celsus (30 BC–25 AD) recognized that certain foods were acidic and recommended that "if the stomach is infested with an ulcer, light and gelatinous food must be used and everything acrid and acid is to be avoided".

The Greeks considered that gastric ulcer complications should best be treated using dietary modifications. Thus the ancient Iatros followed this dictum: "If the stomach is infested with an ulcer, light and gelatinous food must be used and everything acrid and acid is to be avoided".

A millennium later, opinions ranged from there being no acid in the stomach at all, to it originating from the pancreas. Physicians of the 15th and 16th centuries felt that any acid present in the stomach was the result of putrefaction or fermentation and did not in any way reflect an active secretory process of the body or the stomach itself. In the 16th century, Paracelsus (1493–1541), an alchemist-physician and a proponent of chemical pharmacology and therapeutics, however, believed intimately that there was acid in the stomach and that it was necessary for digestion. His proposal that gastric acid was of extracorporeal origin was of course wrong, but nonetheless, he recognized the importance of chemistry and its relation to disease, and rejected Galenism and the mysticism of humors and health. The iatrochemical views propounded by Paracelsus, and thereafter by Jean Baptiste van Helmont (1577–1644) and others, were strongly opposed by the iatromathematical school, which maintained that all physiological happenings should be treated as fixed consequences of the laws of physics. The disciples of this school of thought favored the view that the stomach was little more than a mechanical mill, grinding up its contents into chyme. Their approach to the acid question is exemplified by Mobius, who denied the existence of gastric acid.

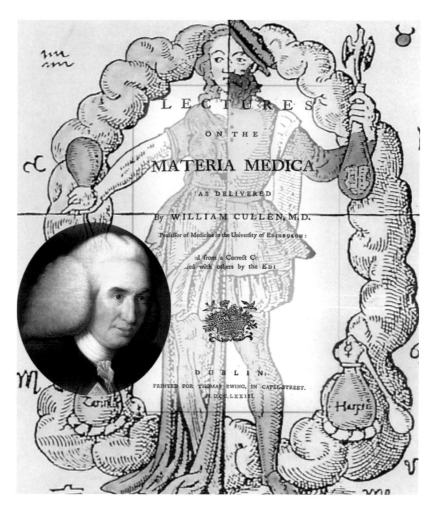

William Cullen (1712–1790) was instrumental in founding the medical school of Glasco in 1744. During his long life, he held the Chairs of Medicine and Chemistry at both Glasco and Edinburgh, and was the first to lecture in the vernacular instead of Latin. An inspiring teacher and a modest clinician, he was particularly noted for his kindness in assisting needy students. However, he introduced few new remedies into practice and his critics have claimed that "he failed to add a single new fact to medical science". Although his finest innovation was the use of hydrotherapy with rapid changes in temperature, he was particularly adept at developing descriptive classifications of disease processes and their therapy. In his synopsis *Nosologiae Methodicae* (1769), he divided diseases into fevers, neuroses, cachexias, and local disorders, even including gout amongst the neuroses and differentiating 34 different varieties of chronic rheumatism.

Caring little for the new science of chemistry, their postulates fermented in corporeal cul-de-sacs, fading into such sterile eccentricities as the proposal by W Pitcairn that the entirety of medical practice could be based on mechanical principles. Ingenious methods for obtaining gastric juice (sponges, hollow tubes, and even emesis), as well as the demonstration and recognition of vegetable dyes to determine acidity or alkalinity, substantially aided the investigation of the precise nature of gastric juice. Such agents possessed the property of color change when exposed to appropriate acids or alkalis and thus facilitated identification of the nature of the material being tested. At this time, while there was some agreement that acid was indeed present in the stomach, there was considerable disagreement about both the chemical nature of the acid and whether it was primarily secreted by the stomach or derived in some way from ingested food.

The Jesuit abbot Lazzaro Spallanzani (1729–1799) (*bottom right*) was a physiologist of considerable skill and insight. His proposal that the stomach produced acid was the source of an acrid debate between himself and John Hunter of London (1728–1793) (*top left*). Hunter was the first surgeon scientist and intellectually explored the structure and function of the body in almost every species available, leaving in excess of 50,000 anatomical specimens at his death. His friend Sir Joshua Reynolds (1723–1792) painted Hunter's portrait and accurately captured his drawn facial features, as he had by this time developed unstable angina. Hunter's comments on digestion were included in his book, *Observations on Certain Parts of the Animal Oeconomy* (London, 1786), which had been translated into Italian by Antonio Scarpa (1752–1832). As a consequence of the views expressed, there arose a degree of tension between he and Spallanzani, who assumed divine support for his digestive position. Their disagreement as to the presence or absence of acid in the gastric juice and whether the process of digestion required heat was finally resolved amicably in the form of a polemic letter (*background*) addressed to Leopoldo Caldani and published in Milan in 1788. Presumably, the limited nature of the chemical techniques available to both Hunter and Spallanzani resulted in a misunderstanding that was subsequently resolved by mutual agreement.

In 1760, Reuss found that even with preliminary alkalization of the stomach, the ingestion of a meal of meat and vegetables resulted in secretion of acid. The vomit had an acid taste and turned an infusion of campanulas a '*feuilles-rondes*' red. Gosse, in 1783, repeated the studies more elegantly. He had, as a child, developed the faculty of aerophagy and self-induced emesis, whereas Reuss needed to take an emetic. By inducing emesis at specific times after eating, Gosse was able to obtain "pure" gastric juice. However, in his studies, he was unable to identify acid or alkaline gastric juice. In 1780, Lazzaro Spallanzani (1729–1799), Professor of Natural History in Pavia, published his extensive observations in this area. He had used the methods of Réaumur on fish, frogs, snakes, cattle, horses, cats, dogs, and even himself, and asserted that gastric juice was probably neutral. Spallanzani was however uncertain about his findings regarding the acidity of gastric juice and therefore undertook collaborative studies in an effort to resolve this question. Thus, in 1785, in conjunction with Carminati, Professor of Medicine at Pavia, they first detected the acidity of the contents of a meal.

Spallanzani was advised to test birds on a meat-free diet; he also found marine acid in the juice squeezed from sponges fed to five ravens that had been fed on vegetables for 15 days. Later, Brugnatelli in 1786 and Werner in 1800 found the contents of the stomachs of sheep, cats, fish, and birds to be acid. Despite the relatively clear evidence produced by Spallanzani and his colleagues that there was acid in the stomach and that it was hydrochloric acid, considerable controversy persisted. Indeed, many of the investigators in this area, including no less a scientist than Hunter, reversed their thoughts a number of times during the study of the subject. Thus, even among the minds of the most eminent physicians of the day, confusion reigned, not only as to the presence of acid, but as to the exact nature of the substance.

Initial human studies

The gastric fistula of Madeline Gore (*center*). At the age of 20 years, she fell down stone stairs and thereafter always walked bent over to the left. Eighteen years later, she developed a lump over her stomach, which broke down and became a fistula through which food passed. Jean Nicholas Corvisart (*left*) was Napoleon's favorite physician and dietician. Although Napoleon received sound French advice, he later developed a gastric tumor that could not be adequately treated and ultimately led to his demise. It is possible that if Corvisart had been more advanced, the gastric examinations of Gore may have culminated in a different (perhaps more conventional) treatment of the Emperor.

The contributions of William Prout

William Prout (1785–1850) provided the final resolution as to the exact nature of acid produced by the stomach in 1823. A brilliant physician with diverse interests outside of medicine, Prout was productive in the fields of chemistry, meteorology, and physiology, as well as clinical medicine. In addition, he was one of the first scientists to apply chemical analysis to biological materials. Prior to Prout, the exact nature of gastric acid had been a controversial issue, and although Johann Tholde had first described the acid known as hydrochloric acid (although it had also been called muriatic acid for many years), its presence in the stomach was debated. In fact, even Prout, at an earlier stage of his studies into the nature of acid had, like JR Young of Philadelphia, believed phosphoric acid to be the acid agent of the stomach.

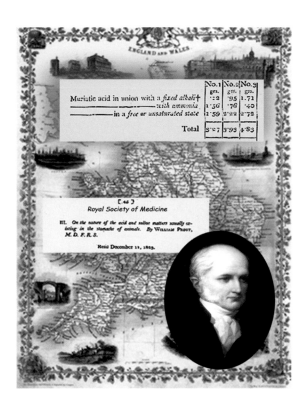

Unfortunately, however, Prout's observations were not readily accepted across *la Manche*. Physiologists as eminent as Claude Bernard were of the opinion that lactic acid (a product of fermentation) was the gastric acid present in gastric contents, while some, such as Montnegre, even believed that there was no gastric secretion of acid. The French Académie des Sciences determined to resolve the exact nature of acid in the stomach, and in 1828, established an essay contest for which they offered a prize of 3,000 francs for the solution to the problem. A panel of distinguished judges was selected to evaluate the essays and one year later, the prize was awarded jointly to Leuret and Lassaigne of Paris, and Tiedemann and Gmelin of Heidelberg. Leuret and Lassaigne declared that the acid in gastric juice was lactic, whilst Tiedemann and Gmelin confirmed Prout's earlier observations that it was hydrochloric acid. When asked to share the prize, the Germans, offended by the contradiction provided by the judges, declined and withdrew from the competition. At this time, Berzelius of Sweden was regarded as the ranking authority on chemistry in Europe, and his arbitration on the matter was anxiously awaited by the authors. Thus Wöhler, in a letter of May 17, 1828, reported to Berzelius how gratified Tiedemann and Gmelin were to have noted in the *Årsberättelser*, 7, 297, his deprecatory comments regarding the "*unbedeutende Arbeit*" of Leuret and Lassaigne.

William Prout (1785–1850) (*bottom right*) was born in Horton, a remote village of Gloucestershire, England. Having studied at Guy's Hospital in London, he became a member of the Royal College of Physicians, as well as a Fellow of the Royal Medical Chirurgical Society. On December 11, 1823, at the Royal Society of Medicine, he presented his landmark paper 'On the nature of acid and saline matters usually existing in the stomach of animals' (*center*). Prout identified hydrochloric acid in the gastric juice of numerous species, including humans, and quantified free and total hydrochloric (muriatic) acid (*top*). In addition, he related the amount of acid to the degree of dyspepsia and also proposed that chloride was secreted from the blood to the lumen by electrical means. In this hypothesis, Prout proposed (more than a century before it could be confirmed) that when gastric acid was secreted, the blood would become alkaline (postprandial alkaline tide). Apart from his definitive resolution of the nature of gastric acid, Prout was the first to propose that the atomic weights of all elements would be multiples of that of hydrogen (Prout's Hypothesis). A further major contribution to the science of gastroenterology was his classification, in 1827, of foods into the subgroups of carbohydrates (saccharinous), fats (oleaginous), and proteins (albuminous), for which he was awarded the Copley Medal.

Edward Stevens (1755–1804) (*right*) was the presumed illegitimate half brother of Alexander Hamilton (1755–1804), the Secretary of the Treasury. Both had been born and raised on the island of St Croix in the Caribbean Leeward Islands before departing to seek their fortunes elsewhere. Stevens graduated from King's College in New York (now Columbia University) in 1774 and thereafter pursued his further medical studies in Edinburgh (*top right*) from 1775. During this time, he became President of the Edinburgh Medical Student Society and wrote one of the first theses (*De Alimentorum Concoctione*) (*left*) that accurately described the process of digestion. It was dedicated to Alexander Monro *tertius*, who was the last member of a family that had held the Chair of Anatomy at Edinburgh for 126 consecutive years (1720–1846). After returning to the United States, Stevens became Professor of Medicine at Columbia University, but soon after lost interest in academia and finally accepted the position of Consul General to the island of Santo Domingo. After his early contributions to the science of digestion, Stevens failed to further pursue an investigative career, choosing rather to follow in the political footsteps of his brother. His description of the course of digestion undertaken by means of the study of the contents of swallowed metal spheres ingested by his "subject," the peripatetic Hussar (*center*), remained a classic until the investigation of William Beaumont (1785–2853) of the gastric fistula of Alexis St Martin at Fort Mackinack, Lake Michigan.

Berzelius indeed may have been too smug in his comment on the work of Leuret and Lassaigne, since he himself had previously reported that gastric acid was lactic! Despite this error, the contributions of Leuret and Lassaigne were not inconsequential, since in separate canine experimental studies, they were the first to demonstrate that acid introduced into the duodenum elicited the secretion of pancreatic juice and bile. Although they failed to explore the mechanism in detail, their observations preceded those of Ivan Petrovich Pavlov (1849–1936) and Ernest Henry Starling (1866–1927). This is explored further in the next section. Nevertheless, the animal experimental data failed to provide conclusive evidence regarding the human physiology of digestion until the contributions of William Beaumont and his patient Alexis St Martin almost half a world away from the sophistication of 19th century Europe.

William Beaumont and Alexis St Martin

William Beaumont (1785–1853) was born in Lebanon, Connecticut, and having trained in medicine by apprenticeship, thereafter became a military doctor. In 1819, after a brief period in practice, his former colleague Joseph Lovell, who had now become Surgeon General, offered Beaumont a commission, and he was assigned to Fort Mackinac on the island of Michel Mackinac at the junction of Lakes Huron and Michigan. As the only physician for 300 miles, Beaumont was busy, and in addition to his military medical responsibilities, was often involved in managing the trauma consequent upon the frequent brawls among Indians and fur traders. One such event resulted in his care of a young man with a musket-induced gastric fistula. Despite his background as a surgeon and no formal training in physiology, Beaumont seized the opportunity to study the patient Alexis St Martin in a manner similar to that previously utilized by Helm of Vienna and Rouilly of Paris to investigate their patients. Albeit unschooled in experimentation and the sophistication of chemistry, Beaumont meticulously studied the physiological basis of human digestion and produced a classic text on the subject in 1833.

The chemical measurement of acid in the stomach involves an interesting tale of three bottles of gastric juice (*center*). Although William Beaumont possessed the intellectual curiosity and perspicacity to use the gastric fistula of Alexis St Martin to study digestion (*top right*), he possessed few scientific skills with which to address the task. To support his endeavors, he secured the support of Robley Dunglison (1798–1869) (*top left*), Professor of Medicine in Virginia, who had initially come to the United States from Edinburgh at the invitation of President Jefferson. Dunglison was trained in science and advised Beaumont as to how he should proceed with his studies. Three bottles of juice were respectively sent for analysis to eminent chemists. Dunglison successfully identified the presence of hydrochloric acid in the first bottle of gastric juice of St Martin and suggested that Beaumont collaborate with Benjamin Silliman (1779–1864) (*bottom left*), Professor of Chemistry at Yale College. Silliman duly confirmed the presence of free hydrochloric acid in the second bottle of gastric juice but thought that a definitive opinion should be sought from the most eminent chemist of the day, Jons Jacob Berzelius (1779–1848) (*bottom right*) of Stockholm. Silliman thus arranged for Beaumont to send the third sample of gastric juice to Berzelius via the diplomatic courier of the Swedish ambassador in New York. Unfortunately, Berzelius never adequately analyzed the sample, pleading problems initially with work overload, then summer heat, and finally inadequate support personnel. As he had already adjudged that gastric juice contained lactic acid, it is likely that he was not keen to confirm his own error!

On the morning of June 6, 1822, a 19-year-old French Canadian voyageur, St Martin, was accidentally shot in the left upper abdomen and chest. Beaumont was called to see the victim, and hearing the extent of the disastrous wound, pronounced that the chances of survival to be slim, remarking: "The man cannot live 36 hours; I will come and see him by and by." Surprisingly, St Martin survived the initial catastrophe, and with the active care provided by Beaumont, had largely recovered after about 10 months, although a gastric fistula remained. By this stage, the ill and unemployed St Martin was penniless and the county authorities, refusing further support, proposed transporting him 1,500 miles back to his birthplace in Canada. Beaumont opposed the proposal, fearing both for the safety of his patient and the loss of his human experimental model. Thus, in April 1823, Beaumont moved St Martin to his own home, where he remained for almost two years under constant care and attention while also being studied. In 1824, Beaumont sent his commanding officer (Surgeon General Joseph Lovell) a manuscript detailing his observations concerning the gastric fistula of St Martin and the results of his preliminary considerations on the nature of digestion. It was published in the *Medical Recorder* as 'A Case of Wounded Stomach' by Joseph Lovell, Surgeon General, USA. The oversight of Beaumont's omission as an author was however soon remedied and Beaumont instated as a co-author.

At this stage, Beaumont, having recognized the unique opportunity that St Martin's gastric fistula presented for formal study, began his epic investigation into gastric function and digestion. Given his lack of knowledge of science, he enlisted the aid of Robley Dunglison (1798–1869), Professor of Medicine in Virginia, and Benjamin Silliman (1779–1864), Professor of Chemistry at Yale College, to support his investigations. Despite the incontrovertible evidence produced by Prout, Tiedemann, Gmelin, and Beaumont, as late as 1885 some German physiologists still had not fully accepted that hydrochloric acid was the critical acid secreted by the stomach. Thus, the doyens of German gastroenterology Carl Anton Ewald (1845–1915) and Ismar Boas (1858–1938) reported that all acid present in the stomach at the beginning of a meal was lactic. It was their theory that hydrochloric acid gradually replaced the lactic acid during eating, with the result that by the end of a meal, only hydrochloric acid was evident!

PEPSIN AND PEPSINOGEN

The story of pepsinogen begins essentially in the Berlin laboratory of Johannes Müller (1801–1858), where Theodor Schwann (1810–1882) had been asked by Müller to attempt to subject the physiological properties of either an organ or a tissue to physical measurement. Schwann initially developed a muscle balance, and became the first to establish the basics of the tension-length diagram. Thereafter, whilst successfully measuring secretion from the gastric gland, he stumbled upon a proteolytic enzyme, whose properties he characterized and soon after published in 1836. In this paper, he described a water-soluble factor in gastric juice that digested egg white and named it "pepsin" after the Greek word for digestion.

In 1835, Theodor Schwann (*bottom right*), while working in the laboratory of Johannes Müller (*top left*), stumbled upon a proteolytic enzyme, whose properties he characterized and soon after published in 1836 (*background*). At the time, they were involved in measuring secretion from the gastric glands (*top*). Both Schwann's and Müller's articles were published sequentially in the same journal; Müller's work was given precedence. It is of interest that the second reference in Müller's work on the artificial digestion of proteins is to William Beaumont's experiments and observations on the gastric juice and physiology of digestion (1830). In his studies, Schwann was able to extract a crude preparation of a digestive enzyme from gastric juice, which he demonstrated to have the ability to convert egg-white albumin to peptones in vitro. He named this water-soluble factor "pepsin" after the Greek word for digestion. In the course of Schwann's studies, both he and Müller noted that no gas evolved during pepsin digestion of food. These findings were thus able to dispel a notion that had been held for three centuries – that digestion was a fermentation-like process. The identification of the cell involved in pepsin secretion (*top right*) would require another half-century, while the identification of the prolate ellipsoid structure of pepsinogen (the protein precursor of this enzyme), required an additional 100 years. Despite the identification of pepsin and its properties in 1836, neither the role of this factor in gastric pathology (peptic ulceration), or its extra-gastric function, have been entirely elucidated.

Three years after the initial identification of pepsin by Schwann, Wasmann was able to isolate the protein and thereby establish the premise for protein digestion. In 1854, the possibility of a pro-enzyme, pepsinogen, was formally postulated by Epstein and P Grützner, but the first evaluation of the protein products of gastric digestion were only described by Meisner in 1859. Rudolf Heidenhain, during his tenure, was able to describe the secretory mechanisms of proteolytic zymogens with the gastric lumen, and noted that pepsin was secreted by the "*Hauptzellen*". The observations of Heidenhain were further extended by Willy Kühne, who theorized that since the stomach itself was not self-digested, that gastric ferments must be produced as inactive protein precursors (for example, pepsinogen). Indeed, such was the prescience of Kühne in defining this area of physiology that he developed the term "zymogen" to describe such precursors, and was the first to use the term "enzyme" having identified the proteolytic pancreatic enzyme, trypsin, in 1868. His influence on the evolution of gastrointestinal physiology was substantial and a number of English physiologists, including Starling and John Langley (1852–1925) of Cambridge, worked in his laboratory.

John Langley

Although the initial contributions to the discovery of pepsin were those of Schwann, his genius led him variously into fermentation, neural cell morphology, the single cell theory of disease, and the design of underwater diving apparatus. It therefore remained for Langley in the 1880s to formalize the study of pepsinogen and the mechanisms of its secretion. Langley's introduction to the gastric gland was driven by chance, since his initial assignment by his mentor, Sir Michael Foster (the first Chairman of Physiology at Cambridge) had been to evaluate the effects of the drug jaborandi on the heart. In pursuit of this goal, by 1874 his work had led him towards the investigation of the drug's effects on secretion. After an initial prelude in the submaxillary gland, Langley addressed the regulation of secretion in the stomach, which he would pursue for the better part of the next 20 years.

Using the salamander as a model, Langley undertook histological studies of the gland structure in activity and at rest, and checked the interpretation of the appearance of killed and stained cells with that of direct observation of living gland cells. He correlated these findings with the effect of nervous influence on the glands, and linked these observations to chemical estimations of the changes in the quality of pepsinogen secretion under different circumstances. Indeed, his drawings and sketches, although now over 100 years old, attest to his clear understanding of the nature of zymogen secretion and the general mechanisms of its stimulation.

The study of pepsinogen and the mechanisms of its secretion were formalized by John Langley (1852–1925) (*bottom right*) of Cambridge. Langley succeeded Sir Michael Foster (1836–1907) as the Editor of the *Journal of Physiology* and trained John Sidney Edkins (1863–1940) (*top left*). He addressed the regulation of secretion in the stomach using the salamander as a model (*bottom left*), and undertook histological studies of the gland structure in activity and at rest, checking the interpretation of the appearance of killed and stained cells with that of direct observation of living gland cells (*background*). He correlated these findings with the effect of nervous influence on the glands, and linked these observations to chemical estimations of the changes in the quality of pepsinogen secretion under different circumstances. These drawings and sketches, although now over 100 years old, attest to his clear understanding of the nature of zymogen secretion and the general mechanisms of its stimulation. In addition, Langley was so impressed with Rudolph Heidenhain's contribution that he was to borrow and translate his terms for the cells in the stomach into English as "border" ("*Haupt*") and "chief" ("*Belleg*") cells, and also coined the term "oxyntic" to identify the role of the acid-secreting cells. In a series of publications between 1879 and 1882, Langley established the basic morphology and secretory characteristics of the pepsin-forming glands of the stomach and esophagus (*center*) and was in addition able to correct Heidenhain by demonstrating that contrary to previous reports, gland cells became less granular as secretion took place.

Sir Arthur Hurst (1879–1944) (*top left*) was born in Bradford, England. The great physicist Heinrich Rudolf Hertz was his father's cousin. In 1908, Hurst (the name change reflected British sensitivities to Germanic origins) published a detailed account of the movement of the stomach, intestine, and colon, having been influenced by the pioneer X-ray studies of WB Cannon. Having been appointed to the staff of Guy's Hospital at the age of 27, he established himself as a general physician with a special interest in gastroenterology. Hurst was particularly interested in ulcer disease, achalasia, and constipation, and wrote definitively on these and diverse gastrointestinal subjects. In 1936, Hurst established the Gastroenterological Club (subsequently the British Society of Gastroenterology) and at its first meeting in 1937, was elected President.

In addition, Langley was so impressed with Heidenhain's contribution that he was to borrow and translate his terms for the "*Haupt*" and "*Belleg*" cells in the stomach into English as "border" and "chief" cells, respectively, and also coined the term "oxyntic" to identify the role of the acid-secreting cells. In a series of publications between 1879 and 1882, he established the basic morphology and secretory characteristics of the pepsin-forming glands of the stomach and esophagus, and was in addition able to correct Heidenhain by demonstrating that contrary to previous reports, gland cells became less granular as secretion took place. Langley demonstrated that granules were stored up during rest and discharged during secretion in not only the pancreas but also the stomach and salivary glands, and that during this event, a chemical change in the zymogen occurred. To quote: "The fresh gastric glands contain no pepsin; they do however contain a large quantity of pepsinogen; consequently the granules of the chief cells consist wholly or in part of pepsinogen."

GASTRIC AND DUODENAL ULCERS, AND GASTRIC HEMORRHAGE

Sir Arthur Hurst claimed that the earliest record of a case of gastric ulcer appeared to be that published in 1586 by Marcellus Donatus of Mantua in his *De Medica Historia Mirabili*. The account as rendered provides a fine example of what, prior to the advent of acid-suppressive therapy, must have been a depressingly familiar tale to many physicians: "Camillus Lacinus, a man of a bilious disposition, suffered at the age of fifty-nine from a certain fever. When that was cured, he was left with a bad colour, and was found to have a swelling of the spleen and an obstruction of the liver. While in this feeble condition, through careless regulation of his habits, he developed the fever once more and was reduced to a bad state of health. On the outbreak of this malady he began vomiting, so that on the third day, after taking food, for three or four hours he vomited what he had eaten and drunk, together with a great quantity of liquid matter, which was repeated on each subsequent day until his death. On every occasion he vomited no less than three pounds of

phlegm, and frequently the amount reached as much as five pounds. During this time he never excreted anything by the lower channels, although purgatives, both violent and mild, were injected, and he took laxative medicines through the upper channels; these, however, he vomited. Meanwhile, he complained of pain about the base of the stomach, and thus he continued, vomiting twice daily, till the fourth day, when he passed from life to death." Donatus, much to his credit, then sought to determine the basis of the malady: "The body was dissected by us with the consent of his wife and son, who were his heirs, and in the lower part of the stomach at the pylorus or lower orifice we found that the inner coating was ulcerated, and we had no doubt that this had been the cause of the malady." Later authors who made contributions to ulceration include Bonetus of Geneva (1700), Littre (1704), and Rawlinson, who provided the earliest detailed report of a perforated gastric ulcer in 1729.

By the turn of the 18th century, the detailed examination and documentation of autopsies enabled Matthew Baillie (Physician at St George's Hospital), in *The Morbid Anatomy of Some of the Most Important Parts of the Human Body*, published in 1793, to provide the first clear description of the morbid anatomy and symptoms of gastric ulcer.

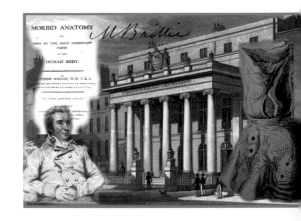

Matthew Baillie (*bottom left*) was the nephew of the more famous John (1728–1793) and William (1718–1783) Hunter. John Hunter was a surgeon who was regarded as one of the most distinguished scientists of his day. In the background is the Royal College of Surgeons of England at Lincoln's Inn Fields. In 1800, the writings and specimen collection of John Hunter, the Hunterian Collection, were collected here. Baillie was educated at the University of Glasgow and Balliol College, Oxford, and following an apprenticeship with William in London, was appointed Physician at St George's Hospital. Baillie's most significant work, *The Morbid Anatomy of Some of the Most Important Parts of the Human Body*, was published in 1793 (*top left*). It established morbid anatomy as an independent science. In this work, Baillie gave the first clinical descriptions of gastric ulcer and chronic obstructive pulmonary emphysema, and presented one of the clearest descriptions ever written on the pulmonary lesions of tuberculosis. At 36, however, he left St George's, ceased writing and lecturing, and spent the rest of his life in private medical practice. Baillie served as Physician Extraordinary to George III (1738–1820), but he accepted patients rich and poor alike. He was the last and most famous owner of the gold-headed cane, the coveted symbol of excellence among London physicians.

Subsequently, in 1799, Baillie published, from the Hunterian Museum of the Royal College of Surgeons of England, a series of engravings of pathological specimens, amongst which was one showing four small ulcers of the stomach, with a larger one of the duodenum and another of a perforating gastric ulcer. Baillie wrote as follows: "Opportunities occasionally offer themselves of observing ulcers of the stomach. These sometimes resemble common ulcers in any other part of the body, but frequently they have a peculiar appearance. Many of them are scarcely surrounded with any inflammation, have not irregular eroded edges as ulcers have generally, and are not attended with any particular diseased alteration in the structure of the stomach in the neighborhood. They

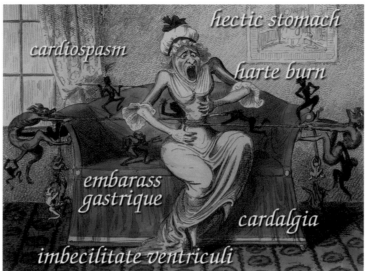

An 18th century British cartoon accurately attests to the wide public awareness and familiarity with the "Demon of Dyspepsia". Confusion as to the source of visceral pain led to the evolution of a nomenclature that confused the origin of the symptoms with the stomach, the heart, or even the brain. Many believed all chest symptoms emanated from the heart, and reflux symptoms were referred to as cardiodynia or cardialgia! Indeed, two centuries later, the basis of esophageal pain is as little understood now as it was then!

In 1828, John Abercrombie of Edinburgh provided an excellent account of the symptoms of gastric ulcer in his *Pathological and Practical Researches on Diseases of the Stomach, the Intestinal Canal, the Liver and other viscera of the Abdomen*. With characteristic Scottish attention to detail, he noted: "The disease may be suspected, when there is pain in the stomach occurring with considerable regularity immediately after meals, and continuing for a certain time during the process of digestion – especially if the pain be distinctly referred to a particular spot and if there be at that spot tenderness on pressure it may be further suspected... We should not be deceived, either by the pain having remarkable remissions and the patient enjoying long intervals of perfect health, or by remarkable alleviation of the symptoms taking place under a careful regulation of diet."

appear very much as if some little time before, a part had been cut out from the stomach with a knife and the edges had been healed so as to present a uniform smooth boundary round the excavation which had been made. These ulcers sometimes destroy only a portion of the inner coat of the stomach at some one part but occasionally they destroy a portion of all the coats forming a hole in the stomach. When a portion of all the coats is destroyed, there is sometimes a thin appearance of the stomach surrounding the hole, which has a smooth surface, and depends upon the progress of the ulceration. At other times the stomach is a little thickened round the hole; and at other times still, it seems to have the common natural structure." Thereafter, Baillie provided an accurate and concise account of the symptoms: "I have reason to believe that ulcers of the stomach are often slow in their progress. They are attended with pain, or an uneasy feeling in the stomach, and what is swallowed is frequently rejected by vomiting. This state continues for a considerable length of time and is very little relieved by medicine which may serve as some ground of distinction between this complaint and a temporary deranged action of the stomach."

Abercrombie was prescient in that he was able to distinguish benign disease from malignant and recognized that cancer of the stomach was a distinct disease, although it should be noted that two of the cases he described under the heading of ulcer appear from his account of the autopsies to have probably been malignant. Of particular interest is his observation of the symptoms that occurred when an ulcer bled or perforated.

As might be predicted given the eternal wrangling between the French and the British, claims and counterclaims were made as to primacy in the elucidation of the nature and treatment of peptic ulcer. Thus, in French literature, gastric ulcer was known as the "ulcer of Cruveilhier" or the disease entity itself as Cruveilhier's disease ("*Maladie de Cruveilhier*"). The Académie de Medicine opined that the investigations of Jean Cruveilhier between 1829 and 1835 were the first to establish the anatomical characteristics and complications, as well as the principal clinical features, of gastric ulcer disease, and maintained that Cruveilhier was the first to

A dramatic example of advanced peptic ulcer disease culminating in fatal hemorrhage was published in 1816 by Benjamin Travers and refers to a patient of Farre. In dealing with the subject of perforated gastric and duodenal ulcer, Travers described a man in whom intractable symptoms of dyspepsia had been present for many years, and at autopsy was found to have an ulcer adherent to the pancreas that had produced an hour-glass contraction of the stomach and had penetrated the splenic artery, resulting in massive bleeding and death.

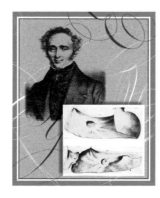

Jean Cruveilhier (1791-1873) was a brilliant pupil of Baron Guillaume Dupuytren and the first incumbent of the Chair of Pathology in the Paris Faculty. He abjured the use of microscopy, but nevertheless produced extraordinarily well-illustrated pathology texts. *La Maladie de Cruveilhier*: the first autopsy that he witnessed so upset Cruveilhier that he returned to his original desire to become a priest and entered the Seminary of St Sulpice. Cruveilhier pondered as to why an ulcer of the stomach might occur in a single place when the rest of the stomach was "in a state of perfect integrity". Details of the case notes of the management of hematemesis and the autopsy findings are of interest as regards current therapeutic strategies. In the case of the unfortunate carpenter on autopsy, he noted a deep ulceration "6 lines in dimension". A stylet introduced into the coronary artery of the stomach pushes a clot out of the center of the ulcer and enters the stomach.

In 1960, Geoffrey Watkinson (*bottom right*) from the Department of Medicine at Leeds (*background*) published his study (*bottom left*) which detailed the frequency of gastric, duodenal, and stomal ulcers at necroscopy in 20,000 examinations. In the work, he concluded that the incidence of ulcers determined at necroscopy accorded closely with clinical experience in life!

definitively distinguish chronic ulcer from cancer and to suggest a viable method of treatment. Hurst, as the founder of the British Society of Gastroenterology, staunchly maintained that as "admirable as was his work it was quite clear that Abercrombie had already done all of this although perhaps he had not distinguished ulcer from growth with quite the same definition". It is certainly clear that Abercrombie had described duodenal ulcer, which is not even mentioned by Cruveilhier in his two memoirs *Anatomie Pathologique* (1829–1842), which he presented in 1856 to the Academy of Sciences in Paris. These two documents summarized the clinical and anatomical observations he had carried out during the preceding 30 years on "simple, generally chronic, ulcers of the stomach". In fairness to the balance of this comment, it should be noted that Cruveilhier had clearly described a case of perforation of a chronic ulcer of the duodenum and provided a very fine drawing of the specimen.

An equally fine assessment of the subject of gastric ulcer was imparted in 1857 by William Brinton of St Thomas' Hospital in London in his monograph on *Gastric Ulcer* and his subsequent larger work on *Diseases of the Stomach* in which he analyzed 1,200 reported autopsies and 200 of his own clinically observed cases. Brinton too was somewhat remiss in failing to evaluate duodenal ulcer, although in fairness it should be noted that he clearly stated that he chose to "carefully avoid discussion of the ulceration of the duodenum, which often follows severe burns, because its situation, cause, and appearance, alike seem essentially different from ulcer of the stomach".

In 1838, Abercrombie, in the second edition of his *Pathological and Practical Researches on Diseases of the Stomach, the Intestinal Canal, the Liver and other viscera of the Abdomen*, described the classic presentation of the disease as follows: "The food is taken with relish and the first stage of digestion is not impeded: but pain then continues, often with great severity sometimes for several hours, and generally extends obliquely backwards in the direction of the

right kidney. In some instances it gradually subsides after several hours, and, in others, is relieved by vomiting." In respect of the relationship to bleeding, he described a patient that had been reported by Broussais in whom death had occurred as a consequence of hemorrhage that followed erosion of the hepatic artery by a duodenal ulcer. In addition, he referred to a specimen in the Museum of the Royal College of Surgeons of Edinburgh in which a patient whose disease had culminated in a perforated duodenal ulcer had perished within 24 hours. To further amplify the dreaded sequelae of duodenal ulceration, Robert Carswell, in his *Pathological Anatomie* of 1838, published a colored illustration of a posterior duodenal ulcer that at autopsy was noted to have caused the death of the patient from massive hemorrhage.

George Budd (1808–1882), an English internist better known for his hepatic contributions, believed chronic hepatomegaly to be caused by intestinal intoxication and coined the term Budd's cirrhosis, which was later named the Budd-Chiari syndrome. Budd was the son of the surgeon Samuel Budd at North Taunton and received private education there before attending Caius College, Cambridge, from where he graduated in 1831. He then went to Paris and studied medicine and pathology before returning to London to become a student at the Middlesex Hospital. He subsequently became Physician at the Dreadnaught Hospital Ship, where he encountered innumerable instances of liver disease in sailors returning home from the tropics, which became a basis for his classical work *On Diseases of the Liver*. In 1840, Budd resigned his commission to become Professor of Medicine at King's College, where he described the syndrome in 1845. In 1855, Budd described "the chief symptom of ulcer in the duodenum" as "pain in the situation of the ulcer, which is seldom constant, and which, in most cases, is felt only two or three hours after a meal". Budd opined with considerable prescience that "some cases heal, but others may cause hemorrhage, which can prove fatal, or they may perforate and lead to death from general peritonitis".

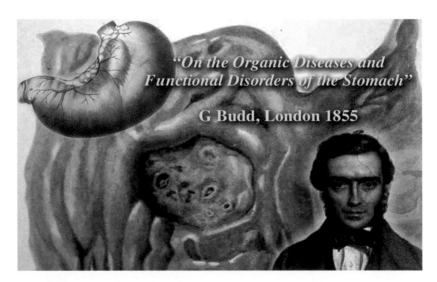

George Budd (*bottom right*) described the chief symptom of ulcer in the duodenum as "pain in the situation of the ulcer, which is seldom constant, and which, in most cases, is felt only two or three hours after a meal". This work was published in 1855, and included his comments that "some cases heal, but others may cause hemorrhage, which can prove fatal, or they may perforate and lead to death from general peritonitis".

CLINICAL TRIAL OF A TRITERPENOID LIQUORICE COMPOUND IN GASTRIC AND DUODENAL ULCER

R. DOLL
M.D., D.Sc. Lond., F.R.C.P.

Richard Doll, at the Middlesex Hospital in London, and his co-authors published a clinical trial (*top*) describing the effects of liquorice compounds (*left and right*) in patients with gastric and duodenal diseases. This work, published in the *Lancet* (1962), demonstrated some clinical efficacy, but the method of action was unclear and edema was noted as a side effect in about 20% of patients.

subservient to one or other of the following purposes. To remove all local obstacles to the 'cicatrisation' of the ulcer; to support the constitution in effecting this process; to remedy the results the lesion may have already brought about; and to limit or arrest some of the more prominent symptoms by which these results are usually betrayed."

In terms of his overall strategy, Brinton chose to separate medicines from diet and suggested that "the mitigation of symptoms which they can certainly effect is generally the first step towards the slow and progressive cure of the malady". He was particularly concerned about bleeding and noted: "...the question of bleeding consisted of a process of destructive absorption and resulted in a dangerous or fatal loss of blood which was generally attended by symptoms of extenuation and cachexia and especially affects the poor, the intemperate, the ill-fed, the wretched, and the aged, is not one in which any presumable local benefit counterpoised the obvious mischief producible by even a moderate loss of blood." Despite an apparently scientific bent, Brinton opined that "a few leeches to the epigastrium will often afford relief to the gnawing pain which torments the sufferer from gastric ulcer".

Up until the early 19th century, the treatment of bleeding peptic ulcer relied largely on gastric rest. In the 1820s–1830s, Abercrombie made the following suggestions for treatment of bleeding ulcers: "The food must be in very small quantity, and of the mildest quality, consisting chiefly or entirely of farinaceous articles and milk; and it would appear to be of much consequence to guard against any degree of distension of the stomach, that can be possibly avoided, even by the mildest articles. The patient should abstain in a great measure from bodily exertions... In the early stages, little probably is gained by medicine given internally, beyond what is required for the regulation of the bowels. In the more advanced stages... benefit may be obtained by some internal remedies, such as the oxide of bismuth, lime water and nitric acid." Brinton in 1857 suggested a wide range of agents to achieve gastric health in the patient with a bleeding ulcer. These included opiates; tartar emetic; vegetable astringents; tris-nitrate of bismuth; milk and raw eggs; a mixture of brandy, water, and opium; ice; gallic acid; and aperients. Of these, probably ice was the most effective!

In 1830, Brinton noted: "...the means by which we endeavor to effect the cure of this disease may be all grouped together as

William Brinton (*top right*) published his monograph on *Gastric Ulcer* in 1857. Apart from his analysis of 1,200 reported autopsies and 200 of his own clinically observed cases, he also commented upon a wide range of agents which he thought would be useful in achieving gastric health in patients with bleeding ulcers. These included opiates; tartar emetic; vegetable astringents; tris-nitrate of bismuth; milk and raw eggs; a mixture of brandy, water, and opium; ice; gallic acid; and aperients (*left*). Of these, probably ice was the most effective!

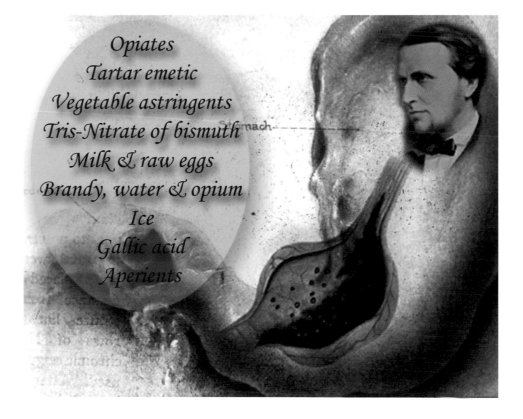

Opiates
Tartar emetic
Vegetable astringents
Tris-Nitrate of bismuth
Milk & raw eggs
Brandy, water & opium
Ice
Gallic acid
Aperients

The British view of the effects of bleeding did not apply to other forms of that revulsion which French authors characteristically termed "the moiety of medicine" ("*La revulsion, c'est la moitie de la médecine*"). Indeed, Gallic medicine favored blisters, turpentine stupes, mustard poultices, dry cupping, and hot formentations, considering them to be exceedingly useful adjuncts to internal remedies. Brinton noted that the symptom that seemed to most demand the application of such means of revulsion was pain, "especially of that continuous gnawing pain which, in severe cases, sometimes occupies even the intervals of taking food". Such remedies were generally applied to epigastrium, and blisters were considered to be most effective in young and well-nourished subjects. Tartar emetic was rarely or never advised since it was painful and troublesome, and in addition, often produced adverse antimonial effects on the system. A mixture of turpentine and mustard was preferable in the old and chronically ill, since it decreased blood loss involved in the serous effusion of a blister. In those patients in whom "the powers of the system were already exhausted by constant vomiting and where pain still was a prominent symptom, dry cupping was considered the best means of mitigation".

The relief of severe and continuous pain was undertaken by sedatives, and especially by opiates. Of the diverse types of bitter infusion available, Brinton found calumba to be the most beneficial in the treatment of flatulent nausea, and his most frequent prescription for the flatulent dyspepsia of gastric ulcer was as follows:

- Bx Pot assii iodidi, gr. j.
- Potassae bicarbonatis, grs. xv.
- Tincturae aurantii, 3ss.
- Infusi calumbae 5viiss.
- M. Horä secunda postcibum sumitur.

In regards to food, there was much less agreement: "There are instances in which the patient is already so much exhausted by the inanition which protracted vomiting implies, that any severe plan of diet – such as involves simple food in very small quantities, or protracted abstinence – becomes quite inadmissible. Indeed, the patient is not infrequently in a state which would itself demand the urgent administration of food and stimulants, if these were not contra-indicated by the state of the stomach."

Hemorrhage was required to be treated with especial reference to the pathology of the lesion that produced it: "The scanty flux that occurs in the earlier stages of gastric ulcer, such as often amounts to little more than a streak or two of blood in the vomit, or a dark coloration of the stools, scarcely demands any special treatment, beyond that which it is necessary to adopt in all cases of gastric ulcer. But where it occurs in a more advanced stage of the ulcer, or amounts to a considerable quantity of blood, physicians were justified in directing a more special (if not exclusive) attention to it. Under such circumstances the stomach was considered amenable to the local action of astringents introduced into it, as well as to that general action which their absorption into the system might induce. A more frequent and moderate oozing justifies (and demands) a more styptic plan of treatment, especially where there is no great tendency to vomiting

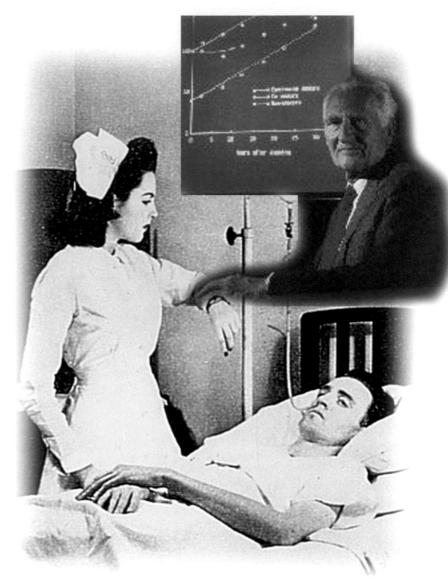

Richard Doll (*top right*) in the 1950s proposed that ulcers could be cured by instilling milk in a continuous fashion through a nasogastric tube into the stomach of a patient. This work revitalized both the observations of B Sippy (1915) and Asher Winkelstein (1935).

present. In such circumstances turpentine, and the sesquichloride of iron which were often used often excited nausea and vomiting, even in moderate doses and dilution." Brinton recommended about 10 grains of gallic acid that were dissolved in 1oz of distilled water by the use of 10 minims of the dilute sulfuric acid. In some cases associated with pain, an astringent combination of bismuth and compound kino powder were noted to arrest the bleeding.

Irrespective of the nature or amount of the hemorrhage, the internal and external application of cold by means of ice and the rigid observance of dietary strictures were regarded as an indispensable part of the treatment. All physicians were concerned about the use of mercury under any pretence whatsoever. Brinton noted two instances in which the ulcer had definitely been produced by the administration of mercury for other maladies and instances of relapse that could only be attributed to it.

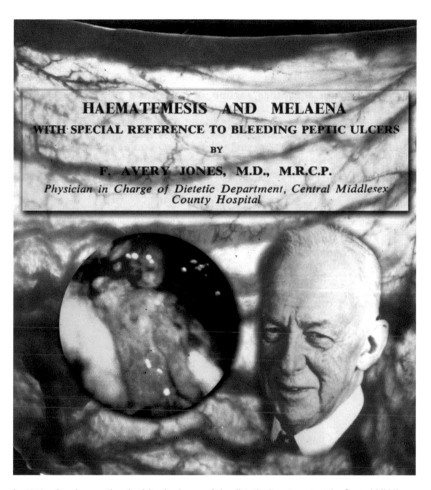

In 1943, when he was the physician in charge of the dietetic department at the Central Middlesex County Hospital, Sir Francis Avery Jones (*right*) published his treatment findings on 171 patients admitted with frank hematemesis (*left*) or melena over a two-and-a-half year period (*top*). Avery Jones treated the patients with prompt feeding and liberal blood transfusions, and noted that this regimen decreased the incidence of recurrent bleeding.

The fact that stigmata of recent hemorrhage (upper GI) was superior to any other single factor or combination of factors in predicting rebleeding and the need for surgery was identified by Losowsky's (*bottom left*) group. This work was performed at St James's Hospital in Leeds and was published in the *British Medical Journal* in 1978. The figure (*bottom right*) identifies stigmata as the best outcome predictor in patients with either duodenal or gastric ulcers.

THE EVALUATION OF THE STOMACH

Although esophagoscopic endoscopy would naturally lead onto gastric endoscopy, the danger of perforation with rigid instruments and the limited visibility provided by the mirror and lens systems left some physicians dissatisfied. Thus, the turn of the 19th century led to the development of a number of interesting and innovative devices designed to provide further information about the stomach.

The development of the stomach tube

The concept of access to the interior of the gut had long fascinated both patients and their physicians. At first, the requirements were simple and based upon the need to either remove *per os* foreign objects that had lodged or to open up the lower passages when feelings of distention and obstruction were perceived to be present. Thus, early attempts at medication were targeted at either promotion of emesis or acceleration of defecation, and purges and clysters were the order of the day.

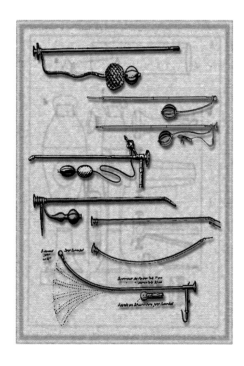

Some examples of the diversity of gastroscopes available between 1911 and 1933. The Elsner scope (1911) (*top*) was the most widely used prior to the introduction of the Schindler rigid gastroscope (*second from top*) in 1922. The Sternberg instrument (*third from top*) introduced in 1923 was claimed to have a size advantage (9mm as compared to 11mm of the preceding two) as well as better visibility, but patient fatalities diminished its appeal. The Korbsch instrument (1926) (*third from bottom*) had an even smaller diameter of 5–8mm, but was supplanted in 1932 by the Schindler flexible instrument (*second from bottom*). The disadvantage of its relatively large diameter (12mm) was far outweighed by the unique introduction of flexibility. Korbsch subsequently produced an elastic metal instrument (1933) of smaller diameter (*bottom*), but the Schindler design became the accepted gastroscope of the decade.

With time, however, the frustration and impatience of physicians with such unpredictable intervention led to efforts to gain more direct access to the interior of the gut. The ingenious development of a diverse variety of tubes was first aimed at therapy either for removing blockages, dilating strictures, or providing sustenance. After recognizing the limitations of the finger or the feather, the concept of using tubes to enter the alimentary tract represented the initial early and important impetus in promoting access to the interior. At first, these were rigid and introduced blindly, but the discovery of more pliable agents, functional light sources, and thereafter lenses led to increased flexibility and better visibility. Thus, therapeutic applications initially preceded diagnostic usage, and only after the advent of fiberoptic technology was parity regained. The evolution of the science of endoscopy was thereafter determined by the introduction of light sources, lenses, mirrors, and flexibility, as physicians moved from blind bougies to flexible fiberoptics.

Emptying the stomach

A simple introduction of the finger into the back of the throat was deemed immodest, and from the time of the Emperor Claudius, dinner guests were either provided with a "pinna" or a vomiting feather at the completion of each banquet course. A further utility of such self-induced emesis was in the rapid evacuation of covertly administered poisons. The application of such ingenuity to obviate the effects of covertly administered poison was circumvented by Agrippina, who poisoned the Emperor Claudius by applying the agent to the feather itself! In the 4th century, the master physician Oribasius described a number of methods utilized to produce emesis. These included swinging an individual in a suspended bed, goose feathers dipped in iris or cypress oil, and a variety of herbal combinations. More direct intervention included a "digital vomitorium" that consisted of a long feather glove, 10–12in in length, of which the lower two thirds were filled with wood fiber, while the upper third remained empty to receive the directing finger of the physician. Presumably, this novel device might be regarded as the earliest form of "gastric sound". Although the utility of such instruments decreased as Roman gluttony abated, they were still of some use to physicians, who were employed to protect royal personages from would-be poisoners. By the 16th century, Hieronymus Mercurialis had described a more elegant device for the induction of vomiting. This *lorum vomitorium* had initially been described for the treatment of opium poisoning by Scribonius Largus in the 1st century, and consisted of a leather strap treated with a nauseating tannic acid-containing substance. The combination of the strap and the chemical when introduced into the esophagus resulted in emesis.

A "Magenkratzer" or "Magenraumer" (circa mid-17th to 18th century). Desperate to alleviate the ill-understood symptoms of dyspepsia, even notable physicians such as L Heister supported rigorous brushing of the stomach, with a view to attaining a state of gastric cleanliness.

A wide variety of tubes, dilators, probangs, and whalebone-based devices were developed over the course of centuries. Thus, the hollow sounds and graspers of Sculetus and Arculanus were replaced by the dilators of Thomas Willis and the eelskin-covered contraptions of William Hunter as physicians sought access to the esophagus and stomach. A late 17th century example of the most dramatic type was the "*Magenkratzer*".

Early devices

Magenkratzer

The first mechanical devices, or stomach brushes, to cleanse the stomach were recorded in the 17th century, and despite their almost fearsome description, achieved great popularity. A stomach brush usually consisted of either a long, smooth, flexible arched whalebone, 2–3ft in length, tipped with an ivory button, to which a tuft of silk cord, horse hair, or linen was firmly attached. Introduction of the instrument was normally facilitated by slight bending and careful soaking in water, as well as the imbibing of copious quantities of diluted brandy prior to the introduction. Once through the mouth and esophagus into the stomach, appropriate cleaning maneuvers were undertaken. Copious vomiting (of the brandy and gastric residue) usually ensued and was regarded as tangible evidence of gastric emptying and cleansing. For a time, these devices were often found hidden in monasteries or convents, where usage was regarded as a sacred secret or "*arcanum*". Such instruments proved so effective in the hands of certain physicians that they were proposed for usage in even healthy individuals as a prophylactic measure by which means a long life could be attained and all stomach troubles avoided. Indeed, the concept acquired such vogue that men of considerable medical stature, including Lorenz Heister, supported outrageous statements made by the likes of Socrates, who claimed, "it appears as if death had laid aside its scythe and instead has had the stomach cleanser placed in its hands".

Such digestive therapy was not limited to rich Europeans and is described in the journals of Dapper, who traveled with the Dutch West Indies fleet in 1673. In these he describes a novel treatment personally witnessed amongst the South American Indians: "The Tapagus, a Brazilian tribe, have a remarkable method of cleansing the stomach. They pass a rope made of padded sharp leaves down the throat and into the stomach and then turn and twist it until vomiting and a bloody discharge occurs. The rope is then withdrawn and the stomach is cleansed."

Aspiration pumps

Stomach pumps for the removal of noxious substances were the next technological innovation in the field. An analysis of the literature of the time suggests that while John Hunter had been interested in this possibility, it was Alexander Monro *tertius* (1773–1859) who first introduced the application in 1797. This was followed by the work of Baron Guillaume Dupuytren (1777–1835) and C Renault of Paris, who in 1803 not only suggested the use of a flexible tube of sufficient length to reach the stomach, but also connected it to a syringe to aspirate swallowed poison. Philip S Physick (1768–1837), who had been a pupil of Hunter, first introduced the application in America in 1812. The unfortunate and contentious rival claims of pump priority (though not technological priority) established in England in 1822 and 1823 may be regarded as modifications of a general principle that had been earlier established by Hunter.

In his inaugural medical thesis, *Disputatio Medica Inauguralis de Dysphagia*, Monro *tertius* provided the first description of the use of a tube and syringe in cases of poisoning. He proposed that a tube could be utilized not only for the extraction of poison from the stomach, but also for the introduction of food into the stomach of individuals with severe dysphagia and an inability to swallow. His observations were however to a large extent based upon the work of his father Monro *secundus*, who had employed a flexible tube to remove fermenting fluids and gasses from the stomach of distended cows in 1767.

Physick, who was Professor of Surgery at the University of Pennsylvania and a former student of Hunter, provided the American contribution. The gastric contents of two three-month-old twins, who had accidentally been given an overdose of laudanum, were washed out utilizing a large flexible catheter. This was accomplished after firstly injecting a drachm of diluted ipecac into the stomach with a syringe and then withdrawing the fluid contents of the stomach repeatedly with warm water. Only one of the children was saved, however, but Physick noted the tragic length of time that had elapsed between imbibing the laudanum and the aspiration.

Alexander Monro *tertius* (1773–1859) (*bottom right*) was the third successive member of the Monro family to hold the Chair of Anatomy in Edinburgh. His thesis *Disputatio Medica Inauguralis de Dysphagia* elegantly described the design and use of a tube, syringe, siphon, and expandable mouthpiece/tongue depressor (*bottom left*) that had been designed to empty the stomach of ingested poison. This device represented an extrapolation of a similar piece of apparatus first utilized by his father to decompress Highland cattle (Black Angus) suffering from acute gastric distention.

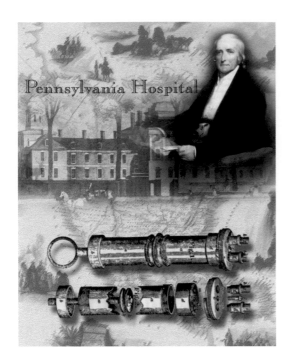

Although the eminent medical historian Fielding Garrison was of the opinion that Philip S Physick (1768–1837) (*top right*) "wrote nothing of consequence," posterity has nevertheless accorded him the honorific of "Father of American Surgery". An Edinburgh graduate of 1792 and a pupil of John Hunter, he subsequently became Professor of Surgery at the Pennsylvania Hospital in Philadelphia. In 1812, he published 'An Account of the New Mode of Extracting Poisonous Substances from the Stomach' and in so doing, claimed to have described a novel method of treatment. A year later, he was forced to recant this claim, when it became apparent that Alexander Monro *tertius* of Edinburgh was the rightful author. Nevertheless, he was the first American to use a syringe and tube to wash out the stomach in a case of poisoning. Since the case described was that of twins accidentally overdosed with laudanum by their mother and one died, his mortality was 50%. The syringes and pumps (*bottom*) used for the purpose of extracting gastric contents underwent a series of modifications and a series of London physicians, including F Bush (1822), E Jukes (1822), and Mathews (1826), each laid their claim to priority of the invention.

These observations were published in 1812 in an article entitled 'Account of the New Mode of Extracting Poisonous Substances from the Stomach'. Interestingly, Monro *tertius* was disingenuously acknowledged the following year with the following statement: "I, therefore, am happy in having called the attention of the profession to a mode of treatment not before used in this country, at least within my knowledge; but I have now an act of justice to perform, in describing the merit of the invention to Dr Alexander Monro, Jr, of Edinburgh who published it in his inaugural thesis in AD 1797. Of this circumstance I was entirely ignorant when I sent you my paper."

Such machinations were but a part of the fully-fledged academic squabble that subsequently developed regarding the priority of the discovery of the stomach tube. In May 1822, E Jukes, an English surgeon, published a paper in the *London Medical and Physical Journal* entitled 'New Means of Extracting Opium from the Stomach' in which he described an instrument called a "stomach pump" for "removing by mechanical agency, poison from the stomach". This consisted of a flexible tube 2.5ft in length and 0.25in in diameter, tipped with an ivory globe containing several perforations. An elastic bottle filled with warmed water was attached to the other end. Following successful introduction of the tube into the stomach, the water could be forced in and out. Jukes initially experimented on dogs, into whose stomachs he had introduced laudanum, which was thereafter irrigated until the water cleared. However, to confirm the efficacy of his treatment,

Sir Astley Paston Cooper (1768–1841) (*top right*) was a distant relative of Sir Isaac Newton and his uncle William Cooper was Senior Surgeon at Guy's Hospital. As a pupil of John Hunter, Cooper soon became regarded as the greatest surgeon and teacher of his time. Although quick tempered and imperious, his sartorial elegance, keen intellect, and remarkable surgical skills earned him widespread respect and admiration. Cooper became a luminary of the Royal College of Surgeons of England and his lectures formed the basis of much surgical education of the time. He was particularly forceful in applying the dictum that "operating is not all a surgeon ought to know" and insisted that "without knowledge it is impossible to adopt a proper remedy". It was Cooper who used a gastric aspirator (*bottom right*) to provide the gastric juice from his patients at Guy's Hospital (*background*) for William Prout (*bottom left*) to analyze for the presence of muriatic acid. In so doing, he thus facilitated the initial identification of hydrochloric acid in humans.

he himself swallowed 10 drachms of laudanum and allowed his colleague, a Mr James Scott, to undertake a successful lavage. This performance was repeated in public at Guy's Hospital, to the wonder of Sir Astley Paston Cooper (1768–1841).

Unfortunately for Jukes, the very similar observations had been published in the same journal two months previously by F Bush, who although utilizing a flexible tube to enter the stomach, employed a syringe rather than a wash bottle to generate a wash. Bush termed his apparatus a "gastric exhauster". As a result of the widespread acceptance of the efficacy of the device, an acrimonious debate regarding primacy immediately ensued. Unfortunately for Jukes and Bush, gastric aspiration using a similar mechanical device had previously been described by D Evans in 1817 (although not published until 1823). A bivalve syringe system that represented a design advance since it obviated the need for repetitive removal of the syringe during the process of gastric lavage was thereafter demonstrated by a W Reed. This was followed, in 1825, by Weiss's small, sophisticated pump, which had the advantages of being used for the emptying of the stomach of poisons, water from drowned persons, or for the presentation of enemata. The latter design became widely used throughout Europe and Weiss was lauded (wrongly) as the inventor of the stomach pump. In 1826, Mathews also described a syringe and provided certificates from three other physicians supporting his primacy. In a publication entitled 'Description of an Improved Instrument for Extracting Poison from the Stomach with some Statements tending to establish the Validity of Dr Physick's title to the credit of having invented the Stomach Tube' Mathews spared no one and criticized Jukes, Bush, Evans, and Reed for falsely claiming priority for the discovery. At this stage, Physick became re-embroiled in the saga and claimed that after initially recommending the introduction of the tube into the stomach as early as 1802, he had thereafter, in 1805, demonstrated the insertion of a tube covered with elastic gum. He alleged that such a tube had not originated in London but had been acquired in Paris and brought to America by his nephew, Dr John Dorsey.

As a result of this unfortunate series of events, the issue of the primacy of discovery of the gastric pump and its usage waxed and waned for years, as the various protagonists vied with each other for recognition.

Gastrodiaphany (gastrodiaphanoscopy)

Ismar Boas, in his 1907 textbook *Diseases of the Stomach*, wrote: "…even though transillumination or illumination of the human stomach is not applicable to general practice, these methods are of much interest. They point towards the road which, when improvement and simplification have taken place, would have to be followed." In the same text, he also stated, "gastroscopy has hitherto been found only of slight practical use… that it might undoubtedly play as important a role in the future, provided it is simplified, as cystoscopy has done in the diagnosis of the diseases of the bladder."

Cazenave in 1845 was the first to devise the technique of diaphanoscopy in order to view the inner urethral walls. He employed a funnel-shaped metallic tube, which was introduced into the urethra by means of a mandarin. The light, which was reflected from a lamp and made more powerful by means of a glaciating lens, was directed against the lower surface of the penis. In this manner, it was possible to plainly see the inner wall of the urethra, in spite of the thickness of the tissue. In 1860 two groups, Czermak and Gerhardt, and Störk and Voltolini, similarly sought to transilluminate the larynx with sun and gaslight. In the same year, Fonssagrives reported on the transillumination of the cavities of the human body by means of Geissler's tubes. It is however Julius Bruck, a dentist in Breslau, to whom the credit should be given for employing galvanic light for transillumination in 1867. In 1889, Max Einhorn of New York, stimulated by the work of Voltolini on electrical transillumination of the larynx, undertook to do this in the stomach. He utilized a Nelaton tube, to the lower end of which was attached an Edison hard glass incandescent lamp containing carbon filaments.

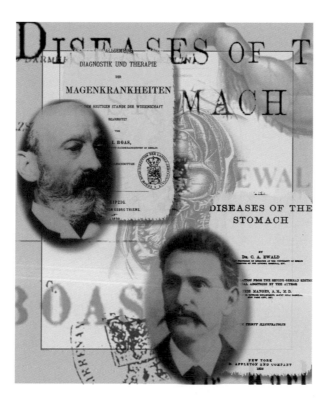

Max Einhorn of New York (*top left*) sought to illuminate the interior of the stomach by introducing a tube to which an incandescent lamp was attached. By viewing the brightly illuminated stomach in a dark room, its size, shape, and masses in its anterior wall could be appreciated. Gastrodiaphany however failed to gain widespread acceptance.

Ismar Boas (1858–1938) (*left*) was the founder of the specialty of gastroenterology and the Editor of the first medical journal for digestive diseases. From 1885 to 1910, he directed a clinic in Berlin, where he trained numerous physicians from many countries. In 1895, he founded, and thereafter edited until 1933, the first medical journal for digestive diseases, Boas' *Archiv für Verdauungskrankheiten*. Although he was a founder of the German Society for Gastroenterology and Metabolic Diseases, he was hounded from the country and committed suicide in Vienna in 1938 as a result of the Nazi Anschluss. As the author of several textbooks and the founder of a clinic devoted to gastroenterology, Boas and his colleague Carl Anton Ewald (1845–1915) were the established authorities on ulcer disease at the turn of the century. Ewald (*bottom*) was not only a pioneer in gastroenterology, but together with Boas, developed the first gastric function test (the Ewald Boas test meal). His monographs on diseases of the stomach and intestine (1886) and the gallbladder and biliary tract (1904) defined the state of the art.

The gastrograph

Einhorn constructed an apparatus to assess the mechanical function of the stomach in the living patient. Prior to developing the device, he had utilized laparotomized experimental animals to determine the appropriate site of placement and mode of introduction. The apparatus consisted of a ball, electric cells, and a ticker. The procedure consisted of swallowing the ball and its connected wires and thereafter monitoring the movements of the stomach. Once placed in the stomach, the motions of the former, which were caused by active and passive motions of the stomach, could be recorded. Einhorn labeled the apparatus a "gastrokinesograph" or "gastrograph" and stored the information to provide objective record of the alterations in the motility of the stomach.

JC Hemmeter of Baltimore devised a slightly different but equally ingenious method for also testing gastric peristalsis. The essential part of the apparatus consisted of a deglutible elastic stomach-shaped bag of very thin rubber attached to an esophageal tube. Since the stomach-shaped pouch only adopted the shape of the stomach when it was blown up and occupied little space when collapsed, it could be introduced without difficulty. Once the bag was in place in the stomach, it was filled with air and connected either with a water manometer or tambour on the Ludwig kymograph.

The gastrograph designed by JC Hemmeter of Baltimore as a test for measuring gastric peristalsis. The patient swallowed a stomach-shaped elastic bag connected by a thin rubber tube to a kymograph. Once in place, the bag was filled with air and then connected with a water manometer to the kymograph. Movement of the stomach altered the pressure within the bag and enabled a record of gastric peristalsis to be derived.

Thus, the slightest contraction of the gastric muscle layer compressed the elastic intragastric bag and distended the tambour, to which a glass bulb ink pin was attached to record the gastric peristalsis on the kymographion. Similarly, a pen connected to a chronometer indicated seconds on the record by small dots so that it was possible to determine the time, occurrence, and duration of gastric peristalsis. Subsequently, AJ Carlson utilized the Hemmeter-Moritz method for studying the normal contractions of the stomach and was able to deduce at least three different rhythms. These included periods of powerful rhythmic contractions altering with periods of relative quiescence (the 32 rhythm). Carlson also described a second rhythm of constant uniformity of about 20 seconds, which increased in intensity during periods of powerful rhythmical contractions of the fundus. The last rhythm type was that of powerful episodic contractions identical with the "hungry contractions" that had also been noted by both Cannon and Washburn. Hemmeter commented

that "in making studies on the kymograph on the gastric motility only such patients are taken as have become accustomed to the stomach tube as the nausea and vomiting first attending the initial introduction of the tube make an exact record impossible". His opinion summarized the difficulty of utilizing apparatus of this kind to determine gastric function.

Gastrogalvinization

The concept of inducing direct electrization of the stomach reflected the belief in the early, middle, and late 19th century that the application of electricity to a damaged part was of therapeutic benefit. The *Handbuch der Elektrotherapie* stated that "the first maxim to observe is the treatment in loco morbio" (that is, the application of electricity to the morbid part itself) and "…there is no doubt that it is best in the great majority of cases to operate directly on the diseased spot". Indeed, so well regarded was the therapy that authorities including Pepper of Philadelphia, Kussmaul, and Canstatt proposed that dilation of the stomach could be combated by direct electrization. This was achieved by the introduction of one electrode into the stomach itself and the other into the stomach region. No less an individual than Duchenne was the first to make use of this method!

In 1877, Adolf Kussmaul began to practice direct electrization of the stomach using a copper wire that ended in an olive point fastened to the cut-off end of a gastric tube. In 1881, Balduino Bocci, in experiments on animals, was persuaded: "the indirect faradization of the stomach through the abdominal walls produced in the stomach even when applied in a very energetic way, phenomenon of very little importance and of dubious curative effect!" This proposal of gastric electrization was further advanced by G Bardet in 1884, who filled the entire stomach with water to facilitate the passage of the electric current between the stomach wall and the electrode, thus establishing contact for the entire organ.

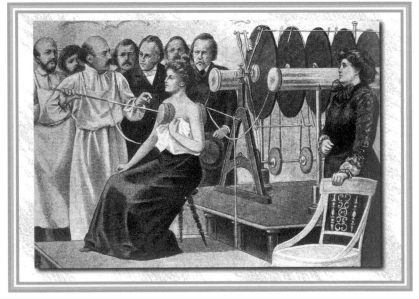

The concept of "electric therapy" as a remedial modality was considered seriously in many reputable medical establishments. For a period of time, its efficiency in the cure of pulmonary tuberculosis was widely accepted.

Einhorn facilitated the process of internal direct electrization by constructing an electrode on the same principle as the stomach bucket. He named this device "the deglutible stomach electrode". The electrode once swallowed reached the stomach without further artificial aid and the silk thread of the bucket was represented in the electrode by a very fine (1mm) rubber tube, through which an even finer soft conducting wire ran to the external battery. After an extensive study of the physiological effects of direct electrization of the stomach, Einhorn published a number of papers, in which he concluded that direct faradization of the stomach with the positive electrode increased gastric secretion, whereas with the negative pole electrode within the stomach, gastric secretion was diminished. In individuals with severe and "obstinate gastralgia" he regarded this therapy as "the sovereign means" for combating the disease. In fairness, it must be stated that Einhorn was quite honest in concluding that he had little understanding of what role was played by faradization.

Gastroscopy

Johann von Mikulicz-Radecki in 1881 provided the nexus of endoscopic development within the 19th century by developing a unifying concept that embraced the three critical components of an endoscope, namely an electric light source, an optical system,

Basil Hirschowitz endoscoping a patient (circa 1990). His seminal work on his fiberoptic technique was published in the *Lancet* in 1961. Much to the chagrin of the Luddites of his era, Hirschowitz was correct in his assessment that "the conventional gastroscope is obsolete on all accounts".

and a tubular endoscope body. In the early part of the 20th century, although Hans Elsner, Theodore Rosenheim, and Sussman of Berlin made further progress, rigidity and a lack of illumination continued to be problematic issues. Most gastroscopists accepted these limitations and by 1922, there were five well-accepted models available: Sussman, Loening-Stieda, Elsner, Schindler, and Kausch, and until 1932, the field was dominated by rigid endoscopes. At that stage, Rudolph Schindler (1888–1868), in conjunction with George Wolf (1873–1938), introduced the semiflexible endoscope and revolutionized gastroscopy. This device remained the prototype of all instrument design until the introduction of the fiberoptic endoscope by Basil Hirschowitz in 1957.

The Schindler modification of the Elsner rigid gastroscope introduced in 1922 and modified by others was the most extensively used instrument of the decade until 1932, when the Schindler-Wolf semiflexible gastroscope first became a reality. Most of the fundamental observations of gastroscopy were undertaken with this device and its contributions to the understanding of various diseases of the stomach probably make this instrument one of the great biotechnical devices of the century.

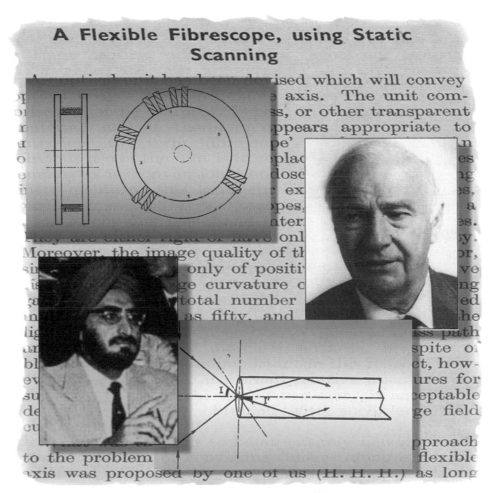

H Hopkins (*right*), Professor of Applied Optics at Imperial College, London, and subsequently the University of Reading, England, was a gifted scientist who, apart from his contributions to the establishment of fiberoptic systems, was responsible for the development of the diffraction theory of image formation. Although initially recognized for his invention of the zoom lens (1945), his work on the rod-lens optical system (1959) which he patented (Great Britain #954629) is now recognized as of fundamental importance. NS Kapany (*bottom left*), while a graduate student at Imperial College, was able to demonstrate that a glass fiber of one micron could successfully convey light. Together with Hopkins, an optical unit was designed (*bottom right*) that could convey images along a flexible axis.

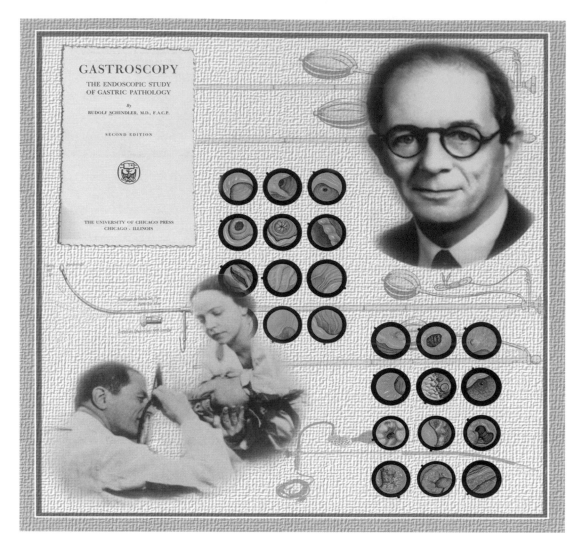

Mrs Gabriele Schindler (*bottom left*) holding the head of a patient while her husband performs an upper gastrointestinal endoscopy (circa 1940). Although she was not medically trained, Rudolph Schindler regarded her expert assistance as paramount to the success of any gastroscopic procedure. Indeed, her unavailability for any reason would prompt him to instantly cancel all scheduled patients. An indefatigable worker and rigid taskmaster, he was capable of performing more than 10 gastroscopies every two-and-a-half hours. Thus, by 1947, Schindler had personally examined 2,500 patients with gastritis and published a monograph on the subject. So effective was the husband and wife team that the Chicago clinic was soon overwhelmed with visiting physicians seeking to learn the methodology of the master. Indeed, such was the national interest that by 1941, Schindler had recognized the need for a formal gastroscopic organization and taken steps to establish a society.

Despite his early success and acclaim, it was apparent to Schindler that the potential problem of stomach perforations and esophageal tears with rigid instruments would be the rate-limiting factor in the development of the discipline. The first attempts to construct a flexible gastroscope were based on the awareness that an optical image could be conducted by a number of movable prisms. Schindler, who had acquired more than a decade of experience in both instrument use and design, was not slow in perceiving what needed to be done. Collaboration with Wolf, a Berlin instrument-maker who had considerable familiarity with the field, resulted in the construction and patenting (Germany patent #662,788; United States patent #1,995,196) of a flexible gastroscope in 1932 (after six versions).

The flexible part was also made elastic and could straighten itself, and the rubber fingertip was retained and modified from the original rigid instrument to facilitate safe passage. The final model of the instrument consisted of a straight, rigid proximal part and a distal flexible segment that contained a number of lenses of short focal length capable of transmitting the optical image even when the instrument was flexed. Driven by the belief that gastroscopy would provide a unique diagnostic window to the resolution of gastric disease, Schindler displayed such enthusiasm and commitment to the subject that by 1923, he had already published an atlas of gastroscopy, *Lehrbuch und Atlas der Gastroskopie*.

Unfortunately, the work of Schindler in Germany was halted by the advent of the Third Reich, and his incarceration in Dachau led him to the conclusion that emigration was the only possible salvation. Fortunately, Marie Ortmayer, a gastroenterologist at the University of Chicago, obtained Schindler a faculty appointment, and with the generous support of some former patients, both he and his family escaped Nazi Germany in 1934. Schindler subsequently established gastroscopy in the United States and in 1941 became the founder of what is now the American Society for Endoscopy.

During his lifetime, Schindler produced more than 170 manuscripts and five books. The *Lehrbuch und Atlas der Gastroskopie* was published in 1923 and his classic monograph on gastroscopy was published in 1937. This was followed in 1957 by the widely accepted *Synopsis of Gastroenterology*, which detailed not only the contributions of endoscopy but also placed Schindler's own views in perspective. At his death in 1968, his exemplary record as a skilled gastroenterologist and innovator deservedly earned him the sobriquet of "The Father of Gastroscopy".

Biopsy

The necessity of gastric biopsy to confirm visual pathology identified either by radiology or gastroscopy was well recognized. As early as 1940, a forceps for tissue sampling that could be successfully used in combination with the Schindler semiflexible gastroscope had been devised by Bruce Kenamore. These forceps, however, were not actually a true component of the gastroscope, but were clamped onto the shaft of the endoscope ("piggy back") and could therefore only be utilized in conjunction with it. As might be predicted, the instrument was subject to mechanical problems and failure.

In 1948, Edward B Benedict, who in collaboration with the American Cystoscope Makers Corporation had developed a fully operational gastroscope for the acquisition of gastric tissue, overcame the Kenamore problem. This device consisted of an operating gastroscope in which both a biopsy forceps and a suction tube had been incorporated (within the housing of the gastroscope itself). Benedict maintained that while gastroscopy itself should not be regarded as a routine diagnostic procedure, if a gastroscopic examination were to be performed, it could not be regarded as complete unless the gastroscopist had some means of biopsy readily available.

Fiberoptic gastroscopy

The rate-limiting factor, however, at this stage of endoscopy was the critical spacing of the optical lenses, which affected both the flexibility as well as the visual acuity of the instrument. Aware of the advances in fiberoptics that had been made by H Hopkins and NS Kapany of Imperial College, London, Hirschowitz attempted to relate the potential applications of fiberoptics to endoscopy. The first step in this venture was the need to perfect the fibers by producing a glass-coated fiber with the optical qualities adequate for gastroscope bundles; this was achieved between 1954 and 1957. Despite the obvious potential of this application to gastroscopy, numerous optical and medical instrument-manufacturing corporations declined to participate in the venture.

Hirschowitz demonstrated his new gastroscope that he called a "fiberscope" at a meeting of the American Gastroscopic Society on May 16, 1957, at Colorado Springs. This presentation was remarkable, since the President of the Society JT Howard actually yielded the podium and declined to give his Presidential address in favor of Hirschowitz. Howard's statement – "I shall forego my prerogative of boring you with a Presidential address so that Dr Hirschowitz may at half past 8 o'clock tell you about what I

Sir Francis Avery Jones (*left*) and his student Basil Hirschowitz (*right*) both contributed significantly to the advancement of the diagnosis and therapy of peptic ulcer disease.

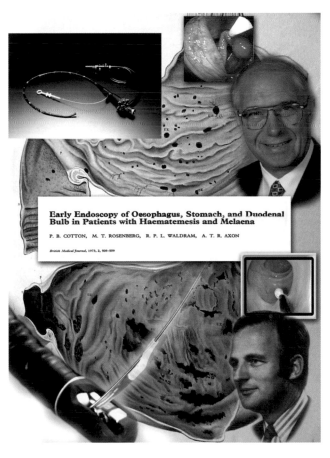

The St Thomas' Hospital group, including Peter Cotton (*bottom right*) and Anthony Axon (*top right*), were able to demonstrate as early as 1973 that upper gastrointestinal endoscopy led to a more accurate diagnosis of upper gastrointestinal bleeding than more traditional techniques.

understand to be a new principle of gastroscopy. I hear that fiberglass conducts light around corners and that Dr Hirschowitz has used this material in a new type of gastroscope" – would usher in an entirely new era of medical and gastroenterological practice. Acceptance of the device, however, was not as rapid as might have been predicted. Initial reports comparing the fiberscope and the conventional gastroscope were guarded in their pronouncements and noted that while the fiberscope provided a better view of the duodenum, the gastroscope resulted in a better quality visual image! The first marketable prototype, the Hirschowitz ACMI 4990 fiberscope, was detailed in a 1961 article in the *Lancet* entitled 'The Endoscopic Examination of the Stomach and Duodenal Cap with the Fiberscope'. This seminal publication was the harbinger of a new world of gastroscopy and documented the introduction of what would prove to be one of the greatest contributions of gastroenterology to the world of medicine. Hirschowitz commented within the publication that it was his considered opinion that "the conventional gastroscope has become obsolete on all counts".

Despite these early optimistic predictions, the ACMI Hirschowitz FO-4990 gastro-duodenoscope proved less than ideal in its ability to pass the pylorus into the duodenum. One report in the *American Journal of Digestive Diseases* in 1966 stated that they had been "unable to enter the duodenum with certainty in any examination" in 1,000 fiberscope examinations. Nevertheless, with the passage of time, gastroenterologists came to recognize the unique advance that fiberoptic endoscopy had conferred upon them. Indeed, such was the enthusiasm of the field that in much the same way as computer technology in the 1990s altered on an almost monthly basis, endoscopy in the 1970s generated technical advances at such a pace that gastroenterologists were barely able to stay abreast of the new possibilities.

Percutaneous endoscopy gastrostomy (PEG)
A wide variety of procedures had been developed in the late 19th and early 20th centuries to provide access to the stomach. The surgical procedures had supplanted the chronic use of stomach tubes and were of particular utility in feeding patients who could not swallow or decompressing the stomachs of those with pyloric obstruction. The earliest percutaneous access to the human stomach was provided by either incidental trauma or disease. Although the Russian physiologist W Bassow was the first to propose the utility of the human gastrostomy, Charles Sedillot in 1849 was the first to successfully undertake the procedure. Thereafter, A Vernuil (1876), Charles Richet (1878), and K Lennander (1908) variously demonstrated the efficiency of the procedure to either provide nutrition to or drain an obstructed stomach, and popularized the operation. Over the next three decades, gastrostomy became regarded as a popular and useful technique, and a wide variety of surgical modifications were developed in the early 20th century to provide long-term access to the stomach.

In 1980, Jeffrey Ponsky and Michael WL Gauderer described an "incisionless gastrostomy" that had been developed for long-term internal feeding of pediatric patients at the Children's Hospital in Cleveland. So effective and safe has this procedure become that in 1990 it was estimated to be the second most common indication for upper endoscopy in hospitalized patients in the United States. Indeed, the efficacy of the maneuver has been such that surgical gastroscopy has virtually become a technique of the past.

MUCOSAL BARRIERS

The question of why the stomach does not autodigest was often posed, and the iatromathematician Archibald Pitcairn asked, "Why upon the digestion of food upon the stomach, which is as easily digestible as the food, yet the stomach itself should not be dissolved?"

Jeffrey Ponsky, General Surgeon and Endoscopist (*right*), and Michael WL Gauderer, Pediatric Surgeon (*left*), conceived and perfected a novel technique (1980) to obviate the need for open surgical construction of a gastrostomy. Although initially contemplated as a pediatric procedure, it was soon widely adopted in adults as a well-tolerated, efficacious, and low risk intervention. Standard operative gastrostomy, like peptic ulcer surgery, thereafter faded for the most part from the armamentarium of the general surgeon. The insert (*bottom right*) is the original tube used in the first PEG. (Courtesy of Jeffrey Ponsky.)

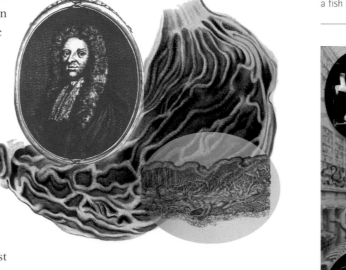

Archibald Pitcairn (*top left*), the noted Iatromathematician, questioned why the stomach (*background*) failed to digest itself. An intact gastric mucosa demonstrating viable arterial and venous blood supplies is indicated (*bottom right*).

No reasonable answer was forthcoming and pundits such as Hunter could only perseverate upon the existence of a putative vital force that maintained the gastric wall intact under the circumstances of digestion. The invocation of "vital spirit" however was of little satisfaction and represented a regression to pre-Paracelsian views on the nature of digestion. Issues such as the existence of a "*locus minoris resistentia*" were entertained to explain ulceration and embraced the concept that this was indeed local digestion of the stomach mucosa. Further reflection on the matter resulted in the recognition that the stomach wall itself must harbor an intrinsic "force" capable of resisting digestion. Indeed, the attractive concept that a breakdown of such an intrinsic mechanism might be responsible for the development of ulcers or even neoplasia became a source of considerable speculation.

A drawing of the Hunterian Surgical Museum at the Royal College of Surgeons of England (circa 1890). During his lifetime, John Hunter amassed a collection of more than 50,000 specimens and wrote exhaustively on physiology, pathology, and clinical medicine. Among the vast collection of stomachs are specimens of considerable interest: a microinjection specimen (*bottom right*), a camel stomach with its water sacs (*bottom left*), an example of extensive postmortem digestion (*top left*), and a fish stomach with its sizable antral organ (*top right*).

In the early 1930s, the issue had arisen as to whether acid was neutralized within the lumen or after diffusion into the mucosa in the interstitial fluid. Torsten Teorell suggested that the back diffusion of H+ ions through the mucosa in exchange for Na+ ions might define the permeability characteristics of gastric mucosa. An alternative hypothesis was that the bicarbonate content of gastric secretion might be responsible for neutralization of some of the acid. Nevertheless, the ability of the stomach to retain the acid it secreted under normal circumstances without digesting itself produced a compelling consideration to define the concept of the existence of a "gastric mucosal barrier". Teorell began the delineation of the barrier properties by demonstrating that unionized organic acids, but not ionized mineral acids, would disappear rapidly from the gastric contents by diffusing into the mucosa. Whilst not fully resolving the issue, his concept of a diffusion process in the mucosa had by 1947 initiated the formal evaluation of the intrinsic mechanisms available to deal with back diffusion of acid into the interstitium of the stomach.

The first formal usage of the term "barrier" arose in 1955 in the work of Davenport and Code, who had published a series of experiments under the title 'The Functional Significance of Gastric Mucosal Barrier to Sodium'. Davenport in later work examined this concept further by seeking to evaluate the effects of damage with various agents, including eugenol, fatty acids, and alcohol, and was able to prove that back diffusion into the mucosa of acid occurred under such conditions. He provided further substantiation of his observations of increased mucosal permeability by demonstrating anatomical evidence of damage to the surface epithelial cells and underlying tissues, including vessels. Considerable substance was thus provided for the important association of barrier breaking and its relationship to acute mucosal ulceration and stress bleeding. Following the initial contributions of Davenport, an immense and tedious body of work was undertaken by diverse investigators, who variously identified the noxious effects of hypoxia, acid, bile salts, aspirin, nonsteroidal anti-inflammatory agents, prostaglandins, and numerous other agents on the integrity of the barrier.

This achieved little except to support the existence of the mucosal barrier and the ability of a variety of agents to break it, and failed for the most part to establish either the precise site or mechanism of the phenomenon. The more recent usage of sophisticated techniques to investigate cell function has determined the relevance of tight junctions and identified the specific property

A comparison of the smoking habits of patients with and without peptic ulcer was undertaken by Richard Doll, Sir Francis Avery Jones, and Pygott in the late 1950s in order to establish whether nicotine intake affected the natural history of this disease. This 1958 *Lancet* publication (*top*) determined that smoking, in some patients, interfered with the healing of a peptic ulcer and helped to maintain the chronicity of the disease.

In 1986 in the *Lancet* (*center*), Kevin Somerville and colleagues from the University of Nottingham, England, were able to demonstrate a significant association between NSAIDs and bleeding peptic ulcer. Their data indicated that non-aspirin NSAIDs were associated with a relative risk of 4.4–6.4 of ulcer bleeding in patients who were over the age of 60 years.

of the apical membrane of the gastric mucosal cells as being of vital importance in maintaining barrier function. Further elaboration of this line of work generated much discussion about the "unstirred layer" and held that under such conditions even a modest concentration of bicarbonate would produce a barrier of both functional and physical significance to acid.

MEASUREMENT OF ACID

Early measurements of gastric acid were qualitative and mostly involved the use of indicator dyes or litmus preparations. However, since Prout first measured muriatic acid in 1823, definitive quantification became possible and a number of techniques were introduced. In the latter part of the 19th century, however, a confusing terminology developed around the inability to adequately quantify low levels of gastric acid secretion. Thus, the term "achylia" was used by Einhorn to describe the absence of both enzymes and acid in the stomach, while "achlorhydria" was used to denote the absence of free acid as determined by Topfer's reagent. The latter term, however, may have been misleading given the fact that very low levels of acid secretion may have been obscured by bicarbonate secretion. This biochemical confusion spilled over into the clinical arena and the use of the term "hypochlorhydria" to denote low levels of acidity further obfuscated the assessment of the secretory status of the stomach.

Wilfred Card and colleagues at the Western General Hospital and Edinburgh University determined the effects of intravenous histamine infusions on gastric secretion in human subjects (*center*). This work was undertaken to determine, mathematically, the effects of histamine on acid secretion. A graph of acid output in one of the three volunteers (WIC) demonstrated that this strongly correlated with increasing doses of intravenous histamine. This 1954 work suggested a close relationship between histamine and acid release.

In 1952, Wilfred Card and Sircus proposed that any gastric pH of more than 6.0 should be denoted as an "anacidity". This resulted in an evolution of the definition of achlorhydria to be a persistent failure of intragastric pH to fall below 6.0 in the presence of any stimulation of gastric acid secretion. The subsequent evolution of quantitative measurements of gastric acid

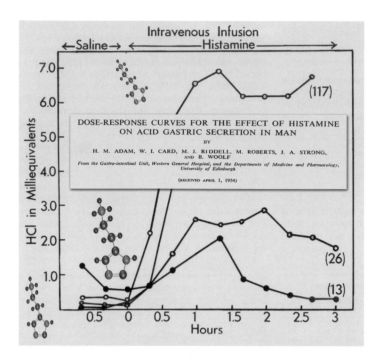

This work amplified that of Leon Popielski, who had initially experimentally established the relationship in the second decade of the 20th century, and G Katsch, who had undertaken similar studies in Germany in 1925. Kay measured the ability of histamine to stimulate acid secretion at a dose of 0.1mg/10kg body weight and derived the values for maximal acid secretion in a number of different groups of patients, while administering mepyramine maleate to block the systemic effects of histamine. Card and IN Marks of the Western General Hospital in Edinburgh subsequently determined the dose-response curves for acid secretion in human subjects in response to intravenous infusions of histamine.

secretion played a pivotal role in the resolution of the role of histamine as an acid stimulant, as well as providing further information necessary to define the physiology of acid secretion. In this respect, the development of the augmented histamine test by Sir Andrew Watt Kay of Glasgow was particularly useful in establishing the precise relationship of histamine to acid secretion in humans.

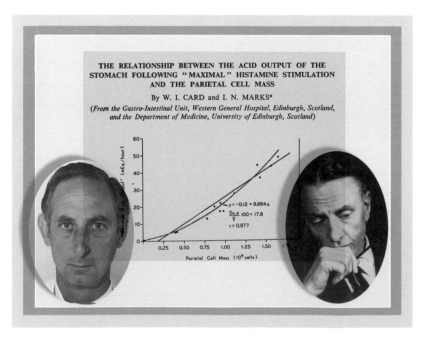

The establishment of the role of acid in the genesis of peptic ulceration was supported by studies undertaken jointly by IN Marks (*left*) and Wilfred Card (*right*) of Capetown and Edinburgh, respectively, who concluded that acid secretion was a function of parietal cell mass. They established that histamine stimulation could be utilized to assess the function of the parietal cell mass. This work facilitated the recognition that acid output, parietal cell mass, and peptic ulceration were inextricably linked. As a result of these physiopathological observations, a rational basis was provided for the consideration of acid reduction, initially surgically and subsequently by pharmacotherapeutic means, as a definitive intervention in the management of acid peptic disease.

Sir Andrew Watt Kay (*center*) of Glasgow was instrumental in developing the histamine stimulation test of gastric acid secretion as a diagnostic tool with predictive application in defining the extent of gastric surgery. This 1953 publication (*top*) attempted to determine the effects of a maximal stimulus to parietal cells following the removal of any "endogenous" histamine. The graph (*left*) shows the maximal acid-dose response curves in five cases of duodenal ulcer, while the figure on the right indicates the frequency of maximal acid output in male subjects.

Marks and Card then applied their method of estimating parietal cell mass to gastrectomy specimens of patients with duodenal ulceration, chronic gastric ulceration, or carcinoma of the stomach, and established that the maximal acid output correlated with the parietal cell mass. Thereafter Marks, working with Simon Komarov and Harry Shay at the Fels Research Institute of the Temple University of Philadelphia, was able to correlate the maximal secretory response of dogs to the estimated total parietal cell mass of each stomach. The subsequent development of an analog of histamine (3-beta-aminoethyl pyrazole) by CE Rosiere was particularly useful, since it enabled stimulation of acid secretion without generating the side effects of histamine. The widespread availability of the standardised augmented histamine test was useful both for experimental studies and for the evaluation of the therapeutic efficacy of various medical agents and surgical procedures.

ACID SUPPRESSION

The role of histamine antagonists

It had long been recognized that acid and ulcer were related and the Schwartz dictum of "no acid, no ulcer" was widely accepted. The exploration of the pathogenesis of peptic ulcer disease suggested a further corollary, namely that hyperchlorhydria (hyperacidic secretion) might play a pivotal role. Since histamine has been identified as a critical secretory agent, the exploration of the pharmacology of histamine evoked considerable interest, with the objective of identifying appropriate blocking agents. Indeed, it was proposed that the identification of such drugs would likely alter the natural history of the disease. Nevertheless, by 1950, numerous antihistaminic agents (produced by modification of the imidazole ring) had been studied without identification of an agent effective in the inhibition of acid secretion. In 1966, ASF Ash and HO Schild of the University College London stated with some degree of frustration: "At present, no specific antagonist is known for the secretory stimulant action of histamine in the stomach." They suggested the symbol H_1 for receptors that are specifically antagonized by low concentrations of antihistaminic drugs (H_1-receptor antagonists were first synthesized by Boivet in the 1950s) and proposed that another class of histamine receptors existed, which might mediate the acid secretory action of histamine.

The first series of gastric-specific histamine-receptor antagonists were soon after synthesized in Welwyn Garden City, England, at a site of a stately home occupied by Smith, Klein and French, a pharmaceutical corporation. Although the site had been initially used for development of diving gear during the Second World War, since it possessed a deep pond, Smith, Klein and French had acquired it for research purposes. A group led by the Uddingston-born pharmacologist Sir James Black was sponsored by the pharmaceutical corporation to identify a molecule that exhibited an H_2-receptor activity.

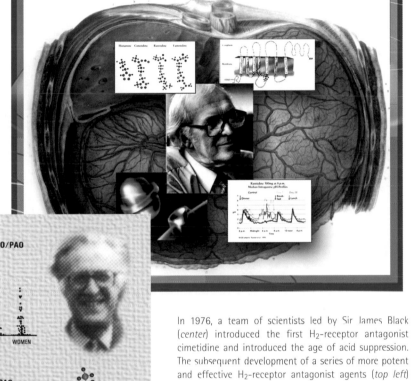

An assessment of the augmented histamine test in the diagnosis of peptic ulcer

Correlations between gastric secretion, age and sex of patients, and site and nature of the ulcer

J. H. BARON[1]
From the Institute of Clinical Research, Middlesex Hospital Medical School, London

In 1976, a team of scientists led by Sir James Black (*center*) introduced the first H_2-receptor antagonist cimetidine and introduced the age of acid suppression. The subsequent development of a series of more potent and effective H_2-receptor antagonist agents (*top left*) revolutionized the treatment of acid-related diseases and provided a highly attractive and safe alternative to surgical therapy, with its significant morbidity and mortality. Although relatively free of adverse effects, H_2-receptor antagonists have nevertheless proved to have some significant drawbacks. In particular, their action as competitive inhibitors of the H_2-receptor-binding site did not block or inhibit other parietal cell stimulatory mechanisms. Furthermore, the nature of receptor antagonist pharmacology (*bottom right*) was such that prolonged usage resulted in tachyphylaxis and tolerance. Such problems became particularly evident in patients undergoing long-term maintenance therapy, particularly in the management of reflux esophagitis or gastrinoma.

In 1963, JH Baron (*top right*), the doyen of acid secretion, assessed the diagnostic value of the augmented histamine test in the diagnosis of peptic ulcer disease. Baron demonstrated a gradient in peak acid outputs in patients with ulcers from different sites and indicated that patients with abnormally high basal or peak acid outputs who had dyspepsia but were negative on barium meal examination may have peptic ulceration.

Black had previously achieved success with the synthesis of the first beta-blockers for the treatment of heart disease. Before embarking on a pharmaceutical career, he had received his medical degree from the University of St Andrews, Scotland, in 1946. Thereafter, he taught a decade before accepting a position at Imperial Chemical Industries as Senior Pharmacologist. In 1956, when Black began work at Imperial Chemical Industries, several substances were known that could selectively stimulate the alpha- and beta-receptors or inhibit the alpha-receptors in heart smooth muscle. At the time, the standard therapy for angina pectoris and other forms of heart disease was to use drugs that increased the supply of oxygen to the heart. Black hypothesized that blocking the beta-receptors would effectively relax the heart, reducing its need for oxygen and the strain on the muscle, and thus retarding any degenerative process. He therefore set out to design a drug that could accomplish this effect. As several analogs of norepinephrine were available, Black and his team used isoprenaline (isoproterenol) to create propanolol, the first specific beta-blocker.

Black then moved to the Smith Kline Group and devoted 14 years to his quest for finding a second specific receptor antagonist that was clinically viable. After synthesizing and testing "about 700 compounds" his group announced in 1972 that a compound (burimamide), which possessed an imidazole ring with a side chain much bulkier than that of histamine, was a potent suppresser of acid secretion. By focusing on the side chain rather than the imidazole group itself, they were able to generate a drug which antagonized the responses to histamine that were not antagonized by drugs acting on the H_1-receptor. Included in these responses were the inhibition of the secretion of acid. The screen used by this group was inhibition of histamine-induced acid secretion in the perfused rat stomach in the Gosh-Schild preparation, an eminently suitable screen for the discovery of a gastric-targeted antihistaminic. Black therefore proposed that there existed a homogenous population of non-H_1-receptors that he chose to term "H_2-receptors". It was

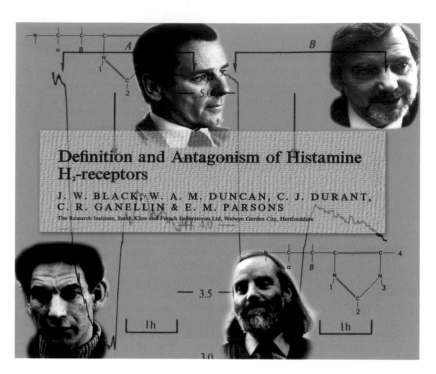

The seminal *Nature* paper (1972) (*center*) from Sir James Black's group. In the background is a graphical depiction of rat gastric secretion and its response to burimamide. Injection of the antagonist reversed 90% of acid output that could be maintained over the experimental period. Black's co-authors included (*clockwise from top left*) Duncan, Durant, Parsons, and Ganellin.

evident that burimamide inhibited pentagastrin as well as histamine stimulated acid secretion, and Black suggested that H_2 blockade might resolve the long-debated question of whether histamine was the final common mediator of acid secretion.

Metiamide and cimetidine followed this first success, and cimetidine was introduced for treatment of acid-related diseases in 1977. It is of interest in each case that Black began with a known chemical substance. He is quoted as stating that "the most fruitful basis for the discovery of a new drug is to start with an old drug" – a paradigm that forms the basis of any rational drug development. Black was knighted in 1981 and then shared the Nobel Prize in 1988 with George Hitchings and Gertrude Elion for their work on developing drugs for the treatment of critical diseases.

George Sachs (originally of Edinburgh and later to be responsible for critical advances in the field of parietal cell proton pump inhibition) noted that Black, Project Leader; Bill Duncan, Site Director; and Bryce Douglas, Head of Research at Smith, Klein and French (then based in Philadelphia) were all Glaswegian Scots.

During the 1980s, the H_2-receptor antagonists became first-line therapy in peptic ulcer disease and led to an improvement in quality of life for a large number of patients. They were found to be superior to any other form of medication at the time, giving good inhibition of night-time secretion and lesser inhibition of daytime acid secretion. After the first successes with the short-acting H_2-receptor

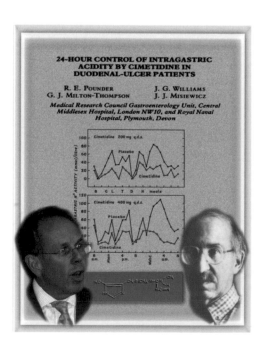

Roy Pounder and John Misiewicz determined that the H_2-receptor antagonist cimetidine (*bottom*) 0.8–1.6g/day resulted in a decrease of intragastric acidity that was compatible with successful medical treatment of patients with duodenal ulceration! The mean hourly intragastric values are given in the graph (*center*). Cimetidine decreased acidity in 44 out of 46 of the hourly sampling periods.

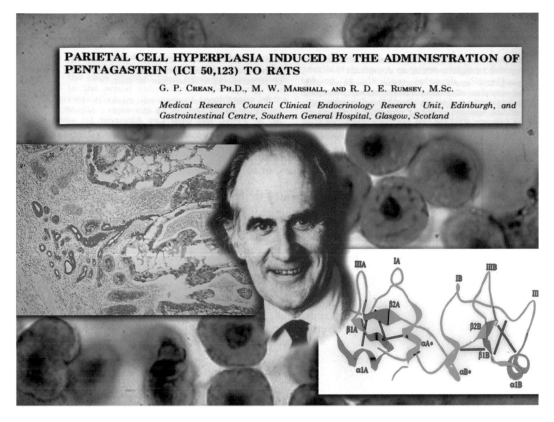

PARIETAL CELL HYPERPLASIA INDUCED BY THE ADMINISTRATION OF PENTAGASTRIN (ICI 50,123) TO RATS

G. P. CREAN, PH.D., M. W. MARSHALL, AND R. D. E. RUMSEY, M.SC.

Medical Research Council Clinical Endocrinology Research Unit, Edinburgh, and Gastrointestinal Centre, Southern General Hospital, Glasgow, Scotland

In 1969, Gordon Crean (*center*) and collaborators in Glasgow and Edinburgh determined that chronic pentagastrin stimulation altered the mucosal structure and function of rats. They specifically noted increases in the average count of parietal cells per unit area of the mucosa and in the total parietal cell population of the stomach. This parietal cell hyperplasia is now recognized to have been driven by trefoil factors (*right*), which also play an important role in ulcer repair (*left*).

effective way of controlling acid secretion. Although work towards this end began at Smith, Klein and French in Philadelphia, it was terminated with the launch of cimetidine.

The development of the first of this series of drugs was due to a combination of serendipity, mechanism, and conviction that the ATPase was the best target for control of acid secretion. A compound, pyridine-2-acetamide, had been acquired by Hassle, a company in Goteborg, Sweden, for possible use as an antiviral agent. Although this compound was found ineffective, it was surprisingly noted to possess some antisecretory activity. Modification to a pyridine-2-thioacetamide in order to improve its antiviral efficacy proved ineffective, although it retained its antisecretory activity. In 1973, Smith, Klein and French announced the development of cimetidine, the world's first clinically useful H_2-receptor antagonist. Based on the structure of cimetidine, a benzimidazole ring was added to the antisecretory drug (pyridine-2-thioacetamide), based on the belief that the mechanism of action of these forerunners was H_2 antagonism. Antisecretory activity was retained. Finally, the sulfide was modified for stabilization to a sulfoxide and timoprazole was born.

antagonists, considerable effort was next expended on identifying compounds that were longer acting, hence relatively irreversible or insurmountable, in order to improve the acid inhibitory profile of this class of drug. The Smith, Klein and French patent was bypassed by a group of chemists working at Allen and Hanbury led by David Jack, also from Glasgow. The imidazole ring was exchanged for a furan and a small side chain modification was made. This generated ranitidine, famotidine with a thiazole ring, and nizatidine.

It was soon apparent that the introduction of the H_2-receptor antagonist class of agents revolutionized the management of acid-peptic-related disease and provided a major increase in the quality of life for innumerable patients. The recognition that further improvement in the regulation of the acid secretory process would yield better clinical results, especially for erosive esophagitis, led to further efforts to amplify acid suppression. Thus, the identification of the proton pump as the final step in the pathway of parietal cell acid secretion provided a unique opportunity for better control of parietal cell secretion.

The development of proton pump inhibitors

The concept that drove the development of alternatives to H_2-receptor antagonists was the recognition that these would have limited efficacy. Indeed, it seemed that inhibition of the pump itself would be a more

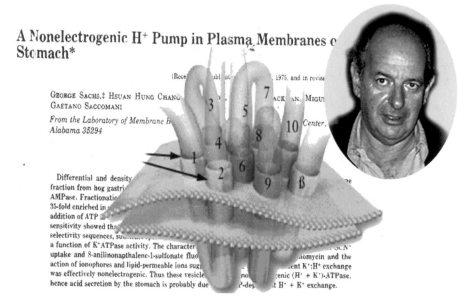

George Sachs (*top right*) of Vienna, Edinburgh, New York, Birmingham, Los Angeles, and La Jolla, with his conceptualization of the three-dimensional structure of the H^+,K^+-ATPase (*center*). The identification and characterization of an H^+,K^+-ATPase specific to the parietal cell provided a therapeutic target for the development of acid suppressive agents. Modifications of the initial proton pump inhibitor drug structure abrogated concerns that it might interfere with thyroid or thymic function.

This compound had rather remarkable anti-secretory properties: it inhibited gastric acid secretion whatever the stimulus. In experimental studies, it inhibited secretion in isolated gastric glands irrespective of the stimulus, but was relatively acid unstable and showed inhibition of iodide uptake by the thyroid; it was also thymotoxic. The first polyclonal antibody against the H^+,K^+-ATPase reacted with cells in the stomach, but also mysteriously with the thyroid and thymus. This suggested that perhaps the ATPase was the target of timoprazole. By 1977, a compound picoprazole had been made which retained the core structure of timoprazole. It was shown that this compound inhibited the gastric H^+,K^+-ATPase only when this ATPase was making acid, and that there was a lag phase before inhibition of transport activity occurred. Since the compound was a weak base, a number of steps that were thought to result in inhibition of ATPase activity and acid secretion were determined. These included accumulation of the compound in the acid space of the isolated gastric vesicle during H^+ transport (or the parietal cell canaliculus), followed by conversion to an active compound. It was postulated that this class of compound acted as pro-drugs that only reacted with the ATPase after acid-catalyzed conversion to an active form, perhaps the sulfenic acid. Later, it was proven that this active form in solution was a rearranged planar tetracyclic compound containing a highly reactive sulfenamide group.

In order to optimize the acid stability of the parent compound and generate absolute selectivity for accumulation in the acid space of the parietal cell, omeprazole was synthesized in 1979 and became the compound that was launched in 1988 at the Rome World Congress of Gastroenterology. The name coined for this class of drug was "proton pump inhibitor" (PPI). Following publication in 1981 of the first of a series of papers on the mechanism of action of these drugs, a variety of derivatives were synthesized that also led to the introduction of other drugs, including pantoprazole, with generally similar properties to this first clinically effective PPI. The next generation of drugs which suppress gastric acidity will most likely be acid-pump antagonists. While the PPIs have a unique mechanism of action based on their chemistry, acid-pump antagonists have a structural specificity for their target, the K^+ binding region of the H^+,K^+-ATPase. Although they have been actively pursued for almost 15 years, thus far none has reached the market place. They promise a more rapid onset of inhibition than the PPIs and an inherent stability that will allow design of more flexible formulations.

General reaction mechanism of the proton pump inhibitors with the H^+,K^+-ATPase in the membrane of the parietal cell canaliculus, showing passive diffusion across the canalicular membrane, accumulation of the protonated form, conversion to the sulfenamide, and reaction with one or more cysteines in the catalytic subunit of the H^+,K^+-ATPase. (Courtesy of IM Modlin and G Sachs.)

SURGERY OF THE STOMACH

Until the mid-19th century, the techniques of surgery were mostly confined to the extremities and usually related to the management of trauma. No surgeon would reasonably consider the violation of a body cavity prior to the introduction of anesthesia and antisepsis. Even under the latter conditions, both the morbidity and mortality were such that incursions into the peritoneal cavity were undertaken with considerable trepidation. Even Galen was aware that injuries to the stomach were relatively less dangerous than injuries to the intestines. For the most part, this reflected the fact that due to the bactericidal properties of the gastric juice, few bacteria were present compared to the large and small bowel.

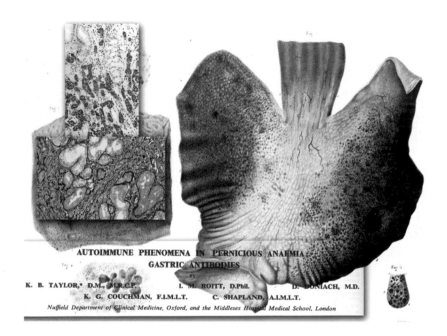

AUTOIMMUNE PHENOMENA IN PERNICIOUS ANAEMIA. GASTRIC ANTIBODIES

BY

K. B. TAYLOR,* D.M., M.R.C.P.   I. M. ROITT, D.Phil.   D. DONIACH, M.D.
          K. G. COUCHMAN, F.I.M.L.T.   C. SHAPLAND, A.I.M.L.T.
Nuffield Department of Clinical Medicine, Oxford, and the Middlesex Hospital Medical School, London

The phenomenon of autoimmune gastritis in pernicious anemia was examined in some detail by KB Taylor and colleagues from Oxford and London (bottom). In this 1962 study, the authors demonstrated the presence of two distinct types of autoantibodies in the sera of patients with pernicious anemia. One antibody was directed against intrinsic factor, the second against a "particulate component" in the cytoplasm of the gastric parietal cell. Pernicious anemia and autoimmune gastritis (right) are also associated with enterochromaffin-like (ECL) cell pathology (top left). The biological relationship remains unclear.

Parietal Cell Cytoplasm
Inhibition of Acid Secretion by PPI's

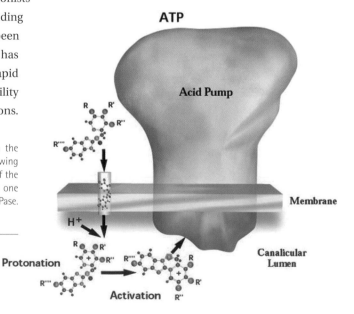

ATP

Acid Pump

R   R'
    R''
R''''

R''''

Membrane

H^+

R   R'
    R''   R''''   R
+   R'
R''''   R''
                    R'

Canalicular Lumen

Protonation

Activation   R''

Gastrostomy

Florian Mathias, Imperial Surgeon in Prague, performed the first recorded gastric procedure in 1602 on a 36-year-old peasant. This individual, who was accustomed to earning free beer and a few pennies in an inn by inserting a long knife into his throat and drinking down the beer past it, on this occasion had swallowed the knife as well. Although this initially resulted in no particular discomfort, it subsequently caused severe pain, presumably as the point began to erode through a part of the gastric wall. Mathias applied plasters to the spot where the point of the knife could be felt under the skin, and 51 days after the knife had been swallowed, successfully incised and extracted the 21cm-long blade with full recovery of the patient.

A considerably greater feat was performed by Daniel Schwalbe in 1635 on a 22-year-old waiter. This individual, while attempting to relieve his dyspepsia by using an 18cm-long knife to tickle his throat and induce vomiting, inadvertently swallowed the blade. Although he reported no serious symptoms, the medical faculty at Konigsberg decided that the knife should be removed from the stomach. Schwalbe, having fastened the patient to a door in an upright standing position, operated upon the unfortunate in the presence of the faculty and the medical students.

In this case, there were no adhesions between the stomach and the abdominal wall and the free abdominal cavity was opened up at surgery. Having identified the stomach, Schwalbe exposed it by inserting a curved needle and linen for traction, and at the point where he could palpate the knife, made an incision and removed the object. Of note is the fact that he did not suture the gastric incision and allowed the stomach to fall back into the abdomen before suturing the abdominal wall with five stitches. Quite surprisingly, the patient recovered from the first open gastrostomy.

For the most part, the early reports of stomach surgery reflected the consequences of either military action with war wounds or incidental trauma. A therapeutic gastrostomy was reported in 1819 to remove a silver fork that had been 'inadvertently' swallowed by a 26-year-old female servant. Jacques Mathieu Delpech (1777–1832) of Montpellier confirmed the diagnosis of a penetrating fork upon noting a red inflamed mass on the anterior abdominal wall five months after the fork had been ingested. He was a shrewd enough clinician to persuade a colleague, Cayroche of Mende, to remove this foreign body (May 1, 1819) via an anterior abdominal incision. Despite this feat, Delpech was subsequently assassinated by a former patient, who believed that a varicocele operation had rendered him impotent.

A case of particular physiological interest was that of the traumatic gastrostomy of the Canadian voyageur St Martin. Although the biological significance of the gastrostomy has been described earlier in this text, the possibility of using it for

A 1635 woodcut depicting the first surgical gastrostomy undertaken by Daniel Schwalbe. The patient was fastened to a door in the upright standing position (*right*). After inserting linen stay sutures into the anterior wall of the stomach, the swallowed knife was removed and the anterior abdominal wall closed with sutures. Although no gastric sutures were placed, the patient recovered uneventfully!

therapeutic purposes was never fully explored by Beaumont. In 1837, Christian Egeberg, a surgeon in Baerum in Norway, drew attention to the fact that patients with cancer of the esophagus could be maintained in reasonably good health by gastrostomy. The first gastric fistulas were made for instructive purposes on dogs by the Russian W Bassow in 1842 and thereafter by the French physiologist Blondlot. Sedillot performed the first gastrostomy on a human (the patient died) on November 13, 1849, and proposed the name gastrostomy. A similar fate met the next 27 patients, who perished from peritonitis. Credit is due to Sidney Jones, surgeon of St Thomas' Hospital in London, for undertaking the first successful gastrostomy (the 29th patient). This individual survived for 40 days after the operation!

Baron Guillaume Dupuytren, although revered as a surgeon and teacher, was much disliked by his colleagues for his arrogance and immodesty. His technical skills were legendary, as were his powers of observation. Although he was well aware of gastroduodenal ulceration and its sequelae, he did not perceive operative intervention to be feasible.

Despite random contributions by diverse practitioners, the principal contributions in gastric surgery at that time emanated from the work of Baron Guillaume Dupuytren of Paris. Few surgeons have evoked more controversy and divergent opinions. He was variously known as "the first of surgeons and the least of men" or a "genius but of unprecedented unkindness and coldness". Born on October 5, 1777, to a family of modest means, his extraordinary intelligence was apparent from an early age. In 1802, at the age of 25, he was appointed to the Hotel Dieu, and by 1815, he was Chief Surgeon, a post he held until his death some 20 years later. Despite the fact that he dressed with appalling taste and that his personal habits left much to be desired, he was highly regarded not only as a teacher but also as a surgeon of extraordinary intellectual and technical proficiency. His workload was extraordinary and it is reported that at the apogee of his career, he would see some 10,000 private patients a year.

Although Dupuytren's fame as a surgeon and teacher was prodigious, he wrote little and most of his work is recollected by renditions of his lectures in notebook form. The majority of his teachings were collated in a book entitled *Leçons Orales de Clinique Chirurgicale* and published by his students. His teachings cover a diverse range of conditions, ranging from anorectal problems to chronic bleeding, arterial aneurysms, urinary calculi, and cataract management. Amongst his most notable contributions are his observations on duodenal ulceration. Although Sir Thomas Blizzard Curling, in 1841, had called attention to the connection between cases of burn and acute ulceration of the duodenum, it was

Dupuytren who had first made this observation. In 1836, Dupuytren drew attention to the congestion of various mucous membranes in the alimentary canal in the early stages of burns. He described in detail the ulceration and bleeding of the stomach and duodenum consequent upon such an event, some five years before Curling provided the definitive description of duodenal ulceration associated with cutaneous burns.

Resection and anastomosis

Overview

Once gastrostomy had been accomplished, the concept of resecting the stomach was next considered. Charles Tivadar Daniel Merrem wrote in his dissertation, published in Giessen in 1810, that he had excised the part of the stomach nearest to the pylorus of three dogs. Of the three, only one died of peritonitis; another lived for 22 days, but perished due to unceasing vomiting. The dissection demonstrated that the peritoneum was undamaged and that the suture at the site of the resection of the stomach had healed well. Although the third dog was well for 27 days, it was stolen and could thereafter no longer be observed. Merrem's experiment demonstrated that resection of the stomach could be achieved and the resection wound heal without any special problems. In spite of this, for many decades the operation of Merrem was spoken of as an item of curiosity or even folly, and even the usually genial Johann Dieffenbach (1792–1847) of Konigsberg was fond of referring to it as "Merrem's dream". In 1874, two pupils of Christian Albert Theodore Billroth, Charles Gussenbauer, who later became Professor of Surgery in Liege, Prague, and Vienna, and Alexander Winiwater, later Professor in Liege, demonstrated by experimental work in dogs that the operation could be successfully performed.

In 1842, Sir Thomas Blizzard Curling (1811–1888) (*bottom left*) described a series of severe duodenal ulcers (some of them bleeding) (*background*) associated with burns. He was careful to point out in his manuscript (*top left*) that the association between burns and inflammation, congestion, and ulceration of the intestine (but not specifically the duodenum) had previously been noted by Baron Guillaume Dupuytren (1777–1835) and even earlier, in 1823, by Cumin.

Johann von Mikulicz-Radecki and Christian Albert Theodore Billroth in the operating room of the General Hospital, Vienna (circa 1886). Early in 1881, Billroth (*top left*) successfully resected the pyloric tumor of Theresa Heller. His report (*background*) documenting the first successful gastrectomy was annotated by the Editor of the journal in which it was published with the comment, "and hopefully the last!" The resected specimen (*bottom center*) and the autopsy specimen (*bottom right*) may both still be seen at the Josephinum Museum in Vienna. On November 16, 1880, Ludwik Rydygier of Chelmo (*top right*) preceded Billroth in undertaking a gastrectomy, but unfortunately his patient had perished.

Jules Emile Péan, a Parisian surgeon, was the first to perform a gastrectomy on a human (April 19, 1879); the second was undertaken by Ludwik Rydygier, then a practicing surgeon in Kulm, later Professor of Surgery in Cracow and Lember. Unfortunately, both of these patients died and it remained for Billroth in Vienna to successfully undertake the first resection of the stomach on a young woman with pyloric obstruction due to a neoplasm in 1881. Unfortunately, she too perished a few months later from metastatic disease.

In the course of time, the technique of gastrectomy underwent many modifications and became a common procedure for most of the 20th century as the definitive cure for peptic ulcer disease. In addition, it was amplified considerably as a radical operation used in the management of gastric cancer. Charles Schlatter of Zurich first carried out a complete removal of the stomach with complete success in 1897, and the concept that survival without a stomach was possible attained medical reality. In 1881, Anthony Wolfler, while an assistant to Billroth (he later became Professor of Surgery in Graz and Prague), during an operation for a tumor obstructing the pylorus, found that it was irresectable. At the suggestion of Charles Nicoladoni, who was an assistant at the operation (later Professor of Surgery in Innsbruck and Graz), Wolfler established a communication (gastroenterostomy) between the stomach and the small intestine. This enabled food to bypass the obstructed pylorus and enter the small intestine, as well as obviating the dramatic symptoms of obstruction and the vomiting of stagnant material.

Gastrectomy

The first gastrectomy was performed by Péan of Paris. Born in 1830 to the family of a miller, Péan attended medical school in Paris in 1855 and in 1868, after training with Denon Villiers and Nelaton, was awarded a doctor of medicine degree in surgery. Péan's reputation as a clinician and a surgeon was prestigious. Although his initial contributions to abdominal surgery were in the area of ovarian cystectomy, in 1867 he undertook the first successful splenectomy during a laparotomy for an ovarian cyst in which incidental damage to the spleen had occurred. A further major contribution in 1868 was the development of a special hemostatic clip made by Gueride, which he successfully utilized for hemostasis. On April 8, 1879, Péan undertook what was to be his most epic contribution to surgery in resecting a pyloric gastric cancer. The operation lasted two-and-a-half hours and the patient initially recovered successfully.

Dr Jules Emile Péan operating. Painting by Henri de Toulouse-Lautrec (1891–1892). In 1891, Toulouse-Lautrec shared an apartment with his friend Dr Henri Bourges and became friendly with other physicians. Gabriel Tape de Celeyran was a cousin of Toulouse-Lautrec and had trained with Péan. It is likely that Toulouse-Lautrec had thus been invited to observe an operation and recorded it (oil on cardboard). Péan is operating on an oral lesion, presumably a forerunner of his epic contribution to gastric surgery (Sterling and Francine Clark Institute, Williamstown, MA). Toulouse-Lautrec's medical interest was not confined to surgery. He utilized pharmacological compounds (thujones) contained in high concentration in absinthe to amplify his creativity and color perception.

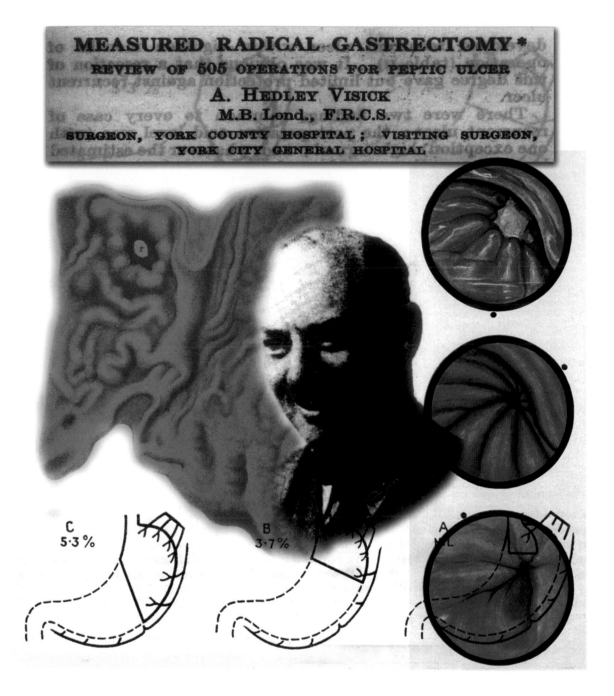

MEASURED RADICAL GASTRECTOMY*

REVIEW OF 505 OPERATIONS FOR PEPTIC ULCER

A. HEDLEY VISICK
M.B. Lond., F.R.C.S.
SURGEON, YORK COUNTY HOSPITAL; VISITING SURGEON,
YORK CITY GENERAL HOSPITAL

A Hedley Visick's grading of the results of gastroduodenal surgery was the first attempt to assess the results of gastrectomy for peptic ulcer, an operation that had become increasingly popular after the Second World War as anesthesia, blood transfusion, and postoperative fluid balance began to improve. Although impressed by the results after gastrectomy, many surgeons had high mortality rates and Visick (center) proved to be no exception. Although he considered abandoning the operation (he had nine deaths in his first 75 operations), he continued, but only after paying close attention to the selection of patients. The next 250 gastrectomies were done without a death, and surgeons from all over the world came to York County Hospital to view his procedure. A recapitulation of the first 500 patients was published in the *Lancet* (1948) and included his emphasis of the need to divide most of the vasa brevia. This resulted in a very small gastric remnant which then became a narrow tube allowing safe anastomosis on the surface of the abdomen using straight, handheld needles. The remnant was always measured and was usually 1.5in on the lesser and 3in on the greater curvature. How little remained appeared to be more important than how much stomach had been removed. Visick coined the phrase "measured radical gastrectomy". His meticulous review of his results were also published in 1948 in a Hunterian Lecture aptly named 'Study of the failures after gastrectomy'! It is of interest that his own Chief at Bart's, Sir Charles Gordon-Watson, was cured by Visick's knife.

Unfortunately, over the subsequent three days, the patient received two blood transfusions of 50mL and 80mL, and died on the fifth postoperative day prior to a further transfusion. Although the cause of death is unknown, the recognition of blood groups did not occur for some 40 years later and it seems likely that either sepsis or transfusion incompatibility may have contributed to this fatality. Nevertheless, to Péan goes the credit for having undertaken the first (albeit unsuccessful) gastrectomy.

On November 16, 1880, Rydygier of Chelmo performed the second documented but also unsuccessful gastrectomy. Like Péan, he undertook a partial resection of the prepyloric portion of the stomach in a patient with gastric cancer. Some two months later in Vienna, Billroth became the first surgeon to successfully undertake a gastrectomy. This third reported gastrectomy was also for a pyloric tumor, but in this instance the patient Theresa Heller survived to be discharged home three weeks postoperatively. The cumulative operative survival from gastrectomy in the two decades following Péan's initial operation rarely exceeded 50%. As a result of the substantial mortality involved in gastrectomy in the pre-antiseptic era, lesser procedures were usually contemplated in an attempt to deal with diseases of the stomach thought to require surgical intervention.

The most popular operation was the gastroenterostomy pioneered by Mathieu Jaboulay of France, but Mikulicz-Radecki of Vienna and Wolfler were also protagonists of the procedure. Jaboulay was born on July 5, 1860, and educated in the Lyon area, where he achieved wide renown as a surgeon of considerable intellectual and technical skill. One of his early accomplishments had been to remove the vagi, coeliac ganglion, and sympathetic chains of the upper abdomen in an attempt to deal with the discomfort induced by the lightning pains of tabes dorsalis. His later development of the gastroenterostomy procedure to obviate problems generated by the gastric outlet obstruction (some consequent upon vagotomy) achieved widespread popularity in Europe.

In the era before the introduction of acid suppression, chronic peptic ulceration resulted in considerable morbidity and mortality. The only effective remedy for intractable pain and complications, such as perforation, bleeding, and gastric outlet obstruction, was surgery. The results, however, were so terrible that many eminent physicians (Bernard Naunyn) regarded surgery as little more than an autopsy *in vivo*. The introduction of anesthesia (inhaler) by William Morton allowed for surgery to be performed in an unhurried fashion on a patient protected from pain. The subsequent advent of antisepsis (carbolic spray), as introduced by Lord Joseph Lister, significantly decreased infectious complications and facilitated the performance of cautious and meticulous surgery. In addition, advances in hemostatic technique (the first-time use of gloves), as instituted by William Halsted of Baltimore, and technical efficiency, as promulgated by Sir Berkeley Moynihan of Leeds, facilitated the development of relatively safe gastric surgery. Nevertheless, the morbidity of postgastrectomy syndromes engendered by such operations resulted in patients being cured of their peptic ulcer, only to acquire a series of lifetime disabilities. Thus, the consequence of the anatomical and physiological derangement attendant upon gastric resection, pyloric ablation, and a variety of gastrojejunal and duodenal anastomoses was as debilitating as, if not worse than, the original disease.

Gastroenterostomy remained the standard of choice for the first decades of the 20th century as the preferred surgical treatment of either peptic ulcer or gastric neoplasia. Thereafter, better techniques developed to ensure the safety of the anastomosis after gastric resection; and with the advent of Listerian antisepsis, the era of the gastrectomist supervened.

SIR BERKELEY MOYNIHAN AND PEPTIC ULCER DISEASE SURGERY

The tide of management in gastric diseases had turned dramatically and gastroenterologists and internists alike were fascinated with the exciting surgical possibilities presented by the dawning era of gastrojejunostomy, gastrectomy, vagotomy, and pyloroplasty. No less a medical icon than Sir William Osler opined, "physicians have been napping, and what the modern gastroenterologist needs is a prolonged course of study at such surgical clinics as Leeds or Rochester, Minnesota". Despite pioneering work in Europe, it fell to Sir Berkeley Moynihan of Leeds, who in the years between 1901 and 1915 published the results of his pioneering surgical work, in which he gave for the first time a complete account of the symptoms now known to be characteristic of duodenal ulcer.

Sir Berkeley Moynihan was born in the British Possession of Malta (*background*) on October 2, 1865, the only son of Captain Andrew Moynihan, a musketry instructor. Malta had been occupied by the British since 1800 and was used as a base for British soldiery. Moynihan's father, who had served in the Army his entire adult career, had been awarded one of the first Victoria Crosses for bravery at the battle of Sebastopol, and fought with the British Forces to put down the Indian mutiny. The fact that he died when his son was only two years of age probably precluded the young man from following an exclusively military career. Nevertheless, during the First World War, he served in France for two years as a consulting surgeon, and reached the rank of Major-General in the Army Medical Corps (*bottom left*).

Moynihan was born in Malta in 1865, but after his father's early demise (Malta fever from goat's milk), his family returned to Britain. After a mixed upbringing, Moynihan entered medical school in 1883 and started by attending courses at Yorkshire College, which later became the University of Leeds. After four years as an undergraduate, he qualified (MD) at the University of London in 1887, and passed the Primary FRCS of the Royal College of Surgeons of England (1890). As a young surgeon, he initially worked as a surgical dresser to AF McGill, who then arranged that he be appointed house surgeon to the great Sir Arthur William Mayo-Robson, who thereafter became Moynihan's mentor. After a brief stint in Berlin to learn the work and methods of the leading German surgeons, Moynihan concentrated on abdominal surgery, which then became his lifelong interest. He succeeded to a surgical consultancy at the Leeds Infirmary (1896), and thereafter his surgical and medical careers blossomed, and he was appointed Professor of Surgery in 1909.

During his lifetime, Moynihan became a pioneer in Britain of gastroenterological surgery, and this is reflected in his work and writings. He was a skilled operator who "threw open the abdomen to all surgeons," but he also was no stranger to mammon and commanded high fees. As a researcher, he made a special study of surgical pathology and promoted applied and clinical research by careful case descriptions, analysis, and resulting conclusions. As a writer, he exerted a substantial influence on his contemporaries on both sides of the Atlantic. His published papers covered topics ranging from appendicitis, tuberculosis of the skin, ruptured kidney, subclavian aneurysm, mesenteric cysts, rarer forms of hernia, pancreatic cysts, surgery of the spleen, and cancer of the stomach. His first two books, *Diseases of the Pancreas and their Treatment* and *Diseases of the Stomach and their Treatment*, were written jointly with Mayo-Robson and published in 1901 and 1902, respectively. They became widely acknowledged by American surgeons

and this led to an American surgical delegation visit to Leeds in 1903. Moynihan also wrote *The Surgical Treatment of Gastric and Duodenal Ulcers* (1903) and the seminal *Abdominal Operations* (1905). A book, *Duodenal Ulcer*, appeared in 1910, and commenting on the clinical picture of duodenal ulcer drawn by Moynihan, Hurst noted in his Harveian Oration on the physiology of the stomach in 1937: "It is as much a piece of original research as the discovery of a new element or a new star, equally deserving of recognition."

As an orator, Moynihan delivered two sets of Arris and Gale Lectures – in 1897 on 'The Anatomy and Surgery of the Peritoneal Fossae' and in 1900 on 'The Pathology of Some of the Rarer Forms of Hernia'. He delivered a Hunterian Lecture in 1920 on 'The Late Surgery of Gun Shot Wounds of the Chest' and the Bradshaw Lecture in the same year on 'The Spleen and Some of its Diseases'; in 1927, he gave a second Hunterian Oration. As an organizer, he instigated the *British Journal of Surgery*, the first national journal in this field.

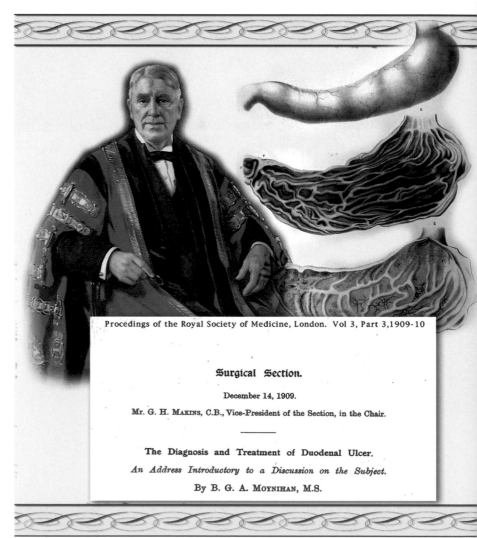

Procedings of the Royal Society of Medicine, London. Vol 3, Part 3, 1909-10

Surgical Section.

December 14, 1909.

Mr. G. H. MAKINS, C.B., Vice-President of the Section, in the Chair.

———

The Diagnosis and Treatment of Duodenal Ulcer.

An Address Introductory to a Discussion on the Subject.

By B. G. A. MOYNIHAN, M.S.

As a member of the Army Medical Advisory Board and Chairman of the Council of Consultants, Sir Berkeley Moynihan toured the United States, lecturing on behalf of the war effort. His relationship with American surgeons had been established earlier (he had been invited to Philadelphia in 1903 to attend and speak at a surgical conference), and he had made friendships with a number of important surgeons. These included William James Mayo, JB Murphy, and G Crile (*right*). In addition, Moynihan was admitted as an Honorary Fellow of the American College of Surgeons (1919).

Sir Berkeley Moynihan (1865–1936) (*top left*) wrote extensively on the surgical management of duodenal ulcer disease. His contributions to the scientific foundation of gastric surgery were internationally recognized. As President of the Royal College of Surgeons of England, he was the prime mover in the introduction of science into surgical training programs.

Moynihan gained the reputation during his lifetime as the most accomplished surgeon in England and certainly one of the greatest exponents of the art in the world. For his efforts to British medicine, he received a knighthood in 1912 and a CBE for his wartime service in 1917. Thereafter, he was awarded a CMG in 1918, created a baronet in 1922, and elevated to the peerage in 1929 as Baron Moynihan of Leeds. He spoke on a few subjects in the House of Lords, such as osteopathy and euthanasia.

The early use of gastrectomy in peptic ulcer disease focused on the management of complications such as obstruction and bleeding. Initial problems related to the leakage of the anastomosis between the duodenum and the gastric remnant led to the popularization of the gastrojejunal anastomosis known as the Billroth II. The significant disturbances in physiology consequent upon this procedure (dumping syndromes, and afferent and efferent loop syndromes) were thought tolerable as compared to the invariable mortality associated with a leak from a Billroth I type anastomosis. In order to obviate the development of such symptomatology, a great number of modifications of the procedure involving the construction of valves or different bowel loop lengths were introduced, almost to no avail.

In assessing the role that Moynihan had played in the elucidation of the rationale for operative intervention in acid peptic disease, Hurst, in a clinical lecture delivered at Guy's Hospital in 1909 after a visit to Moynihan in Leeds, recognized the new era of abdominal surgery in the management of the

Sir Berkeley Moynihan (*bottom left*) received the Fellowship for the Royal College of Surgeons of England (*background*) in 1890 and was thereafter closely associated with its work. He was elected President of the Society in 1926 and held this office for six years following annual re-election. During the period that he was at the helm, the College achieved international prestige. It was also during this time that science was introduced into surgical training programs – Moynihan being one of the principal proponents.

THE ATTITUDE OF SURGERY TO HÆMATEMESIS

The early part of the 20th century represented the glory days of gastric surgery. Surgeons such as Sir Gordon Gordon-Taylor (*center*) of the Middlesex Hospital in London and the Mayo brothers (*right and left*) of Rochester were acclaimed for their heroic surgical efforts in the treatment of peptic ulcer disease. In his attitude to the surgical therapy of gastrointestinal hemorrhage, Gordon-Taylor sided with Finsterer of Vienna, and in his 1954 publication (*bottom*), presciently noted that "Finsterer's first 48 hours is still the optimum period for surgical attack in hematemesis and the golden age of gastric surgery will have been attained only when all cases of hemorrhage from chronic ulcer come to operation within that space of time"!

condition. The technical genius of Moynihan and the Mayo brothers, combined with their compelling personalities, exhibited a profound effect on physicians who had long been baffled and frustrated by peptic ulcer disease and its bleeding, perforation, and stenotic complications.

Hurst was particularly impressed that "Moynihan and other surgeons had confirmed, and modern improvements in radiological technique had made it possible to diagnose with certainty the vast majority of cases of duodenal ulcer without exploratory operation". It is of interest that some British gastroenterologists, mostly influenced by Hurst, believed that advances in understanding gastroduodenal ulcers had actually been delayed by the introduction of the stomach tube, as gastric disorders came to be described in terms of altered secretion and motility rather than structure, especially in France and Germany, where duodenal ulcer was still regarded as a very rare condition as late as 1913. Indeed, there was much acrimony amongst the British physicians and the physicians of continental Europe regarding the relevance of duodenal ulcer. Thus, the eminent German authority Ewald stated his belief that only one duodenal ulcer occurred for every 45 gastric ulcers and regarded duodenal ulcer as a "British disease". Fortunately, the advent of radiological examination of the upper gut in the second and third decades of the 20th century convinced continental physicians that duodenal ulcer was not a disease peculiar to England and America, or a by-product of the "too" vivid imagination of the surgeons of those countries.

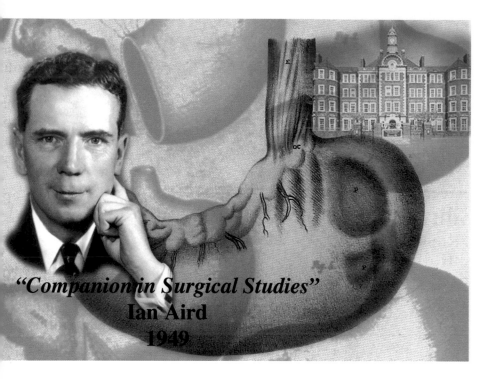

"Companion in Surgical Studies"
Ian Aird
1949

In his 1949 classic surgical text (*bottom*), Ian Aird (*left*) of the Hammersmith (*top right*) still regarded chronic peptic ulceration as responsible for 85% of all gastroduodenal hemorrhage. Indeed, he maintained that "in the serious massive hemorrhage from peptic ulcer in middle-aged and elderly patients the question of differential diagnosis seldom arises; nearly all have been treated for many years on medical lines for proved chronic gastroduodenal ulceration, and the records of numerous and repeated opaque meal investigations are usually available to attest to the accuracy of the diagnosis".

In 1922, Andre Latarjet (*bottom left*) reported his results on 24 patients to the French Academy of Surgery. Like Exner before him, he found delayed gastric emptying in many of these vagotomized patients and as a result, later added a gastrojejunostomy to this operation. He explained: "Indeed, in all of our cases, gastroenteroanastomosis was done at the same time as denervation, either for reasons of promoting mechanical order or to avoid the possibility of an aggravated ulcer evolution as a consequence of the prolonged journey of the food in a stomach which has been rendered hypertonic by denervation." Forty-two years later, CG Clark, Senior Lecturer in Surgery at the University of Aberdeen, was able to demonstrate in a 1964 paper that gastric function returned after denervation of 90% of vagal fibers in the cat stomach. The author presciently observed that a satisfactory vagotomy in the patient must divide more than 90% of these fibers to minimize recurrent ulcer!

Vagotomy

Although the role of the vagus in the regulation of gastrointestinal secretion and motility was incompletely understood, there was general awareness of the fact that it might in some way be implicated in gastric disease processes. The first vagotomy on a human was conducted by Jaboulay, who undertook this in the process of excising the celiac plexus of a man suffering from the lightning pains of tabes dorsalis.

A few years later, Exner similarly divided the vagi in a number of patients afflicted with tabes, but presciently noted that a percentage of these individuals subsequently suffered from the effects of gastric atony. As a result of this observation, he thereafter combined vagotomy with a gastrojejunostomy to promote gastric emptying. In time, other surgeons, including Kuttner, Borchers, and Podkaminsky, attempted vagotomy on patients for a variety of diagnoses that ranged from dyspepsia to gastric ptosis and neurasthenia. Thus, by 1920, the results of 20 subdiaphragmatic vagotomies for treatment of gastric ptosis were reported by Bircher, who commented upon decreased acidity and curiously improved tonus in 75% of his patients. Some years later, Alvarez, in reviewing the work of Bircher, concluded: "His vagotomies were probably incomplete because, aside from some lowering of acidity, he did not seem to obtain the usual effects of a complete nerve resection."

Latarjet

The outcome of these early clinical vagotomies inspired Andre Latarjet of Lyon to further evaluate the procedure. Latarjet made the most detailed investigations into the anatomy of the vagi to date and applied his findings to the surgical patients he treated. The eponymous attribution of the anterior and posterior vagal nerves of the gastric lesser curve attest to his profound influence and excellent work in this area.

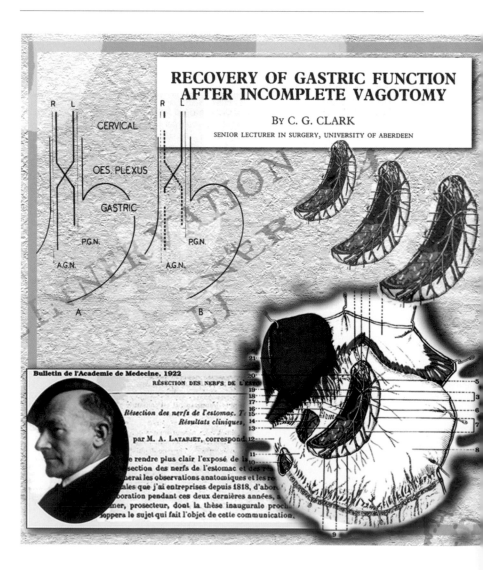

RECOVERY OF GASTRIC FUNCTION AFTER INCOMPLETE VAGOTOMY

BY C. G. CLARK

SENIOR LECTURER IN SURGERY, UNIVERSITY OF ABERDEEN

Bulletin de l'Académie de Medecine, 1922

RÉSECTION DES NERFS DE L'ESTOMAC

Résection des nerfs de l'estomac. T...
Résultats cliniques,

par M. A. LATARJET, correspond...

Latarjet was born on August 20, 1877, in Dijon and studied medicine in Lyon. Because of financial pressures, Latarjet was forced to choose between a career in surgery or anatomy. Since a surgical practice was difficult to establish in the hospitals of Lyon and Latarjet was not financially able to support himself in private practice, he chose a career based principally in anatomy. Probably his most important contribution relates to the work undertaken with his colleague Pierre Wertheimer. In 1921, Wertheimer completed his thesis 'De l'Enervatione Gastrique'. This study documented both anatomical and experimental work in regard to the vagal innervation of the stomach and reported that cutting the vagus nerves significantly impaired gastric motility and emptying as well as producing a substantial inhibition of acid secretion.

The principal difference between the work of Latarjet and his predecessors was his decision to perform vagotomy in a systematic manner for patients with dyspepsia. His operation, first reported in 1921, entailed denervation of the greater and lesser curvatures and the suprapyloric region, with partial circumcision of the serosa and muscularis down to the level of the submucosa. He designed this operation to sever all the extrinsic nerves to the stomach and pylorus, leaving intact the large branch of the right gastric nerve that accompanies the left gastric artery to the celiac plexus. In 1922, Latarjet reported his results on 24 patients to the French Academy of Surgery. Like Exner before him, he found delayed gastric emptying in many of these vagotomized patients and as a result, later added a gastrojejunostomy to this operation. He explained: "Indeed, in all of our cases, gastro-enteroanastomosis was done at the same time as denervation, either for reasons of promoting mechanical order or to avoid the possibility of an aggravated ulcer evolution as a consequence of the prolonged journey of food in a stomach which has been rendered hypotonic by denervation." Almost 30 years later, Lester R Dragstedt of Chicago would come to a virtually identical conclusion.

As early as 1927, Charles Mayo was aware that operations not based on sound physiological principles have no place in the surgical repertoire: "If anyone should consider removing half of my good stomach to cure a small ulcer in my duodenum, I would run faster than he." Since one theory of ulcerogenesis popular during the 1920s was that ulcers were caused by gastric stasis, skeptics proposed that the excellent results of his procedure might be attributed to the concomitant gastroenterostomy – not the vagotomy.

Dragstedt

On 18 January, 1943, Dragstedt performed a subdiaphragmatic vagal resection upon a patient with an active duodenal ulcer and so ushered in the modern era of vagotomy. Born in Anaconda, Montana, of Swedish immigrant parentage, Dragstedt had first trained as a physiologist with A Carlson in Chicago before accepting the invitation of D Phemister to join his department of surgery at Rush University. Given his basic training in science, he brought a different focus to his research on the pathogenesis of peptic ulcer disease and was fascinated by the work of Hunter and Bernard that showed that

normal stomachs do not digest themselves. The operation he initially proposed was a total vagotomy, much like that originally undertaken by Latarjet some decades earlier. The first patient to receive a Dragstedt vagotomy was a 35-year-old man who had a bleeding ulcer necessitating multiple blood transfusions, despite medical therapy. The young man underwent a bilateral vagotomy by way of a left thoracotomy approach and his abdominal pain immediately subsided. Dragstedt, always the physiologist, intermittently instilled 0.1 normal hydrochloric acid into the stomach of the patient for the next couple of weeks. For the first eight days, he was able to reproduce the abdominal pain of the patient. On the ninth day, however, acid infusion no longer caused discomfort. Dragstedt took this to indicate that the ulcer had healed!

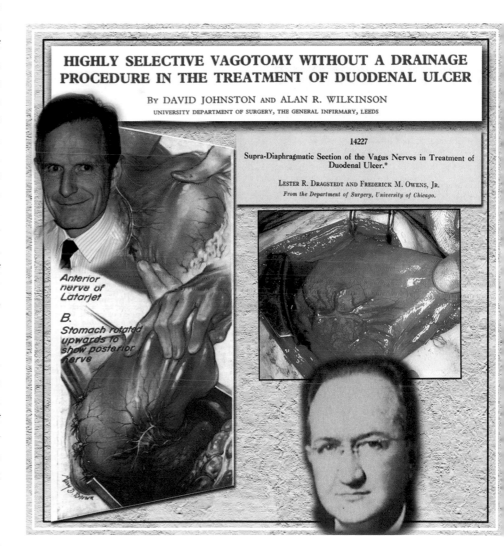

Lester R Dragstedt (*bottom right*) in the 1940s, as a result of his study of the ability of gastric denervation to decrease acid secretion, resuscitated Latarjet's 1923 concept of vagotomy. David Johnston (*top left*) and Alan Wilkinson of Leeds modified this approach, introducing a highly selective vagotomy without a drainage procedure. Their 1970 publication (*top*), which included the anatomical drawings of Mary Brown (*left*), described this approach in a series of 25 patients with chronic peptic ulceration and demonstrated that this was as effective as truncal or a bilateral selective vagotomy (with drainage) in reducing gastric acid output. While these results were encouraging, the authors candidly noted that the follow-up was relatively short, three to 11 months, and 10% of patients were not clinically well!

Dragstedt went on to perform more than 200 vagotomies during the next four years because of its physiological basis and clinical success. Since one third of these patients developed gastric stasis severe enough to necessitate a gastroenterostomy as a secondary procedure, an abdominal approach to the vagi was developed in order to perform the procedures simultaneously. Initially, the drainage procedure of choice was a gastroenterostomy, but during the next decade, the technique of pyloroplasty was perfected and became the drainage method of choice. Later, as the role of the antrum in the physiology of gastric secretion became better understood, vagotomy combined with antrectomy was the procedure used to reduce the secretion of gastric acid maximally. Surgeons from the Mayo Clinic, a relatively conservative institution, had performed about 80 of the Dragstedt procedures that they termed a "gastric neurectomy" and observed with concern that "the results are inconstant, variable, and in most cases unpredictable". The most serious complication they encountered was gastric stasis. In an attempt to establish a reasonable answer, the American Gastroenterological Association formed the National Committee on Peptic Ulcer in 1952. In a 200-page report, the Committee concluded that

gastroenterostomy was the operation of choice for peptic ulcer disease and emphasized that it "should not be concluded from this study that gastroenterostomy plus vagotomy is superior to gastroenterostomy alone". Fortunately, not all surgeons were persuaded and the usefulness of vagotomy continued to be investigated.

Gradually, more favorable reports appeared. In 1952, Farmer and Smithwick from Boston University recommended that vagotomy be combined with hemigastrectomy for treatment of duodenal ulcer disease. By 1956, Weinberg and his colleagues from the Veterans Hospital in Long Beach, California, described an improved single layer pyloroplasty. The single layer method contrasted with the double layer closure of the Heinecke-Mikulicz procedure, which the authors contended could "cause an infolding of the tissues which constricts the lumen and thus jeopardizes the patency of the canal". Nevertheless, it was apparent that better methods of preventing gastric stasis were necessary to obviate the side effects of truncal vagotomy. Griffith and Harkins published the theoretic basis for a more selective vagotomy in 1957.

They incised the branches of the nerves of Latarjet, which were thought to "supply clusters of parietal cells". As a result, they concluded in their experiments on dogs that the cephalic phase of gastric secretion was eliminated and that the dogs experienced minimal to no gastric stasis. Even though they proposed that "clinical application appears feasible," 10 years elapsed before the first selective vagotomy was performed upon a human.

Holle and Hart performed the first highly selective vagotomy in 1967. Their procedure was combined with a pyloroplasty. By 1969, it became apparent that a drainage procedure was unnecessary. Experience from Britain, Scandinavia, and the United States demonstrated only 17 deaths after 5,539 highly selective vagotomies and documented decreased dumping, gastritis, and duodenal reflux as compared with the more traditional operations. Although the initial ulcer recurrence rate was reported at about 5%, a result similar to that after truncal vagotomy and drainage, subsequent authors reported substantial increases in recurrence rates over time, even after the learning curve for this procedure had been overcome.

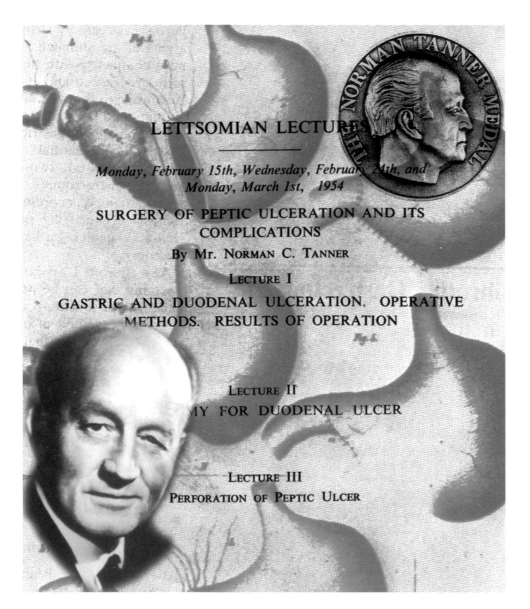

LETTSOMIAN LECTURES

Monday, February 15th, Wednesday, February 24th, and
Monday, March 1st, 1954

SURGERY OF PEPTIC ULCERATION AND ITS
COMPLICATIONS

By Mr. NORMAN C. TANNER

LECTURE I

GASTRIC AND DUODENAL ULCERATION. OPERATIVE
METHODS. RESULTS OF OPERATION

LECTURE II
...MY FOR DUODENAL ULCER

LECTURE III
PERFORATION OF PEPTIC ULCER

Norman Tanner (*bottom left*) was born in Bristol in 1906, educated at the Merchant Venturers School, and obtained his medical degree from the University of Bristol. He was then appointed Senior Resident Surgeon at St James's Hospital, Balham (1939), where he thereafter gained an international reputation as a gastric surgeon. In 1953, he was also invited to join the staff at Charing Cross Hospital. His capacity to teach excellence in standard procedures led to the development of the informal (but international) Tanner school of surgery. He was recognized by the number of lectures he gave, including the Lettsomian Lectures of 1954 (*background*). In 1990, a medal bearing his likeness (*top right*) was introduced to bring recognition to a surgeon in training for original ideas and individual effort.

Numerous individuals had undertaken a wide variety of vagotomies in an attempt to both study vagal function and treat peptic ulcer disease. Early attempts at vagotomy alone had resulted in pyloric dysfunction, requiring the addition of gastric drainage procedures. Although such operations resulted in technical success, recurrent ulceration was also a problem. More extensive procedures involving partial gastrectomies and antrectomy were introduced, but the morbidity from surgical complications and postgastrectomy syndromes diminished enthusiasm for such procedures. Selective operations that sought to denervate the parietal cell mass without interfering with the innervation of the antrum, pylorus, and other gastrointestinal organs proved to be of merit, but their efficiency was subsumed by the introduction of effective acid suppressive medications.

Unfortunately, the therapeutic relevance of vagal section soon became overshadowed by the introduction of acid suppressive agents in the mid-1970s, and by 1985, the use of the procedure had significantly declined in developed countries. In 1993, at a conference at Yale University School of Medicine held to memorialize Dragstedt, the first American surgical scientist, a consensus was reached that vagotomy was no longer a relevant therapeutic procedure in the management of peptic ulcer disease. Indeed, except in conditions of dire emergency surgery, vagotomy should not be considered any more as a means of inhibiting acid secretion.

The gastric pathogen – Helicobacter pylori

Although the association between *Helicobacter pylori* and ulcers was discovered by Robin Warren in 1979 and the organism cultured by Barry Marshall in 1982, resulting in their seminal publications in the *Lancet* in

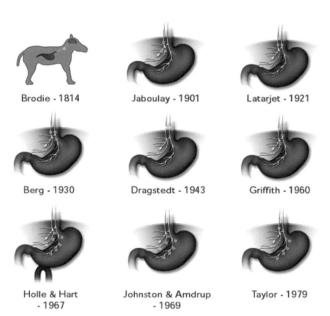

Surgical Evolution of Vagotomy

Brodie - 1814   Jaboulay - 1901   Latarjet - 1921

Berg - 1930   Dragstedt - 1943   Griffith - 1960

Holle & Hart - 1967   Johnston & Amdrup - 1969   Taylor - 1979

1983, the historical origins of its discovery are rooted in the latter half of the 19th century. It was during this period that the eminent German bacteriologist Robert Koch proved scientifically that bacteria were the cause of certain diseases. Almost simultaneously, the Frenchman Louis Pasteur, having been galvanized by Koch's contributions, was in the process of developing vaccines against the microbes causing cholera and rabies. In Sicily, in a small homemade laboratory in Messina, the Russian émigré Elie Metchnikoff had discovered phagocytosis, thus initiating an entirely new vista of biological investigation – host defense mechanisms.

Early observations

One of the first gastric bacteriologists was the German G Bottcher, who along with his French collaborator M Letulle (1853–1929), demonstrated bacterial colonies in the ulcer floor and in its mucosal margins. Their convictions in regard to the disease-causing potential of ingested organisms were so ardent that by 1875 they attributed the causation of ulcers to such bacteria. This view was however not popular. Indeed, in spite of an 1881 report by the pathologist C Klebs of a bacillus-like organism evident both free in the lumen of gastric glands and between the cells of the glands and the tunica propria, with corresponding "interglandular small round cell infiltration," the "bacterial hypothesis" fell into disuse. Bottcher was, however, probably the first to report the presence of spiral organisms in the gastrointestinal tract of animals, although spiral organisms were already well known and had been described as early as 1838 by Ehrenburg. In 1889, Walcry Jaworski, Professor of Medicine at the Jagiellonian University of Cracow, Poland, was the first to describe in detail spiral organisms in the sediment of washings obtained from humans. Amongst other things, he noted a bacterium with a characteristic spiral appearance, which he named "*Vibrio rugula*". He suggested that it might play a possible pathogenic role in gastric disease. Jaworski supposed that these "snail" or "spiral" cells were only to be found in rare cases.

Anthony van Leeuwenhoek (1632–1723) (*top left*) was the enthusiastic pioneer of the biological microcosmos. He was also the first to see gastrointestinal bacteria (from the mouth and colon), but due to his lack of medical training, ascribed no pathological importance to this new world. Once microscopes had sufficiently evolved, order was brought to the vague Linnaean genus of 'Chaos' by the morphological classification of bacteria by Ferdinand Cohn of Breslau (*bottom left*). Cohn's protégé, Robert Koch (1843–1910) (*top right*), along with the Russian émigré Elie Metchnikoff (*bottom right*), laid the foundation for the elucidation of bacterial cause of disease, as well as the fundamental understanding of the defense mechanism of the body. In addition to being one of the founders of modern bacteriology, Koch was also one of the first to develop the correct theory of species-specific infectious diseases. It is of note that the discovery of phagocytosis by Metchnikoff that initiated an entirely new vista of biological investigation – host defense mechanisms – was made in a small homemade laboratory in Messina, Sicily.

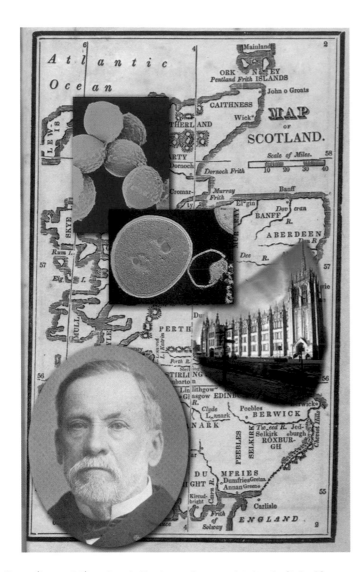

Sir Alexander Ogston (*bottom left*) was born in Aberdeen and was appointed to the Chair of Surgery at the University (*right*) in 1882, holding this post until he retired in 1909. He was one of the most illustrious graduates of medicine at this university, complementing his medical training with ventures at various European Universities. His research into the cause of hospital infection and suppuration led him in 1881 to observe grape-like clusters of bacteria in pus from human abscesses (*center*). He termed these organisms "*Staphylococcus*"; they were cultured by Rosenbach in 1884, and named "*Staphylococcus aureus*" because of their golden pigmentation. In addition to his surgical career, Ogston also had a distinguished military career, serving in the Egyptian War (1884), the South African War (1899–1900), and the First World War (1914–1918). In 1892, he was appointed Surgeon in Ordinary to Queen Victoria, and then to Edward VII and George V. He received a knighthood for his many achievements in 1912.

However, Boas, already a luminary for his gastrointestinal contributions and for the discovery of the "Oppler-Boas" *Lactobacillus*, found these cells quite constantly in all "fasting" gastric contents containing hydrochloric acid. Further detailed analysis by Boas' assistant, P Cohnheim, indicated that such "cells" could be induced by the reaction of bronchial or pharyngeal mucus and hydrochloric acid. This led to the suggestion that Jaworski had consistently observed acid-altered myelin and that similar secondary structures, threads, and small masses could also be induced by these simple chemical reactions. Cohnheim and Boas therefore inferred from their experiments that Jaworski's "cells" were most probably the product of gastric mucus and acid chyme.

The observations of Bottcher and Letulle had suggested a causative bacterial agent in ulcer disease and by 1888, Letulle was actively searching for this postulated entity. A few years earlier, in 1881, the Scottish surgeon and bacteriologist Sir Alexander Ogston (1844–1929) had identified *Staphylococcus pyrogenes aureus* both in acute and chronic abscesses. Letulle was never able to experimentally discriminate between these different agents and was therefore not able to conclusively prove a role for bacteria in ulcer disease. Nevertheless, the experimental work of Letulle inspired a number of other scientists to follow his lead and similar results were attained with *Lactobacillus*, diphtheria toxin, and *Pneumococcus*.

Camillo Golgi (*left*) was the first to depict the differences between the resting (*bottom left*) and stimulated (*bottom right*) gastric glands. Giulio Bizzozero (*center right*) was able to differentiate large parietal cells whose stained mitochondria produced a granular appearance from chief cells that possessed a flat peripheral nucleus. In addition, he noted a novel cell in the neck of the glands of the acid-secreting part of the stomach, as well as organisms adherent to the surface of the gastric cells. Although he proposed that the chief and surface epithelial cells might be produced by proliferation of the neck cells, he did not further explore the nature of the organisms and turned his attention to the discovery of blood platelets. Hugo Salomon (*top right*) was the first to experimentally prove the infectiousness of gastric *Helicobacter* species.

In a time frame contiguous to these sophisticated experiments, the Italian anatomist Giulio Bizzozero (1846–1901) was busily engaged in the extensive study of the comparative anatomy of vertebrate gastrointestinal glands with his adept and capable pupil, the future Nobel Prize winner Camillo Golgi. In the specimens of the gastric mucosa of six dogs, Bizzozero noted the presence of a spirochete organism in the gastric glands and both in the cytoplasm and vacuoles of parietal cells. He commented that this organism affected both pyloric and fundic mucosa, and its distribution extended from the base of the gland to the surface mucosa. Although he neglected to ascribe any clinical relevance to these observations, he did however remark upon their close association with the parietal cells.

Three years later, in 1896, in a paper entitled 'Spirillum of the mammalian stomach and its behavior with respect to the parietal cells', Hugo Salomon reported spirochetes in the gastric mucosa of dogs, cats, and rats, although he was unable to identify them in other animals, including man. In this early paper, Salomon undertook a series of somewhat bizarre experiments, in which he tried to transmit the bacterium to a range of other animal species by using gastric scrapings from dogs. He failed to transmit it to owls, rabbits, pigeons, and frogs; however, the feeding of gastric mucus to white mice resulted in a spectacular colonization within a week, as evidenced by the series of drawings of infected gastric mucosa reproduced in the original paper. The lumen of the gastric pits of the mice was packed with the spiral-shaped bacteria and invasion of the parietal cells was also noted. Almost two decades later, in 1920, Kasai and Kobayashi successfully repeated these experiments, and using spirochetes isolated from cats, demonstrated pathogenic results in rabbits. Histological examination indicated both hemorrhagic erosion and ulceration of the mucosa in the presence of masses of the spirochetes.

The 20th century

By the beginning of the 20th century, physicians involved in the treatment of gastrointestinal disease were generally familiar with some infective processes of the digestive tract: the ulcerative processes of typhoid fever, a variety of dysenteric conditions, and tuberculosis. In 1906, Krienitz identified spirochetes in the gastric contents of a patient with a carcinoma of the lesser curvature of the stomach and commented that upon microscopic examination, three types of spirochetes, including *Spirochete pallidum*, could be identified. He did not address the question of etiology. Spirochetal dysentery, as well as the presence of spirochetes in the stool of healthy individuals, were known, and Muhlens and independently Luger and Neuberger had all reported these organisms to be evident in the stomach contents of patients with ulcerating carcinomas of the stomach. The latter authors also noted the rarity of these organisms in the gastric mucosa and gastric juice of healthy individuals.

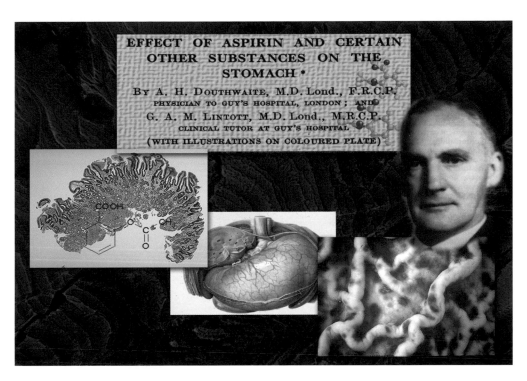

Aspirin was synthesized by chemists from Bayer Corp in 1899, but it was not until a report by AH Douthwaite (*right*) and GAM Lintott from Guy's Hospital in 1938 that the first evidence of gastric injury secondary to aspirin was provided. Their gastroscopic (*bottom right*) and endoscopic observations (*left*) have been corroborated by large studies that have documented a clear association between the use of NSAIDs and gastroduodenal mucosal ulcerations. In addition, evidence has accumulated over the last three decades of the clear relationships between NSAIDs and multiple types of mucosal injury to the distal small intestine and colon. This includes findings of both new lesions as well as exacerbations of pre-existing disease.

Experimental biology, however, dominated gastric research and in the same year, Turcke had undertaken an experiment in which he fed broth cultures of *Bacillus coli* to dogs for a number of months. This resulted in the development of chronic gastric ulceration. In an attempt to establish cause and effect, he thereafter cultured *B coli* from the feces of ulcer patients, which where then injected intravenously into dogs, without effect. However, when the animals ingested the microorganism, every single dog reacted with a spectrum of nonspecific gastric and duodenal alterations, which Turcke loosely called "ulcers". When Gibelli attempted to repeat this work, he could not confirm the results obtained by Turcke.

In Cincinnati, Ohio, the American bacteriologist, EC Rosenow, over a decade from 1913 to 1923, vehemently maintained that ulceration of the stomach could be reproduced in laboratory animals by *Streptococcus*. He isolated this bacterium from foci of infection in humans with ulcer disease and injected the culture into a wide range of animals, including rabbits, dogs, monkeys, guinea pigs, cats, and mice. Based upon these observations, Rosenow postulated that "gastric ulcer-producing *Streptococci*" had a selective affinity for the gastric mucosa and produced a local destruction of the glandular tissue. He further proposed that consequent upon such damage, ulcers would thereafter form, given the autolytic capacity of gastric acid. Rosenow thought that the reservoir for these bacteria were carious teeth, and advanced the idea that a hematogenous bacterial invasion would result in the formation of an ulcer.

296

SPIRELLA REGAUDI IN THE CAT[1]

By J. S. EDKINS.

(From the Physiological Laboratory, Bedford College.)

(With Plates VIII—X including Figs. 1–23.)

THE spiral organism found in the stomach of various carnivora has been investigated by several observers (see the references at the end of this paper). Such studies have been mainly directed to the morphology of the organism, its infectivity and the part it plays in producing a pathological condition. In the present paper I have been concerned rather with the physiological condition of its host as influencing the prevalence and location of the organism in different regions of the stomach. I was anxious further to ascertain if the organism affected the normal processes of digestion in the stomach either to the advantage or the disadvantage of the animal entertaining it.

The frontispiece of John Sidney Edkins' communication documenting his investigations on spiral organisms present in the gastric mucosa of cats. Apart from his epic manuscript documenting the existence of a novel antral stimulant of acid secretion gastrin (1905), Edkins had studied pepsin with John Langley, defined the effects of phosgene on lung function, and developed chemical techniques for destroying weevils without damaging flour. His investigation of the presence of bacteria in the gastric mucosa and the changes they underwent during digestion were, like his studies of gastrin, unappreciated during his lifetime.

from which he recovered gram-negative, fine slender rods which, when inoculated into another guinea pig, once again produced the same lesions. He modestly named his organism "*Bacillus hoffmani*," but it was evident after further study that the lesion-producing capabilities of this bacterium were nonspecific. In 1930, Saunders demonstrated that the *Streptococcus* organism isolated from peptic ulcers in humans was of the alpha variety, and identified specific antibodies against this agent in serum from patients. However, he was unable to produce ulcers in animals by injecting the inoculum and proposed that laboratory animals do not spontaneously form gastric ulcers, since they exhibited an innate resistance to this organism.

One of the early scientific interests of Dragstedt was the causation of gastroduodenal ulceration, although he would subsequently (1943) achieve renown as the surgeon who established the "physiological" rationale for vagotomy as a treatment for duodenal ulcer disease. As early as 1917, as a young physiologist, he had attempted to define the different mechanisms by which gastric juice could affect healing of acute gastric and duodenal ulcers. Fifteen years later, at the Mount Sinai Hospital, A Berg utilized partial vagotomy to reduce "secondary" infections in ulcer margins. Soon after, however, he turned his attention to the colon, and along with his collaborator Burrell Crohn, became more famous for his role in the discovery of the etiology of this disease.

John Sidney Edkins, of London, had made a significant contribution to the elucidation of gastric physiology with the discovery of gastrin. Although the scientific doyens of the time declared it to be humbug, time would vindicate Edkins. Motivated by his disappointment in the investigation of gastrin, Edkins still maintained his enthusiasm for the exploration of gastric pathophysiology. In contrast to the inoculation mode of experimental studies, he proceeded to investigate how the host itself might affect the prevalence and location of the spirochete organisms in different parts of the stomach. The organisms were named "*Spirochete regaudi*" after Regaudi, who considered that the organisms of the gastric mucus layer of cats were morphologically analogous to the syphilis spirochete.

In 1925, Moritz Hoffman investigated whether the causative agent of ulcer disease was a member of the bacillus family by the injection of 5cc of gastric contents from a peptic ulcer patient into guinea pigs. He successfully produced gastric ulcers,

Based to a certain extent on the recognition of the widespread scourge of luetic disease, at around the beginning of the Second World War, spirochetes returned to gastric prominence. JL Doenges observed the organisms to invade the gastric glands of every single one of the *Macacus* rhesus monkeys he studied and to be present in 43% of human gastric autopsy specimens. In contrast to the monkeys, the organisms appeared to be difficult to identify in human gastric mucosa and only 11 of the 103 specimens showed appreciable numbers of spirochetes. These reports prompted Freedberg and Barron in 1941 to further investigate the presence of spirochetes in the gastric tissue of patients who had undergone partial resection surgery. Both authors were familiar with the methods of identifying the organism and used the silver-staining method of DaFano, which they had previously successfully used (but not published) to identify spirochetes in dogs. In spite of such expertise, they were not able to identify the organisms, although they could demonstrate that spirochetes were more frequently present in ulcerating stomachs as compared to non-ulcerated stomachs (53% versus 14%). Based upon their own difficulties with adequate identification and the apparent histological differences noted in Doenges' observations in the *Macacus* mucosa, they concluded that no absolute etiopathological role for these organisms could be defined.

It is with almost tragic irony that one reads that, in the report of the discussion of this paper, Frank D Gorham of St Louis, Missouri, noted "I believe that a further search should be made for an organism thriving in hydrochloric acid medium (and variations of hydrochloric acid are normal in all stomachs) as a possible factor of chronicity, if not an etiological factor, in peptic ulcer". Of interest is that Gorham also wrote that he had, over the previous 10 years, successfully treated patients who had refractory ulcer disease with intramuscular injections of bismuth! Although Gorham may have seemed to be ahead of his time, as early as 1868, Kussmaul had advocated the use of bismuth subnitrate for the treatment of gastric ulcer. In fact, the oral use of bismuth for gastrointestinal symptoms was well accepted, and as early as the late 18th century, reports of the therapy had begun to appear in English literature. In fact, R Sazerac and C Levaditit had already successfully exploited the antibacterial properties of bismuth in 1921 when they reported the cure of experimental syphilis in rabbits.

Whilst ammonia was noted in gastric juice as early as 1852, it was not until 1924 that Luck discovered gastric mucosal urease. His subsequent work and the work of others, especially the Dublin biochemist EJ Conway, who specialized in investigations of the redox mechanism of acid secretion, confirmed the presence of gastric urease in a number of mammals. O Fitzgerald (Conway's medical colleague) postulated a clinical role for urea in gastric physiology and proposed that gastric urease functioned as a mucosal protective agent by providing ions to neutralize acid.

This led to a number of studies in which the ingestion of urea-containing solutions was utilized to alter histamine-stimulated gastric acid secretion. Notwithstanding the unpleasant side effects of this administration (diarrhea, headache, polyuria, and painful urethritis), Fitzgerald further applied his hypothesis by treating ulcer patients with this regimen in 1949. Although he charitably summarized his results as "in general, satisfactory," no further therapeutic studies were undertaken with this particular agent.

The negative results of Freedberg and Barron, the ambivalent results of Doenges, and the fact that the gastric urease story was still being unraveled prompted ED Palmer, in the early 1950s, to investigate spirochetes in human gastric samples. He obtained gastric mucosal biopsies from 1,180 subjects using a vacuum tube technique, but using standard histological techniques failed to demonstrate either spirochetes or any structures resembling them. Although Palmer did not

attempt to identify the organisms with the more reliable silver stain, he concluded (confidently) that the results of all previous authors could be best explained as a postmortem colonization of the gastric mucosa with oral cavity organisms. He also postulated that such spirochetes were normal commensals of the mouth and essentially debunked the concept of bacterial involvement in peptic ulcer disease. Palmer's work may thus be credited with the envious distinction of setting back gastric bacterial research by a further 30 years.

In 1975, Steer, while studying polymorphonuclear leukocyte migration in the gastric mucosa in a series of biopsy materials obtained from patients with gastric ulceration, identified bacteria in close contact with the epithelium and suggested that white cells' migration was a response to these bacteria. By 1980, reports concerning a disease entity broadly referred to as "epidemic gastritis associated with hypochlorhydria" had been published. These observations, coupled with Steer's findings of an apparent association between "active gastritis" and gram-negative bacteria, suggested that the simultaneous occurrence of bacteria in the stomach and peptic ulceration might represent more than a correlatable epiphenomenon. Robin Warren, a pathologist at the Royal Perth Hospital, had for many years observed bacteria in the stomach of people with gastritis. Although convinced that they somehow played a role in gastric disease, in the light of the prevailing dogma of acid-induced ulceration and the skepticism of his colleagues, he had been reluctant to discuss this controversial observation in the wider gastroenterological community.

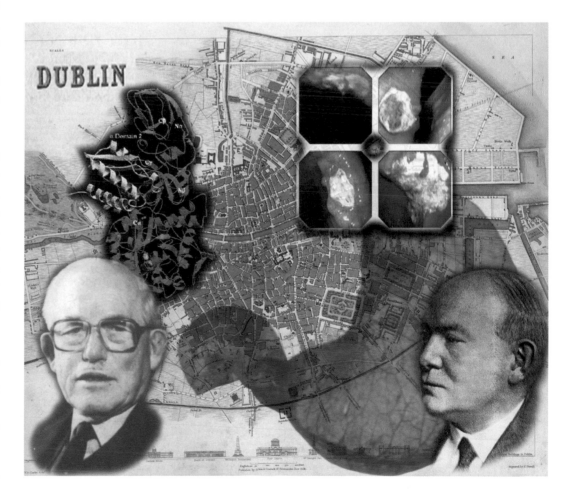

O Fitzgerald (*bottom left*) of Dublin used urea solutions in the clinical setting of the 1940s to treat patients with ulcer disease (*top right*). This was based on the proposal by his colleague EJ Conway (*bottom right*) that gastric urease (*top left*) functioned as a mucosal protective agent by providing ions to neutralize acid. Fitzgerald postulated that the ingestion of urea would alter histamine-stimulated gastric acid secretion by changing the gastric ionic milieu. While Fitzgerald considered this therapy satisfactory, the unpleasant side effects of administration (diarrhea, headache, polyuria, and painful urethritis) prevented any further studies with this agent.

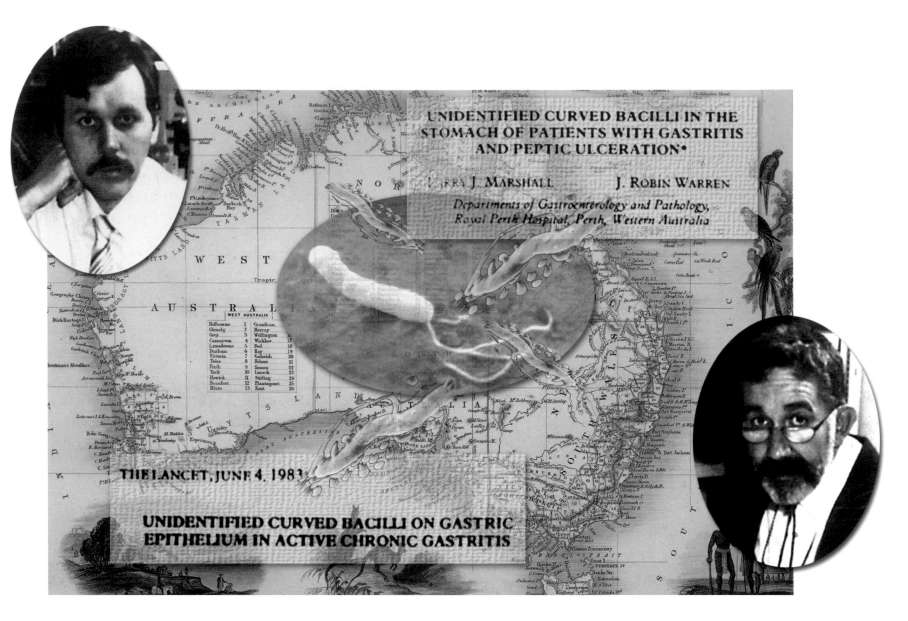

Robin Warren (*bottom right*), a pathologist at the Royal Perth Hospital in Australia, was convinced that the bacteria he noted in the gastric biopsies of patients with gastritis were relevant to the condition. In 1982, Barry Marshall (*left*), a gastroenterology fellow working with Warren, was able to demonstrate the clinical relevance of *Campylobacter* in the pathogenesis of the condition previously known as acid peptic disease.

In 1982, a young gastroenterology fellow in Perth, Australia, Barry Marshall, was looking for a project to complete his fellowship. The iconoclastic hypothesis of Warren attracted Marshall, who persuaded Warren to allow him to investigate this further in the appropriate clinical setting. Later in the year, Marshall submitted an abstract detailing their initial investigations to the Australian Gastroenterology Association. It was flatly rejected, along with a handful of other abstracts on the same subject prepared by him. Young and unfazed, and seeking an alternative audience for the work, Marshall submitted the same abstract to the International Workshop on Campylobacter Infections, where it was accepted. Although the audience was skeptical of Marshall and Warren's results, some members became interested enough to attempt to repeat some of their observations.

Soon after this meeting, both Warren and Marshall published their initial results as two modest letters in the *Lancet*. In the introduction to his seminal article on an S-shaped *Campylobacter*-like organism, Warren noted the constancy of bacterial infection, as well as the consistency of the associated histological changes, which he had identified in 135 gastric biopsy specimens studied over a three-year period. He commented that these microorganisms were difficult to see with hematoxylin and eosin, but stained well in the presence of silver. Furthermore, he observed the bacteria to be most numerous in an "active chronic gastritis," where they were closely associated with granulocyte infiltration. It is a mystery, he wrote, that bacteria in numbers sufficient to be seen by light microscopy were almost unknown to clinicians and pathologists alike! He presciently concluded: "These organisms should be recognized and their significance investigated." Koch's second postulate states that "the germ should be obtained from the diseased animal and grown outside the body". In the same issue of the *Lancet*, Marshall described the conditions necessary to fulfill this requirement.

In 1926, the Nobel Prize in Physiology or Medicine was awarded to Johannes Andreas Grib Fibiger (*top left*) for the subsequently refuted discovery that gastric carcinoma in rats was scored by the nematode *Spiroptera carcinoma*. Fibiger was born in Silkeborg, Denmark, in 1867 and received a medical degree in 1890 from the University of Copenhagen, where he subsequently also earned a doctoral degree in bacteriology. At 33 years of age, he was named Director of the Institute of Pathological Anatomy of the University of Copenhagen and held this position until 1928, when he died. In 1907, Fibiger noted, while studying gastric papillomas in three wild rats, the presence of nematodes, which he believed to be the cause of the tumors.

In order to substantiate that the microorganism was actually a disease-causing agent, it was necessary to demonstrate that it could colonize normal mucosa and induce gastritis (Koch's third and fourth postulates). To prove pathogenicity, Marshall, looking back in time for guidance, decided to be his own guinea pig. Marshall, who had a histologically normal gastric mucosa and was a light smoker and social drinker, received, per mouth, a test isolate from a 66-year-old, non-ulcer dyspeptic man. Over the next 14 days, a mild illness developed, characteristic of an acute episode of gastritis, and was accompanied by headaches, vomiting, abdominal discomfit, irritability, and "putrid" breath. The infectivity of the agent was thereafter successfully confirmed, when after 10 days, histologically proven gastritis was endoscopically documented. The disease process later resolved of its own accord by the 15th day. Marshall went on to describe the urease of the organism and recognized its role in enabling survival of the organism in acidic media.

Of particular interest was the observation that *H pylori* was associated with the development of lymphoid follicles in the stomach and that such histological changes could even progress to neoplasia. Indeed, the description of MALT lymphomas of varying degrees of malignancy led to a renaissance of the old belief that infection and malignancy were related. This conclusion was further bolstered by complex epidemiological and statistical analyses that purported to demonstrate that geographical areas of *H pylori* infection exhibited a far greater incidence of gastric cancer. So dramatic was this information considered that the World Heath Organization declared the bacterium to be a Class 1 pathogen, and many physicians declared worldwide eradication of the organism as a certain means by which the holy grail of peptic ulcer disease obliteration might be achieved. Few remembered that an organism responsible for the cause of gastric cancer had already been previously discovered in the 20th century.

3 PANCREAS

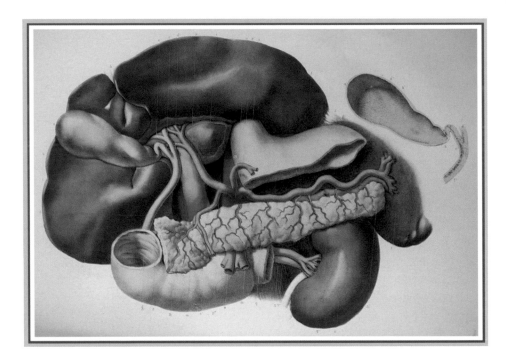

An 1832 illustration of the pancreas from the anatomy text of NH Jacob of Paris (*L'anatomie de L'Homme*, illustrated by JM Bougery).

Vesalius, in his monumental seven books of anatomy, referred to the pancreas in the fifth book as a "glandulous organ or kannelly body of substance growing in the neather pannicle of the caule (omentum)". Despite his anatomical skill, he possessed little understanding of its function and his illustrations deal chiefly with its vascular structure. Vesalius considered the pancreas to provide a protective function (*Schutzorgan*) for the stomach. A subsequent translation of the Vesalian anatomy text by the London astrologer Nicholas Culpeper (1616–1654) in 1653 was the first to use the lay term "sweetbread" to describe the organ.

Nicholas Culpeper, the herbalist and quacksalver, who in 1649 translated the *Pharmacopoeia Londinensis* into English. Culpeper was an enigmatic intellect possessed of an admixture of sound common sense, prescience, and a substantial tincture of entrepreneurial skill.

The derivation of the word pancreas or sweetbread originated with Homer, who broadly used the term to describe edible animal flesh. About 300 BC, Herophilus of Chalcedon named the organ for its meaty or fleshy character, and the term was used both by Aristotle and Rufus of Ephesus (100 AD), although it was the opinion of Andreas Vesalius (1514–1564) that the ancients had not adequately distinguished between the mesenteric glands and the pancreas itself. Although it is believed that the Greeks were the first to recognize the pancreas as a distinct organ, arcane references in the even earlier Babylonian *Talmud* refer to a structure designated by the rabbis as the "finger of the liver". Galen provided a modest description of the organ, but neither he, nor Hippocrates and Erasistratus, were able to identify a relationship to disease. Herophilus, one of the first scholars to have the opportunity to dissect humans, described the pancreas in his diverse deliberations on the structures and functions of the body. Since the ancient anatomists regarded the pancreas as unusual, given that it had no cartilage or bone present, they considered it to be literally "all flesh or meat". Thus Rufus named the organ "pancreas" (the Greek "*pan*" means "all" and "*kreas*" is "flesh or meat").

Culpeper was a well-known writer, and although he was variously considered by his detractors as a charlatan or quack, he achieved a fine reputation as a writer and his *Herbal* became familiar to many generations as a family medicine book. Given that he lived during the English Civil War, much of his time was spent attempting to survive the political vagaries of the times and it is not certain whom he supported. Indeed, judging from the frequent pious expressions in his works, it may be considered that he was ultimately a Parliamentarian. Nevertheless, the conflict seriously involved him such that he was severely wounded in the chest during a battle and it is probable that this wound caused the lung disease from which he later died. Such information as we have of Culpeper's career is gathered from his own works and from some brutal attacks on him in certain public prints. He describes himself on the title pages of some of his larger books as "MD" but there is no evidence that he ever graduated.

Culpeper lived, at least during his married life, at Red Lion Street, Spitalfields, and there established a large medical practice. Although many of those who studied his works formed the idea that he was a bent old man with a long gray beard who eternally busied himself with the collection of simples (herbal medicaments), he was in fact originally a soldier and his early demise at the age of 38 was undoubtedly due to the sequela of his military wound. The portraits and descriptions of him by his astrological friends represent him as a smart, brisk young Londoner, fluent in speech and animated in gesture, good in company, although with frequent fits of melancholy. As might be expected, it appears that his opinion of himself was far in excess of that held by others of his skill.

Culpeper had initially been apprenticed to an apothecary in Great St Helen's, Bishopsgate, at the same time as a certain Marchmont Nedham became a solicitor's clerk in Jewry Street. Nedham subsequently rose up to become the most notorious journalist in England, and founded and edited in turn the *Mercurius Britannicus*, an anti-royalist paper; the *Mercurius Pragmaticus*, which was violently anti-Commonwealth; and the *Mercurius Politicitis*, subsidized by Oliver Cromwell's government and supervised by no less a personage than the eminent poet John Milton (1608–1674). This publication, amalgamated with the *Public Intelligencer*, its principal

rival, lived on for years as the *London Gazette*. Although Nedham and Culpeper were friends in their early days, and may even have been comrades in arms when the war broke out, they subsequently became fierce enemies. In *Mercurius Pragmaticus*, Nedham, pretending to review Culpeper's translation of the official *Dispensatory*, took the opportunity of pouring on him a tirade of scurrilous abuse. The translation, he said, was "filthily done" which was not true and represented the only piece of reasonable criticism in the article of which the rest consisted of a personal diatribe against the author. Nedham informed his readers that Culpeper was the son of a Surrey parson, "one of those who deceive men in matters belonging to their most precious souls". That meant that he was a Nonconformist. Culpeper himself, according to Nedham, had been an Independent, a Brownist, an Anabaptist, a Seeker, and a Manifestationist, but had ultimately become an Atheist. During his apprenticeship, he "ran away from his master upon his lewd debauchery"; afterwards, he became a compositor, then a "figure-flinger" and lived about Moorfields on cozenage. After making further sundry accusations and some appalling personal insinuations about Culpeper's wife, Nedham stated that in two years of drunken labor, Culpeper had "gallimawfred the *Apothecaries' Book* into nonsense"; that he wore an old black coat lined with plush which his stationer (publisher) had got for him in Long Lane to hide his knavery, having been till then a most despicable ragged fellow; and that he looked "as if he had been stewed in a tan pit; a frowzy headed coxcomb". He also claimed that Culpeper was aiming to "monopolise to himself all the knavery and cozenage that ever an apothecary's shop was capable of".

Nicholas Culpeper (*center*) gained a considerable reputation for his purported introduction of the term "sweetbread" (*top*) as a descriptor of the pancreas. Although culinary lore opines that there are two forms of sweetbread – the thymus gland (known as throat sweetbread) and the pancreas (stomach sweetbread), derived from calf or lamb – most physicians referred to the latter in their opinions. Irrespective of the mode of preparation or the nature of the Madeira used in their preparation, pancreas has long been considered a delicacy and the beneficial effects of its consumption attributed both to taste and to the fact that it is rich in mineral elements and vitamins. Since sweetbreads are highly perishable, it is imperative that they should be soaked and parboiled, then creamed, curried, braised, or otherwise prepared for serving (*bottom*), lest their nutritive value be diminished. It is of interest to note that similar complex preparative instructions became obligate in preparing the gland as a therapeutic agent. Aficionados of the gustatory nature of the organ (*left*) are, much like gastroenterologists, united in their belief that the pancreas is preferable to the thymus!

Culpeper's works however themselves answer this spiteful caricature, for he was a man of considerable attainment, and of immense industry. By virtue of his personality and knowledge, he attained almost legendary status in the field of herbal medicine, and worked with ardor to transform medicinal treatments from a mysterious and arcane science to a form comprehensible to laymen. His philosophical thrust was to educate the common people to minister to themselves by providing them with the tools and knowledge for self-health. In so doing, as might be expected, he garnered much approbation and disdain from the established medical profession. Despite this, his writings acquired considerable popularity, best proven by the fact that after his death, it was regarded good business to forge materials that resembled them and then pass them off as Culpeper's work!

WIRSÜNG

Since little was known of the function of the pancreas, in spite of Culpeper's culinary exposition, scientific attention was directed to the subject of the duct and the structure of the gland. In 1642, Johann George Wirsüng (1589–1643), the Prosector to Veslingus in Padua, was the first to describe the main duct of the human pancreas. Wirsüng had studied anatomy in Paris under Professor Jean Riolan before enrolling at Padau University (1629), graduating from the Sacro Collegio on March 23, 1630, with a Doctorate in Philosophy and Medicine.

Johann George Wirsüng's plate of his pancreatic duct discovery is shown. It is evident from this reproduction that Wirsüng was an expert copperplate engraver. He printed his engraving of the pancreas onto a small, oblong folio that clearly indicated the pancreas and both the bile and pancreatic ducts, as well as part of the duodenum and spleen. The 21 branches of the pancreatic duct can also be clearly identified. Included with this drawing is a precise explanatory "epistle" describing his discovery. This copperplate is still on display in the Palazzo del Bo at the University of Padua.

As a young graduate, he was strongly supported by Johann Wesling, Professor of Anatomy at Padua. While working under his direction on March 2, 1642, during the autopsy of Zuane Viaro della Badia, a 30-year-old man guilty of murder and executed by hanging in the Piazza del Vin on the previous day, Wirsüng discovered a duct in the pancreas. Since the dissection was undertaken privately at the San Francesco Hospital, Wesling and the Register of the Deceased provided confirmation of the event. Present at the dissection were Thomas Bartholin (1616–1680) of Denmark and Moritz Hoffman (1622–1698) of Germany. Five years after the death of Wirsüng, Hoffman claimed to have discovered the pancreatic duct in a turkey rooster in September of 1641 and to have informed Wirsüng, who then sought to identify this duct in man!

Wirsüng had no understanding of the function of the pancreatic duct, but recognized its significance and sought further information. He therefore personally engraved his findings on a single copper plate and made seven identical impressions which he then sent to famous anatomists throughout Europe, seeking their opinion as to the function of the ductal structure. These authorities included Dr Ole Worm of Copenhagen (brother-in-law of Bartholin), Kasper Hoffman of Altdorf, and Jean Riolan Jr of Paris. In addition, the pictures were also sent to Professor Severino of Naples and to anatomists at Gena, Hamburg, and Nuremberg. As might have been predicted, none of the authorities at the various institutions were able to offer any specific insight into the function of the duct. Worm thought it might be involved in lymphatic drainage. Riolan, having no answer, did not reply, and Hoffman believed it was somehow related to chyle transport.

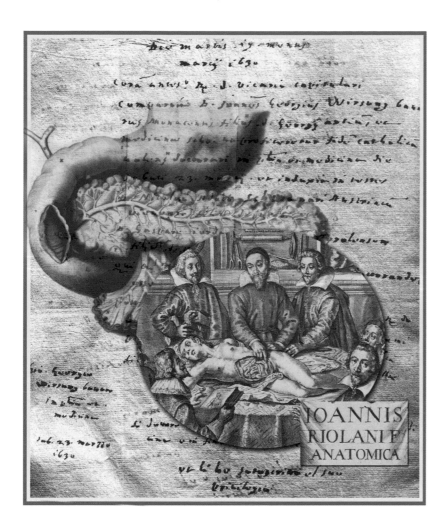

On March 2, 1642, Johann George Wirsüng first identified the pancreatic duct and being unaware of its function, engraved his findings on a single cooper plate, seven impressions of which he sent to the most famous anatomists of Europe, including Jean Riolan (1580–1657) (*center, dissecting*), his Parisian mentor, seeking their opinion regarding the function of the ductal structure. Riolan and the rest of the letter recipients, disappointingly, did not recognize Wirsüng's discovery, and felt the duct was a funnel!

SYLVIUS AND DE GRAAF

The nature of the functional role of the pancreas was first investigated by Franciscus de la Boe Sylvius (1614–1672) of Amsterdam, who proposed that digestion was a multi-step process divided into three principal stages. The first involved fermentation by saliva in the mouth and the stomach, while the second involved the pancreas. In the elucidation of this issue, a brilliant pupil, Regnier de Graaf (1641–1673) of Delft, ably supported Sylvius.

Regnier de Graaf (1641–1673) was the first to scientifically address the nature of pancreatic secretion. In order to facilitate his studies, he developed an ingenious method for the creation of canine pancreatic fistulae (*bottom right*) and was thereby able to elucidate the nature of pancreatic juice. His publication *De Succi Pancreatici* (1662) (*top left*) defined the nature of the juice and detailed the preparation of the canine fistula model. De Graaf is also credited with his anatomical investigations of the female reproductive system, but his tragic early demise precluded his further elucidation of pancreatico-follicular function.

A decade later, Thomas Wharton (1610–1673) of York, in his 1656 text *Adenographia Sive Glandularum Totius Corporis Descriptio*, not only identified and named the thyroid gland, but also commented upon the general similarity between the structure of the pancreas and the submaxillary gland. Wharton had been educated at Cambridge and Oxford, and obtained his medical degree from Trinity College in 1647 before focusing on establishing a medical practice in York. In addition, however, he maintained a serious scholastic interest and continued as a lecturer and dissector at Gresham College. Wharton was widely acknowledged as a skilled anatomist and is credited with being the first to undertake a systemic study of the glands of the human body.

Despite the pioneering work of Wharton and Wirsüng, the function of the pancreatic duct was utterly misunderstood, since contemporary views considered that "chyme" from the duodenum ascended into the pancreas to provoke secretion of a "sharp juice not unlike to the gall". It remained however for the anatomist Samuel von Sommering (1755–1830) to first employ the vernacular term "*Bauchspeicheldrüse*" (abdominal salivary gland) in the medical and scientific literature. Subsequently, in his 1797 thesis on the salivary system, Karl von Siebold (1804–1885) of Jena presciently considered that the three glands might be regarded as analogous to the pancreas. Indeed, as a result of this work, the pancreas was until the late 19th century considered as an abdominal salivary gland!

De Graaf ingeniously developed a method for the direct investigation of the nature of pancreatic juice utilizing canine pancreatic fistula, through which he inserted feather quills into the pancreatic ductal orifices to obtain succus pancreaticus. Both de Graaf and Sylvius believed that the function of pancreatic juice was to effervesce with bile and that the combination of acids and alkalis that occurred was a critical component of digestion. They further postulated that pancreatic juice exhibited a dual function by both "attenuating the mucous lining of the gut as well as initiating segregation of the useful food elements". Unfortunately, de Graaf's conclusion that pancreatic juice was acidic was incorrect and reflected not only the relatively limited chemical knowledge of the time, but also the fact that some of the experiments were undertaken in fish, and the complex gastric pyloric ceca were mistaken as part of the pancreas. Nevertheless, emboldened by his pancreatic contributions, de Graaf ventured forward to his seminal work on ovarian structure and function.

By the end of the 17th century, Johann Bohn had revised Sylvius' doctrine and successfully demonstrated that the pancreatic juice was not acid. Sylvius maintained that the third stage of digestion represented the passage of chyle into lymphatics, which was then conveyed to the venous system by the thoracic duct, which bore it to the right side of the heart. His innovative theories on digestion were subsequently modified by the discovery of Peyer's patches and the duodenal glands named after Johann Conrad Brunner (also known as the Swiss Hippocrates).

Johann Conrad Brunner (1653–1727) discovered Brunner's glands in the duodenum of dog and man in 1672 and published his results in 1687. He believed that they secreted a juice similar to that of the pancreas and undertook experimental excision of the spleen and pancreas to examine the importance of these organs. After such a pancreatic resection in 1683, he noted that one of the surviving dogs developed extreme thirst and polyuria. Had Brunner further pursued this observation, he might well have been regarded not only as the Swiss Hippocrates but also the first to elucidate the pancreatic basis of diabetes!

Willy Kühne (1837–1900) (*bottom left*) of Heidelberg was one of the first scientists to study the changes (*top left and right; bottom left*) seen under the microscope in the living, secreting gland cells of the pancreas (*background*). In addition, he was able to observe and recognize the differences between the active and resting gland cells in the live pancreas. His observations were reflected by similar work in the morphological study of secretion that was respectively applied by Rudolf Heidenhain and John Langley to salivary and peptic glands. In addition to this work, Kühne was a chemist of considerable skill and is credited with being among the first to recognize the concept of chemical catalysis and use the term "enzyme" (1876). In regard to the pancreas, he coined the term "trypsin" to define what he considered to be the major proteolytic enzyme of the pancreas. Of particular relevance to understanding the basis of subsequent therapeutic developments in regard to pancreatin, Kühne also realized that in the normal gastric milieu, "pepsin actually destroys trypsin, but trypsin does not destroy pepsin". He was thus able to recognize that the use of a gastric route for pancreatic enzyme supplementation would require that such enzymes be protected.

During the 18th century, Albrecht von Haller (1708–1777) studied pancreatic physiology (and almost everything else, including botany, astronomy, color spectra, and poetry). He noted the close relationship of the pancreatic duct to the bile duct and with his customary perspicacity, proposed that pancreatic juice and bile interacted in the process of digestion. Further 18th century contributions included that of Giovanni Domenico Santorini, Professor of Anatomy and Medicine in Venice. Girard published his identification of the accessory duct of the pancreas in *Observationes Anatomicae* (1742) many years after Santorini's demise, since the latter was concerned that the Venetian authorities would consider his work heretical. In 1806, Meckel provided a detailed description of the embryology of the pancreas and in 1861, Goette initiated the study of the comparative anatomy of the pancreas.

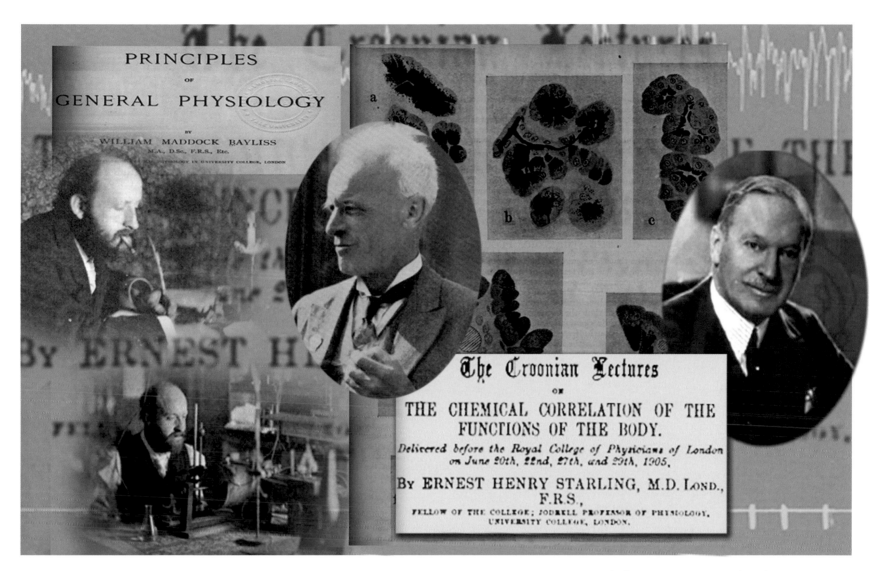

Although the neural regulation of digestive activity was initially defined by Ivan Petrovich Pavlov, the discovery of secretin by Sir William Bayliss (*left*) and Ernest Henry Starling (*center*) and the elucidation of the concept of a chemical messenger system ushered in a new era of understanding of the regulation of gastrointestinal function. Bayliss' text *Principles of General Physiology* (1914) (*top left*) was regarded as a monumental classic of general physiology and earned him high regard. The presentation of the Croonian Lectures of 1905 (*bottom*) by Starling led directly to the development of an entirely novel discipline – endocrinology. Amidst the veritable cornucopia of scientific discoveries made by Bayliss and Starling, the masterful understatement of Charles Martin (*right*), in describing the experiment that first demonstrated a chemical messenger, best sums up the tenor of the time and the individuals. His meticulous experimental notes of January 16, 1901, close with the immortal line: "It was a great afternoon." Thus was born endocrinology!

Further elucidation of pancreatic physiology was provided by Willy Kühne (1837–1900) of Germany, who identified trypsin and evaluated its role in the digestion of protein. In 1815, Alexander Marcet (1770–1822) identified lipase. Between 1849 and 1856, Claude Bernard (1813–1878) of Paris investigated pancreatic physiology in detail and conclusively demonstrated its clinical relevance to digestion as a whole. Over a seven-year period, Bernard unified the concepts of pancreatic digestion, demonstrating that gastric digestion "is only a preparation act" and that pancreatic juice emulsified fatty foods, splitting them into glycerin and fatty acids. In addition, he demonstrated the power of the pancreas to convert starch into sugar and its solvent action upon the "proteides that have not been cleaved in the stomach". Further work by Johann N Eberle in 1843 demonstrated that pancreatic juice emulsified fat and a year later, Gabriel Valentin demonstrated its activity on starch.

The regulation of pancreatic secretion was a vexatious question, which Ivan Petrovich Pavlov (1849–1936) and his pupils addressed with vigor at the turn of the 19th century. Utilizing novel pancreatic fistula preparations, they demonstrated the role of the vagus nerve in the neural regulation of pancreatic secretion and proposed that pancreatic function fell within the doctrine of nervism. Dolinski, a pupil of Pavlov, noted that acid introduced into the duodenum stimulated pancreatic secretion and interpreted this as indicative of a local neural reflex.

In 1902, Sir William Bayliss and Ernest Henry Starling of University College London demonstrated that this phenomenon was in fact not a neural reflex, but the effect of a chemical messenger or regulator. They termed the substance a hormone, derived from the Greek "*hormonos*" ("arouse to excitement") and proposed the putative agent in the duodenal mucosa be called secretin.

Although pancreatic diseases had been neglected since the time of Galen, the work (1664) of Regnier de Graaf (*top right*) in the laboratory of the Leiden Professor Franciscus de la Boe Sylvius (*bottom left*), led to a resurgence of interest in this organ (*center*) in the latter half of the 17th century. De Graaf was the first to address the nature of pancreatic secretion scientifically, and to facilitate his studies, he developed ingenious canine pancreatic fistulas. His mentor Sylvius directed these studies, but was also interested in the clinical importance of the pancreas. He thus determined that the organ was responsible for the fevers associated with malaria, while Nathaniel Highmore (*top left*) considered the pancreas to be the source of apoplexy, palsy, and hysteria. This acme of interest in the pancreas was, however, destroyed by the work of Johann Conrad Brunner (*bottom right*), who in 1683, was able to demonstrate that the pancreas was not an "essential" organ when his pancreatectomized dogs survived for a number of months following the procedure.

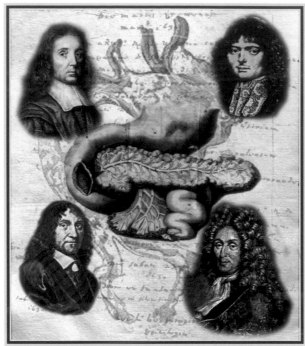

Despite the subsequent debunking of nervism as the sole regulator of gut function, Pavlov's book *The Work of the Digestive Glands* represented a significant contribution to the physiology of digestion and provided a fitting accompaniment to the Nobel Prize awarded to him for his contributions to the field. Further work on pancreatic juice itself was produced by yet another of Pavlov's pupils, Chepovalnikov, who demonstrated that pancreatic juice acquired and exerted a powerful solvent action on proteids only after contact with either the duodenal membrane or extracts thereof. This observation enabled him to deduce that the duodenum produced a unique enzyme (enterokinase) responsible for the activation of pancreatic juice.

In Manchester, some 41 years after the discovery of secretin, in a publication in the *Journal of Physiology*, AA Harper and HS Raper reported a substance (pancreozymin) derived from the small intestine mucosa that upon intravenous injection caused an increased secretion of pancreatic enzymes (amylase). Raper, a Yorkshireman, was the Brackenbury Chairman of Physiology at the University of Manchester. Although his biochemical research dealt largely with fatty acid oxidation, he is probably best remembered for a series of elegant and illuminating publications on tyrosinase and the early stages of melanin formation. Despite this primary focus, he and Harper also investigated the role of the pancreas in fat digestion. The preparation identified by these two co-workers was identical to one stimulating gallbladder contraction that had been discovered by AC Ivy and Eric Oldberg in 1926. The conundrum of a gallbladder- and pancreas-stimulating hormone was cleared up in 1966 when Jorpes, a fugitive Russian general turned biochemist, and Viktor Mutt in Stockholm, chemically determined that this was a common messenger for a common action: pancreaticobiliary digestion.

ONE MECHANISM FOR GALL-BLADDER CONTRAC-
TION AND EVACUATION

A. C. IVY AND ERIC OLDBERG
Department of Physiology, Northwestern University Medical School

Received for publication June 20, 1928

Ivy

J. Physiol. (1943) 102, 115-125

PANCREOZYMIN, A STIMULANT OF THE SECRE
OF PANCREATIC ENZYMES IN EXTRACTS
OF THE SMALL INTESTINE

A. A. HARPER AND H. S. RAPER, *From the Department*
Physiology, University of Manchester

(*Received 9 January 1943*)

Harper

Raper

In 1927, AC Ivy (*top left*) and Eric Oldberg described their experiments, demonstrating that in anesthetized dogs or cats, the intravenous injection of a purified preparation of secretin resulted in a rise in the intra-gallbladder pressure that could not be inhibited by atropine. They commented: "We propose the term 'cholecystokinin' [that which excites or moves the gallbladder] to designate the active principle which causes the gallbladder to contract." In 1943, AA Harper (*bottom left*) and HS Raper (*bottom right*), following up on these earlier observations, demonstrated that extracts of the mucosa of the upper intestine contained a substance that on intravenous administration stimulated the pancreas to secrete enzymes, as opposed to secretin, which stimulated water and bicarbonate secretion. The British researchers therefore proposed the name "pancreozymin" to describe the former. In the center of the collage is a reproduction of Figure 2 from their 1943 paper, indicating the minute output of amylase (y-axis) versus time (over a two-hour period) in cats whose splanchnic and dorsal vagal trunk had been cut. The amylase response to pancreozymin injection (P and P) is clearly evident, as is the inhibitory effect of an atropine sulphate injection (A). In addition, no effect on volume output was noted. Thereafter, Morton Grossman (1919–1981), a pupil of Ivy, was able to demonstrate in dogs with subcutaneously transplanted pancreatic glands that the luminal agents that were effective in releasing pancreozymin were the same as those found to release CCK (1951). In 1966, the peptide chemists Jorpes and Mutt demonstrated that CCK and pancreozymin shared the same chemical structure and that the two biological effects – gallbladder contraction and pancreatic enzyme secretion – were induced by CCK. Thus, six decades after the identification of secretin, a second chemical messenger regulating pancreatic secretion was defined.

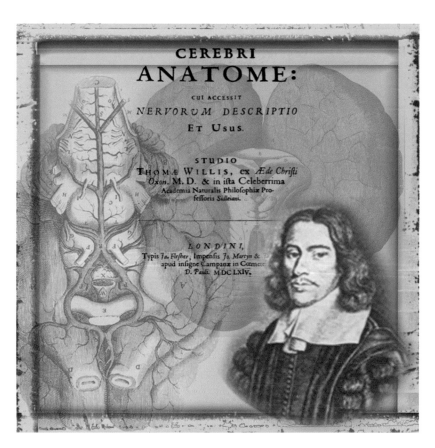

Thomas Willis achieved immortality for his description of the arterial circle at the base of the brain. His friend Sir Christopher Wren, who initially practiced as a physician before becoming an architect of hospitals and St Paul's cathedral, undertook the actual drawings of the eponymous circle. In the field of diabetes, Willis devised the first dietary regimen for diabetics in the 17th century, and the practice of undernutrition he set was to be followed in diabetic diets for the next 200 years. Willis believed that salts were being lost in the urine and advised limewater replacement. In addition, other remedies such as antimony and opium concoctions were also prescribed, and remained in vogue for more than 100 years after Willis' death in 1675.

PANCREATIC DISEASE

Diseases of the pancreas appear to have been largely neglected in antiquity, although Galen (130–201 AD) was aware of pancreatic problems and even termed inflammatory diseases of the pancreas as a "scirrhous". He is quoted as stating: "Scirrhous is a hard, heavy immobile and painful tumor; cancer is a very hard malignant tumor, with or without ulceration." This scirrhous term thereafter encompassed a multitude of pancreatic disorders. While diabetes was known, it was not recognized as a pancreatic disease, largely because of Galen's view that it was due to metabolic alterations in the kidney. Since the anatomical location of the organ was not well known and its physiological functions ill defined, pathological conditions of the pancreas were therefore difficult to delineate.

A pancreatic disease renaissance occurred 1,300 years later when most diseases of the 16th century were ascribed to the pancreas. The English physician Nathaniel Highmore (1613–1685) considered the pancreas to be the seat and source of apoplexy, palsy, and hysteria, while Sylvius himself thought he had identified the cause of malaria.

Highmore was born in Fordingbridge, Hampshire, into a family of clerics (his father was the Rector of Purse Caundle, Dorset) and was educated at Oxford, where he attained an MD in 1643 by Royal mandate (it is thought that he may have attended the young Prince Charles (1630–1685) during a bout of measles in 1642). Highmore was known as an excellent anatomist and his most important work, *Corporis humani disquisitio anatomica* (1651), was the first anatomical textbook to accept the circulation of the blood. In it he described the antrum of Highmore. Thereafter, *The History of Generation* (1651), which was the result of Highmore's collaboration with William Harvey (1578–1657) in Oxford, contained references to a microscope, which the former used in his work on embryology. Highmore also wrote a number of medical works, including *Discourse of the Cure of Wounds by Sympathy* (1651), *De passione hysterica et de affectionae hypochondriaca* (1660), a work which engaged Highmore in a controversy with Willis, and *Short Treatise of Dysenteria* (1658). Although he was largely isolated from the rest of the English scientific circle (despite his correspondence with Harvey), he was able to financially support himself by his medical practice at Sherborne (1651) until his death.

Two decades after Highmore's pancreatic postulate, Thomas Willis (1621–1675) in 1674 noted the urine of diabetics to be "wonderfully sweet as if it were imbued with honey or sugar." Willis, a doctor at Oxford and (later) London, was the leading English exponent of chemistry of his time and an excellent experimentalist as well as clinician. He coined the word "neurology" and is immortalized in the eponym of "The Circle of Willis" – the arteries that form a circle at the base of the brain. Willis was amongst the first to undertake a systematic dissection of the nervous system and in 1664, produced his book *Cerebri Anatomi*, notable not only for its originality and scope, but also for the anatomical drawings of Sir Christopher Wren (1632–1723). In relation to the search for the brain correlates of the mind, Willis extended the concepts proposed by the Roman physician Galen that the brain was the organ responsible for the excretion of animal spirits (which were thought to originate from the cribriform plate, a bone in the base of the skull overlying the nasal cavity). Willis proposed that the choroid plexus was responsible for the absorption of cerebrospinal fluid. Later, in *De Anima Brutorum*, he proposed that the corpus striatum received all sensory information, while the corpus callosum was associated with imagination, and the cerebral cortex with memory.

As a member of the iatrochemical school, which believed that chemistry was the basis of human function, rather than mechanics, Willis attempted to correlate the current knowledge of anatomy, physiology, and biochemistry with clinical findings in neuropathology. In the field of diabetes, Willis devised the first dietary regimen for diabetics in the 17th century, and the practice of undernutrition he set was to be followed in diabetic diets for the next 200 years. Willis believed that salts were being lost in the urine and advised limewater replacement. In addition, other remedies such as antimony and opium concoctions were also prescribed, and remained in vogue for over a century after the death of Willis in 1675.

Once the general concepts of anatomical structure and physiological function were established, attention was directed at the anatomical basis of disease – pathological anatomy. Giovanni Battista Morgagni was amongst the earliest to identify such events and his seminal descriptions provide some of the first images of organ pathology and its relationship to clinical symptomatology and disease. Morgagni was a distinguished Italian physician and investigator in medicine, and was dubbed the "Father of Modern Pathology" by Rudolf Virchow. While at Padua, he wrote his famous *On the Seats and Causes of Disease*, which subsequently laid the foundation of modern pathology. The majority of his observations regarding the pancreas were taken from the work of the Genevan physician Theophile Bonet (1620–1689), who had published an extensive treatise on pathology, *Sepulchretum*, following postmortem findings from 3,000 cases in 1679. While Morgagni is considered as being the first to accurately identify carcinoma of the pancreas, he insisted that though it was the custom to try many remedies, the knife was the only remedy that gave fruitful results!

postmortem examination, was noted to have a pancreas replete with calculi. Descriptions of pancreatic abnormalities from antiquity refer mostly to "scirrhous" disease, without any specific identification of pathology.

As early as at the beginning of the 19th century, Christopher Pemberton (1765–1822), Physician Extraordinary to George III (1738–1820), in 1807 was able to point out that severe emaciation frequently occurred in diseases of the pancreas. His text *A practical treatise on various diseases of the abdominal viscera* provided considerable detail in regard to abdominal disease and clearly noted some instances of pancreatic abnormalities. It is of interest that Pemberton, like the royal monarch, also suffered from a "pain" in the head. In Pemberton's case, however, it was tic douloureux (trigeminal neuralgia with severe, stabbing pain to one side of the face) and not the celebrated madness of George III. This medical problem proved insurmountable and despite being operated upon by Sir Astley Paston Cooper (1768–1841), Pemberton withdrew from his medical work in 1808, and died of apoplexy in 1822. Two years previously, in 1820, Kuntzmann had drawn attention to the relationship between fatty stools and diseases of the pancreas, a feature missed by Pemberton. This observation was however not

Despite the best efforts of Sylvius, Willis, and Highmore, the work of Brunner (1653–1727) in 1683, which demonstrated that dogs could survive without a pancreas, completely discouraged any subsequent interest in the pancreas as a potential site of disease. The Galenic scirrhous differentiation, based on the hardness of the tissue, in the absence of the microscope and histological sections, therefore persisted until the 19th century. Until this time, both experimental physiology and the basic disciplines of physics and chemistry were starting to develop into recognizable disciplines. Clinical medicine too was making progress. Giovanni Battista Morgagni's (1682–1771) *De causa et sedibus morborum* (*On the Seats and Causes of Disease*), which marked the beginning of the end of humoral pathology (the four humors theory of the Ancients), had appeared as early as 1761. After this publication, anatomists increasingly looked for diseases in particular parts of the body, and this led to the gradual systematic autopsy examination of deceased patients to identify disease/pancreas correlations.

These subtle observations marked the beginning of the clinical correlation of pancreatic disease and diabetes, but no specific relationship was recognized until 1788, when Thomas Cawley broadly alluded to such a disease entity. Cawley described a "free living young man" who had died of diabetes and emaciation, and at

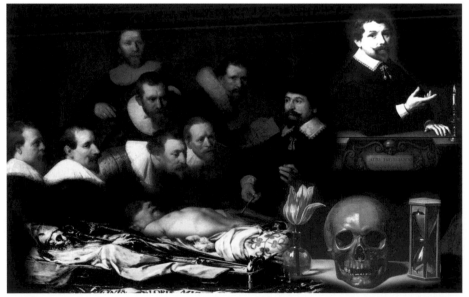

Nicolaas Tulp (1593–1674) portrayed in Rembrandt's 'Anatomy Lesson' demonstrating the flexors of the fingers. Tulp was both a fine surgeon and a politician of Amsterdam. As an anatomist, he believed that anatomy was the "very eye of medicine" and that a knowledge of the subject was a direct path to knowledge of God. His personal philosophy is adequately captured in a contemporary poem by the Neo-Latinist poet and professor at the Athenaeum Illustre in Amsterdam, Caspar Barlaeus (1584–1648): "On the place for anatomies which has recently been constructed at Amsterdam Evil men, who did harm when alive, do good after their deaths: Health seeks advantages from Death itself. Dumb integuments teach. Cuts of flesh, though dead, for that very reason forbid us to die. Here, while with artful hand slits the pallid limbs, speaks to us the eloquence of learned Tulp: 'Listener, learn yourself! And while you proceed through the parts, believe that, even in the smallest, God lies hid.'"

entirely novel, since Nicolaas Tulp (1593–1674) had reported two patients with such symptoms as early as 1652, and in fact one patient was reported to have eliminated large quantities of fat with stools for months. Unfortunately, Tulp also failed to make the connection to the pancreas and became better remembered for his principal role in identifying the ileocecal valve and his dramatic depiction in Rembrandt's great portrait.

PANCREATITIS

Tulp can also be credited with the description of a diffuse pancreatic abscess of pyemic origin. The identification of the etiology of pancreatitis has frustrated physicians since the very earliest observations of the entity. Initially, the pathological examination of the pancreas was the most defining focus in the diagnosis, with clinical assessment of the patient as the only available diagnostic tool for the physician. As early as 1788, Cawley became the first to suggest a link between lifestyle and pancreatic disease. His patient, "a 34-year-old man accustomed to free living and strong corporeal exertions in the pursuit of country living," was noted as having extensive pancreatic disease at autopsy. Twenty years later in 1804, Portal described a case of acute suppurative pancreatitis following an attack of gout in the feet, and Percival recorded a well-marked case of pancreatic abscess associated with jaundice in 1818.

Thereafter, Matthew Baillie (1761–1823), in a work entitled *Morbid Anatomy* (1833), identified a "hard pancreas with distinct lobules". This would now be considered an example of chronic pancreatitis. In the same work, Baillie indicated in a drawing a pancreas in which concretions were discovered in the ducts at post mortem, and demonstrated the associated pancreatic alterations. He also indicated the relationship of the bile and pancreatic ducts to the pathology in this specimen. The first reports of pancreatic calculi as curious manifestations of the disease date as far back as the work of de Graaf in 1667 and Morgagni in 1765. However, prior to 1883, such case reports were for the most part confined to the realm of fascinating observations noted at postmortem study. The relationship of stones and chronic pancreatitis was not specifically evident, and a liberal interpretation of stones as abnormal matter, and therefore likely to be the source of pain and disease (as found in kidney, salivary gland, and gallbladder pathology), was speculated upon.

One of the earliest reports of pancreatitis was by Edwin Klebs, who reported a case of hemorrhagic pancreatitis in 1870. This was followed by many scattered reports throughout the medical literature, without much focus towards a diagnosis before the patient's demise. Thereafter, Friedreich and Claasen in Germany were prominent in establishing the role of alcohol in pancreatitis and defined its clinical and pathological sequel in the 1880s.

Matthew Baillie, in his *Morbid Anatomy* (1833), identified what would now be considered an example of chronic pancreatitis – a "hard pancreas with distinct lobules". In addition, he demonstrated pancreatic concretions in the diseased organ and indicated the relationship of the bile and pancreatic ducts to the pathology. Despite Baillie's prescience, there has been little progress in the elucidation of either the etiology or therapy of pancreatitis. Despite its relative rarity and the usual benign course, in some instances the pancreas virtually implodes (*center*) and the consequent damage is dramatically amplified when proteolytic and lipolytic digestive enzymes are activated and begin to self-destruct both the organ and surrounding structures (*top: CT*). In severe cases, such pancreatitis can result in serious bleeding (hemorrhagic pancreatitis) (*top left*) as micro- and macrovascular structures undergo dissolution. Broadly speaking, the two forms of pancreatitis – acute and chronic – appear to have little in common except the ability to destroy the gland at different rates, with often fatal consequences. The acute form (*bottom left*) occurs suddenly and even though its onset may in some cases be subtle, the evolution of the process may result in life-threatening complications, although in the majority of patients (80%), recovery is complete. Chronic pancreatitis as identified by Baillie (*bottom and top right*) is usually the result of longstanding damage to the pancreas associated with alcohol ingestion and a suboptimal diet. In this variety of pancreatic disease, demise may take decades and is characterized by severe pain and the sequela of loss of both endocrine and exocrine pancreatic function. Suffice to say that little is known of the genesis and biological basis of pancreatitis, and the nosology of the disease process, even in the 21st century, is reflective of distant times when the nature of a disease was little more than a subject for guesswork, gesticulation, and wild conjecture.

THE SYMPTOMATOLOGY AND DIAGNOSIS OF DISEASES OF THE PANCREAS.[1]

BY REGINALD H. FITZ, M.D., BOSTON.[2]

THE consideration of the symptomatology and diagnosis of diseases of the pancreas may appropriately be introduced by referring to the memorable communication on this subject by Friedreich[3] nearly thirty years ago. According to this authority "a single symptom which may occur in diseases of the pancreas is pathognomonic, and the ... several does not always result in a ... Fatty stools, mellituria, ... with the characteristics of celiac ... a palpable tumor lead among the ... t useful in diagnosis;"

BY REGINALD H. FITZ, M.D.,
... OF PATHOLOGICAL ANATOMY IN HARVARD UNIVERSITY.

As the Shattuck Professor of Pathological Anatomy at Harvard University, Reginald H Fitz represented the ninth generation of the Fitz family in America and was descended from the original 1639 settlers of the Massachusetts Bay Colony. Named after the British hymnologist Reginald Heber, Fitz was educated at Harvard and thereafter spent two years in Europe, where he studied at hospitals in Paris, London, Glasgow, Vienna, and Berlin. As a student of Rudolf Virchow, he was fully aware of cellular pathology and on his return to Boston in 1870, introduced the use of the microscope for study at Harvard Medical School. Apart from his seminal contributions to appendicitis in 1886, in 1889 he produced a definitive work on pancreatitis and in so doing, assured himself of a place in the pantheon of gastrointestinal pathology.

Subsequently, Reginald H Fitz of Boston, who had studied with Claasen, defined the signs and symptoms of pancreatitis and categorized the disease in terms of its gangrenous, hemorrhagic, and suppurative forms. This assessment resulted in some prejudicial views, since cases described by pathologists represented advanced and fatal forms of pancreatitis. Thus, many early attempts at classification resulted in contradictions, as physicians and pathologists differed on the nature of the process and in addition lacked scientific data to address the question of etiology. Nevertheless, Fitz's reflections on the nature and causes of the disease, which were published in the *Boston Medical and Surgical Journal* of 1889, have remained little changed in the century since their initial proposal.

Eugene L Opie in 1901 further elucidated the pathogenesis of pancreatitis and proposed a "common channel" hypothesis, whereby acute pancreatitis was the aftermath of the flow of infected bile into the pancreatic duct through the common bile duct. He proposed that this clinical circumstance occurred when a gallstone became impacted in the ampulla of Vater and caused obstruction.

Sir William Osler (*top left*) is probably the best-known physician in the English-speaking world, and at the turn of the century, when Eugene L Opie (*center*) worked in pathology at the Johns Hopkins Hospital, Osler was known as the "most influential physician in history". Osler was trained in medicine at the University of Toronto and McGill (1872) and became the first Professor of Medicine at Johns Hopkins University in 1889. He was an expert in diagnosis of diseases of the heart, lungs, and blood, and wrote the textbook *The Principles and Practice of Medicine* in 1892, which was considered authoritative for more than 30 years. Opie entered this distinguished world in 1899 when he received his MD in the first graduating class of the medical school. While working as an instructor in the pathology department under Welch, Opie autopsied a 47-year-old man (*background*) who had admissions to Osler's service for jaundice and abdominal complaints. At autopsy, Opie was able to identify numerous gallstones (*bottom right*), including one stone that was wedged in the ampulla of Vater. Further examination of the pancreas led Opie to identify hemorrhage, necrosis, and some fibrosis. These findings allowed Opie to postulate a "common channel" between the biliary and pancreatic duct systems, which when impacted (by a stone) would lead to pancreatitis. This work was written up (*right*) as a case report and was supported by 37 similar cases from the literature.

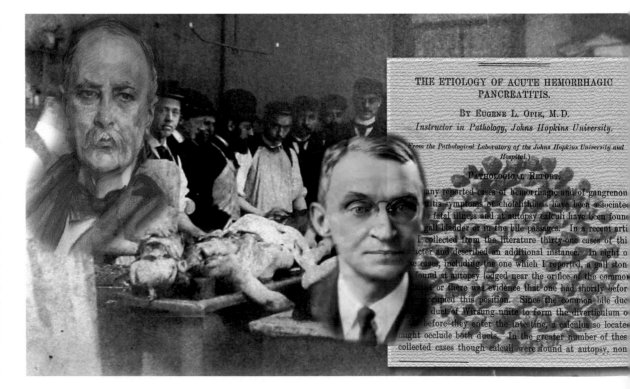

THE ETIOLOGY OF ACUTE HEMORRHAGIC PANCREATITIS.

BY EUGENE L. OPIE, M.D.
Instructor in Pathology, Johns Hopkins University.

(From the Pathological Laboratory of the Johns Hopkins University and Hospital.)

PATHOLOGICAL REPORT.

... many reported cases of hemorrhagic and of gangrenous ... titis symptoms of cholelithiasis have been associated ... fatal illness and at autopsy calculi have been found ... gall bladder or in the bile passages. In a recent arti ... I collected from the literature thirty-one cases of thi ... acter and described an additional instance. In eight o ... e cases, including the one which I reported, a gall ston ... found at autopsy lodged near the orifice of the commo ... or there was evidence that one had shortly befor ... occupied this position. Since the common bile duc ... duct of Wirsung unite to form the diverticulum o ... before they enter the intestine, a calculus so locate ... might occlude both ducts. In the greater number of thes ... collected cases though calculi were found at autopsy, non

SIR ARTHUR WILLIAM MAYO-ROBSON OF LEEDS

At the turn of the 19th century, Sir Arthur William Mayo-Robson (1853–1933), in keeping with contemporary intellectual practice of assigning all disease causality to bacteria, presumed the etiology of pancreatitis to be due to bacterial infection. However, the distinction between acute, sub-acute, and chronic was still controversial. Mayo-Robson was born on April 17, 1853, at Filey in Yorkshire, where his father John Bonnington Robson was a chemist, but only assumed the double-barreled surname in middle age. Mayo-Robson was educated at Wesley College, Sheffield, and entered the Leeds School of Medicine, where from 1870 onwards he provided ample demonstration of his intellectual gifts, becoming medallist in medicine, surgery, forensic medicine, midwifery, anatomy, physiology, practical chemistry, and materia medica. In addition, he won the Thorpe Scholarship in forensic medicine, the Hardwicke Prize for medicine, and the surgical clinical prize! In 1874, presumably having exhausted all further prize-winning opportunities, he qualified MRCS and was appointed Demonstrator of Anatomy at Leeds. In 1876, Mayo-Robson was promoted to the lectureship, took the Fellowship in 1879, and in 1882, was elected to the newly established office of Assistant Surgeon to the General Infirmary at Leeds, where he became Surgeon in 1884. Not content with the practice of clinical surgery alone, from 1886, he became a lecturer in pathology and a teacher of operative surgery from 1888. From 1890 to 1899, he was Professor of Surgery at the Yorkshire College, Victoria University, the forerunner of the University of Leeds. Lured by the greater possibilities of London and based on his surgical reputation (which at that time was substantial), he subsequently made an ill-determined move to the capital in 1902, which resulted both in the loss of his north country connection, as well as a degree of anonymity.

In 1908, Mayo-Robson joined the territorial force on its formation and went to France with a field ambulance in 1914, but was detached at the request of the French authorities to organize a hospital for them based on British principles. Thereafter, he served in Gallipoli and Egypt, where he attained the rank of Temporary Colonel, Army Medical Service, was twice mentioned in despatches, and was created a Companion of the Order of the Bath (military division) in 1916 and a Knight Commander of the Order of the British Empire in 1919 (he had already been knighted in 1908, and was made a Companion of the Royal Victorian Order in 1911). For his services to the French military,

he was also nominated a Chevalier in the French Legion d'Honneur in 1921! On his return home from Egypt, Mayo-Robson became a member of the consultative medical council at the War Office, and was appointed Consulting Surgeon to the King Edward VII Hospital at Windsor and to the Dreadnought Hospital at Greenwich. As a consequence of his Yorkshire youth, Mayo-Robson was also a keen sportsman and an excellent shot, and over a period of years visited Africa and other parts of the world for big game shooting. It is recorded that during one of his expeditions, when shooting buffalo near Nairobi, he was accidentally shot in both thighs by his gun carrier!

Initially devoted to gynecological surgery, Mayo-Robson soon enlarged his sphere of activity to include abdominal surgery, and was amongst the first to undertake experimental procedures such as nerve grafting. He was also responsible for notable advances in the surgery of the extremities and was widely recognized for his scrupulous surgical technique. Although Leeds was already the center of a famous surgical tradition, Mayo-Robson's presence and prescience raised it to a pre-eminence that was unrivalled outside of London. In 1902, he authored a book entitled *Diseases of the Pancreas and their Surgical Treatment* with his protégé and successor at Leeds, Sir Berkeley Moynihan. Thereafter, in 1907, his publication, *The Pancreas: Its Surgery and Pathology*

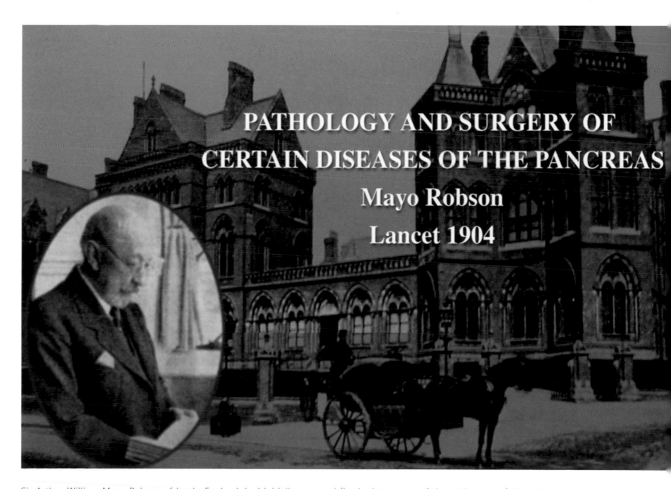

PATHOLOGY AND SURGERY OF CERTAIN DISEASES OF THE PANCREAS
Mayo Robson
Lancet 1904

Sir Arthur William Mayo-Robson of Leeds, England, had initially proposed (in the latter part of the 19th century) that diseases of the pancreas should be nonoperatively managed, but thereafter became the first surgeon to perform a trans-pancreatic stone extraction early in the 20th century.

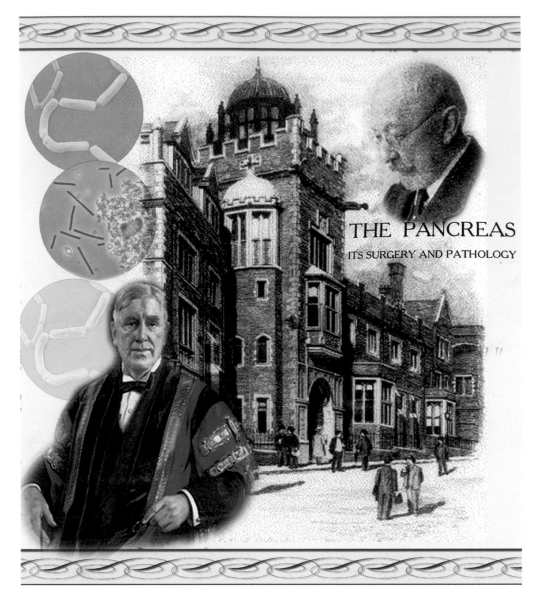

THE PANCREAS
ITS SURGERY AND PATHOLOGY

Sir Arthur William Mayo-Robson (*top right*), following a medal-filled medical studentship, became a surgeon at the General Infirmary at Leeds (*background*) in 1884. Initially devoted to gynecological surgery, he soon enlarged his sphere of action to include abdominal surgery, being amongst the first to undertake nerve grafting. He made notable advances in the surgery of the extremities and was noted for his scrupulous techniques. Leeds was already the center of a famous surgical tradition when Mayo-Robson joined the school, but he was able to raise it to pre-eminence by his forward looking practice. His publication *The Pancreas: Its Surgery and Pathology* (1907) was preceded by a similar book that he wrote with his protégé and successor at Leeds, Sir Berkeley Moynihan (*bottom left*), entitled *Diseases of the Pancreas and their Surgical Treatment* (1902). Each of these books was considered "the last word" at the time of their publication. At the Royal College of Surgeons, Mayo-Robson was three times a Hunterian Professor of Surgery, and his third lecture in 1904 was on 'The pathology and surgery of the pancreas'. In it he considered that bacterial infection may be a cause of pancreatitis. Bacterial etiology of disease was then peaking in medical circles. It is of interest that this idea resurfaced in the last decade of the 20th century, largely because of the rediscovery of *Helicobacter pylori* in peptic ulcer disease. Moynihan, who is most famous for his surgical "cures" of duodenal ulcers, stated: "As I look back dispassionately upon the growth of the science and art of surgery in the last fifty years, I can truthfully say that Mayo-Robson must rank among the very greatest surgeons of all time. At one period he was, I feel sure, indisputably the greatest surgeon in Europe."

fifty years, I can truthfully say that Mayo-Robson must rank among the very greatest surgeons of all time. At one period he was, I feel sure, indisputably the greatest surgeon in Europe." Few who operated with Mayo-Robson would have quibbled at this generous assessment and those who might have are themselves now long forgotten. Together, Mayo-Robson and Moynihan engendered for Leeds a surgical and medical reputation that has endured for more than a century, such that even today its physicians are regarded as primus inter pares in the farthest corners of the earth.

further adumbrated upon his wealth of experience in the management of pancreatic disease. Each of these texts was considered "the last word" on the subject at the time of their publication and they remained authoritative icons in the field for more than three decades after their publication. The Royal College of Surgeons, in recognition of his virtuoso skills, bestowed upon Mayo-Robson its highest honors, and he was on three occasions appointed Hunterian Professor of Surgery. In 1904, Mayo-Robson's third lecture, 'The pathology and surgery of the pancreas', addressed his belief that bacterial infection might be a cause of pancreatitis. Indeed, given the current vogue for attributing all disease to infection, this position was well in keeping with the dogma of the day. It is of interest that almost a century later, this idea once again resurfaced, largely due to the renaissance of *Helicobacter pylori* as a cause of peptic ulcer disease.

Moynihan, who was trained by Mayo-Robson and also succeeded him at Leeds, was renowned both as a surgeon and visionary, and achieved widespread fame for his surgical "cures" of duodenal ulcers that now may be safely managed by acid suppression and bacterial eradication with antibiotics. Of his teacher, Moynihan, with his customary elegance and graciousness, stated: "As I look back dispassionately upon the growth of the science and art of surgery in the last

Following Mayo-Robson's forays into the etiology of pancreatic diseases, E Archibald in 1919 experimentally demonstrated that spasm of the sphincter of Oddi increased biliary pressure and culminated in the development of acute pancreatitis. Although alcohol and gallstones remain the common denominator of the etiology of acute pancreatitis to this day, Rich and Duff in 1936 proposed that a combination of pathological vascular changes and local pancreatic enzyme damage was responsible for the pathogenesis. The diagnosis of acute pancreatitis, which had initially been purely clinical, was subsequently supported by the work of R Elman of St Louis, who in 1929 described the quantitative determination of blood amylase using a viscometer. Subsequent investigation has concluded that the cytokine cascade of acute pancreatitis may be a consequence of disorganized intracellular trafficking of the zymogen granules.

20th century conceptions of pancreatitis

In 1946, Comfort provided a significant analysis of the clinical entity of chronic pancreatitis and in so doing, produced the seminal manuscript on the subject that has remained the critical commentary on the disease for more than 50 years. Although there had been references to the relationship between alcohol and chronic pancreatitis, there were no clinical studies and proof remained anecdotal until Comfort described in detail the connection between alcohol abuse and chronic pancreatitis.

Comfort's study added considerable credibility to the much earlier description of the "drunkard's pancreas" by Friedrich in the 19th century. The criteria utilized by Comfort to characterize the diagnosis included recurrent attacks of abdominal pain, disturbances of acinar function, and alterations in endocrine function. During the last 50 years, despite the fact that much has been learned from studies of alcoholic pancreatitis, the definitive

mechanisms are for the most part obscure. The relative increase in the diagnosis of pancreatitis probably reflects a wide variety of factors, including increased awareness, greater diagnostic skill, and more sophisticated technology, as well as an increase in alcohol consumption. Considerable debate has centered round the question of whether pancreatic lithogenesis is a diagnostic criterion of chronic pancreatitis or whether it merely represents a correlatable epiphenomenon. Prior to the 20th century, pancreatic stones were thought of as exceedingly rare. Indeed, the correlation between the mere presence of pancreatic calculi and the diagnosis of chronic pancreatitis itself remains debated. Thus, in the condition of "senile pancreatitis" described by Amman, the relationship between the presence of idiopathic asymptomatic pancreatic calculi found in the elderly suggests that the chronicity and calculi may not necessarily occur pari passu. There is, however, little disagreement that pancreatic stones may obstruct the ducts and play a part in the development of pancreatic pain. This observation has resulted in efforts to remove stones either by medical dissolution (including HCl) or mechanical intervention. Thus lithotripsy, endoscopic sphincterotomy with or without stent placement, and a wide variety of ductal and pancreatic surgical techniques have been proposed to eliminate calculus disease of the pancreas.

In 1959, Zuideman labeled dietary factors as an additional etiological agent and proposed that the entity known as "tropical pancreatitis" in underdeveloped countries was associated with the standard low-protein, fat-deficient diet prevalent in such areas. Subsequent reports have suggested that the Cassava root (manioc) might be the agent implicated in tropical pancreatitis, but rigorous confirmation of this theory is still required. Despite considerable attention to the identification of the basis of chronic pancreatitis, approximately 30% of patients diagnosed with the disease are still regarded as idiopathic with no known evidence of any associated disease or inciting event. In the absence of minimal evidence for etiology, the identification of a mechanistic explanation of the disease process has been similarly frustrating. Various theories have been propounded to explain the pathology and include the necrosis-fibrosis concept of Kloppel, the obstruction theory of Sarles, the toxic metabolic hypothesis of Bordalo, and the oxidative stress hypothesis of Braganza.

In 1946, Comfort published a clinical paper that provided the first coherent assessment of the nebulous entity of chronic pancreatitis.

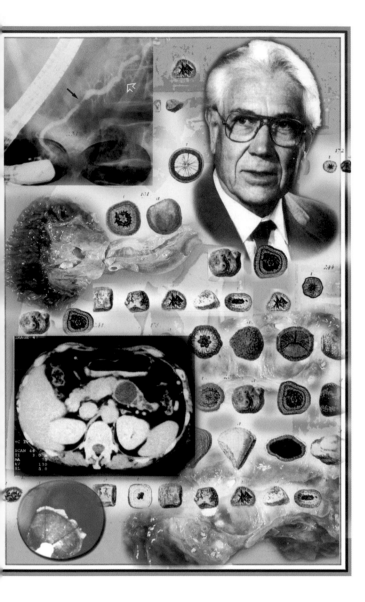

In the past, pancreatic calculi have only been diagnosed at autopsy or during serendipitous surgery of the organ. The ability to satisfactorily image the pancreas and identify calculi has been useful to clinicians, but has added little to the understanding of the nature of the disease process responsible for these pathological findings. Indeed, pancreatic calculi are manifestations of a dying pancreas and little more than tombstones commemorating the demise of functional elements of the gland, despite the influential work of Sarles (*top right*). Nevertheless, the ability to image the pancreas and define the site of the stones by ERCP (*bottom left*) or by CAT scan (*left: an enlarged stone-filled pancreas*) has provided some insight into the anatomical location of disease. Although considerable enthusiasm exists amongst some physicians to remove pancreatic calculi either endoscopically or by open surgery, there is little evidence that such intervention either provides symptomatic relief or alters the course of the disease process. Nevertheless, "cutting for stone" has a long history in medicine, and old traditions die hard among the guild of the barber-surgeons.

the Marseilles (morphological criteria) and Cambridge (imagery of the ductal system) classifications, but neither has adequately resolved the dilemma. In 1976, Ransom described the prospective evaluation of multiple clinical, biochemical, and hematological indices in the prediction of severity of acute pancreatitis (Ransom score). The acute physiological assessment of chronic health evaluation (APACHE) II score, although initially devised as a system for evaluating the expected outcome in patients requiring intensive care, has been successfully used in patients with acute pancreatitis (1985), while a modified version of the Ransom system was later successfully used by the Glasgow group of Clement Imrie (1989). Overall, however, the definition and clinical pictures of both acute and chronic pancreatitis intertwine, and separation often remains obscure. Since no definitive treatment exists, the evolution of therapy has perforce been directed at dealing with the symptomatic manifestations of the disease.

The evolution of management

The definition of chronic pancreatitis and its classification has changed with the advance of biochemical and scientific technology over the last 50 years. The natural history of chronic pancreatitis, with the development of endocrine and exocrine insufficiency, leading to diabetes and steatorrhea, provides further supportive clinical evidence. There exist no pathognomonic criteria for the disease, but rather a constellation of symptoms and signs corroborated with radiographic, ERCP, and biochemical data.

Despite numerous attempts, no particular classification system has proved entirely satisfactory and the field of chronic pancreatitis has been troubled in the area of categorization. Recent attempts include

In this 1999 paper published in the *Surgical Clinics of North America*, Clement Imrie (*top left*) and CJ McKay explored the then currently available methods for grading the severity of pancreatitis. In this useful adjunct to the literature, the authors concluded that despite the utility of a number of systems (particularly the APACHE II score, which provided the best accuracy at an early stage in illness), no one system had sufficient predictive power to facilitate clinical decision making.

Medical treatment

Pain

The first and predominant treatment regime of pancreatitis was pain control, although in the early part of the 20th century, the lack of accurate diagnosis often resulted in treatment delay. For the most part, measures employed included high-dosage opiates, especially morphine. Other strategies included the use of calomel to lessen distention and as a potential intestinal antiseptic. Overall, the extent of the medical treatment in the early part of the 20th century included little more than observation, although in dire circumstances such as shock, hot saline enemas were advocated. The dominant therapy however relied upon pain management, thus the introduction of intravenous agents greatly enhanced the ability to ameliorate acute discomfort. Orr in 1950 established the efficacy of the epidural technique and its application to the management of pancreatic pain proved quite efficacious. Although pain relief was predominantly a pharmacotherapeutic strategy, in 1946, Fontaine achieved some moderate success by resection of splanchnic nerves to relieve the pain associated with chronic pancreatitis and as a result, a wide variety of neural denervations enjoyed some vogue.

Exocrine deficiency

Aside from pain, complaints of chronic diarrhea and fatty stools proved to be issues of considerable discomfort to individuals with chronic pancreatitis. Complaints varied from simple "unrest in the abdomen" to major and even uncontrollable attacks of diarrhea. In 1907, Mayo-Robson, in chapter 10 of his seminal surgical treatise on the pancreas *The Pancreas: Its Surgery and Pathology*, opined that the most important pancreatic digestive disturbances arose from "absence or diminution of its secretion". Furthermore, he stated that the digestive disturbances likely to result from this could be inferred from an understanding of its physiological functions. Thus, since the pancreas produced the most important of all the digestive fluids and exerted an action upon each of the three principal classes of food material, any interference with its activities could be predicted to lead to defective assimilation of fats, proteids, and carbohydrates, and an examination of the feces should show "that an abnormally high proportion of the food is passed in an undigested state". Presumably when he wrote the last sentence, Mayo-Robson had recalled the pioneering work of the Dutchman Joseph Alexander Fles (1819–1905) from Breda. Fles, in 1868, had treated a diabetic patient with oral extracts of calf pancreas and identified a decrease in stool fat and protein, as well as a marked increase in the patient's appetite. A year later, John Langdon-Down, FRCP (1828–1896), Lecturer in Materia Medica and Therapeutics at the London Hospital, treated a patient with "pancreatin" and achieved similar results. Langdon Down would later become better known for his efforts at disease classification undertaken at the Royal Earlswood Asylum in Surrey – he described Monglian idiocy (later renamed Down's syndrome) in some of the patients.

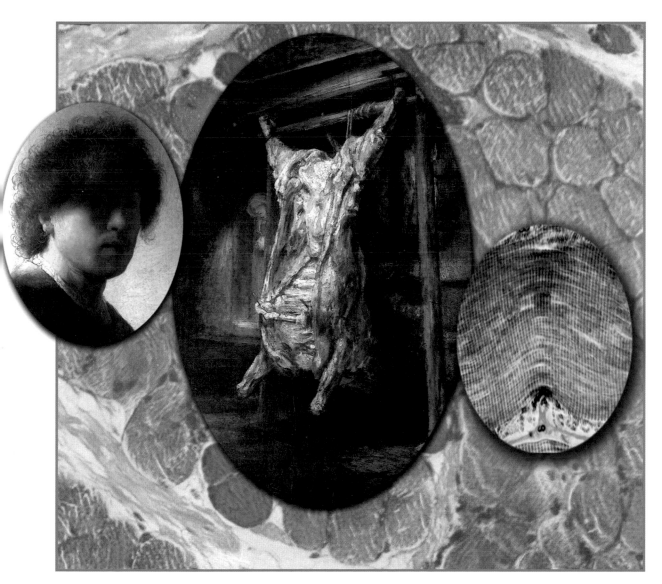

In 1859, the Dutchman Joseph Alexander Fles treated a diabetic patient by the oral administration of calf pancreatic extract and immediately noted a decrease in the amount of muscle fibers (*background*) in the feces of the patient. Withdrawal of the extract resulted in a return of the fibers in the fecal waste. The diet of Dutch hospital patients consisted largely of protein (meat, often beef) extract. Rembrandt, a countryman of Fles, although from Leiden and not Breda, painted a remarkable still life in 1655, 'The Slaughtered Ox' (*center*). Rembrandt aspired to the ethos that truth was the ultimate beauty and like Fles, often lavished his sympathetic art on outcasts, the sick, the miserable, and even the deformed. In the 1629 self-portrait (*left*) at the age of 23, the look is bold and unrepentant in expression, a picture of a romantic as well as a realist. However, contemporary views of his work, as with the response of the medical community to Fles' pioneering work, were lukewarm.

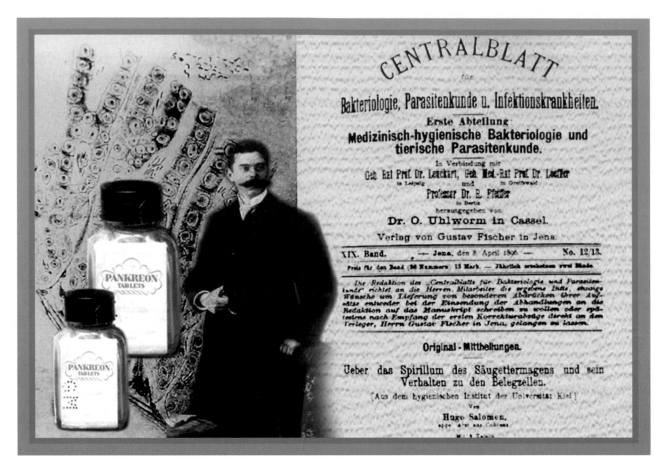

Hugo Salomon (*center*) in 1896 reported spirochetes in the gastric mucosal of numerous animals, but was unable to identify them in man. After his gastric peregrination, he moved into the world of digestive metabolism and in 1900, while working at Carl von Noorden's laboratory, initially tried treating patients suffering from "pancreatogenic" fatty stools with raw pancreas in wafers. Presumably, this was regarded by some as a mere extension of steak tartare, while others simply accepted it as another example of the obscure art of the physician. Salomon was more successful in 1901 when he prescribed non-acid resistant pancreatin (tablets) (*left*) and noted not only greater patient acceptance, but also considerable therapeutic efficacy.

many years. The early institution of appropriate dietary and pharmacotherapeutic (insulin) measures thus became an important prophylactic strategy in stabilizing the adverse metabolic events noted during the evolution of chronic pancreatitis.

The limitations of surgical strategies

The development of a rationale for surgical intervention in chronic pancreatitis has been hindered by numerous difficulties. Firstly, there was little appreciation of pancreatic disease itself. Secondly, the inflammatory condition of acute pancreatitis was often so violent and rapidly terminal that little explicit surgical therapy other than simple exploration, incision, and drainage was ever possible. The notion that various gradations of this disease process were related or even amenable to specific therapy was to a large extent obviated by the technical difficulties encountered in operating upon the pancreas itself. Nevertheless, when faced with the relentless progress of the disease and the ravages inflicted by pain, narcotics, and organ dysfunction, physicians have been driven to seek a therapeutic, albeit symptomatic, intervention. Thus, despite the lack of any discernible cause for chronic pancreatitis, since the latter part of the 19th century, surgeons have applied themselves vigorously and in diverse fashions to the treatment of the disease. The solutions seemed initially obvious. Thus a damaged and dysfunctional gland causing pain might be best removed. Needless to say, the technical aspects of this endeavor soon resulted in reconsideration of this concept. Biliary or pancreatic calculi capable of causing both pain and obstruction should be extracted, but this obvious remedy appeared to be relatively ineffective. The obvious target of a sphincter in "spasm" or fibrosed was attractive as a solution, but its ablation once again appeared to effect little relief. The observation of a massively dilated duct system suggested that drainage would bring relief, but neither disease amelioration nor pain abeyance appeared either to be predictable or occur with any acceptable regularity. Indeed, for the most part, the surgery of chronic pancreatitis has today come to rest in the hands of stalwarts determined to do what best they can, fully aware of the absolute limitations of their procedures, and those who confine their activities to the elimination of pain effected by means of nerve injection or ablation.

Thirty years later, in 1902, Hugo Salomon effectively used a more defined role of diet and "fresh pancreas" with moderate success. This substitution of exocrine production, or organotherapy, was the precursor of later efforts to "cool" the pancreas to both alleviate pain and restore exocrine function. Although the oral supplementation of zymogens has proved to be highly beneficial in the symptomatic management of disordered digestion, rigorous data regarding the effects of "pancreatic cooling" has not been forthcoming. Similarly, the usage of subcutaneous octreotide (an analog of somatostatin) that inhibited acinar secretory activity has been without significant benefit in decreasing the progress of the disease, although some amelioration of pain has been claimed.

Endocrine deficiency

The progressive pancreatic fibrosis associated with the inexorable progress of chronic pancreatitis culminates in diabetes in approximately 15% of patients. Although the overt manifestations of diabetes are not usually evident until the destruction of approximately 90% of the gland, subtle alterations in glucose homeostasis may predate such events by

The general advances in surgery of the late 19th and early 20th century heralded the introduction and refinement of surgical treatment for pancreatic disease, but as might have been predicted, there were misadventures. Intervention in pancreatic disease was regarded as extremely dangerous, and even the most experienced of the gastrointestinal surgeons, such as Mayo-Robson of Leeds, advocated the surgical approach of "waiting until collapse of the patient with presumed pancreatitis" before surgery was undertaken. In fact, Mayo-Robson – an arbiter on such matters – maintained that "until collapse no surgery [was] justifiable". Out of therapeutic strategies of this type would grow the justifiably cynical medical comments of men such as Bernard Naunyn, who described such surgery as little more than an autopsy *in vivo!* The lack of technical expertise and knowledge limited the ensuing surgery to a mere evacuation of the septic material, and given the non-availability of antibiotics and the primitive state of knowledge of fluid and electrolyte balance, the outcome was invariably fatal. Indeed, the early 20th century tenet of Theodor Kocher of Bern seemed most applicable when directed to the subject of pancreatic surgery: "A surgeon is a doctor who can operate and knows when not to."

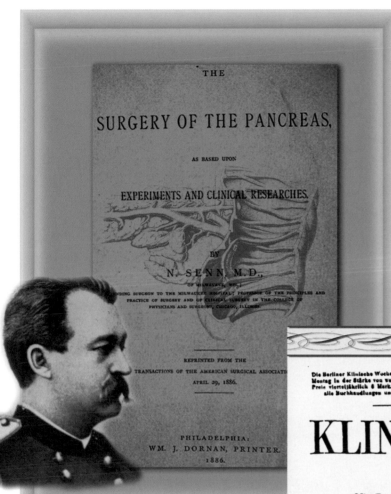

Nicholas Senn of Chicago was an early surgical pioneer of experimental pancreatic surgery. His evaluation of current work in the field led him to a pessimistic conclusion regarding the outcome of surgery on the pancreas. As a result, he cautioned his colleagues regarding the utility of surgery for pancreatic disease.

Aware of the problems of pancreatic disease, Nicholas Senn in 1886 commented in one of his earliest papers, 'The surgery of the pancreas, as based upon experiments and clinical research', on what he recognized as a vexatious problem. Senn demonstrated that experimental extirpation of the pancreas in animals was "invariably followed by death," although prior separate experiments by both Brunner and Meiring had not drawn so absolute a conclusion. Nevertheless, it was evident to most surgeons of any experience that the vast majority of pancreatic surgery (whether major or minor) resulted in fatal consequences.

On July 15, 1882, Carl Langenbuch (*bottom right*) operated upon a 43-year-old accountant who for 16 years had suffered so badly from biliary colic that he had become a morphine addict. After five days of preliminary enemas, Langenbuch removed the gallbladder without difficulty and noted the presence of two cholesterol stones. One day after the surgery, the patient had no fever or pain and smoked a cigar. He was allowed to walk on the 12th day, and after six weeks, was discharged from the hospital. The lengthy hospital stay reflected the current belief that removal of the gallbladder was incompatible with life!

Sphincterotomy

As early as 1884, Carl Langenbuch of Berlin proposed that biliary disease was related to sphincter stenosis and actually proposed division of the muscle fibers as a method of treatment.

In 1901, Opie described the common channel theory as a mechanism of pancreatitis secondary to bile reflux and in so doing, was the first to provide a rationale linking biliary disease to pancreatic pathology. Archibald provided the critical experiments that established a definitive link between the resistance of the sphincter and pancreatitis in 1913. Proof of concept was demonstrated by application of the theory when sphincteric ablation by Archibald of a patient with recurrent pancreatitis was reported to have successfully relieved the symptoms. An extrapolation of this concept led to the notion that long-standing sphincter dysfunction (stenosis) might be an etiological factor (reflux of bile into the pancreas) in the development of chronic pancreatitis and that the condition could be ameliorated by sphincterotomy. Support for this notion was provided by the work of Henry Doubilet and Ralph Colp, who in 1935, undertook a series of studies, which confirmed the theories of Archibald.

Although the classic initial sphincterotomy was credited to Archibald in 1919, the most active proponents of this concept were Doubilet and John H Mulholland, who pursued the subject over the course of many years. In 1956, they published the 'Eight Year Study of Pancreatitis and Sphincterotomy'. In addition to performing a sphincterotomy, they mandated the surgical removal of the gallbladder due to alteration of dynamics of the biliary tree. Unfortunately, the efficacy of sphincterotomy did not live up to these miraculous claims. A further diversion on the sphincterotomy odyssey was based upon a fanciful notion that sphincter spasm reflected the effects of acid from the stomach. Thus, removal of acid by gastrectomy would decrease secretory function of the pancreas, diminish spasm, and relieve pain. This theory accorded well with the then current ill-conceived understanding of the basis of chronic pancreatitis, and Colp thus became a proponent of gastrectomy as a means of treating pancreatic disease of the "chronic pancreatitic type". The introduction of endoscopic retrograde cholangiopancreatography in 1968 by a surgeon, McCune, failed to excite initial interest in chronic pancreatic disease, but subsequent advances in the development of sphincterotomy by M Claasen and K Kawai led to a further re-examination of the clinical efficacy of sphincterotomy, first reporting on this approach in 1974. This technique became rapidly popular for the management of retained or recurrent bile duct stones, especially in elderly or frail patients judged to be poor candidates for a surgical approach. Peter Cotton was an early adept in the application of this novel modality to the treatment of pancreatitis,

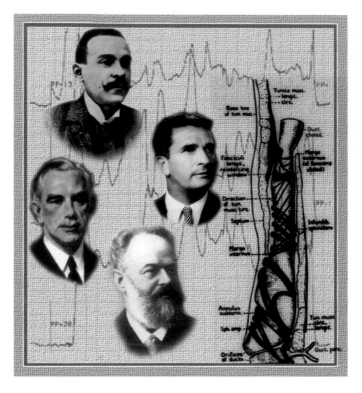

At the turn of the 19th century, Rugerro Oddi (*top left*), a fourth-year medical student in Perugia, Italy, described the choledochal sphincter (*right*), accurately defined its role in the regulation of bile flow, delineated its pressure modulatory effects, and drew attention to its potentially important role in the digestive process (1887). Five years prior to this seminal work, Carl Langenbuch (*bottom*), on July 15, 1882, successfully operated upon a 43-year-old accountant who had suffered from biliary colic for 16 years. In the fourth decade of the 20th century, Ralph Colp (*left*) and Henry Doubilet (*center*) examined the effect of the infusion of diverse substances on pressure in the common bile duct using a kymograph (*background*). They noted the immediate, sustained high pressure resulting from the administration of morphine. This laid the basis for the avoidance of its usage in pancreatitis. The demonstration of the nature of sphincteric resistance by Colp and Doubilet led to the conclusion that it must be of relevance to pancreatic (as well as biliary) disease in humans.

M Claasen (*right*) and K Kawai (*center*) in 1973 independently developed endoscopic papillotomy in Osaka and Munich, respectively. Their contributions were pivotal in facilitating diagnostic and therapeutic access to the biliary and pancreatic ductular system. Thus, once the papilla could reliably be cannulated for diagnostic purposes, a wide variety of devices were implemented to broaden the therapeutic horizon. The sphincters of Oddi and Boyden were breached by papillotomes, balloons, baskets, stents, and coils as the new generation of endoscopists led by Peter Cotton (*left*) and instrument-makers colluded to transluminally supplant the hepatobiliary surgeon. Despite the widespread application of this technique, which has effectively removed sphincterotomy from the armamentarium of the gastrointestinal surgeon, consensus on how these techniques are evaluated remain difficult but necessary (*top right*).

culminating not only in the relief of putative obstruction by papillotomy but also the introduction of stents and even the extraction of calculi, which were deemed to play a role in obstruction and pain.

The extraction of pancreatic calculi

In 1891, A Pearce Gould was the first to remove pancreatic calculi from the duct of Wirsüng. Almost a decade later, in 1902, the first diagnosis and transduodenal surgical removal was undertaken by Moynihan and in 1908, Mayo-Robson performed the first transpancreatic stone extraction. For the most part, such surgical expeditions were random occurrences and not part of a recognizable management strategy. Indeed, the entity of chronic pancreatitis was barely recognized at that time. A more interesting anecdote was provided by the interesting case of a baroness with an epigastric abscess, which after surgical drainage by Capparelli, resulted in the development of a pancreatic fistula that produced hundreds of stones, as observed over the subsequent six-year period.

Ductal drainage

After the failure of sphincterotomy to adequately improve the condition of chronic pancreatitis, it was proposed that the problem might lie with the inability of the former procedure to adequately decompress and allow drainage of a damaged and or dilated distal ductal system.

This inadequacy of sphincterotomy was accepted by many surgeons, who thereupon embarked upon the development of strategies designed to adequately address the presumed distal component of the disease. In 1909, Robert C Coffey reported the effects of a variety of experimental techniques utilizing pancreaticoenterostomy and established the possibility of pancreatectomy and pancreatic anastomosis as a viable procedure. A report in 1921 by Walter Ellis Sistrunk was deemed important, since it claimed that the successful achievement of a direct drainage procedure on the "pancreas proper" without complication had resulted in an improvement in the diabetic condition. In 1954, Merlin K Duval and Robert M Zollinger separately and almost simultaneously published their innovative descriptions of experience using a caudal pancreaticojejunostomy. Duval stated that he did not accept Opie's common channel theory as *sine qua non* of pancreatitis and claimed that current information confirmed the presence of a bidirectional flow of pancreatic juice. Driven by this reasoning, Duval (1954) proposed and implemented the procedure of caudal pancreaticojejunostomy drainage as an alternative treatment for chronic pancreatitis. In his published experience, he gracefully acknowledged that the final result would require the "tincture of time" before definitive conclusions could be drawn.

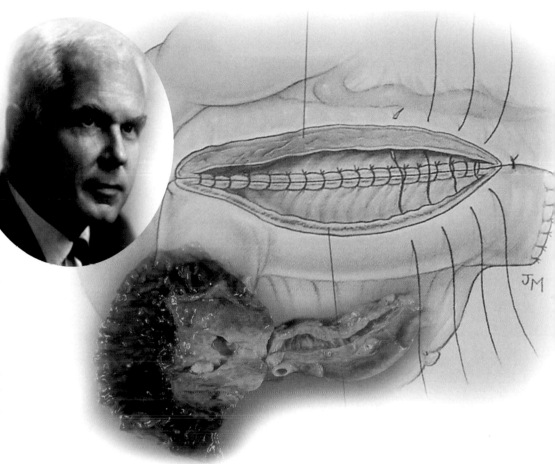

Merlin K Duval (*left*) described an innovative technique for the procedure of caudal pancreaticojejunostomy. He proposed that this procedure would not only decompress the gland, but in addition, obviate the deleterious effects of pancreatic calculi (*bottom*).

Robert C Coffey of Portland, Oregon, proposed that chronic pancreatitis could be treated by pancreatoenterostomy for drainage of the duct and pancreatic resection of irreversibly damaged components of the gland.

Charles Puestow (*left*) devised the procedure of lateral pancreaticojejunostomy as a surgical treatment for "dilated duct chronic pancreatitis" in 1958.

In 1958, Charles Puestow proposed an extension of the efficacy of drainage by opening the dilated duct of Wirsüng lengthwise (filleting) and anastomosing the filleted duct to a loop of jejunum that had been similarly treated. This mechanical arrangement was proposed as beneficial, since each ductal branch was now able to drain directly into a new, widely patent jejunal lumen, rather than a single narrow distal anastomosis.

Biliary

Despite the conclusion of the majority that a pancreatic drainage problem was the crux of the issue in chronic pancreatitis, some surgeons clung steadfastly to the concept of biliary tract disease as the modus operandi in chronic pancreatitis. A body of literature therefore accumulated during the mid-20th century as attempts at relief were directed at the purported biliary component. Thus cholecystostomy, cholecystectomy, common bile duct exploration, bile duct drainage, and sphincterotomy continued to be explored as avenues through which the disease could be dealt with.

Excisional surgery

Since the progress in the surgery of pancreatic carcinoma had resulted in a drastic reduction in morbidity and mortality, it was soon accepted that an "excisional cure" for a malignant disease might have considerable merit if applied to even a "benign disease" such as chronic pancreatitis. Thus, in 1946, OT Clagget performed a total pancreatectomy for chronic pancreatitis, and in so doing, became the first of a long line of surgeons who would undertake extensive and radical surgery for this "benign" condition. Unfortunately, the complications of the procedure and the severe metabolic

consequences for the most part persuaded the majority that this course was less than effective and the procedure did not gain widespread acceptance. A further problem noted was that even in those who survived the operation and could come to terms with the disastrous metabolic sequelae, "phantom pain" still remained a major issue. Indeed, the concept of a diabetic with no exocrine pancreatic function and dependent upon narcotics for pain relief proved to be a daunting specter for even the most hardened pancreatic surgeon.

In 1965, William J Fry and Charles G Child realized that the superfluity of surgical operations for the cure of pancreatitis was a result of the lack of an ideal treatment. Seeking to ameliorate this state of affairs, they proposed an alternative to complete resection and reported the results following a 95% distal pancreatectomy. The rationale for their procedure was well conceived and addressed many of the concerns raised by previous attempts to derive a solution for the surgical management of chronic pancreatitis. They proposed a procedure that would encompass the strong points of the previous excisional techniques, yet obviate the disadvantages.

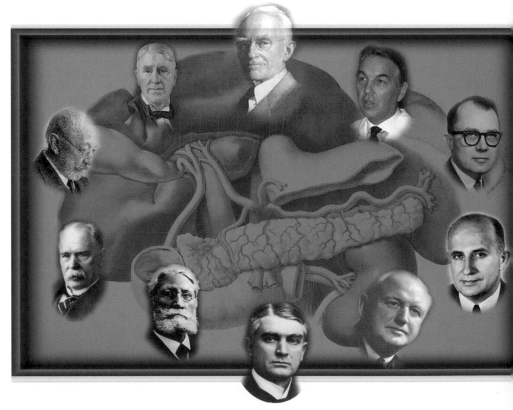

Modern pancreatic surgery to a large extent evolved from the work of Allen Whipple (*top center*), who successfully performed major resections, initially as two- and subsequently as one-stage resections. This could not, however, have been accomplished without the foundation provided by the writings and abdominal surgical techniques of (*counterclockwise from top left*) Sir Berkeley Moynihan and Sir Arthur William Mayo-Robson at the end of the 19th century. Other major contributors to the evolution of pancreatic surgery included the work of Trendelenburg, who excised a tumor of the pancreas in 1882; Louis Theodore Courvoisier, who pioneered much of the early surgery of the gallbladder and biliary system; William James Mayo, who established the basis of visceral and abdominal surgery at the Mayo Clinic and revolutionized American medicine; Roscoe R Graham, who removed the first insulinoma in 1929; and Robert M Zollinger, who described the Zollinger-Ellison syndrome and advanced pancreatic endocrine surgery. Joseph Fortner introduced regional pancreatectomy, and more recently (1985), Hans G Beger devised a head-sparing technique of pancreatic resection and proposed that this might replace the Whipple procedure.

The operation (95% distal pancreatectomy) entailed removal of the spleen, the uncinate process, and the body and the tail of the pancreas (the majority of the diseased tissue), and was designed to be both technically easier, reduce postoperative complications, and have a higher success rate. Regrettably, this surgery also failed to absolutely attain its objectives and provided a further reminder that the surgical therapy for chronic pancreatitis remained an enigma. Although Allen Whipple's original two-stage pancreatico-duodenectomy spared the pylorus, he subsequently revised this and included removal of the distal stomach and entire duodenum in the one-stage procedure. A significant portion of these patients developed jejunal ulceration. Given the limited life expectancy of a patient with pancreatic carcinoma, this was acceptable, but in the more chronic condition of pancreatitis, the issues of mucosal ulceration were significant in a population of this type. However, W Traverso questioned the rationale of not preserving the pylorus for a benign condition and in 1978, applied this technique of preservation of the pylorus to patients with chronic pancreatitis, with acceptable results.

Another refinement of the pancreaticoduodenectomy – the duodenum-preserving resection of the head of the pancreas (DPRHP) – was proposed by Hans G Beger in 1985. Beger, having presciently noted the distinct nature of the discrete inflammatory mass in the head of the pancreas in some patients, devised a technique specifically designed to deal with this apparent subset of patients with chronic pancreatitis. It is of interest that this group of patients had been emphasized as early as 1925 by Mallet-Guy; however, no surgical refinements resulted from his astute observations until the advent of Beger. The proposed surgical goal of this limited resection was relief of pain and decrease of the local complications due to the inflammation, as well as avoidance of the dramatic effects of exocrine and endocrine dysfunction that accompanied massive resection. Beger in fact questioned that this might well represent a separate disease within the broad spectrum of chronic pancreatitis. Dissatisfied with the results of available surgery, Frey proposed a further modification and introduced the combination of local head resection (LRH) of the pancreas with a lateral pancreaticojejunostomy. This operation was designed for a specific subset of patients that had both discrete pancreatic head disease and multiple irregular segments of the pancreatic duct, and initially appeared to have some advantage.

PANCREATIC NEOPLASIA

Given the fact that initial descriptions of pancreatic pathology all fell under the generic heading of scirrhous, it has been difficult to separate early descriptions of what may have been chronic pancreatitis from patients with cancer. It is probable that Morgagni was the first to recognize the condition, although he noted that Theophile Bonet in 1679 had previously described five cases in his text *Sepulchretum*. In his usual impeccably detailed fashion, Morgagni described a variety of autopsy findings that were consistent with a pancreatic neoplasm. These included a patient with jaundice due to obstruction of the common bile duct "as if a ligature had been made upon it... this contraction seemed to have

been brought by a scirrhous and even cancerous tumor of the neighboring pancreas." Despite the recognition of cancer as an entity in other organs, prior to the 18th century some physicians were of the belief that the pancreas did not develop cancer. This confusion was further amplified by the centuries' old difficulty in differentiating between the sequelae of chronic pancreatitis and cancer of the pancreas itself. Thus, Mondiere in the late 18th century commented on patients whom he considered to have perished of cancer of the pancreas, although these were not proven. In 1835, Bigsby was able to collect 28 cases of pancreatic cancer from the literature, although once again the validity of the diagnosis had not been established in all. In 1858, Jacob M Da Costa of Philadelphia provided the records of 35 autopsies of what he claimed to be pancreatic carcinoma, but was only able to provide a microscopic diagnosis of an adenocarcinoma in one. By the end of the 19th century, Bard and Pick had distinguished between ductal and acinar cell cancers as well as noting the possibility that the islet cells themselves might be the source of neoplasia. Such pathological distinctions were, however, not of direct clinical relevance, given the absence of an understanding of the concept of hormones and the possibility of lesions producing symptoms other than those referable to mass effect.

Jacob M Da Costa (1833–1900) of Philadelphia was an accomplished pupil of Trousseau. In 1858, he assembled the first American autopsy series of pancreatic carcinoma and in 1864, wrote a definitive treatise on diagnosis.

Thus, by the end of the 19th century, the clinical signs and symptoms of cancer of the head of the pancreas were well known and a number of cases had also been verified by histological examination. In 1907, Mayo-Robson provided a good appreciation of the overall status of pancreatic disease at the beginning of the 20th century in his book *The Pancreas: Its Surgery and Pathology*, which summarized the current state of knowledge. It is of interest that he noted: "There are as yet many points on which observers are not agreed, and there are questions which still call for elucidation, but the enormous literature of today as compared with that prior to 1886, when Professor Senn of Chicago published his valuable experimental work on the pancreas, shows the great advances that have been, and are being, made in the subject." In addition, he noted: "One of the most important practical results that has followed from the modern observations on the pancreas is the recognition of the very close similarity of the symptoms of cancer and chronic pancreatitis in the head of the gland!" An examination of the postmortem records from Guy's Hospital over a 13-year period (1884–1897) by H White identified that in 6,708 autopsy reports, the pancreas was recognized by the "morbid anatomists" as diseased or injured in 142 (2.1%) of cases. White's findings are included in the table (*below*).

Finding	Number of patients	Percentage
Primary and secondary malignancies	55	38.7
Cirrhosis/atrophy	45	31.7
Fatty changes	9	6.3
Hemorrhage	3	2.1
Calculi	3	2.1
Pancreatic cysts	1	0.7
Hydatid cysts	1	0.7
Suppuration	3	2.1
Tuberculosis	4	2.8
Miscellaneous (not identified)	18	12.7

Pancreatic pathology, Guy's Hospital autopsy reports (1884–1897).

The high prevalence of pancreatic cancers as well as the changes associated with pancreatitis (more than 80% of all cases) is clearly evident.

In 1882, Trendelenburg was probably the first to successfully excise a solid tumor of the pancreas, which was subsequently diagnosed as a spindle cell carcinoma. Unfortunately, this patient died shortly after discharge. In 1883, Carl Gussenbauer, a pupil of Christian Albert Billroth, became the first to diagnose a pancreatic cyst preoperatively and treat it successfully by marsupialization, although Bazeman (1882) had in fact resected a pancreatic cyst under the impression that it was ovarian in origin. In 1887, Kappeler described the first cholecystojejunostomy performed as a palliative procedure

for cancer of the pancreas in a patient who survived 14-and-a-half months. In 1894, Biondi removed a tumor that arose from the head of the pancreas and although a bilious and pancreatic fistula developed, it healed in 25 days and the patient was reported well 18 months after surgery.

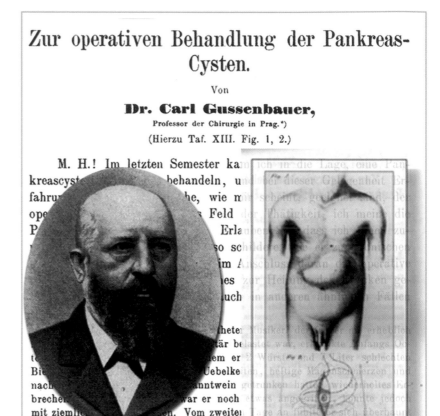

Carl Gussenbauer, a former pupil of Christian Albert Billroth, was the first to describe a successful technique for the management of pancreatic pseudocysts.

In 1893, Menier published an extensive review of pancreatic diseases, including solid tumors, cysts, and pancreatitis, and proposed that many of them would be amenable to surgical therapy. Spurred on by such exhortations, Codivilla in 1898 performed a block excision of the major part of the duodenum and the head of the pancreas for carcinoma of the pancreas. The pylorus was closed, the termination of the duodenum invaginated, and the transected common duct ligated. A Roux-en-Y gastroenterostomy was performed and a "button" cholecystenterostomy constructed for biliary drainage. Unfortunately, the patient died after 24 days and the autopsy revealed disseminated metastases.

The first successful removal of the cancer of the ampulla, with excision of a segment of duodenum and a portion of the pancreas around the ampulla, was undertaken by William S Halsted in 1898. The pancreatic and common duct

William S Halsted (*top right*) of Johns Hopkins Hospital, in 1898 resected the first carcinoma of the "duodenal papilla and diverticulum Vateri" and in so doing, demonstrated that pancreatic surgery was a feasible albeit risky proposition. This, combined with the latter work in 1935 of Allen Whipple, who undertook a radical pancreatic excisional surgery, laid the groundwork for modern pancreatic surgery.

were implanted into the repaired line of incision of the duodenum, but stenosis of the common duct developed after three months and the patient died six months later. Autopsy revealed recurrent carcinoma in the head of the pancreas and the duodenum. In the next decade, a number of surgeons, including Kehr, Coffey, Sauve, and Desjardins, proposed a variety of major operations to remove the head of the pancreas and the duodenum. While some of these were performed in one stage and others in two stages, all were associated with considerable mortality and a substantial morbidity.

In 1912, W Kausch was the first to carry out a successful partial pancreaticoduodenectomy in two stages. He implanted the stump of the resected pancreas at the distal end of the resected duodenum and the patient survived nine months before developing acute cholangitis and dying. In 1914, G Hirschel performed a one-stage partial pancreaticoduodenectomy for an ampullary carcinoma and connected the common bile duct to the duodenum by means of a rubber tube. Although the jaundice was ameliorated, the patient only survived a year. In 1922, O Tetoni reported a successful partial pancreaticoduodenectomy undertaken in two stages. In the first, a gastrojejunostomy was undertaken, the common bile duct divided, and its end connected to the lower part of the duodenum. One month later, the second stage included resection of the duodenum and included the head of the pancreas beyond the limits of the ampullary tumor. The stump of the pancreatic head was then implanted into the lower end of the transected duodenum and the patient reported as cured. Lester R Dragstedt of the Laboratory of Physiology and Pharmacology of the State University of Iowa provided scientific support for this surgery, experimentally demonstrating that dogs could survive total duodenectomy and the physiological consequences of the operation might therefore be tolerable to humans. A further issue in the danger of pancreatic surgery was presented by the problems of excessive bleeding. As a result of prolonged biliary obstruction, the resultant hemostatic diathesis rendered major surgery hazardous. The discovery of vitamin K, its biological effects, and the profound relationship to hepatic function by Henrik Dam initiated a major strategic evaluation of pancreatic surgery. The entire concept of hemostasis in patients with jaundice was reviewed and as a result, hemostasis in pancreatic surgery was addressed from the biliary obstructive perspective.

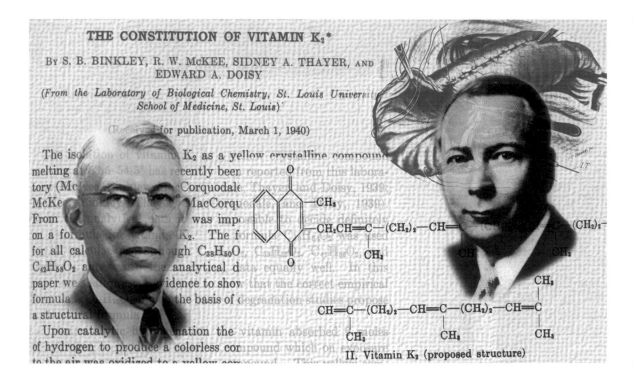

THE CONSTITUTION OF VITAMIN K₂*

BY S. B. BINKLEY, R. W. McKEE, SIDNEY A. THAYER, AND
EDWARD A. DOISY

(From the Laboratory of Biological Chemistry, St. Louis University, School of Medicine, St. Louis)

II. Vitamin K₂ (proposed structure)

The discovery of vitamin K, its biological effects, and the profound relationship to hepatic function by Henrik Dam (*right*) in 1938 and the determination of its chemical structure and synthesis in 1936–1939 by Edward Doisy (*left*) initiated a major strategic evaluation of pancreatic surgery, as hemostasis was effectively resolved. Dam and Doisy received Nobel Prizes in Physiology or Medicine in 1943 for this work. Dam's interest in vitamin K derived from his observations that chicks fed a low-fat diet showed continued bleeding under the skin. By careful addition and elimination diets, he was able to identify that hemp seed, which corrected the bleeding, contained a previously unidentified vitamin. Doisy's interest in vitamin K grew out of the interest his graduate student Ralph McKee had in Dam's antihemorrhagic factor, and the discovery that light had a deleterious effect on vitamin K. With the help of chemists provided by Parke, Davis and Company, Doisy was able to extract pure vitamin K1 from alfalfa and K2 from fishmeal using common water-softening adsorbents to separate the components using chromatography. This was reported in the *Journal of the American Chemical Society* in 1939 (*top left*), and the discovery of the sterol-based structure of vitamin K (*bottom right*) occurred soon after.

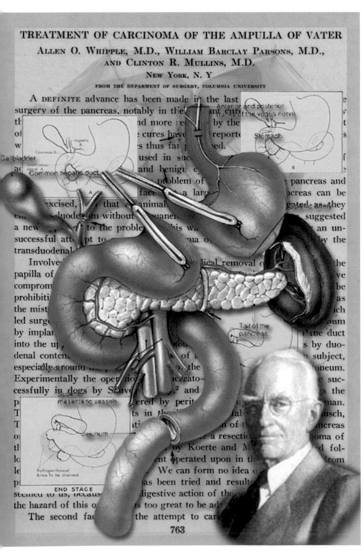

TREATMENT OF CARCINOMA OF THE AMPULLA OF VATER

ALLEN O. WHIPPLE, M.D., WILLIAM BARCLAY PARSONS, M.D.,
AND CLINTON R. MULLINS, M.D.

NEW YORK, N. Y

FROM THE DEPARTMENT OF SURGERY, COLUMBIA UNIVERSITY

763

Thus, improvement of hepatic function consequent upon relief of biliary obstruction became a critical issue in defining a resolution of the bleeding. Armed with this knowledge, Whipple was able to successfully perform a one-stage procedure later that year, modifying the two-stage procedure by re-anastomosis of the pancreatic duct into an enterostomy. By 1940, sufficient experience had been developed in pancreatic carcinoma and resection that other diseases and other areas of the pancreas could be considered amenable to intervention. Also by 1940, Whipple and Nelson had gained further experience and refined the procedure to the extent that they were able to successfully undertake one-stage pancreaticoduodenectomy. By 1945, Whipple could, based upon his own extensive work, advocate the one-stage procedure as the operation of choice for pancreatic carcinoma.

He judged his experience to be substantial and noted that in his initial eight two-stage procedures, the mortality had been 38%, whereas in the subsequent 19 one-stage procedures, the postoperative mortality was only 31%!

These surgical approaches allowed in the succeeding years for the identification that ampullary cancers could be differentiated from cancers of the rest of the gland and that adenocarcinomas behaved biologically very differently from endocrine tumors. Similarly, the observation that cystic, neoplastic lesions of the pancreas were more amenable to extirpation than solid tumors allowed for the further recognition of the need to better understand the genesis of pancreatic neoplasia. Subsequently, the inherited nature of some forms of pancreatic cancer was identified and in 1973, MacDermott and Kramer reported a kindred in which four siblings had developed pancreatic cancer. Thereafter, several large family cancer registries were established and the underlying germline genetic lesion demonstrated in some instances as the cancer-causing genes (BRCA2 – the breast cancer 2, early onset gene; p16 gene – a negative regulator of the cell cycle; and STK11/LKB1 [Serine/threonine kinase 11] – the gene associated with Peutz-Jeghers syndrome).

Allen Whipple successfully resected the pancreas and duodenum for adenocarcinoma in 1934. This 'radical' procedure was thereafter often applied to the management of the 'benign' process of chronic pancreatitis.

LORD RODNEY SMITH OF MARLOW

Despite the more recent recognition of the genetic underpinnings of pancreatic diseases, little effective therapy has as yet emanated from this area and surgical approaches to this organ remain beset with difficulties. One British surgeon who gained substantial international repute for his work dealing with the most difficult cases of pancreatic cancer was Lord Rodney Smith of Marlow (1914–1998). Smith, of St George's Hospital (London), achieved during his lifetime a reputation as a remarkable surgeon, teacher, and administrator. Educated at St Thomas', he embarked on a surgical career, training initially under Philip Mitchener before being appointed Surgical Registrar at the Middlesex Hospital, where he came under the influence of Lord Webb-Johnson and Sir Gordon Gordon-Taylor. From 1941–1945, Smith served as a surgical specialist in the Royal Army Medical Corps, working in field units in Israel, Egypt, and North Africa before being wounded at Anzio. In 1946, he was appointed to the staff at St George's Hospital, where he subsequently established an international reputation in abdominal, but particularly hepatobiliary and pancreatic, surgery. Indeed, his skill in dealing with difficult cases of pancreatic cancer, postoperative biliary fistulae, retained calculi, and bile duct strictures became legendary in his own lifetime. In particular, he became noted for the mucosal hepaticojejunostomy that he devised for hilar biliary strictures. At the height of his career, while producing lectures and manuscripts that were regarded as models of lucidity,

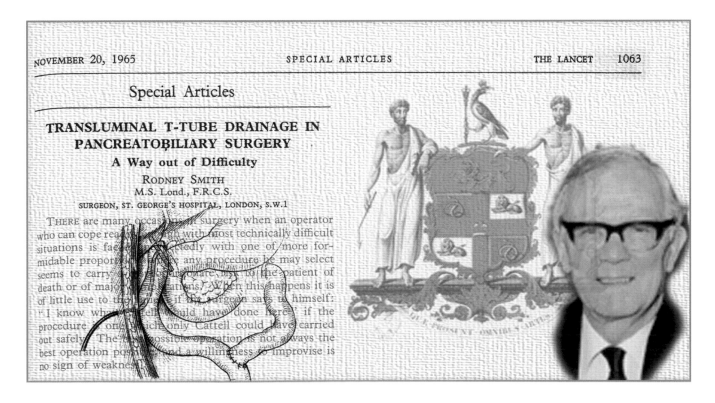

Management of the stump of the pancreas after distal pancreatic resection

Br. J. Surg. 1990, Vol. 77, May, 541–544

S. Shankar, B. Theis and R. C. G. Russell

Department of Gastroenterology, The Middlesex Hospital, London W1N 8AA, UK
Correspondence to:
Mr R. C. G. Russell

In 1990, Chris Russell (*top left*) of the Middlesex Hospital and colleagues published an article in the *British Journal of Surgery* in which they attempted to identify the optimal management for the stump of the pancreas following a distal resection. In their retrospective survey, they identified that caudal pancreatic drainage conferred no significant benefit to patients who had undergone this procedure compared to patients without a drainage procedure.

he edited the multiple-volume *Operative Surgery*, which remained the standard reference text on the subject for decades. Smith also devoted much energy to the Royal College of Surgeons, serving as Penrose May Tutor and Dean of the Institute of Basic Medical Sciences before being elected a councilor in 1965 and subsequently President of the College.

Lord Rodney Smith (*bottom right*) presciently summarized his surgical philosophy in the first paragraph of his 1965 *Lancet* paper. He stated that "the best possible operation is not always the best operation possible, and a willingness to improvise is no sign of weakness". Thereafter, he expanded on the usefulness of a transluminal t-tube drainage (*left*) in obstructed cases of the pancreaticobiliary tract. This special article was commissioned by the publishers to provide a "way out of difficulty" for surgeons engaged in operating on patients with this complication.

4 GASTROINTESTINAL NEUROENDOCRINOLOGY

The majority of the glands and tissues that form the endocrine system were recognized by the end of the 19th century. Although they were initially described and studied individually, like other organs they were later grouped together as the ductless glands and regarded as the source of internal secretions. The gonads were recognized in prehistoric times, with the testes being the most obvious given their location, while the ancient Egyptians later identified the ovaries. Galen described the pituitary in the 2nd century and Andreas Vesalius of Padua the thyroid in 1543.

By the mid-17th century, Thomas Warton had included the thyroid, suprarenals, and pancreas amongst the glands of the body in his classic *Adenographia*, published in 1656. Nevertheless, the function of the endocrine glands was unknown and the subject of much speculation until 1776, when Albrecht von Haller described the thyroid, thymus, and spleen as glands without ducts that poured substances into the circulation. Claude Bernard in 1855 demonstrated this effect experimentally by describing sugar which enters the portal vein as an internal secretion, and bile as an external secretion of the liver. He similarly listed the adrenals, thyroid, lymphatic glands, and spleen as further sources of internal secretion. Although the effects of castration had been recognized from early days, it was John Hunter of London who in 1786 proposed that an internal secretion from the testes was responsible for the development of secondary sex characteristics.

Similarly, Thomas Addison of Guy's Hospital London provided evidence that the absence or destruction of an endocrine gland causes disease when, in 1855, he published his work *On the Constitutional and Local Effects of Disease of the Supra-renal Capsules*. Theodore Kocher, Professor of Surgery at Bern, confirmed this principle in 1883 when he described the condition of "cachexia strumipriva" that supervened after total extirpation of the thyroid gland in man. In 1890, George Oliver, a general medical practitioner from Harrogate, England, extracted a potent vasoconstrictor from the adrenal medulla together with Edward Schäfer (later Sharpey-Schäfer), Professor of Physiology at University College London. The active principal, epinephrine or adrenaline, was isolated in 1897 and in 1901, became the first internal secretion chemically identified.

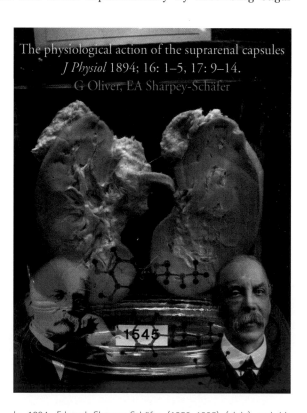

Thomas Addison (*center*) was a brilliant pathological lecturer at Guy's Hospital (*top*) and diagnostician, but possessed of a haughty and repellent manner. In 1849, he described pernicious anemia (20 years before Biermer), as well as disease of the suprarenal capsules (melasma suprarenale). The latter publication is now recognized as of epoch-making importance, since in connection with the physiological work of Claude Bernard, it inaugurated the study of the diseases of the "ductless glands".

In 1894, Edward Sharpey-Schäfer (1850–1935) (*right*) and his co-worker George Oliver (*left*) (1841–1915) discovered that an extract from the central part of an adrenal gland injected into the bloodstream of an animal caused a rise in blood pressure by vasoconstriction (*top*). They also noted that the smooth muscles of the animal's bronchi relaxed. These effects were subsequently identified to have been caused by the action of the hormone adrenaline (*bottom*).

Although the physiological climate of this time was dominated by Ivan Petrovich Pavlov of St Petersburg, who believed that the nervous system controlled all bodily activities, the concept of the ductless gland effects was still regarded as important by some. Thus Sir William Bayliss and Ernest Henry Starling, in a discovery "breathtaking in its elegant simplicity," noted that acid in the gut stimulated secretion of the pancreas when both organs were denervated. They concluded that since acid introduced directly into the circulation failed to cause this response, whereas injection of the jejunal mucosa extract did, that the action of acid on the gut was the effect of a chemical reflex and proposed the name "secretin" as the hypothetical chemical messenger involved. This new class of chemical substances was grouped together under the term "hormone" by Starling, and the use of the colliquation, endocrine, which had previously been attributed to the islets of Langerhans in 1893 by Eduard Laguesse of France, was utilized to describe this discipline of medicine. As a result, the consideration of nervism as the only regulatory mechanism of the body waned as the science of endocrinology achieved dramatic prominence. Thus, in subsequent years, more endocrine tissues and numerous hormones were identified and their functions and complex interrelationships explored. The Leydig cells of the testes, the Kulchitsky cells of the gut, the islets of Langerhans, the parathyroid glands, and the pituitary were thus all recognized as endocrine organs over a relatively short period of time. Thyroxin was isolated from the thyroid by Edward Kendall of the Mayo Clinic in 1914, and in 1921, Fredrick Banting, an orthopedic surgeon and physiologist of London, Ontario, extracted insulin from the pancreatic islets. In 1931, Sir Walter Langdon-Brown of London, England, described the pituitary as "the leader in the endocrine orchestra" and the endocrine glands were regarded as not only sharing a common mode of action but also to be functionally interdependent.

Thus, the endocrine system became regarded as an integrated mechanism for the control of body functions in a fashion that complemented nervism, or the regulation of the nervous system, as proposed by Pavlov. The particular interrelationship between nerves and endocrine cells was of considerable interest in the regulation of gut, motor, and secretory activity. In 1911, Walter Cannon, Professor of Physiology at Harvard University, Boston, using adrenaline as an example, demonstrated that the adrenal medulla functioned not only as an endocrine gland but also as part of the autonomic nervous system. In 1921, Otto Loewi, a pharmacologist at Graz, Austria, established the chemical nature of nerve transmission and in the 1930s, the secretory cells in the hypothalamus were demonstrated to exert neurohormonal control over the anterior pituitary. Thus feedback mechanisms were identified and central nervous system regulation became a recognized part of hormonal regulation. As regards the gastrointestinal tract, Pierre Masson, a pathologist in Montreal, had suggested in 1914 that the Kulchitsky cells in the gut formed a diffuse endocrine organ, and later in 1928 described them as being of neural origin.

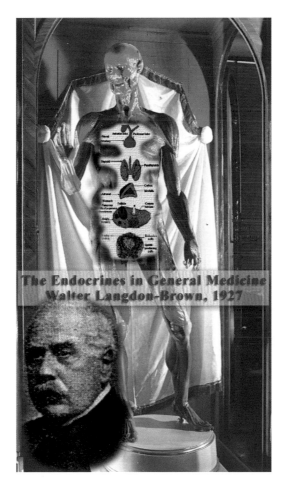

Sir Walter Langdon-Brown (1870–1946) (*bottom left*) was a clinician, teacher, and humanist – a great scholar-physician in the tradition of Thomas Linacre. His interest in medicine covered two broad areas, therapeutics and pharmacology, and the relationship of psychology to medicine. He was most well known, however, for his contributions to endocrinology, and was regarded as the founder of modern clinical endocrinology in Britain. His book, *The Endocrines in General Medicine* of 1927 (*center*), was considered a classic in the application of endocrine science to clinical medicine.

In 1930, Friedrich Feyrter (*left*) of Gdansk, Poland, proposed the existence of a diffuse system of neuroendocrine cells in the gastrointestinal tract (*center*).

In the early 1930s, the Austrian pathologist, Friedrich Feyrter of Gdansk, Poland, described a system of "*helle zellen*" ("clear cells"), which were distributed widely in tissues but were most prominent in the gastrointestinal tract and the pancreas, and proposed that such cells were the source of hormones that acted locally.

This concept later became recognized under the terminology "paracrine" and was subsequently linked to a similar concept that related interaction to nerve cells under the term "neurocrine". The conglomeration of these investigations over a period of three decades led to the conclusion that the nervous and endocrine systems were inseparable, and in the gut formed an interwoven syncytium responsible for regulatory function. The summation of these thought processes was consummated and finally extended in the 1960s by Everson Pearse, a histochemist in London, who demonstrated that the cells described by Masson and Feyrter shared important functional characteristics with cells in many of the major endocrine glands, as well as in the hypothalamus. Thus, all were concerned with the metabolism of amines and the production of peptides, and were conveniently described by the acronym APUD (amine precursor uptake and decarboxylation). While the hypothesis of Pearse failed to completely resolve the cell lineage of the diffuse endocrine system, his work, together with that of Steven Bloom and Julia Polak, confirmed the concept of a single neuroendocrine system that pervaded the tissues of the body and was particularly conspicuous in the gastrointestinal tract.

PAVLOV AND THE VAGUS

The modern era of the study of vagal physiology was initiated and dominated by Ivan Petrovich Pavlov (1849–1938) of St Petersburg. Although he achieved considerable recognition for his investigation of conditioned reflexes, his methods and the results of his observations on vagal function laid the foundation for the subsequent study of the nervous control of gastrointestinal function. Although B Brodie of London had a century earlier identified some of the general effects of vagal nerve function, it was Pavlov and his students who, over the course of three decades, scientifically delineated the role of the vagus in both pancreatic and gastric physiology.

As a graduate of the Medico-Chirurgical Academy in St Petersburg, Russia, in the late l9th century the scientific philosophy of Pavlov had been greatly influenced by the work of Lister and Pasteur. Thus, when given the opportunity to create a laboratory for physiological studies, he established an operating suite for animals that was in fact superior at that time to most European facilities used for operations upon humans!

Ivan Petrovich Pavlov (*center*) was a son of a Russian priest and a pupil of both Heidenhain and Ludwig. He became Director of the Institute for Experimental Medicine at Leningrad in 1890, and in 1904, received the Nobel Prize for his investigations into the neural regulation of gastrointestinal secretion. The success of Pavlov's work was in large measure due to his remarkable surgical skills. A brilliant thinker as well as an ambidextrous surgeon, his development of a diverse variety of gastric and pancreatic fistulae allowed him to elucidate the neuroregulatory mechanisms of gastric and pancreatic secretion.

Indeed, the care given to the animals in Pavlov's laboratory was exemplary, and combined with his own ambidextrous and superb surgical skills, considerably facilitated his experimental studies. Pavlov's theory of "nervism" was a momentous postulate for the times in which he lived and he was fond of explaining it as "a physiological theory which tries to prove that the nervous system controls the greatest possible number of bodily activities". Using this proposal as a basis, Pavlov sought to prove the hypothesis that the neural regulation of gastric secretion (nervism) was mediated via the vagus nerves.

BAYLISS, STARLING, AND SECRETIN

While the central regulation of gastric digestive activity was initially delineated by Pavlov, the discovery by Sir William Bayliss (1860–1924) and Ernest Henry Starling (1866–1926) in 1902 of the hormone secretin and the establishment of the concept of "chemical messengers" ushered in a new era of gastrointestinal physiology. Indeed, the description of the stimulatory effect of secretin on pancreatic secretion would not only establish the hormonal basis for the regulation of gastric secretion, but also directly inaugurate the field of endocrinology. The work on the movement and innervation of the intestine and on the nature of the peristaltic wave (1898–1899) led Bayliss and Starling on to what was probably their most fecund investigation, the concept of the existence of "chemical messengers". In actuality, the story of secretin however had begun as early as 1825, when F Leuret and J-L Lassaigne wrote that they had "opened the abdomen of a living dog: incised the first part of the small intestine along its length; applied vinegar diluted with water to the villi. Instantly a serous liquid was produced in abundance… At the same time the openings of the biliary and pancreatic ducts were dilated, and bile and pancreatic juice flowed for several minutes… If an acid stimulates duodenal secretions and dilates the ducts of the liver and pancreas, chyme ought to do the same thing, for it is always acid." Although Leuret and Lassaigne are more often remembered for their ill-fated studies demonstrating that gastric acid was lactic, in spite of William Prout (1823) and Friedrich Tiedeman and Leopold Gmelin's proof that it was hydrochloric, the relevance of this seminal observation was for the most part ignored.

Unfortunately, the exposure to the bias of Pavlov's beliefs led Popielski to an erroneous conclusion of a peripheral reflex through these nerves. Indeed, the exhaustive experiments he described quite clearly indicate the need to have considered the presence of a chemical reflex.

The next stage of the saga of the identification of a "secretin" took place in Lille, France, in 1901, where Pierre Wertheimer had developed an interest in the role of nerves in both physiological and pathological processes. Indeed, his subsequent work with André Latarjet would explore the effects of innervation and denervation on numerous gastrointestinal and gynecological organs, and finally led to the development of vagotomy for the treatment of acid peptic disease. Wertheimer conducted a series of experiments to further investigate Popielski's thesis. He found that despite cutting the junction of the pylorus and duodenum, ablating the celiac and mesenteric plexuses, sectioning the vagi as well as the thoracic sympathetic chains, and destroying the spinal cord in a curarized dog, he could not abolish the pancreatic secretory response to acid in the duodenum. Wertheimer, accepting only neural regulation as an explanation for these phenomena, concluded that the response to acid in the jejunum was mediated by the abdominal sympathetic ganglia – a reflex operating in nerves directly connecting the duodenum with a center in the pancreas itself.

Since Bayliss had been interested in secretion since 1890, he engaged Starling in studying the mechanisms by which acid introduced into the upper intestine was followed by secretion of pancreatic juice.

Seventy years later in 1895, IL Dolinsky, a student of Pavlov in St Petersburg, rediscovered the fact that acid in the duodenum stimulates pancreatic secretion. Dolinsky, as an acolyte of the "master of nervism" believed that the nervous apparatus of the pancreatic gland was responsive to specific irritants, including acid and fat, and had postulated that such a neural reflex could be proven. This proposal reflected the firmly-held belief of the time that all glandular secretion was nerve-operated and was for the most part based on the work of Carl Ludwig, who had initially demonstrated this phenomenon in salivary glands in 1851. Pavlov had inherited and thereafter expanded the doctrine of nervism – the belief that all physiological responses are mediated by the nervous system. Since the pancreas was regarded by physiologists of the time as the equivalent of an abdominal salivary gland, Pavlov proposed that the pancreatic response to acid in the duodenum was regulated by a local neural reflex. Given this background to the issue of the regulation of pancreatic secretion, Leon Popielski in Pavlov's laboratory was given the task of elucidating the nervous connections between the mucosa of the upper small intestine and the pancreas that had previously been postulated by Dolinsky. In all these experimental scenarios, Popielski noted that the pancreas secreted when he infused hydrochloric acid or acetic acid in the duodenum. Applying the dogma of nervism, he therefore concluded that if the central and autonomic nervous systems are unnecessary for reflex regulation of pancreatic secretion, that control must be the function of local nerves connecting the intestine and pancreas. These nerves, he thought, were processes of the 25–30 nerve cells he found in several ganglia contained within the pancreas.

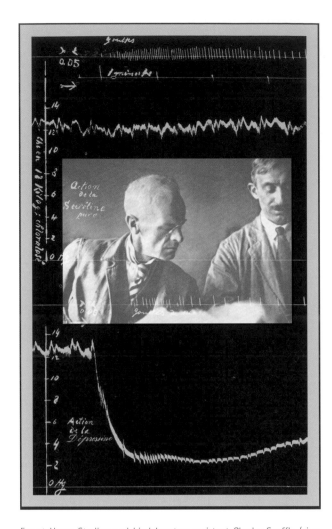

Ernest Henry Starling and his laboratory assistant Charles Scuffle (circa 1925). In 1902, Sir William Bayliss and Starling demonstrated that a chemical agent present in jejunal mucosa when administered intravenously stimulated a denervated pancreas to secrete (*background*).

introduction of acid to this area of the bowel did not lead to any secretion of pancreatic juice. As Martin afterwards wrote: "I happened to be present at their discovery. In an anesthetized dog, a loop of jejunum was tied at both ends and the nerves supplying it dissected out and divided so that it was connected with the rest of the body only by its blood vessels. On the introduction of some weak HCl into the duodenum, secretion from the pancreas occurred and continued for some minutes. After this had subsided a few cubic centimeters of acid were introduced into the enervated loop of jejunum. To our surprise a similarly marked secretion was produced. I remember Starling saying: 'Then it must be a chemical reflex.' Rapidly cutting off a further piece of jejunum he rubbed its mucous membrane with sand in weak HCl, filtered and injected it into the jugular vein of the animal. After a few moments the pancreas responded by a much greater secretion than had occurred before. It was a great afternoon." Six days after their first experiment, Bayliss and Starling read a paper before the Royal Society describing their work. They published the same story in the March 22, 1902 issue of the *Lancet* and a longer summary in German in the February 1, 1902 issue of *Centralblatt für Physiologie*. This paper provoked Wertheimer to perform the experiment of irritating the jejunal mucosa with mustard oil and thereafter re-injecting the collected venous blood. On two occasions, this stimulated pancreatic secretion and as a consequence, Wertheimer unwillingly edged towards accepting a hormonal hypothesis. E Pfluger (1829–1910), who edited his own archives (*Pfluger's Archives*), was however still unconvinced. In a more critical analysis, he suggested that the denervation performed by Bayliss and Starling had not been complete and that the effect was non-specific, since it was well recognized that the extracts of many tissues stimulated glands to secrete.

Bayliss and Starling completed their work in March 1902 and when their complete paper was published in the September issue of the *Journal of Physiology*, they apologized for the long delay, citing the need to completely validate their novel proposal. The interval however also provided the opportunity to cite Wertheimer and Pfluger, and in so doing, to rebut their criticisms. In a masterful riposte, they agreed that denervation had probably not been complete, and intimated "that it does not matter whether the nerves were all cut or not; the only fact of importance is that it was the belief that all nerves were cut that caused us to try the experiment of making an acid extract of the mucous membrane that led to the discovery of secretin".

As the first step in evaluating the question, they therefore decided to repeat the work of Wertheimer. Thus, on January 16, 1902, they performed their crucial experiment witnessed by Starling's friend Charles Martin. A loop of jejunum was tied off and carefully denervated so that its only connection with the rest of the body remained the mesenteric vessels. Dilute hydrochloric acid introduced into the loop of jejunum resulted in a steady flow of pancreatic juice, just as it had previously done in the control experiment when introduced into the intact duodenum. The mucosa was then scraped from some jejunum, ground with 0.4% hydrochloric acid, filtered, and injected intravenously, and within minutes a free flow of pancreatic juice ensued. In the same set of experiments, they then demonstrated that the active substance was not destroyed by boiling, and that it was absent from the lower ileum. This further supported the observation that the

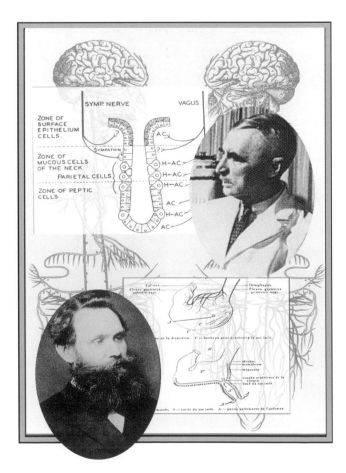

B Babkin (*right*), a pupil of Ivan Petrovich Pavlov (*bottom left*), translated the Russian scientist's views into English and was responsible for disseminating many of his ideas in North America. Babkin himself developed novel theories regarding the parasympathetic innervation of the gastric glands (*background*).

Pavlov, after some inner turmoil, accepted the evidence presented in support of the existence of the chemical control of pancreatic secretion. His compatriot, B Babkin (1877–1950) summarized the conflict thus: "Pavlov radically changed his opinion about the new fact discovered by the English physiologists probably in the fall or winter of 1902–3 after reading Bayliss and Starling's complete and excellent paper on secretin in the *Journal of Physiology* (1902)… I think it was in the fall of 1902 that Pavlov asked VV Savich to repeat the secretin experiments of Bayliss and Starling. The effect was self-evident. Then, without a word, Pavlov disappeared into his study. He returned half an hour later and said: 'Of course, they are right. It is clear that we did not take out an exclusive patent for the discovery of truth'." Having effectively rebuffed the critique of their European counterparts, Bayliss and Starling demonstrated remarkable alacrity at not only following up their discovery but also expanding the applications. Such was the impact that Bayliss was elected to the Royal Society in 1903. In 1904, they gave a joint Croonian Lecture to the Royal Society and also published in German one account of the chemical coordination of bodily functions. It was Starling, however, who was most effective in placing the work in the broader scientific domain and expanding upon its possible extrapolation. In 1905, at the suggestion of William B Hardy, he used the general name of "hormone" from the Greek "to excite" to describe the chemical messengers as a class of agents. In his Croonian address to the Royal College of Physicians, he took the opportunity to outline his concepts of what the general outlines of endocrinology might become. As examples, he utilized the then recent studies of adrenaline by John Langley (1852–1925) in 1901 and by HK Elliot in 1904. Starling also adumbrated upon his considerations of the theory of humoral transmission with the following words: "We are dealing here with a problem which, betraying, as it does, an intimate relationship between nerve excitation and excitation by chemical messengers, promises by its solution to throw a most interesting light on the nature of the nerve process and of excitatory processes in general."

In the same lecture, he also considered the possible role of sex hormones, the antidiabetic hormone of the pancreas, and a probable gastric hormone (gastrin), which had recently been proposed by John Sidney Edkins (1863–1940). The discovery of histamine by Sir Henry Hallett Dale (1875–1968) in 1910, as well as the demonstration that extracts from other tissues had a similar physiological effect to gastrin, led many to seriously question the validity of Edkins' observation. As a result, gastrin, although originally acknowledged and accepted, subsequently fell into disfavor and a further half-century was required before Simon Komarov (1892–1964) produced incontrovertible proof of its existence.

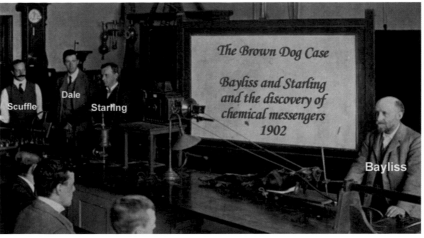

Sir William Bayliss (*right*) demonstrating an experiment on a dog at University College to Sir Henry Hallett Dale and Ernest Henry Starling (*far left*). Considerable controversy fueled by the antivivisectionist movement arose surrounding the experimental work of Bayliss and Starling. In a court case for libel, Bayliss was adjudged the victor and donated the settlement to the physiology research fund.

JOHN SIDNEY EDKINS AND GASTRIN

The observations of Bayliss and Starling stimulated John Sidney Edkins, a physiologist working with Sir Charles Scott Sherrington, to evaluate the control of gastric secretion. Even prior to the presentation of the data regarding secretin, Edkins had harbored the idea that absorbed peptones might liberate a chemical messenger, but had lacked the support to pursue the matter. His deliberations in this area led him to conclude that since there was now evidence for an agonist for pancreatic secretion, there might well be a "gastric secretin". He thus proposed the critical hypothesis that there might be in the gastric mucosa a preformed substance that is absorbed into the portal stream and returned to the circulation to stimulate the fundic oxyntic glands. On May 18, 1905, he obtained sufficient evidence to make a preliminary communication to the Royal Society on this matter. In a modest paper entitled 'On the Chemical Mechanisms of Gastric Secretion', he described how various extracts of antral mucosa potently stimulated gastric secretion in anesthetized cats.

The frontispiece of John Sidney Edkins' epic communication (*center*), which documented the existence of a novel antral stimulant of acid secretion – gastrin (1905). Edkins (*top left*) entered Cambridge University as a scholar of Caius College in 1881. Such was his ability that he was awarded two scholarships, one in mathematics and the other in natural sciences. After Cambridge, he worked with Sir Charles Scott Sherrington (*right*) in Liverpool (later to attain a Nobel Prize for his work in neurophysiology), who initially communicated the gastrin abstract in 1905. Apart from his fundamental observations in regard to gastrin, Edkins worked with John Langley on the study of pepsin, defined the effects of phosgene on lung function, and developed a chemical technique for destroying weevils without damaging flour.

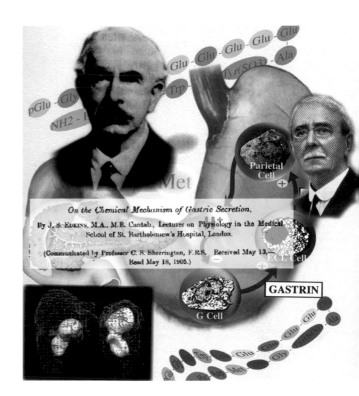

On the Chemical Mechanism of Gastric Secretion.

By J. S. Edkins, M.A., M.B. Cantab., Lecturer on Physiology in the Medical School of St. Bartholomew's Hospital, London.

(Communicated by Professor C. S. Sherrington, F.R.S. Received May 13, Read May 18, 1905.)

GASTRIN

It was unfortunate for Edkins that a large number of distinguished investigators, including Dale, provided substantial and "apparently incontrovertible" evidence in support of the theory that the active principal in his antral extract was histamine. More than a quarter of a century was to elapse before Komarov, a Russian émigré in Canada, in 1938 recognized the sad trick that nature had played on Edkins. In antral mucosa there is both histamine and a protein-like substance with a bioactivity that mimics the action of histamine on gastric acid secretion. Komarov, a meticulous chemist, undertook the task of demonstrating the existence of gastrin. After numerous tedious repetitions of precipitation, extraction, salting out, and further extraction, a powder that was a protein in nature was obtained. Komarov said it was free of choline and "organic crystalloids," but could say nothing further about its chemical nature. Since the product did not lower the blood pressure of anesthetized cats when injected intravenously, he reasoned that it therefore did not contain histamine and therefore believed that he was justified in calling it gastrin: "In all cases without exception the pyloric preparation, injected in quantities equal to 5gm of mucosa, elicited a copious secretion of gastric juice, which was characterized by high acidity and low peptic power and which was not affected by atropine even in large doses."

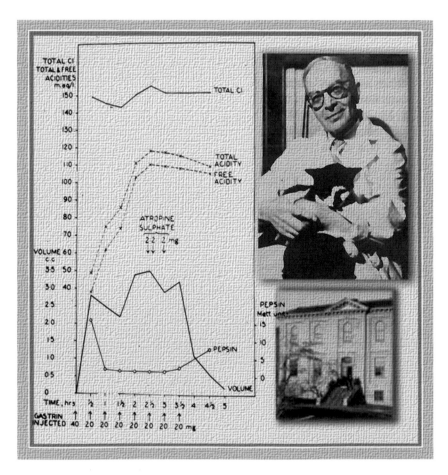

The graph (*left*) from the original publication (1942) of Simon Komarov (*top right*) from McMaster University (*bottom right*) in the *Rev Can Biol*. The demonstration of the acid response of an anesthetized cat to an intravenous injection of histamine-free antral mucosal extract and the effect of atropine on the response confirmed the existence of "gastrin" and vindicated John Sidney Edkins.

Rod Gregory and his assistant Hilda Tracy of Liverpool were the first to devise a method of extracting gastrin using trichloroacetic acid in acetone. Early in his career, Gregory had worked at the Mayo clinic and having mastered German, read all the early physiology texts in the original. Despite the fact that he was a British citizen working in Liverpool, he was on good terms with his American counterparts and thus received a substantial grant from the United States Public Health Service. This support enabled him on his return to Britain to purchase numerous items of capital equipment necessary to fully undertake the isolation and characterization of gastrin. In addition, he and Tracy signed a contract with a Liverpool firm that made pork pies and as a result, they were able to acquire for extraction purposes up to 600 hog antrums weekly for six months. Despite this huge load of material, the system worked well enough that by the end of 18 months, they had accumulated hundreds of milligrams of pure gastrin.

In collaboration with George W Kenner, a Manchester and Cambridge trained peptide chemist, who was then the Head of the Department of Organic Chemistry at Liverpool, they set out to identify the structure of gastrin. On Christmas Day, 1962, Gregory and Tracy noted that they had identified not one but two gastrins that they imaginatively proceeded to name "gastrin I" and "gastrin II". Of interest was the observation that the tyrosine on gastrin II was sulfated. Gregory subsequently presented this work on April 26, 1962, at a meeting in New York at which Komarov was chairman.

It now remained to fully determine the precise clinical and biological relevance of gastrin. In 1958, Solomon Berson and Rosalyn Yalow published a manuscript documenting the use of radioimmunoassay (RIA) to measure plasma insulin. Using this principle, James McGuigan in 1967 developed a similar strategy to devise an RIA for gastrin by developing a double antibody technique and was able to measure gastrin in human serum.

HISTAMINE AND SIR HENRY HALLETT DALE

In 1911, Sir Henry Hallett Dale, while working with the chemist George Barger, applied Kutscher's silver method to a specimen of ergot dialysatum and "isolated a few centigrams of the picrate of an intensively active base, which produced a characteristic action on the cat's non-pregnant uterus in a minute dose". Barger and Dale identified the base as beta-imidazolylethylamine and compared it with an authentic sample that had been obtained by the putrefaction of histidine. Many years later in his life, commenting on the early days of histamine research, Dale wrote: "Beta-1 as we called it, is, of course, the now almost too familiar histamine; and this was always the obvious name for it. Somebody, however, had objected to its use, as infringing his trademark rights in a name to which its resemblance was, in fact, only distant. Later somebody called it histamine and then the road was clear." In fact, the supplement of the *Oxford English Dictionary* attributes the first use of the term "histamine" to the *Journal of Chemistry*, circa 1913.

Rod Gregory (*top right*) of Liverpool was responsible, with Hilda Tracy (*bottom left*), for the elucidation of the structure of gastrin.

The circle of Sir William Bayliss and Ernest Henry Starling fostered a number of high-profile individuals. These included Charles Code (*left*), Sir Henry Hallett Dale (*center right*), and Charles Lovatt-Evans (*bottom right*). Dale was responsible for the discovery of histamine and received the Nobel Prize for his contribution with Otto Loewi to the chemical transmission of nerve impulses (acetylcholine). Code carefully defined the role of histamine as a principal physiological regulator of parietal cell secretion, while Lovatt-Evans was responsible for some of the early work conducted with Starling's heart-lung preparations. In the background is a photograph of Starling with the heart-lung preparation of a dog (1920), and top left to right are the original illustrations for the different heart-lung preparations that evolved in the Starling laboratory at the University College of London from 1910–1914.

Dale worked extensively in the area of the pharmacological and physiological actions of histamine between 1910 and 1927, but despite an exhaustive evaluation of its properties, failed to detect its role in promoting acid secretion by the glands of the stomach. This unique property of stimulating acid secretion was to be discovered by Popielski, a student of Pavlov. After leaving Pavlov's laboratory in 1901, Popielski had been placed in charge of the military bacteriological laboratory in Moscow, where his initial work was on the mechanism by which intravenous injection of Witte's peptone (a peptic digest of fibrin) caused a fall in blood pressure. This research continued after he had become Professor of Pharmacology at the University of Lemberg, and Popielski believed that he had identified a substance, "vaso-dilantine," as a component of Witte's peptone distinct from histamine or choline. On October 28, 1916, in the course of experiments on the effect of the injection of an extract of the pituitary gland upon gastric secretion, Popielski injected 32mg of beta-imidazolylethylamine hydrochloride subcutaneously into a dog with a gastric fistula. Over the next 5.75 hours, the dog secreted 937.5ml of gastric juice, having a maximum acidity of 0.166N.

Because similarly stimulated secretion was unaffected by section of the vagus or by atropine, Popielski concluded that beta-imidazolylethylamine acted directly on the gastric glands to stimulate acid secretion. Unfortunately, the First World War delayed the publication of Popielski's paper describing these results until 1920.

The key protagonist in the elucidation of the role of histamine and its clinical relevance in gastric secretion would be Charles Code. Code had grown up in Winnipeg and received an MD degree from the University of Manitoba in 1933 before joining Frank Mann at the Mayo Clinic. Thereafter, he obtained support to study in London, where he first worked with Charles Lovatt-Evans at the University College of London and later with Dale at the National Institutes for Medical Research. There, Code demonstrated that 70–100% of histamine in unclotted blood is in the white cell layer and that clotting liberates 60–90% of this into the serum. He further determined that granular lymphocytes contained most of the histamine in the buffy coat and that the white cells leaving the marrow carry histamine with them. Although Code, on his return to the Mayo Clinic in 1937, continued to work with Mann as his first assistant at the operating room table, he remained fascinated by the effect of histamine and its bioactivity.

Charles Best (depicted at various stages of his life), having participated in the discovery of insulin, subsequently investigated the physiology of histamine.

In 1882, Kühne and Lea noted the complex capillary network that embraced the collection of islets and in considering the physiological implications, failed to divine the relationship to glucose homeostasis. Laguesse eponymously attributed the islet structures that Langerhans had identified to him in 1893. In 1902, the latter further amplified the histological characteristics of these microorgans by studying the atrophied pancreas after duct ligation and proposed a putative relationship with diabetes.

The regulation of pancreatic secretion was a vexatious question, which Pavlov and his pupils addressed with vigor at the turn of the 19th century. Pavlov's pupil, Dolinsky, noted that acid introduced into the duodenum stimulated pancreatic secretion and interpreted this as indicative of a local neural reflex. In 1902, Bayliss and Starling of University College London demonstrated that this phenomenon was in fact not a neural reflex but the effect of a chemical messenger or regulator.

It soon became apparent to the group that with increasing doses of histamine and increasing acid secretion, duodenal ulcers could be initiated not only in dogs but in a number of other animal species, including chickens, woodchucks, calves, monkeys, and rabbits. Code concluded that the experiments incriminated gastric juice as the factor in the production of peptic ulcer and noted the relationship of histamine to this event. A series of meticulous studies conducted over many years led to his determination of the critical role of histamine in the stimulation of parietal cell acid secretion. In addition, Code proposed the existence of an intermediate cell that he called a "histaminocyte" responsible for the regulation of gastric histamine secretion. Indeed, the validity of his observations were borne out by the subsequent identification of the histamine 2 receptor on the parietal cell and the profound inhibitory effects of the histamine 2 class of antagonists in generating acid suppression.

In his medical student doctoral thesis (1869), Paul Langerhans (*right*) of Berlin described microscopic structures in the pancreas, which he termed "*Zellhauschen*" ("little heaps of cells"). Despite the seminal nature of this observation, he attributed no function to these cells and it remained for Hedon (*top left*) to suggest that these cells may play a role in the "internal" secretion of the pancreas. Thereafter, Eduard Laguesse (*bottom left*) in 1893 proposed their relationship to diabetes and named the cells after Langerhans.

The subsequent integration of the neural and hormonal mechanisms provided by the two schools of physiological thought regarding the modulation of gastrointestinal function proved to be a major contribution to 20th century gastroenterology.

Further work on pancreatic juice itself was produced by yet another of Pavlov's pupils, Chepovalnikov, who demonstrated that pancreatic juice acquired and exerted a powerful solvent action on proteids only after contact with either the duodenal membrane or extracts thereof. This observation enabled him to deduce that the duodenum produced a unique enzyme (enterokinase) responsible for the activation of pancreatic juice.

THE PANCREATIC ISLETS

In 1869, Paul Langerhans, while a medical student, published his inaugural thesis 'Contributions to the Microscopic Anatomy of the Pancreas', and utilizing staining and transillumination, became the first to note the differences between the exocrine and endocrine pancreas.

Joseph von Mering (1849–1908) (*bottom left*) and Oskar Minkowski (1858–1931) (*right*) noted that extirpation of the pancreas of a dog resulted in diabetes (*background*). This dramatic observation resulted from the étude observation of a laboratory attendant, who noted that the urine of a pancreatectomized dog attracted flies!

DIABETES

Although the relationship between the pancreas and diabetes is seemingly self-evident at this time, it was only in 1889 that Joseph von Mering and Oskar Minkowski noted that extirpation of the pancreas of a dog resulted in diabetes. This observation escaped Johann Conrad Brunner, who almost two centuries previously, had resected the canine pancreas, and despite noting the onset of polydipsia in the surviving animals, had failed to relate it to diabetes. A vignette of interest in the von Mering/Minkowski experiments was the seminal observation of an astute laboratory attendant, who noted that the urine of the pancreatectomized dogs attracted flies, whereas the urine of the non-pancreatectomized animals exhibited no such effect. Although Langerhans had initially described the islets of the pancreas in 1869, it remained for Laguesse to suggest that they were related to the genesis of diabetes. This proposal was supported by Eugene L Opie, who described hyaline changes in islets of diabetic patients, and Sobelow and Schulze. The latter investigators demonstrated that although ligation of the pancreatic duct atrophied the exocrine component of the pancreas, the islets remained unchanged and diabetes did not supervene. Similar observations were subsequently made by both WG MacCullen of Johns Hopkins and Moses Baron of Minnesota. The latter succinctly noted that in instances of pancreatic disease without islet involvement, no diabetes was evident.

A wide variety of fistula dogs (*center*) created by Ivan Petrovich Pavlov and his students facilitated the elucidation of the neural regulation of gastric and pancreatic secretion. The different types of fistula modeled after Rudolf Heidenhain and used to access the gastric juice are depicted (*top right and bottom left*). Pavlov sold some of the Russian canine juice to Germany as an aphrodisiac to finance his work!

In 1922, Banting, working with Charles H Best at the University of Toronto, Canada, responded to Baron's observations on the relationship between islet cell damage and diabetes. Their relatively simple two-phase experiment provided information that earned Banting a Nobel Prize and forever altered the management of diabetes. Having initially ligated the pancreatic duct of a dog, they waited 10 weeks before sacrificing it and producing a crude preparation of "islets and isletin" in Ringer's solution from its atrophic pancreas. This extract was then injected into a second dog that had been pancreatectomized some days previously and thereafter allowed to lapse into diabetic coma. As a result of the insulin (isletin) injection, the dog recovered from its coma and the clinical relevance of insulin became apparent. Subsequently, JB Collip standardized insulin and the widespread use of this agent in the treatment of diabetes revolutionized the management of the disease.

GASTROENTEROPANCREATIC TUMORS

Islet cell tumors

Although Bard and Pick in 1888 had proposed that the islet cell was a potential candidate for the development of neoplastic lesions, it was 1908 before AG Nichols became the first to report a solitary adenoma of the pancreas arising directly from the islet tissue. The lesion was noted at autopsy as a small, round, flattened nodule located on the anterior side of the pancreas approximately at the junction of the middle and the terminal third. Other reports included that of Cecil in 1909, who while studying the islets of Langerhans and diabetes, noted an "enormous adenomatous hypertrophy of an islet of Langerhans." Over the next decade, several reports of islet cell adenoma were generated both in Europe and America, but the functional effects of such lesions were not noted. However, in 1927, Russell M Wilder reported the first case of hyperinsulinism in a 40-year-old physician whose episodic unconsciousness was related to hypoglycemia. The unsuccessful surgical attempt at removal undertaken in December 1926 revealed metastatic disease of the liver, lymph nodes, and mesentery. Histology indicated a striking resemblance to the cells at islet of Langerhans and alcoholic extracts of the "cancer" tissue injected into rabbits generated hypoglycemia. On March 15, 1929, Roscoe R Graham of Toronto undertook the first successful removal of an islet cell tumor from a 52-year-old woman suffering from repeated hypoglycemic episodes of coma and convulsion. Successful enucleation of the tumor from the body of the pancreas resulted in cure. Recognition of the disease allowed Allen Whipple in 1938 to describe an eponymous clinical triad for the diagnosis of insulinoma and by 1950, the literature contained descriptions of more than 400 such patients.

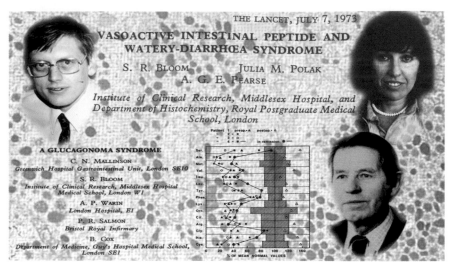

In 1995, Robert M Zollinger (*top right*) and Edwin H Ellison (*bottom left*) identified the relationship between non-beta islet cell tumors of the pancreas and a peptic ulcer diathesis (*background*). The subsequent identification of gastrin as the cause of the increased acid secretion and the trophic effect on the gastric mucosa led to a further understanding of the secretory and trophic roles of peptide hormones. Although gastrinomas were initially believed to be of pancreatic origin, the subsequent identification of the duodenum as a major site of the tumor led to reconsideration of the biology of the disease process.

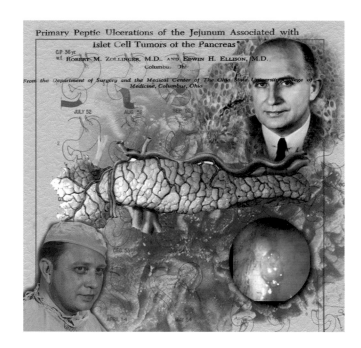

Steven Bloom (*top left*), Julia Polak (*top right*), and Everson Pearse (*bottom right*) of the Hammersmith Hospital, London, were instrumental in establishing the concept of the Apudoma and elucidating the peptide secretion and histopathology of neuroendocrine tumors of the gut. In a 1973 *Lancet* paper (*top*), this group identified elevated plasma and tumor vasoactive intestinal polypeptide (VIP) in six patients with watery-diarrhea syndrome. They suggested that VIP was the hormone causing the Verner-Morrison syndrome and proposed that the radioimmunoassay that they had developed should be used as the definitive diagnostic test for the disease. The following year, a glucagonoma syndrome (*bottom*) was established and verified by this group.

In 1955, Robert M Zollinger and Edwin H Ellison proposed that lesions of the non-beta islet cells might have the capacity to produce an "ulcerogenic humoral factor" and reported two patients with jejunal ulceration and pancreatic non-beta islet cell tumors. Having duly noted the massive gastric hypersecretion, it remained for Gregory to subsequently isolate and identify gastrin as the causal agent of the "Ulcerogenic Syndrome". In 1958, Verner and Morrison similarly reported a non-beta islet cell syndrome associated with diffuse diarrhea and hypokalemia that Said and Mutt subsequently identified as due to tumor secretion of vasoactive intestinal polypeptide (VIP). The identification of VIP in neural tissue and the recognition that a similar series of clinical symptoms could occur with adrenal or sympathetic chain tumors resulted in the elucidation of the Vipoma syndrome. Further work by Bloom, Polak, and R Mallinson led to the identification of a number of different endocrine tumors of the pancreas, including glucagonoma, somatostatinoma, and pancreatic polypeptidoma. Such lesions were recognized to sometimes form part of the Multiple Endocrine Neoplasia Type I syndrome (MEN I) and the concept of linked neural, endocrine, and gastrointestinal disease attained widespread acceptance by the 1970s.

Carcinoid disease

In 1867, Langerhans first described a tumor of the gut that on later review, seems almost certain to have been a carcinoid lesion. Otto Lubarsch of Breslau provided the first detailed description of such a tumor in 1888, when he reported autopsy findings on a patient with multiple carcinoids of the ileum. Two years later, William Ransom of Nottingham described in detail a patient with diarrhea and wheezing secondary to an ileal carcinoid tumor with liver metastases, thus providing the first identification of the classical symptomatology of the carcinoid syndrome. At about this time, the development of diverse staining techniques enabled numerous additional endocrine cell types, including Nussbaum cells, Ciaccio cells, Schmidt cells, Feyrter cells, and Plenk cells, to be identified and aroused a widespread interest in their location, function, and relation to disease. Given the distinct histological appearance and particular staining properties, these cells could be codified as enterochromaffin, argentaffin, argyrophil, pale, or yellow cells, and recognized simply as being morphologically different to other intestinal mucosal cells.

The first appendiceal neoplasm that may have been a carcinoid tumor was reported by L Glazebrook in 1895. He noted during the autopsy of a 55-year-old man who had died of a cerebral hemorrhage a primary appendiceal tumor "the size and shape of a pigeon's egg," found in the anterior wall about 3in from the appendiceal base. Microscopic evaluation demonstrated that the tumor consisted of nests of irregular cuboidal and cylindrical cells, and no metastases were evident. In 1907, Siegfried Oberndorfer, noting the "benign course of the tumors that resemble carcinomas," first coined the term "karzinoid" to describe these tumors. He first used this diminutive at the German Pathological Society meeting of the same year in Dresden, where he sought to signify his appreciation of the more benign biological and clinical course of lesions of this type.

Siegfried Oberndorfer (bottom left) in 1907 described tumors that resembled carcinomas and coined the term "karzinoid".

Ciaccio introduced the term "enterochromaffin" in the same year and six years later, Kull noted that the gastrointestinal tract contained cells with a morphology similar to that of chromaffin cells. Since they were unable to reduce silver nitrate (lacked argentaffinity), he proposed that such cells be considered as the progenitors of the EC cell. A year late (1914), Gosset and Masson of Montreal demonstrated the argentaffin-staining properties of the carcinoid tumors and proposed that such lesions were derived from the enterochromaffin cells or Kulchitsky's cells, which had been earlier discovered in 1897 by Nikolai Kulchitsky within the crypts of Lieberkuhn in the intestinal mucosa.

Subsequent studies have to a large extent confirmed this proposal. Masson in addition suggested that the cells formed a "diffuse endocrine gland" in the intestines, but misguidedly some 14 years later proposed that these cells were neurocrine and that they originated in the intestinal mucosa before subsequently migrating to the nerves. In the 1930s, Feyrter of Gdansk, Poland, also described a diffuse endocrine organ that included the gastroenteropancreatic (GEP) argentaffin cells as well as a number of argyrophilic cells. The ability to stain EC and non-EC cells of the gastrointestinal tract (using silver nitrate) was developed by Dawson in 1948, while the endogenous substance which reduced silver and chromium, 5-hydroxytryptamine, was identified by Erspamer and Asero. In 1963, Williams and Sandler initially classified carcinoid tumors according to their site of origin in the gut as fore-gut, mid-gut, or hind-gut, but this grouping has for the most part been replaced by a histological classification based on the cell of origin and the nature of the secretory product. The term carcinoid is now generally considered archaic, since it is understood to represent a spectrum of very different neoplasms, which originate from different neuroendocrine cell types and produce diverse biochemical agents.

Initially, carcinoid tumors were resected as widely as possible, since it was evident that even if metastatic, this would represent the best means of ameliorating the unpleasant sequelae of the secretion of the diverse biogenic amines and peptides responsible for the symptomatology. Unfortunately, resective techniques were relatively ineffective and pharmacotherapy was directed either at the specific symptoms, including diarrhea, flushing, and bronchospasm, or the causal agent(s) using antiserotonergic agents. While of some benefit, each agent was rarely effective in the long term and patients required polypharmaceutical intervention to maintain even minimal comfort. The discovery of the ovine inhibitory peptide somatostatin by Guillemin and Schally (1977) led rapidly to the elucidation of the somatostatin receptor subtype and the development of a receptor agonist capable of activating the system.

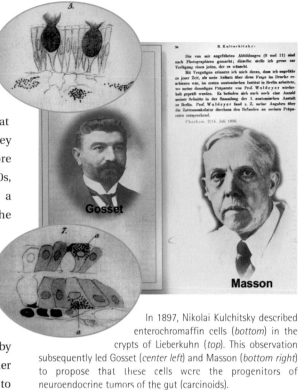

In 1897, Nikolai Kulchitsky described enterochromaffin cells (bottom) in the crypts of Lieberkuhn (top). This observation subsequently led Gosset (center left) and Masson (bottom right) to propose that these cells were the progenitors of neuroendocrine tumors of the gut (carcinoids).

Since neuroendocrine cells expressed significant numbers of such receptors, the further development of a long-acting analogue (octreotide) resulted in a substantial decrease in symptomatology and also life expectancy. The addition of an isotope (indium[111]) to the molecule enabled the development of a sensitive and sophisticated isotopic study (OctreoScan) that greatly facilitated the diagnosis of both primary and secondary neuroendocrine tumors (NETs). A subsequent extrapolation of this concept led to the introduction of somatostatin receptor analogues complexed with other isotopes (yttrium, lutetium) capable of delivering therapeutic dosages of irradiation to the tumor sites when administered intravenously. Thus, somatostatin receptor expressing lesions (the majority of NETs) could be diagnosed with an SST receptor scan, have their symptoms controlled with octreotide (inhibitor of tumor amine and peptide secretion) and irradiated by somatostatin receptor specific targeted intravenous irradiation. Surgery was reserved for mechanical problems of obstruction, perforation, and bleeding, and hepatic resection to a large part replaced by percutaneous hepatic embolization techniques, although very occasionally transplantation was deemed to be of some merit.

5 | HEPATOBILIARY TRACT

THE LIVER

A widespread belief existed for many centuries that the liver was the repository of life. Indeed, ancient poetry and writings referred to it as the seat of emotions and vitality. Thus, in Demotic Greek, the word liver ("*hepar*") was used in place of the word heart. Similarly, the expression "hit in the liver" was equivalent to the phrase "struck in the heart" and was interpreted as a mortal wound. In the Old Testament, the words liver and life are often juxtaposed. Thus in Psalms VII, 5, it is recorded: "Let him tread down my life to the earth and drag my liver to the dust."

The preoccupation of ancient people with the liver provides a long and interesting tale of belief, not only in its ability to predict the future but also its role as the pre-eminent vital organ of the body. During antiquity, it was considered to be one of the most important organs and variously regarded as harboring the soul, the life spirit, or being the source of blood. The Mesopotamians considered it to be the seat of the soul and the very center of life, and used it both to define the future and predict the outcome of disease. During the Assyrian civilization, hepatoscopy was regarded as a skill of considerable importance and individuals capable of interpreting the shape of the liver, its lobes, and the markings on its surface were highly regarded and became personages of considerable influence in the political system. In this context, it is worth noting that liver divination marked the initial stages in the study of anatomy, since to develop appropriate and precise interpretation, novel terminology needed development to facilitate description of the pathological features of the liver. For purposes of both education and consistency of interpretation, clay models demonstrating the gallbladder, porta hepatis, the umbilical vein, right, left, quadrate and caudate lobes, and the pyramidal process were constructed. The portal triads noted on cutting the liver surface were variously designated in Assyrian scripts as either "weapons", "paths" or "holes". Similarly, the port hepatis was known as the gate, and the incisura and "umbilicalis" as the "door to the palace," while the gallbladder was called the "bitter part" and the common bile duct the "outlet". Indeed, the concepts embodied in Babylonian hepatic structure provided a fundamental assessment of liver anatomy that would remain unsurpassed until the advent of Andreas Vesalius in the 16th century.

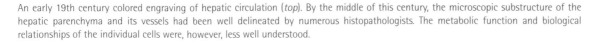

An early 19th century colored engraving of hepatic circulation (*top*). By the middle of this century, the microscopic substructure of the hepatic parenchyma and its vessels had been well delineated by numerous histopathologists. The metabolic function and biological relationships of the individual cells were, however, less well understood.

The liver was regarded in many ancient cultures as a source from which divine prognostication might be derived. Thus, when Sargon (*left*) in 718 BC had destroyed the Urartian and Zikirtian forces and avenged the insult delivered to the Mannean throne, it is likely he sought to placate the gods by sacrificing an animal and inspecting its liver. An awareness of the liver stretches back to time immemorial, as reflected by the comments of the haruspexes (divine interpreters of the future who used the liver as their medium) and augurs. Numerous clay tablets and models have survived to attest to the importance to which ancient civilizations of the Middle East ascribed "hepatoscopy" as a form of prophecy. A liver model (*right*) from Marti in Syria, circa 2000 BC, reflects the accurate understanding of hepatic function and attests to the careful observation necessary for divination. Observations were carefully recorded and correlation sought between previous events and future possibilities. The porta hepatis was known as the "gateway" and the insertion of the ligament arteries as the "door to the palace". The gallbladder was designated "the bitter place".

Even the Greek philosophizers and physicians deemed the liver to be of considerable importance, and Galen (of Phrygia and later Rome) followed the commentaries of Plato, who went so far as to establish the liver as the site of the vegetative part of the soul. The Alexandrian intellects and physicians considered the liver to be the source of the heat of the body and believed that nourishment in the form of chyle reached it from the blood, thus enabling the liver to be the main source of blood formation. There were various considerations as to what bile might represent. Overall, it was considered a waste product of the process by which absorbed food underwent conversion into blood by the liver.

The plates depicting the intestinal lymphatics from the 1622 dissertation of Gasparo Aselli (*bottom left*) of Cremona, who believed that lymphatics passed to the liver. This was the first use of colored plates in an anatomical text. Thomas Bartholin of Copenhagen (*top right*) published his first study on the lacteal vessels in 1652. His studies convinced him that chyle was a different substance to the lymph, which flowed via the thoracic duct into the subclavian vein.

Further confusion as to the role of the liver was engendered by the controversy regarding the discovery of lacteals and the thoracic duct in the 17th century. Thus, despite the argument regarding lymphatic valves and the fanciful notion of a "gyrus" it was apparent to the experimentalists of Amsterdam (Sylvius, Blasius, Ruysch, and van Horne) that chyle moved from the abdominal cisterna chyli into the thoracic duct and then into the venous circulation. Thomas Bartholin in 1657 was not reticent in pointing out that under these circumstances, chyle could not be regarded as providing nourishment for the liver. Although now regarded as a relatively obvious piece of information, this dramatic reinterpretation of liver function led to widespread skepticism and controversy. Bartholin rendered the coup de grace himself by writing an epitaph to the liver, and thus ended centuries of the hepatic hegemony (Bartholin, *Vasa Lymphatica*, Copenhagen, 1653).

Subsequently, in 1669, Francis Glisson gave his name to the capsule of liver and together with Wepfer and Marcello Malpighi, described the glandular structure of the organ and confirmed the role of the lacteals in transmitting intestinal nutrients to the circulation. In so doing, they supported the position of Bartholin and confirmed that since the liver was bypassed by the chylous circulation, it should now be relegated to an inferior position as a simple manufacturing site for bile.

During the 19th century, the further refinement of chemical methodology led to major advances in the study of bile and the delineation of its metabolic and digestive role. Thus, by 1826, the old Galenic concept of the liver being a main organ in the nutritional system had once again achieved popularity as the biochemical work of Friedrich Tiedemann became accepted. Theodor Schwann, as well as Claude Bernard, recognized its important digestive role, and the use of experimental biliary fistula enabled elucidation of the function of bile in fat absorption. Leopold Gmelin had developed a test to identify bile

pigments in 1826, and after prolonged study of the nature of bile cells by a number of individuals, Willy Kühne in 1858 isolated and measured bilirubin in blood.

In 1846, Francois Magendie demonstrated that the portal vein was the recipient of considerable venous influx from the gut, and together with Gmelin, confirmed the potential central role of the liver in human metabolic function. Bernard in 1853 produced a masterful thesis on the novel functions of the liver relating to its ability to form and store glycogen, and in an epoch-making series of studies, demonstrated experimentally that the body (liver) could not only degrade chemical substances but was also able to synthesize them. In 1877, Nikolai Eck used the experimental model of the Eck fistula to further evaluate the chemical function of bile and to study its relationship to digestive function. S Rosenberg demonstrated that the amount of ingested fat is an important regulator of bile production, while W Balas and Ernest Henry Starling outlined the role of secretin in stimulating bile secretion.

The internal structure of the liver (*top left*) by Francis Glisson (*top center*), who summarized his work (*bottom left*), condensing it into five propositions concerning the movement of bile. As Regius Professor of Physic at Cambridge (*background*) and Reader of Anatomy at the College of Physicians in London, Glisson also contributed substantially to this area of medicine. Glisson believed that the primary function of the sphincter was to prevent chyle from flowing into the bile duct, rather than to regulate the flow of bile into the intestine. Indeed, Glisson was of the opinion that this function was governed by another sphincter at the neck of the gallbladder: "...in the same place where the cystic passage is joined to the gallbladder, it is finished with a fibrous ring; by which it happens that the bile cannot of its own accord flow out; and from there does not move unless a light pressure has been given, or on account of an extraordinary fullness (which amounts to the same)... for the decree of nature seems to be that in bodies possessing favorable health this vesicle is always found full!" Indeed, Glisson felt that the gallbladder was filled at least in part by ducts that emanated from the cavity of the liver.

Nikolai Eck (*top right*) described, in 1877, the surgical creation of a fistula between the inferior vena cava and the portal vein in a dog and suggested that this operation may be of use in patients with ascites. Fifty years thereafter, Allen Whipple reported his experience and initiated the "nebulous" surgical era of the portacaval shunt as a treatment for portal hypertension.

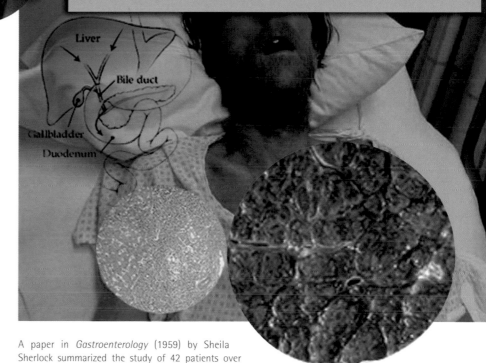

A paper in *Gastroenterology* (1959) by Sheila Sherlock summarized the study of 42 patients over 15 years with primary biliary cirrhosis (*top*). Sherlock demonstrated that hepatocellular failure occurred soonest among the most deeply jaundiced patients and was associated with a falling serum albumin and peripheral edema.

JL Bollmann and FC Mann studied the effects of total hepatectomy on the formation of urea and provided important physiological information regarding the extrahepatic production of bile pigments. BE Lyon (1850–1950) was the first to use a chemical cholagogue to study gallbladder disease and thus used physiological information to elucidate the management of pathology. In 1926, Minot and Murphy demonstrated that the liver also contained a major blood-forming factor, and further confirmed the multiple metabolic functions of the liver in the maintenance of body hemostasis. Indeed, the ability of ingested liver to cure the then fatal disease of pernicious anemia was regarded as further evidence of its vital role in the sustenance of life.

DISEASE OF THE LIVER

Although no clear evidence is available except that evident in old cuneiform scripts and disintegrated mummies, it is likely that ancient Egypt and Mesopotamia were major sites of liver disease, particularly of a parasitic nature. In Greco-Roman antiquity, much indirect evidence is available to support the fact that physicians were aware of jaundice, cirrhosis, abscess, and hepatitis. Indeed, the accounts of jaundice by Aretaeus and Caelius Aurelianus (circa 400 AD) are excellent examples of the general features of liver disease. All of the extant Arab literature of medicine dealt in considerable detail with hepatic disease, but since their religion forbade dissection and autopsy, only broad clinical descriptions of problems are available.

Thomas Willis in 1673, demonstrating his usual intellectual prescience, recognized not only obstructive jaundice but also what are now regarded as either retention or regurgitation as causes. He wrote: "The cause of the Jaundies to consist chiefly in this, that the choler being sever'd in the liver is not by reason of the ways being obstructed… but that it must of necessity regurgitate into the mass of blood to proceed… when… the choler is more plentifully separated or discharged forth by the ordinary ways." The clinical sign of jaundice was a source of considerable anxiety for the people of ancient times and evoked both fear and loathing. Thus, an 11th century Anglo-Saxon text stated: "From gall disease that is from the yellow jaundice, cometh great evil; it is of all disease most powerful when there wax within a man unmeasured humours; these are tokens: that the patient's body all becometh bitter and yellow as good silk; and under the root of his tongue there may be swart veins and pernicious, and his urine yellow."

It was long recognized that an excess of bilirubin (jaundice) was associated with serious illness. In clay tablets from Mesopotamia circa 3000 BC, the condition is well described: "…when a man suffers from jaundice of the eye line and his disease rises in the interior of his eyes, the water of the interior of his eyes is green like copper… his interior parts being raised, return food and drink. The disease desiccates this man's entire body: he will die." Although the Mesopotamians did not specifically recognize jaundice as related to underlying liver disease, the Bible notes that a yellow discoloration of the eyes is a sign of the disease (*left*). The word "jaundice" however did not enter usage in English language until the 14th century. Etymologically, it derives from "*jaundis*" (Middle English), "*jaunisse*" (Middle French), "*galbinus*" (Latin), "*jaune*" (French), "*galbos*" (Celtic), and "*ghel*" (Indo-European). All the roots of these words mean the color yellow. In fact, the synonym icterus is traceable back to the Greek word "*iktis*" that was derived from the name for the yellow-breasted marten that in ancient Greece was kept as a household pet; or to "*iktepos*" the golden oriole, the sight of which was supposed to cure jaundice; and to "*iktivos*," a kite with yellow eyes.

Icterus

In the 5th century BC, Hippocrates had produced an excellent description of icterus and recognized the poor prognosis of individuals with yellow discoloration and a hard liver. Rufus of Ephesus in the 1st century AD had advanced further in his thinking and divided jaundice into three types: that associated with fever, that related to hepatic abscess, and jaundice due to obstruction of the bile duct. Galen in the 2nd century AD wrote that an effusion of yellow bile was related to stone in the biliary tree, but also noted that disease could be unrelated to the liver and that conditions such as snakebite might result in the development of jaundice. Aretaeus in the 2nd century AD was of the opinion that jaundice arose not only from the liver but also the spleen, kidney, colon, and stomach. He was the first to relate the symptom of itching to jaundice and like Galen, believed that such symptoms were due to the failure of the spleen to remove black bile from the blood. Rhazes in the 9th century opined that jaundice originated from obstruction of the bile ducts, while Avicenna, in his *Canon* of 1000 AD, commented that jaundice from duct obstruction was different to other kinds of jaundice.

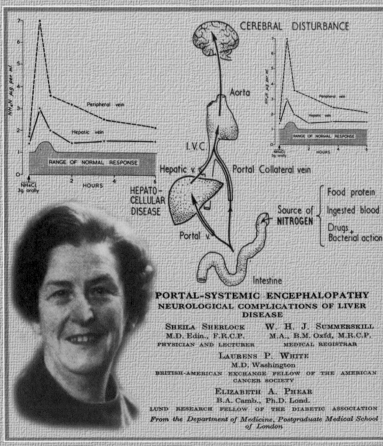

In 1954, Sheila Sherlock (*bottom left*) demonstrated that toxic nitrogenous substances passing via the portal vein into the systemic circulation caused diffuse cerebral disturbances that sometimes culminated in a hepatic coma.

It is probable that the first individual to identify bilirubin as the chromogen in bile was Louis-Jacques Thénard, who in 1827, shortly after the Battle of Waterloo, worked with the yellow magma removed from the dilated biliary tract of an elephant that had died in the Paris zoo. In 1826, Tiedemann and Gmelin used nitric acid to promote the oxidative conversion of bilirubin to biliverdin and observed the change of colors. In 1840, Jons Jacob Berzelius resolved the formula for bilirubin and called the substance "cholephyrrine". A year later, he also identified biliverdin from an ox, and in 1845, Scherer isolated biliverdin from humans. The green pigment was later crystallized by Küster in 1909 and purified by Barcroft and Lemberg in 1932.

Theophile Bonet, in his *Sepulchretum* of 1679, described numerous "jaundice producing conditions," but as late as the 18th century, the ancient Galenic theories of hepatic function would still be utilized to explain hepatic disease. By the early 19th century, however, Laennec's description of cirrhosis (1819) and Bright's (1836) as well as Karl von Rokitansky's (1842) contributions had produced a substantial new amount of clinical pathological information, which allowed for a better understanding of hepatic disease.

Friedrich Theodor von Frerichs in 1860 produced his classic monograph on liver disease, and by focusing attention on the subject in a formal fashion, facilitated the development of a substantially better understanding of hepatic pathology. In 1875, VC Hanot using microscopic technology was able to provide considerable further pathological detail on the underlying processes of hepatic dysfunction. As a result of the fusion of biochemical and pathological information, jaundice became recognized as a common-denominator clinical manifestation of serious liver disease. A Weil, who described the relationship of parasitic infestation to jaundice (leptospirosis), highlighted the role of extrinsic disease in the development of hepatic pathology in 1886. L Lucatello, who first described hepatic biopsy, provided a considerable advance in the assessment of hepatic pathology in 1895, but the technique failed to gain widespread acceptance until many years later. As a result, the widespread introduction of this diagnostic technique did not occur until 1939 with the report of P Iverson and K Roholm. Correlations of hepatic pathology with biochemical function were first established reliably by Hijmans van den Bergh in 1913, and subsequent to this contribution, innumerable biochemical assessments of parenchymal function appeared.

Friedrich Theodor von Frerichs (*left*) is regarded as the "Father of Hepatology" based upon his systematic and scientific contributions to liver disease. His monumental two-volume book on liver disease included an atlas with his own drawings of morphological findings. Josef Disse (*bottom right*) delineated the basis of normal liver anatomy and defined the spaces named after him.

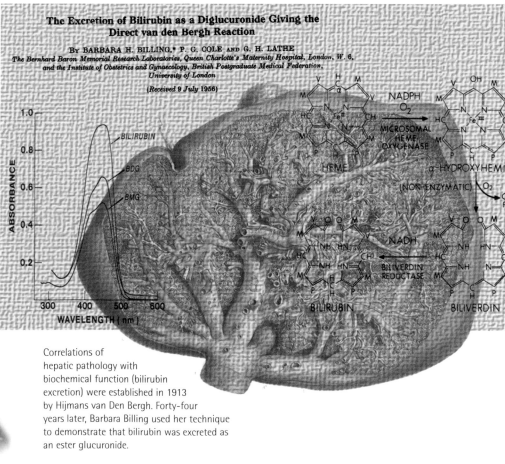

Correlations of hepatic pathology with biochemical function (bilirubin excretion) were established in 1913 by Hijmans van Den Bergh. Forty-four years later, Barbara Billing used her technique to demonstrate that bilirubin was excreted as an ester glucuronide.

Cirrhosis

It is worthy of note that the first commentary on cirrhosis is reflected in the Hippocratic aphorism of the 4th century BC that "in cases of jaundice it is a bad sign when the liver becomes hard". Although a similar remark is apparent in the writings of Celsus (100 AD), as far back as the 3rd century BC Erasistratus had noted that cirrhosis was associated with ascites. He considered the basis of the fluid accumulation "a chronic and scirrhous inflammation of the liver or the spleen which prevented the assimilation of the food in the bowels and its distribution through the body, that changes to water, which, being refrigerated is deposited between the intestines and peritoneum".

It was well known in antiquity that the "hard state" referred to the consistency of the cirrhotic liver, whereas "scirrhous" was used more to describe carcinoma. Thus Aretaeus the Capadocian, a contemporary of Galen, had the following to say in regard to the evolution of a cirrhotic liver: "...but if after the inflammation, the liver does not suppurate, the pain does not go off, its swelling, changing to a 'hard state', settles down into scirrhous; in which case, indeed, the pain is not continued, and when present is dull; and the heat is slight; there is loss of appetite; delight in bitter taste, and dislike of sweets; they have rigors; are somewhat pale, green, swollen about the loins and feet, forehead wrinkled; belly dried up, or the discharge is frequent. A cap of these bad symptoms is dropsy." Aretaeus thus indicated that cirrhosis might evolve from hepatitis and carcinoma from cirrhosis. Little further was added to the assessment of cirrhosis until the Middle Ages, when a salt-poor diet was introduced in the treatment of ascites.

By the 17th and 18th centuries, pathological anatomy had allowed for the postmortem identification of a cirrhotic liver. Thus Vesalius (1543), Nicolaas Tulp (1652), Bonet (1679), and Giovanni Battista Morgagni (1769) all produced reasonable descriptions of the disease process. Of particular interest is the description by Vesalius of an autopsy of a lawyer who died during a meal. The abdomen was found to be full of blood from a ruptured portal vein and the liver pale, indurated, and studded with nodules. Although Morgagni introduced the term "tubercle" to denote a nodule in the liver, he did not differentiate between cirrhotic nodules and those due to neoplasia. In 1685, John Brown, a London surgeon, was the first to describe and publish an illustration of cirrhosis.

On Diseases of the Liver
George Budd, 1845

Although Matthew Baillie was the first to establish cirrhosis as a nosological entity in his 1793 text *Morbid Anatomy*, Robert Carswell (*bottom left*), in his text *Pathological Anatomy*, delineated clearly and elegantly the gross morphology of the disease process (*background*). Thereafter, George Budd (*top right*), in his 1845 publication, described a rare disorder marked by cirrhosis of the liver and ascites due to an obstruction of the hepatic vein by a blood clot or tumor (Budd-Chiari syndrome). In addition, he wrote about Budd's cirrhosis – a condition of chronic hepatomegaly believed to be caused by intestinal intoxication.

Although William Harvey in 1616 had reported the presence of "a gray liver, retracted and hard" in a postmortem examination of a person who had perished of ascites, he had failed to define in detail the nature of the condition. By the end of the 18th century, Matthew Baillie had established cirrhosis as a nosological entity in pathology (1793) and in his text *Morbid Anatomy*, he described the disease in detail: "The tubercles which are formed in this disease occupy generally the whole mass of the liver and are placed very near each other, and are of a rounded shape; they give the appearance of everywhere of irregularity to its surface. If a section of the liver be made in this state, its vessels seem to have a smaller diameter than they have naturally. It very frequently happens that in this state the liver is of a yellow color, arising from the bile accumulating in its substance; and there is also water in the cavity of the abdomen which is yellow from the mixture of bile." Baillie not only described the anatomicopathological nature of cirrhosis, but also noted the relationship of alcohol intake to cirrhosis: "This disease is hardly ever met within a very

As a result of a decrease in alcohol tax, a massive overproduction and consumption of gin resulted in an epidemic of cirrhosis. Gin liver became one of the commonest clinical diagnoses of the 18th century, and numerous cartoons and caricatures of the time, from William Hogarth to Thomas Rowlandson, attest to the vices and diseases of the inebriate.

young person, but frequently takes place in persons of middle or advanced age: it is likewise more common in men than women. This seems to depend on the habit of drinking more common in one sex than the other; for this disease is most frequently found in hard drinkers…" The consequences of the "gin plague" (1720–1750) resulted in a widespread awareness of alcoholic cirrhosis in England and the massive consummation of cheap and contaminated spirit at this time was well documented in the writings of Henry Fielding and the caricatures of William Hogarth and Thomas Rowlandson.

The overindulgence of gin related to a surplus of corn crops on the continent and in England, and in an attempt to stabilize the price of the grain commodity, parliament promoted distilling and consumption of spirits. As a result of the repeal of the old laws governing distillation and the lowering of taxes related to the buying and selling of alcohol, cirrhosis became widespread and was known in England as either "gin liver" or "gin drinker's liver".

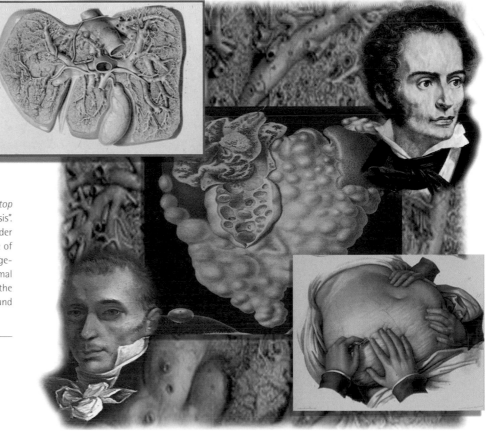

Some 25 years after the publication of Matthew Baillie, Laennec (*bottom left and top right*), the discoverer of the stethoscope, formally introduced the name "cirrhosis". He stated: "This type of growth belongs to the group of those which are confused under the name scirrhus. I believe we ought to designate with the name cirrhosis because of its color". Laennec coined the term from the Greek word "*kirrhos*" meaning orange-yellow, and thought that the disease was due to a new growth that resulted in normal liver tissue reabsorbing and diminishing in size. The case that Laennec described was the postmortem of a 45-year-old man who died of a hemorrhagic pleurisy and was found to have ascites and liver cirrhosis.

Boullard in 1826 considered the yellow granulation to consist of disorganized hepatic parenchyma, but much controversy arose as to the exact nature of the cirrhotic process. Andral in 1829 proposed that the red substance containing blood vessels was converted to fibrous tissue and that this accounted for the atrophic portions of the liver. Hope in 1834 endorsed the concept of hypertrophy of the white substance, but further complicated the matter by stating that there was in addition "an interstitial deposition in that substance, connected with a lesion of secretion". Becqueral in 1840 proposed an alternative hypothesis, stating that the primary lesion in cirrhosis was an infiltration of the yellow substance by an "albumino fibrinous material" that secondarily compressed the red substance. A more sensible approach, however, was adopted by Jean Cruveilhier (1829–1835), who proposed that it was fibrous tissue that resulted in cirrhosis, causing atrophy in one area while the remainder grew in order to compensate for the atrophy. Subsequent to his proposals, F Kiernan of England in 1833 described the appropriate hepatic microanatomy that enabled a better understanding of the disease process.

Robert Carswell in 1838 demonstrated that cirrhosis depended on the growth of interlobular connective tissue, and E Hallman (1839) in Germany became the first to examine cirrhosis microscopically, noting nodules of liver cells surrounded by fibrotic bands. By 1842, von Rokitansky had begun to refer to cirrhosis as a "granular liver". Von Oppolzer claimed that the early gestation of cirrhosis included partial obliteration of the small portal veins due to inflammation and compression by enlarged bile ducts. Von Frerichs of Freiburg in 1861 supported the concept of new capillaries growing into the scar tissue of the liver and referred to the condition as "chronic interstitial hepatitis" rather than cirrhosis. R Kretz in 1905 affirmed the regenerative aspects of cirrhosis and proposed that the nodular appearance of the liver was a consequence of asymmetric degeneration and regeneration of liver cells. By 1911, FB Mallory had written the definitive paper, entitled 'Cirrhosis of the Liver', and placed the disease on solid footing as a clinicopathological syndrome: "To the clinician the term cirrhosis usually means a chronic, progressive, destructive lesion of the liver combined with reparative activity and contraction on the part of the connective tissue. This contraction of the connective tissue may lead to obstruction of bile ducts causing more or less jaundice and to interfere with the flow of the blood through the blood vessels resulting in portal congestion and ascites." In 1928, Archibald H McIndoe produced exquisite vascular injection models of the hepatic circulation.

F Kiernan, in *The Anatomy and Physiology of the Liver* published in 1833, provided the first detailed drawings of the portal triad. The large perforated vessel (*center right*) is the portal vein, accompanied by a smaller artery and bile duct. The triangular spaces (portal triads) subsequently became known as Kiernan's spaces and Kiernan himself wrote: "...the lobules constitute the secreting portion of the liver. A lobule is apparently composed of numerous minute bodies of yellowish color (imparted to them by the bile they contain) and are various forms, connected with each other by vessels. These minute bodies are the acini of Malpighi." Kiernan disposed of the prevalent idea of the time that two types of lobule (red or yellow) existed, which had been termed "cortico medullary substance" by Antoine Ferrein of Montpellier. The Kiernan concept of lobular organization of the liver became the accepted model of hepatic microstructure and has lasted almost 200 years.

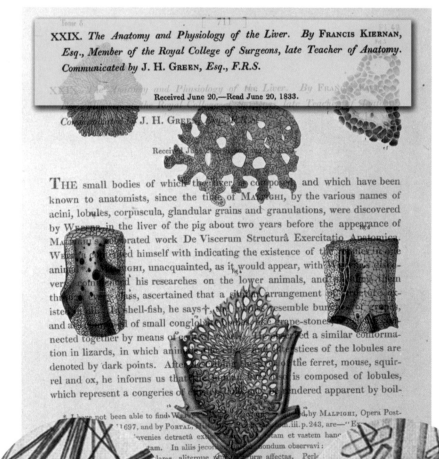

Alcohol

Although the deleterious affects of alcohol had been well recognized from time immemorial, it was only in the 18th century that it became accepted that alcohol was responsible for the development of both a fatty liver and cirrhosis. Thus Thomas Addison in 1836 drew attention to the relationship between fatty liver and alcohol, and wrote that patients with fatty liver may be diagnosed when their skin "presents a bloodless and almost semi-transparent and waxy appearance". About the same period, Justus von Liebig (1842) attempted to provide a chemical explanation for the development of the fatty liver. He drew a powerful analogy between the force-feeding of geese with grain to produce foie gras. Rudolf Virchow in 1860 stated that fatty livers were pathological and distinguished fatty degeneration from fatty infiltration. To further confuse the issue, French clinicians, including F Trousseau (1870), proposed that steatosis in an enlarged liver was an early component in the development of alcoholic cirrhosis. Further support for the dietary origin of cirrhosis was provided by the experimental work of Joseph von Mering and Oscar Minkowski, who in 1889 demonstrated that in animals without a pancreas with experimental diabetes mellitus, increased hepatic fat deposition occurred.

The efficacy of treating patients with Wilson's disease with penicillamine was reported by JM Walshe of Cambridge in the *Lancet* in 1960 (*bottom center*). This work provided the first assessment of the clinical usefulness of this drug in these patients. An improvement in the drawing of a spiral and a signature in one of the treated patients is shown (*bottom right*). Thirty-eight years previously, the entire March 1912 issue of *Brain* was devoted to SA Kinnier Wilson's (*top center*) description of this familial hepatolenticular degenerative disease. On the left is the cut brain of one of Wilson's patients, demonstrating the clear bilateral degeneration of the lenticular nuclei. Prior to 1948, Wilson's disease was considered to be untreatable, but the use of "decoppering agents" (such as penicillamine or ßß-dimethyl cysteine) led to a better management of the disease.

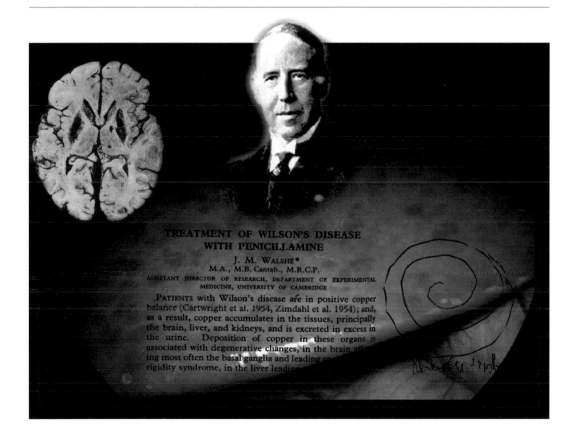

TREATMENT OF WILSON'S DISEASE
WITH PENICILLAMINE

J. M. WALSHE*
M.A., M.B. Cantab., M.R.C.P.
ASSISTANT DIRECTOR OF RESEARCH, DEPARTMENT OF EXPERIMENTAL
MEDICINE, UNIVERSITY OF CAMBRIDGE

PATIENTS with Wilson's disease are in positive copper balance (Cartwright et al. 1954, Zimdahl et al. 1954); and, as a result, copper accumulates in the tissues, principally the brain, liver, and kidneys, and is excreted in excess in the urine. Deposition of copper in these organs is associated with degenerative changes, in the brain affecting most often the basal ganglia and leading to rigidity syndrome, in the liver leading

Thus, a deficiency of lipotrophic agents and experiments with choline deficiency models further supported Laennec's original hypothesis that cirrhosis was due to a dietary deficiency condition provoked by an excessive indulgence of alcohol. By the turn of the century, the major interest in bacteria provoked by the work of Robert Koch and his colleagues stimulated considerable enthusiasm to identify an infectious cause of cirrhosis. Syphilis was the first candidate, followed by malaria and thereafter schistosomiasis. The subsequent identification of hepatitis and its related viral etiology promoted even further interest in the possibility of an initiating infective agent.

Portal hypertension and ascites

The ancient world had noted that liver damage was associated with other abdominal abnormalities, particularly fluid collection. Thus, a study of the Ebers papyrus (1600 BC) revealed that the ancient Egyptians were aware of the relationship between ascites and liver disease. Given the prevalence of schistosomiasis in Egypt, it is likely that parasitic disease may have been the cause. More than 10 centuries later, Erasistratus of Alexandria (300 BC) commented on the presence of ascites with hardness of the liver.

Physicians as diverse as Vesalius, Boerhaave, and Bianchi later reported the occurrence of splenomegaly in diseases of the liver. The early clinical and the later morphological descriptions of cirrhosis as undertaken by Bonet, Morgagni, Rokitansky, and Skoda recognized ascites as an integral component of the disease complex.

Hippocrates associated liver disease with dropsy and stated: "...when the liver is full of fluid and this overflows in the peritoneal cavity so that the belly becomes full of water, death follows." Erasistratus noted that a hard liver and dropsy were related and proposed that ascites is formed by the leakage of fluid into the peritoneal cavity. Galen felt the problem was due to suppression of hemorrhoids or imperfect evacuation with the accumulation of cold humors. Aretaeus of Cappadocia proposed that "dropsy sometimes is occasioned suddenly by a copious cold draught when on account of thirst much cold water is swallowed and the fluid is transferred to the peritoneum"

As early as the 1st century AD, both Celsus and Hippocrates had proposed paracentesis for the relief of ascites. Celsus used a lead or bronze tube with the collar about the middle to avoid fluid loss in the patient's abdomen, but preferred medical therapy, including long walks and the application of "fatty figs bruised with honey". Paul of Aegina in the 7th century AD proposed dehydration as well as paracentesis, but suggested that the latter be undertaken slowly "lest having evacuated the vital spirit with the fluid the patient be killed". In the 14th century, John of Gaddesden advocated salt-poor bread for the use of treatment of dropsy, and in 1728, Richard Lower, an Oxford physiologist, was the first to produce experimental ascites in dogs by ligating the thoracic segment of the inferior vena cava.

By the early 19th century, the clinical detection of ascites was well advanced and R Bright noted that obstruction of the venous system could be the basis of some ascitic effusions. He used cirrhosis of the liver with its obstruction of the portal vein as a classic example of this situation. P Charcot of Paris (1881) astutely noted that ascites would not develop if venous collaterals were present and implicated portal hypertension in the developing of the condition. Starling in 1895 provided a considerable contribution to the physiological understanding of ascites by defining the nature of colloid osmotic pressure.

In 1928, McIndoe opined that hepatic insufficiency was considerably more dangerous than ascites and that once jaundice appeared, it was likely that vascular compromise of the hepatic parenchyma had occurred. Subsequent to the evaluation of the hemodynamic factors involved in the development of ascites, hypoalbuminemia and thereafter excessive intra-abdominal lymph secretion were recognized as further issues involved in the genesis of the disease.

Archibald H McIndoe (*bottom right*) of New Zealand, while a Fellow at the Mayo Clinic in 1928, defined the physiological basis of portal hypertension. In the background is an injection specimen of the liver demonstrating (in green) the portal venous circulation. The latter elucidation of the complex architecture of the individual hepatic segments (*top left*) provided critical information necessary to facilitate surgical intervention in hepatic pathology.

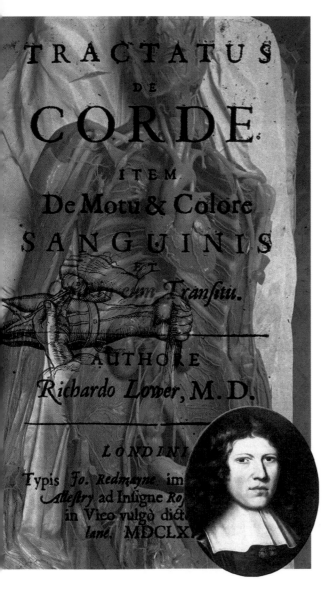

Richard Lower (*bottom right*) was an original thinker whose association with Thomas Boyle and Sir Christopher Wren at Oxford University embraced a triumvirate of the greatest scientific thinkers of the generation. Lower was also a prominent 18th century pioneer of the technique of intravenous injection and explored the concept of transfusion.

The demonstration of sodium retention in the 1940s by EB Farnsworth and the relationship to increased antidiuretic hormone secretion and excessive aldosterone production led to the development of spironolactone diuretics to antagonize the effects of aldosterone. At least three separate theories were developed in regard to the basis of the sodium and water problems in the development of ascites. These included the oldest concept (endocrine changes secondary to the intra-abdominal fluid secretion that resulted from portal hypertension). The second or renal theory was impaired renal ability to excrete salt and water. The third or lymphatic theory maintained that the primary cause of cirrhotic ascites was increased lymph flow into the abdominal cavity due to the portal hypertension and hyperdynamic splenic blood flow.

In 1689, Stahl described a syndrome of portal hypertension that was associated with his theory of plethora. The vague disease involved the portal and splenic veins and the hemorrhoidal venous plexuses, and Stahl reported epistaxis and the salutary effects of rectal hemorrhages in alcoholic individuals. Subsequently, in 1751, Kremff observed engorgement of the portal vein in patients who vomited blood, and

Morgagni (1769) recorded a case of thrombosis of the portal vein in a young man who presented with hematemesis and splenomegaly. Almost a century later, Le Diberder and Fauvel (1857–1858) in France and Power (1840) in America recognized the entity of esophageal varices. Meanwhile, both Retzius (1835) and Sappey (1859) published descriptions of the portacaval anastomotic circulation.

In 1883, Banti published the first systemic treatise on the syndrome, then known as hepatosplenopathy, which was to subsequently bear his name. Banti maintained that the disease ran a chronic course and suggested a toxic cause, believing that the spleen was the organ principally affected and that a toxin released by the spleen secondarily damaged the liver. This proposal was not accepted in Europe, although in England and America it was considered credible, mostly by the fact that Sir William Osler, as one of the most influential clinicians of the time, supported it. Indeed, his articles 'On Splenic Anemia' (1900 and 1902) documented the coexistence of splenomegaly and anemia in 45 cases. Osler however did not consider that the disease was a primary splenic disorder, but simply a "chronic splenic anemia plus features of cirrhosis of the liver".

Treating the putative disease of "splenic anemia" was an interest of surgeons, who claimed that a cure could only be effected by performing splenectomy or omentopexy. Indeed, notable wielders of the scalpel, including Cushing (1898), Halsted (1901), and Mayo (1902), insisted that splenectomy was useful in alleviating recurrent hematemesis.

Reconsideration of the fundamental basis of the problem occurred at the turn of the century. Thus Gilbert in 1899 deduced that portal vein pressure must be high in the patient with ascites after obtaining pressure readings of ascitic fluid as high as 400mm saline, and introduced the term "portal hypertension." The observations in terms of increased pressure were subsequently confirmed by Villaret (1906) and Pichancourt (1913) in patients with ascites.

At that stage, doubts about Banti's hypothesis began to appear when investigators explored the relationship of the hepatic vasculature to portal vein pressure. Thus Herrick in 1907 conducted perfusion studies that correlated the intrahepatic increase of vascular resistance to the cirrhotic process, and demonstrated the backflow of portal venous flow secondary to arteriovenous shunting. Similarly, Dock and Warthin in 1904, on the basis of their clinical studies, thought that the congestion of the portal vein accounted for the congestive splenomegaly.

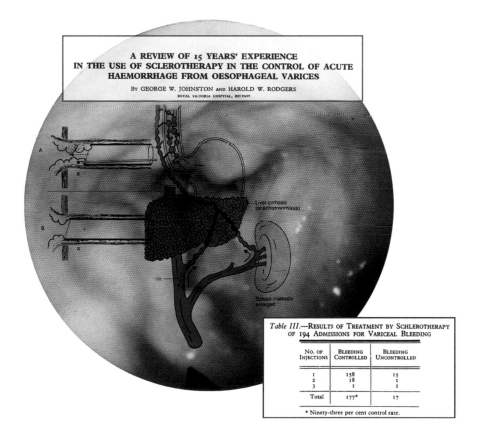

In 1973, in the *British Journal of Surgery*, George Johnston and Harold Rodgers of the Royal Victoria Hospital in Belfast published (*top*) their 15-year experience of controlling hemorrhage from esophageal varices using sclerotherapy. Portal hypertension often led to the development of esophageal varices and the lethal complication of hemorrhage (*background*). They were able to demonstrate a control rate of 93% (*bottom right*), with a mortality per injection of under 12%. A rigid, wide-bore esophagoscope was used to distend the varices (*left: A*) prior to injection and then compress them following this procedure (*left: B*).

The connection between the esophageal varices of portal hypertension and cirrhosis was poorly understood until Preble of Chicago (1900) published his autopsy series of 60 patients with cirrhosis and fatal gastrointestinal hemorrhage. He noted that esophageal varices occurred in 80% of the cases and proposed that the varices developed in response to the blockage of the portal vein, with the obstruction following from the loss of elasticity of the cirrhotic liver. The importance of portal venous stasis in the development of congestive splenomegaly was further recognized by Warthin (1910) and Eppinger (1920), who coined the term "*Staungsmilz*" in his treatise on hepatolienal disease.

A definitive comment, 'Vascular Lesions of the Portal Cirrhosis', was produced in 1928 by McIndoe, who concluded that portal vein pressure is high in cirrhosis with the hemodynamic changes evolving in stages. McIndoe suggested the use of an Eck's fistula as a means of relieving portal hypertension. The use of the term portal hypertension was given further credence by McMichael (1931 and 1934), who extended the concept by relating it to the thickening and narrowing of the portal or splenic vein. Congestive splenomegaly, according to McMichael, might be explained on the basis of increased portal pressure, reasoning by analogy with pulmonary hypertension. In 1930, Carnot reported the initial measurement of portal venous pressure in animals and shortly thereafter, in 1936, Rousselot published the first determination of pressure in the human portal system. Hemodynamic studies of the portal circulation accelerated with the introduction of hepatic vein catheterization (Warren and Brannon, 1944), a method for measuring hepatic blood flow (Bradley *et al*, 1945), and the technique for measuring hepatic wedge pressure (Friedman and Weiner, 1951; Meyers and Taylor, 1951, Sherlock *et al*, 1953).

The repetitive demonstration of hypertension led to surgical enthusiasm to decrease the pressure in the belief that this would ameliorate hemorrhage. Indeed, in America, surgeons seeking to rationalize the therapy performed many of the pioneer investigations. Thus, the revival of surgical therapy for portal hypertension (Blakemore and Lord, 1945; Whipple, 1945) led in addition to an increased recognition of disorders with elevated portal pressure other than cirrhosis. One consequence of the detailed evaluation of the problem was the development of sophisticated radiological examinations as the need for accurate anatomical diagnosis increased. Such procedures included celiac angiography (Seldinger, 1953), splenoportography (Abeatici and Campi), umbilical vein catheterization (Gonzales Carbalhaes, 1955), and hepatic venography (Tori, 1953). During the 1960s, shunt surgery became popular as a method to control the high incidence of variceal hemorrhage in patients with cirrhosis and a diverse range of procedures was introduced as each surgeon claimed advantages for a novel technique. As a result of the disappointing surgical outcomes, the use of pharmacological agents that decreased portal venous pressure was considered a more reasonable approach.

Thus vasopressin was initially demonstrated to provide considerable relief in acute situations, and the subsequent introduction of the somatostatin analogue octreotide provided evidence that long-term pharmacological control of portal hypertension might be a feasible therapeutic option.

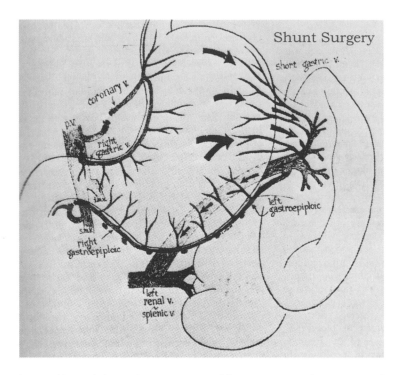

Innumerable surgical procedures were proposed in an attempt to decompress portal hypertension. In general, these were described as "shunts". The morbidity and mortality of such operations was considerable, and the depressing long-term outcome in most cases of cirrhosis resulted in tepid enthusiasm for this strategy.

Viral hepatitis

The concept of infectious jaundice has long plagued physicians. Indeed, for almost two millennia, the catchall phrase "bilious fever" covered a multitude of ill-understood diseases associated with icterus. The further uncertainty about viral hepatitis is reflected in the terminology, which over time has included at least 21 different designations. Up to 1937, the terms "catarrhal jaundice," "epidemic jaundice," and "infectious jaundice" were used. Then the terms "infective hepatitis" (preferred in England, 1939) or "infectious hepatitis" (United States, 1943) replaced catarrhal jaundice. In 1943, the terms "homologous serum jaundice" and "serum hepatitis" appeared. To gain some understanding of the evolution of thought on the subject, it is necessary to reflect on the manner in which icterus was considered over time.

Given the lack of knowledge of the time, it is admirable that the Hippocratic writers and their successors postulated that yellow bile was the cause of jaundice with fever. In addition, they noted that the disease often occurred in epidemics and could end fatally. The humoral concept of yellow bile was extended to cover other clinical entities that featured icterus as a sign and in which it was considered that the primary lesions were neither hepatic nor biliary. Thus the term "bilious fevers" was used to describe diverse illnesses that probably included malaria, typhoid fever, and typhus, as well as viral hepatitis.

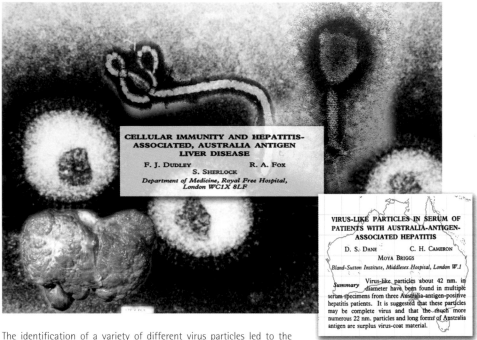

The identification of a variety of different virus particles led to the consideration of their relationship to hepatitis. Thus, the 1970 *Lancet* article (*bottom right*) by DS Dane and co-workers identified virus-like particles of 42nm diameter from serum samples in three patients with Australian-antigen-associated hepatitis. Two years later in the same journal (*top*), Sheila Sherlock's group was able to demonstrate that T-cell competence would play a role in limiting the degree of infection and subsequent liver damage (*bottom left*).

With the demise of the vacuous notion of humoral pathology in the 18th century, thoughtful physicians such as Herman Boerhaave (1721) considered jaundice to be a disorder of the liver and biliary tree, and proposed that icterus was a consequence of a hepatitis-linked duct obstruction. The observations of Morgagni (1761) also supported the mechanical theory of jaundice.

During the 19th century, controversy arose as to whether jaundice was solely a hepatic phenomenon or due to other diseases as well. On the one hand, the identification of infectious diseases such as typhoid fever led to a decline in the use of the generic term "bilious fever" as a catchall diagnosis for uncertain entities. On the other hand, appreciation of other causes of febrile jaundice, such as pneumonia, septicemia, Weil's disease, scarlet fever, relapsing fever, and even phosphorus poisoning enhanced the difficulty of delineating acute viral hepatitis.

The concept of catarrhal jaundice arose around 1825, when the proponents of the disease believed biliary obstruction to be the mechanism of jaundice. For Broussais (1832) of France, "Jaundice almost always depends upon gastroduodenitis or hepatitis, and is removed by the application of leeches". On the contrary, Andral (1829) attributed the icterus to an inflammation ascending from the duodenum and obstructing the biliary ducts. This emphasis on obstruction partly reflected the spirit of "anticontagionism" current at the time, and ignored the infectious nature of diseases. It is noteworthy that a number of significant thought leaders of the time, including Stokes (1833), Budd (1845), von Frerichs (1861), Bamberger (1864), and Virchow (1865), all accepted the causal role of duodenitis and gastroenteritis, and the disease became referred to as "catarrhal jaundice".

The pathogenesis of this entity assumed a more contemporary appearance, with the description of serous hepatitis that both Rossle (1930) and Eppinger (1937) considered to be a "capillaritis". They proposed that the intralobular edema and the capillary permeability were due to damage by toxins absorbed from the intestines, with the exuded serum deposited as albuminous material in the spaces of Disse. Keschner and Klemperer (1936) preferred the term "primary hepatic edema" to serous hepatitis and described the changes as focal and inconstant, interpreting the intact areas as representative of a compensated phase of the serous inflammation and the involved area as the decompensated phase (Zinck, 1941).

Although the diagnosis of catarrhal jaundice was long considered a sporadic disease, by the early 19th century, there emerged a distinct separation from other infectious causes of jaundice, as Weil's disease and relapsing fever were defined. Weil (1886) described a peculiar acute infectious disease accompanied by icterus, splenomegaly, and nephritis in four patients and resolved the diverse etiologies that had been attributed to this entity (ictere grave essential, fievre bilieuse, bilious typhoid, and icterus typhosus). Inada and Ido (1915) of Japan subsequently isolated the causative organism. Another infective jaundice – louse-borne relapsing fever – was also resolved at about this time, when Obermeir discovered the responsible organism in 1868.

The contagious aspects of epidemic jaundice were first appreciated by Pope Zacharias (8th century AD), who advised in a letter to Saint Boniface, Archbishop of Mainz, that patients be segregated from healthy persons. To Cleghorn, however, belongs the credit of providing the first reliable reference to epidemic jaundice. He wrote of its prevalence on Minorca during the summer of 1745. Although Thomas Sydenham (1624–1689) had already identified the clinical features of the disease, it was Herlitz of Göttingen who introduced the term "icterus epidemicus" in 1791.

DIE LEBERKRANKHEITEN

ALLGEMEINE UND SPEZIELLE PATHOLOGIE UND THERAPIE DER LEBER

VON

PROF. DR. HANS EPPINGER
VORSTAND DER I. MEDIZINISCHEN UNIVERSITÄTSKLINIK IN WIEN

MIT III ... ILDUNGEN

WIEN
VERLAG VON JULIUS SPRINGER
1937

Hans Eppinger of Vienna contributed significantly to the study of hepatic disease and proposed that there existed two separate types of hepatitis, a hepatocellular and a cholangitic form. His illustrious scientific contributions were subsequently clouded by well-founded allegations of involvement in the Nazi regime.

Epidemic jaundice actually became best recognized as a military disease in the 17th and 18th centuries, but its full impact and clear symptoms were not appreciated until the 19th century, when army physicians such as Frohlich (1879) reported its high incidence and low mortality. During the American Civil War (1861–1865), the Union army sustained 41,569 reported cases of jaundice, with 161 deaths among a total of just over two million troops. Similar epidemics attacked both the civilian and military population during the Franco-Prussian War of 1870, and the French referred to the disease as "*jaunisse des camps*" while the Germans named it "*Soldatengelbsucht*". The Japanese navy reported large numbers of hepatitis cases in its war with Russia (1904–1905), as did the German navy in the First World War. The Teutonic explanation for this phenomenon was attributed to hunger that had weakened the usually staunch German livers.

In 1886, Louis Kelsch (1841–1911) clarified the relationship of catarrhal jaundice, acute yellow atrophy, and epidemic jaundice by analyzing clinical and epidemiological data currently available, and concluded that they were all forms of the same disease, as Frohlich had already suggested somewhat earlier. Although Carl Anton Ewald (1913) raised doubts as to the nature of the obstructive element in catarrhal jaundice, he offered no new thoughts on the pathogenesis. Bernard Naunyn (1911) replaced the concept of an obstructive catarrh with the proposal of infectious cholangitis, thus expanding the earlier view of Strumpell (1883), who had differentiated catarrhal jaundice from acute yellow atrophy. Hans Eppinger (1922), who autopsied four icteric soldiers killed in the First World War, found no obstruction but "an acute destructive hepatitis" and concluded that the disease represented a milder and nonfatal form of the massive necrosis in acute yellow atrophy.

Although Eppinger was well aware of the identity of catarrhal jaundice and acute yellow atrophy, he refuted the concept that they were of infectious origin. In his classic textbook *Die Leberkrankheiten* (1937), Eppinger was prescient in distinguishing two clinical and histological types of hepatitis, the hepatocellular and cholangitic forms. The concept of cholangitic hepatitis was particularly seminal and initiated the concept of cholangiolitic cirrhosis later proposed by Watson and Hoffbauer in 1946.

Sir William Osler (*top right and bottom left*) is probably the best known physician in the English-speaking world, and at the turn of the 19th century he was known as the "most influential physician in history". Osler was trained in medicine at the University of Toronto and McGill (1872) and became the first Professor of Medicine at Johns Hopkins University in 1889. He was an expert in diagnosis of diseases of the heart, lungs, and blood and wrote the textbook *The Principles and Practice of Medicine* in 1892, which was considered authoritative for more than 30 years. This definitive text, however, included the mistaken assumption by Osler that "catarrhal jaundice" was a disease of the bile passage, which he also thought was probably not an infectious problem. In 1905, he moved to England to take up the Regius Chair of Medicine at Oxford (*background*), which he held until his death in 1919.

Similarly, this proposal also instigated Popper in the 1950s to consider the entity of cholangiolitis or intrahepatic cholestasis. A similar ambivalence toward catarrhal jaundice prevailed among the English and Americans. Thus, although Cockayne (1912) recognized the composite nature of hepatitis – which was clearly infectious in nature – he considered that epidemic jaundice was transmitted by an airborne route. On the other hand, traditionalists such as Osler differed and in the first edition of his famous textbook of medicine (1892), Osler placed catarrhal jaundice among "diseases of the bile-passages," explaining that the disease was "due to swelling and obstruction of the terminal portion of the duct".

Although the earliest recorded epidemic of serum (type B) hepatitis struck shipyard workers in Bremen in 1883 (Liirman, 1885), it must have been present before the 19th century, its survival ensured by the practices of venesection, scarification, and tattooing. Findley reported jaundice following accidental exposure to infective serum in a laboratory worker, and hepatitis complicated the use of yellow fever vaccine, while Beeson in 1943 noted its occurrence after whole blood transfusion.

McDonald (1908) was the first to postulate a virus as the cause and as a result, during the first half of the 20th century, there were numerous efforts to detect the specific etiology of viral hepatitis. However, as late as 1940, Lainer maintained categorically that hepatitis was due to toxins and not an icterogenic organism!

The advent of techniques for viral culture facilitated study of the issue, as did the Second World War, when military needs accelerated the necessity to understand the disease. In 1942, after inoculation of yellow fever vaccine containing human serum, 28,505 American soldiers in the African theater developed jaundice, with 62 deaths. Yoshibumi and Shigemoto (1941) gave filtered samples of blood, urine, and pharyngeal secretions from infected patients to children. Voegt (1942) in Germany carried out similar experiments in volunteers, as did Cameron (1943) in Palestine. In fact, the work of Voegt confirmed the existence of anicteric hepatitis, which had been previously proposed by Mende (1810) and accurately described by Eppinger (1922). Despite their relatively limited scope, the transmission studies did however establish the viral etiology of hepatitis. Subsequent studies undertaken by MacCallum and Bradley in England (1944) and by Havens (1944) and Neefe (1944) in America thereafter characterized two filterable agents responsible for the two types of hepatitis.

Baruch Blumberg (*bottom right*) was born in New York City (1925) and educated at the Flatbush Yeshiva, where he studied the Talmud before completing a medical degree at the College of Physicians and Surgeons (Columbia, 1947). Thereafter, he became interested in genetic polymorphisms following studies undertaken at Moengo in Northern Surinam. Although his initial studies related to the variation in response to infection with *Wucheria bancroftia*, he subsequently became interested in the study of inherited polymorphisms, which culminated in the discovery of the hepatitis B virus (*top left*) and his award of a Nobel Prize in 1976.

23. **PRIMARY HEPATIC CARCINOMA AND HEPATI-TIS B INFECTION. A SUMMARY OF RECENT WORK.**
Blumberg BS, Larouze B, London WT, Lustbader ED, Saimot G, Payet M
Inst. Cancer Res., Fox Chase Cancer Center, Philadelphia, PA
Prevention and Detection of Cancer. Part II. Detection. Vol 2. Cancer Detection in Specific Sites. Proceedings of the Third International Symposium on Detection and Prevention of Cancer held in New York NY April 26 to May 1 1976Nieburgs HE, ed. New York, Marcel Dekker Inc, 1303-2456 pp, 1980.

In 1965, a serendipitous discovery by Baruch Blumberg, a geneticist interested in the genetic basis of polymorphism, of a serological marker for type B hepatitis reignited the further elucidation of viral hepatitis. Blumberg wondered if patients receiving multiple transfusions might develop antibodies against polymorphic serum proteins. The blood of one patient reacted with inherited antigenic specificities on the low-density lipoproteins, a system that Blumberg termed "Ag". In 1963, he examined the reactions of hemophiliac sera that did not commonly have antibodies against the Ag antigen, and noted that one hemophiliac serum precipitated one of 24 test sera in a panel. Since this specimen was quite unlike any of the other Ag precipitins and came from the blood of an Australian Aborigine, the reactant in the Aborigine serum became known as Australia (Au) antigen. The specificity of the marker for type B hepatitis was subsequently confirmed by Prince (1968) and Okochi (1968), and Blumberg received the Nobel Prize in 1976.

The general management of infectious and toxic hepatitis initially was broad and included bed rest, avoidance of hepatotoxins, and a high-protein, high-carbohydrate diet. The rationale for the latter proposal lay with the reasoning that "a high glycogen content in the liver cell acted as a protective substance for the essential cell proteins and lessened necrosis". The era of high-protein diets lasted until the late 1950s, by which time it had become apparent that protein overload had little effect upon the morbidity and mortality of patients with chronic liver disease and on the contrary might even precipitate hepatic coma. The use of specific amino acid mixtures was promulgated by J Fisher, but rigorous analysis of the data and evidence of only marginal clinical efficacy led to a loss of enthusiasm.

The introduction of purified adrenal hormones into everyday practice by Hench in 1949 marked a pivotal point in the history of liver therapy. Although, as Eppinger had proposed, they had been used in liver disease as early as 1937, purified preparations were unavailable. The overwhelmingly fatal course in fulminant hepatitis forced the utilization of alternative heroic measures, including hemodialysis, peritoneal dialysis, exchange blood transfusion, cross-circulation, total body washout, hemoperfusion with artificial exchange columns or membrane, and even extracorporeal liver perfusion (Eiseman 1965). Few met with any predictable success, although recently liver transplantation has proved of some utility. More recently, the development of specific vaccines directed against the individual hepatitis viruses has led to a major therapeutic advance.

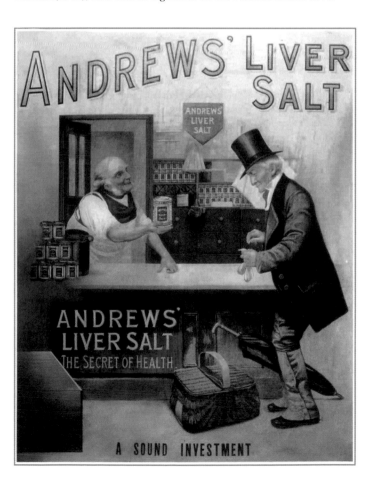

The widespread uncertainty as to the specific cause and appropriate therapy for liver disease led to the development of numerous remedies of dubious efficacy. The remedy offered by the pharmacist appears to have had little effect on his own condition!

A major advance in the therapy of liver disease was hepatic transplant. Although this was introduced by Starzl, Calne (*bottom left*) advanced the subject such that long-term survival of recipients became a reality. More recently, the age of biotechnology has spawned the development of numerous devices capable of substituting for organ and cell function (*background*). The quest for an artificial liver, however, remains the Holy Grail of hepatology.

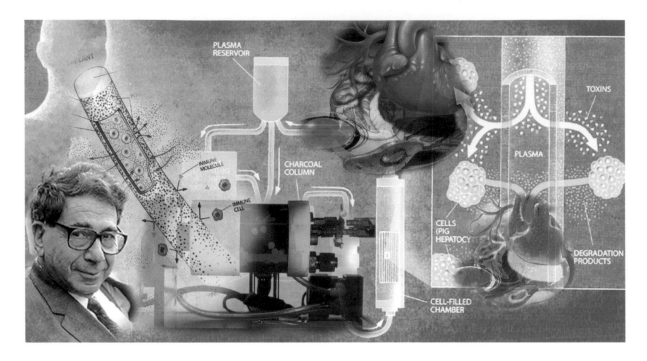

A major advance in the annals of hepatic therapeutics and surgery was provided by the successful introduction of liver transplantation. Although Welch in 1955 had undertaken the first attempts in heterotopic transplantation of the liver in dogs, the difficulties of maintaining vascular inflow and adequate biliary drainage soon forced abandonment of this procedure. In 1959, Starzl at Denver successfully undertook orthotopic liver transplantation and thereafter, in 1963, he performed the first successful liver grafting in man. Thereafter Calne, at Cambridge and King's College Hospital in England, further advanced the subject and the long-term survival of recipients became noteworthy.

The exigencies of 19th century fashion resulted in the development of significant anatomical distortions of the waist and even spine. In some women, the exaggeration of high fashion produced dramatic contortion of the liver and provided surgeons with difficulty in establishing whether symptoms were related to hepatic pressure effects or structural aberrations of the liver. Since it was thought not unreasonable that the monstrously contorted livers might be a good reason for the cause for complaints, and since ladies could not be induced to abandon their foundation garments, the surgeons (as might be predicted) took out the scalpel. Indeed, no less a savant than Christian Albert Theodore Billroth (1829–1894) carried out ventral fixation of a corset lobe in 1884! Other surgeons were less inhibited in their response and actually undertook complete resection of corset lobes. Few successful reports exist to document the efficacy of this therapy.

An even more exotic disease was provided by descriptions of the wandering liver, which appeared to be a forme fruste of the visceroptosis mania that afflicted both medical and surgical diagnosis at the turn of the 20th century. Such was the belief in this condition – known as Glenard's disease – that eminent surgeons including Kolliker (1906) and Eugene Bircher in 1918 operated on what they described as genuine wandering livers.

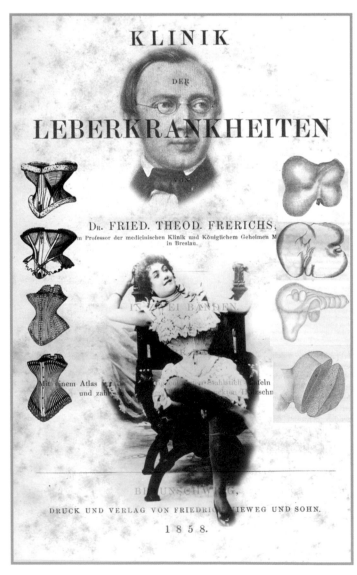

The use of complex corsets (*left and center*) to define the waists of women was a fashion statement that led to major alterations of the hepatic architecture, as can be noted (*right*). These abnormalities were at one stage thought to be responsible for disease, and no less a person than Friedrich Theodor von Frerichs (*top*) wrote on this 'medical' condition. Interestingly, surgery was occasionally undertaken in a misguided attempt to remedy the disorder!

THE GALLBLADDER

The early anatomists described the gallbladder accurately, but had little idea of its function, although Albrecht von Haller had in 1736 proposed that it played a role in the digestion of fat. In 1720, Abraham Vater was the first to describe the ampulla, and thereafter in 1887, Ruggero Oddi of Perugia described the sphincter and its function. Although this mechanism had been previously recognized by Glisson in 1654, the contributions of Oddi represented a significant advance in attempting to elucidate the physiological role of the sphincter in digestion. The earliest examples of gallstones were demonstrated in an Egyptian mummy from 1500 BC, but apart from a passing mention of the subject by Alexander of Tralles (525–605 AD), there is little clear evidence that their relationship to disease was recognized.

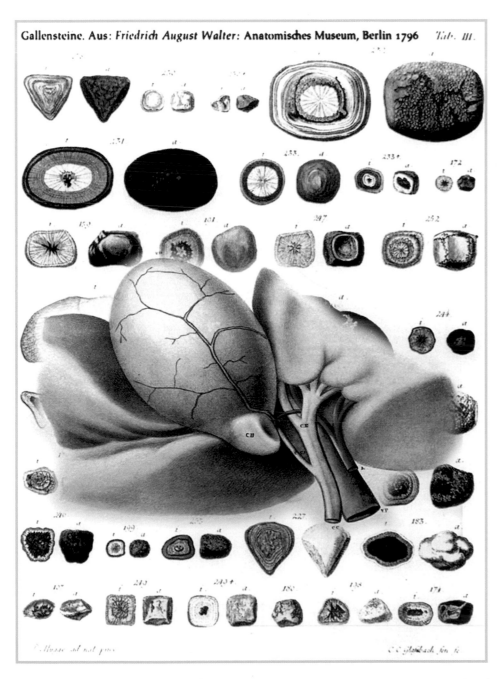

A gallbladder and its principal vessels (*center*) in the text of Jean Cruveilhier. In the background is the collection of gallstones assembled by Friedrich August Walter and exhibited in the Anatomical Museum of Berlin in 1794.

The fact that gallstones may be formed was known since the 14th century, and indeed, the first description of these was attributed to Gentilis di Foligno, who died of the plague in Perugia in 1349. For the most part, gallstones were obtained post mortem and used like bezoars as talismans capable of exerting powerful therapeutic effects themselves. A Benivieni (1443–1502) was the first to relate the presence of gallstones with clinical and pathological findings in 1507. Thereafter, numerous individuals, including Morgagni, as well as Johannes Müller and Naunyn, to cite a few, produced important information and detail regarding the relationship of gallstones to hepatic disease and their ability to produce jaundice by duct obstruction. The correct diagnosis of the symptoms produced by stones, however, remained an enigma and a considerable interest in gallbladder disease and duct obstruction was evident in the early 19th century as frustration with the postmortem detection of such stones grew. The French surgeon Jean Louis Petit as early as 1837 had proposed that in cases of gallbladder disease, the organ should be drained. Fortunately, the introduction of safe and effective surgery to effect cure of gallbladder disease was not possible until more than a century later, when Marion Sims performed the first planned cholecystostomy in 1878. Thereafter, in 1882, C Langenbuch (1846–1901) of Berlin undertook the first successful cholecystectomy. Unfortunately, the clinical symptomatology was such that in many incidences misdiagnoses occurred, until the introduction of appropriate radiological techniques in 1924 by EA Graham and WH Cole.

Although A Buxbaum had as early as 1898 been able to demonstrate the presence of gallstones, the development of reliable techniques for the clinical identification of such pathology required a further 20 years and the development of appropriate radio-opaque dyes.

Stone removal

The first gallstone was removed from a live person by William Fabry, a surgeon in Bern, known under the name of Fabricius Hildanus (1618). Cornelius Stalpart van der Wyl, a surgeon in The Hague, also performed these operations and there is record of two operations from the 18th century in which gallstones were removed from abscesses caused by ruptured gallbladders that contained stones. The first deliberate operation to deal with gallstones was carried out by Petit of Paris in 1743. He considered such surgery permissible only in cases where the gallbladder adhered to the wall of the abdomen, and used a trocar through which he inserted long pliers to discharge the contents of the gallbladder and extract the stones from the bladder.

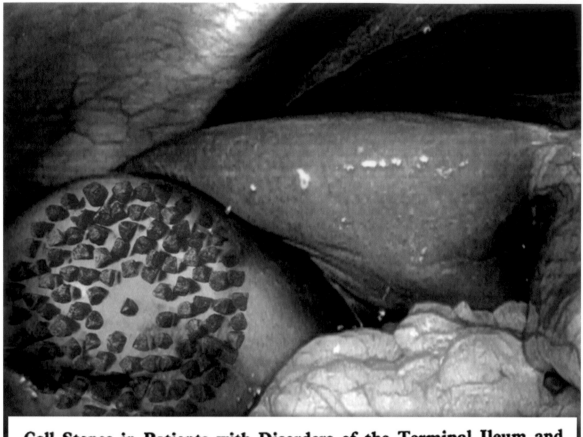

Gall Stones in Patients with Disorders of the Terminal Ileum and Disturbed Bile Salt Metabolism*

K. W. HEATON,† M.D., M.R.C.P. ; A. E. READ,‡ M.D., F.R.C.P.

KW Heaton and AE Read of Bristol University presented data at the British Society of Gastroenterology (April 25, 1969) that was subsequently published in the *British Medical Journal* in the same year. In this work, they described a four- to five-fold increase in cholelithiasis (32%) in patients with disorders of the terminal ileum. They also noted the abnormally high ratios of glycine/taurine conjugation in 90% of the patients examined. The authors suggested that both an impaired bile salt recirculation, as well as the absorption of poorly soluble bacterially degraded bile salts, may play etiological roles in these patients.

Since there was great anxiety of opening the abdominal cavity, much effort was directed at generating adhesion of the expanded gallbladder to the peritoneum of the anterior wall of the abdomen. In order to achieve this end, stimulants were applied to the skin of the frontal wall of the abdomen. Bloch, a Berlin physician, advocated the use of radishes, onions, and even the notorious aphrodisiac Spanish fly for this purpose! Others made an incision in the abdominal wall as far as the peritoneum and then placed various stimulants into the wound. August Gottlieb Richter (1742–1812) of Göttingen advocated the crushing of the stone in order to facilitate their elimination through a smaller opening and proposed that the adhesion of the peritoneum to the gallbladder could be achieved by leaving the inserted trocar in the gallbladder. More in keeping with current surgical principles was a procedure recommended in 1859 by Thudichum, who proposed opening the abdominal cavity and palpating the gallbladder to determine whether it contained any stones; should this be the case, the gallbladder should be sutured to the wall of the abdomen and once adherent, opened after six days and the stones removed. This operation in this form was only performed in 1882 by Francis Konig, Professor of Surgery in Göttingen and later in Berlin.

In 1867, Bobbs in Indianapolis operated in the belief that he was dealing with an ovarian cyst. He identified a large gallbladder, which he opened, and he removed the stones before proceeding to suture the bladder to the abdominal wall. This was the first single-stage gallbladder operation, albeit an unintended one. In 1877, Sims, a gynecologist in New York, performed this operation deliberately, but the patient died within 11 days. The American William Williams Keen and Robert Lawson Tait of Birmingham also proceeded along the lines of the gallbladder, while Theodor Kocher of Bern preferred to place tampons around the gallbladder and only opened it after six days when it had already adhered to its surroundings.

As a result of this success, this procedure soon became widely accepted and Louis Theodore Courvoisier first performed the procedure in France in 1885, followed }soon after in the United States in 1887. In England, however, the operation was strongly opposed by Tait, who regarded it as a complete absurdity! Indeed, Tait considered that Sims had already written everything that could be written about gallbladder surgery and stones and therefore considered the "experimentation of Langenbuch" to be completely superfluous! The problem of stones in the duct system itself became the next issue that required resolution. Langenbuch was aware of the problem and wisely stated that in such cases, the bile ducts required exploration (choledochotomy) and stone removal. Although Hermann Kummel of Hamburg performed the first choledochotomy in 1884, the patient died and it remained for Courvoisier of Switzerland to successfully undertake the procedure shortly thereafter. Knowsley Thornton in 1889 introduced the operation to England, while the German surgeon Hans Kehr was instrumental in disseminating the technique, as well as drainage of the liver ducts, throughout Europe.

The sphincter of Oddi

Early recognition of such a structure began with Vesalius, who in his *Fabrica* (1542 AD) referred to the ancient controversy as to where the meatus of the bile vesicle was inserted. Even in his day, he wrote, some physicians still thought it was divided into two portions: one inserting into the stomach, the other into the intestine. However, Vesalius noted, some of those defending that assertion had never personally observed the organs. He himself by dissection was able to confirm "that not the smallest portion of the bile vessicle was extended into the stomach except in one oarsman of a pontifical trireme".

An important question at this stage was the nature of the anatomical relationship of the bile duct to the intestinal wall. In 1561, in his *Observationes Anatomica*, Fallopius established that the common bile duct took an oblique course through the intestinal wall. Roughly 100 years later (1654), Glisson, in his *Anatomica Hepatis*, gave what is thought to be the first description of a sphincter mechanism at the orifice of the common bile duct; however, history has somewhat overlooked Glisson's discovery. In his *De Meatu Cystico* (1681), Glisson presented considerable further discussion of the sphincter and the gallbladder.

The ampulla of Vater

In 1720, Abraham Vater, Professor of Anatomy at Wittenburg, presented the first description of the tubercle or diverticulum that was later to be named the ampulla of Vater. Of particular note was the fact that he appeared to recognize that there was no simple combination of the pancreatic and bile duct, but that they were fused in a complex fashion and ended as an elevation of the mucosa (later referred to as an ampulla).

In 1685, Godefridus Bidloo (*center right*) of Leyden, Physician to William III of England (*top left and background*) produced what is probably the first pictorial representation of the union of the pancreatic duct (*ductus pancreaticus*) and the bile duct (*ductus bilis*) within the membranes of the intestine (*top right*). It is unclear exactly when the theory originated that proposed that gallbladder filling is initiated by contraction of a special muscle at the distal end of the common bile duct in the duodenum.

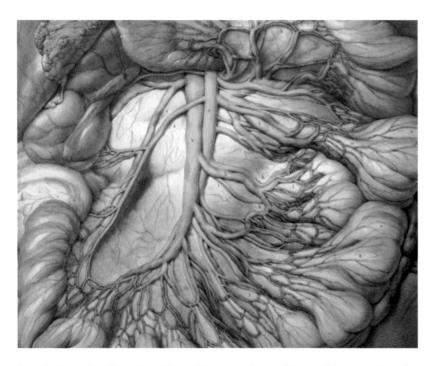

An early 18th century illustration of the small bowel and its vasculature by JP Bougery of Paris. The proximal portion was named duodenum since it was 12 fingerbreadths ("*duo decima*") in length. The jejunum was so called as it is the Latin term for empty. The term "ileum" was designated for the latter part of the small bowel, meaning to twist or writhe (Greek derivation).

ANATOMY

The first part of the small intestine was referred to as duodenum, since it was estimated by Herophilus to be 12 fingerbreadths in length. This Greek terminology was subsequently translated into Arabic and thereafter into "barbarous Latin" from the *Canon of Avicenna* by Gerard of Cremona as "duodenum" meaning "twelve" (the correct Latin translation would have been "*duodecim digitorum*"). The portion of the small intestine that followed the duodenum was noted by the ancients as always being empty, even after death. So apparent was this observation that even Aristotle commented upon it. The basis of the name jejunum is a derivation of the Latin for "vacant" since this part of the intestine was always empty and regarded as the hungry part of the gut. In fact, jejunum was the first breakfast among the Romans. Galen is credited with declaring it to be "fasting" and this became translated into Latin

as "*jejunus*" ("*jejunum intestinum quia ubique est vacuum*" – "the jejunum is that part of the intestine that is always empty"). The term was first popularized by Celsus and by the 14th century, had appeared in English literature.

The original use of the word intestine derived from "*intus*" meaning internal or within, but when used in the plural was taken to refer to the "guts" or internal organs. In the medical sense, it was first used by Celsus, who, in *De Medicina*, referred to "*intestinum tenue et crassum.*" The origin of the word gut is not as clear, although in Latin "*guttus*" was a narrow-necked jug and "*guttar*" referred to the throat. In Anglo Saxon, gut meant a drain or channel, while the common origin of both words may derive from the Aryan "*ghud*" meaning to pour. After the 14th century, the word gut was generally regarded as inclusive of the alimentary tract between the pylorus and anus.

In contradistinction, "*intestinum ileum*" meant the colicky part of the gut, since it was always in contraction and derived from the Greek meaning "to twist". Hence the ileum was regarded as the twisted gut. Galen did not distinguish between the two parts to the small intestine and it was known by him as tenue or gracile, and the term was retained as "*vasa intestini tenuis*". Although Galen was responsible for using the term ileum, he used it mostly in the pathological sense. The first recognized use of the term appears in a 1618 text entitled *Anonymous Introduction to Anatomy*.

The division between the ileum and the colon was known as the "ileocecal valve". It was first observed by Diocles and various early anatomists, and recorded by Fallopius in an unpublished manuscript *Anatomia Simiae* that currently resides in the Göttingen library. This report of 1553 not only identified the bowel but also noted its action in delaying the passage of food into the colon. Vidius, a pupil of Fallopius, proposed that the valve function was to delay the passage of material through the intestine, and similarly Varolius was aware of the action of this valve and considered it an invagination of the ileum into the cecum. A detailed description of the structure is contained in his work *De Resolution Corporis Humani,* published in 1591. Subsequently, in 1592, Caspar Bauhin of Basel published *Theatrum Anatomicum* and claimed to have previously described the valve in Paris as early as 1579. The Dutch physician Nicolaas Tulp subsequently redescribed the ileocecal valve in the 17th century and thus it variously became known as the valve of Tulp or Bauhin.

CELIAC DISEASE

The background and precise nature of celiac disease was ill understood for almost 2,000 years until Willem Karel Dicke of the Netherlands noted the remarkable decline of the disease during the war when bread was unavailable. It is, however, likely that the condition was known as early as the 2nd century AD, since Aretaeus the Cappadocian described in detail a condition that seems quite likely to have been celiac disease. The 1856 translation of his work by Francis Adams on behalf of the Sydenham Society reads as follows: "…the stomach being the digestive organ labors in digestion when the diarrhea seizes the patient. If this diarrhea does not proceed from a slight cause of only one or two days duration, and if, in addition, the patient's general condition be debilitated by atrophy of the body, the celiac disease of a chronic nature is formed."

Of interest is Aretaeus' suggestion that "drinks be taken before meals, for otherwise bread is very little conducive to trim vigor". His description of the disease, however, was reasonably accurate and he claimed that the inability to adequately digest failed to convert the food into its "proper chyme," leaving the work of digestion "half finished". As a result of this flaw in the digestive process, "the food then being deprived of this operation is changed to a state which is bad in color, smell, and consistence. For its color is white and without bile, it has an offensive smell and is flatulent; it is liquid and wants consistence from not being completely elaborated".

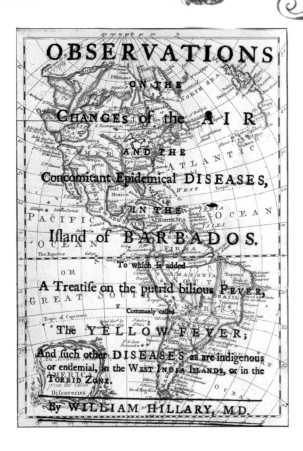

Aretaeus of Cappadocia provided an early description of celiac disease.

In 1699, a Dutch physician, Vincent Ketelaer, wrote a text, *De Aupthsis nostratibus, seu Belgarium Sprouw*, in which, whilst describing the oral aphthous ulceration associated with sprue, he devoted little attention to its intestinal manifestations. In 1759, William Hillary of Yorkshire produced the first description of tropical sprue in *Observations on the Changes of the Air and the Concomitant Epidemical Diseases in the Island of Barbados*.

William Hillary (1697–1763), an English physician, received his MD in 1722 from the University of Leiden, where he studied under Herman Boerhaave. He is best known for his systematic studies of the effect of weather on prevalent diseases in Ripon from 1726 to 1734 and in the colony of Barbados from 1752 to 1758. This, his most important work, contains accounts of lead colic and infective hepatitis, as well as the first description of the tropical variety of sprue or diarrhea alba, which chiefly attacks adults.

Thereafter, Manson in China in 1880 and van der Burg in Java made major contributions by delineating the clinical features of tropical sprue. Probably the next significant contribution to the subject was provided in October 1887, when Dr Samuel Jones Gee lectured on the subject of "the celiac affection" and subsequently published his observations in the St Bartholomew's Hospital report of 1888. Gee drew attention to the fact that the disease affected all ages, and particularly children between the ages of one and five years. He similarly reiterated Aretaeus' earlier observations, noting "the feces being loose, not formed but watery; more bulky than the food taken which seemed to account for; paling color as if devoid of bile; yeasty, frothy, and appearance probably due to fermentation, stinking, stench often very great, the food having undergone putrefaction rather than concoction".

OBSERVATIONS ON THE AETIOLOGY OF IDIOPATHIC STEATORRHOEA

JEJUNAL AND LYMPH-NODE BIOPSIES

BY

J. W. PAULLEY, M.D., M.R.C.P.

Physician to the Ipswich Hospitals

Br Med J 1954; ii: 1318-21

I have previously reported the finding of emotion factors influencing the onset and relapses of idiopath steatorrhoea, and of personality traits much like tho found in ulcerative colitis and Crohn's disease (Paulle 1949a, 1949b, 1950, 1952a, 19... 1952... This was u expected, and led me to wond... ...ight cause such a disturbance of s... ...ction. Wi colitis and ileitis in mind, the ... ...w. a form of ... That ... ...cos oedema ... from ... ...ow meals, which ... broa... ...va... con... ...es in ... ...torrhoea. ... ne inter... obs... by ... 1950...) and ... (19... cause of ... henomen... in ... ...rium ... ...tions ... occu... the ... ...s ... seemed to ...end su... the ... ...e ...lic infla...ation of ...ta... tion ... ... The chief di...culty ... his theory ... ...aysen's (193... ... i had been, a... ...s, accepted that th... ...cosa is normal in sprue and idiopathic steato...hoea ...d that

In 1887, Dr Samuel Jones Gee (*bottom right*) provided a clinical description of celiac disease. Seventy years later (*background*), JW Paulley still lamented the fact that the normal appearance of the human jejunum was virtually unknown, given the absence of any technique by which a live biopsy could be undertaken.

Not surprisingly, Gee proposed that the best form of treatment would be to regulate the diet and quite presciently instructed that the allowance of farinaceous foods should be minimal, although he supported the use of thin toasted bread and rusks (a well-versed Victorian dietetic remedy). As was the custom of the time, he proposed a variety of diets to treat children afflicted with the disease process. One in particular has remained a source of interest to the gastroenterological fraternity. Gee claimed: "...a child who has fed upon a quart of the best Dutch mussels daily, throve wonderfully but relapsed when the season for the mussels was over; next season he could not been prevailed upon to take them. This is an experiment I have not yet been able to repeat... but if the patient can be cured at all, it must be by means of diet."

A year later, RA Gibbons contributed two papers on 'The Coeliac Affection in Children' to the *Edinburgh Medical Journal* and described four patients managed according to the dictates of Gee. Although Gibbons undertook postmortem studies of his patients (Gee's diet was obviously less than efficacious), he was able to demonstrate no obvious abnormalities. As a result, he contented himself by claiming that the disease represented "a functional disturbance of the nervous supply of the liver, pancreas, glands of Brunner, and the follicles of Lieberkuhn, possibly also those of the stomach and salivary glands".

The manifestations of celiac disease continued to remain an issue of considerable concern to physicians of the turn of the century. Thus, in 1903, Dr WB Cheadle published in the *Lancet* a copy of a lecture that he had delivered in the previous year at St Mary's Medical School. Although Cheadle was able to add little to the understanding of the disease process, he somewhat changed the focus by publishing his description of it under the title of 'Acholia'. He noted that although there was no jaundice, "the stools are as white as though of obstructive jaundice when the bile is absolutely shut out from the intestine." Of particular note, however, was his important observation that the stools contained an excess of fat and that this could be quantified by fat estimation.

Christopher Booth (*bottom right*) was educated at St Andrews and trained thereafter at the Postgraduate Medical School (London), where he showed a natural flair for identifying clinical problems and then solving them using the available technology. During the 1960s, he produced a number of interesting papers focusing on the small intestine. In one in particular (*top*), Booth and Soad Tabaqchali were able to demonstrate that an alteration of bile salt metabolism by bacterial activity was responsible for steatorrhea in patients with stagnant-loop syndrome. In the graph (*bottom left*), treatment of patients with antibiotics reduced free bile acids in jejunal fluid, which was associated with a reduction in the degree of steatorrhea.

The advent of the late 19th and early 20th century focus on microbiology and the influence of this discipline resulted in considerable attention being directed to bacteria as the cause of diverse disease processes. Thus, in 1908, when CA Herter published his text *Infantilism from Chronic Intestinal Infection*, he proposed that celiac disease was due to an inflammation of the intestine caused by the persistence and overgrowth of intestinal flora derived during nursing. He claimed to have identified *Bacillus bifidus* and *B infantilis* in such patients, and therefore proposed that the term "intestinal infantilism" be utilized to describe the condition.

The frontispiece of George Frederic Still's text on childhood diseases. Still (1868–1941) was England's first Professor of Childhood Medicine. It is noted that while he loved children, and particularly little girls with long hair, he generally could not stand their mothers! His name is associated with a rare chronic inflammatory systemic disease that may cause joint or connective tissue damage and visceral lesions throughout the body. In addition, "Still's murmur" is an early systolic murmur heard near the left sternal edge in children and young adolescents.

COMMON DISORDERS AND DISEASES OF CHILDHOOD

BY

GEORGE FREDERIC STILL

M.A., M.D. (Cantab.), F.R.C.P. (Lond.)

PROFESSOR OF DISEASES OF CHILDREN, KING'S COLLEGE, LONDON
PHYSICIAN FOR DISEASES OF CHILDREN, KING'S COLLEGE HOSPITAL
PHYSICIAN TO THE HOSPITAL FOR SICK CHILDREN, GREAT ORMOND STREET
HONORARY MEMBER OF THE AMERICAN PÆDIATRIC SOCIETY

LONDON

HENRY FROWDE   HODDER & STOUGHTON
OXFORD UNIVERSITY PRESS   WARWICK SQUARE, E.C.

1912

Unfortunately, little progress was made in the further evaluation of the problem, when in 1918, George Frederic Still in his Lumleian Lectures on the subject to the Royal College of Physicians of London was able to add no new information. Six years later in 1924, Sidney Haas, writing in the *American Journal of Diseases of Children*, reported his successful management of celiac disease using a banana diet. Having successfully treated patients with anorexia nervosa using this fruit, he concluded that the anorexia of celiac disease might be similarly amenable to banana therapy, which he claimed to function as some kind of "hormone". The initial rationale of the therapy was based upon evidence emanating from Puerto Rico, where it had been noted that town dwellers in this island who ate bread suffered from sprue, whereas farmers who lived on bananas were protected from the disease process. Even during the Second World War, children with celiac disease were provided with an extra ration of bananas.

Although Haas had been prescient in recognizing that celiac disease was connected to carbohydrate metabolism, he had failed to identify the critical role of gluten. This observation was elegantly derived by Dicke of the Netherlands and subsequently became the basis of his medical thesis. On May 30, 1950, 'Celiac Disease An Investigation of the Harmful Effects of Certain types of Cereal on Patients Suffering from Celiac Disease' was successfully defended by Dicke and his proposal soon received international acceptance. In a modest 97-page monograph, Dicke, with extraordinary accuracy and skill, delineated the clinical and biochemical basis of celiac disease and proposed a successful therapy.

THE VALUE OF THE BANANA IN THE TREATMENT OF CELIAC DISEASE *

SIDNEY V. HAAS, M.D.
NEW YORK

Some years ago I treated a child, aged 3 years, who suffered from a severe case of anorexia nervosa. She had reached a serious state of depletion and weakness from her self imposed starvation, refusing all food and regurgitating that fed to her by gavage. She finally accepted a banana, with the result that other food was taken in a more or less normal amount within forty-eight hours. There was a conscious ... when the banana was withheld, and food was taken no longer ... bananas.

This experiment was repeated to test the validity ... always with the same result, until a time came ... normal whether bananas were included in the di ... was such as is attributed to a hormone. It wa ... test bananas in a case of celiac disease where ... nent symptom.

Sidney Haas (*bottom right*) in 1924 claimed that celiac disease could be successfully treated using a banana diet. Although the clinical and scientific evidence provided by Willem Karel Dicke was unequivocal, Haas, as late as 1963, continued to propound the success of his banana diet. He claimed that "Dicke's demonstration was an excellent achievement scientifically and of immense value for the study of the celiac syndrome, but clinically it was a possible disservice since he ignored other carbohydrates as etiological factors".

Born in 1905 in Dordrecht, it was as a relatively young pediatrician in The Hague in 1936 that Dicke first became alerted to the etiology of celiac disease. It is claimed that the statement from a young mother that her celiac child's rash improved rapidly when she removed bread from the diet directed his attention to the possible etiology of the condition. In addition, he noted that the improvement of the condition of many celiac children seemed to be associated with the scarcity of bread in The Netherlands during the Second World War. Thus, in 1941, he published a brief report in *Nederlands Tijdschrift voor Geneeskunde*. In this article, he proposed that a wheat-free diet be utilized in place of either the Haas "banana diet or the Fanconi vegetable" diet. In 1950, his thesis detailed meticulous dietary studies of children with celiac disease and demonstrated unequivocally that a strict regimen of a wheat-free diet had a favorable and normalizing effect on such patients.

The development and introduction of the gluten-free diet and the consequent dramatic improvement in the prognosis of the disease rapidly achieved international acceptance. In a subsequent publication with van de Kamer and Weyers, Dicke published that the alcohol soluble or the gliadin component of the water insoluble protein or gluten moiety of wheat produced the fat malabsorption in patients with celiac disease.

Willem Karel Dicke (*right*) of the Netherlands provided the clinical and scientific information fundamental to the elucidation of the diagnosis and therapy of celiac disease. Dicke was recognized as an outstanding clinician, scientist, and administrator possessed of exceptional personal qualities. Born in 1905 in Dordrecht, it was as a relatively young pediatrician in The Hague in 1936 that he first became alerted to the etiology of celiac disease. It is claimed that the statement from a young mother that her celiac child's rash improved rapidly when she removed bread from the diet directed his attention to the possible etiology of the condition. In addition, he noted that the health of many celiac children improved significantly during the bread scarcity prevalent in the Netherlands during the Second World War.

BIOPSY

A potential problem, however, in the diagnosis and management of small bowel disease was the lack of the availability of jejunal histological material. Although the development by Rudolph Schindler had allowed visualization of the stomach, little progress had been made with the acquisition of histological material for diagnosis. Early attempts at developing biopsy techniques had been proposed by Benedict of Boston and Bruce Kenamore in the late 1930s and 1940s.

Unfortunately, the modifications of the gastroscope to accommodate the biopsy channel rendered it clumsy and even more difficult to use. Nevertheless, such material was valuable in that it obviated the need for diagnostic laparotomy and enabled gastric biopsies to be undertaken under direct vision.

In 1949, IJ Wood and RK Doig of Melbourne published in the *Lancet* the design of a simple flexible biopsy tube that could be used for gastric biopsies without the use of the gastroscope or an X-ray screen. Such was the state of affairs that in 1954, JW Paulley, writing in the *British Medical Journal*, stated that the normal appearance of the human jejunum was actually unknown: "The difficulty of obtaining satisfactory postmortem material and the possibility of autolytic changes before death which suggest that biopsy material is necessary to further research on the subject." His remarks, published under the title of 'Observations on the Etiology of Idiopathic Steatorrhea' reflected the frustration of both gastroenterologists and pathologists in establishing the nature of any disease process occurring within the small bowel. Fortunately, in 1955, the further technological development of Woods' original flexible gastric biopsy tube by M Royer of Argentina and Margot Shiner of England enabled the fluoroscopically directed biopsy of the duodenum. So confident was Shiner of her technique that she proposed that with minor modifications, it would be likely that biopsies of the jejunum might be obtained.

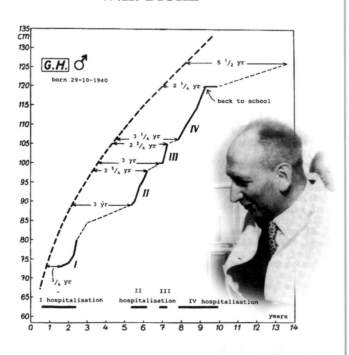

COELIAC DISEASE

INVESTIGATION OF THE HARMFUL EFFECTS OF CERTAIN TYPES OF CEREAL ON PATIENTS SUFFERING FROM COELIAC DISEASE

W.K. DICKE

THESIS

FOR DEGREE OF DOCTOR OF MEDICINE AT THE STATE UNIVERSITY OF UTRECHT, UNDER THE AUSPICES OF THE RECTOR MAGNIFICUS DR. H.J.M. WEVE, PROFESSOR IN THE FACULTY OF MEDICINE, ACCORDING TO THE UNIVERSITY SENATE'S DECREE TO BE DEFENDED IN PUBLIC ON TUESDAY 30 MAY 1950 AT 4 P.M.

The development of a small intestinal biopsy system by Margot Shiner in 1956 led to the subsequent establishment of the histological characteristics of celiac disease in conjunction with I Doniach and Jack Sakula in London.

Despite its success, the Shiner biopsy tube was cumbersome and as a result, Lieutenant Colonel WH Crosby of the United States Army improved the design. As part of the American army sprue team stationed in Puerto Rico, Crosby was aware of the need for a more flexible instrument to obtain jejunal biopsies. Together with HW Kugler, he therefore developed a series of modifications, including a spring-loaded knife, a timer, solenoids, and magnets before settling on an air pressure mechanism for biopsy. In 1957, Crosby and Kugler published in the *American Journal of Digestive Diseases* the first successful series of intraluminal biopsies of the small intestine using a device which subsequently became known as the Crosby Capsule.

CROHN'S DISEASE

Although the disease ultimately bears the name of the man (Burrell Crohn) responsible for documenting it, his colleagues Leon Ginzburg and Gordon D Oppenheimer were intimately involved in its delineation. A name not often included is that of Alexander Berg, the surgeon who was responsible for the first successful resections performed in the early cases and declined inclusion in the authorship of the original manuscript.

There is little known about the earliest reports of the condition and although Soranus of Ephesus described a Crohn's-like proctitis, most of the conditions involving rectal bleeding and weight loss reported by the early Greek and Alexandrian physicians were probably various forms of parasitic disease or dysentery. The postmortem of a 34-year-old man recounted by Giovanni Battista Morgagni in 1769 in *De Sedibus et Causis Morborum* refers to an inflamed terminal ileum and colon with ulceration stricture and large mesenteric lymph nodes. Although this was probably intestinal tuberculosis, the description is consistent with non-specific enteritis and has long been regarded as one of the earliest possible reports. In the subsequent two centuries, a number of descriptions of diseases of this kind appeared under synonyms that included "non-specific granuloma of the intestine" and "chronic cicatrizing enteritis". No less a personage than Louis XIII was felt to suffer from an anal variant of the disease process and much speculation has accrued regarding the royal posterior and its management.

Although a wide variety of anatomicopathological texts and presentations alluded to the existence of a number of ill understood conditions of the small bowel, these were mostly regarded as manifestations of tuberculosis or syphilis. Furthermore, the widespread use of the non-specific term "dysentery" led to even further confusion regarding the precise nature of the disease processes in the area of the ileocecal valve. In 1813, Charles Combe and William Saunders (*top right*) described what appears to have been the first accurately identifiable case of terminal ileitis, although there is no evidence to indicate that this may not have been tuberculosis. On the other hand, the condition of diffuse polyposis was well recognized as a separate entity.

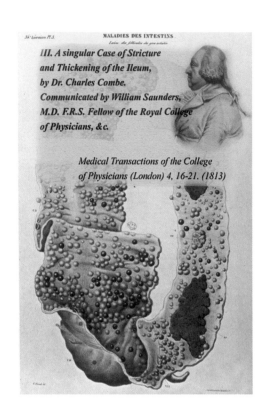

III. A singular Case of Stricture and Thickening of the Ileum, by Dr. Charles Combe. Communicated by William Saunders, M.D. F.R.S. Fellow of the Royal College of Physicians, &c.

Medical Transactions of the College of Physicians (London) 4, 16-21. (1813)

In 1882, N Moore, in the *Transactions of the Pathological Society of London*, was amongst the first to describe the microscopic and macroscopic features of Crohn's disease in a patient with intestinal obstruction and reported on the presence of chronic inflammatory cell infiltrates. The surgeons AWM Robson and Sir Berkeley Moynihan of Leeds in 1907 and 1908, respectively, reported their experience with chronic inflammatory masses causing intestinal obstruction. A year later, H Braun adumbrated further in the *Deutsche Zeitschrift für Chirugie* upon the origin of chronic inflammatory disease of the large intestine and proposed that tuberculosis, syphilis, and actinomycosis were separate diseases from idiopathic chronic inflammatory changes and could be distinguished by microscopic examination of the resected bowel.

In 1913, Sir Kennedy Dalziel described the entity of chronic intestinal enteritis in the *British Medical Journal*. He reported nine patients (two fatalities) with the disease and noted involvement of the jejunum, and middle and lower ileum, as well as the transverse and sigmoid colon: "The affected bowel gives the consistency and smoothness of an eel in a state of rigor mortis and the glands, though enlarged, are evidently not caseous." Dalziel considered the prognosis to be generally poor unless the disease was localized and could be treated surgically: "As far as I am aware the prognosis is bad except in cases where the disease is

In 1813, Charles Combe and William Saunders, writing in the *Medical Transactions of the College of Physicians* (London), reported a case of stricture and thickening of the ileum that they had demonstrated at the Royal College of Physicians of London. In so doing, they may have provided the first verifiable documentation of the disease. A similarly well described case was that of John Abercrombie, who in 1828, in his *Pathological and Practical Researches on Diseases of the Stomach, the Intestinal Canal, the Liver and other viscera of the Abdomen*, reported a 13-year-old girl with inflammatory thickening of the terminal ileum, proximal colonic involvement, and skip lesions. In 1859, Samuel Wilks proposed that idiopathic colitis should be considered a disease different from that of specific epidemic dysentery. Subsequently, he and W Moxon (1875), in *Lectures on Pathological Anatomy*, described "severe acute ileitis in the shape of the thickening of the whole of the coat including the valvulae conniventes". They noted the condition to be evident in a circumscribed patch 6in to 2 or 3ft in the ileum and "the whole wall was thick with inflammatory lymph, the microscope showing a generalized charging of the whole tissue with pyoid corpuscles".

The term "intestinal pseudo-obstruction" was introduced in 1958 by HAF Dudley and co-workers in a study of 13 patients (*top*). They had identified cases where neither mechanical intestinal obstruction nor "spastic ileus" were present. Ten years previously, however, Sir Heneage Ogilvie had described two patients with metastatic cancer and retroperitoneal spread to the celiac plexus who also had signs and symptoms of colonic obstruction, but with no evidence of organic obstruction to the intestinal flow. Ogilvie hypothesized that the etiology of their conditions was an imbalance in the autonomic nervous system, with sympathetic deprivation to the colon leading to unopposed parasympathetic tone, regional contraction, and thus a functional obstruction. In contrast, Dudley's group suggested that an antecedent period of hypoxia may have been the etiological agent.

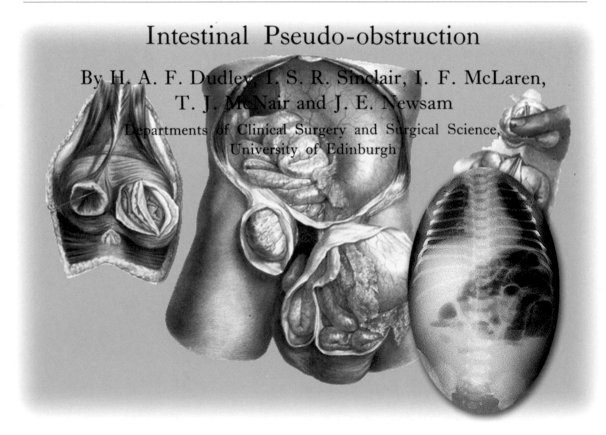

Intestinal Pseudo-obstruction
By H. A. F. Dudley, I. S. R. Sinclair, I. F. McLaren, T. J. McNair and J. E. Newsam
Departments of Clinical Surgery and Surgical Science, University of Edinburgh

Sir Kennedy Dalziel (*top left*) of Edinburgh, who described "chronic intestinal enteritis" in 1913 (*bottom*).

In 1932, however, Crohn, Ginzburg, and Oppenheimer published their paper entitled 'Regional Ileitis: a Pathological and Clinical Entity' in *The Journal of the American Medical Association*. They described their experiences with 14 cases of terminal ileitis, which they termed a pathological and clinical entity. A series of meticulous clinicopathological studies subsequently laid the basis for the establishment of a "novel" disease process, although its exact nature is still far from being understood. Crohn's original article described a disease "affecting mainly young adults, characterized by a subacute or chronic narcotizing and cicatrizing inflammation". They declared the disease to exhibit a relatively optimistic course: "...the course is relatively benign, all the patients who survive operation being alive and well."

Subsequent progress in the elucidation of regional ileitis involved the assessment of its course, a delineation of its histological profile, and a consideration in regard to whether the colonic form was different to the ileal component. Thus, in 1951, H Rappaport, in 100 patients with regional ileitis, noted that in more than half there existed a similar but less severe disease in the colon. A year later, C Wells, writing in the *Annals of the Royal College of Surgeons of England*, proposed that certain types of ulcerative colitis closely resembled regional enteritis of the small intestine and suggested that segmental colitis might represent a colonic form of Crohn's disease without an associated ileitis. S Warren and SC Sommers subsequently in 1954 noted that regional enteritis was restricted to the small intestine in almost 85% of individuals, but in 10%, skip areas of involvement coexisted in the large intestine.

In 1932, Burrell Crohn (*left*) and colleagues at Mount Sinai Hospital, New York City (*background*), defined the condition of regional ileitis.

localized and even then seems to be rather hopeless unless operation be had recourse to." Of interest is the preoccupation at this time of physicians to differentiate the disease from tuberculosis, which was already well recognized as capable of mimicking almost every known condition.

MOUNT SINAI HOSPITAL, NEW YORK

In 1923, Moschowitz and Wilensky, in the *American Journal of Medical Sciences*, produced an overview of non-specific intestinal granulomas. They described the presence of the giant cells and their resemblance to hyperplastic ileocecal tuberculosis, but emphasized the unknown etiology of this disease process given the absence of bacteria and caseation. Indeed, their analysis of the contemporary literature of ileocecal tuberculosis led them to conclude that in many instances, this pathology was novel and represented a simple inflammatory process and not tuberculosis itself. Their conclusions were thus consistent with the original proposals of Lawen in regard to the nature of fibroplastic appendicitis.

Basil Morson (*center*) and Sir HE Lockhart-Mummery focused attention on the criteria necessary to confirm the diagnosis of ulcerative colitis, as well as the issues related to neoplastic transformation.

The English surgeon Sir Brian Brooke (*bottom right*) was responsible for developing an improved ileostomy procedure that substantially augmented the quality of life of patients who underwent a pan-proctocolectomy as therapy.

A significant advance in the thought processes relating to this disease process was provided by Sir Brian Brooke in 1959 in a *Lancet* article. He considered that regional enteritis was not limited to the small intestine and that not all disease considered as idiopathic colitis was ulcerative. The basis for his observations was derived from information contained in the Birmingham Crohn's disease register.

His second proposal, namely that ulcerative colitis and Crohn's disease of the colon should be differentiated from each other because they varied in their response to medical therapy and in progress after surgery, was of critical clinical importance. Brooke was prescient in his recognition that Crohn's disease recurred after total colectomy and ileostomy, whereas in the instance of ulcerative colitis, such procedures were usually curative. Further observations in the early 1960s by Basil Morson and Sir HE Lockhart-Mummery provided further information on the histological and clinical nature of the disease process, but shed little light on its etiology. Although little progress has been made in defining the etiology, the development of a number of different anti-inflammatory agents, including steroids, has considerably facilitated therapy. Similarly, the development of appropriate surgical procedures has greatly improved the quality of life of many individuals suffering from regional ileitis.

An ancient Greek depiction of a physician seeking to define the site of abdominal pain.

DIARRHEA, PARASITES, AND BACTERIA

It is likely that the earliest symptom appreciated as being of gastrointestinal significance was abdominal pain. Almost certainly, this would have been followed by an appreciation that vomiting and diarrhea were similarly related to gut function. The recognition that something ingested might engender emesis was relatively straightforward, but the recognition of the causation of diarrhea was more complex. Intuition suggested that contamination of food might be involved and certainly decomposed products were obvious, but the understanding of toxins and invisible organisms awaited the development of the microscope, bacteriology, and the science of chemistry. However, for centuries prior to this, most diarrheal diseases were generically referred to as dysenteries, and if associated with bleeding, as bloody dysenteries.

Indeed diarrhea, or dysentery, is one of the oldest diseases known to mankind, and references to this uncomfortable and dangerous condition are found in the most ancient writings. In fact, the modern word "cholera" derives from the Hebrew "*cholira*" and in Second Chronicles, XXI, 19, the first recorded references to this disease bear witness to the fact that "Jehoram died of an incurable flux lasting two years". Later in the Bible, Acts XXVIII, 8, the intractable diarrhea besetting the father of Publius is described and is probably the first recorded psychiatric approach to the treatment of the problem as Paul cured the venerable patient with the laying on of hands.

In 1970, Leslie Turnberg (*top right*) of the Manchester Royal Infirmary (who at that time was working in Dallas, Texas) demonstrated using a triple-lumen constant perfusion system that ileal electrolyte transport (*right*) occurred via a simultaneous double exchange of Cl/HCO₃ and Na/H. The authors suggested a unitary model of ion exchange.

Hippocrates commented extensively on diarrhea and noted the influence of the weather: "For when suffocating heat sets in all of a sudden, while the earth is moistened by vernal showers... men's bellies are not in an orderly state, for it is impossible, after such a spring, but that the body and its flesh must be loaded with humors. Dysenteries are also likely to occur..." Hippocrates was also aware of different types of this illness and that diarrhea could accompany other diseases "when they are set with fever" or "with inflammation of the liver," and commented that under such circumstances, the prognosis might be worse. Similarly, he noted that cases "attended with blood and scrapings of the bowels"

(bacillary dysentery?) enjoyed a better prognosis. In addition to these observations, Hippocrates noted the relationship of diarrhea to teething as well as the significance of anuria in severe diarrhea: "...those who pass from below humors and scarcely urinate... are sickly."

In the 3rd and 4th centuries immediately following the birth of Christ and the beginning of the disintegration of the Roman Empire, very little was written on either medicine or diarrhea. The Talmudists stressed that sudden changes in living habits, particularly overeating, were apt to cause diarrhea, and Rabbi Samuel stressed the importance of fluids: "He who eats without drinking, eats blood from his own body... and this is the beginning of diarrhea."

The ancient Jewish physician/rabbi was well aware of the potentially harmful effects of certain kinds of food. A complex set of dietary laws was thus developed to protect the populace from infection or infestation. Although some of the edicts of Kashrut reflected mysticism and superstition, many even to this day demonstrate a sound understanding of the principles of food hygiene.

Although descriptions of early therapy appear odd to us today, the treatment recorded by the Talmudic scholars remained essentially unchanged for over 1,000 years. They advised external applications to the abdomen – usually heat of some sort or irritants such as wine and oil, as well as cupping to the navel. In the diet, they advised old apple or grape wine, or lemons, and to drink much water. In severe cases of tenesmus, as with the daughter of Rabbi Asche, pepper seeds in wine were administered. It is possible that the rabbis were aware of the contagiousness of dysentery.

During the Greek period, Soranus of Ephesus (circa 98–117 AD) wrote a pediatric text consisting of 23 chapter headings, amongst them 'On flux of the Belly'. The latter is notable in that it contains the first description of the fingernail test for purity of milk.

This test continued in use for over 1,600 years and was repeated almost verbatim in the first English book on diseases of children, written by Thomas Phaer in 1515: "That mylke is goode that is whyte and sweete; and when ye droppe it on your nayle and do move your finger, neyther fleteth abrod at every stiring nor will hange faste upon your nayle, whex ye turn it downeward, but that whvche is betwene bothe is best." This ancient test for the palatability of milk is repeated even as late as 1752 in William Smellie's *Treatise on the Theory and Practice of Midwifery*.

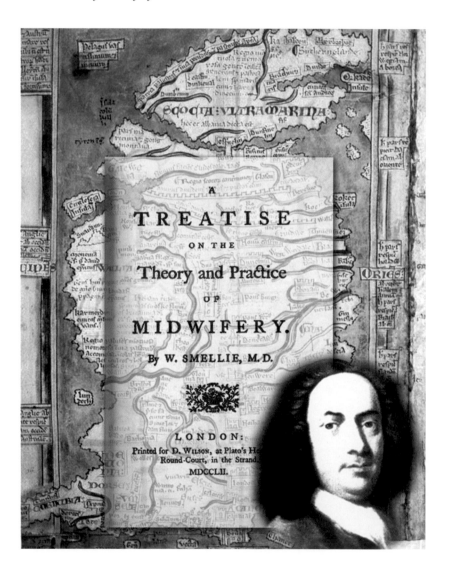

The first work in English on childcare, *The Boke of Chyldren*, was published by Thomas Phaer (1510–1560). Phaer was educated at Oxford and at Lincoln's Inn before obtaining an MD at Oxford in 1559. In addition to his medical works, he was the English translator of Virgil and also published the *Natura Brevium* in 1535 and in 1543, the *Newe Boke of Presidents*.

William Smellie (1697–1762) (*bottom right*) of Lanark, Scotland, was the first to teach obstetrics and midwifery on a scientific basis. After 20 years of practicing in Lanark, Smellie moved to London, where he established a teaching course for midwives and medical students. To facilitate education, he would deliver poor women free of charge if his students were allowed to attend the delivery and thus learn the principles of the practice of obstetrics. In addition to being a superb teacher, he developed an obstetric forceps, described and detailed the mechanism of labor, and provided much useful information in regard to the care of babies after their birth.

forms an interesting background to contemporary use of pancreatic extracts in chronic diarrhea. The other admonition was "instead of milk let him take… some barley soaked in water". The prohibition of milk and the use of barley water are little different to contemporary therapy in many parts of the world.

The "Father of Pediatrics" in England, Thomas Phaer, earned his title by writing *The Boke of Chyldren* in 1584, but the text was little more than another compilation of the classic authors and its chief importance is historical, since its existence illustrates the Renaissance tendency to translate the classic authors into the vernacular. The ideas of Phaer in regards to the etiology of diarrhea were conventional and his treatment standard, although it is interesting that he stressed abstention from milk for two-hour periods during the disease and then advised heating it when its use was resumed. Subsequently, neither Robert Penells nor Franciscus de la Boe Sylvius of Amsterdam (Sylvan fissure, 1641; the aqueduct of Sylvius, 1650) added anything new to the subject. In France, Simon de Vallembert (1565) published a treatise, *Cinq Bares de la maniere de nourrier et souvener les infants des leur naissance*. Although he had little novel to add to the subject, his description of the different forms of the illness is worthy of consideration: "…food is passed much as when eaten (the Greek, lientery); the condition is accompanied by skinning of the intestines (the Greek, dysentery); and lastly, neither of these two (called diarrhea by the Greeks)."

The treatment of disease was a source of considerable skepticism, as expressed by British cartoonists of the 18th century. Caricatures of this kind ridiculed not only the neurosis and hypochondriases of the patients, but also the absurdity of the therapies provided by the local quack.

The disintegration of the Roman Empire was followed by the Dark Ages, unenlightened for medicine as well as it was for other sciences and arts. Medical writing was confined chiefly to the Arabian physicians, who devoted themselves to translating the ancient Greeks and in so doing, perpetuated the ancient Galenic concepts. The translations were later reintroduced into Europe by Hebrew authors, who retranslated the Arabians into Latin. One of the best-known manuscripts on pediatrics of this period is *Liber de Passionibus Puerorum Galeni*, attributed to Galen but in reality more a compendium of many classic medical essays gathered together during the 6th to the 9th centuries. Indeed, the text contained little new information regarding the treatment of diarrhea. However, Rhazes (852–932 AD), a Persian of a somewhat later period, in referring to diarrhea bridged the ancient with the most modern by attributing the disease to teething, to catching cold (parenteral infection), and to spoiled milk. A compatriot of Rhazes, Avicenna, attributed diarrhea to teething, and reaffirmed the need for belly fermentations and fruit seeds, but added two new ideas. The first was the advice to "drink five grains of kids rennet in cold water". In fact, this suggestion to ingest the secretion of glandular organ was repeated in succeeding literature on the subject until the modern era, and

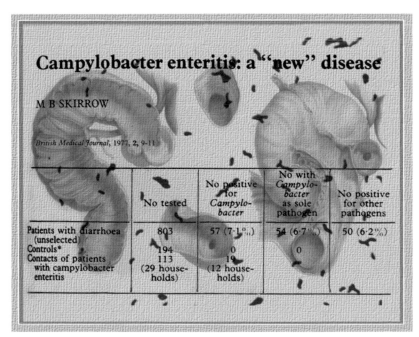

In 1977, MB Skirrow of the Public Health Laboratory in Worcester demonstrated a close association between *Campylobacters* in feces and a distinctive clinical enteritis. He suggested that *C jejuni* and *C coli* (which required a selective culture medium that was developed in his laboratory) were important enteric pathogens.

In 1886, Theodor Escherich (*left*) described *Bacillus coli*. Subsequently, Kiyoshi Shiga (*right*) in 1897 identified the cause of dysentery (*Shigella*).

In this respect, the development of the microscope and the subsequent work of Kocher, Pasteur, Cohnheim, and Escherich would prove to be of fundamental importance. Studies of parasites that were identified first in the skin and thereafter the gut led to an understanding of the biological processes involved in their diseases. They were regarded as organisms that lived in or on another animal and in obtaining food from the host, might or might not cause damage. Their presence certainly conferred no benefit. The diverse parasites identified in man included bacteria, viruses, fungi, protozoa, and metazoa, as well as worms.

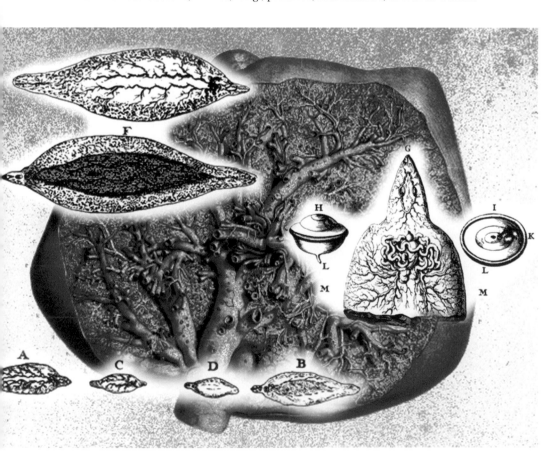

As a result of its widespread prevalence, an almost separate scientific discipline arose to deal with the effects of the association of two organisms. The term "parasite" is derived from the Greek word meaning "situated beside" and was used in ancient times to describe people who ate beside or at the tables of others. In spite of this "social" background of the word, scientists have used the term to define parasites as organisms residing on or within another living organism.

From the medical point of view, parasitism and potential harm to the host have become synonymous. Further restriction of the domain of parasitology occurred between the 17th and 19th centuries, when parasitology became the science dealing with zooparasites, that is, organisms that belong to the animal kingdom. Thus, parasites such as bacteria, viruses, and fungi that have been classified as of plant origin are dealt with in the discipline of microbiology.

Anthony van Leeuwenhoek was credited with seeing the first protozoon using a simple microscope, and between 1674 and 1716, he described many free-living protozoa and also the first parasitic protozoan *Eimeria stiedae*. In 1681, van Leeuwenhoek described the first human parasitic protozoon by the identification of *Giardia lamblia* in his own diarrheic stools. The major discoveries of parasitic protozoa were however delayed until the 19th century, when trypanosomes, amoebae, and malaria parasites were identified. Indeed, prior to the 1870s, worms or flukes had comprised almost all known parasites. In retrospect, evidence for several worm infections have been found in ancient Egyptian mummies (1210–1000 BC), reflecting the long-standing relationship between man and parasites. The Ebers papyrus of 1550 BC indicates that in ancient Egypt, at least four worm infections were recognized, including *Ascaris lumbricoides*, *Taenia saginata*, *Dracunculus medinensis* (guinea worm), and *Schistosoma haematobium* (bilharzia). The papyrus also includes information on arthropods such as fleas, flies, and lice. More recently, evidence was obtained from examining tissue sections of ancient Egyptian mummies that *Trichinella spiralis* existed as an infection during that period. Worms also were mentioned by Assyrian, Babylonian, and Greek physicians.

The liver fluke (*Clonorchis sinensis*) was recognized to be a major source of liver disease in the East. In 1911, Harujiro Kobayashi discovered the second intermediate host of the liver fluke and in so doing, facilitated the eradication of the disease. Indeed, the elucidation of the trematode worm diseases was to a large extent the province of Japanese bacteriologists and microbiologists. Thus, in 1904, S Katsurada had discovered *Schistosoma japonicum* and in 1914, K Nakagawa had identified the intermediate host of *Paragonimus westermani*. Similarly, the migratory course of human ascaris was demonstrated by S Yoshida and the experimental production of cancer from continuous simulation noted by K Yamagaw and K Ithikaw in 1915.

Theodor Maximilian Bilharz (*bottom left*) was a young German pathologist from the University of Tubingen. As a pupil of Karl von Siebold, he developed an interest in helminthology. As a result, in 1815 he accompanied Professor Wilhelm Griesinger of Kiel, who had been appointed Director of the Kasr-el-aimi Medical School in Cairo, to Egypt. Here he discovered the "*Distomum hematobium*" which was subsequently renamed "*Schistosoma hematobium*". Unfortunately, the medical school declined and Bilharz and Griesinger returned to Germany after two years. In 1862, on an expedition to Massawa with the Duke of Saxe-Coburg-Gotha, Bilharz contracted typhus and perished.

vector control and chemotherapy were thought to be effective measures against the spread of malaria. Short-term successes were achieved, but soon drug resistance developed in the mosquito vectors and in the parasite.

Francisco Redi (1626–97) (*center*) of Arezzo, Italy, confounded the current idea of its time that grubs and maggots developed spontaneously in decaying matter. This refutation of the theory of spontaneous generation, as well as the observation by Anthony van Leeuwenhoek of bacteria, led to the understanding that disease processes could be transmitted by living agents (bacteria, fungi, parasites). The further use of histology allowed the identification of the different lifecycle forms of parasites in various hosts and the subsequent elucidation of a wide variety of parasitic diseases that involve humans.

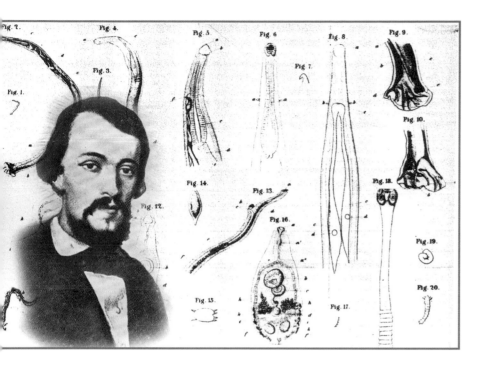

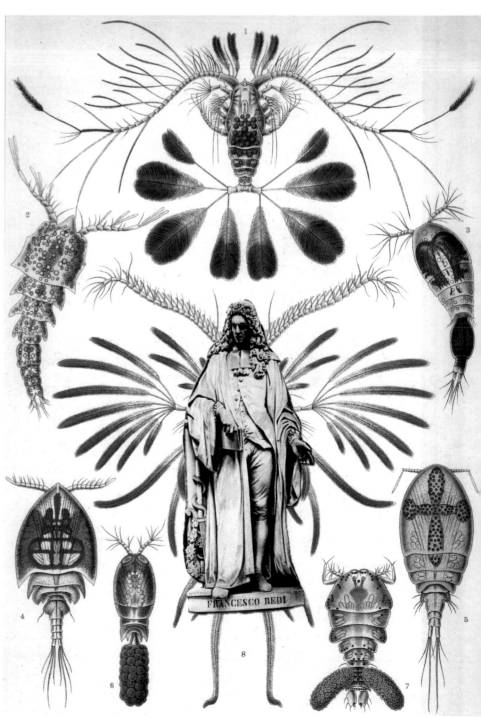

The two most prominent historical discoveries of worms occurred in 1379 (*Fasciola hepatica*) and in 1558 (*Cysticercus cellulosae*), but it was not until the 18th century and first half of the 19th century that many species of worm and arthropod were identified and classified. Thus, by the latter part of the 19th century and early 20th century, a consolidation of the discoveries of many human parasites had occurred, and in general, the identification of their lifecycle and recognition of their related disease syndromes had been established.

The host–parasite relationship is a dynamic process and although the host may exhibit several natural (innate) and acquired protective mechanisms, the complex structure of zooparasites in contrast to bacteria and viruses poses a significant challenge to host immune responses. A byproduct of some host responses is a chain of immunopathological reactions that ultimately results in significant morbidity. Whether diseases such as ulcerative colitis or Crohn's disease represent examples of such events is a matter of considerable controversy. The prevalence, intensity, and clinical significance of parasitic infections vary in different parts of the world. They are generally more prevalent in warm climates, in less developed areas, and in the socially deprived sections of any given society. Environmental and economic factors are prominent among those responsible for endemicity of parasitic infections in many parts of the world. Attempts to control the major parasitic infections have yet to demonstrate the effectiveness of any given strategy. In the 1940s and 1950s,

7 | COLON

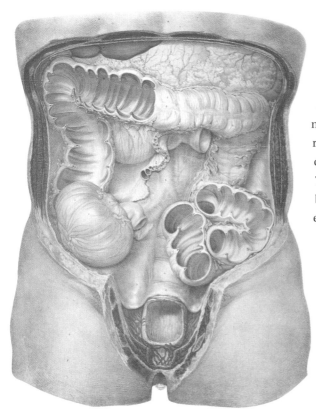

An 1832 illustration of the colon from the anatomy text of NH Jacob of Paris (*L'anatomie de L'Homme*), illustrated by JM Bougery.

The colon has since time immemorial been an object of both medical and social concern, as the passage of gaseous and noxious effluent constantly remained a source of concern as well as humor. The ancient Egyptians believed that the very essence of life resided in the anal area, while even thousands of years later in the elegant and sophisticated city of Vienna, Sigmund Freud asserted that issues relating to the colon and fecal retention were as pertinent to the health of the mind as to the body. Although the physicians of the Nile valley maintained that health depended upon a clean colon, their notion extended far beyond the immutable secrets of Thebes and Luxor, such that throughout history, both the physician and the patient have exhibited an obsessional requirement to clean the bowels by purgatives, cathartics, or enemata. Indeed, emptying of the bowel is regarded to this day as one of the most salubrious of sensations, recorded across all cultures. Given the fact that medications were often unpalatable or the patient too ill to swallow and retain them, the nether route of administration attained widespread popularity and acceptance amongst both physicians and patients. Enema administration became regarded not only as an appropriate medical intervention, but indeed a requisite daily exercise necessary to ensure maintenance of good health.

Disturbances of bowel function when associated with pain or obstruction led to obvious discomfort, rapidly apparent by way of either distention or loss of flatal or fecal effluent. The dreaded disease of appendicitis was completely misunderstood for years and in a world deficient of antibiotics and surgery, resulted in extensive loss of life. However, by the early 1900s, the prohibition against surgery declined to the extent that reasonable intervention became possible. Large bowel obstruction, however, remained the bane of physicians, as surgery represented a formidable challenge, given the problems of sepsis and the difficulties associated with resection and anastomosis. Thus, the most critical challenges in the development of large bowel therapy related firstly to the advance of methods to amplify visibility and secondly to the evolution of techniques that could be used to safely resect obstructions or inflammatory or neoplastic masses and facilitate the restoration of bowel continuity.

A novel clyster (*center*) designed by Regnier da Graaf. De Graaf's innovative mind ranged from the pancreas to the posterior with equally skillful results. This unique design allowed the patient to undertake self-administration of the enema. The flexibility of the tube was generated by using either leather or a length of intestine supported by a flexible cylinder of copper wire. Ingress was facilitated by the use of candle breeze, although a French modification of the procedure claimed an advantage for foie gras!

Given the early lack of knowledge of the interior of the system, a considerable preponderance of attention was paid to external manifestations, thus bleeding or prolapsed hemorrhoids figure amongst the earliest descriptions of disease and therapy. Therapy ranged from ointments to pessaries and even cautery. Excision was a dramatic intervention and particularly so prior to the development of analgesia and anesthetic agents. A particular problem was also posed by the difficulty of adequate visibility of the area, and thus early considerations were directed at the development of specula, whose utility was amplified first by mirrors and subsequently by candles, lamps, and eventually even lenses. Turck is believed to have been the first to X-ray the rectum in order to confirm the position of metallic tubes that he had inserted. The first radiographic observations of the colon were however recorded by Walsh (circa 1905), who identified a faint outline in an abdominal radiograph of a patient receiving therapeutic bismuth. Unfortunately, he and numerous other radiologists of the time failed to recognize the potential value of this observation in obtaining contrast studies of the large intestine.

IMAGING THE COLON

The first formal opaque enema examination of the colon was undertaken in 1904 by Schule, who published radiographs of patients who had received 300–400ml of an oily suspension of bismuth subnitrate, administered in the knee/chest position. By 1910, George Fedor Haenisch had described a more sophisticated fluoroscopic technique for the examination of the colon utilizing a novel horizontal fluoroscopy table – the trochoscope – and the retrograde instillation of a mixture of bismuth carbonate, bolus alba, and water. A decade later in 1923, AW Fischer first utilized the double contrast technique, and noted with enthusiasm that "the contours and lumen of the intestine are very clearly recognizable, so that any stenosis or tumor is certain not to pass unnoticed". By the 1930s, Kirkland and Weaver of the Mayo Clinic had further modified and improved Fischer's double contrast examination of the colon to produce radiographs that were able to detect the very smallest of intraluminal tumors. The subsequent use of gastrografin enemas and the introduction by Cook and Margulis of the silicon foam enema for the examination of the rectum and the sigmoid produced novel information, but was superseded by the introduction of colonic endoscopy.

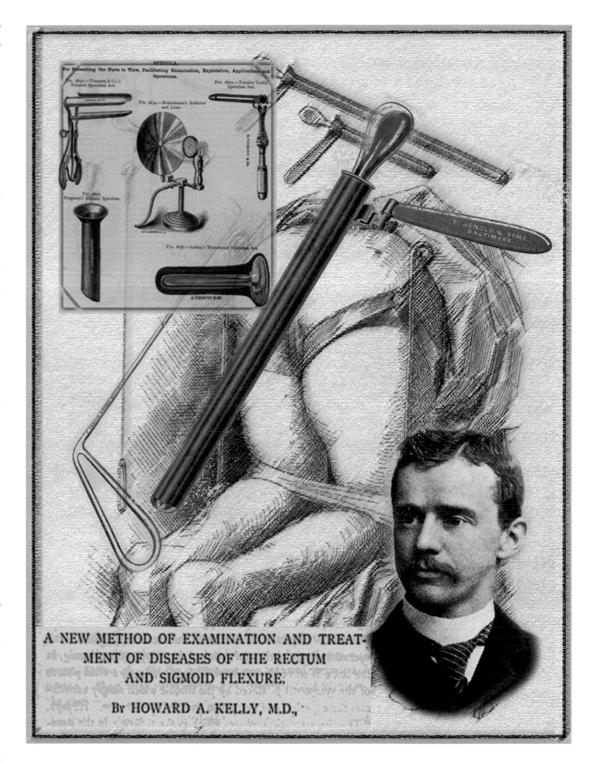

A NEW METHOD OF EXAMINATION AND TREATMENT OF DISEASES OF THE RECTUM AND SIGMOID FLEXURE.

By HOWARD A. KELLY, M.D.,

In 1895, Howard A Kelly (*bottom right*), Professor of Gynecology and Obstetrics at Johns Hopkins University, published in the *Annals of Surgery* the description and drawings of his instruments for proctosigmoidoscopy (*top and bottom left*). Kelly was not the first to perform examinations of this sort, as the care of the nether region had been of considerable concern to humans since the distant times of the Egyptians. Thus, the Chester Beatty papyrus is devoted solely to anorectal disease and the great physician Irj Or-en Akhty of the 10th dynasty is recorded as carrying the illustrious title of "Shepherd of the Anus". Examples of a wide variety of rigid instruments were developed over the centuries, ranging from the hollow wooden pipes of African tribes to the diverse specula of Greece and Rome. Nevertheless, irrespective of material or design, inadequate lighting and flexibility proved critical obstacles to ingress beyond the rectosigmoid junction. In addition, the length and tortuosity of the colon further accentuated the limitations of rigid devices prior to the widespread introduction of fiberoptic technology in the early 1960s.

Although a variety of endoscopic devices and tubes had been inserted into the colon for centuries prior to the introduction of X-rays, little visibility was possible beyond the rectum due to lighting problems and the inability of rigid tubes to circumvent the rectosigmoid flexure. The ability to pass a flexible tube as far as the cecum had been demonstrated as early as 1928 by HC Hoff. Although this blind procedure was of little diagnostic use to endoscopists, it did indicate that transmission of a device from the anus to the cecum was possible. F Matsunaga utilized a modified gastro camera to intubate the colon, but the procedure was difficult and provided only limited information. However, the advent of the Hirschowitz gastroscope in 1957 paved the way for applications of a similar type to the colon, and by the early 1960s, both the Machida and Olympus Corporations had developed prototype models for colonic examination. In 1963, Robert Turell of New York reported his experiences with colonoscopy in the *American Journal of Surgery* and detailed his use of a Hirschowitz gastroscope adapted to function as a colonoscope.

Luciano Provenzale and Antonio Revignas of Cagliari University, Sardinia, Italy, reported the first total colonoscopy in a human subject in the same year. In a highly innovative fashion, their subject was induced to swallow a long, polyvinyl tubing, which over a period of days emerged from his anus.

Provenzale and his colleague then attached the tubing to a side-viewing Hirschowitz gastroscope and gently pulled it northwards through the entire colon up to the cecum. Although this succeeded in its goal of achieving total colonoscopy, the technique was generally regarded as unacceptable for routine usage. In May 1967, Bergein F Overholt, working in conjunction with the Eder Instrument Company, developed a flexible fiberoptic sigmoidoscope whose application he presented at the ASGE meeting in Colorado Springs, Colorado. Convinced that better illumination, adequate flexibility, and deeper penetration would all be to the advantage of both the endoscopist and the patient, Overholt enthusiastically generated the supporting data and within two years, reported favorably on the newly introduced Olympus colonoscope.

The ability to place a wire snare into an endoscope considerably amplified the utility of the endoscope as a therapeutic device. One of the applications of the use of such a reconfigured endoscope was the successful removal of colonic polyps with a wire loop snare in the biopsy channel of a fiberoptic colonoscope. William I Wolff and Hiromi Shinya undertook this at the Beth Israel Hospital in New York, and within a year, were able to report a further 300 polypectomies with minimal complication rates and zero mortality.

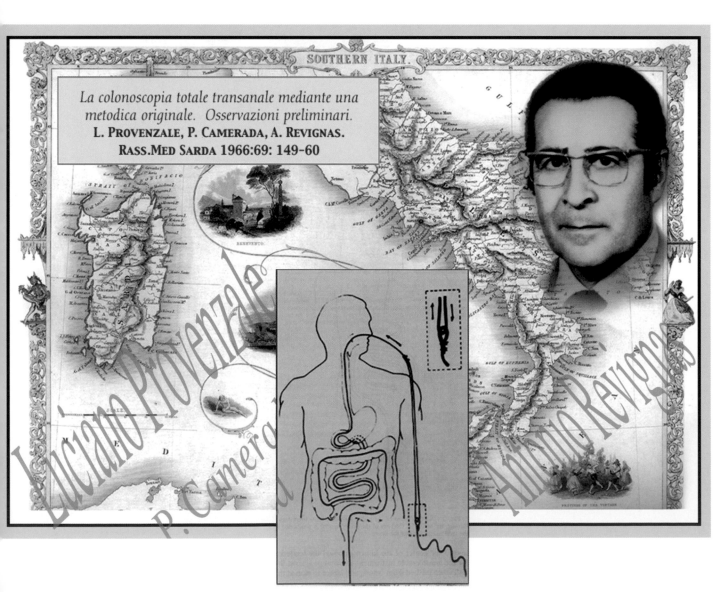

SOUTHERN ITALY.

La colonoscopia totale transanale mediante una metodica originale. Osservazioni preliminari.
L. PROVENZALE, P. CAMERADA, A. REVIGNAS.
RASS.MED SARDA 1966:69: 149-60

Although the island of Sardinia (*left*) had languished in relative obscurity since the departure of the Carthaginians, the innovative contributions in 1966 of Luciano Provenzale (*top right*) and Antonio Revignas (*top left*) of the University of Cagliari to the development of colonoscopy once again reminded the world of the power of the heirs of the Caesars. Using the 1955 technique of Blankenhorn for end-to-end intestinal intubation with a small-caliber swallowed tube, they positioned a pulley system of thin polyvinyl tubing arranged in tandem in the digestive tract and attached it to a lateral-viewing, non-steerable Hirschowitz gastroscope. The application of a light pulling or pushing force enabled the gastroscope to progress endoluminally in a retrograde fashion along the length of the colon (*center*).

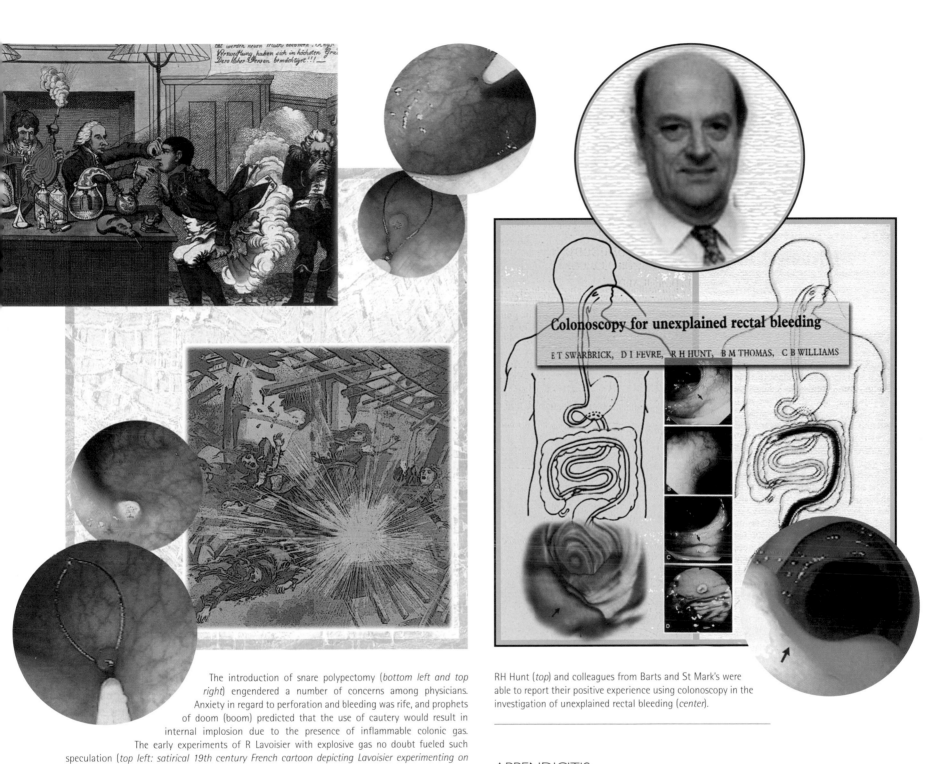

The introduction of snare polypectomy (*bottom left and top right*) engendered a number of concerns among physicians. Anxiety in regard to perforation and bleeding was rife, and prophets of doom (boom) predicted that the use of cautery would result in internal implosion due to the presence of inflammable colonic gas. The early experiments of R Lavoisier with explosive gas no doubt fueled such speculation (*top left: satirical 19th century French cartoon depicting Lavoisier experimenting on Napoleon*). Such concerns were soon dispelled and for the most part represented long-standing societal concerns (mostly of Freudian origin) regarding scybala and flatus.

RH Hunt (*top*) and colleagues from Barts and St Mark's were able to report their positive experience using colonoscopy in the investigation of unexplained rectal bleeding (*center*).

More cautious individuals and some surgeons with a vested interest in colectomy, however, insisted that colonoscopic polypectomy was being practiced overenthusiastically and that bleeding, perforation, and gas explosions were or could be common complications. Such conclusions were not supported by the available data and were effectively rebuffed by an article, in 1973, in the *New York State Journal of Medicine*, in which Wolff noted that he had undertaken 1,600 polypectomies without complication.

APPENDICITIS

Although now regarded as an organ of only modest medical and surgical interest, 100 years ago, inflammation of the appendix was a highly morbid condition, often leading to death. The elucidation of the pathogenesis of the disease process and the development of a rational therapeutic strategy remain important milestones in the successful management of patients presenting with abdominal pain. The history of appendicitis includes examples of considerable resistance to change, prescient but unacceptable early observations, and emotional support of often-insupportable views, leading finally to the development of an acceptable therapeutic strategy.

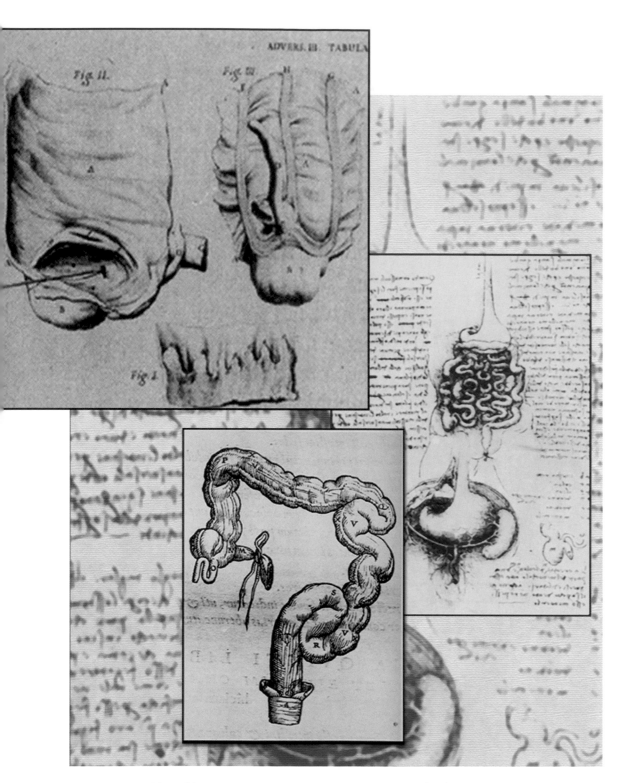

A series of early depictions of the appendix. Leonardo da Vinci accurately drew the organ (*right*), but made no reference to its possible function. Andreas Vesalius (*bottom image*) indicated its position at the base of the cecum, but similarly failed to remark upon its nature.

Background

Although the physician-anatomist Berengario da Carpi was the first to describe the appendix in 1521, Leonardo da Vinci had clearly depicted the organ in his anatomical drawings that date back to 1492. By 1543, Andreas Vesalius in *De Humani Corpis Fabrica*, although clearly delineating the existence of the appendix, failed to discuss the organ in any detail in the text. The publication of the drawings of Leonardo da Vinci of the peritoneal cavity in the 18th century and thereafter the work of Giovanni Battista Morgagni published in 1719 provided further details of the gross anatomy of the appendix. The first description of appendicitis is that of Jean Fernel, published in 1544.

Jean Fernel was born in Montdidier in 1497 and attended school at Clermont before entering the College of Saint Barbe at Paris in 1516, where he studied philosophy and eloquence. In 1519, he became a Master of Arts, a student of mathematics, and in 1530, at the age of 33, acquired his degree in medicine. Uninterested in the subject, he focused chiefly on mathematical work and became the first to determine the exact measurement of a degree of the meridian, as well as making other contributions in mathematical and astronomical research. Unfortunately, despite his intellect, he was unable to support his family by research in science and at the advanced age of 38, undertook the practice of medicine, thereafter rapidly achieving a considerable reputation.

IOANNIS
FERNELII
AMBIANI

De luis Venereæ curatione
perfectissima
LIBER,

M. D. LXIX.

Although the appendix was not much referred to in early anatomical studies (since these were mostly undertaken in animals that did not possess the vestigial organ), by 1889, almost 2,500 articles or books relevant to the subject had been published. By 1950, this number had risen to more than 13,000, and the subjects of appendicitis, appendiceal abscess, antibiotics, and surgery had become major issues amongst both gastroenterologists and surgeons.

Such was Fernel's success that he became Chief Physician to the Dauphin of France and garnered further acclamation upon the latter's accession to the throne as Henry II, being appointed the first Court Physician and Doctor to Catherine de Medici. In Book 6, Chapter 9, of *The Causes and Signs of Diseases in the Intestines*, Fernel described a case of a seven-year-old child with acute appendicitis and perforation. Since he used the term "*cecum intestinum*" controversy has existed as to whether the diagnosis actually was a perforated appendicitis. A similar case published by von Hilden, a German surgeon, in 1652, is somewhat dubious, but the account of Lorenz Heister of 1711 presented a very clear description of perforated appendix and appendicitis.

In this text, Heister described the appendix as the seat of acute inflammation and drew attention to the surgical significance of such disease. In November 1711, Heister, while dissecting the body of a criminal, noted the small bowel to be diffusely erythematous and commented that even the smallest vessels were filled with blood "as if they had been injected with red wax after the manner of Ruysch". In phraseology that carries weight even three centuries later, he noted: "...when I was about to demonstrate the situation of the great guts, I found the vermiform of process of the cecum pre-naturally black adhering closer to the peritoneum than usual. As I now was about to separate it, by gently pulling it asunder the membranes of this process broke not withstanding the body was quite fresh and discharged two or three spoonfuls of matter."

In 1759, M Mestivier of Paris reported an autopsy on a 54-year-old man who died shortly after surgical drainage of a right lower quadrant abscess. Despite the surgeon having opened the abdomen and drained the pus, the patient

Lorenz Heister was born in Frankfurt in 1683 and after studying initially at Giessen and Wetzlar, he travelled to Holland, where he became a docent in Amsterdam and taught surgical courses using cadavers. In 1708, he received a medical degree at Harderwyk and enrolled in the Dutch army as a surgeon. Relinquishing his military obligations after a year, he thereafter continued his studies in Strasbourg, Paris, and London, before accepting a Professorship of Surgery at Altdorf in Franconia in 1710. After 10 productive years at Altdorf, he moved to the University of Helmstedt, where he remained until 1758, dying at the age of 75. An extraordinarily industrious man and indefatigable student, his reputation was such that during his lifetime, he declined professorships at Göttingen, Kiel, Würzberg, and St Petersburg. His major opuses, *Institutiones Chirurgicae* and *Chirurgische Warnehmungen*, are the source of the first authoritative account of appendicitis.

subsequently perished and at the autopsy, Mestivier noted that the abdomen was sprinkled with gangrenous sloughs and that a pin had penetrated the vermiform appendix! Almost a decade later in 1767, John Hunter described a gangrenous appendix encountered at the autopsy of a Colonel Dalrymple, but failed to pursue the subject with his usual vigor. Of particular interest is the report of James Parkinson in 1812 in respect of disease of the appendix vermiformis. At autopsy, he described an ulcerated and perforated appendix with an aperture sufficient to insert a crow quill. Parkinson had attended Hunter's lectures in surgery and was regarded as a reformer and radical, and was known to be a member of several secret political societies. Although he is best remembered for his 1817 'Essay on Shaking Palsy', he also authored several political and medical pamphlets, including *Revolution without Bloodshed* as well as *Hints for the Improvements of Trusses*.

The French consideration of appendicitis was significantly inhibited by the fact that the premiere surgeon of the time, Baron Guillaume Dupuytren, did not accept the appendix as a cause for right lower quadrant inflammatory disease, but believed that the cecum itself was the origin. Thus, when Louyer-Villermay demonstrated the presence of gangrenous appendix in the autopsies of two young men in 1824, there was little enthusiasm for its acceptance as a novel disease process. Indeed, as early as 1827, Melier had suggested that the disease might be ameliorated by early surgical intervention. Nevertheless, the primacy of Dupuytren as the Chief of Surgery at the Hotel Dieu prevailed and Melier's suggestion fell upon deaf ears. A further confounding problem of the era was the confusion provided by an abundant literature seeking to define the differences between the putative entities of "typhlitis" and "perityphlitis".

Nevertheless, in 1839, Richard Bright and Thomas Addison of Guy's Hospital, in their text *Elements of Practical Medicine*, clearly described the symptomatology of appendicitis and opined that the appendix was the cause of most of the inflammatory processes described as arising in the right iliac fossa. Since both were physicians (internists), they failed to propose surgical intervention. Thomas Hodgkin (also of Guy's Hospital) had similarly commented on the clinical symptomatology of appendicitis, but likewise failed to support surgical intervention.

Surgical treatment

The advent of anesthesia in 1846 and the introduction of antisepsis by Lord Joseph Lister in 1867 produced a more acceptable environment for the consideration of surgery. Thus on June 18, 1886, at the first meeting of the Association of American Physicians at Washington, DC, Dr Reginald H Fitz read a paper entitled 'Perforating Inflammation of the Vermiform Appendix: with Special Reference to its Early Diagnosis and Treatment'. In a monumental contribution to the subject, Fitz emphasized that most inflammatory disease of the lower quadrant began in the appendix and urged early surgical removal of the organ as the only treatment likely to yield a favorable outcome.

Fitz was the first to actually use the term "appendicitis" and in so doing, was in fact criticized by the classically educated audience for the use of a word consisting of a Greek suffix and a Latin stem. As a result of his pathological contributions to the study of the appendix, the terms "typhlitis" and "perityphlitis" declined in usage, and much of the confusion around the disease was abolished.

Thomas Guy (1644–1724) founded Guy's Hospital in London (*background*) and in so doing established one of the great medical centers of the 19th century. Thomas Addison (adrenal disease) (*top right*), Thomas Hodgkin (lymphoma) (*bottom right*), and Richard Bright (nephritis) (*bottom left*) had all opined that the appendix was the cause of most inflammatory processes in the right iliac foci. Given the high morbidity and mortality of surgical intervention and their training as physicians, they opposed any consideration that Sir Astley Paston Cooper (*top left*), one of the finest surgeons of the time, would contemplate surgical intervention.

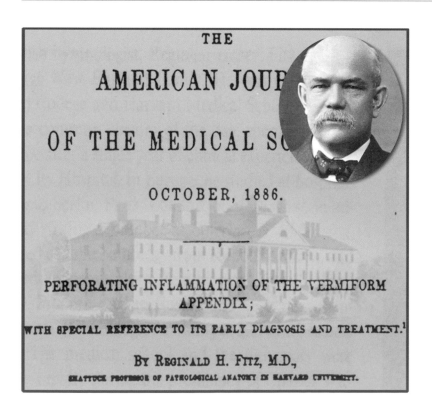

THE

AMERICAN JOUR

OF THE MEDICAL SC

OCTOBER, 1886.

PERFORATING INFLAMMATION OF THE VERMIFORM APPENDIX;

WITH SPECIAL REFERENCE TO ITS EARLY DIAGNOSIS AND TREATMENT.[1]

BY REGINALD H. FITZ, M.D.,

SHATTUCK PROFESSOR OF PATHOLOGICAL ANATOMY IN HARVARD UNIVERSITY.

As the Shattuck Professor of Pathological Anatomy at Harvard University, Reginald H Fitz (*top right*) represented the ninth generation of the Fitz family in America and was descended from the original 1639 settlers of the Massachusetts Bay Colony. Named after the British hymnologist Reginald Heber, Fitz was educated at Harvard and thereafter spent two years in Europe, where he studied at hospitals in Paris, London, Glasgow, Vienna, and Berlin. As a student of Rudolf Virchow, he was fully aware of cellular pathology, and on his return to Boston in 1870, introduced the use of the microscope for study at Harvard Medical School. Apart from his seminal contributions to appendicitis in 1886, in 1889 he produced a definitive work on pancreatitis and in so doing, assured himself a place in the pantheon of gastrointestinal pathology.

Surgical evolution

Claudius Amyand, a Huguenot refugee and founder of St George's Hospital in London, is attributed with the first surgical removal of appendix in December 1735. He operated on an 11-year-old boy with a longstanding scrotal hernia and a fecal fistula of the thigh. Having opened the hernia through a scrotal incision, he noted an appendix wrapped in omentum and perforated by a pin, with a resultant fecal fistula. Amyand amputated the omentum and appendix, opened the fistula, and a satisfactory recovery ensued. No further accounts of such surgery occurred for a further century, with abdominal pain and inflammation being for the most part treated by opium administration. This therapy had been initially introduced by C Stokes of Dublin in 1838 and was regarded as the standard therapy, based on its ability to relieve pain, inhibit peristalsis, and presumably allow localization of the inflammatory process.

The strategy was first challenged in 1848 when Henry Hancock, the President of the Medical Society of London, presented a paper describing the successful treatment of a 30-year-old woman with acute peritonitis drained via a right lower quadrant incision. The subsequent removal of a fecolith from the wound two weeks after the operation was followed by recovery of the patient. Similarly, in 1867, Willard Parker of New York reported his experiences with four patients whom he had treated over 10 years with successful drainage of appendiceal abscesses.

Although Robert Lawson Tait of Birmingham successfully removed a gangrenous appendix from a 17-year-old girl in 1880, he failed to report the procedure until 1890, concentrating his activities mostly on gynecological surgery. Abraham Groves of Fergus, Ontario, undertook a similar case of unreported successful appendectomy in 1883. Groves, educated at the University of Toronto, was a friend of Sir William Osler and highly regarded as a clinician and scholar. Despite the fact that the 12-year-old boy, on whom he operated on May 10, 1883, recovered successfully, Groves failed to mention the condition until its inclusion in his autobiography, published in 1934. A series of further reports of appendectomy included a failed instance by Johann von Mikulicz-Radecki in 1884, a successful intervention by Kronlein of Zurich in 1885, and an additional success by Charter Symonds of London in 1885. In America,

RJ Hall performed the first appendectomy at the Roosevelt Hospital in New York in 1886, while Henry Sands, an assistant to Parker, reported operating on a patient with appendicitis and removing two fecoliths.

It is of interest that Charles McBurney, a subsequent major contributor to the subject of the management of appendicitis, was an assistant to Sands. In 1887, Thomas G Morton of Philadelphia reported a successful appendectomy with the drainage of an abscess in a 27-year-old patient. Sadly for Morton, both his brother and son would die of acute appendicitis. By 1889, McBurney had

Robert Lawson Tait of Birmingham, although amongst the first to successfully remove an appendix, subsequently became a vehement opponent of cholecystectomy.

published the first of several important papers on the subject of appendicitis and his clinical description of the process would assure him a place in the history of the disease.

In 1889, Dr Edward Cutler reported his successful experiences with a number of patients with appendicitis and described one of the first instances of an appendectomy for unruptured acute appendicitis. By this stage, the level of enthusiasm for surgical intervention had considerably increased and attention was now directed not only to the type of surgery but also to its timing. Thus, by 1898, Bernays had reported 71 consecutive appendectomies without death and in 1904, John B Murphy of Chicago reported a personal experience of 2,000 appendectomies. AJ Ochsner of Chicago in 1902 published a text on the management of appendicitis and advocated nonoperative treatment in circumstances where evidence of spreading peritonitis could be determined.

Technique

Although the earliest incisions were simply for drainage of the most inflamed, tender, or fluctuant areas, the most commonly used incision at the turn of the century was that described by William Henry Battle of St Thomas' Hospital in London in 1897. This constituted a vertical incision through the lateral edge of the right rectus sheath and often resulted in denervation of the rectus muscle with subsequent incisional hernia formation. In 1894, McBurney of New York described the lateral muscle splitting or "grid iron" incision at almost the same time that an identical incision was described by Lewis L McArthur of Chicago. Unfortunately for McArthur, the presentation of his paper at the Chicago Medical Society of June 1894 was postponed due to time constraints and the prior publication of McBurney's manuscript in the *Annals of Surgery*, July 1894, resulted in priority being incorrectly ascribed to the latter. Despite McBurney's generous and open acknowledgment of McArthur's primacy, the term "McBurney incision" has remained in common usage. Two years later in 1896, JW Elliot of Boston advocated a transverse skin incision, but this excited little attention until 1905, when AE Rockey of Portland, Oregon, once again proposed a transverse skin incision with vertical division of the muscle layers for lower abdominal operations.

The appendicitis of Edward VII (*bottom left*) was successfully treated by the surgical intervention of Sir Frederick Treves (*bottom right*). The delay of the coronation is reported to have cost the British government many millions of pounds and represents one of the first documented instances of lost revenue based upon delay of therapeutic intervention.

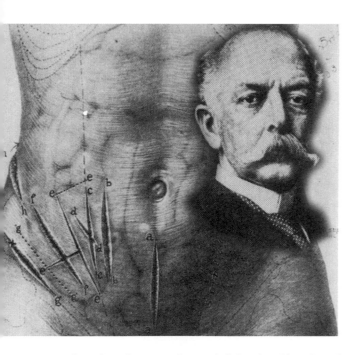

An early 20th century diagram depicting the wide variety of abdominal incisions proposed to facilitate appendectomy (*background*). Charles McBurney (*top right*) is eponymously remembered for his incision – a lateral incision for appendicitis.

THE KING'S APPENDIX

Of particular interest is the operation performed upon Edward VII by Sir Frederick Treves. Edward VII was the first male child of Queen Victoria and given his irresponsible behavior, was little thought of in terms of subsequent regal responsibilities. On the death of Victoria in 1901, the coronation of Edward VII was scheduled for June 26, 1902. On June 14, the King developed abdominal discomfort and was examined by Sir Francis Laking, the Physician in Ordinary to the monarchy. By midnight, the abdominal pain had worsened to the extent that Laking summoned Sir Thomas Barlow as his consultant the following morning, seeking to confirm his diagnosis. Despite his declining condition, the King proceeded by carriage to Windsor on June 16, but such was his ill health, that on June 18, Treves was asked to examine him. At this stage, the clinical presentation was of swelling and tenderness in the right iliac foci with elevated body temperature. Fortunately, these findings appeared to improve over the next 48 hours and by Monday, June 23, Edward felt sufficiently recovered to travel to London to host a large dinner party for the coronation guests.

As a result, a relapse occurred and by 10 o'clock the next morning, Treves, Sir Thomas Smith, Lister, Barlow, and Laking all agreed that an operation was necessary. Edward, however, was unwilling to delay his coronation and declined to have the procedure, preferring as he told his physician to attend the coronation rather than a surgery. When Treves informed him "then Sir you will go as a corpse," the King capitulated and the operation was undertaken in a room in Buckingham Palace on June 24 at half past twelve. Sir Frederic Hewitt provided anesthesia and a large abscess was opened and pus evacuated. The appendix was not removed and Edward made an uninterrupted recovery, enabling the coronation to take place some weeks later. Although Treves was not an advocate of early operations for appendicitis, he nevertheless was successful in his therapy of Edward VII and as a result of the successful outcome, was made a baron. Ironically, the daughter of Treves would subsequently die of acute appendicitis.

ULCERATIVE COLITIS

Introduction

It is uncertain when it actually became apparent that there was a difference between the wide variety of dysenteries and a more specific disease entity that could be characterized as ulcerative colitis. Certainly, the recognition by Robert Koch of bacteria and their relationship to specific disease entities was an important advance, but the wide variety of gut flora obfuscated the identification of causal pathogens for many decades. Indeed, it can be inferred from the historical texts that the idiopathic inflammatory bowel diseases (IBDs), ulcerative colitis, and Crohn's disease are, as J Kirsner noted, "old" rather than "new" diseases. Matthew Baillie, in his 1793 text *Morbid Anatomy of Some of the Most Important Parts of the Human Body*, provided enough descriptive material for Basil Morson to conclude that "patients were dying from ulcerative colitis during the latter part of the 18th century". The first "impact" description of "ulcerative colitis" by Samuel Wilks of London in 1859 concerned a 42-year-old woman who died after several months of diarrhea and fever. Autopsy demonstrated a transmural ulcerative inflammation of the colon and terminal ileum, originally designated as "simple ulcerative colitis" but a century later identified as Crohn's disease. The 1875 case report of Wilks and Moxon of extensive ulceration and inflammation of the entire colon in a young woman who had succumbed to severe bloody diarrhea also was labeled "simple ulcerative colitis".

By 1907, 317 patients had been admitted to seven London hospitals with an inflammatory and ulcerative disease of the colon. Although precise details of all were not available, almost half of the patients perished from perforation of the colon and peritonitis, hemorrhage, and complications, including "nephritis, infective endocarditis," sepsis, hepatic abscess, fatty liver, and pulmonary embolism.

At the turn of the 20th century, similar clinical reports emanated from both Europe and the United States. Thus, in 1902, R F Weir performed an appendicostomy in a patient to facilitate colonic irrigation with a 5% solution of methylene blue alternating with a 1:5000 solution of silver nitrate or bismuth, presumably to eliminate an "infection." Sir HE Lockhart-Mummery of London, in 1907, diagnosed carcinoma of the colon in seven of 36 patients with ulcerative colitis and recommended use of the recently developed electrically illuminated proctosigmoidoscope to facilitate diagnosis.

An example of a colon demonstrating the severe inflammatory changes of ulcerative colitis.

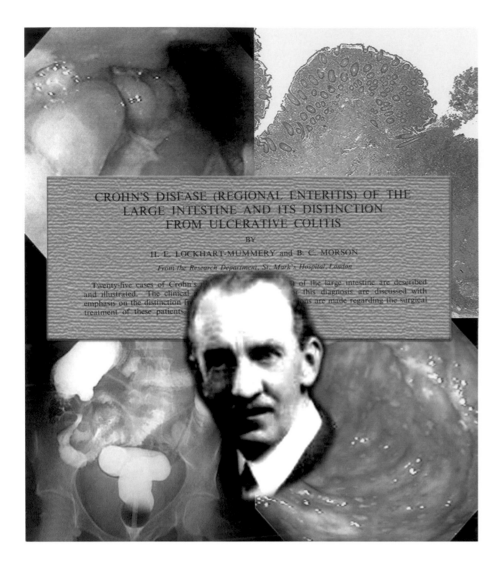

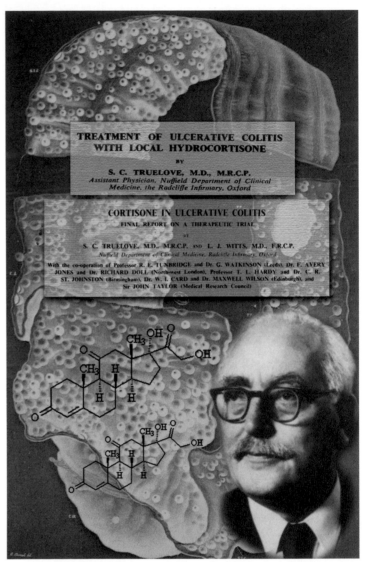

The clinical and radiological manifestation of Crohn's disease, and the frontispiece of the seminal text by HE Lockhart-Mummery (*bottom and center*).

Awareness of the condition resulted in an increased number of reports of ulcerative colitis from France, Germany, Italy, and England during the early years of the 20th century and ulcerative colitis was a major subject of the 1913 Paris Congress of Medicine. During the second quarter of the 20th century, AF Hurst of London implicated an organism "related to *B dysenteriae*," as being the causative agent and recommended as treatment daily irrigations of the colon with dilute solutions of silver nitrate or tannic acid, and the intravenous administration of a "polyvalent anti-dysenteric serum".

During the 1930s through the 1950s, etiological speculation was rampant and included food and pollen allergy, deficiency of an "intestinal protective substance," and a wide variety of aerobic and anaerobic intestinal bacteria, as well as an underlying psychiatric disorder (the so-called "ulcerative colitis personality"). Given the current vogue for Freudian intervention, many patients actually underwent extensive psychiatric scrutiny and prolonged psychotherapy without apparent sustained benefit. The introduction of the sulfanilamide agents in 1938 facilitated treatment, and similarly management improved with the availability first of penicillin in the 1940s, and subsequently adrenocorticotropic hormone (ACTH) adrenal steroids and their related compounds in 1950. Thus, by 1951, Kirsner of Chicago was able to document the complete clinical and radiological reversibility of ulcerative colitis in a group of patients who had responded promptly and consistently to therapy.

Gastroenterology in Oxford was developed by Sidney Truelove (1913–2002) (*bottom right*), who was appointed First Assistant to the Nuffield Professor of Medicine in 1937 and subsequently Reader in Medicine. His contribution to academic and clinical gastroenterology was outstanding, especially in advancing the understanding and management of ulcerative colitis and Crohn's disease. Together with Leslie Witts, who initially recruited him to Oxford, Truelove undertook the first clinical trial in the history of gastroenterology. These authors (with a large number of physicians in the field) demonstrated that cortisone was more effective than placebo in ulcerative colitis (*top: British Medical Journal 1955; 2: 1041*). Thereafter, Truelove introduced intravenous treatment of a severe attack of ulcerative colitis with glucocorticosteroids, which subsequently became known as the "Truelove regimen". In addition to his perceptive clinical examinations, Truelove introduced the practice of collaborating from the beginning with surgeons in order to optimize therapy and indications for surgery in the treatment of severe ulcerative colitis patients!

In 1933, Buie and Bargen of the Mayo Clinic implicated vascular "thrombotic phenomena" as the pathological basis for ulcerative colitis and in 1937, Bargen actually went so far as to designate the disease as "thrombo-ulcerative colitis." Despite the fact that a review of 120 surgical patients and 60 autopsied cases by S Warren and SC Sommers of Boston in 1949 re-emphasized the mucosal involvement, none of the prevailing etiological hypotheses seemed acceptable. However, the focus on a vascular pathogenesis was further accentuated in 1954 when Warren and Sommers reclassified 10% of their 1949 series as "colitis gravis" with inflammatory necrosis of arteries, veins, or both, leading to vascular occlusions and infarction of a part or all of the adjacent colon. However, the presence of a "damaging substance" in the fecal stream was acknowledged as a significant possibility, as had been suggested by P Manson-Bahr in 1943, and even earlier by B Dawson in the 1909 London Symposium.

RT Stoughton in 1953 isolated a substance that was thought to possibly be a proteolytic enzyme, probably originating in the gut microflora (bacterial endotoxin), from fecal filtrates of patients with ulcerative colitis. Since it was demonstrated to be capable of digesting epidermal cells even after the skin had been fixed in formalin, it was considered a likely candidate agent until the "acantholysis" was noted to also occur with fecal extracts from individuals without any evidence of colonic disease.

Salicylazosulfapyridine (*bottom right*) was originally proposed as a treatment for rheumatoid arthritis, a disorder in which it produces modest benefit, but its greatest effect has been in inflammatory bowel disease. It has now become the mainstay of outpatient medical management for patients with mild to moderately active ulcerative colitis or Crohn's colitis, and is effective in maintaining remissions in those with ulcerative colitis. It inhibits cyclooxygenase and lipoxygenase enzymes in arachidonic acid metabolism, thereby preventing formation of proinflammatory prostaglandins and leukotrienes. The efficacy of sulfasalazine for the treatment of active ulcerative colitis was initially demonstrated by JE Lennard-Jones (*top right*) and colleagues in 1962. In this article (*top*), they demonstrated a significant improvement in symptoms ($p < 0.02$) (*bottom left*) in patients compared to the control group. More recently, the effective dose range for this drug has been determined as 2–6g/day, which induces a remission in 50–80% of patients.

Little more progress was made in defining the etiology of the disease and clinicians could do little but content themselves with a description of the pathology, as provided by Morson: "In active ulcerative colitis, the mucous membrane shows diffuse infiltration with chronic inflammatory cells, mainly lymphocytic and plasma cells but also eosinophils. There is also a variable degree of vascular congestion and intra-mucosal hemorrhage. The epithelium shows goblet cell depletion and reactive hyperplasia, and some of the tubules contain an accumulation of polymorphonuclear leukocytes, so called crypt abscesses."

A five-day intensive intravenous regimen for the treatment of severe attacks of ulcerative colitis was developed by Sidney Truelove and DP Jewell (*right*) from the Radcliffe Infirmary (*bottom*) (Jewell took over the running of the unit after the retirement of Truelove in 1980). Their paper in the *Lancet* (1974) outlined this regimen and determined that patients who did not respond to treatment were immediate candidates for surgery. Up to two thirds of patients who went into remission with their regimen (3L saline with prednisolone-21-phosphate or rectal administration of hydrocortisone in a saline drip) remained symptom free for three years, a higher remission rate than had heretofore been demonstrated.

The etiological concepts of the 1950s and 1960s, which included "vascular disease," infection, allergy, "non-specific damage" to colonic epithelium, and a locally "injurious agent" in the fecal stream, produced little reliable data to suggest that any progress in determining the nature of the disease had been made. An examination in the 1950s as to the possibility of naturally occurring animal counterparts of the disease that were known to veterinarians was undertaken. In fact, the only animal colitis that appeared relevant to the human disease was that observed in captive cotton-top tamarin monkeys (*Saguinus oedipus*). Its clinical and histological features were almost identical in that it responded to sulfasalazine and if untreated, was complicated by colonic carcinoma. Furthermore, since the colitis was absent among the wild cotton-top tamarins of the Colombian rainforest, the findings suggested an environmental (for example, infection, "cold stress") cause for the colitis of the captive tamarins.

Numerous attempts were made during the 1920s through 1960 to reproduce ulcerative colitis in animals (rabbits, guinea pigs, hamsters, dogs, mice, rats) but none succeeded. In some circumstances, the small and large intestine were readily damaged by these manipulations, but the lesions healed rapidly and in no fashion resembled the human condition. In 1969, ulcerations in the right colon were produced in guinea pigs and rabbits given orally a 5% aqueous solution of carrageenan, a sulfated polysaccharide of high molecular weight extracted from red seaweed (*Chondrus crispus, Eucheuma spinosum*). The reaction was enhanced immunologically by a component of the outer cell wall of *Bacteroides vulgatus*, inhibited by the addition of metronidazole, and was not reproducible in germ-free animals.

The elucidation of the disease or diseases broadly classified as ulcerative colitis has been difficult, since few experimental models for study exist. The only relevant animal colitis model available is the disease identified in captive cotton-top tamarin monkeys (*bottom*) from South America. These animals are part of the marmoset New World monkey species and although primarily insect-eaters, take fruit as well as other small animals. Of interest is the fact that the female of the species generally bears twins. While tamarins normally exhibit little colonic disease, it appears to affect only those in captivity. The issue of a stress response or infestation by agents not present in the tropical jungle has been raised. An examination of the taxonomy of the marmoset and tamarin families broadly classified as part of the *Leontopithecus* genus provides little clue as to why this animal might develop an acute colonic infection. Of further interest is the fact that the catarrhine family, or Old World monkey, which also forms part of the *Cercopithecidae*, does not exhibit this disease, even when maintained in captivity.

Treatment

In 1938, a study of 871 patients with ulcerative colitis suggested physical fatigue and emotional distress as "predisposing circumstances" and as a result, psychotherapy was regarded as an important form of treatment. However, by the mid 1940s, Dr Nana Svartz, a Swedish rheumatologist, became the first physician to use sulfasalazine to treat ulcerative colitis and the compound soon became the most widely prescribed drug for people with the disease. The subsequent development in the 1950s of ACTH and cortisone led to their utilization as the standard treatments for IBD. With the advent of relatively effective pharmacotherapy, the emphasis on the role of psychogenic factors began to diminish. Nevertheless, uncontrollable disease required surgical management, and in 1954, BN Brooke, who had been responsible for developing the ileostomy, concluded that there were three distinct forms of colitis with more than one cause.

The confusion regarding the precise nature of the disease and whether there was more than one type was further obfuscated by clinicians in the United States acknowledging that Crohn's disease could also affect the colon, as had been previously reported in England. The advent of the concept that an immune disorder might be the cause of the disease led to the utilization in the 1960s of immunosuppressive drugs, such as 6-mercaptopurine and azathioprine. The positive results led to clinical enthusiasm and such agents were recognized as effective in treating Crohn's disease. Despite advances in medical therapy, a substantial number of patients still required surgery, and the development in 1969 by Dr Nils Kock, a Swedish surgeon, of the continent ileostomy ("Kock pouch"), was regarded as a major advance, since it eliminated the need for an external pouch. Unfortunately, the patency of the pouch and complications related to it led to disenchantment, with the result that alternatives were sought.

Intra-abdominal "Reservoir" in Patients With Permanent Ileostomy

Preliminary Observations on a Procedure Resulting in Fecal "Continence" in Five Ileostomy Patients

Nils G. Kock, MD, Goteborg, Sweden

uring recent years much progress has been made in creating functioning ileostomies in patients after panproctocolectomy. The development of the adherent stomy has to a great extent ted problems in patients. of a in management of the y, and in the most of the the pa are very pleased with the ostomy after a long disabling dis-

troublesome skin irritation. Some patients do not tolerate the glue used for fixation of the bag and for these patients the management of the skin is laborious and time-consuming. Skin irritation seems to be one of the most frequent late complications omy and occurs, at le 26% to 70% y patien and its co blem.

Nils Kock of Gothenburg, Sweden, in 1959 developed a continent ileostomy pouch, which allowed patients to discard the ileostomy bag. Unfortunately, technical problems with the long-term management of the pouch led to discontinuation of the procedure.

Modifications of the ileoanal anastomosis, or "pull through" procedure, were undertaken and construction of an internal pouch subsequently became an acceptable alternative to the external ostomy. In 1988 in the United States, the first 5-ASA drugs received FDA (Food and Drug Administration) approval for the treatment of ulcerative colitis, but despite substantial efficacy, failed to resolve all instances of the disease. At this stage, there remain more questions than answers regarding the genesis of the disease and the ideal method to treat it. The possibility that the use of genetic technology may provide a more appropriate molecular target remains to be determined.

OBSTRUCTION

Although surgery of the colon and rectum had originally developed to manage either trauma or obstruction induced by tumor, increasing technical skill and safety allowed its application to other conditions. Thus, the treatment of

diverticular disease, Hirschsprung's disease, inflammatory bowel disease, and prolapse of the rectum moved from the province of medical therapy into the surgical arena. It was, however, in the management of obstruction that the greatest progress was made. Although the clinical description of intestinal obstruction with its distention, vomiting, and failure to pass feces and flatus may be noted in the earliest of literature, there was little except homeopathic remedies that could be directed at its remedy. Prior to the advent of anesthesia and antisepsis, treatment was expectant and mortality almost uniform. In the case of obstruction due to strangulated hernias, Sir Astley Paston Cooper and others would suspend the patient in the upside-down position on an attendant's shoulders as a preliminary to taxis and reduction.

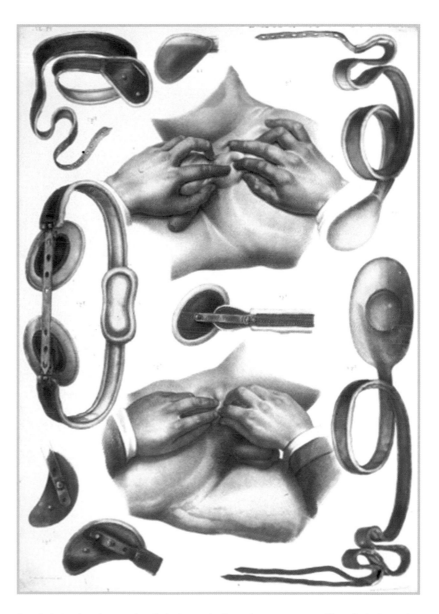

Bowel obstruction due to a hernia is shown. In the early management of intestinal obstruction (uniformly considered fatal), treatment had focused on the use of opiates, mercury, and expectancy. The repair of strangulated hernias, although undertaken, was associated with major morbidity and mortality due to peritonitis, gangrene, and sepsis. Physicians were thus hesitant to allow surgeons to operate and ignored commentary by luminaries such as Robert Lawson Tait, who complained: "Is it not better to perform exploration before rather than after death?"

Percutaneous intestinal puncture had been proposed in 1756, and as late as 1880, was still used by the Boston physicians Blake and Bigelow, although patients usually perished of sepsis and inanition.

The operative treatment of intestinal obstruction was first proposed by Treves of London Hospital, who wrote: "It is less dangerous to leap from the Clifton suspension bridge, 250 to 275ft above the Avon River near Bristol, than to suffer from acute intestinal obstruction and decline operation." Treves believed that the use of the stethoscope allowed for some differentiation between small and large bowel obstruction, but such a distinction could not be accurately or reliably ascertained prior to the 1930s.

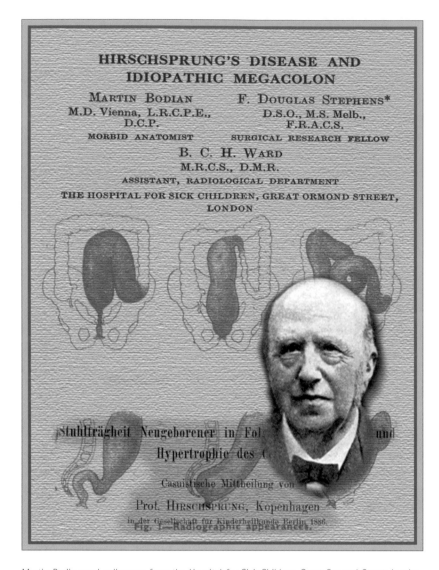

Martin Bodian and colleagues from the Hospital for Sick Children, Great Ormond Street, London, reviewed 73 cases of "idiopathic colon". In this 1949 *Lancet* paper, the authors were able to offer evidence that re-established the original conception of Hirschsprung's disease as a separate entity. Indeed, Harald Hirschsprung (*bottom right*) of Copenhagen had first identified this entity, a previously ill understood cause of bowel obstruction in young children and neonates, in 1886 (*bottom*).

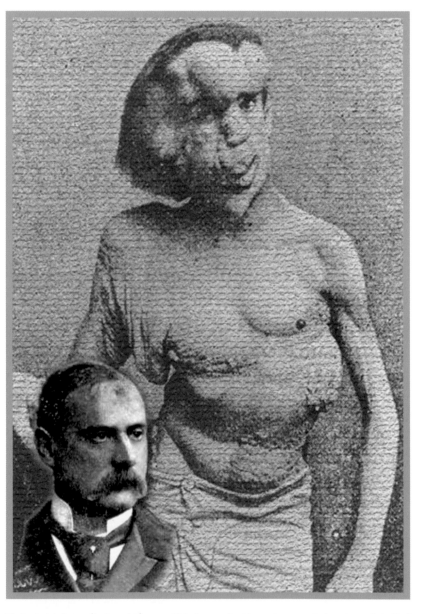

Sir Frederick Treves (*bottom left*) was widely known for his work on surgical anatomy, intestinal obstruction, appendicitis, and peritonitis. As surgeon to the British army in the Transvaal War (Boer), he made important contributions to military surgery and wrote fascinating travel sketches of the area. His care and concern for the "Elephant man" earned him a place of distinction as a man of both intellectual skill and exquisite sensitivity.

Thomas Sydenham of London favored opium as a universal panacea, and even two centuries later, this form of therapeutic nihilism was defended as reasonable by Hugh Owen Thomas of Liverpool. The use of mobile metallic mercury had long been favored, given the concept that the freely flowing substance would make its way past an obstruction and re-establish intestinal *continuity*. Indeed, this method was widely advocated, since mercury had achieved a substantial reputation as a therapeutic agent. In one recorded instance, the French surgeon Pillore, using a cecostomy, had met with some success, but the 21lbs of metallic mercury that also had been administered to his patient resulted in their demise. Physicians as eminent as Begin, Broussais, and Dupuytren had all vainly attempted to intervene in intestinal obstruction. Purges, enemas, ice packs, electrical stimulation, leeches, and even the use of esophageal sounds were of little use, and even colostomy, while an obvious remedy, usually proved fatal due to leakage and peritonitis when employed.

Heschl, the successor of Karl von Rokitansky as the Professor of Pathology at the Allgemeine Krankenhaus in Vienna, proposed that the ileocecal valve might act as a check valve and preclude regurgitation of the distended colon back into the ileum. Hence, for a period of time, some physicians believed that small and large bowel obstruction were completely separate events.

The development of the intestinal or nasogastric tube facilitated the diagnosis of obstruction, as well as being of considerable therapeutic value. In 1883, at a meeting of the British Medical Association, Tait of Birmingham, in his usual forthright fashion, protested the protracted palliative management of intestinal obstruction, commenting: "Was it not better to perform exploration before rather than after death?" His frustration reflected the prevailing medical view that it was better to ease the patient into oblivion with sedatives and opium rather than permit operation.

Substantial interest in the surgical relief of intestinal obstruction was provided in 1885 when Greves of Liverpool invited Mr Pue, a local surgeon, to operate on a patient with obstruction. The division of a loop of ileum close to the cecum resulted in the patient's survival. Such enthusiasm, however, for intervention was tempered by the reports of Madelung of Rostock and von Mikulicz-Radecki of Breslau at the German Surgical Congress of 1887. They noted that in their experience, early operative invention for intestinal obstruction resulted in a high operative mortality rate and urged caution. Indeed, as late as 1929, C Jeff Miller of the New Orleans Charity Hospital reported that the mortality rate for small bowel obstruction was 65%, and for obstruction of the colon, 88%. By 1930, the important role of decompression, whether achieved by indwelling duodenal suction or by aseptic operative decompression, had demarcated the first significant advances in the reduction of mortality and the management of intestinal obstruction.

COLOSTOMY

Although the first proposal that an enterostomy or colostomy be considered a formal procedure was made by Littre (1658–1726), the operation would not be performed for another 66 years until undertaken by the French surgeon Pillore. Pillore made a lower transverse incision to enter the abdomen and thereafter, having created a transverse incision of the cecum, secured it to the edges of the wound. Unfortunately, the patient perished 20 days after the operation from erosion of the intestine due to large quantities of mercury, which had been previously administered in the fond belief that this would ease the obstruction. Duret, who undertook a left ileal colostomy in the case of imperforate anus in a three-day-old child, is accorded credit for the first successful elective colostomy in 1793. It is noteworthy that the patient survived until the ripe old age of 45 years.

Although the concept of a colostomy made obvious sense, the operation met with little success in its initial stages. Dessault (1744–1795) of the Hotel Dieu in Paris performed a similar operation on a two-day-old child in 1774, but he omitted to suture the edge of the bowel to the wound and the patient died.

In 1810, Callisen, Professor of Surgery at Copenhagen, described his experience with colostomies and Freer, a surgeon of Birmingham in England, performed the first colostomy in Britain in 1815. By 1826, Philip S Physick (1768–1837) of Philadelphia had written a paper describing colostomy under the title 'An operation for artificial anus' and the inimitable Dupuytren (1777–1835) of Paris had extended the procedure by developing a clamp for the exteriorized bowel. Although this technique was highly regarded and widely practiced for a period of time as a result of the great surgical reputation of Dupuytren, it was associated with considerable morbidity and mortality. Its further evolution, however, was considerably amplified by the French surgeon Amussat (1856), who had been greatly influenced by the tragic death of his friend Broussais, who perished of intestinal obstruction due to a carcinoma of the rectum. After evaluating the technique and results of colostomy as currently practiced, Amussat recognized that the fatalities were due to peritonitis, and therefore proposed that a lumbar colostomy should be undertaken. As such, the technique developed by Amussat was both logical and eminently clinically sensible. First, he determined the location of obstruction by rectal examination, and when the exact site of the tumor could not be determined, punctured the distended bowel with a small trocar. He proposed that the operation should be undertaken on the right side if the tumor was proximate to the site of operation, and on the left side when the obstruction was either distant from the anus or if its precise site could not be determined. A true diplomat and scholar, Amussat cautiously noted that the operation he proposed was difficult and required considerable skill: "An artificial anus, it is true, is a grave infirmity but it is not insupportable. To be able to practice it a surgeon ought to fear to be surprised by pressing occasion and he should be prepared to support himself by repetitions of the operation upon the cadaver."

Ischemic colitis is the most common ischemic injury of the gastrointestinal tract and one of the most common disorders of the large bowel in the elderly. The disease was first described by Boley and associates as a "reversible vascular occlusion" of the colon. Thereafter, Adrian Marston and colleagues in 1966 (in *Gut*) published an important paper that brought a conceptual unity to this disease process, and suggested three syndromes that may occur. They detailed the gangrenous, stricturing, and transient forms. Recent advances in endoscopy have revealed the venous vessel origin of ischemic colitis and other new types of ischemic colitis, and nowadays, a more in-depth definition has emerged that includes a broad spectrum of ischemic injury to the colon, from benign reversible colonopathy to fulminant colitis and colonic gangrene.

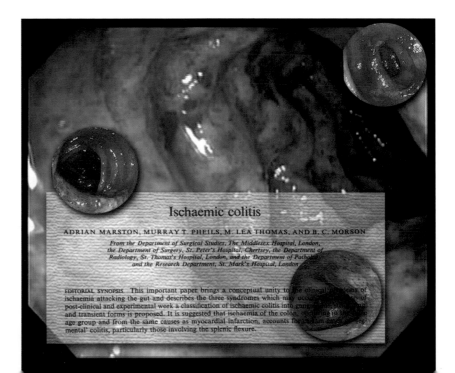

Ischaemic colitis

ADRIAN MARSTON, MURRAY T. PHEILS, M. LEA THOMAS, AND B. C. MORSON

From the Department of Surgical Studies, The Middlesex Hospital, London, the Department of Surgery, St. Peter's Hospital, Chertsey, the Department of Radiology, St. Thomas's Hospital, London, and the Department of Pathology and the Research Department, St. Mark's Hospital, London

EDITORIAL SYNOPSIS This important paper brings a conceptual unity to the clinical anatomy of ischaemia attacking the gut and describes the three syndromes which may occur. From post-clinical and experimental work a classification of ischaemic colitis into gangrenous, stricturing, and transient forms is proposed. It is suggested that ischaemia of the colon, occurring in the elderly age group and from the same causes as myocardial infarction, accounts for segmental colitis, particularly those involving the splenic flexure.

While most attention was directed to the construction of a colostomy for rectal obstruction, some surgeons actually attempted to excise the lesion itself. Jacques Lisfranc (1790–1847) of La Pitie Hospital in Paris was the first to perform a successful peritoneal or posterior resection of the rectum in 1826. By 1833, he had reported nine cases and proposed that only those lesions palpable on digital examination should be removed. The procedure as described by him was more an anal excision, and only palliative, since the majority of the patients reported died of general carcinomatosis within two years. Nevertheless, physicians were now fully aware that conditions of the bowel and the rectum were amenable to surgical intervention. Formal attention was therefore devoted to the subject of the anus and the rectum, and in the first half of the 19th century, several textbooks were variously published by John Kirby, John Hawship, Fredrick Salmon, William White, Thomas Copeland, and George Calvert. The 1810 text of Copeland described cancer of the rectum in terms not much different to those employed by John Arderne. In 1836, Bushe published the first American textbook on rectal diseases. Of particular relevance was the establishment by Salmon (1796–1868) in 1835 of a seven-bed infirmary known as the "Infirmary for the relief of the poor afflicted with the fistula and other diseases of the rectum". In 1854, this institution was renamed St Mark's Hospital, and over the next century, established itself as a center for the treatment and investigation of colorectal disease.

With the advent of colostomy as an acceptable and successful operation, surgeons then turned their interest to methods whereby colostomy might be avoided. Thus, the treatment of intestinal wounds, resection of the bowel, and the suturing of intestines became areas of considerable interest. In 1812, Benjamin Travers (1783–1858) reported on his work with intestinal repair in *An inquiry into the process of Nature in repairing injuries of the Intestines*, and demonstrated the successful experimental use of intestinal sutures.

Resection and anastomosis

While gallbladder surgery reflects a history of less than 200 years, the origins of surgery of the intestines recapitulates many thousands of years of vain experiment and fruitless intervention. Thus sepsis, soilage, and the lack of sutures defeated even the most ardent of surgical enthusiasts. Intervention ranged from the attempts of the Samhita of Susruta (2nd century AD), who effected intestinal suturing utilizing large red ants, to Galen's use of hairs drawn from the tails of horses.

Given the frequency of abdominal wounds and the use of spears, daggers, and swords, the question of managing prolapsed or perforated intestines had exercised the minds of surgeons since ancient times. It was well recognized that something had to be done and in particular, the need to replace the prolapsed abdominal viscera was obvious. The problem of suturing the intestine was less easily addressed. It was the teaching of Abukaszim that raising the pelvis of the patient could facilitate the relocation of the intestines

in cases of injuries to the lower abdomen. Almost 2,000 years later, a similar position was advocated by Frederic Trendelenburg, Professor of Surgery in Leipzig, for the purpose of operating within the pelvis, and nowadays, almost all abdominal procedures undertaken for gynecological surgery are carried out in this position. The concept of actually enlarging the abdominal incision to replace abdominal contents was initially advocated by Rhazes and thereafter supported in the writings of both Celsus and Galen. Subsequently, the Alsatian army surgeon Hans von Gersdorff (circa 1450–1530), dubbed "Schyllhans" (cross-eyed Johnny) of Strasbourg popularized the notion that if the intestine prolapsed into the abdominal wound and could not be put back, the wound should be extended to ensure complete replacement prior to suturing the abdominal wall.

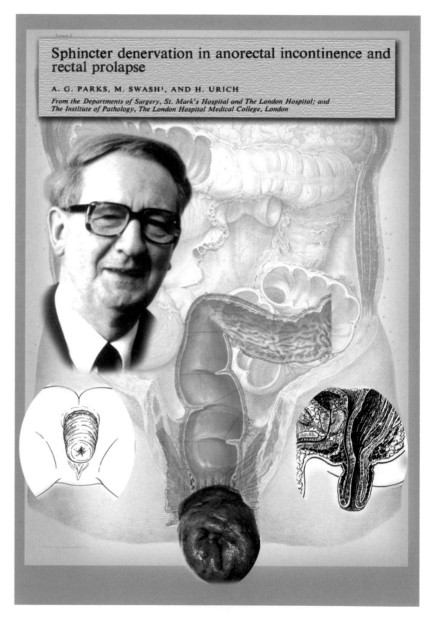

In a seminal article in *Gut* in 1977, Alan Parks (*left*) of St Mark's was able to demonstrate that idiopathic anal incontinence was associated with denervation of the muscles of the anorectal sling and of the anal sphincter mechanism.

This proposal was far more effective than the suggestion that the intestines be punctured and their contents drained prior to replacement. Indeed, this concept was surprising, since it had been accepted since very ancient times that feces harmed the peritoneum and that the flow of excrement into the abdominal cavity was dangerous.

In fact, it was the acceptance of these considerations that had been responsible for the earliest attempts to suture intestines. The failure of reliable intestinal repair led to the recognition that the abdominal cavity could be prevented the peril of the influx of excrement by leaving the damaged intestine outside the abdominal cavity. Although this created an unpleasant situation, since leaking feces would soil the body, it was preferable to an internal leak with peritonitis and death. The concept of an artificial anus was unattractive, but in desperate circumstances, there was often little alternative.

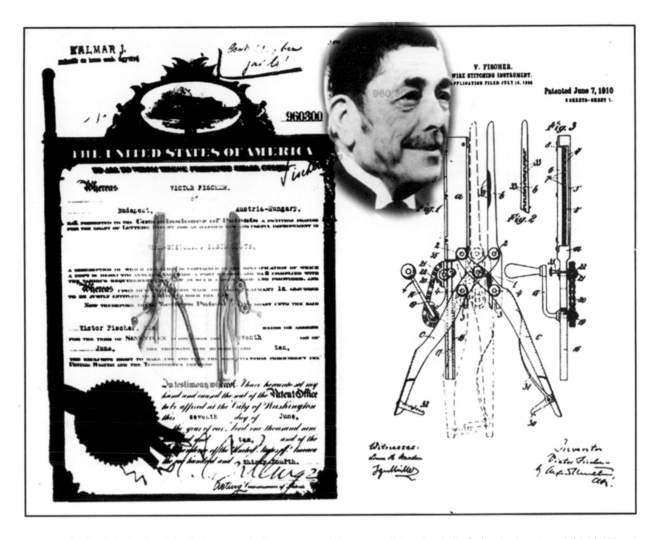

Humer Hültl (*top*) of St Rochas Hospital in Budapest was the first surgeon to design a successful stapling device for intestinal anastomosis (*right*). Although the original patent (*left*) was held by him for many years, subsequent design modifications superseded the earlier device, which was heavy, clumsy to use, and required hand loading.

The history of the suturing of intestines provides one of the most interesting chapters of surgery and undying proof of the creativity of physicians. A wide variety of fibers of animal (hair) and plant origin were tried before the use of silk thread and catgut, which are still in use. The primary concern, apart from leakage, was the problem posed by constriction of the intestine. In order to avoid this problem, a number of diverse measures were advocated. Roger Frugardi (12th century) sutured the intestine over a tube made of elder pith, while William of Saliceto used animal gut inserted into the two cut ends of the intestine (endoprosthesis) to support the suture. The Four Masters (13th century) used the trachea of an animal over which they sutured the ends of the intestine and indeed this technique proved so effective that it was renewed by Duverger as late as 1744. Sabatier in 1760 proposed the formation of an internal tube by rolling a membrane and uniting the two ends of the intestine over this. Experienced surgeons such as Treves supported this technique, and even Thienot as late as 1899 applied his name to this procedure. Similarly, William Halsted of Baltimore accepted this idea and his least favorite pupil Cushing, in 1898, even advocated the suturing of

the ends of intestines over inflatable rubber balloons. Lanfranco and Purman and other older surgeons declared these aids dispensable and the concept soon fell into disfavor.

At about the beginning of the 19th century, it became apparent that the healing of intestinal sutures was dependent on the cohesion of the serous and mucous membrane surfaces of the two ends of the intestine. As a result, it was realized that healing of the sutures of the intestine could only be effected if sutures provided adequate apposition of these two layers. Credit for the recognition of this critical observation is due to two Parisian surgeons, Antoine Jobert de Lamballe and Antoine Lembert. Jobert de Lamballe reported his procedure in 1824, Lembert in 1826. Although Ramdohr, a surgeon of Wolfenbüttel, had described a similar procedure to that of Jobert de Lamballe in 1727, it was inferior in respect of safety and accuracy. Overall, the Lembert technique was more acceptable, since it did not penetrate the mucous membrane of the intestine, and in fact the procedures in use today remain very similar to the original procedure described by Lembert. A number of alternative devices for intestinal apposition were developed, including the Murphy button, as proposed by the Chicago surgeon John Benjamin Murphy in 1892, and the Senn plate. By the first two decades of the 20th century, although suturing was still the standard technique, T Hertzel of Budapest had developed the first automatic stapling device and the subsequent advance of this technique would dramatically alter intestinal anastomosis.

John Benjamin Murphy in his study (note the two desk telephones – unusual for the turn of the century) developed the Murphy button (*inset*) to facilitate intestinal anastomosis.

In ancient times, sutures of intestines were used exclusively for the treatment of accidental injuries and remarkably, in spite of the imperfections of the sutures, many successes were recorded. As noted by Felix Platter (1536–1614), Professor in Basle, most were due to the good fortune of the development of adhesions around the damaged intestines that resulted in the leaking contents of the intestines being evacuated outward and not inward. Subsequent external fistulas would often heal, whereas an internal leak resulted in sepsis and death. The principal beneficiaries of the advance of intestinal sutures were those operated on for strangulated hernia, since the development of strangulated bowel had previously been a death sentence. The earliest advances in this area reflected the contributions of Francois de la Peyronie (1678–1747) of Montpellier, who worked diligently on the promotion of better training for surgeons and in 1731 founded the Academie de Chirurgie of Paris.

Once the precedent for successful bowel resection had been established, operations were undertaken for other causes, including obstruction and tumors. The first such procedure was performed by Balthasar Anselme Richerand in Paris in 1829, but the patient did not survive. Thereafter, Reybard (1793–1863) of Lyons was the first to excise a colon cancer (1833) with survival. Charles Thiersch of Leipzig repeated this operation 42 years later in Germany, but his patient died. As might be predicted, the mortality for colon resection at the beginning of the 20th century fluctuated between 70–80%. The subsequent development of colonic lavage, colostomy, the early antibiotics, and better anastomotic techniques reduced this to less than 10% by the 1940s. A particular challenge was however provided by lesions of the anus and rectum. Since the transanal excision of rectal tumors was difficult and often incomplete, rectotomy had been used, but this often resulted in disastrous leakage.

Restorative proctocolectomy is now the operation of choice for the definitive management of ulcerative colitis and familial adenomatous polyposis coli. AG Parks and RJ Nicholls first described restorative proctocolectomy as the operation of choice for the definitive surgical treatment of ulcerative colitis. This approach avoids the need for a permanent ileostomy. The original Parks pouch has largely fallen out of favor and has been replaced by the "J" pouch or the four-limbed "W" pouch, the former being easier to construct and the latter having superior function because of larger capacity. About 50% of the patients with the "S" pouches require catheterization to empty their pouches because of the long efferent ileal limb. By anastomosing the pouch directly to the anal canal ("J", "W"), the need for catheterization is however completely eliminated.

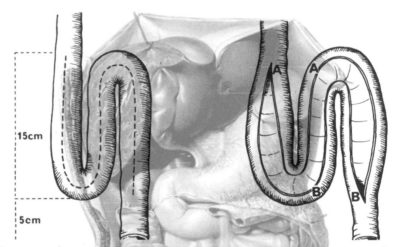

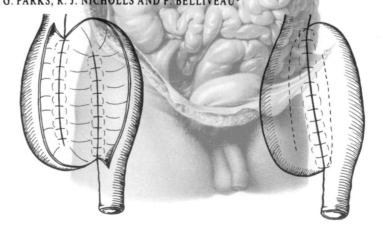

Proctocolectomy with ileal reservoir and anal anastomosis
A. G. PARKS, R. J. NICHOLLS AND P. BELLIVEAU*

The surgery of intestinal obstruction where there was no external hernia was late in development, since diagnosis was difficult and abdominal exploration risky. Hilton almost succeeded with such a case practice (obstruction by a band) as early as 1846, but for many years after this, patients with intestinal obstruction were left to die in the hands of physicians. Towards the end of the 19th century, such cases began to be handed over to surgeons, and Treves made clear the possible causes that might lead to such obstruction. Unfortunately, for many years, the results of surgery for obstruction were poor, since cases were generally referred for surgery too late and operations upon toxic and dehydrated patients with septicemia produced unsatisfactory results. In 1912, Hartwell and Hoguet showed the importance of replacing fluid lost by vomiting, and in 1923, Haden and Orr demonstrated the metabolic problems resulting from a loss of chlorides.

Intravenous replacement led to a rapid improvement in mortality, and in 1953, Wangensteen demonstrated the beneficial effect following decompression of the small intestine line by means of a small rubber tube swallowed into the stomach and allowed to pass into the small bowel. Aspiration of intestinal and gastric contents led to a great improvement. Conservative management of intestinal obstruction became possible and surgery was only necessary in situations involving strangulation.

When resection of distended or obstructed large bowel was attempted, it was soon found that similar methods to those used in cases of resection of small gut were inapplicable. Sutures did not hold and peritonitis resulted. It was found necessary to develop methods of external drainage of the bowel and to close the resulting fistula at a later date. Von Mikulicz-Radecki, Paul, and Bloch each independently devised techniques whereby the affected portion of the bowel was brought outside the abdomen, the loop excised, and temporary bowel drainage instituted.

Rectal surgery of a minor character had been performed for many centuries, but the major operation of excision of the rectum for cancer only became possible after the introduction of anesthesia and antisepsis. Those surgeons who first made the attempt adopted the perennial route, and even under such circumstances, were only able to undertake a limited excision. Of particular note in the development of this procedure are the names or Cripps, Allingham, and Langenbeck, though each described different aspects. In 1874, Kocher advised removal of part of the sacrum to facilitate approach to the rectum, and in 1886, Paul Kraske of Freiburg developed this technique and the sacral approach, which is still known by his name. As early as 1883, Czerny had tried a combined abdominal and perineal approach and after him, numerous surgeons in a variety of different countries tried to expand this technique. W Ernest Miles, however, was the first individual to develop the abdominoperineal method to a high degree of technical efficiency. George Grey Turner first practiced and Gabriel subsequently extended the usefulness of starting excision from the perineum and then finishing through the abdomen. Finally, the work of Devine demonstrated that results were better when the operation was performed by two surgeons working simultaneously – one from the perineum and the other through the abdomen.

In 1885, Paul Kraske (*bottom left*) at the 14th Congress of the German Surgeons presented his major contribution to the field. He described in detail his resection of the sacrum, extensive resection of the rectum, and anastomosis of the bowel to the anus (*bottom*). W Ernest Miles (1869–1947) (*right*) was born in Trinidad and educated at Queen's Royal College Port of Spain, at which his father was headmaster. He undertook his clinical training at St Bartholomew's Hospital and St Mark's Hospital for Diseases of the Rectum. In 1899, Miles was appointed to the Royal Cancer Hospital, where in 1907 he introduced the abdominoperineal resection for rectal carcinoma. Not only a doyen of rectal surgery, Miles was a keen horse racer and maintained a box at Ascot, where he was highly regarded as an equinophile.

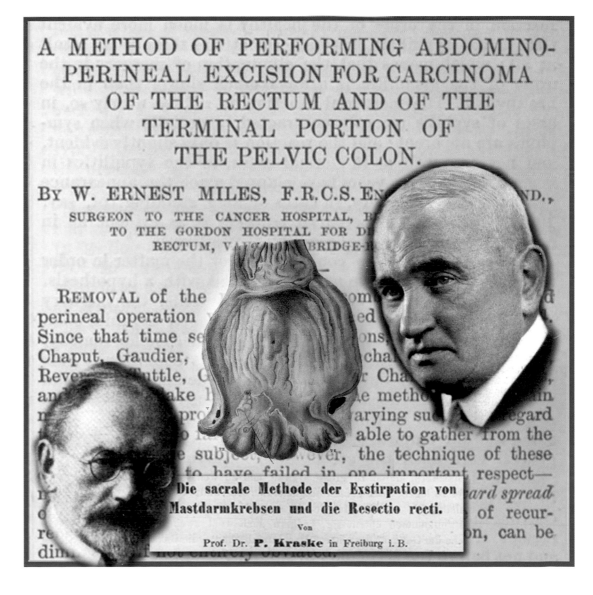

A METHOD OF PERFORMING ABDOMINO-PERINEAL EXCISION FOR CARCINOMA OF THE RECTUM AND OF THE TERMINAL PORTION OF THE PELVIC COLON.

BY W. ERNEST MILES, F.R.C.S. EN...ND.,
SURGEON TO THE CANCER HOSPITAL, ...
TO THE GORDON HOSPITAL FOR D...
RECTUM, ...BRIDGE-...

Die sacrale Methode der Exstirpation von Mastdarmkrebsen und die Resectio recti.
Von
Prof. Dr. P. Kraske in Freiburg i. B.

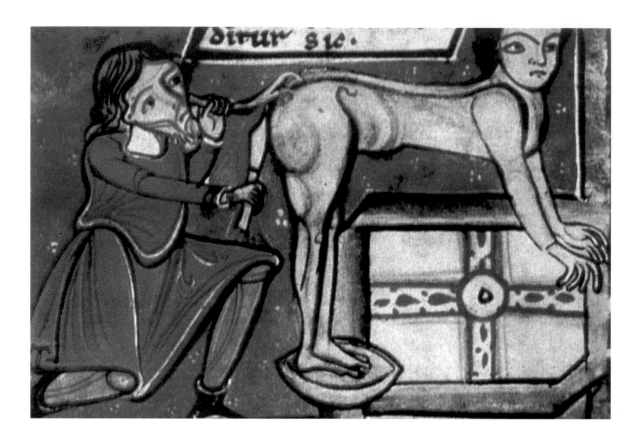

Early English medicine, particularly as practiced by John Arderne, focused heavily on the management of anorectal disease.

ANORECTAL DISEASE

The Ebers Papyrus of circa 1700 BC provides more than 33 prescriptions or recipes for treatment of anal and rectal disease. These include liniments, enemas, ointments, and suppositories, as well as prescriptions for vermifuges and cathartics. Similarly, the Beatty Medical Papyrus of the 12th and 13th centuries BC consists almost entirely of methods and remedies for the treatment of anal, rectal, and colonic disease. Its prescriptions contain ingredients such as myrrh, honey, flour, ibex fat, and rectal injection with honey and sweet beer. The conditions described include pruritus and painful swelling (thrombosed hemorrhoids) and prolapsed rectum. Between 460–177 BC, Hippocrates wrote a number of dissertations on the subjects, including 'On fistula' and 'On hemorrhoids'. He proposed treatment of the disease by ointment, enemas, and suppositories, but in an advance on Egyptian medicine, he also discussed surgical therapy. This included excising, sewing, binding, and cautery of hemorrhoids. The directions given to the surgical novice for treatment of such conditions using cautery were to "force out as much anus with fingers as possible make the irons red hot and burn the pile until it be dried up, so that no part may be left behind".

Hippocrates described the relationship between anorectal abscess and fistula, and his treatment using a stent or ligature remains in practice to this day in various somewhat updated forms. In addition to surgery, however, Hippocrates proposed the use of astringent dressings as well as suppositories to control bleeding.

In 1983, John Alexander-Williams (*bottom right*) published a leading article on pruritus ani in the *British Medical Journal*. In an addendum (*top*) to that article, in response to requests for his "Ten rules" for patients attending his proctology clinic, he published *Causes and management of anal irritation*. In essence, these 10 commandments attempted to keep the anal skin clean and dry, and further to limit damage by scratching or rubbing.

Although Greek medicine was transmuted to the Romans after their conquest of Athens, even Galen could contribute little to the management of anorectal disease. Celsus, who was in effect little more than an assimilator (albeit a very fine one) of information, as late as 50 AD proposed that wounds of the intestine should be sutured in all layers, and suggested that the knife and ligature be used to treat anal fistulas. During the Byzantine period, Paul of Aegina, in the 7th century AD, recounted a slightly more sophisticated method for the management of hemorrhoids and anal fistulas, proposing the use of frequent clysters to clean the intestine before everting the anus and using a strong ligature to tie off the hemorrhoids. Leonides avoided the ligature, preferring to first cauterize the hemorrhoids before excising them with a scalpel. Maimonides (1138–1204), in his treatise on hemorrhoids, proposed a light diet and the frequent usage of baths. By the close of the 12th century, the preoccupation with anorectal disease had diminished somewhat, as surgeons began with some temerity to approach the bowel itself.

In the 14th century, the dominant influence on anorectal disease was provided by Arderne, who served in the Hundred Years War under the Duke of Lancaster John of Gaunt. On discharge from the army, he established a practice in anorectal disease and developed a great reputation, becoming immensely rich in the process. Nevertheless, he insisted that his followers be charitable and live a chaste life, providing them with strict rules of conduct which would ensure their health. Arderne was advanced for his time and wrote extensively on appropriate follow-up of patients, reporting both his successes and his failures. Although he was effective in the treatment of ischiorectal abscesses and fistulas and described their care in great detail, he recognized the inadequacy of treatment for rectal cancer: "I never saw or heard of any man that was cured of cancer of the rectum but I have known many that died of the afore said sickness." His description of the condition is noteworthy: "Bubo is an apostem breeding within the anus in the rectum with great hardness but little aching. This I say, before it ulcerates, it is nothing else than a hidden cancer, that may, not in the beginning of it be known by the sight of the eye, for it is always hidden within the rectum; and it is therefore called a bubo, for as a bubo, that is an owl, is always dwelling and hiding so that this sickness lurks within the rectum in the beginning; but after a passage of time it ulcerates and eroding the anus comes out."

St Fiacre was a 7th century acolyte. Originally the patron saint of gardeners, he subsequently became the patron saint of hemorrhoid sufferers. The inn at which numerous patients were treated stood opposite the church commemorating St Fiacre and was named after him. As a result, the numerous horsedrawn carriages waiting for their patients to be treated outside this establishment eventually became known as fiacres.

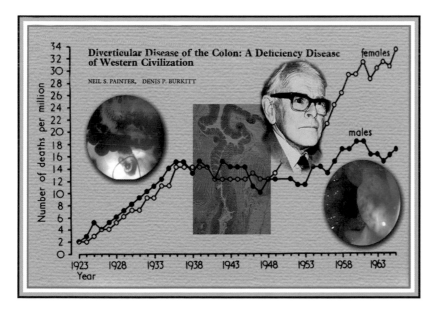

In 1971, Denis Burkitt (*right of center*) and his colleague Neil Painter presented the hypothesis that diverticular disease (*left: radiology*) was a deficiency disease caused by a lack of vegetable fiber (increases in refined carbohydrates) in the diet. Diverticular disease was uncommonly encountered at the beginning of the 20th century, but the prevalence increased from 5–10% 80 years ago to 35–50% in an autopsy series published in 1969. Westernized nations have prevalence rates of 5–45%, depending upon the method of diagnosis and age of the population, while in Africa and Asia, the prevalence is less than 0.2%. Burkitt and Painter demonstrated no change in the death rate (*background*) during the Second World War, when white bread was not available and refined sugars strictly rationed. The rise however continued when these dietary exigencies were removed. In addition, there may be a relation between diverticulosis and colon cancer (*bottom right*) – both diseases have a similar etiology. Burkitt considered both diseases preventable.

SAINT FIACRE,
Patron de MM. les Jardiniers et de MM. les Pépiniéristes.

Although the 16th century provided surgery with Andreas Vesalius and Ambroise Paré (1510–1590), they contributed little of interest to the management of intestinal disease, although Paré did produce a text dealing with wounds of the intestine under the title of *The Gut:* "When the guts are wounded the whole body griped and pained, the excrements come out of the wound, where often times the guts break force with great violence." His description of an enterocutaneous fistula was accurate, but unfortunately, he could provide no adequate therapy. Given the inability to safely enter the peritoneal cavity, intestinal surgery languished well into the 17th century, until Charles Francois Felix operated on Louis XIV and with this success, initiated the renaissance of French surgery. In 1685, Louis developed a small but painful lump in the rectum. Despite numerous remedies, the court doctors and apothecary failed to successfully cure the condition and as a last resort, his surgeon Felix was summoned. Felix explained to the King how the surgery would bring relief and proposed that a date six months later be set for the operation. This provided Felix with the time to operate on more lowly patients, of whom it is rumored a substantial number perished under his knife as he perfected his technique.

Finally, on November 18, 1686, Felix had the temerity to perform the operation at Versailles in the presence of Madame de Maintenon and the court medical staff. Fortunately for both himself and the King, it proved a complete success. As Louis recovered, his sycophantic courtiers paraded around Versailles with bandaged bottoms to show their sympathy with the King's posterior discomfort.

In recognition of his services to the royal posterior, Felix received 300,000 livres, which represented a sum equivalent to three times the annual salary of the chief court physician. In addition, he was ennobled, and cynics of the time referred to the year 1686 as "*L'Année de la Fistule*".

By the 18th century, Morgagni (1682–1771) had not only described the crypts and columns of the anus, but also proposed an operation for cancer of the rectum. Indeed, in 1739, Fajet performed a posterior resection of the rectum, but the subsequent uncontrollable sacral anus proved impossible to deal with and as a result, the procedure evoked considerable criticism. The aftermath of this catastrophe served to focus more attention on the development of a colostomy procedure, since much experience had been inadvertently gained in this area by virtue of accidental fistulas caused by either trauma or disease. In the early 18th century, Heister produced a report on 'The spontaneous or operative creation of an external intestinal fistula in injuries or gangrene of the bowel'. In this he proposed that in the case of a damaged intestine, it should be "stitched to the external wound either by continued or interrupted suture for by this means the patient is not only saved from instant death but there have been instances where the wounded intestine has been so far heated that the feces which used to be voided per anum have been voided by the wound in the abdomen". Heister went on to describe a series of techniques whereby bowel that had been inadvertently damaged might be fashioned into a colostomy, stating quite pragmatically: "It is surely far better to part with one of the conveniences of life than to part with life itself. Besides the excrements that are voided by this passage arc not altogether so offensive as those that are voided per anum."

Given the lack of sanitary facilities in Versailles and the debauched lifestyle that he lived, it was little surprise to Charles Francois Felix (*top right*) that Louis XIV (*center*) developed a perianal abscess. The successful incision and drainage of the royal posterior is claimed by many to have provided the initial impetus for the development of French surgery.

Frederick Salmon (*top right*) in 1835 established a seven-bed infirmary in London, known as "The infirmary for the relief of the poor afflicted with a fistula and other diseases of the rectum". When the institution was enlarged, its new benefactors insisted that it be called "St Andrew's Hospital of the Lower Intestine" since it was located in the parish of St Andrew's. Salmon declined and accepted an offer to locate the hospital in the parish of St Luke's, provided it could be called "The Fistula Hospital". The benefactors objected, claiming that it would be "difficult to raise public funds for an institution with this name". Since the parish already contained a St Luke's Hospital, a compromise was reached by renaming the institution "St Mark's Hospital for Fistula". The new name was determined by designating the opening day as August 25, 1852 – St Mark's Day! Over the next century, St Mark's Hospital established itself as an epicenter for the study of colorectal disease.

Rectal prolapse had been well recognized since the earliest medical literature and Hippocrates had even described it: "...eversion of the gut takes place in middle aged persons having piles, of children afflicted with stone and in protracted and intense discharge of the bowel, and in old persons having mucous concretions (Scybale)." Although the first therapy involved the application of fomentations and reductions, curative treatments included cauterization, excision, and even incision. By 1843, Chelius was able to record a list of more than a half-dozen notable surgeons, including Heister (1745), Copeland (1814), Hawship (1820), Bushe (1827), Senn (1828), Dupuytren (1831), and Velpeau (1841), who had described a surgical methodology for dealing with the condition.

Cuthbert Esquire Dukes (1890–1977) (*right*), a pathologist, was Director of the Research Laboratory at St Mark's Hospital in London. In 1932, he developed a classification or staging system for colorectal cancer that described the staging of rectal carcinoma only, but could also be applied to carcinomas of the colon. It was divided into three simple stages, A to C, based on the local spread of the cancer. Stage D was subsequently introduced and several modified versions now exist. In 1958, he published his seminal application of this approach in almost 2,500 patients with rectal cancer. The utility of the system was demonstrated by the marked differences in five-year survival in the different stages. This ranged from 97.7% (A – limited to rectum, no spread) to 77.6% (B – spread to extra-rectal tissue) to 32.0% (C – lymphatic metastases).

BIBLIOGRAPHY

SECTION I: THE ORIGINS OF BRITISH MEDICINE AND GASTROENTEROLOGY

1 INTRODUCTION

Brockbank W. *Ancient Therapeutic Arts*. Springfield: Thomas, 1954.

Dioscorides Pedanius of Anazarbos. *The Greek Herbal of Dioscorides*. Gunther RT (ed). Oxford: Oxford University Press, 1934.

Friedenwald H. *The Jews and Medicine*. Baltimore: John Hopkins Press, 1967.

Garrison FH. *Contributions to the History of Medicine*. New York: Hafner Publishing Company, 1966.

The Genuine Works of Hippocrates, translated from the Greek with a preliminary discourse and annotations by Francis Adams. New York: W Wood, 1891.

Mettler CC. *History of Medicine: a correlative text, arranged according to subjects*. Philadelphia: Blakiston Company, 1947.

Norman J (ed). *Morton's medical bibliography: an annotated checklist of texts illustrating the history of medicine*. 5th edn. Brookfield: Gower, 1991.

2 ANGLO-SAXON ENGLISH MEDICINE

Bonser W. *The Medical Background of Anglo-Saxon England; a study in history, psychology and folklore*. London: Wellcome History of Medicine Library, 1963.

Cameron ML. Anglo-Saxon medicine and magic. *Anglo Sax Engl* 1988; 17: 191–215.

Cockayne TO. *Leechdom, Wortcunning and Starcraft of Early England*. London: Longmann, 1864–1866.

Meaney A. The practice of medicine in England about the year 1000. *Soc Hist Med* 2000; 13(2): 221–37.

Moore Sir N. *English Medicine in Anglo-Saxon Times*. Oxford: Clarendon Press, 1908.

Payne JF. *English Medicine in Anglo-Saxon Times*. Oxford: Clarendon Press, 1904.

Power Sir D'A. *Medicine in the British Isles*. New York: PB Hoeber, 1930.

Vrebos J. Cleft lip surgery in Anglo-Saxon Britain: the Leech Book (circa AD 920). *Plast Reconstr Surg* 1986; 77(5): 850–3.

3 THE EVOLUTION OF MEDICINE IN ENGLAND

Albutt TC. *The Historical Relations of Medicine and Surgery to the End of the Sixteenth Century*. New York: Macmillan & Company Ltd, 1905.

Crawfurd Sir RHP. *Plague and Pestilence in Literature and Art*. Oxford: Clarendon Press, 1914.

Power Sir D'A. *Medicine in the British Isles*. New York: PB Hoeber, 1930.

Rawcliffe C. *Sources for the History of Medicine in Medieval England*. Kalamazoo: Medieval Institute Publications, 1995.

Richardson R (ed). *English Hospitals, 1660–1948: a survey of their architecture and design*. Swindon: Royal Commission on the Historical Monuments of England, 1998.

Rubin S. *Medieval English Medicine*. New York: Barnes & Noble Books, 1974.

Wear A. *Knowledge and Practice in English Medicine, 1550–1680*. New York: Cambridge University Press, 2000.

4 OXFORD AND CAMBRIDGE

Cumberledge J. *Science, Medicine, and History*. London: Oxford University Press, 1953.

Garrison FH. *Contributions to the History of Medicine*. New York: Hafner Publishing Company, 1966.

Gottfried RS. *Doctors and Medicine in Medieval England 1340–1530*. Princeton: Princeton University Press, 1986.

Moore Sir N. *The Physician in English History*. Cambridge: Cambridge University Press, 1913.

Rawcliffe C. God, Mammon, and the physician: medicine in England before the College. *J R Coll Physicians Lond* 2000; 34(3): 266–72.

Siraisis NG. *Medieval and Renaissance Medicine*. Chicago: University of Chicago Press, 1990.

Talbot CH. *Medicine in Medieval England*. London: Oldbourne Press, 1967.

5 THE DARK AGE – MAGIC AND MEDICINE

Bauer WW. *Potions, Remedies, and Old Wives' Tales*. Garden City: Doubleday, 1969.

Biedermann H. *Medicina Magica*. Birmingham: Gryphon Editions, 1978.

Brockbank W. *Ancient Therapeutic Arts*. Springfield: Thomas, 1954.

Darby JC. *Science and the Healing Art, or A new book on old facts*. Louisville: JP Morton & Company, 1880.

Mathison RR. *The Eternal Search: the story of man and his drugs*. New York: GP Putnam, 1958.

Alchemy and the Occult: a catalogue of books and manuscripts from the collection of Paul and Mary Mellon given to Yale University Library. Compiled by Ian MacPhail. New Haven: Yale University Library, 1977.

Roob A. *The Hermetic Museum: Alchemy and Mysticism*. Cologne: Taschen America Llc, 1997.

Rubin S. The medical practitioner in Anglo-Saxon England. *J R Coll Gen Pract* 1970; 20(97): 63–71.

Wootton AC. *The Chronicles of Pharmacy*. Boston: Milford House Inc, 1910.

6 LEECHCRAFT

Cameron ML. Anglo-Saxon medicine and magic. *Anglo Sax Engl* 1988; 17: 191–215.

Cockayne TO. *Leechdom, Wortcunning and Starcraft of Early England*. London: Longmann, 1864–1866.

Hart FD. Anglo-Saxon cures. *Br J Clin Pract* 1988; 42(6): 250–1.

Moore Sir N. *English Medicine in Anglo-Saxon Times*. Oxford: Clarendon Press, 1908.

Payne JF. *English Medicine in Anglo-Saxon Times*. Oxford: Clarendon Press, 1904.

Singer CJ. *Early English Magic and Medicine*. London: Oxford University Press, 1920.

Singer CJ. *From Magic to Science: essays on the scientific twilight*. New York: Dover Publications, 1958.

Voigts LE. Anglo-Saxon plant remedies and the Anglo-Saxons. *Isis* 1979; 70(252): 250–68.

7 ELIZABETHAN MEDICINE

Cope Z. *The Royal College of Surgeons of England: a history*. London: Anthony Blond, 1959.

Copeman WSC. *Doctors and Disease in Tudor Times*. London: W Dawson, 1960.

Cosman BC. All's Well That Ends Well: Shakespeare's treatment of anal fistula. *Dis Colon Rectum* 1998; 41(7): 914–24.

Dobson J, Milnes WR. *Barbers and Barber-Surgeons of London*. Oxford: Blackwell Scientific Publications, 1979.

Ellis H. The Hunterian Professors and Arris and Gale Lecturers. *Ann R Coll Surg Engl* 1979; 61(1): 71–2.

McNee J. Barber-Surgeons in Great Britain and Ireland. *Ann R Coll Surg Engl* 1959; 24(1): 1.

Metcalfe R. The rise and progress of hydrotherapy in England and Scotland. London, 1906. In: *Health and Healing in Early Modern England: studies in social and intellectual history*. Wear A (ed). Brookfield: Ashgate, 1998.

Modlin I. The surgical legacy of Arris and Gale. *J Med Biogr* 1996; 4(4): 91–199.

Richardson RG. Dr John Hall, Shakespeare's son-in-law. A vignette of Elizabethan medicine. *Practitioner* 1981; 225(1354): 593–5.

Young S. *The Annals of the Barber-Surgeons of London*. London: Blades, East & Blades, 1890.

8 THE ROYAL SOCIETY

Bonnabeau RC Jr. The Royal College of Physicians and the apothecaries in the 17th century. A dispute for all seasons. *Minn Med* 1983; 66(9): 565–7.

Clark Sir GN. *A History of the Royal College of Physicians of London.* Oxford: Clarendon Press, 1964–1972.

Cooper DB. The Royal College of Physicians of London during the reign of the House of Stuart (1603–1714). *Trans Stud Coll Physicians Phila* 1983; 5(3): 191–211.

Davidson M. *The Royal Society of Medicine: the Realization of an Ideal 1805–1955.* London: Royal Society of Medicine, 1955.

Hooke R. *Micrographia, or, Some physiological descriptions of minute bodies made by magnifying glasses: with observations and inquiries thereupon.* London: John Martyn & James Allestry, 1665.

Porter R. *The Biographical Dictionary of Scientists.* 2nd edn. New York: Oxford University Press, 1994.

Sakula A. Founding of the Athenaeum and Fellows of the Royal College of Physicians. *J R Coll Physicians Lond* 1983; 17(3): 206–7.

Wall C. *A History of the Worshipful Society of Apothecaries of London.* London: Wellcome History of Medicine Museum, 1963.

9 MEDICINE AND ROYALTY

Chaplin A. *Medicine in England during the Reign of George III.* London: Henry Kimpton, 1919.

Crawfurd Sir RHP. *The King's Evil.* Oxford: Clarendon Press, 1911.

Dirckx JH. Dr John Arbuthnot – physician to royalty and creator of "John Bull". *Pharos Alpha Omega Alpha Honor Med Soc* 1979; 42(3): 20–6.

Kirkup J. The historical instrument collection at the Royal College of Surgeons of England. *J Med Biogr* 1993; 1(1): 52–8.

Miller JM. Vignette of medical history: porphyria in royalty. *Md Med J* 1993; 42(10): 1015–7.

Rogal SJ. *Medicine in Great Britain from the Restoration to the Nineteenth Century, 1660–1800: an annotated bibliography.* New York: Greenwood Press, 1992.

Sloan AW. *English Medicine in the Seventeenth Century.* Durham: Durham Academic Press, 1996.

10 THE GREAT MEN OF GUY'S

Addison T. *A Collection of the Published Writings of the Late Thomas Addison, MD, Physician to Guy's Hospital.* London: The New Sydenham Society, 1860.

Coley NG. Medical chemistry at Guy's Hospital (1770–1850). *Ambix* 1988; 35(3): 155–68.

Cooper A. *Surgical Essays.* London: Cox, 1818–1819.

Daws JJ. Thomas Hodgkin and the museum at Guy's Hospital. *Cancer Treat Rev* 1999; 25(3): 145–9.

Dubovsky H. Hilton's rest and pain, Guy's Hospital personalities and Guy's South African rugby connection. *S Afr Med J* 1997; 87(7): 898–900.

Jacoby MG. Mr Guy's Hospital: 263 not out. *JAMA* 1989; 262(15): 2092.

Peitzman SJ. Bright's disease and Bright's generation – toward exact medicine at Guy's Hospital. *Bull Hist Med* 1981; 55(3): 307–21.

11 ADVANCES IN SCIENCE AND MEDICINE

Fulton JF. *Selected Readings in the History of Physiology.* 2nd edn. Springfield: Thomas, 1930.

Holmes FL. *Claude Bernard and Animal Chemistry: the emergence of a scientist.* Cambridge: Harvard University Press, 1974.

Lister J. *The Collected Papers of Joseph Baron Lister.* Oxford: Clarendon Press, 1909.

The Collected Essays of Sir William Osler. Birmingham: Classics of Medicine Library, 1985.

Snow J. *On Chloroform and Other Anesthetics.* London: John Churchill, 1858.

Stirling W. *Some Apostles of Physiology; being an account of their lives and labours that have contributed to the advancement of the healing art as well as to the prevention of disease.* London: Waterlow & Sons Ltd, 1902.

Weatherall M. *Gentlemen, Scientists, and Doctors: Medicine at Cambridge 1800–1940.* Rochester: Boydell Press, 2000.

Youngson AJ. *The Scientific Revolution in Victorian Medicine.* New York: Holmes & Meier Publishers, 1979.

12 THE FOUNDING OF THE GASTROENTEROLOGICAL CLUB

Avery Jones Sir F. Gastroenterology in Britain before 1937 and the founding of the Gastro-Enterological Club. *Gut* 1987; 28(Suppl): 3–6.

Hobsley M. The Meetings. British Society of Gastroenterology. *Gut* 1987; 28(Suppl): 10–13.

Sladen GE. Memberships 1937–1987. British Society of Gastroenterology. *Gut* 1987; 28(Suppl): 16–17.

13 BRITISH GASTROENTEROLOGY – THE EARLY YEARS

Aird I. *Companion in Surgical Studies.* Edinburgh: Livingstone Ltd, 1949.

Baron JH. History of the British Society of Gastroenterology. British Society of Gastroenterology. *Gut* 1987; 28(Suppl): 1.

Robin IG. My reminiscences of Sir Arthur Hurst. *Postgrad Med J* 1999; 75(889): 643–4.

14 SIR ARTHUR HURST (1879–1944)

Anon. Centenary of Sir Arthur Hurst. *Br Med J* 1979; 2(6183): 160–1.

Hurst AE, Stewart MJ. *Gastric and Duodenal Ulcer.* London: Oxford University Press, 1929.

Sakula A. Sir Arthur Hurst (1879–1944): master of medicine. *J Med Biogr* 1999; 7(3): 125–9.

15 GASTROENTEROLOGY AS A SPECIALTY

Alexander-Williams J, Baron JH. British Society of Gastroenterology 1937–87: an overview. British Society of Gastroenterology. *Gut* 1987; 28(Suppl): 53–5.

Cockel R. Regional societies groups and committees: BSG specialty committees and related but independent societies. British Society of Gastroenterology. *Gut* 1987; 28(Suppl): 42–5.

Lenard-Jones JE. The Society promotes gastroenterology as a national speciality. British Society of Gastroenterology. *Gut* 1987; 28(Suppl): 29–31.

Losowsky MS. Research, education, science, training. Work of the committees. British Society of Gastroenterology. *Gut* 1987; 28(Suppl): 25–6.

Sarner M. The British Digestive Foundation. *Gut* 1987; 28(Suppl): 46–7.

Watkinson G. Role of the BSG in the development of international gastroenterology. British Society of Gastroenterology. *Gut* 1987; 28(Suppl): 49–52.

16 THE BRITISH SOCIETY FOR DIGESTIVE ENDOSCOPY

Truelove SC. British Society for Digestive Endoscopy. *Gut* 1987; 28(Suppl): 49–52.

17 THE PROCEEDINGS OF THE SOCIETY – *GUT*

Misiewicz JJ. Publication of the Society's proceedings – Gut. *Gut* 1987; 28(Suppl): 20–2.

18 HONORS

Turnberg LA. Awards, lectureships and medals. British Society of Gastroenterology. *Gut* 1987; 28(Suppl): 39–41.

SECTION II: THE EVOLUTION OF GASTROENTEROLOGY IN BRITAIN

1 ESOPHAGUS

Allison PR, Johnstone AS, Royce GB. Short esophagus with simple peptic ulceration. *J Thorac Surg* 1943; 12: 432–57.

Allison PR. Peptic ulcer of the oesophagus. *J Thorac Surg* 1946; 15: 308.

Allison PR. Reflux esophagitis, sliding hiatal hernia, and the anatomy of repair. *Surg Gynecol Obstet* 1951; 92: 419–31.

Barrett NR. Chronic peptic ulcer of the oesophagus and "oesophagitis". *Br J Surg* 1950; 38: 175–82.

Cruise FR. The utility of the endoscope as an aid in the diagnosis and treatment of disease. *Dublin QJ Med Sci* 1865; 39: 329–63.

Kirsner JB (ed). *The Growth of Gastroenterologic Knowledge During the Twentieth Century.* Philadelphia: Lea & Febiger, 1994.

Mackenzie M. *Diseases of the Throat and Nose, Vol II.* Philadelphia: P Blankston, Son & Company, 1884.

Modlin IM. *A Brief History of Endoscopy.* Milan: Multi Med, 2000.

Shaldon S, Sherlock S. The use of vasopressin (pitressin) in the control of bleeding from esophageal varices. *Lancet* 1960; 2: 222–5.

Skinner DB, Belsey RH. Surgical management of esophageal reflux and hiatal hernia: long-term results with 1030 patients. *J Thorac Cardiovasc Surg* 1967; 53(1): 33–54.

2 STOMACH AND DUODENUM

Avery Jones F. Haematemesis and melaena with special reference to bleeding peptic ulcer. *Br Med J* 1947; 2: 441–6.

Avery Jones F, Gummer JWP, Lennard-Jones JE. *Clinical Gastroenterology.* 2nd edn. Edinburgh: Blackwell Scientific, 1968.

Bircher E. Die Resektion von Aesten der N. Vagus zur Behandlung gastrischer Affektionen. *Schweiz Med Wochenschr* 1920; 50: 519–28.

Black J, Duncan W, Durant C *et al.* Definition and antagonism of histamine H$_2$ receptors. *Nature* 1972; 236: 385–90.

Boas II. *Diagnostik und Therapie der Magenkrankheiten.* Leipzig: G Thieme, 1890.

Brinton W. *Ulcer of the Stomach.* London: 1857.

Card WI, Marks IN. The relationship between the acid output of the stomach following "maximal" histamine stimulation and the parietal cell mass. *Clin Sci* 1960; 19: 147–63.

Code C, Scholer JE. Barrier offered by gastric mucosa to absorption of sodium. *Am J Physiol* 1955; 183: 604.

Curling TB. On acute ulceration of the duodenum in cases of burn. *Med-Chirurg Trans* 1842 (2nd series); 25: 260–81.

Dragstedt L. Section of the vagus nerves to the stomach in the treatment of peptic ulcer. *Ann Surg* 1947; 126: 687–708.

Ewald O. *Klinik der Verdauungskrankheiten* (3 vols). Berlin: A Hirschwald, 1879–1902.

Gussenbauer C, Winiwarter A. Die partielle Magenresektion: eine experimentelle operative Studie. *Arch kim Chit* 1876; 19: 347–80.

Heidenhain RP. Über die Pepsinbildung in den Pylorusdruesen. *Pflüg Arch ges Physiol* 1878; 18: 169–71.

Hirschowitz BI, Curtiss LE, Peters CW *et al.* Demonstration of a new gastroscope, the 'fiberscope'. *Gastroenterology* 1958; 35(1): 50–3.

Kirsner JB (ed). *The Growth of Gastroenterologic Knowledge During the Twentieth Century.* Philadelphia: Lea & Febiger, 1994.

Koch R. *Untersuchungen ueber die Aetiologie der Wundinfektionskrankheiten.* Leipzig: FCW Vogel, 1878.

Kocher ETh. Über die Radicalbehandlung des Krebses. *Deutsch Z Chir* 1880; 13: 134–166.

Langley JN. *Pepsin-forming Glands.* London: 1881.

Latarjet A. Resection du nerfs de l'estomac: technique operatoire; resultats cliniques. *Bull Acad Natl Med Paris* 1922; 87: 681–91.

Modlin IM. *From Prout to the Proton Pump.* Konstanz: Schnetztor-Verlag GmbH, 1995.

Modlin IM, Sachs G. *Acid-related Diseases.* Konstanz: Schnetztor-Verlag GmbH, 1998.

Moynihan B. *Duodenal Ulcer.* Birmingham: Classics of Medicine Library, 1991.

Polya EA. Zur Stumpfversorung nach Magenresektion. *Zbl Chit* 1911; 38: 532–5.

Prout W. On the nature of the acid and saline matters usually existing in the stomach of animals. *Philos Trans* 1824; 114: 45–9.

Rutkow IM. *Surgery: An Illustrated History.* St Louis: Mosby-Year Book Inc, 1993.

Rydygier L. First extirpation of carcinomatous pylorus: death after 12 hours. *Deutsch Z Chir* 1881; 14: 252–60.

Sawyer Sir J. *Clinical Lecture on the Treatment of Gastralgia.* London: 1887.

Sedillot C. Operation de gastrostomie pratique pour la premiere fois le 13 Novembre 1849. *Gaz Med Strasbourg* 1849; 9: 366–77.

Tanner NC. The diagnosis and management of massive haematemesis. *Br J Surg* 1964; 51: 754–6.

Von Mikulicz-Radecki J. Chirurgische Erfährungen über das Darmcarcinom. *Arch kim Chir* 1903; 69: 28–47.

Warren JR, Marshall B. Unidentified curved bacilli on gastric epithelium in active chronic gastritis. *Lancet* 1983; 1(8336): 1273–5.

3 PANCREAS

Banting FG, Best CH. The internal secretion of the pancreas. *J Lab Clin Med* 1922; 7(5): 465–80.

Bartholin I. *De lacteis thoracicis in homine brustique.* Hafinae: M Martzan, 1652.

Brunner JC. *De glandulis in intestino duodeno hominis desectis.* Heidelberg: CE Buchta, 1687.

Howard JM, Hess W, Traverso W. Johann Georg Wirsung (1589–1643) and the pancreatic duct: the prosector of Padua, Italy. *J Am Coll Surg* 1998; 187(2): 201–11.

Langerhans P. Beitraege zur mikroskopischen Anatomie der Bauchspeicheldrüse. Berlin: Gustav Lange, 1869. English translation by Morrison H. *Bull Hist Med* 1937; 5: 259–97.

Nyhus LM. Surgical sketch on Wirsung. *World J Surg* 1999; 23(5): 528.

Opie E. *Disease of the Pancreas, its Cause and Nature.* Philadelphia: JB Lippincott, 1903.

Rudbeck O. Nova exercitatio anatomica, exhi hens ductus hepaticos aquosos, et vasa glandulorum serosa, 1653. English translation. *Bull Hist Med* 1942; 11: 304–39.

Whipple AD. Treatment of carcinoma of the ampulla of Vater. *Ann Surg* 1935; 102: 763–79.

Zollinger RM, Ellison EH. Primary peptic ulcerations of the jejunum associated with islet cell tumors of the pancreas. *Ann Surg* 1955; 142(4): 709–28.

4 GASTROINTESTINAL NEUROENDOCRINOLOGY

Babkin BP. *Die aussere Sekretion der Verdauungsdrüsen.* Berlin: J Springer, 1914.

Bayliss W, Starling F. Preliminary communication on the causation of the so-called 'peripheral reflex secretion' of the pancreas. *Lancet* 1902; 2: 810–13.

Best C, McHenry F. The inactivation of histamine. *J Physiol Lond* 1930; 70: 349–72.

Code C. Histamine and gastric secretion. In: *Histamine.* Wolstenholme G, O'Conner C (eds). Boston: Little, Brown & Company, 1956.

Dale H. *Adventures in Physiology.* London: Pergamon Press, 1953.

Edkins J. The chemical mechanism of gastric secretion. *J Physiol Lond* 1906; 34: 133–44.

Gregory R, Tracey H. The preparation and properties of gastrin. *J Physiol Lond* 1959; 149: 70–1.

Komarov S. Gastrin. *Proc Soc Exp Biol Med* 1938; 38: 514–16.

Mann FC, Ballman JL. Experimentally produced peptic ulcer: development and treatment. *JAMA* 1932; 99: 1576.

McGuigan JE. Gastric mucosal intracellular localization of gastrin by immunofluorescence. *Gastroenterology* 1968; 55(3): 315–27.

Modlin IM, Kidd M, Marks I *et al*. The pivotal role of John S Edkins in the discovery of Gastrin. *World J Surg* 1997; 21(2): 226–34.

Pavlov I. *The Work of the Digestive Glands*. London: Griffin, 1902.

Pearse AG. The cytochemistry and ultrastructure of polypeptide hormone-producing cells of the APUD series and the embryologic, physiologic and pathologic implications of the concept. *J Histochem Cytochem* 1969; 17(5): 303–13.

Starling EH. The Croonian Lectures on the chemical correlation of the functions of the body. *Lancet* 1905; 2: 339–41, 423–5, 501–3, 579–83.

Welbourn RB. *The History of Endocrine Surgery*. New York: Praeger, 1990.

5 HEPATOBILIARY TRACT

Browne J. A remarkable account of a liver, appearing glandulous to the eye. *Phil Trans* 1685; 15: 1266–8.

Burnett JC. *The Diseases of the Liver: jaundice, gall-stones, enlargements, tumours, and cancer and their treatment*. 2nd edn. Philadelphia: Boericke & Tafel, 1895.

Clunics Ross I. *Liver Fluke Disease in Australia: its treatment and prevention*. Melbourne: HJ Green, Government Printer, 1928.

Frerichs FT. *Klinik der Leberkrankheiten*. Braunschweig: F Vieweg, 1858.

Glisson F. *Anatomia hepatis: cui praemittuntur quaedam ad rem anatomicam universe spectantia*. London: Typis Du-Gardianis, impensis Octaviani Pullein, 1654.

Graham E, Cole H. Roentgenologic examination of the gallbladder. *J Am Med Assoc* 1924; 82: 613–14.

Hounsfield Sir GN. Computerized transverse axial scanning (tomography). 1. Description of system. *Br J Radiol* 1973; 46(552): 1016–22.

Laennec RI. *De l'auscultation mediate*. Paris: JA Brosson & JS Chude, 1819.

Langenbuch C. Em Fall von Exstirpation Jet Gallen blase wegen chronischer Cholelithiasis. *Berl kim Wschr* 1882; 19: 725–7.

Muraskin WA. *The War Against Hepatitis B: a history of the International Task Force on Hepatitis B Immunization*. Philadelphia: University of Pennsylvania Press, 1995.

Naunyn B. *Klinik der Cholelithiasis*. Leipzig: ECW Vogel, 1892.

Oddi R. D'une disposition a sphincter speciale de l'ouverture do canal choledoque. *Arch Iral Bid* 1887; 8: 317–22.

Schaffner F, Sherlock S, Leevy CM (eds). *The Liver and its Diseases*. New York: Intercontinental Medical Book Corp, 1974.

Sherlock S. *Diseases of the Liver and Biliary System*. Oxford: Blackwell Scientific Publications, 1955.

6 SMALL BOWEL

Abercrombie J. *Pathological and Practical Researches on Diseases of the Stomach, the Intestinal Canal, the Liver and Other Viscera of the Abdomen*. Edinburgh: Waugh and Innes, 1828.

Begos DG, Modlin IM, Ballantyne GH. A brief history of intestinal surgery. *Col Rect Surg* 1994; 7: 133–57.

Chapman J. *Diarrhoea and Cholera: their nature, origin, and treatment through the agency of the nervous system*. 2nd edn. London: Trubner, 1866.

Crohn BB, Ginzburg L, Oppenheimer G. Regional ileitis: a pathologic and clinical entity. *JAMA* 1932; 99: 1323–9.

Crosby WH, Kugler HW. Intraluminal biopsy of the small intestine; the intestinal biopsy capsule. *Am J Dig Dis* 1957; 2(5): 236–41.

Dalzeil K. Chronic interstitial enteritis. *BMJ* 1913; 2: 1068–70.

Fitz RH. Perforating inflammation of the vermiform appendix: with special reference to its early diagnosis and treatment. *Am J Med Sci* 1886; 92: 321–46.

Fowler GR. *A Treatise on Appendicitis*. 2nd edn. Philadelphia: JB Lippincott Company, 1900.

Gee S. On the coeliac affection. *St Barth Hos Rep* 1888; 24: 17.

Hall R. Arthur Hedley Clarence Visick FRCS 1897–1949. *Ann R Coll Surg Engl* 1986; 68(3): 147.

Halsted WS. Circular suture of the intestines: an experimental study. *Am J Med Sci* 1887; 94: 436–61.

Jaboulay H. La gastro-enterostomie. La jejunoduodenostomie. La resection du pylore. *Arch Prov Chir* 1892; 1: 1–22.

McBurney C. The incision made in the abdominal wall in cases of appendicitis, with a description of a new method of operating. *Ann Surg* 1894; 20: 38–43.

Meckel JE. Über die Divertikel im Darmkanal. *Arch Physiol (Halle)* 1809; 9: 421–53.

Murphy JB. Cholecysto-intestinal, gastro-intestinal, entero-intestinal anastomosis, and approximation without sutures. *Med Rec (NY)* 1892; 42: 665–76.

Treves F. Inflammation of the vermiform appendix. *Lancet* 1902; 1: 815–1818.

Woelfler A. Gastro-Enterostomie. *Zbl Chit* 1881; 8: 705–8.

7 COLON

Avery Jones Sir F. *Management of Constipation*. Oxford: Blackwell Scientific Publications, 1972.

Bernier O. *Louis XIV: a royal life*. Garden City: Doubleday, 1987.

Hirschprung H. Stuhlträgbeit Neugeborener in Folge von Dilatation und Hypertrophie des Colon. *Jahrb f Kinderh* 1887; 27: 1.

Kelly HA. A new method of examination and treatment of diseases of the rectum and sigmoid flexure. *Ann Surg* 1895; 21: 468–78.

Kraske P. Die sacrale Methode der Extirpation von Mastdarmkrehses und die Resectio recti. *Berlin klin Wschr* 1887; 24: 899–904.

Miles WE. A method of performing abdomino-perineal excision for carcinoma of the rectum and of the terminal portion of the pelvic colon. *Lancet* 1908; 2: 1812–13.

Turell R. Fiber optic coloscope and sigmoidoscope. *Am J Surg* 1963; 105: 133–6.

Wolff WI, Shinya HA. A new approach to colonic polyps. *Ann Surg* 1973; 178(3): 367–78.

"As pines

Keep the shape of the wind

Even when the wind

has fled and is no longer

there –

So words guard the shape of man,

Even when man has fled and is no longer there."

Giorgios Seferiades